WITHDRAWN
DUPLICATE

United States Relations With

China

With Special Reference
to the Period 1944–1949

VOL. II

BASED ON THE FILES OF THE U.S. DEPARTMENT OF STATE

Republished 1971
Scholarly Press, Inc., 22929 Industrial Drive East
St. Clair Shores, Michigan 48080

E
183.8
C5
U53
1971

Library of Congress Catalog Card No. 76-145342
ISBN 0-403-01293-7

66310

United States Relations With China

ERRATA

p. xxxi: Last line: page number should be 662 instead of 622.
p. 52: Date in heading should be 1938–1941 instead of 1938–1931.
p. 92: Last line of footnote should refer to annexes 171 and 185 instead of 171 and 186.
p. 104: 22d line: date should be December 28 instead of 21.
p. 143: End of 2d line: insert reference to footnote 8a, which should read: "See annex 71."
p. 227: 7th line from bottom: insert after "in large measure of" the words "small ships and marine equipment, fixed installations,".
p. 321: 22d line: insert after "Government forces" the words "in the Mukden area".
p. 329: 7th line from bottom: first word should be "or" instead of "of".
p. 349: 22d line should read: "Generalissimo's directive initiating such a training program. Though over 17,000 replacements were passed through the center, . . ."
p. 351: 10th line below heading: substitute the word "suggestion" for the word "question".
p. 353: 14th line: insert the word "at" before the word "least".
p. 356: 6th line from bottom should refer to annex 171 instead of 173.
p. 390: 9th line below heading should refer to 36.5 million dollars instead of 37.5.
10th line below heading should refer to 13.5 million dollars instead of 12.5.
p. 399: 6th line should refer to 215.0 million dollars instead of 220.4.
p. 405: Last line: figure should read "$1,596.7".
p. 478: Annex 28 (h): paragraph beginning "Secretary Hull" should be transposed below the list of participants.
p. 561: Date in heading should be 1944–1945 instead of 1944–1946.
p. 945: Table on OFLC shipments: 2d line under "Air Force" should read "Aircraft P47N" instead of "Aircraft P47D".

(1)

p. 946: Table: 15th line under "Ammunition" should read "Bombs, grenades and mines (mixed) . . . L/T5,666".
17th line under "Ammunition" should read "Ammunition—(mixed, bulk) . . . L/T4,125".

p. 953: Section XVII: A (1) a) should refer to Nov. 29 instead of Dec. 1.
A (1) b) should refer to Dec. 1 instead of Nov. 29.

p. 968: 3d column (Weight): wherever the term "metric tons" is used substitute the term "measured tons".

p. 974: 21st line should refer to annex 171 instead of 167.

p. 975: 20th line should refer to OFLC instead of OFIC.

Annexes

Annexes to Chapter I: A Century of American Policy, 1844-1943

1

Treaty of Wánghia (Cushing Treaty), July 3, 1844 [1]

[Extract]

ARTICLE II

Citizens of the United States resorting to China for the purposes of commerce will pay the duties of import and export prescribed in the Tariff, which is fixed by and made a part of this Treaty. They shall, in no case, be subject to other or higher duties than are or shall be required of the people of any other nation whatever. Fees and charges of every sort are wholly abolished, and officers of the revenue, who may be guilty of exaction, shall be punished according to the laws of China. If the Chinese Government desire to modify, in any respect, the said tariff, such modifications shall be made only in consultation with Consuls or other functionaries thereto duly authorized in behalf of the United States, and with consent thereof. And if additional advantages or privileges, of whatever description be conceded hereafter by China to any other nation, the United States, and the citizens thereof, shall be entitled thereupon, to a complete, equal, and impartial participation in the same.

2

Treaty of Tientsin (Reed Treaty), June 18, 1858 [2]

[Extract]

ARTICLE XXX

The contracting parties hereby agree that should at any time the Ta Tsing Empire grant to any nation, or the merchants or citizens of any nation, any right, privilege or favor, connected either with navigation, commerce, political or other intercourse, which is not conferred by this treaty, such right, privilege and favor shall at once freely inure to the benefit of the United States, its public officers, merchants and citizens.

---

[1] Hunter Miller, ed., *Treaties and Other International Acts of the United States of America*, vol. 4, pp. 559, 560.
[2] *Ibid.*, vol. 7, pp. 793, 804.

3

Treaty of Washington (Burlingame Treaty), July 28, 1868 [3]

[Extract]

ARTICLE VI

Citizens of the United States visiting or residing in China shall enjoy the same privileges, immunities or exemptions in respect to travel or residence as may there be enjoyed by the citizens or subjects of the most favored nation; and, reciprocally, Chinese subjects visiting or residing in the United States shall enjoy the same privileges, immunities and exemptions in respect to travel or residence as may there be enjoyed by the citizens or subjects of the most favored nation. But nothing herein contained shall be held to confer naturalization upon citizens of the United States in China, nor upon the subjects of China in the United States.

4

The Open Door Notes

Secretary Hay to the Ambassador in Great Britain (Choate) [4]

WASHINGTON, *September 6, 1899*

SIR: The Government of Her Britannic Majesty has declared that its policy and its very traditions precluded it from using any privileges which might be granted it in China as a weapon for excluding commercial rivals, and that freedom of trade for Great Britain in that Empire meant freedom of trade for all the world alike. While conceding by formal agreements, first with Germany and then with Russia, the possession of "spheres of influence or interest" in China in which they are to enjoy special rights and privileges, more especially in respect of railroads and mining enterprises, Her Britannic Majesty's Government has therefore sought to maintain at the same time what is called the "opendoor" policy, to insure to the commerce of the world in China equality of treatment within said "spheres" for commerce and navigation. This latter policy is alike urgently demanded by the British mercantile communities and by those of the United States, as it is justly held by them to be the only one which will improve existing conditions, enable them to maintain their positions in the markets of China, and extend their operations in the future. While the Government of the United States will in no way commit itself to a recognition of exclusive rights of any power within or control over any portion of the Chinese Empire under such agreements as have within the last year been made, it can not conceal its apprehension that under existing conditions there is a possibility, even a probability, of complications arising between the treaty powers which may imperil the rights insured to the United States under our treaties with China.

This Government is animated by a sincere desire that the interests of our citizens may not be prejudiced through exclusive treatment by any of the con-

---

[3] William M. Malloy, ed., *Treaties, Conventions, International Acts, Protocols and Agreements Between the United States of America and Other Powers*, vol. I, pp. 234, 236.

[4] *Foreign Relations of the United States*, 1899, p. 131. Similar instructions were sent to American Diplomatic Representatives at Paris, Berlin, St. Petersburg, Rome, and Tokyo.

trolling powers within their so-called "spheres of interest" in China, and hopes also to retain there an open market for the commerce of the world, remove dangerous sources of international irritation, and hasten thereby united or concerted action of the powers at Pekin in favor of the administrative reforms so urgently needed for strengthening the Imperial Government and maintaining the integrity of China in which the whole western world is alike concerned. It believes that such a result may be greatly assisted by a declaration by the various powers claiming "spheres of interest" in China of their intentions as regards treatment of foreign trade therein. The present moment seems a particularly opportune one for informing Her Britannic Majesty's Government of the desire of the United States to see it make a formal declaration and to lend its support in obtaining similar declarations from the various powers claiming "spheres of influence" in China, to the effect that each in its respective spheres of interest or influence

First. Will in no wise interfere with any treaty port or any vested interest within any so-called "sphere of interest" or leased territory it may have in China.

Second. That the Chinese treaty tariff of the time being shall apply to all merchandise landed or shipped to all such ports as are within said "sphere of interest" (unless they be "free ports"), no matter to what nationality it may belong, and that duties so leviable shall be collected by the Chinese Government.

Third. That it will levy no higher harbor duties on vessels of another nationality frequenting any port in such "sphere" than shall be levied on vessels of its own nationality, and no higher railroad charges over lines built, controlled, or operated within its "sphere" on merchandise belonging to citizens or subjects of other nationalities transported through such "sphere" than shall be levied on similar merchandise belonging to its own nationals transported over equal distances.

The recent ukase of His Majesty the Emperor of Russia, declaring the port of Ta-lien-wan open to the merchant ships of all nations during the whole of the lease under which it is to be held by Russia, removing as it does all uncertainty as to the liberal and conciliatory policy of that power, together with the assurances given this Government by Russia, justifies the expectation that His Majesty will cooperate in such an understanding as is here proposed, and our ambassador at the court of St. Petersburg has been instructed accordingly to submit the propositions above detailed to His Imperial Majesty, and ask their early consideration. Copy of my instruction to Mr. Tower is herewith inclosed for your confidential information.

The action of Germany in declaring the port of Kiaochao a "free port," and the aid the Imperial Government has given China in the establishment there of a Chinese custom-house, coupled with the oral assurance conveyed the United States by Germany that our interests within its "sphere" would in no wise be affected by its occupation of this portion of the province of Shang-tung, tend to show that little opposition may be anticipated from that power to the desired declaration.

The interests of Japan, the next most interested power in the trade of China, will be so clearly served by the proposed arrangement, and the declaration of its statesmen within the last year are so entirely in line with the views here expressed, that its hearty cooperation is confidently counted on.

You will, at as early date as practicable, submit the considerations to Her Britannic Majesty's principal secretary of state for foreign affairs and request their immediate consideration.

I inclose herewith a copy of the instruction sent to our ambassador at Berlin bearing on the above subject.⁵

I have the honor to be [etc.]

JOHN HAY.

Secretary Hay to American Diplomatic Representatives at London, Paris, Berlin, St. Petersburg, Rome, and Tokyo ⁶

WASHINGTON, *March 20, 1900*

SIR: The —— Government having accepted the declaration suggested by the United States concerning foreign trade in China, the terms of which I transmitted to you in my instruction No. —— of ——, and like action having been taken by all the various powers having leased territory or so-called "spheres of interest" in the Chinese Empire, as shown by the notes which I herewith transmit to you,⁷ you will please inform the Government to which you are accredited that the condition originally attached to its acceptance—that all other powers concerned should likewise accept the proposals of the United States—having been complied with, this Government will therefore consider the assent given to it by —— as final and definitive.

You will also transmit to the minister for foreign affairs copies of the present inclosures,⁷ and by the same occasion convey to him the expression of the sincere gratification which the President feels at the successful termination of these negotiations, in which he sees proof of the friendly spirit which animates the various powers interested in the untrammeled development of commerce and industry in the Chinese Empire, and a source of vast benefit to the whole commercial world.

I am [etc.]

JOHN HAY.

5

Secretary Hay to American Diplomatic Representatives at Berlin, Paris, London, Rome, St. Petersburg, Vienna, Brussels, Madrid, Tokyo, The Hague, and Lisbon ⁸

WASHINGTON, *July 3, 1900*

In this critical posture of affairs in China it is deemed appropriate to define the attitude of the United States as far as present circumstances permit this to be done. We adhere to the policy initiated by us in 1857 of peace with the Chinese nation, of furtherance of lawful commerce, and of protection of lives and property of our citizens by all means guaranteed under extraterritorial treaty rights and by the law of nations. If wrong be done to our citizens we propose to hold the responsible authors to the uttermost accountability. We regard the condition at Pekin as one of virtual anarchy, whereby power and responsibility are practically devolved upon the local provincial authorities. So long as they are not in overt collusion with rebellion and use their power to protect foreign life and property, we regard them as representing the Chinese people, with whom we seek to remain in peace and friendship. The purpose of the President is, as it has been heretofore, to act concurrently with the other

---

⁵ Not printed.
⁶ Foreign Relations, 1899, p. 142.
⁷ Not printed.
⁸ Foreign Relations 1900, p. 299.

powers; first, in opening up communication with Pekin and rescuing the American officials, missionaries, and other Americans who are in danger; secondly, in affording all possible protection everywhere in China to American life and property; thirdly, in guarding and protecting all legitimate American interests; and fourthly, in aiding to prevent a spread of the disorders to the other provinces of the Empire and a recurrence of such disasters. It is of course too early to forecast the means of attaining this last result; but the policy of the Government of the United States is to seek a solution which may bring about permanent safety and peace to China, preserve Chinese territorial and administrative entity, protect all rights guaranteed to friendly powers by treaty and international law, and safeguard for the world the principle of equal and impartial trade with all parts of the Chinese Empire.

You will communicate the purport of this instruction to the minister for foreign affairs.

JOHN HAY.

6

Treaty Between the United States and China for the Extension of the Commercial Relations Between Them, Signed at Shanghai, October 8, 1903 [9]

The United States of America and His Majesty the Emperor of China, being animated by an earnest desire to extend further the commercial relations between them and otherwise to promote the interests of the peoples of the two countries, in view of the provisions of the first paragraph of Article XI of the final Protocol signed at Peking on the seventh day of September, A. D. 1901, whereby the Chinese Government agreed to negotiate the amendments deemed necessary by the foreign Governments to the treaties of commerce and navigation and other subjects concerning commercial relations, with the object of facilitating them, have for that purpose named as their Plenipotentiaries:—

The United States of America—
    Edwin H. Conger, Envoy Extraordinary and Minister Plenipotentiary of the United States of America to China—
    John Goodnow, Consul-General of the United States of America at Shanghai—
    John F. Seaman, a Citizen of the United States of America resident at Shanghai—

And His Majesty the Emperor of China—
    Lü Hai-huan, President of the Board of Public Works—
    Sheng Hsüan-huai, Junior Guardian of the Heir Apparent. Formerly Senior Vice-President of the Board of Public Works—

who, having met and duly exchanged their full powers which were found to be in proper form, have agreed upon the following amendments to existing treaties of commerce and navigation formerly concluded between the two countries, and upon the subjects hereinafter expressed connected with commercial relations, with the object of facilitating them.

---

[9] *Ibid.*, 1903, p. 91.

Article I

In accordance with international usage, and as the diplomatic representative of China has the right to reside in the capital of the United States, and to enjoy there the same prerogatives, privileges and immunities as are enjoyed by the similar representative of the most favored nation, the diplomatic representative of the United States shall have the right to reside at the capital of His Majesty the Emperor of China. He shall be given audience of His Majesty the Emperor whenever necessary to present his letters of credence or any communication from the President of the United States. At all such times he shall be received in a place and in a manner befitting his high position, and on all such occasions the ceremonial observed toward him shall be that observed toward the representatives of nations on a footing of equality, with no loss of prestige on the part of either.

The diplomatic representatives of the United States shall enjoy all the prerogatives, privileges and immunities accorded by international usage to such representatives, and shall in all respects be entitled to the treatment extended to similar representatives of the most favored nation.

The English text of all notes or dispatches from United States officials to Chinese officials, and the Chinese text of all from Chinese officials to United States officials shall be authoritative.

Article II

As China may appoint consular officers to reside in the United States and to enjoy there the same attributes, privileges and immunities as are enjoyed by consular officers of other nations, the United States may appoint, as its interests may require, consular officers to reside at the places in the Empire of China that are now or that may hereafter be opened to foreign residence and trade. They shall hold direct official intercourse and correspondence with the local officers of the Chinese Government within their consular districts, either personally or in writing as the case may require, on terms of equality and reciprocal respect. These officers shall be treated with due respect by all Chinese authorities, and they shall enjoy all the attributes, privileges and immunities, and exercise all the jurisdiction over their nationals which are or may hereafter be extended to similar officers of the nation the most favored in these respects. If the officers of either government are disrespectfully treated or aggrieved in any way by the authorities of the other, they shall have the right to make representation of the same to the superior officers of their own government who shall see that full inquiry and strict justice be had in the premises. And the said consular officers of either nation shall carefully avoid all acts of offense to the officers and people of the other nation.

On the arrival of a consul duly accredited at any place in China opened to foreign trade it shall be the duty of the Minister of the United States to inform the Board of Foreign Affairs, which shall, in accordance with international usage, forthwith cause the proper recognition of the said consul and grant him authority to act.

Article III

Citizens of the United States may frequent, reside and carry on trade, industries and manufactures, or pursue any lawful avocation, in all the ports or localities of China which are now open or may hereafter be opened to foreign residence and trade; and, within the suitable localities at those places which have been or may be set apart for the use and occupation of foreigners, they may rent or purchase houses, places of business and other buildings, and rent or lease in perpetuity land and build thereon. They shall generally enjoy as to their persons and property all such rights, privileges and immunities as are or may hereafter be granted to the subjects or citizens of the nation the most favored in these respects.

ARTICLE IV

The Chinese Government, recognizing that the existing system of levying dues on goods in transit, and especially the system of taxation known as *likin*, impedes the free circulation of commodities to the general injury of trade, hereby undertakes to abandon the levy of *likin* and all other transit dues throughout the Empire and to abolish the offices, stations and barriers maintained for their collection and not to establish other offices for levying dues on goods in transit. It is clearly understood that, after the offices, stations and barriers for taxing goods in transit have been abolished, no attempt shall be made to re-establish them in any form or under any pretext whatsoever.

The Government of the United States, in return, consents to allow a surtax, in excess of the tariff rates for the time being in force, to be imposed on foreign goods imported by citizens of the United States and on Chinese produce destined for export abroad or coastwise. It is clearly understood that in no case shall the surtax on foreign imports exceed one and one-half times the import duty leviable in terms of the final Protocol signed by China and the Powers on the seventh day of September, A. D. 1901; that the payment of the import duty and surtax shall secure for foreign imports, whether in the hands of Chinese or foreigners, in original packages or otherwise, complete immunity from all other taxation, examination or delay; that the total amount of taxation, inclusive of the tariff export duty, leviable on native produce for export abroad shall, under no circumstances, exceed seven and one-half per centum *ad valorem*.

Nothing in this article is intended to interfere with the inherent right of China to levy such other taxes as are not in conflict with its provisions.

Keeping these fundamental principles in view, the High Contracting Parties have agreed upon the following method of procedure.

The Chinese Government undertakes that all offices, stations and barriers of whatsoever kind for collecting *likin*, duties, or such like dues on goods in transit, shall be permanently abolished on all roads, railways and waterways in the nineteen Provinces of China and the three Eastern Provinces. This provision does not apply to the native Customs offices at present in existence on the seaboard, at open ports where there are offices of the Imperial Maritime Customs, and on the land frontiers of China embracing the nineteen Provinces and the three Eastern Provinces.

Wherever there are offices of the Imperial Maritime Customs, or wherever such may be hereafter placed, native Customs offices may also be established, as well as at any point either on the seaboard or land frontiers.

The Government of the United States agrees that foreign goods on importation, in addition to the effective five per centum import duty as provided for in the Protocol of 1901, shall pay a special surtax of one and one-half times the amount of the said duty to compensate for the abolition of *likin*, of other transit dues besides *likin*, and of all other taxation on foreign goods, and in consideration of the other reforms provided for in this article.

The Chinese Government may recast the foreign export tariff with specific duties, as far as practicable, on a scale not exceeding five per centum *ad valorem;* but existing export duties shall not be raised until at least six months' notice has been given. In cases where existing export duties are above five per centum, they shall be reduced to not more than that rate. An additional special surtax of one-half the export duty payable for the time being, in lieu of internal taxation of all kinds, may be levied at the place of original shipment or at the time of export on goods exported either to foreign countries or coastwise.

Foreign goods which bear a similarity to native goods shall be furnished by the Customs officers, if required by the owner, with a protective certificate for each package, on the payment of import duty and surtax, to prevent the risk of any dispute in the interior.

Native goods brought by junks to open ports, if intended for local consumption, irrespective of the nationality of the owner of the goods, shall be reported at the native Customs offices only, to be dealt with according to the fiscal regulations of the Chinese Government.

Machine-made cotton yarn and cloth manufactured in China, whether by foreigners at the open ports or by Chinese anywhere in China, shall as regards taxation be on a footing of perfect equality. Such goods upon payment of the taxes thereon shall be granted a rebate of the import duty and of two-thirds of the import surtax paid on the cotton used in their manufacture, if it has been imported from abroad, and of all duties paid thereon if it be Chinese grown cotton. They shall also be free of export duty, coast-trade duty and export surtax. The same principle and procedure shall be applied to all other products of foreign type turned out by machinery in China.

A member or members of the Imperial Maritime Customs foreign staff shall be selected by the Governors-General and Governors of each of the various provinces of the Empire for their respective provinces, and appointed in consultation with the Inspector General of Imperial Maritime Customs, for duty in connection with native Customs affairs to have a general supervision of their working.

Cases where illegal action is complained of by citizens of the United States shall be promptly investigated by an officer of the Chinese Government of sufficiently high rank, in conjunction with an officer of the United States Government, and an officer of the Imperial Maritime Customs, each of sufficient standing; and, in the event of it being found by the investigating officers that the complaint is well founded and loss has been incurred, due compensation shall be paid through the Imperial Maritime Customs. The high provincial officials shall be held responsible that the officer guilty of the illegal action shall be severely punished and removed from his post. If the complaint is shown to be frivolous or malicious, the complainant shall be held responsible for the expenses of the investigation.

When the ratifications of this Treaty shall have been exchanged by the High Contracting Parties hereto, and the provisions of this Article shall have been accepted by the Powers having treaties with China, then a date shall be agreed upon when the provisions of this Article shall take effect and an Imperial Edict shall be published in due form on yellow paper and circulated throughout the Empire of China setting forth the abolition of all *likin* taxation, duties on goods in transit, offices, stations and barriers for collecting the same, and of all descriptions of internal taxation on foreign goods, and the imposition of the surtax on the import of foreign goods and on the export of native goods, and the other fiscal changes and reforms provided for in this Article, all of which shall take effect from the said date. The Edict shall state that the provincial high officials are responsible that any official disregarding the letter or the spirit of its injunction shall be severely punished and removed from his post.

Article V

The tariff duties to be paid by citizens of the United States on goods imported into China shall be as set forth in the schedule annexed hereto and made part of this Treaty, subject only to such amendments and changes as are authorized by Article IV of the present convention or as may hereafter be agreed upon by the High Contracting Parties hereto. It is expressly agreed, however, that citizens of the United States shall at no time pay other or higher duties than those paid by the citizens or subjects of the most favored nation.

Conversely, Chinese subjects shall not pay higher duties on their imports into the United States than those paid by the citizens or subjects of the most favored nation.

Article VI

The Government of China agrees to the establishment by citizens of the United States of warehouses approved by the proper Chinese authorities as bonded warehouses at the several open Ports of China, for storage, re-packing, or preparation for shipment of lawful goods, subject to such necessary regulations for the protection of the revenue of China, including a reasonable scale of fees according to commodities, distance from the custom house and hours of working, as shall be made from time to time by the proper officers of the Government of China.

Article VII

The Chinese Government, recognizing that it is advantageous for the country to develop its mineral resources, and that it is desirable to attract foreign as well as Chinese capital to embark in mining enterprises, agrees, within one year from the signing of this Treaty, to initiate and conclude the revision of the existing mining regulations. To this end China will, with all expedition and earnestness, go into the whole question of mining rules; and, selecting from the rules of the United States and other countries regulations which seem applicable to the condition of China, will recast its present mining rules in such a way as, while promoting the interests of Chinese subjects and not injuring in any way the sovereign rights of China, will offer no impediment to the attraction of foreign capital nor place foreign capitalists at a greater disadvantage than they would be under generally accepted foreign regulations; and will permit citizens of the United States to carry on in Chinese territory mining operations and other necessary business relating thereto provided they comply with the new regulations and conditions which will be imposed by China on its subjects and foreigners alike, relating to the opening of mines, the renting of mineral land, and the payment of royalty, and provided they apply for permits, the provisions of which in regard to necessary business relating to such operations shall be observed. The residence of citizens of the United States in connection with such mining operations shall be subject to such regulations as shall be agreed upon by and between the United States and China.

Any mining concession granted after the publication of such new rules shall be subject to their provisions.

Article VIII

Drawback certificates for the return of duties shall be issued by the Imperial Maritime Customs to citizens of the United States within three weeks of the presentation to the Customs of the papers entitling the applicant to receive such drawback certificates, and they shall be receivable at their face value in payment of duties of all kinds (tonnage dues excepted) at the port of issue; or shall, in the case of drawbacks on foreign goods re-exported within three years from the date of importation, be redeemable by the Imperial Maritime Customs in full in ready money at the port of issue, at the option of the holders thereof. But if, in connection with any application for a drawback certificate, the Customs authorities discover an attempt to defraud the revenue, the applicant shall be dealt with and punished in accordance with the stipulations provided in the Treaty of Tientsin, Article XXI, in the case of detected frauds on the revenue. In case the goods have been removed from Chinese territory, then the consul shall inflict on the guilty party a suitable fine to be paid to the Chinese Government.

Article IX

Whereas the United States undertakes to protect the citizens of any country in the exclusive use within the United States of any lawful trade-marks, provided that such country agrees by treaty or convention to give like protection to citizens of the United States:—

Therefore the Government of China, in order to secure such protection in the United States for its subjects, now agrees to fully protect any citizen, firm or corporation of the United States in the exclusive use in the Empire of China of any lawful trade-mark to the exclusive use of which in the United States they are entitled, or which they have adopted and used, or intend to adopt and use as soon as registered, for exclusive use within the Empire of China. To this end the Chinese Government agrees to issue by its proper authorities proclamations, having the force of law, forbidding all subjects of China from infringing on, imitating, colorably imitating, or knowingly passing off an imitation of trade-marks belonging to citizens of the United States, which shall have been registered by the proper authorities of the United States at such offices as the Chinese Government will establish for such purpose, on payment of a reasonable fee, after due investigation by the Chinese authorities, and in compliance with reasonable regulations.

Article X

The United States Government allows subjects of China to patent their inventions in the United States and protects them in the use and ownership of such patents. The Government of China now agrees that it will establish a Patent Office. After this office has been established and special laws with regard to inventions have been adopted it will thereupon, after the payment of the prescribed fees, issue certificates of protection, valid for a fixed term of years, to citizens of the United States on all their patents issued by the United States, in respect of articles the sale of which is lawful in China, which do not infringe on previous inventions of Chinese subjects, in the same manner as patents are to be issued to subjects of China.

Article XI

Whereas the Government of the United States undertakes to give the benefits of its copyright laws to the citizens of any foreign State which gives to the citizens of the United States the benefits of copyright on an equal basis with its own citizens:—

Therefore the Government of China, in order to secure such benefits in the United States for its subjects, now agrees to give full protection, in the same way and manner and subject to the same conditions upon which it agrees to protect trade-marks, to all citizens of the United States who are authors, designers or proprietors of any book, map, print or engraving especially prepared for the use and education of the Chinese people, or translation into Chinese of any book, in the exclusive right to print and sell such book, map, print, engraving or translation in the Empire of China during ten years from the date of registration. With the exception of the books, maps, etc., specified above, which may not be reprinted in the same form, no work shall be entitled to copyright privileges under this article. It is understood that Chinese subjects shall be at liberty to make, print and sell original translations into Chinese of any works written or of maps compiled by a citizen of the United States. This article shall not be held to protect against due process of law any citizen of the United States or Chinese subject who may be author, proprietor, or seller of any publication calculated to injure the well-being of China.

Article XII

The Chinese Government having in 1898 opened the navigable inland waters of the Empire to commerce by all steam vessels, native or foreign, that may be specially registered for the purpose, for the conveyance of passengers and lawful merchandise, citizens, firms, and corporations of the United States may engage in such commerce on equal terms with those granted to subjects of any foreign power.

In case either party hereto considers it advantageous at any time that the rules and regulations then in existence for such commerce be altered or amended, the Chinese Government agrees to consider amicably and to adopt such modifications thereof as are found necessary for trade and for the benefit of China.

The Chinese Government agrees that, upon the exchange of the ratifications of this treaty, Mukden and Antung, both in the province of Sheng-king, will be opened by China itself as places of international residence and trade. The selection of suitable localities to be set apart for international use and occupation and the regulations for these places set apart for foreign residence and trade shall be agreed upon by the Governments of the United States and China after consultation together.

Article XIII

China agrees to take the necessary steps to provide for a uniform national coinage which shall be legal tender in payment of all duties, taxes, and other obligations throughout the Empire by the citizens of the United States as well as Chinese subjects. It is understood, however, that all customs duties shall continue to be calculated and paid on the basis of the Haikwan Tael.

Article XIV

The principles of the Christian religion, as professed by the Protestant and Roman Catholic Churches, are recognized as teaching men to do good and to do to others as they would have others do to them. Those who quietly profess and teach these doctrines shall not be harassed or persecuted on account of their faith. Any person, whether citizen of the United States or Chinese convert, who, according to these tenets, peaceably teaches and practices the principles of Christianity shall in no case be interfered with or molested therefor. No restrictions shall be placed on Chinese joining Christian churches. Converts and non-converts, being Chinese subjects, shall alike conform to the laws of China; and shall pay due respect to those in authority, living together in peace and amity; and the fact of being converts shall not protect them from the consequences of any offense they may have committed before or may commit after their admission into the church, or exempt them from paying legal taxes levied on Chinese subjects generally, except taxes levied and contributions for the support of religious customs and practices contrary to their faith. Missionaries shall not interfere with the exercise by the native authorities of their jurisdiction over Chinese subjects; nor shall the native authorities make any distinction between converts and nonconverts, but shall administer the laws without partiality, so that both classes can live together in peace.

Missionary societies of the United States shall be permitted to rent and to lease in perpetuity, as the property of such societies, buildings or lands in all parts of the Empire for missionary purposes and, after the title deeds have been found in order and duly stamped by the local authorities, to erect such suitable buildings as may be required for carrying on their good work.

Article XV

The Government of China having expressed a strong desire to reform its judicial system and to bring it into accord with that of Western nations, the United States agrees to give every assistance to such reform and will also be prepared to relinquish extra-territorial rights when satisfied that the state of the Chinese laws, the arrangements for their administration, and other considerations warrant it in so doing.

Article XVI

The Government of the United States consents to the prohibition by the Government of China of the importation into China of morphia and of instruments for its injection, excepting morphia and instruments for its injection imported for medical purposes, on payment of tariff duty, and under regulations to be framed by China which shall effectually restrict the use of such import to the said purposes. This prohibition shall be uniformly applied to such importation from all countries. The Chinese Government undertakes to adopt at once measures to prevent the manufacture in China of morphia and of instruments for its injection.

Article XVII

It is agreed between the high contracting parties hereto that all the provisions of the several treaties between the United States and China which were in force on the first day of January, A. D. 1900, are continued in full force and effect except in so far as they are modified by the present treaty or other treaties to which the United States is a party.

The present treaty shall remain in force for a period of ten years, beginning with the date of the exchange of ratifications and until a revision is effected as hereinafter provided.

It is further agreed that either of the high contracting parties may demand that the tariff and the articles of this convention be revised at the end of ten years from the date of the exchange of the ratifications thereof. If no revision is demanded before the end of the first term of ten years, then these articles in their present form shall remain in full force for a further term of ten years reckoned from the end of the first term, and so on for successive periods of ten years.

The English and Chinese texts of the present Treaty and its three annexes have been carefully compared; but, in the event of there being any difference of meaning between them, the sense as expressed in the English text shall be held to be the correct one.

This Treaty and its three annexes shall be ratified by the two High Contracting Parties in conformity with their respective constitutions, and the ratifications shall be exchanged in Washington not later than twelve months from the present date.

In testimony whereof, we, the undersigned, by virtue of our respective powers, have signed this Treaty in duplicate in the English and Chinese languages, and have affixed our respective seals.

Done at Shanghai, this eighth day of October in the year of our Lord one thousand nine hundred and three, and in the twenty ninth year of Kuang Hsü eighth month and eighteenth day.

            EDWIN H. CONGER [SEAL.]
            JOHN GOODNOW [SEAL.]
            JOHN F. SEAMAN [SEAL.1

Signatures and seal of Chinese Plenipotentiaries.
 [LÜ HAI-HUAN]
 [SHENG HSÜAN-HUAI]

ANNEX I

As citizens of the United States are already forbidden by treaty to deal in or handle opium, no mention has been made in this Treaty of opium taxation.

As the trade in salt is a government monopoly in China, no mention has been made in this Treaty of salt taxation.

It is, however, understood, after full discussion and consideration, that the collection of inland dues on opium and salt and the means for the protection of the revenue therefrom and for preventing illicit traffic therein are left to be administered by the Chinese Government in such manner as shall in no wise interfere with the provisions of Article IV of this treaty regarding the unobstructed transit of other goods.

            EDWIN H. CONGER [SEAL.]
            JOHN GOODNOW [SEAL.]
            JOHN F. SEAMAN [SEAL.]

Signatures and seal of Chinese Plenipotentiaries.
 [LÜ HAI-HUAN]
 [SHENG HSÜAN-HUAI]

ANNEX II

Article IV of the Treaty of Commerce between the United States and China of this date provides for the retention of the native Customs offices at the open ports. For the purpose of safeguarding the revenue of China at such places, it is understood that the Chinese Government shall be entitled to establish and maintain such branch native Customs offices at each open port, within a reasonable distance of the main native Customs offices at the port, as shall be deemed by the authorities of the Imperial Maritime Customs at that port necessary to collect the revenue from the trade into and out of such port. Such branches, as well as the main native Customs offices at each open port, shall be administered by the Imperial Maritime Customs as provided by the Protocol of 1901.

           EDWIN H. CONGER [SEAL.]
           JOHN GOODNOW [SEAL.]
           JOHN F. SEAMAN [SEAL.]

Signatures and seal of Chinese Plenipotentiaries.
 [LÜ HAI-HUAN]
 [SHENG HSÜAN-HUAI]

ANNEX III

The schedule of tariff duties on imported goods annexed to this Treaty under Article V is hereby mutually declared to be the schedule agreed upon between the representatives of China and the United States and signed by John Goodnow for the United States and Their Excellencies Lü Hai-huan and Sheng Hsüan-huai for China at Shanghai on the sixth day of September, A. D. 1902, according to the Protocol of the seventh day of September, A. D. 1901.

           EDWIN H. CONGER [SEAL.]
           JOHN GOODNOW [SEAL.]
           JOHN F. SEAMAN [SEAL.]

Signatures and seal of Chinese Plenipotentiaries.
 [LÜ HAI-HUAN]
 [SHENG HSÜAN-HUAI]

7

Secretary Hay to American Diplomatic Representatives at Peking, St. Petersburg, and Tokyo [10]

           WASHINGTON, *February 10, 1904.*

You will express to the minister of foreign affairs the earnest desire of the Government of the United States that in the course of the military operations which have begun between Russia and Japan the neutrality of China and in all practicable ways her administrative entity shall be respected by both parties, and that the area of hostility shall be localized and limited as much as possible, so that undue excitement and disturbance of the Chinese people may be prevented and the least possible loss to the commerce and peaceful intercourse of the world may be occasioned.

               JOHN HAY.

8

Secretary Hay to American Diplomatic Representatives at Vienna, Brussels, Paris, Berlin, London, Rome, and Lisbon [11]

           WASHINGTON, *January 13, 1905.*

It has come to our knowledge that apprehension exists on the part of some of the powers that in the eventual negotiations for peace between Russia and Japan claim may be made for the concession of Chinese territory to neutral

---

[10] *Ibid.*, 1904, p. 2.
[11] *Ibid.*, 1905, p. 1.

powers. The President would be loath to share this apprehension, believing that the introduction of extraneous interests would seriously embarrass and postpone the settlement of the issues involved in the present contest in the Far East, thus making more remote the attainment of that peace which is so earnestly to be desired. For its part, the United States has repeatedly made its position well known, and has been gratified at the cordial welcome accorded to its efforts to strengthen and perpetuate the broad policy of maintaining the integrity of China and the "open door" in the Orient whereby equality of commercial opportunity and access shall be enjoyed by all nations. Holding these views the United States disclaims any thought of reserved territorial rights or control in the Chinese Empire, and it is deemed fitting to make this purpose frankly known and to remove all apprehension on this score so far as concerns the policy of this nation, which maintains so considerable a share of the Pacific commerce of China and which holds such important possessions in the western Pacific, almost at the gateway of China.

You will bring this matter to the notice of the government to which you are accredited, and you will invite the expression of its views thereon.

JOHN HAY.

9

Root-Takahira Agreement, November 30, 1908

The Japanese Ambassador (Takahira) to Secretary Root [12]

Washington, November 30, 1908.

SIR: The exchange of views between us, which has taken place at the several interviews which I have recently had the honor of holding with you, has shown that Japan and the United States holding important outlying insular possessions in the region of the Pacific Ocean, he Governments of the two countries are animated by a common aim, policy, and intention in that region.

Believing that a frank avowal of that aim, policy, and intention would not only tend to strengthen the relations of friendship and good neighborhood, which have immemorially existed between Japan and the United States, but would materially contribute to the preservation of the general peace, the Imperial Government have authorized me to present to you an outline of their understanding of that common aim, policy, and intention:

1. It is the wish of the two Governments to encourage the free and peaceful development of their commerce on the Pacific Ocean.

2. The policy of both Governments, uninfluenced by any aggressive tendencies, is directed to the maintenance of the existing status quo in the region above mentioned and to the defense of the principle of equal opportunity for commerce and industry in China.

3. They are accordingly firmly resolved reciprocally to respect the territorial possessions belonging to each other in said region.

4. They are also determined to preserve the common interest of all powers in China by supporting by all pacific means at their disposal the independence and integrity of China and the principle of equal opportunity for commerce and industry of all nations in that Empire.

5. Should any event occur threatening the status quo as above described or the principle of equal opportunity as above defined, it remains for the two

[12] *Ibid.*, 1908, p. 510.

Governments to communicate with each other in order to arrive at an understanding as to what measures they may consider it useful to take.

If the foregoing outline accords with the view of the Government of the United States, I shall be gratified to receive your confirmation.

I take [etc.]
K. TAKAHIRA.

Secretary Root to the Japanese Ambassador (Takahira) [13]

Washington, November 30, 1908.

EXCELLENCY: I have the honor to acknowledge the receipt of your note of to-day setting forth the result of the exchange of views between us in our recent interviews defining the understanding of the two Governments in regard to their policy in the region of the Pacific Ocean.

It is a pleasure to inform you that this expression of mutual understanding is welcome to the Government of the United States as appropriate to the happy relations of the two countries and as the occasion for a concise mutual affirmation of that accordant policy respecting the Far East which the two Governments have so frequently declared in the past.

I am happy to be able to confirm to your excellency, on behalf of the United States, the declaration of the two Governments embodied in the following words:

1. It is the wish of the two Governments to encourage the free and peaceful development of their commerce on the Pacific Ocean.

2. The policy of both Governments, uninfluenced by any aggressive tendencies, is directed to the maintenance of the existing status quo in the region above mentioned, and to the defense of the principle of equal opportunity for commerce and industry in China.

3. They are accordingly firmly resolved reciprocally to respect the territorial possessions belonging to each other in said region.

4. They are also determined to preserve the common interests of all powers in China by supporting by all pacific means at their disposal the independence and integrity of China and the principle of equal opportunity for commerce and industry of all nations in that Empire.

5. Should any event occur threatening the status quo as above described or the principle of equal opportunity as above defined, it remains for the two Governments to communicate with each other in order to arrive at an understanding as to what measures they may consider it useful to take.

Accept [etc.]
ELIHU ROOT.

10

Memorandum by Secretary Knox on the Neutralization of the Manchurian Railways [14]

Now that there has been signed and ratified by an unpublished imperial decree an agreement by which American and British interests are to cooperate in the financing and construction of the Chin Chou Tsitsihar Aigun Railroad, the

---

[13] *Ibid.* 1908, p. 511.
[14] *Ibid.*, 1910, p. 234. The Ambassador at London was instructed, on Nov. 6, 1909, to deliver the memorandum to the British Government. On Dec. 14, 1909, the American Diplomatic Representatives at Paris, Berlin, St. Petersburg, Tokyo, and Peking were instructed to present this proposal to the respective governments to which they were accredited.

Government of the United States is prepared cordially to cooperate with the British Government in diplomatically supporting and facilitating this, so important alike to the progress and the commercial development of China.

The Government of the United States would be disposed to favor ultimate participation to a proper extent on the part of other interested powers whose inclusion might be agreeable to China and which are known to support the principle of equality of commercial opportunity and the maintenance of the integrity of the Chinese Empire.

However, before the further elaboration of the actual arrangement the Government of the United States asks the British Government to give their consideration to the following alternative and more comprehensive projects:

1. Perhaps the most effective way to preserve the undisturbed enjoyment by China of all political rights in Manchuria and to promote the development of those Provinces under a practical application of the policy of the open door and equal commercial opportunity would be to bring the Manchurian highways and the railroad under an economic and scientific and impartial administration by some plan vesting in China the ownership of the railroads through funds furnished for that purpose by the interested powers willing to participate. Such loan should be for a period ample to make it reasonably certain that it could be met within the time fixed, and should be upon such terms as would make it attractive to bankers and investors. The plan should provide that nationals of the participating powers should supervise the railroad system during the term of the loan, and the Governments concerned should enjoy for such period the usual preferences for their nationals and materials upon an equitable basis *inter se*.

The execution of such a plan would naturally require the cooperation of China and of Japan and Russia, the reversionary and the concessionaries, respectively, of the existing Manchurian railroads, as well as that of Great Britain and the United States, whose special interests rest upon the existing contract relative to the Chin Chou Aigun Railroad.

The advantages of such a plan to Japan and to Russia are obvious. Both those powers, desiring in good faith to protect the policy of the open door and equal opportunity in Manchuria, and wishing to assure to China unimpaired sovereignty, might well be expected to welcome an opportunity to shift the separate duties, responsibilities, and expenses they have undertaken in the protection of their respective commercial and other interests for impartial assumption by the combined powers, including themselves, in proportion to their interests. The Government of the United States has some reason to hope that such a plan might meet favorable consideration on the part of Russia, and has reason to believe that American financial participation would be forthcoming.

2. Should this suggestion not be found feasible in its entirety, then the desired end would be approximated if not attained by Great Britain and the United States diplomatically supporting the Chin Chou Aigun arrangement and inviting interested powers friendly to the complete commercial neutrality of Manchuria to participate in the financing and construction of that line and of such additional lines as future commercial development may demand, and at the same time to supply funds for the purchase by China of such of the existing lines as might be offered for inclusion in this system.

The Government of the United States hopes that the principle involved in the foregoing suggestions may commend itself to His Britannic Majesty's Government. That principle finds support in the additional reasons that the consummation of some such plan would avoid the irritations likely to be engendered by the uncontrolled direct negotiations of bankers with the Chinese Government, and also that it would create such community of substantial interest in China as would facilitate a cooperation calculated to simplify the problems, fiscal and monetary—reforms now receiving such earnest attention by the Imperial Chinese Government.

11

Secretary Bryan to the Japanese Ambassador (Viscount Chinda)[15]

WASHINGTON, *March 13, 1915*

EXCELLENCY: On February 8 last your excellency left with me at the Department a memorandum setting forth the demands which the Imperial Japanese Government felt obliged to make upon China, and on the 22d day of the same month your excellency delivered to me an additional memorandum presenting certain "requests" affecting the relations between the two countries which the Imperial Government has urged China to consider.

The American Government is glad to learn from these two communications of the Imperial Government that the "requests" were not presented to China as "demands" but that they were but "wishes" for which "friendly consideration" was asked on the part of China. The American Government understands from this distinction between the "demands" and the "requests" that the latter are not to be pressed if the Chinese Government should decline to consider them.

Inasmuch as these requests appear to have a bearing upon the traditional attitude of both the United States and Japan towards China, I desire to present to your excellency the following considerations of the Government of the United States relative to the effect which, it is thought, these demands and requests may have upon the relations of the United States with the Chinese Republic.

Reciprocating the frank and friendly character of the statements of the Imperial Japanese Government, the Government of the United States of America believes that an expression of its views with respect to these matters will be received by the Imperial Government in the same friendly spirit in which it is offered.

It will be recalled that in the year 1899 the Government of the United States requested the Governments of France, Germany, Great Britain, Italy, Russia and Japan to give their formal consent to three proposals:

First. They will in no way interfere with any treaty port or any vested interest within any so-called "sphere of interest" or leased territory they may have in China.

Second. The Chinese treaty tariff of the time being shall apply to all merchandise landed or shipped to all such ports as are within said "sphere of interest" (unless they be "free ports"), no matter to what nationality it may belong, and that duties so leviable shall be collected by the Chinese Government.

Third. They will levy no higher harbor dues on vessels of another nationality frequenting any port in such "sphere" than shall be levied on vessels of their own nationality, and no higher railroad charges over lines built, controlled, or operated within such "sphere" on merchandise belonging to citizens or subjects of other nationalities transported through such "sphere" than shall be levied on similar merchandise belonging to their own nationals transported over equal distances.

---

[15] *Ibid.*, 1915, p. 105.

On December 26, 1899, the Minister for Foreign Affairs addressed a note to the American Minister at Tokyo assuring the Minister—

> that the Imperial Government will have no hesitation to give their assent to so just and fair a proposal of the United States, provided that all the other Powers concerned shall accept the same.

A similar acceptance was given on behalf of the other Powers approached.

On July 3, 1900, having been consulted by other Powers as to the course to be pursued in China as a result of the Boxer disturbances, this Government expressed its views in a circular communication to Austria-Hungary, France, Germany, Great Britain, Italy, Japan and Russia, stating that—

> the policy of the Government of the United States is to seek a solution which may bring about permanent safety and peace to China, preserve Chinese territorial and administrative entity, protect all rights guaranteed to friendly Powers by treaty and international law, and safeguard for the world the principle of equal and impartial trade with all parts of the Chinese Empire.

In reply the Minister for Foreign Affairs of the Imperial Government expressed through the American Minister at Tokyo views in accord with those of the United States Government.

In the following month Great Britain and Germany signed an agreement defining their mutual policy in China:

> I. It is a matter of joint and permanent international interest that the ports on the rivers and littoral of China should remain free and open to trade and to every other legitimate form of economic activity for the nationals of all countries without distinction, and the two Governments agree on their part to uphold the same for all Chinese territory so far as they can exercise influence.
>
> II. Her Britannic Majesty's Government and the Imperial German Government will not on their part make use of the present complication to obtain for themselves any territorial advantages in Chinese dominions and will direct their policy towards maintaining undiminished the territorial conditions of the Chinese Empire.

This agreement being communicated by those Powers to Japan was acknowledged by the Imperial Government in a note containing the following language:

> The Imperial Government having been assured by the contracting Powers that in adhering to the agreement in question they would be placed in relation to it in the same position as if they had been a signatory thereto, do not hesitate to declare formally their adherence to the said agreement and their acceptance of the principles embodied therein.

In 1901, when the Manchurian Convention was being negotiated by the Russian and Chinese Governments, involving the grant of certain exclusive privileges relating to the opening of mines and the building of railroads in Manchuria, the Japanese Minister called on the Secretary of State of the United States and said that the Japanese Government considered that the convention was a most undesirable thing because it was a violation of the understanding among all the Powers that the integrity of the Chinese Empire should be preserved, and that the Japanese Government was anxious that some means should be taken by the different Powers to induce China to delay the final signature of the convention beyond the period assigned by Russia as an ultimatum for signing.

On the same subject a circular note was sent by the United States to Belgium, China, France, Germany, Great Britain, Italy, Japan, the Netherlands, Russia and Spain, as follows:

An agreement by which China cedes to any corporation or company the exclusive right and privilege of opening mines, establishing railroads, or in any other way industrially developing Manchuria, can but be viewed with the gravest concern by the Government of the United States. It constitutes a monopoly, which is a distinct breach of the stipulations of treaties concluded between China and foreign Powers, and thereby seriously affects the rights of American citizens; it restricts their rightful trade and exposes it to being discriminated against, interfered with or otherwise jeopardized, and strongly tends towards permanently impairing the sovereign rights of China in this part of the Empire, and seriously interferes with her ability to meet her international obligations. Furthermore, such concession on the part of China will undoubtedly be followed by demands from other Powers for similar and equally exclusive advantages in other parts of the Chinese Empire, and the inevitable result must be the complete wreck of the policy of absolute equality of treatment of all nations in regard to trade, navigation, and commerce within the confines of the Empire.

On the other hand, the attainment by one Power of such exclusive privileges for a commercial organization of its nationality conflicts with the assurances repeatedly conveyed to this Government by the Imperial Russian Ministry of Foreign Affairs of the Imperial Government's intention to follow the policy of the open door in China, as advocated by the Government of the United States and accepted by all the Treaty Powers having commercial interests in that Empire.

It is for these reasons that the Government of the United States, animated now, as in the past, with the sincerest desire of insuring to the whole world the benefits of full and fair intercourse between China and the nations on a footing of equal rights and advantages to all, submits the above to the earnest consideration of the Imperial Governments of China and Russia, confident that they will give due weight to its importance and adopt such measures as will relieve the just and natural anxiety of the United States.

The foregoing constitute the beginnings of the policy of the United States and other Powers interested in the welfare of China for the maintenance of the territorial integrity and administrative entity of China, and equal opportunities in commerce and industries in her behalf. To this policy the Powers have generally given their formal acceptance and support.

It is only necessary to refer to the British-Japanese Treaty of 1902, the Japanese Declarations at the opening of the Russo-Japanese war, the British-Japanese Treaty of 1905, the Russo-Japanese Treaty of Portsmouth, of 1905, the Franco-Japanese Entente of 1907, and the Russo-Japanese Treaty of 1907, in which Japan confirmed her special interest in maintaining the political independence and territorial integrity of the Empire of China, and in securing equal opportunities to all nations in the commercial and industrial development of China.

Finally, the United States and Japan declared their policy in the Far East by an exchange of notes on November 30, 1908, between the Honorable Elihu Root, then Secretary of State, and Baron Kogoro Takahira, the Ambassador of Japan. These notes contain the following language:

4. They are also determined to preserve the common interest of all Powers in China by supporting by all pacific means at their disposal the independence and integrity of China and the principle of equal opportunity for commerce and industry of all nations in that Empire.

5. Should any event occur threatening the status quo as above described or the principle of equal opportunity as above defined, it remains for the two Governments to communicate with each other in order to arrive at an understanding as to what measures they may consider useful to take.

I assume that it is because they wish to act in the spirit of this agreement to communicate with each other in reference to any event which may threaten these principles that your excellency's Government has informed this Government of the above-mentioned proposals which have been made to China. It is with the same purpose also, and on the further ground that the United States feels itself under a moral obligation to the Powers whose pledges are deposited with it not to pass over in silence any threatened violation of these pledges, that I address this communication to you with a view to carrying out the agreement of 1908 in accordance with that mutual regard and friendship which inspired it.

The United States, confident that the principle of mutuality will be preserved by Japan, believes that it may rely upon the often repeated assurances of your excellency's Government relative to the independence, integrity and commerce of China, and that no steps will be taken contrary to the spirit of those assurances.

For two generations American missionaries and teachers have made sacrifices in behalf of religious and educational work in China. American capital has been invested and industries have been established in certain regions. The activity of Americans has never been political, but on the contrary has been primarily commercial with no afterthought as to their effect upon the governmental policy of China. As an outgrowth of these two interests Americans have become concerned in the legitimate participation in the economic development of China along broader lines. Many projects which in other countries are left to private enterprise are in China conducted necessarily under government direction. United States citizens and capital are thus engaged in certain public improvements, such as the Huai River conservancy, the Hukuang Railway project, etc. A fourth matter of great moment to the United States is its broad and extensive treaty rights with China. These in general relate to commercial privileges and to the protection of Americans in China. In view of these treaty rights and its increasing economic interests in China, this Government has noted with grave concern certain of the suggestions which Japan has, in the present critical stage of the growth and development of the new Republic, considered it advisable to lay before the Chinese Government. While on principle and under the treaties of 1844, 1858, 1868 and 1903 with China the United States has ground upon which to base objections to the Japanese "demands" relative to Shantung, South Manchuria, and East Mongolia, nevertheless the United States frankly recognizes that territorial contiguity creates special relations between Japan and these districts. This Government, therefore, is disposed to raise no question, at this time, as to Articles I and II of the Japanese proposals. Further, as to Article IV, and Article V, paragraphs 2, 5 and 7, this Government perceives no special menace to the existing rights and interests of the United States or of its citizens in China. On the other hand Article V, paragraph 4, restricting the purchase of arms and ammunition to purchases from Japan, and paragraph 6 contemplating a monopoly of the development of the province of Fukien, the United States Government considers, would, if they should become operative, be violations of the principle of equal opportunity for the commerce and industries of other nations. American citizens may claim a right to share in the commercial development not only in Fukien but in other provinces as well. The United States is not unmindful that many serious disadvantages would result to its commercial and industrial enterprises if special preference is given to one nation in the matter of concessions. An example is shown in the operation of the South Manchuria Railway whereby discriminations have been made for some time against freight brought into Manchuria in other than Japanese vessels. This case indicates the embarrassing results of concessions of a broad preference or option. The United States, as well as every other nation, has the right to have its citizens free to make contracts with the Central and Provincial Governments without having the exercise of their rights interrupted or regarded as unfriendly by a third power; for each American enterprise in China is treated on its own merits as to its usefulness and prospective benefit, and without any regard to the possible effect it might have on China's future political status in the Orient.

The rights and privileges, which are set forth in these two paragraphs and which Japan seeks to obtain from China, are in conflict with rights of Americans secured by treaties between the United States and China.

Article XV of the Treaty of 1844 reads as follows:

> The former limitation of the trade of foreign nations to certain persons appointed at Canton by the Government and commonly called Hong-merchants, having been abolished, citizens of the United States, engaged in the purchase or sale of goods of import or export, are admitted to trade with any and all subjects of China without distinction; they shall not be subject to any new limitations, nor impeded in their business by monopolies or other injurious restrictions.

Article XXX of the Treaty of 1858 reads as follows:

> The contracting parties hereby agree that should at any time the Ta Tsing Empire grant to any nation or the merchants or citizens of any nation, any right, privilege or favor, connected either with navigation, commerce, political or other intercourse which is not conferred by this treaty, such right, privilege and favor shall at once freely enure to the benefit of the United States, its public officers, merchants and citizens.

Article VIII of the Treaty of 1868 reads as follows:

> The United States, always disclaiming and discouraging all practices of unnecessary dictation and intervention by one nation in the affairs or domestic administration of another, do hereby freely disclaim and disavow any intention or right to intervene in the domestic administration of China in regard to the construction of railroads, telegraphs or other material internal improvements. On the other hand, his Majesty, the Emperor of China, reserves to himself the right to decide the time and manner and circumstances of introducing such improvements within his dominions. With this mutual understanding it is agreed by the contracting parties that if at any time hereafter his Imperial Majesty shall determine to construct or cause to be constructed works of the character mentioned within the empire, and shall make application to the United States or any other western Power for facilities to carry out that policy, the United States will, in that case, designate and authorize suitable engineers to be employed by the Chinese Government, and will recommend to other nations an equal compliance with such application, the Chinese Government in that case

protecting such engineers in their persons and property, and paying them a reasonable compensation for their service.

Articles III and VII of the Treaty of 1903 read as follows:

Article III. Citizens of the United States may frequent, reside and carry on trade, industries and manufactures, or pursue any lawful avocation, in all the ports or localities of China which are now open or may hereafter be opened to foreign residence and trade; and within the suitable localities at those places which have been or may be set apart for the use and occupation of foreigners, they may rent or purchase houses, places of business and other buildings, and rent or lease in perpetuity land and build thereon. They shall generally enjoy as to their persons and property all such rights, privileges and immunities as are or may hereafter be granted to the subjects or citizens of the nation the most favored in these respects.

Article VII. The Chinese Government, recognizing that it is advantageous for the country to develop its mineral resources, and that it is desirable to attract foreign as well as Chinese capital to embark in mining enterprises, agrees, within one year from the signing of this treaty, to initiate and conclude the revision of the existing mining regulations. To this end China will, with all expedition and earnestness, go into the whole question of mining rules; and, selecting from the rules of the United States and other countries regulations which seem applicable to the condition of China, will recast its present mining rules in such a way as, while promoting the interests of Chinese subjects and not injuring in any way the sovereign rights of China, will offer no impediment to the attraction of foreign capital nor place foreign capitalists at a greater disadvantage than they would be under generally accepted foreign regulations; and will permit citizens of the United States to carry on in Chinese territory mining operations and other necessary business relating thereto provided they comply with the new regulations and conditions which will be imposed by China on its subjects and foreigners alike, relating to the opening of mines, the renting of mineral land, and the payment of royalty, and provided they apply for permits, the provisions of which in regard to necessary business relating to such operations shall be observed. The residence of citizens of the United States in connection with such mining operations shall be subject to such regulations as shall be agreed upon by and between the United States and China.

Any mining concessions granted after the publication of such new rules shall be subject to their provisions.

It is manifest that these articles including "most favored nation" treatment entitle Americans to claim from China the same rights as those which Japan now seeks to have granted exclusively to her subjects.

It remains to call attention to Article III forbidding the alienation or lease of any port, harbor or island on the coast of China, and to Article V, paragraph 1, requiring China to employ competent Japanese subjects as advisers for conducting administrative, financial and military affairs, and paragraph 3 suggesting the joint policing of China, "where it is deemed necessary."

With reference to the first of these three proposals, Baron Kato has explained to the American Ambassador at Tokyo that Japan has no desire for a naval station on the coast of China, either at Tsingtau, or south of that point, as it would be valueless to her, but that it would however object to another nation having such a station. With reference to the employment of advisers the United States believes it may be assumed that the Chinese Government will not discriminate unfairly in their selection, although it should be pointed out that this Government understands that Japan has six out of twenty-five advisers to the Republic representing eight nations. In respect to the proposed joint policing of certain places where there has been some friction between Japanese and Chinese, this Government feels apprehensive that this plan, instead of tending to lessen such friction might create greater difficulties than those which it is desired to remove.

But what is more important is the fact that these proposals, if accepted by China, while not infringing the territorial integrity of the Republic, are clearly derogatory to the political independence and administrative entity of that country. The same is in a measure true of Paragraph 4 of Article V relative to the purchase of arms. It is difficult for the United States, therefore, to reconcile these requests with the maintenance of the unimpaired sovereignty of China, which Japan, together with the United States and the Great Powers of Europe, has reaffirmed from time to time during the past decade and a half in formal declarations, treaties and exchanges of diplomatic notes. The United States, therefore, could not regard with indifference the assumption of political, military or economic domination over China by a foreign Power, and hopes that your excellency's Government will find it consonant with their interests to refrain from pressing upon China an acceptance of proposals which would, if accepted, exclude Americans from equal participation in the economic and industrial development of China and would limit the political independence of that country.

The United States is convinced that an attempt to coerce China to submit to these proposals would result in engendering resentment on the part of the Chinese and opposition by other interested Powers, thereby creating a situation which this Government confidently believes the Imperial Government do not desire.

The United States Government embraces this opportunity to make known that it has viewed the aspirations of Japan in the Far East with that friendship and esteem which have characterized the relations of the two nations in the past. This Government cannot too earnestly impress upon your excellency's Government that the United States is not jealous of the prominence of Japan in the East or of the intimate cooperation of China and Japan for their mutual benefit. Nor has the United States any intention of obstructing or embarrassing Japan, or of influencing China in opposition to Japan. On the contrary the policy of the United States, as set forth in this note, is directed to the maintenance of the independence, integrity and commercial freedom of China and the preservation of legitimate American rights and interests in that Republic.

Accept [etc.] W. J. BRYAN.

12

Secretary Bryan to the Ambassador in Japan (Guthrie)[16]

WASHINGTON, *May 11, 1915—5 p. m.*

Please call upon the Minister for Foreign Affairs and present to him a note textually as follows:

"In view of the circumstances of the negotiations which have taken place and which are now pending between the Government of Japan and the Government of China, and of the agreements which have been reached as a result thereof, the Government of the United States has the honor to notify the Imperial Japanese Government that it cannot recognize any agreement or undertaking which

---

[16] *Ibid.*, 1915, p. 146.

has been entered into or which may be entered into between the Governments of Japan and China, impairing the treaty rights of the United States and its citizens in China, the political or territorial integrity of the Republic of China, or the international policy relative to China commonly known as the open door policy.

"An identical note has been transmitted to the Government of the Chinese Republic."
BRYAN.

13

Lansing-Ishii Agreement, November 2, 1917

Secretary Lansing to Viscount Ishii, Japanese Ambassador on Special Mission [17]

WASHINGTON, *November 2, 1917.*

EXCELLENCY: I have the honor to communicate herein my understanding of the agreement reached by us in our recent conversations touching the questions of mutual interest to our Governments relating to the Republic of China.

In order to silence mischievous reports that have from time to time been circulated, it is believed by us that a public announcement once more of the desires and intentions shared by our two Governments with regard to China is advisible.

The Governments of the United States and Japan recognize that territorial propinquity creates special relations between countries, and, consequently, the Government of the United States recognizes that Japan has special interests in China, particularly in the part to which her possessions are contiguous.

The territorial sovereignty of China, nevertheless, remains unimpaired and the Government of the United States has every confidence in the repeated assurances of the Imperial Japanese Government that while geographical position gives Japan such special interests they have no desire to discriminate against the trade of other nations or to disregard the commercial rights heretofore granted by China in treaties with other powers.

The Governments of the United States and Japan deny that they have any purpose to infringe in any way the independence or territorial integrity of China and they declare, furthermore, that they always adhere to the principle of the so-called "open door" or equal opportunity for commerce and industry in China.

Moreover, they mutually declare that they are opposed to the acquisition by any Government of any special rights or privileges that would affect the independence or territorial integrity of China or that would deny to the subjects or citizens of any country the full enjoyment of equal opportunity in the commerce and industry of China.

I shall be glad to have your excellency confirm this understanding of the agreement reached by us.

Accept [etc.]
ROBERT LANSING.

Viscount Ishii, Japanese Ambassador on Special Mission, to Secretary Lansing [18]

WASHINGTON, *November 2, 1917.*

SIR: I have the honor to acknowledge the receipt of your note of to-day, communicating to me your understanding of the agreement reached by us in our

---
[17] *Ibid.*, 1917, p. 264.
[18] *Ibid.*

recent conversations touching the questions of mutual interest to our Governments relating to the Republic of China.

I am happy to be able to confirm to you, under authorization of my Government, the understanding in question set forth in the following terms:

In order to silence mischievous reports that have from time to time been circulated, it is believed by us that a public announcement once more of the desires and intentions shared by our two Governments with regard to China is advisable.

The Governments of Japan and the United States recognize that territorial propinquity creates special relations between countries, and, consequently, the Government of the United States recognizes that Japan has special interests in China, particularly in the part to which her possessions are contiguous.

The territorial sovereignty of China, nevertheless, remains unimpaired and the Government of the United States has every confidence in the repeated assurances of the Imperial Japanese Government that while geographical position gives Japan such special interests they have no desire to discriminate against the trade of other nations or to disregard the commercial rights heretofore granted by China in treaties with other Powers.

The Governments of Japan and the United States deny that they have any purpose to infringe in any way the independence or territorial integrity of China and they declare, furthermore, that they always adhere to the principle of the so-called "open door" or equal opportunity for commerce and industry in China.

Moreover, they mutually declare that they are opposed to the acquisition by any government of any special rights or privileges that would affect the independence or territorial integrity of China or that would deny to the subjects or citizens of any country the full enjoyment of equal opportunity in the commerce and industry of China.

I take [etc.]   K. Ishii

14

Nine-Power Treaty Signed at Washington, February 6, 1922 [19]

The United States of America, Belgium, the British Empire, China, France, Italy, Japan, the Netherlands and Portugal:

Desiring to adopt a policy designed to stabilize conditions in the Far East, to safeguard the rights and interests of China, and to promote intercourse between China and the other Powers upon the basis of equality of opportunity;

Have resolved to conclude a treaty for that purpose and to that end have appointed as their respective Plenipotentiaries:

The President of the United States of America:
    Charles Evans Hughes,
    Henry Cabot Lodge,
    Oscar W. Underwood,
    Elihu Root,
        citizens of the United States;

His Majesty the King of the Belgians:
    Baron de Cartier de Marchienne, Commander of the Order of Leopold and of the Order of the Crown, His Ambassador Extraordinary and Plenipotentiary at Washington;

---

[19] *Ibid.*, 1922, vol. I, p. 276.

ANNEXES 439

His Majesty the King of the United Kingdom of Great Britain and Ireland and of the British Dominions beyond the Seas, Emperor of India:
 The Right Honourable Arthur James Balfour, O. M., M. P., Lord President of His Privy Council;
 The Right Honourable Baron Lee of Fareham, G. B. E., K. C. B., First Lord of His Admiralty;
 The Right Honourable Sir Auckland Campbell Geddes, K. C. B., His Ambassador Extraordinary and Plenipotentiary to the United States of America;

and
 for the Dominion of Canada:
  The Right Honourable Sir Robert Laird Borden, G. C. M. G., K. C.;
 for the Commonwealth of Australia:
  Senator the Right Honourable George Foster Pearce, Minister for Home and Territories;
 for the Dominion of New Zealand:
  The Honourable Sir John William Salmond, K. C., Judge of the Supreme Court of New Zealand;
 for the Union of South Africa:
  The Right Honourable Arthur James Balfour, O. M., M. P.;
 for India:
  The Right Honourable Valingman Sankaranarayana Srinivasa Sastri, Member of the Indian Council of State;

The President of the Republic of China:
 Mr. Sao-Ke Alfred Sze, Envoy Extraordinary and Minister Plenipotentiary at Washington;
 Mr. V. K. Wellington Koo, Envoy Extraordinary and Minister Plenipotentiary at London;
 Mr. Chung-Hui Wang, former Minister of Justice.

The President of the French Republic:
 Mr. Albert Sarraut, Deputy, Minister of the Colonies;
 Mr. Jules J. Jusserand, Ambassador Extraordinary and Plenipotentiary to the United States of America, Grand Cross of the National Order of the Legion of Honour;

His Majesty the King of Italy:
 The Honourable Carlo Schanzer, Senator of the Kingdom;
 The Honourable Vittorio Rolandi Ricci, Senator of the Kingdom, His Ambassador Extraordinary and Plenipotentiary at Washington;
 The Honourable Luigi Albertini, Senator of the Kingdom;

His Majesty the Emperor of Japan:
 Baron Tomosaburo Kato, Minister for the Navy, Junii, a member of the First Class of the Imperial Order of the Grand Cordon of the Rising Sun with the Paulownia Flower;
 Baron Kijuro Shidehara, His Ambassador Extraordinary and Plenipotentiary at Washington, Joshii, a member of the First Class of the Imperial Order of the Rising Sun;
 Mr. Masanao Hanihara, Vice Minister for Foreign Affairs, Jushii, a member of the Second Class of the Imperial Order of the Rising Sun;

Her Majesty the Queen of The Netherlands:
 Jonkheer Frans Beelaerts van Blokland, Her Envoy Extraordinary and Minister Plenipotentiary;

Jonkheer Willem Hendrik de Beaufort, Minister Plenipotentiary, Chargé d'Affaires at Washington;

The President of the Portuguese Republic:
Mr. José Francisco de Horta Machado da Franca, Viscount d'Alte, Envoy Extraordinary and Minister Plenipotentiary at Washington;
Mr. Ernesto Julio de Carvalho e Vasconcellos, Captain of the Portuguese Navy, Technical Director of the Colonial Office.

Who, having communicated to each other their full powers, found to be in good and due form, have agreed as follows:

Article I

The Contracting Powers, other than China, agree:
(1) To respect the sovereignty, the independence, and the territorial and administrative integrity of China;
(2) To provide the fullest and most unembarrassed opportunity to China to develop and maintain for herself an effective and stable government;
(3) To use their influence for the purpose of effectually establishing and maintaining the principle of equal opportunity for the commerce and industry of all nations throughout the territory of China;
(4) To refrain from taking advantage of conditions in China in order to seek special rights or privileges which would abridge the rights of subjects or citizens of friendly States, and from countenancing action inimical to the security of such States.

Article II

The Contracting Powers agree not to enter into any treaty, agreement, arrangement, or understanding, either with one another, or, individually or collectively, with any Power or Powers, which would infringe or impair the principles stated in Article I.

Article III

With a view to applying more effectually the principles of the Open Door or equality of opportunity in China for the trade and industry of all nations, the Contracting Powers, other than China, agree that they will not seek, nor support their respective nationals in seeking—
(a) any arrangement which might purport to establish in favour of their interests any general superiority of rights with respect to commercial or economic development in any designated region of China;
(b) any such monopoly or preference as would deprive the nationals of any other Power of the right of undertaking any legitimate trade or industry in China, or of participating with the Chinese Government, or with any local authority, in any category of public enterprise, or which by reason of its scope, duration or geographical extent is calculated to frustrate the practical application of the principle of equal opportunity.

It is understood that the foregoing stipulations of this Article are not to be so construed as to prohibit the acquisition of such properties or rights as may be necessary to the conduct of a particular commercial, industrial, or financial undertaking or to the encouragement of invention and research.

China undertakes to be guided by the principles stated in the foregoing stipulations of this Article in dealing with applications for economic rights and privileges from Governments and nationals of all foreign countries, whether parties to the present Treaty or not.

Article IV

The Contracting Powers agree not to support any agreements by their respective nationals with each other designed to create Spheres of Influence or to provide for the enjoyment of mutually exclusive opportunities in designated parts of Chinese territory.

Article V

China agrees that, throughout the whole of the railways in China, she will not exercise or permit unfair discrimination of any kind. In particular there shall be no discrimination whatever, direct or indirect, in respect of charges or of facilities on the ground of the nationality of passengers or the countries from which or to which they are proceeding, or the origin or ownership of goods or the country from which or to which they are consigned, or the nationality or ownership of the ship or other means of conveying such passengers or goods before or after their transport on the Chinese Railways.

The Contracting Powers, other than China, assume a corresponding obligation in respect of any of the aforesaid railways over which they or their nationals are in a position to exercise any control in virtue of any concession, special agreement or otherwise.

Article VI

The Contracting Powers, other than China, agree fully to respect China's rights as a neutral in time of war to which China is not a party; and China declares that when she is a neutral she will observe the obligations of neutrality.

Article VII

The Contracting Powers agree that, whenever a situation arises which in the opinion of any one of them involves the application of the stipulations of the present Treaty, and renders desirable discussion of such application, there shall be full and frank communication between the Contracting Powers concerned.

Article VIII

Powers not signatory to the present Treaty, which have Governments recognized by the Signatory Powers and which have treaty relations with China, shall be invited to adhere to the present Treaty. To this end the Government of the United States will make the necessary communications to nonsignatory Powers and will inform the Contracting Powers of the replies received. Adherence by any Power shall become effective on receipt of notice thereof by the Government of the United States.

Article IX

The present Treaty shall be ratified by the Contracting Powers in accordance with their respective constitutional methods and shall take effect on the date of the deposit of all the ratifications, which shall take place at Washington as soon as possible. The Government of the United States will transmit to the other Contracting Powers a certified copy of the *procès-verbal* of the deposit of ratifications.

The present Treaty, of which the French and English texts are both authentic, shall remain deposited in the archives of the Government of the United States, and duly certified copies thereof shall be transmitted by that Government to the other Contracting Powers.

IN FAITH WHEREOF the above-named Plenipotentiaries have signed the present Treaty.

DONE at the City of Washington the Sixth day of February One Thousand Nine Hundred and Twenty-Two.

	CHARLES EVANS HUGHES	[SEAL]
	HENRY CABOT LODGE	[SEAL]
	OSCAR W UNDERWOOD	[SEAL]
	ELIHU ROOT	[SEAL]
	BARON DE CARTIER DE MARCHIENNE	[SEAL]
	ARTHUR JAMES BALFOUR	[SEAL]
	LEE OF FAREHAM	[SEAL]
	A. C. GEDDES	[SEAL]
	R. L. BORDEN	[SEAL]
	G. F. PEARCE	[SEAL]
	JOHN W SALMOND	[SEAL]
	ARTHUR JAMES BALFOUR	[SEAL]
	V S SRINIVASA SASTRI	[SEAL]
[SEAL]	SAO-KE ALFRED SZE	
[SEAL]	V. K. WELLINGTON KOO	
[SEAL]	CHUNG-HUI WANG	
[SEAL]	A SARRAUT	
[SEAL]	JUSSERAND	
[SEAL]	CARLO SCHANZER	
[SEAL]	V. ROLANDI RICCI	
[SEAL]	LUIGI ALBERTINI	
	T. KATO	[SEAL]
	K. SHIDEHARA	[SEAL]
	M. HANIHARA	[SEAL]
	BEELAERTS VAN BLOKLAND	[SEAL]
	W. DE BEAUFORT	[SEAL]
	ALTE	[SEAL]
	ERNESTO DE VASCONCELLOS	[SEAL]

15

Statement by Secretary Kellogg, January 27, 1927 [20]

At this time, when there is so much discussion of the Chinese situation, I deem it my duty to state clearly the position of the Department of State on the questions of tariff autonomy and the relinquishment of extraterritorial rights.

The United States has always desired the unity, the independence and prosperity of the Chinese nation. It has desired that tariff control and extraterritoriality provided by our treaties with China should as early as possible be released. It was with that in view that the United States made the declaration in relation to the relinquishment of extraterritoriality in the Treaty of 1903 and also entered into the Treaty of Washington of February 6, 1922, providing for a Tariff Conference to be held within three months after the coming into force of the Treaty.

---

[20] *Ibid.*, 1927, vol. II, p. 350.

The United States is now and has been, ever since the negotiation of the Washington Treaty, prepared to enter into negotiations with any Government of China or delegates who can represent or speak for China not only for the putting into force of the surtaxes of the Washington Treaty but entirely releasing tariff control and restoring complete tariff autonomy to China.

The United States would expect, however, that it be granted most favored nation treatment and that there should be no discrimination against the United States and its citizens in customs duties, or taxes, in favor of the citizens of other nations or discrimination by grants of special privileges and that the open door with equal opportunity for trade in China shall be maintained; and further that China should afford every protection to American citizens, to their property and rights.

The United States is prepared to put into force the recommendations of the Extraterritoriality Commission which can be put into force without a treaty at once and to negotiate the release of extraterritorial rights as soon as China is prepared to provide protection by law and through her courts to American citizens, their rights and property.

The willingness of the United States to deal with China in the most liberal spirit will be borne out by a brief history of the events since making the Washington Treaty. That Treaty was ratified by the last one of the Signatory Powers on July 7, 1925, and the exchange of ratifications took place in Washington on August 6, 1925. Before the treaties finally went into effect and on June 24, 1925, the Chinese Government addressed identic notes to the Signatory Powers asking for the revision of existing treaties. On the first of July 1925, I sent instructions to our Minister in Peking, which instructions I also communicated to all the other Governments, urging that this should be made the occasion of evidencing to the Chinese our willingness to consider the question of treaty revision. I urged that the Powers expedite preparations for the holding of the Special Conference regarding the Chinese customs tariff and stated that the United States believed that this special tariff conference should be requested, after accomplishing the work required by the Treaty to make concrete recommendations upon which a program for granting complete tariff autonomy might be worked out. The Delegates of the United States were given full powers to negotiate a new treaty recognizing China's tariff autonomy. At the same time, I urged the appointment of the Commission to investigate extraterritoriality, with the understanding that the Commission should be authorized to include in its report recommendations for the gradual relinquishment of extraterritorial rights. Prior to this, the Chinese Government urged the United States to use its influence with the interested Powers to hasten the calling of the Conference on Tariff Matters and the appointment of the Extraterritorial Commission and for each Government to grant to its representatives the broad power to consider the whole subject of the revision of the treaties and to make recommendations upon the subject of the abolition of extraterritorial rights. This was in harmony with the views of the United States. Accordingly, on September 4, 1925, the United States and each of the other Powers having tariff treaties with China evidenced their intention to appoint their delegates to the Tariff Conference. By a note which has been published, the Powers informed China of their willingness to consider and discuss any reasonable proposal that might be made by the Chinese Government on the revision of the treaties on the subject of the tariff and also announced their intention of appointing their representatives to the Extraterritorial Commission for the purpose of considering the whole subject of extraterritorial rights and authorizing them to make recommendations for the purpose of enabling the governments concerned to consider what, if any, steps might be taken with a view to the relinquishment of extraterritorial rights. Delegates were promptly appointed and the Chinese Tariff Conference met on October 26, 1925.

Shortly after the opening of the Conference and on November 3, 1925, the American Delegation proposed that the Conference at once authorize the levying of a surtax of two and one-half per cent on necessaries, and, as soon as the requisite schedules could be prepared, authorize the levying of a surtax of up to five per cent on luxuries, as provided for by the Washington Treaty. Our Delegates furthermore announced that the Government of the United States was prepared to proceed at once with the negotiation of such an agreement or agreements as might be necessary for making effective other provisions of the Washington Treaty of February 6, 1922. They affirmed the principle of respect for China's tariff autonomy and announced that they were prepared forthwith to negotiate a new treaty which would give effect to that principle and which should make provision for the abolition of likin, for the removal of tariff restrictions contained in existing treaties and for the putting into effect of the Chinese National Tariff Law. On November 19, 1925, the Committee on Provisional Measures of the Conference, Chinese delegates participating, unanimously adopted the following resolution:

"The Delegates of the Powers assembled at this Conference resolve to adopt the following proposed article relating to tariff autonomy with a view to incorporating it, together with other matters, to be hereafter agreed upon, in a treaty which is to be signed at this Conference.

"The Contracting Powers other than China hereby recognize China's right to enjoy tariff autonomy; agree to remove the tariff restrictions which are contained in existing treaties between themselves respectively and China; and consent to the going into effect of the Chinese National Tariff Law on January 1st, 1929.

"The Government of the Republic of China declares that likin shall be abolished simultaneously with the enforcement of the Chinese National Tariff Law; and further declares that the abolition of likin shall be effectively carried out by the First Day of the First Month of the Eighteenth Year of the Republic of China (January 1st, 1929)."

Continuously from the beginning of the Conference, our delegates and technical advisers collaborated with the delegates and technical advisers of the other Powers, including China, in an effort to carry out this plan,—viz. to put into effect the surtaxes provided for in the Washington Treaty, and to provide for additional tariff adequate for all of China's needs until tariff autonomy should go into effect. Until about the middle of April 1926, there was every prospect for the successful termination of the Conference to the satisfaction of the Chinese and the other Powers. About that time the Government which represented China at the Conference was forced out of power. The delegates of the United States and the other Powers, however, remained in China in the hope of continuing the negotiations and on July 3, 1926, made a declaration as follows:

"The Delegates of the foreign Powers to the Chinese Customs Tariff Conference met at the Netherlands Legation this morning. They expressed the unanimous and earnest desire to proceed with the work of the Conference at the earliest possible moment when the Delegates of the Chinese Government are in a position to resume discussion with the foreign Delegates of the problems before the Conference."

The Government of the United States was ready then and is ready now to continue the negotiations on the entire subject of the tariff and extraterritoriality or to take up negotiations on behalf of the United States alone. The only question is with whom it shall negotiate. As I have said heretofore, if China can agree upon the appointment of delegates representing the authorities or the people of the country, we are prepared to negotiate such a treaty. However, existing treaties which were ratified by the Senate of the United States cannot be abrogated by the President but must be superseded by new treaties negotiated with somebody representing China and subsequently ratified by the Senate of the United States.

The Government of the United States has watched with sympathetic interest the nationalistic awakening of China and welcomes every advance made by the Chinese people toward reorganizing their system of Government.

During the difficult years since the establishment of the new regime in 1912, the Government of the United States has endeavored in every way to maintain an attitude of the most careful and strict neutrality as among the several factions that have disputed with one another for control in China. The Government of the United States expects, however, that the people of China and their leaders will recognize the right of American citizens in China to protection for life and property during the period of conflict for which they are not responsible. In the event that the Chinese Authorities are unable to afford such protection, it is of course the fundamental duty of the United States to protect the lives and property of its citizens. It is with the possible necessity for this in view that American naval forces are now in Chinese waters. This Government wishes to deal with China in a most liberal spirit. It holds no concessions in China and has never manifested any imperialistic attitude toward that country. It desires, however, that its citizens be given equal opportunity with the citizens of the other Powers to reside in China and to pursue their legitimate occupations without special privileges, monopolies or spheres of special interest or influence.

16

Treaty Between the United States and China Regulating Tariff Relations, Signed at Peiping, July 25, 1928 [21]

The United States of America and the Republic of China, both being animated by an earnest desire to maintain the good relations which happily subsist between the two countries, and wishing to extend and consolidate the commercial intercourse between them, have, for the purpose of negotiating a treaty designed to facilitate these objects, named as their Plenipotentiaries:—

The President of the United States of America:

J. V. A. MacMurray, Envoy Extraordinary and Minister Plenipotentiary of the United States of America to China;

and the Government Council of the Nationalist Government of the Republic of China:

T. V. Soong, Minister of Finance of the Nationalist Government of the Republic of China;

who, having met and duly exchanged their full powers, which have been found to be in proper form, have agreed upon the following treaty between the two countries:

---

[21] *Ibid.*, 1928, vol. II, p. 475.

Article I

All provisions which appear in treaties hitherto concluded and in force between the United States of America and China relating to rates of duty on imports and exports of merchandise, drawbacks, transit dues and tonnage dues in China shall be annulled and become inoperative, and the principle of complete national tariff autonomy shall apply subject, however, to the condition that each of the High Contracting Parties shall enjoy in the territories of the other with respect to the above specified and any related matters treatment in no way discriminatory as compared with the treatment accorded to any other country.

The nationals of neither of the High Contracting Parties shall be compelled under any pretext whatever to pay within the territories of the other Party any duties, internal charges or taxes upon their importations and exportations other or higher than those paid by nationals of the country or by nationals of any other country.

The above provisions shall become effective on January 1, 1929, provided that the exchange of ratifications hereinafter provided shall have taken place by that date; otherwise, at a date four months subsequent to such exchange of ratifications.

Article II

The English and Chinese texts of this Treaty have been carefully compared and verified; but, in the event of there being a difference of meaning between the two, the sense as expressed in the English text shall be held to prevail.

This treaty shall be ratified by the High Contracting Parties in accordance with their respective constitutional methods, and the ratifications shall be exchanged in Washington as soon as possible.

In testimony whereof, we, the undersigned, by virtue of our respective powers have signed this Treaty in duplicate in the English and Chinese languages and have affixed our respective seals.

Done at Peiping, the 25th day of July, 1928, corresponding to the 25th day of the 7th month of the 17th year of the Republic of China.

[SEAL]   J. V. A. MacMurray

[SEAL]   Tse Ven Soong

17

Secretary Stimson to the Ambassador in Japan (Forbes)[22]

Washington, *January 7, 1932—noon.*

7. Please deliver to the Foreign Office on behalf of your Government as soon as possible the following note:

"With the recent military operations about Chinchow, the last remaining administrative authority of the Government of the Chinese Republic in South Manchuria, as it existed prior to September 18th, 1931, has been destroyed. The American Government continues confident that the work of the neutral commission recently authorized by the Council of the League of Nations will facilitate an ultimate solution of the difficulties now existing between China and Japan. But in view of the present situation and of its own rights and obligations therein, the American Government deems it to be its duty to notify both the Imperial

---

[22] *Foreign Relations of the United States, Japan,* 1931–1941, vol. I, p. 76.

Japanese Government and the Government of the Chinese Republic that it cannot admit the legality of any situation *de facto* nor does it intend to recognize any treaty or agreement entered into between those Governments, or agents thereof, which may impair the treaty rights of the United States or its citizens in China, including those which relate to the sovereignty, the independence, or the territorial and administrative integrity of the Republic of China, or to the international policy relative to China, commonly known as the open door policy; and that it does not intend to recognize any situation, treaty or agreement which may be brought about by means contrary to the covenants and obligations of the Pact of Paris of August 27, 1928, to which Treaty both China and Japan, as well as the United States, are parties."

State that an identical note is being sent to the Chinese government.

STIMSON

18

Secretary Stimson to Senator Borah, Chairman of the Committee on Foreign Relations of the Senate, February 23, 1932 [23]

You have asked my opinion whether, as has been sometimes recently suggested, present conditions in China have in any way indicated that the so-called Nine Power Treaty has become inapplicable or ineffective or rightly in need of modification, and if so, what I considered should be the policy of this Government.

This Treaty, as you of course know, forms the legal basis upon which now rests the "Open Door" policy towards China. That policy, enunciated by John Hay in 1899, brought to an end the struggle among various powers for so-called spheres of interest in China which was threatening the dismemberment of that empire. To accomplish this Mr. Hay invoked two principles (1) equality of commercial opportunity among all nations in dealing with China, and (2) as necessary to that equality the preservation of China's territorial and administrative integrity. These principles were not new in the foreign policy of America. They had been the principles upon which it rested in its dealings with other nations for many years. In the case of China they were invoked to save a situation which not only threatened the future development and sovereignty of that great Asiatic people, but also threatened to create dangerous and constantly increasing rivalries between the other nations of the world. War had already taken place between Japan and China. At the close of that war three other nations intervened to prevent Japan from obtaining some of the results of that war claimed by her. Other nations sought and had obtained spheres of interest. Partly as a result of these actions a serious uprising had broken out in China which endangered the legations of all of the powers at Peking. While the attack on those legations was in progress, Mr. Hay made an announcement in respect to this policy as the principle upon which the powers should act in the settlement of the rebellion. He said

"The policy of the Government of the United States is to seek a solution which may bring about permanent safety and peace to China, preserve Chinese territorial and administrative entity, protect all rights guaranteed to friendly powers by treaty and international law, and safeguard for the world the principle of equal and impartial trade with all parts of the Chinese Empire."

He was successful in obtaining the assent of the other powers to the policy thus announced.

[23] *Ibid.*, p. 83.

In taking these steps Mr. Hay acted with the cordial support of the British Government. In responding to Mr. Hay's announcement, above set forth, Lord Salisbury, the British Prime Minister expressed himself "most emphatically as concurring in the policy of the United States."

For twenty years thereafter the Open Door policy rested upon the informal commitments thus made by the various powers. But in the winter of 1921 to 1922, at a conference participated in by all of the principal powers which had interests in the Pacific, the policy was crystallized into the so-called Nine Power Treaty, which gave definition and precision to the principles upon which the policy rested. In the first article of that Treaty, the contracting powers, other than China, agreed

1. To respect the sovereignty, the independence and the territorial and administrative integrity of China.

2. To provide the fullest and most unembarrassed opportunity to China to develop and maintain for herself an effective and stable government.

3. To use their influence for the purpose of effectually establishing and maintaining the principle of equal opportunity for the commerce and industry of all nations throughout the territory of China.

4. To refrain from taking advantage of conditions in China in order to seek special rights or privileges which would abridge the rights of subjects or citizens of friendly states, and from countenancing action inimical to the security of such states.

This Treaty thus represents a carefully developed and matured international policy intended, on the one hand, to assure to all of the contracting parties their rights and interests in and with regard to China, and on the other hand, to assure to the people of China the fullest opportunity to develop without molestation their sovereignty and independence according to the modern and enlightened standards believed to maintain among the peoples of this earth. At the time this Treaty was signed, it was known that China was engaged in an attempt to develop the free institutions of a self-governing republic after her recent revolution from an autocratic form of government; that she would require many years of both economic and political effort to that end; and that her progress would necessarily be slow. The Treaty was thus a covenant of self-denial among the signatory powers in deliberate renunciation of any policy of aggression which might tend to interfere with that development. It was believed—and the whole history of the development of the "Open Door" policy reveals that faith—that only by such a process, under the protection of such an agreement, could the fullest interests not only of China but of all nations which have intercourse with her best be served.

In its report to the President announcing this Treaty, the American Delegation, headed by the then Secretary of State, Mr. Charles E. Hughes, said

"It is believed that through this Treaty the 'Open Door' in China has at last been made a fact."

During the course of the discussions which resulted in the Treaty, the Chairman of the British delegation, Lord Balfour, had stated that

"The British Empire delegation understood that there was no representative of any power around the table who thought that the old practice of 'spheres of interest' was either advocated by any government or would be tolerable to this conference. So far as the British Government was concerned, they had, in the most formal manner, publicly announced that they regarded this practice as utterly inappropriate to the existing situation."

At the same time the representative of Japan, Baron Shidehara, announced the postion of his government as follows:

"No one denies to China her sacred right to govern herself. No one stands in the way of China to work out her own great national destiny."

The Treaty was originally executed by the United States, Belgium, the British Empire, China, France, Italy, Japan, the Netherlands and Portugal. Subsequently it was also executed by Norway, Bolivia, Sweden, Denmark and Mexico. Germany has signed it but her Parliament has not yet ratified it.

It must be remembered also that this Treaty was one of several treaties and agreements entered into at the Washington Conference by the various powers concerned, all of which were interrelated and interdependent. No one of these treaties can be disregarded without disturbing the general understanding and equilibrium which were intended to be accomplished and effected by the group of agreements arrived at in their entirety. The Washington Conference was essentially a disarmament conference, aimed to promote the possibility of peace in the world not only through the cessation of competition in naval armament but also by the solution of various other disturbing problems which threatened the peace of the world, particularly in the Far East. These problems were all interrelated. The willingness of the American government to surrender its then commanding lead in battleship construction and to leave its positions at Guam and in the Philippines without further fortification, was predicated upon, among other things, the self-denying covenants contained in the Nine Power Treaty, which assured the nations of the world not only of equal opportunity for their Eastern trade but also against the military aggrandizement of any other power at the expense of China. One cannot discuss the possibility of modifying or abrogating those provisions of the Nine Power Treaty without considering at the same time the other promises upon which they were really dependent.

Six years later the policy of self-denial against aggression by a stronger against a weaker power, upon which the Nine Power Treaty had been based, received a powerful reinforcement by the execution by substantially all the nations of the world of the Pact of Paris, the so-called Kellogg-Briand Pact. These two treaties represent independent but harmonious steps taken for the purpose of aligning the conscience and public opinion of the world in favor of a system of orderly development by the law of nations including the settlement of all controversies by methods of justice and peace instead of by arbitrary force. The program for the protection of China from outside aggression is an essential part of any such development. The signatories and adherents of the Nine Power Treaty rightly felt that the orderly and peaceful development of the 400,000,000 of people inhabiting China was necessary to the peaceful welfare of the entire world and that no program for the welfare of the world as a whole could afford to neglect the welfare and protection of China.

The recent events which have taken place in China, especially the hostilities which having been begun in Manchuria have latterly been extended to Shanghai, far from indicating the advisability of any modification of the treaties we have been discussing, have tended to bring home the vital importance of the faithful observance of the covenants therein to all of the nations interested in the Far East. It is not necessary in that connection to inquire into the causes of the controversy or attempt to apportion the blame between the two nations which are unhappily involved; for regardless of cause or responsibility, it is clear beyond peradventure that a situation has developed which cannot, under any circumstances, be reconciled with the obligations of the covenants of these two treaties, and that if the treaties had been faithfully observed such a situation could not have arisen. The signatories of the Nine Power Treaty and of the Kellogg-Briand Pact who are not parties to that conflict are not likely to see any reason for modifying the terms of those treaties. To them the real value of the faithful performance of the treaties has been brought sharply home by the perils and losses to which their nationals have been subjected in Shanghai.

That is the view of this Government. We see no reason for abandoning the enlightened principles which are embodied in these treaties. We believe that this situation would have been avoided had these covenants been faithfully observed, and no evidence has come to us to indicate that a due compliance with them would have interfered with the adequate protection of the legitimate rights in China of the signatories of those treaties and their nationals.

On January 7th last, upon the instruction of the President, this Government formally notified Japan and China that it would not recognize any situation, treaty or agreement entered into by those governments in violation of the covenants of these treaties, which affected the rights of our Government or its citizens in China. If a similar decision should be reached and a similar position taken by the other governments of the world, a caveat will be placed upon such action which, we believe, will effectively bar the legality hereafter of any title or right sought to be obtained by pressure or treaty violation, and which, as has been shown by history in the past, will eventually lead to the restoration to China of rights and titles of which she may have been deprived.

In the past our Government, as one of the leading powers on the Pacific Ocean, has rested its policy upon an abiding faith in the future of the people of China and upon the ultimate success in dealing with them of the principles of fair play, patience, and mutual goodwill. We appreciate the immensity of the task which lies before her statesmen in the development of her country and its government. The delays in her progress, the instability of her attempts to secure a responsible government, were foreseen by Messrs. Hay and Hughes and their contemporaries and were the very obstacles which the policy of the Open Door was designed to meet. We concur with those statesmen, representing all the nations in the Washington Conference who decided that China was entitled to the time necessary to accomplish her development. We are prepared to make that our policy for the future.

Very truly yours,

HENRY L. STIMSON

19

Statement by Secretary Hull, December 5, 1935 [24]

In reply to inquiries by press correspondents in regard to the "autonomy movement" in North China, Chinese and Japanese activities in relation thereto, and the American Government's attitude, the Secretary of State said:

There is going on in and with regard to North China a political struggle which is unusual in character and which may have far-reaching effects. The persons mentioned in reports of it are many; the action is rapid and covers a large area; opinions with regard to it vary; what may come of it no one could safely undertake to say; but, whatever the origin, whoever the agents, be what they may the methods, the fact stands out that an effort is being made—and is being resisted—

---

[24] *Ibid.*, p. 240.

to bring about a substantial change in the political status and condition of several of China's northern provinces.

Unusual developments in any part of China are rightfully and necessarily of concern not alone to the Government and people of China but to all of the many powers which have interests in China. For, in relations with China and in China, the treaty rights and the treaty obligations of the "treaty powers" are in general identical. The United States is one of those powers.

In the area under reference the interests of the United States are similar to those of other powers. In that area there are located, and our rights and obligations appertain to, a considerable number of American nationals, some American property, and substantial American commercial and cultural activities. The American Government is therefore closely observing what is happening there.

Political disturbances and pressures give rise to uncertainty and misgiving and tend to produce economic and social dislocations. They make difficult the enjoyment of treaty rights and the fulfillment of treaty obligations.

The views of the American Government with regard to such matters not alone in relation to China but in relation to the whole world are well known. As I have stated on many occasions, it seems to this Government most important in this period of world-wide political unrest and economic instability that governments and peoples keep faith in principles and pledges. In international relations there must be agreements and respect for agreements in order that there may be the confidence and stability and sense of security which are essential to orderly life and progress. This country has abiding faith in the fundamental principles of its traditional policy. This Government adheres to the provisions of the treaties to which it is a party and continues to bespeak respect by all nations for the provisions of treaties solemnly entered into for the purpose of facilitating and regulating, to reciprocal and common advantage, the contacts between and among the countries signatory.

20

Press Release Issued by the Department of State on October 6, 1937 [25]

The Department of State has been informed by the American Minister to Switzerland of the text of the report adopted by the Advisory Committee of the League of Nations setting forth the Advisory Committee's examination of the facts of the present situation in China and the treaty obligations of Japan. The Minister has further informed the Department that this report was adopted and approved by the Assembly of the League of Nations today, October 6.

Since the beginning of the present controversy in the Far East, the Government of the United States has urged upon both the Chinese and the Japanese Governments that they refrain from hostilities and has offered to be of assistance in an effort to find some means, acceptable to both parties to the conflict, of composing by pacific methods the situation in the Far East.

The Secretary of State, in statements made public on July 16 and August 23, made clear the position of the Government of the United States in regard to international problems and international relationships throughout the world and as applied specifically to the hostilities which are at present unfortunately going on between China and Japan. Among the principles which in the opinion of the Government of the United States should govern international relationships,

[25] *Ibid.*, p. 396.

if peace is to be maintained, are abstinence by all nations from the use of force in the pursuit of policy and from interference in the internal affairs of other nations; adjustment of problems in international relations by process of peaceful negotiation and agreement; respect by all nations for the rights of others and observance by all nations of established obligations; and the upholding of the principle of the sanctity of treaties.

On October 5 at Chicago the President elaborated these principles, emphasizing their importance, and in a discussion of the world situation pointed out that there can be no stability or peace either within nations or between nations except under laws and moral standards adhered to by all; that international anarchy destroys every foundation for peace; that it jeopardizes either the immediate or the future security of every nation, large or small; and that it is therefore of vital interest and concern to the people of the United States that respect for treaties and international morality be restored.

In the light of the unfolding developments in the Far East, the Government of the United States has been forced to the conclusion that the action of Japan in China is inconsistent with the principles which should govern the relationships between nations and is contrary to the provisions of the Nine Power Treaty of February 6, 1922, regarding principles and policies to be followed in matters concerning China, and to those of the Kellogg-Briand Pact of August 27, 1928. Thus the conclusions of this Government with respect to the foregoing are in general accord with those of the Assembly of the League of Nations.

21

The Ambassador in Japan (Grew) to Prince Konoye, Japanese Prime Minister and Minister for Foreign Affairs [26]

No. 1076   Tokyo, *October 6, 1938.*

Excellency: On the occasion of the interview which Your Excellency accorded me on October 3, when I had the honor to convey orally the views and desires of my Government with regard to conditions in China being brought about by agencies or representatives of the Japanese Government, which are violative of or prejudicial to American rights and interests in China, I undertook to set forth and to extend those views and desires in a note to be presented shortly thereafter. In fulfilment of that undertaking and under instruction from my Government, I now have the honor to address Your Excellency as follows:

The Government of the United States has had frequent occasion to make representations to Your Excellency's Government in regard to action taken and policies carried out in China under Japanese to which the Government of the United States takes exception as being, in its opinion, in contravention of the principle and the condition of equality of opportunity or the "open door" in China. In response to these representations, and in other connections, both public and private, the Japanese Government has given categorical assurances that equality of opportunity or the open door in China will be maintained. The Government of the United States is constrained to observe, however, that notwithstanding the assurances of the Japanese Government in this regard violation by Japanese agencies of American rights and interests has persisted.

As having by way of illustration a bearing on the situation to which the Government of the United States desires to invite the attention of the Japanese

---

[26] *Ibid.*, p. 785.

Government, it is recalled that at the time of the Japanese occupation of Manchuria the Japanese Government gave assurances that the open door in Manchuria would be maintained. However, the principal economic activities in that area have been taken over by special companies which are controlled by Japanese nationals and which are established under special charters according them a preferred or exclusive position. A large part of American enterprise which formerly operated in Manchuria has been forced to withdraw from that territory as a result of the preferences in force there. Arrangements between Japan and the regime now functioning in Manchuria allow the free movement of goods and funds between Manchuria and Japan while restricting rigidly the movement of goods and funds between Manchuria and countries other than Japan.

This channeling of the movement of goods is effected primarily by means of exchange control exercised under the authority of regulations issued under an enabling law which provide expressly that for the purposes of the law Japan shall not be considered a foreign country nor the Japanese yen a foreign currency. In the opinion of my Government equality of opportunity or open door has virtually ceased to exist in Manchuria notwithstanding the assurances of the Japanese Government that it would be maintained in that area.

The Government of the United States is now apprehensive lest there develop in other areas of China which have been occupied by Japanese military forces since the beginning of the present hostilities a situation similar in its adverse effect upon the competitive position of American business to that which now exists in Manchuria.

On April 12, 1938 I had occasion to invite the attention of Your Excellency's predecessor to reports which had reached the Government of the United States indicating that discrimination in favor of Japanese trade with North China was likewise to be by means of exchange control and to ask for assurances that the Japanese Government would not support or countenance financial measures discriminating against American interests. Although the Minister for Foreign Affairs stated then that the Japanese Government would continue to support the principle of equal opportunity or open door in China no specific reply has yet been made by the Japanese Government on the subject of these representations.

The Government of the United States now learns that the Japanese authorities at Tsingtao have in effect established an exchange control, that they are exercising a discretionary authority to prohibit exports unless export bills are sold to the Yokohama Specie Bank, and that the Bank refuses to purchase export bills except at an arbitrary rate far lower than the open market rate prevailing at Tientsin and Shanghai. A somewhat similar situation apparently prevails at Chefoo. Furthermore, reports continue to reach the American Government that a comprehensive system of exchange control will soon be established throughout North China. Control of foreign exchange transactions gives control of trade and commercial enterprise, and the exacting, either directly or indirectly, by the Japanese authorities of control of exchange in North China would place those authorities in position to thwart equality of opportunity or free competition between Japan and the United States in that area. In such a situation, imports from and exports to the United States, as well as the choice of dealers in North China, would be entirely subjected to the dispensation of the Japanese authorities. Notwithstanding the short time that exchange control has been enforced in Tsingtao, two cases of discrimination have already been brought to the attention of the Government of the United States. In one instance an American dealer in a staple commodity has been unable to export to the United

States because Japanese authorities there have insisted that his export bills be sold to a Japanese bank at a price so far below the current rate of exchange of the Chinese currency in the open market that such transaction would involve a loss rather than a profit; but a Japanese competitor recently completed a large shipment invoiced at a price in United States dollars which was equivalent to the local market price calculated at the current open market rate. In the other instance, an American firm was prevented from purchasing tobacco in Shantung unless it should purchase so-called Federal Reserve notes or yen currency with foreign money and at an arbitrary and low rate of exchange, conditions not imposed upon the company's Japanese or Chinese competitors.

The Government of the United States has already pointed out to the Japanese Government that alterations of the Chinese customs tariff by the regimes functioning in those portions of China occupied by Japanese armed forces and for which the Japanese Government has formally assured its support are arbitrary and illegal assumptions of authority for which the Japanese Government has an inescapable responsibility. It is hardly necessary to add that there can be no equality of opportunity or open door in China so long as the ultimate authority to regulate, tax, or prohibit trade is exercised, whether directly or indirectly, by the authorities of one "foreign" power in furtherance of the interests of that power. It would appear to be self-evident that a fundamental prerequisite of a condition of equality of opportunity or open door in China is the absence in the economic life of that country of preferences or monopolistic rights operating directly or indirectly in favor of any foreign country or its nationals. On July 4 I spoke to General Ugaki of the desire of the American Government that there be avoided such restrictions and obstacles to American trade and other enterprises as might result from the setting up of special companies and monopolies in China. The Minister was so good as to state that the open door in China would be maintained and that the Government of the United States might rest assured that the Japanese Government would fully respect the principle of equal opportunity.

Notwithstanding these assurances, the Provisional regime in Peiping announced on July 30th the inauguration as of the following day of the China Telephone and Telegraph Company, the reported purpose of this organization being to control and to have exclusive operation of telephone and telegraph communications in North China. There was organized in Shanghai on July 31st the Central China Telecommunications Company, and the Special Service Section of the Japanese army has informed foreign cable and telegraph companies that the new company proposes to control all the telecommunications in Central China. According to a semi-official Japanese press report, there was organized at Shanghai on July 28 the Shanghai Inland Navigation Steamship Company to be controlled by Japanese the reported object of which is to control water transportation in the Shanghai delta area. According to information which has reached my Government, a Japanese company has been organized to take over and operate the wharves at Tsingtao which have hitherto been publicly owned and operated. Should such a development occur, all shipping of whatever nationality would become dependent upon a Japanese agency for allotments of space and stevedoring facilities. The wool trade in North China is now reported to be a Japanese monopoly and a tobacco monopoly in that area is reported to be in process of formation. Moreover, according to numerous reports which have been reaching my Government, the Japanese Government is proceeding with the organization of two special promotion companies which it has chartered and which it will control with the object of investing in, unifying, and regulating the administration of certain large sectors of economic enterprise in China.

The developments of which I have made mention are illustrative of the apparent trend of Japanese policy in China and indicate clearly that the Japanese authorities are seeking to establish in areas which have come under Japanese military occupation general preferences for, and superiority of, Japanese interests, an inevitable effect of which will be to frustrate the practical application of the principle of the open door and deprive American nationals of equal opportunity.

I desire also to call Your Excellency's attention to the fact that unwarranted restrictions placed by the Japanese military authorities upon American nationals in China—notwithstanding the existence of American treaty rights in China and the repeated assurances of the Japanese Government that steps had been taken which would insure that American nationals, interests and property would not be subject to unlawful interference by Japanese authorities—further subject American interests to continuing serious inconvenience and hardships. Reference is made especially to the restrictions placed by the Japanese military upon American nationals who desire to reenter and reoccupy properties from which they have been driven by the hostilities and of which the Japanese military have been or still are in occupation. Mention may also be made of the Japanese censorship of and interference with American mail and telegrams at Shanghai and of restrictions upon freedom of trade, residence and travel by Americans, including the use of railways, shipping, and other facilities. While Japanese merchant vessels are carrying Japanese merchandise between Shanghai and Nanking, those vessels decline to carry merchandise of other countries, and American and other non-Japanese shipping is excluded from the lower Yangtze on the grounds of military necessity. Applications by American nationals for passes which would allow them to return to certain areas in the lower Yangtze valley have been denied by the Japanese authorities on the ground that peace and order have not been sufficiently restored, although many Japanese merchants and their families are known to be in those areas.

American nationals and their interests have suffered serious losses in the Far East arising from causes directly attributable to the present conflict between Japan and China, and even under the most favorable conditions an early rehabilitation of American trade with China cannot be expected. The American Government, therefore, finds it all the more difficult to reconcile itself to a situation in which American nationals must contend with continuing unwarranted interference with their rights at the hands of the Japanese authorities in China and with Japanese actions and policies which operate to deprive American trade and enterprise of equality of opportunity in China. It is also pertinent to mention that in Japan, too, American trade and other interests are undergoing severe hardships as a result of the industrial, trade, exchange and other controls which the Japanese Government has imposed incident to its military operations in China.

While American interests in the Far East have been thus treated at the hands of the Japanese authorities, the Government of the United States has not sought either in its own territory or in the territory of third countries to establish or influence the establishment of embargoes, import prohibitions, exchange controls, preferential restrictions, monopolies or special companies—designed to eliminate or having the effect of eliminating Japanese trade and enterprise. In its treatment of Japanese nationals and their trade and enterprise, the American Government has been guided not only by the letter and spirit of the Japanese-American Commercial Treaty of 1911 but by those fundamental principles of international law and order which have formed the basis of its policy in regard to all peoples and their interests; and Japanese commerce and enterprise have continued to enjoy in the United States equality of opportunity.

Your Excellency cannot fail to recognize the existence of a great and growing disparity between the treatment accorded American nationals and their trade and enterprise by Japanese authorities in China and Japan and the treatment accorded Japanese nationals and their trade and enterprise by the Government of the United States in areas within its jurisdiction.

In the light of the situation herein reviewed the Government of the United States asks that the Japanese Government implement its assurances already given with regard to the maintenance of the open door and to non-interference with American rights by taking prompt and effective measures to cause,

(1) The discontinuance of discriminatory exchange control and of other measures imposed in areas in China under Japanese control which operate either directly or indirectly to discriminate against American trade and enterprise;

(2) The discontinuance of any monopoly or of any preference which would deprive American nationals of the right of undertaking any legitimate trade or industry in China or of any arrangement which might purport to establish in favor of Japanese interests any general superiority of rights with regard to commercial or economic development in any region of China; and

(3) The discontinuance of interference by Japanese authorities in China with American property and other rights including such forms of interference as censorship of American mail and telegrams and restrictions upon residence and travel by Americans and upon American trade and shipping.

The Government of the United States believes that in the interest of relations between the United States and Japan an early reply would be helpful.

I avail myself [etc.] JOSEPH C. GREW

22

The Japanese Foreign Minister (Arita) to the Ambassador in Japan (Grew) [27]

[Translation]

No. 102, American I [TOKYO,] *November 18, 1938.*

EXCELLENCY: I have the honor to inform Your Excellency that I have carefully perused the contents of Your Excellency's note no. 1076, dated October 6th, addressed to the then Minister for Foreign Affairs Prince Konoye, concerning the rights and interests of the United States in China.

In this note, Your Excellency sets forth, on the basis of information in the possession of the Government of the United States, various instances in which Japanese authorities are subjecting American citizens in China to discriminatory treatment and are violating the rights and interests of the United States.

The views held by the Japanese Government with regard to these instances may be stated as follows:

1. According to the information in the possession of the Imperial Government, the circumstances which led to the adoption of such measures as those at present enforced in Tsingtao concerning export exchange, and the present situation being as set forth below, it is believed that those measures cannot be construed as constituting any discrimination against American citizens.

---

[27] *Ibid.*, p. 797.

A short time ago the Federal Reserve Bank of China was established in North China. This bank's notes, with foreign exchange value fixed at one shilling and two pence to one yuan, already have been issued to an amount of more than one hundred million yuan, and are being widely circulated. These bank notes being the legal currency required by the Provisional Government, the maintenance of their value and their smooth circulation is regarded as an indispensable' basis for the conduct and development of economic activities in North China. Since the Japanese Government has, therefore, taken a cooperative attitude, all Japanese subjects are using those notes, and accordingly, even in their export trade are exchanging them at the rate of one shilling and two pence. On the other hand, the former legal currency still circulating in these areas has depreciated in exchange value to about eight pence per yuan. Consequently those who are engaged in export trade and are using this currency, are enjoying improper and excessive profits, as compared with those who are using Federal Reserve notes and carrying on legitimate transactions at the legally established rate of exchange. Japanese subjects and others who are using Federal Reserve notes have been suffering unreasonable and excessive losses as compared with those persons who use exclusively the former legal currency although residing and carrying on their businesses in the areas under the jurisdiction of the Provisional Government of North China. Furthermore, the existence of the above mentioned disparity between the foreign exchange value of the Federal Reserve notes and that of the former legal currency, which currency the Federal Reserve Bank has been and is exchanging at a rate almost on a par with its own notes, is bound to exert an unfavourable effect upon the exchange value of the Federal Reserve notes, and eventually also upon the exchange value of the Japanese yen. The Japanese Government therefore can not remain indifferent to such a situation.

In order to place the users of the former legal currency who have been obtaining improper and excessive profits on an equal footing with those using the Federal Reserve notes and at the same time to assist in the maintenance of the exchange value of the Federal Reserve Bank notes, represents an objective of those export exchange measures adopted at Tsingtao. Inasmuch as the application of the measures makes no differentiation according to nationality they are not at all discriminatory. As a matter of fact, it is through these measures that those users of the Federal Reserve notes who had in a sense been discriminated against have been placed on an equal footing with the others, and thus, for the first time on equal footing, are enabled to compete on an entirely equitable basis.

2. Some time ago the new regimes in North and Central China revised the Customs tariff rates seeking to secure a rational modification of the former tariff rates enforced by the Nationalist Government, because those rates were unduly high and not suitable for the promotion of the economic recovery and general welfare of the Chinese people. In any case, the schedule adopted is the one that was readily approved by the Powers in 1931, and was not calculated to inure to the benefit of any particular country. Accordingly no complaint has been heard from foreign residents of any nationality in China. The Japanese Government is, of course, in favor of the purpose of this revision, and believes that it will serve to promote effectively the trade of all countries with China.

3. As for the organization of certain promotion companies in China, the restoration and development of China's economic, financial and industrial activities following the present incident is a matter of the most urgent necessity for the welfare of the Chinese people. Moreover, the Japanese Government,

for the sake of the realization of a new order in East Asia, is exceedingly anxious for the prompt inauguration and progress of undertakings looking toward such restoration and development, and is devoting every constructive effort to realize this objective. The fact that the North China Development Company and the Central China Promotion Company were established represents nothing other than an offer to China of the necessary assistance for this restoration, and at the same time, an attempt to contribute to the development of the natural resources of China. It does not in any way impair the rights and interests of nationals of Your Excellency's country or in any way discriminate against their enterprises. The Japanese Government therefore, of course, has no intention of opposing, but rather welcomes heartily, the participation of third Powers which intend to cooperate on the basis of the new conditions.

The telecommunication companies in North and Central China, the inland navigation steamship company at Shanghai and the wharfage company at Tsingtao have also been established to meet the imperative need of an early restoration of communications, transportation, and harbor facilities which were destroyed as a result of the incident. It is proper that the telecommunications enterprise, not only because of its nature as a public utility but also in view of its relation to the maintenance of peace and order and to national defense, should be undertaken by special companies. However, all other enterprises being ordinary Chinese or Japanese juridical persons, do not have the objectives of discrimination against Your Excellency's country or third powers or of the gaining of monopolistic profits. As regards the wool trade, while the control of purchasing agencies was enforced in the Mongolian region, it now has been discontinued. There is at present no plan of any sort for the establishment of a tobacco monopoly.

4. Concerning the return of American citizens to the occupied areas, in North China there is no restriction on their returning, except in special cases where the personal safety of those who return would be endangered. Your Excellency is aware that in the Yangtze Valley large numbers of Americans have already returned. The fact that permission to return has not yet been made general is, as has been repeatedly communicated to Your Excellency, owing to considerations of the danger involved on account of order not yet being restored, or because of the impossibility of admitting nationals of third Powers on account of strategic necessities such as the preservation of military secrets. Further, the various restrictions enforced in the occupied areas concerning the residence, travel, enterprise and trade of American citizens, constitute the minimum regulations possible consistent with military necessities and the local conditions of peace and order. It is the intention of the Japanese Government to restore normal conditions as soon as circumstances permit.

5. The Japanese Government is surprised at the allegation that there exists a fundamental difference between the treatment accorded to Japanese in America and the treatment accorded to Americans in Japan. While it is true that in this period of emergency, Americans residing in this country are subject to various economic restrictions, these restrictions are, needless to say, imposed not upon Americans alone but also equally upon all foreigners as well as upon Japanese subjects. A statement of the views of the Japanese Government concerning the opinion as set forth in Your Excellency's note, regarding the treatment of Japanese subjects in American territory, is reserved for another occasion.

While the Japanese Government with the intention of fully respecting American rights and interests in China, as has been frequently stated above, has been making every effort in that direction, in view of the fact that military operations on a scale unprecedented in our history are now being carried out in East Asia, I am of the opinion that the Government of Your Excellency's country also should recognize the fact that occasionally obstacles arise hindering the effecting of the intention of respecting the rights and interests of Your Excellency's country.

At present Japan, devoting its entire energy to the establishment of a new order based on genuine international justice throughout East Asia, is making rapid strides toward the attainment of this objective. The successful accomplishment of this purpose is not only indispensable to the existence of Japan, but also constitutes the very foundation of the enduring peace and stability of East Asia.

It is the firm conviction of the Japanese Government that now, at a time of the continuing development of new conditions in East Asia, an attempt to apply to present and future conditions without any changes concepts and principles which were applicable to conditions prevailing before the present incident does not in any way contribute to the solution of immediate issues and further does not in the least promote the firm establishment of enduring peace in East Asia.

The Imperial Government, however, does not have any intention of objecting to the participation in the great work of the reconstruction of East Asia by Your Excellency's country or by other Powers, in all fields of trade and industry, when such participation is undertaken with an understanding of the purport of the above stated remarks; and further, I believe that the regimes now being formed in China are also prepared to welcome such participation.

I avail myself [etc.]

HACHIRO ARITA

23

The Ambassador in Japan (Grew) to the Japanese Foreign Minister (Arita) [28]

No. 1153
TOKYO, *December 30, 1938.*

EXCELLENCY: Acting under the instructions of my Government I have the honor to address to Your Excellency the following note:

The Government of the United States has received and has given full consideration to the reply of the Japanese Government of November 18 to this Government's note of October 6 on the subject of American rights and interests in China.

In the light of facts and experience the Government of the United States is impelled to reaffirm its previously expressed opinion that imposition of restrictions upon the movements and activities of American nationals who are engaged in philanthropic, educational and commercial endeavors in China has placed and will, if continued, increasingly place Japanese interests in a preferred position and is, therefore, unquestionably discriminatory in its effect against legitimate American interests. Further, with reference to such matters as exchange control, compulsory currency circulation, tariff revision, and monopolistic promotion in certain areas of China the plans and practices of the Japanese authorities imply an assumption on the part of those authorities that the Japanese Government or the regimes established and maintained in China by Japanese armed forces are entitled to act in China in a capacity such as flows from rights of sovereignty and further in so acting to disregard and even to declare non-

[28] *Ibid.,* p. 820.

existent or abrogated the established rights and interests of other countries including the United States.

The Government of the United States expresses its conviction that the restrictions and measures under reference not only are unjust and unwarranted but are counter to the provisions of several binding international agreements, voluntarily entered into, to which both Japan and the United States, and in some cases other countries, are parties.

In the concluding portion of its note under reference, the Japanese Government states that it is firmly convinced that "in the face of the new situation, fast developing in Asia, any attempt to apply to the conditions of today and tomorrow inapplicable ideas and principles of the past neither would contribute toward the establishment of a real peace in East Asia nor solve the immediate issues" and that "as long as these points are understood Japan has not the slightest inclination to oppose the participation of the United States and other Powers in the great work of reconstructing East Asia along all lines of industry and trade."

The Government of the United States in its note of October 6 requested, in view of the oft reiterated assurances proffered by the Government of Japan of its intention to observe the principles of equality of opportunity in its relations with China and in view of Japan's treaty obligations so to do, that the Government of Japan abide by these obligations and carry out these assurances in practice. The Japanese Government in its reply appears to affirm that it is its intention to make its observance of that principle conditional upon an understanding by the American Government and by other governments of a "new situation" and a "new order" in the Far East as envisaged and fostered by Japanese authorities.

Treaties which bear upon the situation in the Far East have within them provisions relating to a number of subjects. In the making of those treaties, there was a process among the parties to them of give and take. Toward making possible the carrying out of some of their provisions, others among their provisions were formulated and agreed upon: toward gaining for itself the advantage of security in regard to certain matters, each of the parties committed itself to pledges of self-denial in regard to certain other matters. The various provisions agreed upon may be said to have constituted collectively an arrangement for safeguarding, for the benefit of all, the correlated principles on the one hand of national integrity and on the other hand of equality of economic opportunity. Experience has shown that impairment of the former of these principles is followed almost invariably by disregard of the latter. Whenever any government begins to exercise political authority in areas beyond the limits of its lawful jurisdiction there develops inevitably a situation in which the nationals of that government demand and are accorded, at the hands of their government, preferred treatment, whereupon equality of opportunity ceases to exist and discriminatory practices, productive of friction, prevail.

The admonition that enjoyment by the nationals of the United States of non-discriminatory treatment in China—a general and well-established right—is henceforth to be contingent upon an admission by the Government of the United States of the validity of the conception of Japanese authorities of a "new situation" and a "new order" in East Asia, is, in the opinion of this Government, highly paradoxical.

This country's adherence to and its advocacy of the principle of equality of opportunity do not flow solely from a desire to obtain the commercial benefits which naturally result from the provisions of that principle. They flow from a firm conviction that observance of that principle leads to economic and political stability, which are conducive both to the internal well-being of nations and to mutually beneficial and peaceful relationships between and among nations; from a firm conviction that failure to observe that principle breeds international friction and ill-will, with consequences injurious to all countries, including in particular those countries which fail to observe it; and from an equally firm conviction that observance of that principle promotes the opening of trade channels thereby making available the markets, the raw materials and the manufactured products of the community of nations on a mutually and reciprocally beneficial basis.

The principle of equality of economic opportunity is, moreover, one to which over a long period and on many occasions the Japanese Government has given definite approval. It is one to the observance of which the Japanese Government has committed itself in various international agreements and understandings. It is one upon observance of which by other nations the Japanese Government has of its own accord and upon its own initiative frequently insisted. It is one to which the Japanese Government has repeatedly during recent months declared itself committed.

The people and the Government of the United States could not assent to the establishment at the instance of and for the special purposes of any third country of a regime which would arbitrarily deprive them of the long established rights of equal opportunity and fair treatment which are legally and justly theirs along with those of other nationals.

Fundamental principles such as the principle of equality of opportunity which have long been regarded as inherently wise and just which have been widely adopted and adhered to, and which are general in their application are not subject to nullification by a unilateral affirmation.

With regard to the implication in the Japanese Government's note that the "conditions of today and tomorrow" in the Far East call for a revision of the ideas and principles of the past, this Government desires to recall to the Japanese Government its position on the subject of revision of agreements.

This Government had occasion in the course of a communication delivered to the Japanese Government on April 29, 1934, to express its opinion that "treaties can lawfully be modified or be terminated—but only by processes prescribed or recognized or agreed upon by the parties to them".

In the same communication this Government also said, "In the opinion of the American people and the American Government, no nation can, without the assent of the other nations concerned, rightfully endeavor to make conclusive its will in situations where there are involved the rights, the obligations and the legitimate interests of other sovereign states". In an official and public statement on July 16, 1937, the Secretary of State of the United States declared that this Government advocates "adjustment of problems in international relations by processes of peaceful negotiation and agreement".

At various times during recent decades various powers, among which have been Japan and the United States, have had occasion to communicate and to confer with regard to situations and problems in the Far East. In the conducting of correspondence and of conferences relating to these matters, the parties involved have invariably taken into consideration past and present facts and they have not failed to perceive the possibility and the desirability of changes in the situation. In the making of treaties they have drawn up and have agreed upon provisions intended to facilitate advantageous developments and at the same time to obviate and avert the arising of friction between and among the various powers which, having interests in the region or regions under reference, were and would be concerned.

In the light of these facts, and with reference especially to the purpose and the character of the treaty provisions from time to time solemnly agreed upon for the very definite purposes indicated, the Government of the United States deprecates the fact that one of the parties to these agreements has chosen to embark—as indicated both by action of its agents and by official statements of its authorities—upon a course directed toward the arbitrary creation by that power by methods of its own selection, regardless of treaty pledges and the established rights of other powers concerned, of a "new order" in the Far East. Whatever may be the changes which have taken place in the situation in the Far East and whatever may be the situation now, these matters are of no less interest and concern to the American Government than have been the situations which have prevailed there in the past, and such changes as may henceforth take place there, changes which may enter into the producing of a "new situation" and a "new order", are and will be of like concern to this Government. This Government is well aware that the situation has changed. This Government is also well aware that many of the changes have been brought about by the action of Japan. This Government does not admit, however, that there is need or warrant for any one Power to take upon itself to prescribe what shall be the terms and conditions of a "new order" in areas not under its sovereignty and to constitute itself the repository of authority and the agent of destiny in regard thereto.

It is known to all the world that various of the parties to treaties concluded for the purpose of regulating contacts in the Far East and avoiding friction therein and therefrom—which treaties contained, for those purposes, various restrictive provisions—have from time to time and by processes of negotiation and agreement contributed in the light of changed situations toward the removal of restrictions and toward the bringing about of further developments which would warrant in the light of further changes in the situation, further removals of restrictions. By such methods and processes, early restrictions upon the tariff autonomy of all countries in the Far East were removed. By such methods and processes the rights of extraterritorial jurisdiction once enjoyed by Occidental countries in relations with countries in the Far East have been given up in relations with all of those countries except China; and in the years immediately preceding and including the year 1931, countries which still possessed those rights in China including the United States were actively engaged in negotiations—far advanced—looking toward surrender of those rights. All discerning and impartial observers have realized that the United States and others of the "treaty powers" have not during recent decades clung tenaciously to their so-called "special" rights and privileges in countries of the Far East but on the contrary have steadily encouraged the development in those countries of institutions and practices in the presence of which such rights and privileges may safely and readily be given up; and all observers have seen those rights and privileges gradually being surrendered voluntarily through agreement by the Powers which have possessed them. On one point only has the Government of the United States, along with several other governments, insisted: namely, that new situations must have developed to a point warranting the removal of "special" safeguarding restrictions and that the removals be effected by orderly processes.

The Government of the United States has at all times regarded agreements as susceptible of alteration, but it has always insisted that alterations can rightfully be made only by orderly processes of negotiation and agreement among the parties thereto.

The Japanese Government has upon numerous occasions expressed itself as holding similar views.

The United States has in its international relations rights and obligations which derive from international law and rights and obligations which rest upon treaty provisions. Of those which rest on treaty provisions, its rights and obligations in and with regard to China rest in part upon provisions in treaties between the United States and China and in part on provisions in treaties between the United States and several other powers including both China and Japan. These treaties were concluded in good faith for the purpose of safeguarding and promoting the interests not of one only but of all of their signatories. The people and the Government of the United States cannot assent to the abrogation of any of this country's rights or obligations by the arbitrary action of agents or authorities of any other country.

The Government of the United States has, however, always been prepared and is now prepared to give due and ample consideration to any proposals based on justice and reason which envisage the resolving of problems in a manner duly considerate of the rights and obligations of all parties directly concerned by processes of free negotiation and new commitment by and among all of the parties so concerned. There has been and there continues to be opportunity for the Japanese Government to put forward such proposals. This Government has been and it continues to be willing to discuss such proposals, if and when put forward, with representatives of the other powers, including Japan and China, whose rights and interests are involved, at whatever time and in whatever place may be commonly agreed upon.

Meanwhile, this Government reserves all rights of the United States as they exist and does not give assent to any impairment of any of those rights.

I avail myself [etc.]

JOSEPH C. GREW

24

Statement by Secretary Hull, March 30, 1940 [29]

In response to inquiries with regard to the attitude and position of the Government of the United States in the light of the setting up at Nanking of a new regime, the Secretary of State made a statement as follows:

"In the light of what has happened in various parts of China since 1931, the setting up of a new regime at Nanking has the appearance of a further step in a program of one country by armed force to impose its will upon a neighboring country and to block off a large area of the world from normal political and economic relationships with the rest of the world. The developments there appear to be following the pattern of other regimes and systems which have been set up in China under the aegis of an outside power and which in their functioning especially favor the interests of that outside power and deny to nationals of the United States and other third countries enjoyment of long-established rights of equal and fair treatment which are legally and justly theirs.

"The Government of the United States has noted statements of high officials of that outside power that their country intends to respect the political independence and the freedom of the other country and that with the development of affairs in East Asia this intention will be demonstrated. To this Government

[29] *Ibid.*, vol. II, p. 59.

the circumstances, both military and diplomatic, which have attended the setting up of the new regime at Nanking do not seem consistent with such an intention.

"The attitude of the United States toward use of armed force as an instrument of national policy is well known. Its attitude and position with regard to various aspects of the situation in the Far East have been made clear on numerous occasions. That attitude and position remain unchanged.

"This Government again makes full reservation of this country's rights under international law and existing treaties and agreements.

"Twelve years ago the Government of the United States recognized, as did other governments, the National Government of the Republic of China. The Government of the United States has ample reason for believing that that Government, with capital now at Chungking, has had and still has the allegiance and support of the great majority of the Chinese people. The Government of the United States of course continues to recognize that Government as the Government of China."

25

Document Handed by Secretary Hull to the Japanese Ambassador (Nomura) on November 26, 1941 [30]

Strictly Confidential,
Tentative and Without
Commitment

WASHINGTON, *November 26, 1941*

OUTLINE OF PROPOSED BASIS FOR AGREEMENT BETWEEN THE UNITED STATES AND JAPAN

SECTION I

Draft Mutual Declaration of Policy

The Government of the United States and the Government of Japan both being solicitous for the peace of the Pacific affirm that their national policies are directed toward lasting and extensive peace throughout the Pacific area, that they have no territorial designs in that area, that they have no intention of threatening other countries or of using military force aggressively against any neighboring nation, and that, accordingly, in their national policies they will actively support and give practical application to the following fundamental principles upon which their relations with each other and with all other governments are based:

(1) The principle of inviolability of territorial integrity and sovereignty of each and all nations.
(2) The principle of non-interference in the internal affairs of other countries.
(3) The principle of equality, including equality of commercial opportunity and treatment.
(4) The principle of reliance upon international cooperation and conciliation for the prevention and pacific settlement of controversies and for improvement of international conditions by peaceful methods and processes.

The Government of Japan and the Government of the United States have agreed that toward eliminating chronic political instability, preventing recurrent economic collapse, and providing a basis for peace, they will actively support and practically apply the following principles in their economic relations with each other and with other nations and peoples:

[30] *Ibid.*, p. 768.

(1) The principle of non-discrimination in international commercial relations.
(2) The principle of international economic cooperation and abolition of extreme nationalism as expressed in excessive trade restrictions.
(3) The principle of non-discriminatory access by all nations to raw material supplies.
(4) The principle of full protection of the interests of consuming countries and populations as regards the operation of international commodity agreements.
(5) The principle of establishment of such institutions and arrangements of international finance as may lend aid to the essential enterprises and the continuous development of all countries and may permit payments through processes of trade consonant with the welfare of all countries.

SECTION II

Steps To Be Taken by the Government of the United States and by the Government of Japan

The Government of the United States and the Government of Japan propose to take steps as follows:

1. The Government of the United States and the Government of Japan will endeavor to conclude a multilateral non-aggression pact among the British Empire, China, Japan, the Netherlands, the Soviet Union, Thailand and the United States.

2. Both Governments will endeavor to conclude among the American, British, Chinese, Japanese, the Netherland and Thai Governments an agreement whereunder each of the Governments would pledge itself to respect the territorial integrity of French Indochina and, in the event that there should develop a threat to the territorial integrity of Indochina, to enter into immediate consultation with a view of taking such measures as may be deemed necessary and advisable to meet the threat in question. Such agreement would provide also that each of the Governments party to the agreement would not seek or accept preferential treatment in its trade or economic relations with Indochina and would use its influence to obtain for each of the signatories equality of treatment in trade and commerce with French Indochina.

3. The Government of Japan will withdraw all military, naval, air and police forces from China and from Indochina.

4. The Government of the United States and the Government of Japan will not support—militarily, politically, economically—any government or regime in China other than the National Government of the Republic of China with capital temporarily at Chungking.

5. Both Governments will give up all extraterritorial rights in China, including rights and interests in and with regard to international settlements and concessions, and rights under the Boxer Protocol of 1901.

Both Governments will endeavor to obtain the agreement of the British and other governments to give up extraterritorial rights in China, including rights in international settlements and in concessions and under the Boxer Protocol of 1901.

6. The Government of the United States and the Government of Japan will enter into negotiations for the conclusion between the United States and Japan of a trade agreement, based upon reciprocal most-favored-nation treatment and reduction of trade barriers by both countries, including an undertaking by the United States to bind raw silk on the free list.

7. The Government of the United States and the Government of Japan will, respectively, remove the freezing restrictions on Japanese funds in the United States and on American funds in Japan.

8. Both Governments will agree upon a plan for the stabilization of the dollar-yen rate, with the allocation of funds adequate for this purpose, half to be supplied by Japan and half by the United States.

9. Both Governments will agree that no agreement which either has concluded with any third power or powers shall be interpreted by it in such a way as to conflict with the fundamental purpose of this agreement, the establishment and preservation of peace throughout the Pacific area.

10. Both Governments will use their influence to cause other governments to adhere to and to give practical application to the basic political and economic principles set forth in this agreement.

26

Master Lend-Lease Agreement Between the United States and China, Signed at Washington June 2, 1942 [31]

Whereas the Governments of the United States of America and the Republic of China declare that they are engaged in a cooperative undertaking, together with every other nation or people of like mind, to the end of laying the bases of a just and enduring world peace securing order under law to themselves and all nations;

And whereas the Governments of the United States of America and the Republic of China, as signatories of the Declaration by United Nations of January 1, 1942, have subscribed to a common program of purposes and principles embodied in the Joint Declaration made on August 14, 1941 by the President of the United States of America and the Prime Minister of the United Kingdom of Great Britain and Northern Ireland, known as the Atlantic Charter;

And whereas the President of the United States of America has determined, pursuant to the Act of Congress of March 11, 1941, that the defense of the Republic of China against aggression is vital to the defense of the United States of America;

And whereas the United States of America has extended and is continuing to extend to the Republic of China aid in resisting aggression;

And whereas it is expedient that the final determination of the terms and conditions upon which the Government of the Republic of China receives such aid and of the benefits to be received by the United States of America in return therefor should be deferred until the extent of the defense aid is known and until the progress of events makes clearer the final terms and conditions and benefits which will be in the mutual interests of the United States of America and the Republic of China and will promote the establishment and maintenance of world peace;

And whereas the Governments of the United States of America and the Republic of China are mutually desirous of concluding now a preliminary agreement in regard to the provisions of defense aid and in regard to certain considerations which shall be taken into account in determining such terms and conditions and the making of such an agreement has been in all respects duly authorized, and all acts, conditions and formalities which it may have been necessary to perform, fulfil or execute prior to the making of such an agreement in conformity with the

---

[31] 56 Stat. 1494.

laws either of the United States of America or of the Republic of China have been performed, fulfilled or executed as required;

The undersigned, being duly authorized by their respective Governments for that purpose, have agreed as follows:

Article I

The Government of the United States of America will continue to supply the Government of the Republic of China with such defense articles, defense services, and defense information as the President of the United States of America shall authorize to be transferred or provided.

Article II

The Government of the Republic of China will continue to contribute to the defense of the United States of America and the strengthening thereof and will provide such articles, services, facilities or information as it may be in a position to supply.

Article III

The Government of the Republic of China will not without the consent of the President of the United States of America transfer title to, or possession of, any defense article or defense information transferred to it under the Act of March 11, 1941 of the Congress of the United States of America or permit the use thereof by anyone not an officer, employee, or agent of the Government of the Republic of China.

Article IV

If, as a result of the transfer to the Government of the Republic of China of any defense article or defense information, it becomes necessary for that Government to take any action or make any payment in order fully to protect any of the rights of a citizen of the United States of America who has patent rights in and to any such defense article or information, the Government of the Republic of China will take such action or make such payment when requested to do so by the President of the United States of America.

Article V

The Government of the Republic of China will return to the United States of America at the end of the present emergency, as determined by the President of the United States of America, such defense articles transferred under this Agreement as shall not have been destroyed, lost or consumed and as shall be determined by the President to be useful in the defense of the United States of America or of the Western Hemisphere or to be otherwise of use to the United States of America.

Article VI

In the final determination of the benefits to be provided to the United States of America by the Government of the Republic of China full cognizance shall be taken of all property, services, information, facilities, or other benefits or considerations provided by the Government of the Republic of China subsequent to March 11, 1941, and accepted or acknowledged by the President on behalf of the United States of America.

Article VII

In the final determination of the benefits to be provided to the United States of America by the Government of the Republic of China in return for aid furnished under the Act of Congress of March 11, 1941, the terms and conditions thereof shall be such as not to burden commerce between the two countries, but to promote mutually advantageous economic relations between them and the betterment of world-wide economic relations. To that end, they shall include provision for agreed action by the United States of America and the Republic of China, open to participation by all other countries of like mind, directed to the expansion, by appropriate international and domestic measures, of production, employment, and the exchange and consumption of goods, which are the material foundations of the liberty and welfare of all peoples; to the elimination of all forms of discriminatory treatment in international commerce; to the reduction of tariffs and other trade barriers; and, in general, to the attainment of economic objectives identical with those set forth in the Joint Declaration made on August 14, 1941, by the President of the United States of America and the Prime Minister of the United Kingdom.

At an early convenient date, conversations shall be begun between the two Governments with a view to determining, in the light of governing economic conditions, the best means of attaining the above-stated objectives by their own agreed action and of seeking the agreed action of other like-minded Governments.

Article VIII

This Agreement shall take effect as from this day's date. It shall continue in force until a date to be agreed upon by the two Governments.

Signed and sealed at Washington in duplicate this second day of June, 1942.

FOR THE GOVERNMENT OF THE UNITED STATES OF AMERICA

       CORDELL HULL   [SEAL]
       Secretary of State
        of the United States of America

FOR THE GOVERNMENT OF THE REPUBLIC OF CHINA

       TSE VUNG SOONG [SEAL]
       Minister for Foreign Affairs
        of China

27 (a)

Secretary Stimson to the Chinese Minister for Foreign Affairs (Soong)

WASHINGTON, *January 29, 1942*

MY DEAR MR. SOONG: In furtherance of the plan for sending to the Generalissimo a high ranking United States Army officer to act as his Chief of Staff and as Commanding Officer of United States Army forces in that region, it is necessary to have certain points quite clearly understood, so that essential arrangements with the British Chiefs of Staff may be completed. In accordance with our previous conversations and correspondence on this subject, it is my understanding that the functions of the United States Army Representative are to be generally as follows:

To supervise and control all United States defense-aid affairs for China.

Under the Generalissimo to command all United States forces in China and such Chinese forces as may be assigned to him.

To represent the United States Government on any International War Council in China and act as the Chief of Staff for the Generalissimo.

To improve, maintain and control the Burma Road in China.

If the above represents the understanding and agreement of the Generalissimo on the functions of the United States Army Representative, the British will agree to cooperate in Burma and India so as to promote the effectiveness of the United States Army Representative's efforts.

A particular point involving personnel on which clarification is sought is as follows:

The message from the Generalissimo dated January 21st stated that the United States representative should bring with him an Air officer of high rank. We were prepared to make such an assignment but have since learned, informally, that the Generalissimo might like to retain Colonel Chennault as the highest ranking American Air officer in China. If this should be the case, the arrangement will be quite agreeable to the War Department and Chennault's promotion to the grade of Brigadier General will be accomplished at the proper time.

I request that you give me an early reply since we are making every effort to place the general plan into prompt execution.

Sincerely yours,

HENRY L. STIMSON

27 (b)

The Chinese Minister for Foreign Affairs (Soong) to Secretary of War Stimson

WASHINGTON, *January 30, 1942*

MY DEAR MR. STIMSON: I have to acknowledge with thanks the receipt of your letter of January 29th and wish to confirm our understanding that the functions of the United States Army Representative are to be generally as follows:

To supervise and control all United States defense-aid affairs for China.

Under the Generalissimo to command all United States forces in China and such Chinese forces as may be assigned to him.

To represent the United States Government on any International War Council in China and act as the Chief of Staff for the Generalissimo.

To improve, maintain and control the Burma Road in China.

With reference to the appointment of an Air officer of high rank, the Generalissimo would indeed like if possible to retain Colonel Chennault as the highest ranking American Air officer in China, because of his signal services to both our countries, and much appreciates your kind consideration in the matter.

I am glad to learn of your intention to promote Colonel Chennault to the grade of Brigadier General in due course.

Yours sincerely,

T. V. SOONG

28

Five Hundred Million Dollar Financial Aid of 1942 and Other Wartime Financial Relationships

INTRODUCTION

The documents and other materials appearing in this annex provide background (a) on the negotiations and discussions leading up to the passage of the Joint Resolution of February 7, 1942, authorizing financial aid to China (Public Law 442, 77th Cong., 56 Stat. 82) and the signing of the financial aid agreement of March 21, 1942, pursuant thereto by the Governments of the United States and the Republic of China, (b) on the uses of the financial aid provided by the United States and (c) on negotiations concerning the financing of expenditures in Chinese currency by or on behalf of the United States Army in China during the war.

Transfers to Chinese accounts from the financial aid authorized in 1942 were as follows:

Date of Transfer	Purpose	Amount (millions)
1. April 15, 1942	Establishment of fund for redemption of U. S. dollar security issues.	$200
2. February 1, 1943	Purchase of gold	20
3. March 2, 1943	Purchase of bank notes and supplies	20
4. October 13, 1944	Purchase of gold	20
5. May 22, 1945	Purchase of gold	60
6. June 12, 1945	Purchase of gold	60
7. July 18, 1945	Purchase of textiles	10
8. July 27, 1945	Purchase of gold	60
9. August 3, 1945	Purchase of bank notes	35
10. February 7, 1946	Purchase of textiles	1.5
11. March 13, 1946	Purchase of raw cotton	13.5
	TOTAL	500.0

On March 24, 1941, the Chinese Government announced in Chungking its plan to issue U.S. $100 million of 4 percent ten year National Government Allied Victory Bonds and U.S. $100 million of one, two and three year savings certificates with interest at 3 percent, 3½ percent and 4 percent, respectively. Following the announcement the Chinese Government requested the immediate transfer of 200 million dollars for the establishment of a fund for the redemption of these issues. As noted above, the transfer was made on April 15, 1942.

These issues were denominated in United States dollars, were sold for Chinese currency and were repayable at maturity in United States dollars or in Chinese currency at the option of the holder. It is believed that the most of the savings certificates were redeemed in United States dollars. Provision for U.S. dollar redemption of the ten year Allied Victory bonds, however, was revoked in 1946, except for registered bond holders outside China. It is not known how many bonds of this issue have been redeemed in United States dollars.

Of the 220 million dollars in gold purchased by China from the 500 million dollar credit of 1942, 158.6 million dollars had been shipped to China by V–J Day. Shipments in 1943 amounted to 10.5 million dollars and in 1944 to 15.2

million dollars, and the remainder was shipped in the first eight months of 1945. From late 1943 to June 30, 1945, the Chinese Government sold gold to the public for Chinese currency in an effort to combat inflation. Approximately 100 million dollars in gold (valued at $35 per ounce) was sold up to June 30, 1945, when gold sales were temporarily suspended. Some gold was sold on an advance basis. On June 30, 1945, the Chinese Government imposed a tax, payable in gold or Chinese currency on such sales as had not then been completed. Data are lacking as to how much gold was retained by this device.

Gold sales were resumed in September 1945 and terminated in February 1947 and were resumed intermittently in 1948 and 1949. Data are unavailable as to the amount of gold sold since September 1945.

Payments to the Chinese Government for Chinese currency supplied to or expended on behalf of the United States Army during the war were as follows:

(Millions of dollars)
1. Through February 1944 at the official rate of 20 yuan equals US $1 155
2. Lump sum settlement for advances in 1944 through September 210
3. Lump sum settlement for fourth quarter, 1944 45

Settlement for advances of Chinese currency in 1945 and up to August 30, 1946, was provided in the Surplus Property Sales Agreement of the latter date between the United States and China.

The documents which follow are arranged substantially in chronological order.

28 (a)

The Ambassador in China (Gauss) to Secretary Hull

CHUNGKING, *December 30, 1941*

Today I called on General Chiang at his request. After briefly reviewing recent measures for political and military collaboration with the United States and Great Britain, he passed on to the economic situation in substantially the following terms:

While there is no lack of confidence on the part of intelligent Chinese that the anti-Axis Powers will be victorious in the end, there is such lack of confidence among the uninformed masses, the sceptics, and the associates of the Chinese traitors. Morale has been affected by the early Japanese successes and by the way the Japanese have exploited them for purposes of propaganda. Specific mention was made of the radio appeal for Asiatic solidarity against westerners which was recently made to Chiang by the Prime Minister of Thailand. China can contribute fighting man power to the common cause but the United States and Great Britain must give China financial help in order to prevent further deterioration in economic fundamentals, loss of confidence in the Chinese currency, etc. Such help would do much toward strengthening morale and to silence the critical and doubtful elements. The credit he wants is about one billion United States dollars, of which he has through the British Ambassador asked the British Government to provide about one-half or one hundred million pounds, expecting America to provide the rest or about five hundred million dollars.

Chiang asked that in transmitting his request to my Government I should emphasize the importance such aid at this time would have to Chinese morale in overcoming Japanese propaganda and because of the needed support it would give to the economic structure of China. He pointed out that the present currency issue exceeds thirteen billion paper dollars and that the 1942 budget shows a deficit of at least nine billion Chinese dollars, and said that the proposed loan would be used partially to support a domestic bond issue intended to curb inflation.

I replied that of course I would faithfully and immediately report his request and his discussion to my Government which I was confident would be disposed to consider with sympathy any reasonable proposals to aid China in resisting Japan. However, I suggested that to assist consideration of his request and in approaching Congress for legislation necessary to authorize participation by the United States in a credit or loan to China, a carefully prepared outline of the needs of the situation on the basis of the studies and recommendations of the financial advisers and experts of the Chinese Government should be submitted together with an outline of the measures contemplated to be undertaken to meet the situation including the measures which China will take to help herself. I explained that what I was suggesting was not an outline of the terms of any proposed loan but an outline of the needs of the situation and of the definite measures which should be taken to meet these needs.

Chiang said that experts and advisers were working out plans for the use of the proposed credit or loan but that he desired me in the meanwhile to make the proposal to my Government. The proposals for application of the loan could be put forward when the loan is assured.

I learned from the British Ambassador that he was approached for a loan of one hundred million pounds from Great Britain and has referred the matter to his Government. He equally lacked any specific proposals as to how the loan, if granted, would be applied to the difficulties of the economic situation of China; Chiang had said that he considered it an urgent necessity that he should be enabled to demonstrate to the Chinese people and armies that the British Government had sufficient faith in victory to give quick and effective aid to China.

28 (b)

A. Manuel Fox, U.S. Member on the Chinese Stabilization Board, to Secretary of the Treasury Morgenthau

CHUNGKING, *January 3, 1942*

(A) In Yunnanfu and Chungking I find a great deal of talk of a loan to China by Great Britain and the United States. I am informed that the subject has already been raised with each of the Governments by the Generalissimo. In Chinese Government circles the talk is of a loan by Britain of one hundred million pounds and a loan of the United States amounting to five hundred million United States dollars.

(B) For some time prior to the outbreak of the war I have felt that a new loan to China was needed due to the extreme gravity of the internal economic situation here. My feeling has been reinforced since December 8 in view of (1) the effect on Chinese political opinion of the initial Japanese successes; and (2) the perceptible strengthening of defeatist elements in Chinese Government circles; and (3) the probable effect of temporary Japanese successes in southeast Asia in the near future. In this situation in order to keep China going as an Anti-Axis power a substantial loan (the bigger the better) would be invaluable. An argument in favor of making the loan as big as possible is the very fact that the larger portion of such a loan could not be used.

(C) The internal economic effects of such a loan would be beneficial, after the first psychological effects have worn off, although because of the physical difficulties in the importing of goods they might not be commensurate with its size. The fact that the political advantages would be very great is of more importance. A loan might make all the difference between a Chinese defeatist victory (lukewarm as they are) and the neutralization of the defeatists. The actual outlay would be much smaller than the nominal amount of the loan, as already indicated. It would be desirable to use the loan as an occasion for insisting on strengthening and improving the Central Bank and the Chinese banking system, but the political effects of the loan could be reinforced by not requiring any specific guarantees.

(D) The following uses could be made of the loan: (1) To retard the inflationary spiral by guaranteeing an attractive issue of Government bonds to absorb fapi and make it unnecessary for the future that the Government of China issue more currency to cover its budgetary deficit; (2) To insure the maintenance of an inflow of imports by promoting trade with India (as long as the Burma Road remains open) and with Russia. I am not in a position to evaluate from a political standpoint the aspects of financing trade with Russia but certainly there would be an accrual of economic advantages; (3) the financing of loans, if possible, for the promotion of the internal small scale production which is greatly needed and for agricultural production. Retardation of rise in prices would be aided by the effects of both (2) and (3) in increasing the supply of goods; and perhaps (4) the provision of foreign exchange backing for the note issue which would temporarily affect beneficially internal confidence in the currency. If it were possible to link the Stabilization Board in some way with the loan it might be desirable to do so because, if for no other reason, it might be easier for the Board than for the Chinese Government itself to secure confidence.

(E) The Board has received a scheme submitted by the Ministry of Finance which proposes that its remaining U.S. dollar and sterling assets be used as a guarantee fund for an issue of Chinese Government bonds on the lines of I (D). I see three objections to this: 1. The amount involved would not be sufficient to contribute substantially to the absorption of fapi; 2. taking into consideration the terms of agreements instituting the fund, there is some doubt as to the legality of the suggested procedure; 3. The Board would be deprived of its function of providing foreign exchange for imports. (This function must be performed so long as imports are possible.)

28 (c)

The Ambassador in China (Gauss) to Secretary Hull

CHUNGKING, *January 8, 1942*

I have the honor to refer to my message on the subject of finance-economic conditions in China and to my earlier messages in regard to the Chinese Government's request for an American credit of half a billion dollars and a British credit for one hundred million pounds, and to enclose for the Department's information (1) a memorandum of my conversation with General Chiang on December 30 when he asked me to place his request for a loan before the American Government,[32] (2) paraphrase of a telegram sent by the British Ambassador to his govern-

---

[32] See annex 28 (a).

ment on the reference subject,[22] (3) copy of a memorandum of Mr. Vincent's conversation with Mr. Hall-Patch, financial attache of the British Embassy,[22] and (4) copy of a confidential memorandum prepared by Mr. Chang Chia-ngau, Minister of Communications, for General Chiang and Dr. Kung in regard to the financial situation in China.[22]

I had suggested previously that the Congress might be asked to authorize a credit to China up to a specified amount for utilization under agreements or arrangements to be made by the executive branch of the Government after the presentation and consideration of definite proposals to be put forward by the Chinese Government.

I am convinced that credits of the magnitude requested by General Chiang (a total of about one billion U. S. dollars) are out of all proportion to the needs of the situation viewed from the political-psychological or the finance-economic standpoint—or both. While, in the absence of any definite proposals supported by factual data, only a rough estimate can be made, I feel that credits (American and British) of at most no more than a half billion dollars would generously satisfy all the requirements of the situation, psychological and financial, and that credits in excess of such an amount would be misleading and invite attempts at misuse. They would be misleading in that they might lead to popular expectation of practical results commensurate with the size of the credits, which would not be the case, because in present circumstances there is no practicable way in which such large credits could be effectively and legitimately utilized. They would invite attempts at misuse on the part of self-seeking banking and government elements who would find it difficult to resist the temptation to draw on such excessive credits for their own gain.

Aside from the broad idea of supporting government credit and retarding currency inflation, I am not informed with regard to any program for using the credits requested. Conversations with Dr. Fox and with Sir Otto Niemeyer lead me to believe that the Chinese Government has not formulated plans for coping with the serious internal situation and is therefore hardly in a position to indicate with any exactness the use it expects to make of desired foreign credits. Mr. Chang Chia-ngau sets forth in very general terms the need and usefulness of an internal bond issue supported by foreign credits and the Vice Ministers of Finance speak of "reconstruction" even more vaguely, and unconvincingly in so far as immediate needs are concerned. These, I fear, are examples illustrative of the government approach to the problem. The attitude and ideas of the Minister of Finance and the Minister of Economics are no more encouraging.

In the absence of technical studies on the subject, it is difficult for the Embassy to arrive at even a relatively precise idea of the reasonably constructive uses to which the credit might be put. However, it may serve some purpose to indicate in purely suggestive terms the Embassy's thoughts in the matter based on general observation.

A domestic bond issue, supported by foreign credits, would seem to be theoretically sound and advisable. No approximately definite figures as to the amount of such bonds that might be marketed are obtainable. The figure of two billion Chinese dollars is the one most often mentioned and under favorable conditions the amount might increase to four billions. Distribution primarily among the investing public would seem to be essential to accomplish the ends desired; that is, the withdrawal of currency from circulation and the release of goods now being hoarded. Obviously no public benefit would result from the

---
[22] Not printed.

government banks' exchanging currency in their vaults and newly issued currency for bonds backed by foreign currency at a fixed rate.

Encouragement of agricultural and small industrial production is wanting and badly needed. If it is feasible to do so, a portion of the credit might be used to support loans or grants to agricultural interests for the reclamation and improvement of farm land and to home and community industrial enterprises. The Chinese Government, notwithstanding the obvious advantages of such action, has been slow and reluctant to give assistance but it might be induced to do so if credits were set aside available only to support loans or grants of the kind. Only a very rough guess can be made as to the amount that might be earmarked for this purpose. Although there is slight likelihood that it would all be used, one hundred million dollars might be designated for the purpose of supporting grants or loans up to a billion Chinese dollars for small scale production and a like amount for agricultural improvement.

Dr. Fox, suggests,[34] inter alia (to the Secretary of the Treasury), use of a portion of the credit to promote imports from Russia into China. (He makes a similar suggestion with regard to imports from India). I am not in a position to evaluate the practical features of such a plan but I know that any opportunity to encourage the inflow of goods into China at this time should not be overlooked. One hundred million dollars of the credit might be set aside for this purpose in the hope that some portion could be used to accomplish the desired results.

The Central Executive Committee of the Kuomintang, at its meeting in December last, passed a resolution calling for "The execution of a land policy and the institution of government machinery to deal exclusively with land registration and the equalization of land ownership. . .". Various Kuomintang organs and committees have in the past passed similar resolutions, the effect of which has been inconsequential. To encourage implementation of the resolution quoted above, a practical step would seem to be the earmarking of a portion of the credit (one hundred million dollars is suggested as a generous estimate) for the support of the necessary financing of the agrarian reform contemplated.

The Generalissimo stresses the psychologically beneficial effect of a large political loan or credit at this time but he offers no program for its use, stating that a program will be forthcoming after the credit is given. I concur in his statement as to the need and the effect of a credit (while differing with regard to the amount) but I am convinced of the advisability, from the Chinese point of view as well as our own, of earmarking portions of the credit for certain purposes. Designation of portions of the credit for support of measures suggested above may be ill-received in banking and some governmental quarters but I believe that, viewing the situation as a whole from the standpoint of general public welfare and from the standpoint of strengthening the country's economic structure for continued resistance to Japan, it will produce more constructive results than the granting of a large lump credit or loan without designation as to use. It is well not to overlook the beneficial psychological effect upon the Chinese people of support for measures mentioned above (in particular measures for increased production and agrarian reform); and the practical effects of even partial application and implementation of such measures would fully justify our support. Probably no more than half the amounts suggested would be effectively used for the purposes mentioned and no doubt there would be administrative difficulties and inefficiencies, but even so, urgent requirements would at least be partially met—production of commodities would be increased (thereby remov-

---

[34] See annex 28 (b).

ing some of the curse from currency inflation) and a start towards long overdue agrarian reform would be made. And those elements in China which have been urging such measures and the infinitely greater number that would benefit therefrom would be encouraged and strengthened in their resolve to support active prosecution of the war against Japan, having received a practical demonstration that they are fighting *for* something. The alternative is purchase of the support of the retrogressive, self-seeking, and, I fear, fickle elements in and intimately associated with the government through the granting of a "free" credit, for I am convinced that a substantial credit should be granted.

I cannot too strongly emphasize my feeling that we should clearly and forcefully make known to the Chinese Government, in connection with financial aid that we may extend to China, our opposition to the use of any portion of such aid, directly or indirectly for the financing of expensive and harmful monopolies. This is a matter which calls for no clarification on my part in as much as I am sure that the Department is fully aware of the dangers of the situation.

28 (d)

The Chinese Minister of Finance (Kung) to Secretary of the Treasury Morgenthau

CHUNGKING, *January 9, 1942*

China has been fighting a war of resistance with heavy strain on her resources and with untold sacrifices for four and one-half years. At the present time, China's economic and financial situation is in a precarious condition. The livelihood of the people is difficult, because of increasing prices; and the brave soldiers at the front are ill-clothed and ill-fed. It is necessary to retain control of currency and prices without production being curtailed. It would be impossible to carry on the war if the already very critical economic and financial front should collapse.

Since the survival and existence of democratic countries are interdependent, present world war developments render it imperative for these countries to pool their economic and military resources. Consequently, I appeal to you for a political war loan of five hundred million dollars. Great Britain has also been approached by us for a loan of one hundred million pounds for the purpose of covering the total sum required. We are awaiting a reply from Great Britain. If you will lead, I am confident they will follow your example. This loan is requested for the purpose of replenishing reserve so as to restore confidence in currency, to offset diminished imports by increased production, to restrain prices, and to meet additional urgent war requirements. There are sound justifications for the loan on economic grounds, and also from the standpoint of joint military front. Frankly, however, my reason for approaching you is political above all; and the import of a loan of this nature is even more important than the Lend-Lease Bill's import. The essence of such a move is timeliness, so as to demonstrate that China's confidence in the allied powers is matched by equal confidence in China of the allied powers, in the most crucial months of emergency immediately before us. In addition to electrifying public opinion, early announcement of the loan would have an immediate effect throughout Asia, including our common enemy, Japan. My appreciation of your continuing keen interest in China provides me with confidence in sending you this message.

28 (e)

Secretary Hull to Secretary of the Treasury Morgenthau

WASHINGTON, *January 10, 1942*

MY DEAR MR. SECRETARY: Reference is made to Generalissimo Chiang Kai-shek's request of December 30, 1941 that the United States Government provide China with $500,000,000 of financial help in order to support Chinese morale and prevent the effects of further depreciation of the Chinese currency and deterioration of the fundamental economic situation in China.

The Generalissimo's proposal has been given very careful consideration. I feel that, as an act of wartime policy and to prevent the impairment of China's military effort which would result from loss of confidence in Chinese currency and depreciation of its purchasing power, it is highly advisable that the United States extend financial assistance to the Government of China in amounts up to $300,000,000 at the present time. I believe that a determination of this Government's policy to this effect need not await ascertainment of the attitude to be taken by Great Britain on the similar Chinese proposal with reference to sterling credits.

I feel that the greatest possible expedition in reaching a position where an announcement can be made is highly important. I feel also that it would seem to be highly desirable that the British Government be kept currently informed of our views and decisions in regard to this matter in order that the British Government may be afforded opportunity, should it so desire, to take simultaneous and comparable action.

Sincerely yours,

CORDELL HULL

28 (f)

Generalissimo Chiang Kai-shek to Secretary of the Treasury Morgenthau

CHUNGKING, *14th January, 1942*

DEAR MR. SECRETARY: I have requested Mr. Fox to inform you in person of China's present financial and economic realities and needs. Throughout these critical years your support of China's cause has been most enthusiastic and sympathetic. You are now naturally more than ever concerned with our problems and difficulties, especially at the moment when our interests and destiny are absolutely identical.

If China's finance and economics fail to be improved and strengthened, our power of resistance against Japanese aggression will be so adversely affected that the entire war front of the allied Powers will inevitably suffer. My Government and people earnestly hope that your Government will give us the speediest and most effective assistance, and that, in compliance with my request and in accordance with the plan prepared by our Minister of Finance, you will exert your utmost to procure the desired loan for China. In view of actual war-time requirements this loan is not large.

I feel certain that in his verbal report Mr. Fox will enter fully into the military, financial and economic situations in China, and will explain in detail what bearing they have in the attainment of our common victory.

With best wishes,

Yours sincerely,

CHIANG KAI-SHEK

28 (g)

The Chinese Minister for Foreign Affairs (Soong) to Secretary of the Treasury Morgenthau

[WASHINGTON,] *January 21, 1942*

MY DEAR MR. SECRETARY: During your absence from Washington I received the enclosed message for you from the Generalissimo.

Since Mr. Fox is due to arrive in Washington shortly, it occurs to me that you may like to have an opportunity of seeing him and hearing from him of the situation in China before you renew discussions with me. However I am at your disposal at any time, should you wish to see me earlier.

Sincerely yours,

T. V. SOONG

[Enclosure]

The Generalissimo deeply appreciates Secretary Morgenthau's efforts which have materialized in a proposal that the U. S. Government would undertake to pay for the maintenance of part of the Chinese army in U. S. Dollar notes. After careful consideration, however, he doubts whether this scheme is practicable. Payment of Chinese soldiers in U. S. currency would tend to create a cleavage between the army and the general economic structure in China which may actually hasten the collapse of the Chinese currency. Before Mr. Fox left Chungking the Generalissimo had a long discussion with him in which he pointed out a number of reasons why he considered the scheme difficult of application and which he asked Mr. Fox to convey to Secretary Morgenthau.

The Generalissimo urgently requests that careful consideration be given to his original proposal that the United States grant to China a political loan of 500 million U. S. dollars, which would be the only means to prevent an impending economic collapse. This loan should be regarded in the light of an advance to an ally fighting against a common enemy, thus requiring no security or other pre-arranged terms as to its use and as regards means of repayment.

28 (h)

Minutes [35] of a Meeting in the Office of the Secretary of State, January 30, 1942

[Extract]

Secretary Hull asked for opinions as to which of the several methods suggested by the Treasury would be the best medium for giving help. He said he himself was not interested in the method. He said that should be the Treasury's business.

Present: Secretary Hull
Secretary Morgenthau
Dr. Viner
Mr. White
Later Joined By: Mr. Berle
Mr. Hornbeck
Mr. Hamilton
Mr. Feis

---

[35] Prepared at the Treasury Department.

ANNEXES 479

He was solely interested in seeing that China did get aid in the present critical situation.

Mr. Hornbeck stated that he thought the ideal method of helping would be a Congressional statute providing for an extension of financial aid to China. He said that might, however, cause undue delay. He was not certain that legislation was the most practical method of approaching the problem. He stated that he did not think the matter was so urgent or acute that a matter of days were critical, but that if it were to take several weeks for Congress to pass such legislation, it would be too late. If legislation could be passed in a few days he favored legislation.

Mr. Hornbeck went on to say that he thought that the sum should be $500 million instead of the $300 million which Secretary Hull had indicated in his letter to Secretary Morgenthau. Mr. Hornbeck thought that a reduction in the portion which the United States was prepared to give to $300 million would be too great a reduction from the sum which Chiang-Kai-Shek was asking. He felt Chiang-Kai-Shek should be given what he asked for, namely $500 million from the United States. Secretary Morgenthau agreed with Hornbeck, as did the others, and it was therefore decided that the sum which they would recommend would be $500 million.

28 (i)

Secretary of the Treasury Morgenthau to Generalissimo Chiang Kai-shek

WASHINGTON, *February 16, 1942.*

DEAR GENERALISSIMO CHIANG: I read with great interest your letter of January 14, 1942, transmitted to me in person by Mr. Fox. The unanimity and promptness with which my Government responded to the appeal for financial assistance is evidence that your confidence in the support of the United States is well founded. It also demonstrated that the American people have faith in the Chinese people and know that you and your Government will continue to play a vital part in the common effort against our foes.

I wish you to know that here in the United States Generalissimo Chiang Kai-shek is looked upon as the personification of the heroism and courage of the Chinese people who, under the most difficult circumstances and at tremendous odds, have successfully defended their country against invasion. No one doubts in the United States that your leadership has secured for China the unity of purpose and will, without which China would have fallen victim to the Japanese aggressor. Moreover, the people of the United States clearly understand that China's unceasing resistance will not only bring freedom and independence to itself, but will play a major part in achieving victory and peace for free men everywhere.

Sincerely yours,

H. MORGENTHAU, Jr.

28 (j)

Initial Draft of United States-China Financial Aid Agreement [36]

WHEREAS, the Governments of the United States of America and of the Republic of China are engaged, together with other nations and peoples of like mind, in a

---

[36] Handed to the Chinese Minister for Foreign Affairs, T. V. Soong, by the Treasury Department, Feb. 21, 1942.

cooperative undertaking against common enemies, to the end of laying the bases of a just and enduring world peace securing order under law to themselves and all nations, and

WHEREAS, the United States and China are signatories to the Declaration of United Nations of January 1, 1942, which declares that "each government pledges itself to employ its full resources, military or economic, against those members of the Tripartite Pact and its adherents with which such government is at war"; and

WHEREAS, the Congress of the United States, in unanimously passing Public Law No. 442, approved February 7, 1942, has declared that financial and economic aid to China will increase China's ability to oppose the forces of aggression and that the defense of China is of the greatest possible importance, and has authorized the Secretary of the Treasury of the United States, with the approval of the President, to give financial aid to China, and

WHEREAS, such financial aid will enable China to strengthen greatly its war efforts against the common enemies by helping China to

(1) strengthen its currency, monetary, banking and economic system;
(2) finance and promote increased production, acquisition and distribution of necessary goods;
(3) retard the rise of prices, promote stability of economic relationships, and otherwise check inflation;
(4) prevent hoarding of foods and other materials;
(5) improve means of transportation and communication;
(6) effect further social and economic measures which will safeguard the unity of the Chinese people; and
(7) meet military needs and take other appropriate measures in its war effort.

In order to achieve these purposes, the undersigned, being duly authorized by their respective Governments for that purpose, have agreed as follows:

ARTICLE I.

The Secretary of the Treasury of the United States agrees to establish forthwith on the books of the United States Treasury a credit in the name of the Government of the Republic of China in the amount of 500,000,000 U.S. dollars. The Secretary of the Treasury shall make transfers from his credit, in such amounts and at such times as the Government of the Republic of China shall request, to an account or accounts in the Federal Reserve Bank of New York in the name of the Government of the Republic of China or any agencies designated by it. Such transfers may be requested by and such accounts at the Federal Reserve Bank of New York may be drawn upon by the Government of the Republic of China either directly or through such persons or agencies as it shall authorize.

ARTICLE II.

China desires to keep the Secretary of the Treasury of the United States informed as to the use of the funds herein provided and to consult with him from time to time as to such uses. The Secretary of the Treasury of the United States desires to make available to the Government of the Republic of China technical and other appropriate advice as to ways and means of effectively employing these funds to achieve the purposes herein described. Technical problems that may from time to time arise in effectuating the financial aid herein provided will be subjects of discussion between the Secretary of the Treasury of the United States and the Government of the Republic of China.

ANNEXES 481

ARTICLE III.

The final determination of the terms upon which this financial aid is given, including the benefits to be rendered the United States in return, is deferred until the progress of events makes clearer the final terms and benefits which will be in the mutual interest of the United States and China and will promote the establishment of lasting world peace and security. In determining the final terms and benefits no interest charges shall be made for the financial aid herein provided and full cognizance shall be given to the desirability of maintaining a healthy and stable economic and financial situation in China in the post-war period as well as during the war and to the desirability of promoting mutually advantageous economic and financial relations between the United States and China and the betterment of world-wide economic and financial relations.

ARTICLE IV.

This Agreement shall take effect as from this day's date.

Signed and sealed at Washington, District of Columbia, in duplicate this _____ day of _____, 1942.

On behalf of the United States of America

Secretary of the Treasury

On behalf of the Republic of China

----

28 (k)

The Ambassador in China (Gauss) to Secretary Hull

CHUNGKING, *March 1, 1942.*

Strictly confidential information has reached the Embassy that a draft Sino-American loan agreement has been received from Washington by the Ministry of Finance and has been discussed. It is said that the Ministry resents on the ground that a measure of control is contemplated the provision for consultation by the Government of China with the Treasury Department concerning expenditures under the loan. The Ministry has been disappointed to find that the loan is not granted, as the Press has stated, as an absolute gift in recognition of China's contribution to the War effort in general.

I am not prepared to express an opinion on the question of policy whether or not we should provide for some means of repayment. I have been privately told by a prominent and intelligent Chinese banker that the obtainment of the loan was too easy for the loan to be appreciated or for provision for its effective use to be insured. There is a perceptible assumption on the part of Chungking officials and bankers that it is a compensation which was due to China for its past and present resistance to Japan and for what the Chinese regard as our past and present shortcomings.

It is my conviction that for the purpose of having some measure of control over the matter in which so large a loan is expended we should firmly insist on retaining the provision for consultation. It is my opinion as I have indicated in previous telegrams that the best interests of China and our own best interests as well would be served by controls and allocation of parts of the loan for specific purposes.

28 (l)

The Chinese Minister for Foreign Affairs (Soong) to Under Secretary of the Treasury Bell

[WASHINGTON,] *March 3, 1942*

DEAR MR. BELL: I am in receipt of a reply on the draft of the Loan Agreement from the Generalissimo dated February 25th, which I delayed presenting to you owing to a visit to Canada.

The Generalissimo is very appreciative of the generous spirit that characterized the draft Agreement and desires me to convey his grateful appreciation to the Secretary.

As to details he suggested the following points:

1. Reactions in Chungking as to Article II appear to be that the U. S. Government will in some way pass judgment on the uses to which the Loan may be put, and thereby limits in some degree the freedom of making disbursement.

As China in any case would like to keep the Secretary informed, and as the Secretary has in the past without any agreement always exerted himself on every occasion to help China, he suggests that Article II is unnecessary, since it makes of such voluntary acts mandatory. He therefore hopes that Article II may be dropped.

2 (a) As the whole energy of the people is concentrated on winning the war, he hopes that the final determination of the terms upon which the financial aid is given should be left until after the war. He suggests that the phrase "after the war" should appear in Article III, coming after the phrase "deferred until the progress of events" in the opening sentence.

2 (b) Although greatly appreciative of the United States waiving interest, he believes that the lofty plane of cooperation between the United States and China would be aided by dropping all reference to interest through deleting the clause "no interest charges shall be made for the financial aid herein provided".

2 (c) For the purpose of clarification that the final determination of the terms upon which the financial aid is given should be a bilateral and not a unilateral measure, he would suggest that in the final sentence of Article III the words the "United States and China shall take full cognizance of" should come after the words "In determining the final terms and benefits".

In order to make the suggestions clearer I am enclosing the draft Agreement with such alterations as are suggested in the telegram.

The Generalissimo again bids me to say that such textual changes as he suggested are only to heighten the impression of the Chinese people at this unprecedentedly generous act of the American Government and people.

Would you be good enough to pass on the suggestions to your colleagues for their kind consideration.

Yours sincerely,

T. V. SOONG

ANNEXES 483

28 (m)

Acting Secretary Welles to Secretary of the Treasury Morgenthau

WASHINGTON, *March 11, 1942.*

MY DEAR MR. SECRETARY: I refer to your letter of March 10 on the subject of the draft of the proposed agreement regarding the extension of financial aid to China.

All parties concerned are in agreement that the purposes of the extension of this financial aid are predominantly political, diplomatic, and military.

The draft which you submitted to Dr. T. V. Soong for consideration contains in its four articles provisions which make readily available to the Chinese Government without restrictive commitments the $500,000,000 which the Congress appropriated for the making of a loan, the extending of a credit or the giving of other financial aid to China. It does not in fact impair or restrict the Chinese Government's freedom of action in the making of disbursements.

In his letter to Mr. Bell of March 3 Dr. Soong suggests, on behalf of Generalissimo Chiang Kai-shek, the making of a number of changes. In my opinion, we can readily accept most of these suggestions and proceed accordingly. With regard, however, to the suggestion that Article II be omitted in its entirety, it seems to me that there is ample warrant for a discussion of the matter and that we should endeavor to cause Dr. Soong and the Generalissimo to realize that provisions such as appear in the draft of that article are desirable from point of view not only of this Government but of the Chinese Government.

With regard to procedure, I would suggest that there first be made a redraft of the proposed Article II and that there then be communicated to Dr. Soong a statement by you that we are in complete concurrence with his comments and the changes which he has suggested except as regards that article, and that, in the light of his comments on that article, there is submitted to him for his consideration a possible alternative form.

Toward facilitating procedure along that line, I submit here attached for your consideration a draft of a possible substitute for Article II.

Another possible line of procedure which might be considered would be that of putting the substance of this suggested alternative draft of Article II into letters which might be exchanged between you and Dr. Soong.

In as much as the only delay which has occurred in connection with the attention which has been given this matter has been delay on the part of the Chinese, I would further suggest that, in whatever communication you make to Dr. Soong, you indicate to him that all officers of this Government who are concerned with the negotiating of this agreement are eager to bring the matter to a mutually satisfactory conclusion with the utmost possible expedition.

Sincerely yours,

SUMNER WELLES

[Enclosure—Draft]

ARTICLE II

As a manifestation of the cooperative spirit which underlies the common war effort of China and the United States, appropriate officials of the two Governments will confer from time to time regarding technical problems which may arise in connection with the financial aid herein provided and will exchange information and suggestions regarding ways and means of most effectively applying these funds toward achieving the purposes which are envisaged by the two nations.

28 (n)

The Chinese Minister for Foreign Affairs (Soong) to Under Secretary of the Treasury Bell

[WASHINGTON,] *March 19, 1942*

DEAR MR. BELL: Confirming our conversation, I have to inform you that I have received a reply from the Generalissimo with reference to your proposal to reinsert Article II of the proposed loan agreement in a modified form.

The Generalissimo states that after carefully consulting his colleagues he feels that even in the modified form Article II is generally construed as limiting the freedom of action in the use of the proceeds, and would therefore adversely affect the public response to bonds, savings deposits and other measures that are to be based on the loan.

In addition, among his soldiers, who have been tremendously heartened by the generous and unconditional assistance as revealed in the exchange of messages between the President and himself, the inclusion of Article II would create the impression that the terms are not as clear-cut as they envisaged.

The Generalissimo therefore feels that the civilian and military reactions are such as to justify his request that Article II be dropped completely, and I shall be grateful if you will transmit his message to your colleagues for their consideration.

With kind regards,
Yours sincerely,

T. V. SOONG

28 (o)

The Chinese Minister for Foreign Affairs (Soong) to Secretary of the Treasury Morgenthau

[WASHINGTON,] *March 21, 1942*

MY DEAR MR. SECRETARY: In connection with the Agreement concluded today between the Governments of the United States of America and the Republic of China regarding financial aid to China, as a manifestation of the cooperative spirit which underlies the common war effort of our two countries, I wish to inform you that it is the intention of my Government, through the Minister of Finance, to keep you fully informed from time to time as to the use of the funds provided in the said Agreement.

Sincerely yours,

T. V. SOONG

28 (p)

[*For the Joint Statement by Secretary of the Treasury Morgenthau and the Chinese Minister for Foreign Affairs (Soong), March 21, 1942, see post, annex 29 (b).*]

28 (q)

The Chinese Minister of Finance (Kung) to Secretary of the Treasury Morgenthau

[CHUNGKING,] *April 20, 1942*

With reference to keeping the Treasury informed on all developments relating to the loan I have done so and intend to do so in the future. For example, I told Adler on the 18th of March about the plan to put out savings certificates and bonds and he must have cabled this to the Treasury. I welcome any counsel the Treasury is willing to offer and if the Secretary cares to make any suggestions every consideration will be given to them. It was essential to request the shift of funds to the Central Bank in order to convince the people that use was being made of the loan without delay to prevent inflation.

28 (r)

Secretary of the Treasury Morgenthau to the United States Treasury Representative, American Embassy at Chungking

WASHINGTON, *December 29, 1942*

One. With reference to your cable in which you report that Dr. Kung is willing to accept any decision the Treasury may desire to make in connection with the amount of gold which should be purchased from the Treasury by China, whether it be twenty, thirty, forty, or fifty million dollars, due to the considerations set forth in the following, the Treasury believes that the more appropriate sum would be the amount already agreed upon, U.S. twenty million dollars.

A. Treasury does not perceive in what manner the Chinese government would benefit by purchasing additional gold on which the required charges would have to be paid by the government of China.

B. It would seem to be indicated by the information received from Mr. Hsi and from you with respect to the attitude of Dr. Kung on purchasing additional gold that Dr. Kung does not feel any urgent requirement for additional gold exists.

C. Additional gold purchase by the government of China would entail raising funds to purchase the additional gold by the United States Treasury. It would be necessary for the Government of the United States to pay interest on the funds raised at a time when the Government is already engaged in the task of borrowing tremendous amounts in order to meet its current fiscal requirements.

D. The Treasury would have difficulty in justifying to the public an increase in the indebtedness of the United States Government so as to render it possible for the Chinese government to buy gold for earmarking here, unless China would benefit in some way by the purchase of additional gold.

Two. Kindly advise Dr. Kung of the foregoing.

28 (s)

Message Received from the Chinese Minister of Finance (Kung), July 8, 1943

During the six years of our war of resistance China's military expenditure has been increasing continuously. According to the national budget of the current year, the estimated expenditure was originally placed at 36,200,000,000 yuan, while the estimated income was given as 23,200,000,000 yuan, representing about 65% of the total expenditure. The remaining 35% is entirely met by increased note issue.

Owing to military requirements and the requests made by the American Military Mission, the Chinese Government has undertaken to build, or improve, the airfields in various parts of the country and to increase their equipment, as well as to improve the Yunnan-Burma highway and other necessary highways and railways. Each enterprise often necessitated the expenditure of 4,000,000,000 to 5,000,000,000 yuan, making a total of additional requirements amounting to over 30,000,000 yuan.

Furthermore, owing to the difficulties of transportation and the small volume of supplies received under the American Lend-Lease Act, the Chinese Government has been obliged to provide ways and means of increasing the production of military supplies in order to meet the demands of the war. All such expenses are beyond what is provided by the budget, and the Chinese Government is compelled to further increase its note issue in order to meet the situation. For these reasons there has been constant tendency toward inflation. In order to remedy the situation and to stabilize the price of commodities, it is necessary to adopt measures having the effect of checking inflation. Through increased taxation and other means, the Government has withdrawn a certain portion of the notes in circulation, but there is still by far the larger portion in the hands of the people which is being used toward the purchase and accumulation of commodities, resulting in the further rising of prices and in making livelihood increasingly difficult.

The chief purpose for the proposed purchase and sale of gold is to withdraw large quantities of notes now in circulation. The fact that each ounce of gold is worth now about 8,000 yuan shows the psychology of Chinese people toward gold. To obtain the desired result, it is only necessary for the time being to have bullion which can be handled easily. However, the question of coinage is being given careful study and can be best taken up at the time of reorganization of Chinese currency.

According to Madam Chiang, the proposal which we are making—that is, the purchase of 200,000,000 dollars' worth of gold with the United States loan—has received the approval of President Roosevelt and Secretary Morgenthau in principle. It is earnestly hoped that it can be realized at an early date. We always appreciate and welcome suggestions and advices from Secretary Morgenthau and Dr. White, but in this particular case we are influenced by actual conditions in China, and we feel that it has to be done in the way we suggested in order to reap the desired benefits. It is earnestly hoped that we shall not lose this good opportunity of checking inflation.

28 (t)

Memorandum to President Roosevelt from Secretary of the Treasury Morgenthau

[WASHINGTON,] *July 15, 1943*

On July 14, 1943, we sent a message to Dr. H. H. Kung, the Chinese Minister of Finance, informing him that the Treasury is prepared in principle to agree to the Chinese request to purchase $200 million of gold out of the $500 million financial aid as a means of helping to check inflation in China. Dr. Kung was also informed that a formal request was, of course, necessary before any definitive decision and action could be taken.

The Chinese Government has already drawn on the Treasury to the extent of $240 million out of the $500 million financial aid:—$200 million has been set aside as backing for Chinese Government savings certificates and bond issues; $20 million was used to purchase gold, and $20 million is being used for the printing of banknotes and the purchase of relative materials. The purchase of gold with an additional $200 million will mean that in total the Chinese will have used $440 million out of the $500 million financial aid.

In the message to Dr. Kung, as well as in discussions with the representatives of the Chinese Government in Washington, it has been made clear that the Treasury is acquiescing to the Chinese proposal because the Government of China deems that the sale of gold to the public will aid its war effort by helping to fight inflation and hoarding and that, therefore, the decision to purchase the gold is primarily the responsibility of the Chinese Government. Furthermore, the Chinese have been urged to give careful consideration to the best ways of using the gold, particularly because of the great costs, difficulties and dangers inherent in the use of gold as a means of checking inflation under conditions existing in China at present. We especially stressed the fact that the Chinese Government will by this step be sacrificing large amounts of foreign exchange, which could be used in the post-war period to pay for imports needed for reconstruction and rehabilitation.

The use of gold coins as against bullion for the purpose was carefully considered. It was felt both by us and by the Chinese Government that this technique for selling the gold to the public would not be feasible in the present instance, primarily because it would be necessary to give the gold coins a fixed monetary value, while it is contemplated that the price of gold in terms of yuan will change frequently and substantially as time goes on.

The suggestion was therefore made to the Chinese representatives in Washington that the gold might be sold to the public in China in small bars of one or two ounces in order to reach the widest possible section of the Chinese public and such bars might have some engraving which might suggest the United States origin of the financial aid, if the Government of China so wished.

28 (u)

Secretary of the Treasury Morgenthau to the Chinese Minister of Finance (Kung)

WASHINGTON, *July 27, 1943*

The Treasury agrees to the request of the Government of China transmitted to me by Ambassador Wei Tao-ming that $200 million be made available from the credit on the books of the Treasury in the name of the Government of the Republic of China for the purchase of gold.

In order to avoid unnecessary raising of funds by the United States Treasury, it is suggested that transfers from the credit of the Chinese Government for the purchase of gold be made at such time and in such amounts as are allowed by existing facilities for the transportation to China of the equivalent amount of gold. Since it is intended that this gold will be sent to China for sale to the public, this procedure should not interfere with the program outlined in your message of July 23, 1943.

On receipt of requests from the Government of China that a specific amount should be transferred from the credit of the Government of China on the books of the Treasury and be used for the purchase of gold, the necessary action will be taken to consummate these requests. The details of the arrangements will be discussed with Dr. P. W. Kuo and Mr. Hsi Te-mou.

Sincerely yours,

H. MORGENTHAU, Jr.

28 (v)

Memorandum to President Roosevelt from Secretary of the Treasury Morgenthau

[WASHINGTON,] *December 18, 1943*

You have spoken of the request of Generalissimo Chiang-Kai-Shek for an additional $1 billion of financial aid to China to be used to help control inflation and for postwar reconstruction.

I

The facts regarding inflation in China and the possibility of its control through the use of dollar resources are as follows:

Inflation in China, as you well know, arises from the grave inadequacy of production for war needs and essential civilian consumption. Supplies have been drastically reduced by enemy occupation and the cutting off of imports except the small amounts that come by air or are smuggled from occupied territory.

The Chinese Government cannot collect sufficient taxes or borrow from the people in adequate amounts. As a consequence, the Government has been issuing 3.5 billion yuan a month, twice the rate of a year ago.

The official exchange rate for yuan is now 5 cents; before China entered the war it was 30 cents. The open market rate for yuan in U. S. paper currency is one cent and in terms of gold one-third of a cent.

You have suggested the possibility of our selling dollar currency for yuan to be resold to China after the war at no profit to us. No doubt something could be done to alleviate inflation through the sale of gold or dollar currency in China. I have received the following message from Dr. Kung dated December 14:

"You will be pleased to hear that the recent gold shipment is one of the outstanding factors contributing to the strengthening of fapi, because people believe that the arrival of gold has increased the much needed reserve of our currency, thereby influencing the stability of prices. The action of the United States Government re-affirms to the Chinese people that, despite difficulties arising from the blockade and the cumulative effects of over six years of war against the invasion, China has a powerful friend desirous of strengthening China's economy as conditions permit."

However, while something could be done to retard the rise in prices, the only real hope of controlling inflation is by getting more goods into China. This, you know better than I, depends on future military operations.

ANNEXES 489

II

China has tried two similar monetary remedies for alleviating inflation without marked success.

1. The Chinese Government issued and sold dollar securities for yuan, setting aside $200 million of the aid granted by this country for the redemption of the securities. (These securities were sold at exorbitant profit to the buyers. For instance, a person holding $100 in United States currency could have quadrupled his money in less than two years by selling the currency for yuan on the open market and buying the dollar securities issued by the Chinese Government.) I believe that the program made no significant contribution to the control of inflation.

2. The Chinese Government has recently been selling gold at a price in yuan equivalent to $550 an ounce, about fifteen times the official rate. We have shipped to China more than $10 million of gold and they have sold about $2 million of gold for yuan. This program has not been tried sufficiently to warrant any definite conclusion as to its possible effect.

China now has $460 million of unpledged funds in the United States and is getting about $20 million a month as a result of our expenditures. China could use these funds in selling gold or dollar assets for yuan, although in my opinion such schemes in the past have had little effect except to give additional profits to insiders, speculators and hoarders and dissipate foreign exchange resources that could be better used by China for reconstruction.

Under the circumstances, a loan to China for these purposes could not be justified by the results that have been obtained. It is my opinion that a loan is unnecessary at this time and would be undesirable from the point of view of China and the United States. Large expenditures on ineffective measures for controlling inflation in China would be an unwise use of her borrowing capacity which should be reserved for productive uses in other ways. On reconstruction, it is too soon for us to know the best use or the best form of the aid we might give to China.

RECOMMENDATIONS

For the past five years I have had a deep admiration for the valiant fight that the Chinese people, under the leadership of Chiang-Kai-Shek, have waged against Japanese aggression. Therefore, I am in complete sympathy with your position that no stone be left unturned to retard the rise in prices. Using the tools we have at hand, I recommend the following:

1. All United States expenditures in China, currently $400 million yuan a month and rising rapidly, be met through the purchase of yuan with gold or dollar currency at whatever price we can get them for in the open market. This is equal to more than 10 percent of the present rate of issue.

2. Accelerate the shipment of gold purchased by China to twice the amount we have previously planned to send. It should be possible to raise gold shipments from $6 million a month to about $12 million. At the present price for gold in the open market this would be equal to the present 3.5 billion of yuan currency that is being issued.

The impact of this two-fold program should contribute to retarding inflation, always bearing in mind that the basic reason for inflation in China is the shortage of goods.

28 (w)

The Ambassador in China (Gauss) to Secretary Hull

CHUNGKING, *December 23, 1943*

I called last evening in company with Atcheson upon President and Madame Chiang at their request. The only other person present was Wang Chung Hui who had been with them at Cairo. In reply to Chiang's question, which he asked significantly, whether I had received any telegrams recently I said none of importance. The Generalissimo then asked my opinion of the situation in China, especially economic developments, and he observed that he would welcome any advice that I might offer and hear any plan I might suggest.

In referring to the seriousness of economic conditions, he reiterated his suggestion that I put forward any plan for amelioration. He then went on to say that in his country the coming year would be most crucial and that the faith of the Chinese people in China's national currency had so far prevented an economic collapse. Chiang said that it was essential that there be an early reopening of the Burma Road for so long as this road remains unopened the desperate economic situation of China renders it essential to support the value of the currency of China and maintain the rate of exchange.

In reply to Chiang's question as to whether I have studied the problem of the financial difficulties of China, I said that we try to keep up with the financial situation in the light of whatever information is available and that from the American point of view one aspect which has lately been causing me much concern is the effect which the rate of exchange is having on the expenditures by the American Government for the American military forces with which China is being assisted; those expenditures are now attaining high figures and when converted at the artificial rate of exchange are costing the American Government twenty million dollars and over a month in American currency, which, while benefitting China by accumulating a currency reserve in the United States, make for expenditures by the United States eight to ten times as great as we would have to spend in the United States or elsewhere for services and facilities of a comparable character such as advance airbase facilities which our forces urgently require. I expressed my concern that as this became known in our country it might cause serious criticism that the American Government and Army are being exploited and that such criticism would operate to the injury of China as well as of our war effort in China.

The Generalissimo firmly affirmed that the exchange rate for Chinese currency cannot be altered. I replied that I entirely understood his position on that point. I suggested however that there might be adopted without involving a change in the exchange rate other proposals toward a solution of the problem, such as reverse Lend-Lease, or the proposal that the Secretary of the Treasury had made to Dr. Kung regarding the sale of gold. Madame Chiang observed that as there was no market for gold, the efforts of the Chinese Government to sell gold had proved a failure. The Generalissimo affirmed that he had given study to the question of reverse Lend-Lease, that the whole financial situation had been causing Kung and himself much anxiety, that it is not possible to change the exchange rate and that support must be given to the value of Chinese currency. He asked that I see Dr. Kung again and just before leaving the room in the way that is his custom requested with a manifestation of some exasperation and emphasis that I make it known to our Treasury and military authorities that both the economic and military collapse of China would result from a failure to support the currency of China.

Madame Chiang indicated during the course of the conversation that the President had been made acquainted at Cairo with the Generalissimo's views on the seriousness of the situation. After Chiang had left she expressed herself emphatically in regard to China's economic difficulties and remarked with some bitterness that about 200 Chinese dollars were being paid by China for the maintenance of every American soldier in China. She indicated that as our forces are augmented the cost would become intolerable and added that it is becoming more and more impossible to find sufficient pigs, chickens, and cattle to feed the American troops (needed to supplement the amounts of supplies which we ourselves bring in). She said that it was imperative that sufficient backing be accorded Chinese currency.

Two. It is my belief that last evening's stage was set for soliciting the support of the Department of State for request of an additional American loan and that such a request was not put forward because of the diversion made to the subject of our expenditures for military purposes. On December 20 I was informed by Stilwell that a billion dollar loan had been requested by Chiang and that an answer was expected by Chiang that day. That he told me and no more. I assume that the request was made through military channels and in connection with military talks.

It is unfortunate that the Embassy is not kept fully advised of developments occurring in relations between the United States and China.

In my recent telegram there was carefully set forth the Embassy's view in regard to a further loan to China at this time. It is my firm opinion that we should take a firm stand at this time on this question. In regard to military plans for a Burma campaign calculated to restore overland transportation to China, believed by experts here to be the only possible measure for bettering the abnormal economic situation, I have no information. I am ready to believe that although the foreign exchange rate is not of concern to the masses of the people, hoarders and speculators would avail themselves of any substantial change in that rate to accelerate rising prices still further.

Nothing substantial has actually been done by the Chinese Government to find and deal with these speculators and hoarders. Nevertheless, I am of the opinion that China possesses substantial reserves of U. S. currency at this time and there might be taken, without reference to exchange rate as such, probably within the framework of the sale of gold and reverse Lend-Lease, reasonable measures to cope with the situation affecting our military expenditures in China.

Although I do not pretend to pass judgment in matters of a military character, I should stress what we have repeatedly reported previously, namely, that economic and military conditions in China are deteriorating so fast that, in order to prevent collapse of China in due course, military measures to restore the Burma Road and reopen land transportation to China are imperative at an early date. The economic situation in China will not be helped by a loan from the United States at this juncture. It can only be helped by successful military operations on an extensive scale.

28 (x)

Secretary of the Treasury Morgenthau to Secretary Hull

WASHINGTON, *December 31, 1943*

MY DEAR MR. SECRETARY: This is to acknowledge receipt of your letter of December 29th enclosing a report of December 23, 1943 from Ambassador Gauss. I appreciate your sending me this telegram and have found it of considerable interest.

I see that Ambassador Gauss is in agreement with the views expressed in our Memorandum to the President, a copy of which I sent to you in letter dated December 20, 1943.

It would seem that no further steps can be taken regarding the Chinese request for a loan until we have received a reply to our Memorandum which, as you probably know, the President said he was going to forward to President Chiang Kai-shek.

Sincerely yours,

H. MORGENTHAU, Jr.

28 (y)

Generalissimo Chiang Kai-shek to President Roosevelt [37]

I have received your recent telegram forwarded through Ambassador Gauss and am happy that you have recovered from your indisposition. I appreciate the fact that you have been endeavoring to find a solution to the economic problems of China even during your illness.

To my mind the proposals made by the Treasury Department are not those of one allied nation to another but rather are in the nature of a commercial transaction. If put into practice these proposals would not increase China's economic strength in the prosecution of the war. On the contrary the impairment of the Chinese people's confidence in *fapi* would only add to her economic difficulties. I would not make this urgent appeal to you were it not for the fact that we are entering a most critical stage. I have reached the following conclusions after giving mature consideration to the future perilous economic situation in this war theater:

(1) An out and out loan of one billion dollars from the United States would enable us partly to meet the deficit of the coming war budget and also through reciprocal aid to meet a part of American military expenses in China, such as the repair and construction of airfields and necessary installations, the feeding of American troops and the transportation of war materials, et cetera.

(2) If it is the opinion of the Treasury Department that it is not able to accept the above proposal I suggest that such expenditures as are incurred by United States forces in China should be borne by the American Government. The Central Bank of China will facilitate exchange at the official rate of US$1 equals 20 yuan. The rate is unalterable in as much as we cannot afford to shake the confidence of the people in *fapi*, which is a stabilizing factor amidst a world of uncertainty brought about by the vicissitudes of war. It is only thus that we can directly maintain the credit of *fapi* and indirectly save China from economic collapse. Such collapse would seriously affect the whole military posi-

---

[37] Transmitted by the Ambassador in China from Chungking, Jan. 16, 1944.

tion of the Allies because of China's inability to continue resistance for any considerable length of time.

The second of these proposals is outright help which the Chinese people and army would appreciate and when it is considered that the United States has been feeding even British and Russian civilians this would be entirely in accordance with the Allied strategy of pooling resources. As an example, I might point out here that following the battle of Changteh 300,000 houses in that area were left in ruins and less than 10 buildings still remain. In this respect the people of China have suffered incalculable losses since the commencement of our war of resistance seven years ago. Our sacrifice in men and materials both civil and military is convincing proof of our willingness to give all that we are and everything that we have to the Allied cause. One of the crack units of China, 57th Division, has been entirely sacrificed.

I felt keenly when I saw you in Cairo that with your vision and wisdom you completely comprehended the critical situation which now faces this country and that you were eager to extend to our people every means of practical help in order to enable them to march forward shoulder to shoulder with the American people to common victory. I was so encouraged that I hastened to reassure the Chinese people of the solidarity and strength of our united efforts. I still feel sure that as leader of the Allied nations you will do all in your power to help China to continue her resistance and to do her full part in the global war. You realize, I am sure, that I will do all in my power to rally the support of the Chinese nation to bring about speedy victory and that I have even gone to the length of delaying the reopening of the Burma route so that essential amphibious equipment might be diverted to the European theater, thereby disappointing all classes of my countrymen who still bear in their memories the scar of the defeat suffered in the last Burma campaign as a result of which China lost large quantities of men and equipment through no fault of her own.

In the event that the Treasury Department feels unable to agree to either of the above two proposals then China will be compelled to pursue the only course open to her, namely, to continue resistance against our common enemy Japan with all her available strength and for as long as possible, thus in a way discharging her responsibilities as a member of the United Nations. In that eventuality she would have to permit her wartime economy and finances to follow the natural course of events. In such a case the Chinese Government would have no means at its disposal to meet the requirements of United States forces in China and consequently the American Army in China would have to depend upon itself to execute any and all of its projects, for to our great regret we would be placed inevitably in a position in which we could not make any further material or financial contribution, including the construction of works for military use.

28 (z)

The Ambassador in China (Gauss) to Secretary Hull

CHUNGKING, *January 16, 1944*

The Generalissimo requested that the Ambassador inform the Departments of State, Treasury and War that China would not be asking for anything were it not for the critical military and economic situation because China has pride in helping herself and in being self-sufficient; that the Generalissimo assured the Ambassador that any financial or material assistance rendered China by the

United States would not be hoarded for post-war purposes; that China would not take advantage of any situation to profit thereby and that China is neither a petty thief nor a robber baron. The Generalissimo said China had not asked for assistance last year or the year before. But the situation now is very much worse than a year ago and the cost of assisting American forces in China has become such a great strain that China is unable to keep up such assistance and that if the Treasury Department cannot help China financially, the American Army in China will have to depend on itself after March 1. The Generalissimo said that the United States forces have six weeks to make preparations and that after March 1 China could not be of material or financial assistance in connection with any project the American forces might have in mind. The Ambassador inquired whether this meant China would be unable to cooperate militarily with the United States forces in China. The Generalissimo replied that what he meant was that after March 1 American forces must look after themselves. Mr. Atcheson said he assumed this meant that the American forces must finance themselves and also make necessary arrangements for the purchase of supplies, construction materials and labor. The Generalissimo replied in the affirmative and said that China would of course continue to fight as long as she could and that as indicated in the latter part of his message to the Press she will carry on until the inevitable military and economic collapse and then will do the best possible under existing circumstances. Generalissimo Chiang said that within the past two weeks he had approved requests of United States Army headquarters that China undertake airfield projects which would cost the enormous sum of 13 billion dollars and that China simply could not finance such projects. (Madame Chiang said as an interesting sidelight that every American soldier in China cost the Chinese Government three hundred Chinese dollars per day; that there are several thousand American soldiers and that a great increase in the number of these is contemplated. She said furthermore that at the current cost of military rice 300 Chinese dollars would feed a Chinese soldier for a month; that after March 1 the United States Army would also have to feed its own soldiers and that the United States will have to depend upon itself. Madame Chiang said that date of March first was an implementation of the Generalissimo's statement set forth in the last paragraph of his message to the President.)

The Ambassador stated that it was his impression that it is the view of American economists that no amount of American money to the credit of China in the United States could remedy China's economic and financial situation any more than would be the case if our entire output of machine guns were hypothecated to China but remained in the United States. The Generalissimo replied that American economists know American economy and world economy in general but do not understand Chinese economy or Chinese psychology, the latter having a great deal to do with the situation in China. The Generalissimo said that the exchange rate is absolutely unalterable; that a maintenance of *fapi* is necessary to maintain public confidence; that a loan even though the actual cash remained in the United States would be regarded by the Chinese people as a reserve for *fapi*.

In reply to Mr. Atcheson's inquiry the Generalissimo said that the question of the Commission proposed by Mr. Morgenthau was covered in that section of his message referring to the Treasury's proposals. Mr. Atcheson pointed out that this was a suggestion made by the President. The Generalissimo replied that the Commission would be acting under directions of the Treasury and along the lines of the proposals made by the Treasury.

ANNEXES   495

The Ambassador reported further that after his return to the Embassy Madame Chiang telephoned him to say that if the Commission planned to discuss the proposals made by the Treasury there was no use in its coming but if it was sent out to discuss the two proposals made by the Generalissimo it would be welcome. Among various arguments advanced by Madame Chiang was one to the effect that the expenditures of the United States forces in China amounting to approximately U. S. $20,000,000 per month could not be dumped on the black market in a day and that dumping of even U. S. $1,000,000 would swiftly and extensively lower the black market rate.

The Ambassador added that his comments would follow.

The Ambassador reported that while the Generalissimo rejected the suggestion of sending a commission to China to confer on the proposals made by the Treasury, he has not closed the door entirely to such a commission provided it comes to discuss the Generalissimo's proposals, namely, a loan or assumption by our Army of all expenses incurred by it in the China theater without financial or material assistance from the Chinese Government.

The Ambassador stated that if he knew of any possible means which the United States could utilize to provide aid to China at this time either to transform her contribution to the general war effort into something affirmative or to support the present economic situation which continues rapidly to deteriorate he would heartily advocate it. The Ambassador said he would at all times prefer to see us operate in China without Chinese aid; that we could completely justify our heavy expenditures in China on the basis of spiraling prices which China must also meet in her own operations; but to be compelled to increase these heavy expenditures another five times because of the unrealistic attitude on the exchange rates creates a situation which might readily lead to a charge of exploitation and react unfavorably for China if it became known in the United States.

The Ambassador said that since he had not been informed in regard to commitments or military and other plans he could not suggest how far if at all pressure might be brought to bear upon China, but expressed the opinion that, however unpleasant these developments may be, and however unfortunate it may be that disagreements with China over money matters should have arisen, we should maintain a firm position declining to be coerced by petulant gestures or threats.

The Ambassador concluded his message by stating that the conversation held the preceding evening was calm and friendly on both sides and that the Generalissimo and Madame Chiang were most cordial throughout.

28.(aa)

Message From General Stilwell to General Somervell, March 27, 1944

[Extract]

We are now hoping that the Chinese may take a more realistic attitude on money matters. The Generalissimo is pressing Kung to effect agreement although mention of the phrase "exchange rate" sends the Generalissimo into a tailspin. We would like to have permission to explore the possibilities of the following plan, the only one which has a chance of success at the present time.

That the Chinese continue to advance CN to U. S. Army according to our needs and their ability. At the beginning of each three-month period, the U. S. to decide on a sum of U. S. dollars which will be advanced to the Chinese during the period.

For the next three-month period this sum to be figured between 100 and 200, probably between 125 and 165, U. S. requirements in CN to be kept secret, while the Chinese may publicize our "contribution" if they think wise for stabilization purposes. The rate of exchange will not come into the transaction, and the decision on final benefit derived by the Chinese and U. S. respectively will be left to postwar negotiation.

We think that the "tri-monthly ratio" between the two contributions will become the de facto rate of final settlement, since postwar stabilization of rate must certainly be at a much lower figure. To raise a portion of their contribution to U. S. in the least inflationary manner the Chinese to be urged to sell gold and U. S. dollars on joint account. This procedure is preferable to our sale on our own account since the sales will probably produce only 20 percent of our requirement. We fully realize the disadvantage of postwar negotiation on final rate, but think that the dangers are more imaginary than real.

28 (bb)

Secretary of War Stimson to President Roosevelt

WASHINGTON, *May 26, 1944*

DEAR MR. PRESIDENT: I submit herewith a chronological résumé of the negotiations with the Chinese Government with respect to the rates of exchange covering our expenditures in China. Since the résumé necessarily is somewhat long, I am also summarizing herewith its context.

When our troops first arrived in China they found an agreed exchange rate of $20 (Chinese) for $1 (U.S.), which even then had no realistic relationship to the purchasing value of the Chinese yuan. However, our requirements for food and housing were small and the expenditures were assumed by the Chinese Government which also undertook the requisite airport construction. In the fall of 1943 when General Somervell visited Chungking, this situation had changed and important construction was delayed, as the Chinese Government had not provided sufficient funds. General Stilwell was making direct expenditures to obtain necessary speed in completing urgently needed facilities.

General Somervell proposed to Dr. Kung the establishment of a more favorable exchange rate. He suggested a rate of 100 to 1 in comparison with the then black market rate of 120 to 1. He proposed that we continue to procure $20 (Chinese) for each $1 (U.S.) with the Chinese either to donate or to make available under reverse lend-lease $80 (Chinese) for each $1 (U.S.).

At the Cairo Conference the United States agreed to finance further construction expenditures. However the exchange rate was not discussed. The Generalissimo on his return cabled you requesting either a loan of $1,000,000,000 (U.S.), or the payment of Chinese expenditures at a 20 to 1 rate. As this would have made our expenditures in China astronomical, you disapproved the proposal and urged the Generalissimo to accept proposals offered by our representatives.

The Chinese had been threatening to discontinue construction. With the receipt of your message, they agreed to provide $2,500,000,000 (Chinese) and we in turn agreed to deposit $25,000,000 to Chinese account in this country. This was in effect a 100 to 1 rate, but the Chinese would not continue the arrangement on a monthly basis. We also forwarded $20,000,000 (U.S.) at Chinese request for purchase by the Chinese in the black market to lower the rate. There was little confidence in this proposal and the money has not as yet been turned over to the Chinese. Nevertheless, the Chinese continued to advance funds for the construction program subject to our shipment of $5,000,000,000 (Chinese) per month into China. This is continuing and work to date has not been held up.

The Chinese have advanced us $7,000,000,000 (Chinese) and have received in partial payment the one deposit of $25,000,000. Manifestly, they are worried as to the rate for repayment. For the first time we occupy the favorable position. We have advised the Chinese consistently of our willingness to bear these expenditures at a reasonable exchange rate. The 60 to 1 rate recently proposed by Dr. Kung with $20 (Chinese) to be purchased for each $1 (U.S.) and $40 (Chinese) to be provided under reverse lend-lease is not realistic in view of the present black market rate. We are not adverse to a reverse lend-lease arrangement of this type, though we do object to an unrealistic rate; and although it would result in the Chinese obtaining a greater credit for future settlement, it would appear most unlikely that funds received under reverse lend-lease at any rate approaching realism would at any time even closely approach the dollar value of direct lend-lease aid.

Perhaps our war program in China has contributed somewhat to inflation. However, the number of our troops and the magnitude of our construction are not sufficient to have a major effect. The Chinese report expenditures at approximately $10,000,000,000 (Chinese) for support of our troops and for construction prior to the Cairo Conference. They have advanced $7,000,000,000 (Chinese) for construction authorized at Cairo. In turn the United States has lend-leased goods valued at $413,000,000 (U.S.). The Treasury Department granted a credit to the Chinese Government of $500,000,000 (U.S.), against which it drew $243,000,000. The FEA has purchased goods for $48,000,000 (U.S.) at a 20 to 1 rate. Our forces in China have expended through February 1944 a total of $155,000,000 (U.S.) at the rate of 20 to 1. The financial contribution of the United States has been most substantial and greatly in excess of the Chinese expenditures even at the 20 to 1 rate. A settlement of the $7,000,000,000 (Chinese) construction advance alone at the 20 to 1 rate would involve a premium payment of over $300,000,000 (U.S.) compared with a rate of 150 to 1, and the latter is below current black market.

The black market is continuing to rise. The rate at the present time should not be less than 150 to 1 and even this rate should be revised periodically unless the Chinese Government controls inflation.

The War Department believes that our representatives should continue to stand firm for a realistic rate. In view of the effect of any rate on military planning, commitments should not be made in Chungking without clearance in Washington by the Treasury Department and your approval.

Respectfully yours,

HENRY L. STIMSON

[Enclosure]

RÉSUMÉ OF CHINESE EXCHANGE SITUATION, 19 MAY 1944

1. The exchange situation in China first was brought to the attention of the War Department by General Stilwell early in 1943, at which time he reported that the official rate of exchange of 20 to 1 was not realistic, inasmuch as the open market rate at that time was around 40 to 1 and increasing rapidly. He called attention to the fact that with the large expenditures contemplated by the Army, definite steps should be taken to have a new official rate established.

2. The official rate of exchange of 20 to 1 was established in August 1941 and has been supported by the U. S. Government as a measure of making effective the stabilization agreement entered into with China at the same time. This stabilization agreement expired in January 1944.

3. When the matter of the rate was first reported by General Stilwell the Treasury Department was requested to give some consideration to having the Chinese effect a change in the rate and during the latter part of 1943, that department endeavored to obtain some relief in the matter. These efforts included a change in the official rate, the granting of a special rate to the United States or the sale of gold at an advantageous price to use the proceeds to decrease the excessive costs of the War Department's expenditures in China because of the unrealistic rate.

4. With a knowledge of the State and Treasury Department and undoubtedly with the full knowledge of the Chinese Government, the War Department has been paying its personnel in China U. S. currency and permitting that personnel to go into the open or black market and purchase Chinese currency at any available rate. Later, the State and Treasury Department requested the War Department to ship United States currency to China for use in paying personnel and operating expenses. The War Department has been reluctant to having its soldiers dealing in black market operations, but for morale purposes, it could not do other than authorize such a procedure in view of its failure to find other means of giving its men in China sufficient local currency to offset the unrealistic exchange rate. In addition to the morale factor, there has been the ever increasing expenditures by the War Department for supplies and construction.

5. Failing to secure relief through a change in the official rate, the War Department, early in 1943 felt the need for a reciprocal Lend-Lease agreement with China and the Chinese Government indicated that they may be willing to enter into such an agreement. Accordingly, an agreement was drafted for submission to the Chinese. In view of the exchange situation and the fact that the Treasury Department expressed the view that efforts up to that time to secure a better official rate of exchange had proved fruitless, it was decided to include in the reciprocal Lend-Lease agreement, in addition to the provisions to direct aid in kind, a section to the effect that the Chinese Government would provide funds in Chinese currency to be used by the U. S. in direct purchase of supplies, materials, facilities and services in lieu of reciprocal aid in kind and to meet the essential governmental and military needs for Chinese currency. The understanding was that this currency received under the agreement could be used in reducing the excessive cost to the U. S. of expenditures for personnel and other purposes on account of the unrealistic Chinese exchange rate. This reciprocal Lend-Lease agreement was presented to Dr. Soong, Foreign Minister of the Chinese government by the State Department in Washington in May 1943 with a memorandum explaining the purpose of the financial provisions thereof. The agreement was submitted to General Stilwell in China and was concurred in by him in view of the apparent impossibility of securing a proper exchange rate.

6. In October 1943 General Somervell visited Chungking. He was advised by General Stilwell that delays occurring in construction necessitated direct contractual expenditures by United States forces. The artificial exchange rate of 20 to 1 as compared with a black market rate of 120 to 1 was resulting in exorbitant costs. General Stilwell believed that a better arrangement was essential to our planned operations. General Somervell, with the knowledge and consent of the Ambassador, proposed to Dr. Kung, subject to ratification

by the U. S. authorities in Washington, that the Chinese Government make available to our forces the requisite Chinese currency to support these forces and the military construction under one of two alternatives:

  a. The United States would deposit to Chinese account in the United States $1 U. S. for each $100 CN furnished, this deposit to be credited against an official exchange rate of 20 to 1, with the remaining $80 CN to be a contribution of the Chinese Government to our joint war effort (this arrangement would protect publicly the 20 to 1 official rate) ; or,

  b. The Chinese Government would provide the requisite funds with the United States depositing to Chinese account $1 U.S. for $20 CN of each $100 CN made available, the remaining $80 CN to be provided under a reverse lend-lease agreement.

Dr. Kung appeared to view these proposals as feasible and promised to place them before the Generalissimo for approval.

7. Shortly after General Somervell's return to the United States in November, and before the proposals could be carried further, the Cairo Conference was held. The Generalissimo attended this conference. It is understood that he was advised that the United States was prepared to bear the cost of its military effort in China. It is not understood that the question of exchange rates was considered. Subsequent to the conference, as indicated in the report of Ambassador Gauss, January 16, 1944, the Generalissimo in a message to the President urged that a loan of $1,000,000,000 U.S. be made to China, or that, otherwise, the United States assume full responsibility for its expenditures in China at a 20 to 1 rate.

8. The Treasury Department was then negotiating with the Chinese Government with a view to transporting gold to China for purchase of Chinese currency in the open market to control inflation and to secure a better exchange rate. These negotiations did not appear to be progressing rapidly. The Secretary of Treasury recognizing the urgency of the airport construction program authorized the War Department to proceed with its own negotiations.

Representatives of the State Department concurred in this arrangement. Our military representatives were authorized to advise the Chinese that the United States was prepared to accept full responsibility for its military expenditures subject to the establishment of a reasonable exchange rate which would have some relationship to the actual purchasing power of the Chinese dollar. On 15 January our Commanding General in China and State Department representatives were advised to press for an early completion of a reverse lend-lease agreement concurrently with an agreement to be presented by military representatives with respect to the funds to be made available by the Chinese Government to cover our military expenditures. The military representatives were advised to keep in constant touch with the State Department and Treasury Department representatives so that any action taken in Chungking would be jointly understood. Mr. Edward C. Acheson was sent to China to assist the Commanding General in presenting the proposed fiscal arrangement.

9. In reply to the Generalissimo's request, referred to above, the President urged the acceptance of the proposal submitted by our military and diplomatic representatives. It is to be noted that the authorities in this country were in agreement that there was little merit in the proposed loan to China.

10. Our military and diplomatic representatives proceeded with the negotiations. In the latter part of January estimates became available with respect to the substantial construction costs involved in the new airport projects. Meanwhile the black market exchange rate had continued to advance and payments in

American dollars at a 20 to 1 rate would have become astronomical in comparison to the value received in work. The War Department would have found it necessary to have requested additional funds for the purpose from Congress and was apprehensive that the exorbitant costs would have serious repercussions. Again on 24 January our military representatives were advised to maintain a firm stand, but to inform the Chinese Government that the United States was prepared to place to Chinese account the U.S. dollar equivalent of any Chinese funds made available under general arrangements which they would suggest to the Chinese Government.

11. Dr. Kung was designated by the Generalissimo to receive the United States' proposals. Our representatives proposed as an interim measure that the United States would purchase $1,000,000,000 CN at the rate of 40 to 1 through the deposit of $25,000,000 U.S. to Chinese account in this country. The Chinese Government would add $1,500,000,000 CN to this account. This proposal would have established an interim exchange rate of 100 to 1. The Chinese Government did advance the first funds and the $25,000,000 U.S. in payment thereof was deposited to Chinese account. However the Chinese Government did not accept the proposal as a continuing measure. On 3 February Dr. Kung made a counter-proposal to continue the official exchange rate of 20 to 1 with the Central Government contribution $10 CN more for each $1 U.S. under reverse lend-lease. Our representatives turned down this proposal. They advised us on 12 February that they could see no benefit in further proposals. However, Dr. Kung was asked to advance $1,000,000,000 CN per month during the remainder of the negotiations with the repayment rate to be decided during negotiations.

12. Report of expenditures at this time indicated that our own expenditures in China had increased from $400,000 in January 1943 to $23,000,000 in December. Estimates for airport and other construction indicated a requirement of approximately $2,500,000,000 CN monthly. Payment for these funds at a 20 to 1 rate as compared with the proposed 100 to 1 rate would have resulted in an annual premium to the Chinese Government in excess of $1,000,000,000. However, the proposed rate of 100 to 1 was still below the real purchasing value which was more adequately expressed by the black market rate which had reached 150 to 1. On February 20 General Stilwell was advised that he must continue to take a firm stand while still expressing the willingness of the United States to bear full costs at a reasonable exchange rate. On February 25 we were advised by our military representatives that Dr. Kung had asked for $20,000,000 U. S. to be flown to China as an advance to the Chinese account with the rate to be determined later. These funds Dr. Kung proposed to use for the purchase of Chinese currency in the black market in an effort to drive down the black market rate. At the suggestion of our representatives, and with the approval of the Treasury Department, this money was flown to India in the understanding that $5,000,000 U. S. was to be made available to the Chinese Government to test the effect of the proposed purchases prior to utilizing the full amount. These funds have not as yet been turned over to the Chinese Government as our representatives on the ground felt that the transfer might prove detrimental in view of the existing status of negotiations.

13. On March 2 our representatives advised us that the Chinese Government had agreed to furnish not to exceed $5,000,000,000 CN per month to our forces provided the requisite money in Chinese currency was shipped from the United States, with March and April requirements to be shipped by air. Arrangements were made to meet this request.

14. During the period of negotiations the construction work has been proceeding satisfactorily. As our proposal with respect to the deposit of $25,000,000 U. S. per month to the Chinese account in the United States in exchange for $2,500,000,000 CN had not been accepted by the Chinese Government, only the initial deposit was made. Since we are obtaining all of the funds needed without an exchange commitment, our representatives in China believed it undesirable to submit further proposals to the Chinese. They awaited counter-proposals from the Chinese Government. On May 7 our representatives advised us that the Chinese were pressing hard for a financial agreement at a 60 to 1 rate, $40 CN of each $60 CN furnished to be credited as reverse lend-lease. As the black market was continuing to rise, our representatives were unwilling to accept this offer and insisted on a three months' agreement for a rate of 150 to 1. Our representatives in the field reported that the Chinese Government would make a direct appeal to the United States.

15. It is important to note that the Chinese Government has receded considerably from its stand taken in 1943, and from its even more adamant stand taken in December 1943 and January 1944, as a result of the firm position taken by the United States. While the work undertaken by the American forces and payment therefor may aggravate the distress of the Chinese economy, it is very doubtful if its influence on the inflation difficulties is a major contributing factor. In local areas where work is being carried on, our expenditures will have more serious effect on inflationary difficulties than elsewhere, but even there our expenditures are not the primary cause of their economic disturbance. In any event, it is difficult to understand the effect of the rate of exchange on this economy as the United States funds made available to China would accumulate as a credit to be drawn against after the war. It would be difficult to justify an artificial exchange rate which would make the cost of American participation in the war in China out of all proportion to the actual value of the work received, particularly taking into consideration the relatively low cost of labor in China as compared with the United States.

16. The extent of United States aid to China must also be taken into consideration in determining the exchange rate which is to be accepted. Lend-Lease aid to China has aggregated more than $400,000,000 U.S., although some of the Lend-Lease material is still stock piled in India as transportation has not been available for its movement to China. At a realistic rate, this Lend-Lease expenditure alone is equivalent to $60,000,000,000 CN.

In addition thereto, the Treasury Department granted a credit to the Chinese Government of $500,000,000 U.S. in March 1942 against which $243,000,000 has been drawn at the end of 1943.

The Foreign Economic Administration will have purchased in China from 1941 through June 1944 approximately $48,000,000 U.S. which at the official rate would purchase $960,000,000 CN worth of merchandise (strategic materials). At a realistic rate of 100 to 1 as a conservative average for the period, these purchases would have cost only $9,600,000 U.S. This means that over the period the Chinese Government had been benefited as a result of the unrealistic exchange rate by a premium of $38,400,000 U.S.

Likewise, our forces in China have expended for the period 1 January 1943 to include February 1944 a total of $155,550,000 U.S. which at the official rate of exchange total $3,111,000,000 CN. Expenditures during the month of March and April 1944 have been on the basis of the new agreement, whereby the Chinese advanced to us the currency required for our needs and we in turn deposited U. S. currency to the credit of the Chinese Government in such amount as the

Commanding General, U. S. Forces reports as properly due. The total amount reported by the Commanding General, U. S. Forces under this agreement to have been received up to April 23 is $7,680,000,000 CN. (How much of this should be credited as a Chinese contribution to the war effort, and how much the United States Government is expected to reimburse the Chinese cannot be determined in Washington at this time in view of the fact that negotiations in this respect are being carried on by General Stilwell in China.) This is a total expenditure in Chinese currency to date of $10,791,000,000 CN. This would cost the U. S. at the official rate of 20 to 1 $539,550,000 U.S. whereas at a realistic rate of 150 to 1 it would cost only $72,000,000. This means that the U. S. pays a premium on these expenditures of $467,550,000 due to the unrealistic rate.

Dr. Kung in a letter to the Secretary of War has reported Chinese expenditures during part of February and all of March and April as aggregating $7,016,000,000 CN. The Chinese state, however, in addition to this amount the Chinese Government has paid out since September 1942 for construction of airfields, barracks, air force supplies and improvement of roads at the request of the United States authorities a total of $10,878,260,457 CN.

While the cost of the services furnished the United States forces in China cannot be verified, his estimate of construction cost in 1944 of $7,000,000,000 CN is in agreement with our own figures. The United States has deposited against this advance of $7,000,000,000 CN the sum of $25,000,000 U.S. to Chinese credit in the United States.

17. In view of the large sums involved and the continuing expenditures, it is apparent that the agreed exchange rate may have a decided influence on military operations and on military planning. While it is desirable for a firm agreement to be effected at the earliest possible date, the importance of such agreement to contemplated military operations warrants its careful consideration in Washington before it is accepted formally. It is suggested, therefore, that any arrangements which may be proposed in Chungking be tentative until their effect on military operations can be studied by our Government in Washington so that all factors may be taken into consideration. It is apparent that the American position has constantly improved during the progress of the negotiations as a result of the firm stand taken by all of our representatives working in close agreement. Meanwhile, military construction has proceeded without delay.

28 (cc)

Minutes of a Meeting on Chinese Gold Purchases [38]

Present: Mr. White
Mr. Bernstein
Mr. Hsi te-mou
Mr. T. L. Soong
Mr. Y. C. Koo
Mr. Adler

Mr. Hsi gave Mr. White a copy of the following telegram from K. K. Kwok:

"As Federal Reserve Bank of New York advised having shipped balance by plane thus exhausting our $20 million and as sales still extremely heavy and recent arrivals far from being adequate to meet outstanding contracts, please request

---

[38] Held in the office of Mr. H. D. White, Director of the Division of Monetary Research, Treasury Department, on Oct. 2, 1944.

U. S. Treasury immediately transfer US$20 million or if possible more out of $200 million and ship by plane. Please contact Adler and give him my best regards."

Mr. White raised the general question of the merits of selling US$200 million of gold in the existing situation. He pointed out that China's gold would be an enormous asset to her after the war if still conserved as it could provide a base for economic reconstruction as well as for reorganization of the currency. If it were sold now it might have some little psychological effect but could not substantially retard rising prices or the basic economic situation which was due to the acute scarcity of goods. Moreover, much of the gold would disappear into hoards and might emerge from those hoards either very slowly or not at all. Mr. White asked who was buying the gold and Mr. Koo replied that it was distributed from Chungking to Sian, Lanchow, Chengtu, etc. where it was bought by farmers and amahs.

Mr. Y. C. Koo indicated that sale of gold had had some beneficial effect and that the cessation of the sale of gold would send prices skyrocketing. The question was then raised of the discrepancy between the price at which gold was sold by the Central Bank and the black market price. Mr. White pointed out that with the existence of such a spread sometimes amounting to CN$5–6,000 somebody was making a profit and it was not the government. The Secretary had shown some interest in this question. Mr. Soong expressed surprise that the spread had been so high, Mr. Adler adding that it had been as much as 60% of the official price in the early part of September and then had dropped to CN$1,500 with the arrival of gold. There was some discussion of the relationship between spot and forward prices, Messrs. Koo and Soong claiming that the main reason for the discrepancy between the price at which the Central Bank sold and the black market price was the non-availability of supplies in Chungking. If there were sufficient supplies of gold, the discrepancy could be obliterated. Mr. Hsi pointed out that even with current arrivals, forward sales exceeded Central Bank's supplies of gold. It was also pointed out that the existence of high rates of interest might explain part of the discrepancy between spot and forward but after some comment by Mr. White and Mr. Bernstein, Messrs. Soong and Koo emphasized that the market's lack of confidence in the Central Bank's ability to procure adequate supplies was apparently the main reason.

Mr. White pointed out that it was cheaper for the Central Government to print fapi than to absorb fapi in exchange for gold at a time when the dent that was being made by the sale of gold was not significantly large. Mr. Koo stated that in the month of July two billion fapi had been absorbed by the sale of gold, Mr. Adler adding that the note issue in July was 9 billion fapi. Mr. Y. C. Koo mentioned that U.S. Army expenditures had been the major factor in the deterioration of the economic situation and alluded to the good relations that had existed between the Treasury and the Ministry of Finance during the past ten years. Mr. White said there was no question of that; in fact were it not for these good relations the Treasury would not be interested in how China utilized her gold. He was anxious to see that she got the maximum advantage from such utilization.

He asked how much gold China had left. Mr. Hsi replied that she had US $10 million left from a previous account and that Dr. Kung was anxious to get more gold through use of the half billion dollar loan. In fact, Dr. Kung was asking for $50 million of gold for sale of gold bullion and $100 million of gold for minting token coins. Mr. Koo and Mr. Soong stressed the fact that the cessation of the sale of gold would have very serious effects at this time. Mr. White asked whether people who bought forward could receive cash for their delivery certificates and the answer was in the affirmative. Mr. White pointed out this fact should reduce the spread between spot and forward. Mr. Adler asked why the price of gold had been lowered in July. Mr. Koo and Mr. Hsi said they would cable to Chungking for an explanation, Mr. Hsi confessing that it appeared to have been a mistake.

Mr. Hsi expressed the desire to take up the question of the minting of coins. Mr. White indicated that it should be taken up with Mr. Adler and the people from the Mint.

Mr. White concluded the meeting by saying that he would take up the matter with the Secretary and get in touch with the Chinese again.

28 (dd)

Memorandum by Secretary of the Treasury Morenthau [39]

1. This memorandum does not deal with the questions of textiles and trucks which were included in the program which was presented to this Government. The urgency of China's need for these items and their bearing upon inflation are recognized. They are omitted because our supply authorities are in the process of making an over-all determination of requirements and supplies and are not yet in a position to make a decision respecting China's requests.

2. We are agreed that any program to stabilize the currency and to check inflation should comprise a broad series of measures in the following categories:
    (a) Monetary and banking rehabilitation.
    (b) Foreign exchange stabilization.
    (c) Fiscal and administrative reforms.
    (d) Increase of supplies and improvement in their distribution.

3. We are anxious to give full support to an effective anti-inflationary program for China. It is therefore recommended that a Currency Stabilization Fund of $500 million be constituted for this purpose from the remaining $240 million of the United States loan to China and from China's existing dollar balances. Such an allocation of this remainder of the United States loan would be in strict accordance with the spirit and the letter of the 1942 financial agreement. The Fund would be set aside with firm mutual commitment on the part of China and the United States as to its purposes and availability.

It is envisaged that the uses to which this Currency Stabilization Fund would be put would be part of a broad concerted program for combatting inflation and for currency stabilization and these uses would be subject to joint agreement. The time at which the Fund's operations would start would be discussed at a later date.

The Treasury stands ready to advise and consult with the Chinese Government on the content and timing of such anti-inflationary and stabilization program. We are strongly of the opinion that the initiation of a Currency Stabilization Fund would strengthen the financial position of the Chinese Government and would inspire confidence both at home and abroad in its future economic and financial stability. The existence of such a Fund would give the Chinese people a real sense of security with respect to their ability to cope with their grave problems of reconstruction.

---

[39] Handed to Dr. T. V. Soong on May 8, 1945.

It should be noted that this proposal relates to only one portion of the foreign exchange assets presently available to China and that it would leave a relatively large amount of dollar exchange for helpful intermediate measures and for meeting China's current foreign exchange requirements.

4. We believe that the Chinese Government should terminate the program of forward sales of gold. As you know, the U. S. Treasury was not consulted when this program was initiated. In view of the difficulties of shipping gold, the limited effects of sales upon price rises in China, the public criticism of such sales and the desirability of using foreign exchange resources to achieve maximum effects, this program is ill-advised.

5. The Treasury will endeavor, as in the past, to make available limited quantities of gold for shipment to China during the next few months, having due regard to the need for restricting gold shipments where these endanger lives or use scarce transport facilities. However, in consideration of points 2 and 3 above, it is believed that further shipments should be financed out of foreign exchange assets other than those proposed to be earmarked for currency stabilization.

6. China should investigate and cancel sales to speculators and illicit purchasers and insure that only bona fide purchasers will receive such gold as is available. If gold arrivals are still not sufficient to meet past commitments, it is suggested that China may offer to place dollar credits (at about $35 per ounce) for the time being from her existing assets to the accounts of purchasers of gold to whom she cannot temporarily make delivery.

7. It is most unfortunate that the impression has arisen in the United States that the $200 million of U. S. dollar certificates and bonds and the gold sold in China have gone into relatively few hands with resultant large individual profits and have failed to be of real assistance to the Chinese economy.

28 (ee)

Minutes of a Meeting on Gold Fund for China [40]

Present: Secretary Morgenthau
Mr. D. W. Bell
Mr. Coe
Mr. Adler } Treasury
Mr. Friedman
Mr. Clayton
Mr. Collado } State
Mr. T. V. Soong
Mr. Tsu-yee Pei } China
Mr. W. Y. Lin

Before Dr. Soong, Mr. Pei and Mr. Lin joined the meeting, there was a brief discussion of what the Chinese would be told. In this discussion Mr. Coe made the point that he still favored the establishment of the $500 million fund and pointed out that our memorandum was not inconsistent with our commitment to the Chinese. The Secretary indicated that he was prepared to give them the remainder of the $200 million of gold.

When Dr. Soong, Mr. Pei and Mr. Lin joined the meeting, the Secretary asked Dr. Soong for the answer to his questions on how much gold China would need

---

[40] Held in the office of the Secretary of the Treasury, Mr. Morgenthau, on May 9, 1945.

for the next three months. Dr. Soong replied that in addition to the outstanding commitments the Chinese planned to sell about 1 million ounces during the next three months. The Secretary asked the "experts" to agree on the figures after the meeting.

Dr. Soong then read a memorandum proposing a reconstruction fund which, in effect, indicated that the Chinese wanted much larger loans from the United States.

The Secretary replied that we would give their proposal our careful consideration. He then went on to say that the establishment of a $500 million Fund would assist him in furthering China's interest before Congress. At this time, he said he was asking Dr. Soong to reconsider their decision to see whether they could not see their way clear to the establishment of such a Fund.

Dr. Soong replied that he could not do it; that he could only consider it if the Fund was established out of new loans. He, moreover, could not be responsible for the mistakes made in his absence and these mistakes were now being overcome. He, Dr. Soong, had not objected to the publicity on the mishandling of the Funds. He had not opposed sale of U.S. dollar savings certificates and bonds, but it had been stupid to stick to the original 20 to 1 rate.

The Secretary pointed out that he would like to be helpful and that, in effect, it was merely a matter of re-arrangement of Chinese bookkeeping in order to set up this Fund. If Dr. Soong decided not to accept the proposal on the $500 million Fund, the Secretary would obviously be disappointed. However, the commitment to make available the remainder of the $200 million of gold was not tied up with the fund proposal and the Treasury would study ways of accelerating gold shipments.

28 (ff)

The Chinese Minister for Foreign Affairs (Soong) to Secretary of the Treasury Morgenthau

[WASHINGTON] *May 9, 1945*

MY DEAR MR. SECRETARY: May I express my appreciation of the frank talk we had at luncheon, and the helpful attitude you showed at the conference this afternoon.

I have cabled to the Generalissimo your suggestion of setting up a $500 million Reconstruction Fund, and will let you know as soon as I have his reply. I added that you recognized that the above suggestion and the question of gold delivery are two separate matters; that there is no question of the validity of your prior commitment; that you are ready to meet it; and that gold will be made available.

In view of the urgency of the situation, I shall appreciate it if you will kindly designate some member of your Department to discuss the details with my assistants, Mr. Tsu-yee Pei and Dr. W. Y. Lin, so that the necessary shipments could be made at once.

As Mr. Clayton said this afternoon, I have to return to San Francisco to meet my engagements there, accordingly I shall be grateful for your prompt reply.

Faithfully yours,

T. V. SOONG

28 (gg)

Acting Secretary of State Grew to Secretary of the Treasury Morgenthau

WASHINGTON, *May 16, 1945*

MY DEAR MR. SECRETARY: The Department has given careful attention to the request of the Chinese Foreign Minister, Dr. T. V. Soong, for the delivery during the remainder of 1945 of about $190,000,000 of gold from the unused balance of the $500,000,000 credit approved by the Congress in January 1942.

It is the Department's view, which it understands is shared by the Treasury, that the sale of gold by China has not proved and is not likely to prove a very effective anti-inflationary device. Moreover, it believes that the establishment of a $500,000,000 fund for combating inflation and stabilizing the Chinese currency which you proposed last week to Dr. Soong would, if adopted by the Chinese Government, be of considerable short and long run benefit to China.

The Chinese Government believes, however, that the immediate political and psychological as well as real economic effects of a continued and accelerated gold sale policy will have a vital importance in the critical situation confronting it, and strongly requests the delivery of the gold in question in accordance with the terms of the understanding between the two governments of July 1943. Since there appears to be no doubt that the Chinese Government attaches a greater importance to the immediate delivery of the gold than to the longer run benefits which might result from the establishment of the fund which you have proposed and since the continued stability of China and her increasing military efforts in the war against the common enemy are of great concern to the United States, the Department recommends that the Treasury, if transportation is available, deliver the gold to China in accordance with the time schedules put forward by Dr. Soong.

Sincerely yours,

JOSEPH C. GREW

28 (hh)

Secretary of the Treasury Morgenthau to the Chinese Minister for Foreign Affairs (Soong)

WASHINGTON, *May 16, 1945*

DEAR MR. SOONG: This is to confirm what I told you today. In accordance with your memorandum of May 11, the Treasury is prepared to authorize the shipment of the balance of the $20 million of gold which is on earmark with the Federal Reserve Bank of New York for the Central Bank of China and to transfer the balance of $180 million to the account of the Central Bank of China with the Federal Reserve Bank of New York, in three equal monthly installments of $60 million from May to July 1945. The Treasury accepts the schedule of gold shipments contained in your memorandum of May 11, 1945 and is making arrangements with the Army to carry out the shipments of the gold according to that schedule. The preliminary arrangements to ship the requested amount for the month of May have already been made. These steps are being taken in accordance with our Financial Aid Agreement of March 1942 and my letter to Dr. Kung of July 27, 1943.

At this time it seems to me necessary and desirable to point out that the purpose of the $500 million of financial aid to China, and particularly my agreement in July 1943 to ship gold to China, was to assist in an anti-inflationary program which would strengthen confidence in the Chinese Government and its finances and thereby help maintain the Chinese economy. As you know, it is my opinion that the sale of gold by China has not proved effective in combating inflation, and I am doubtful that it will prove effective. Also as I have told you, the manner in which the gold sales have been conducted and the consequent public criticism of them in China are not conducive to achieving the purposes for which our financial aid was granted.

Therefore, I would respectfully ask the Chinese Government to consider carefully the matters proposed to you in my memorandum of May 8, 1945. In particular I would reiterate my suggestion that China constitute a $500 million fund for combating inflation and stabilizing the currency from its foreign exchange assets. I think that this step would be of considerable short and long-run benefit to China and would inspire confidence in the Chinese Government's handling of its difficult economic situation.

The Treasury has noted with great interest the intention of the Chinese Government, as stated in your memorandum to the Secretary of State, to effectuate reforms relating to financial and economic matters. We think that the carrying out of these reforms will do more to insure confidence among the people and give a measure of stability to the present economic and financial situation than the gold program.

I know that you and your Government will take these friendly suggestions in the spirit in which they are offered. As I told you, we intend to carry out faithfully our financial agreement of 1942. However, the Chinese Government's response to our proposal to institute a $500 million fund and her conduct of the gold sales program will be important considerations in our financial relations with China.

This Government has as prime objectives the defeat of Japan and the liberation of China. As an old friend of China, I believe that our faith and confidence in China will be justified.

Very truly yours,

H. MORGENTHAU, Jr.

28 (ii)

Information Requested in Connection with the Uses of the 1942 $500 Million China Aid Credit [41]

I. U. S. dollar allocations of the $500 million aid by purpose and amount.
   A. Redemption of U. S. dollar securities issued in China in 1942.
      1. Types of securities issued, maturity, rate of interest, exchange rate at which sold and at which redeemed, whether or not negotiable, and the pertinent regulations, if any, concerning their use as collateral from 1942 to date.
      2. Breakdown with respect to each type of security issued of:
         a. The U.S. dollar value of sales to date.
         b. The U.S. dollar face value of the securities redeemed to date.

---

[41] Enclosure in a letter from J. Burke Knapp, Director, Office of Financial and Development Policy, Department of State, to Dr. Shao-Hwa Tan, Minister, Chinese Embassy at Washington, June 9, 1948. To date, the information requested has not been received.

c. The actual amount of U.S. dollars paid out for the redemption of securities by months and the total to date.

e [d]. The actual amount of U.S. dollars paid out in interest on the securities by months and the total to date.

f [e]. The amount of U.S. dollars the Chinese Government expects to pay out in interest and principal in the future on outstanding securities.

g [f]. The U.S. dollar value of purchases of securities by foreigners from the Central Bank of China and from other banks authorized to market the securities.

3. Breakdown with respect to each type of security of:
   a. The U.S. dollar value of sales to government and semi-government institutions by months and the total to date.
   b. The actual amount of U.S. dollars paid out to government and semi-government institutions for the redemption of securities owned by these institutions.

B. Sales of gold purchased by the Chinese Government out of the $500 million financial aid.
   1. Breakdown of the amount of gold sold in the form of spot gold, forward gold, and gold certificates by months and the total to date, with prices at which sold.
   2. The amount of gold delivered to purchasers by months and the total to date, with details of the proceeds of the tax in gold and Chinese currency and of the impact on deliveries of gold to purchasers of the 40 percent tax on undelivered gold imposed in July 1945.
   3. Breakdown of the amount of gold sold in the form of spot gold, forward gold, and gold certificates to government and semigovernment institutions and the amount delivered by months and the total to date.
   4. Regulations, if any, concerning the status of gold as collateral from 1943 to date.

C. Breakdown of all other dollar expenditures by the Chinese Government out of the $500 million financial aid by purpose, by amount and by months and total to date.

II. Chinese currency proceeds of the sales of U. S. dollar securities, gold, and other assets procured from the 1942 financial aid.

A. Amount of Chinese currency receipts.
   1. Breakdown of amount of Chinese currency receipts by source (U.S. securities, gold, etc.), by months and by fiscal years and the total to date.
   2. Percentage of total government revenue constituted by Chinese currency receipts of sales of U.S. securities, gold, etc. by months and fiscal years to date.

B. Uses of Chinese currency receipts.
   1. Amounts of government expenditures financed by these Chinese currency receipts by months and the total to date.
   2. Percentage of total government expenditures constituted by B. 1 by months and fiscal years to date.

C. Amounts of Chinese currency, if any, paid out for interest on and for the redemption of U. S. dollar securities.

29(a)

President Roosevelt to Generalissimo Chiang Kai-shek, February 7, 1942 [42]

It is a source of great gratification to me and to the Government and people of the United States that the proposal which I made to the Congress that there be authorized for the purpose of rendering financial aid to China in the sum of $500,000,000 was passed unanimously by both the Senate and the House of Representatives and has now become law.

The unusual speed and unanimity with which this measure was acted upon by the Congress and the enthusiastic support which it received throughout the United States testify to the wholehearted respect and admiration which the Government and people of this country have for China. They testify also to our earnest desire and determination to be concretely helpful to our partners in the great battle for freedom. The gallant resistance of the Chinese armies against the ruthless invaders of your country has called forth the highest praise from the American and all other freedom loving peoples. The tenacity of the Chinese people, both armed and unarmed, in the face of tremendous odds in carrying on for almost five years a resolute defense against an enemy far superior in equipment is an inspiration to the fighting men and all the peoples of the other United Nations. The great sacrifices of the Chinese people in destroying the fruits of their toil so that they could not be used by the predatory armies of Japan exemplify in high degree the spirit of sacrifice which is necessary on the part of all to gain the victory toward which we are confidently striving. It is my hope and belief that use which will be made of the funds now authorized by the Congress of the United States will contribute substantially toward facilitating the efforts of the Chinese Government and people to meet the economic and financial burdens which have been thrust upon them by an armed invasion and toward solution of problems of production and procurement which are essential for the success of their armed resistance to what are now our common enemies.

I send you my personal greetings and best wishes. I extend to you across land and sea the hand of comradeship for the common good, the common goal, the common victory that shall be ours.

29 (b)

Joint Statement by Secretary of the Treasury Morgenthau and Dr. T. V. Soong, Chinese Minister for Foreign Affairs, March 21, 1942

The United States and China have today entered into an Agreement giving effect to the Act of Congress unanimously passed by the Senate and House of Representatives authorizing $500,000,000 of financial aid to China. The Agreement, approved by the President and by Generalissimo Chiang Kai-shek, was signed by Secretary Morgenthau on behalf of the United States and by Dr. Soong on behalf of China.

This financial aid will contribute substantially towards facilitating the great efforts of the Chinese people and their government to meet the financial and

---

[42] *Department of State Bulletin*, Feb. 7, 1942, p. 142.

economic burdens which have been imposed upon them by almost five years of continuous attack by Japan.

This Agreement is a concrete manifestation of the desire and determination of the United States, without stint, to aid China in our common battle for freedom.

The final determination of the terms upon which this $500,000,000 financial aid is given to China, including the benefits to be rendered the United States in return, is deferred until the progress of events after the war makes clearer the final terms and benefits which will be in the mutual interest of the United States and China and will promote the establishment of lasting world peace and security.

The text of the Agreement is as follows:

"WHEREAS, The Governments of the United States of America and of the Republic of China are engaged, together with other nations and peoples of like mind, in a cooperative undertaking against common enemies, to the end of laying the bases of a just and enduring world peace securing order under law to themselves and all nations, and

"WHEREAS, The United States and China are signatories to the Declaration of United Nations of January 1, 1942, which declares that 'Each government pledges itself to employ its full resources, military or economic, against those members of the Tripartite Pact and its adherents with which such government is at war'; and

"WHEREAS, the Congress of the United States, in unanimously passing Public Law No. 442, approved February 7, 1942, has declared that financial and economic aid to China will increase China's ability to oppose the forces of aggression and that the defense of China is of the greatest possible importance, and has authorized the Secretary of the Treasury of the United States, with the approval of the President, to give financial aid to China, and

"WHEREAS, such financial aid will enable China to strengthen greatly its war efforts against the common enemies by helping China to

"(1) strengthen its currency, monetary, banking and economic system:

"(2) finance and promote increased production, acquisition and distribution of necessary goods;

"(3) retard the rise of prices, promote stability of economic relationships, and otherwise check inflation;

"(4) prevent hoarding of foods and other materials;

"(5) improve means of transportation and communication;

"(6) effect further social and economic measures which promote the welfare of the Chinese people; and

"(7) meet military needs other than those supplied under the Lend-Lease Act and take other appropriate measures in its war effort.

"In order to achieve these purposes, the undersigned, being duly authorized by their respective Governments for that purpose, have agreed as follows:

ARTICLE I.

"The Secretary of the Treasury of the United States agrees to establish forthwith on the books of the United States Treasury a credit in the name of the Government of the Republic of China in the amount of 500,000,000 U. S. dollars. The Secretary of the Treasury shall make transfers from this credit, in such amounts and at such times as the Government of the Republic of China shall request, through the Minister of Finance, to an account or accounts in the Federal Reserve Bank of New York in the name of the Government of the Republic of China or any agencies designated by the Minister of Finance. Such transfers may be requested by and such accounts at the Federal Reserve Bank of New York may be drawn upon by the Government of the Republic of China either directly or through such persons or agencies as the Minister of Finance shall authorize.

ARTICLE II.

"The fiinal determination of the terms upon which this financial aid is given, including the benefits to be rendered the United States in return, is deferred by the two contracting parties until the progress of events after the war makes clearer the final terms and benefits which will be in the mutual interest of the United States and China and will promote the establishment of lasting world peace and security. In determining the final terms and benefits full cognizance shall be given to the desirability of maintaining a healthy and stable economic and financial situation in China in the post-war period as well as during the war and to the desirability of promoting mutually advantageous economic and financial relations between the United States and China and the betterment of world-wide economic and financial relations.

ARTICLE III.

"This Agreement shall take effect as from this day's date.

"Signed and sealed at Washington, District of Columbia, in duplicate this 21st day of March, 1942.

"On behalf of the United States of America
HENRY MORGENTHAU, Jr.
Secretary of the Treasury

"On behalf of the Republic of China
T. V. SOONG
Minister for Foreign Affairs."

30

Statement by Acting Secretary Welles, July 19, 1940 [43]

In response to inquiries from press correspondents with regard to the British Prime Minister's comments upon the question of extraterritoriality in China included in his statement of July 18, the Acting Secretary of State, Mr. Sumner Welles, commented as follows:

"The most recent statement of this Government on this subject is contained in a note presented on December 31, 1938, to the Japanese Government, which mentions *inter alia* the progress made toward the relinquishment of certain rights of a special character which the United States together with other countries has long possessed in China. In 1931 discussions of the subject between China and each of several other countries, including the United States, were suspended because of the occurrence of the Mukden incident and subsequent disrupting developments in 1932 and 1935 in the relations between China and Japan. In 1937 this Government was giving renewed favorable consideration to the question when there broke out the current Sino-Japanese hostilities, as a result of which the usual processes of government in large areas of China were widely disrupted.

"It has been this Government's traditional and declared policy and desire to move rapidly by process of orderly negotiation and agreement with the Chinese Government, whenever conditions warrant, toward the relinquishment of extra-

---

[43] *Foreign Relations of the United States, Japan,* 1931–1941, vol. I, p. 927.

territorial rights and of all other so-called 'special rights' possessed by this country as by other countries in China by virtue of international agreements. That policy remains unchanged."

31

Secretary Hull to the Appointed Chinese Minister for Foreign Affairs (Quo Tai-chi) [44]

WASHINGTON, *May 31, 1941.*

MY DEAR MR. MINISTER: I acknowledge the receipt of and thank you for your letter of May 26, 1941 in regard to your visit to Washington and to our conversations during your short sojourn here.

We greatly enjoyed your visit.

It is very gratifying to receive in your letter reaffirmation of the endorsement by the Chinese Government and people of the general and fundamental principles which this Government is convinced constitute the only practical foundation for an international order wherein independent nations may cooperate freely with each other to their mutual benefit.

As you know, the program in which the Government and people of the United States put their trust is based upon and revolves about the principle of equality of treatment among nations. This principle comprehends equality in international relations in a juridical sense, nondiscrimination and equality of opportunity in commercial relations, and reciprocal interchange in the field of cultural developments. Implicit in this principle is respect by each nation for the rights of other nations, performance by each nation of established obligations, alteration of agreements between nations by processes not of force but of orderly and free negotiation, and fair dealing in international economic relations essential to peaceful development of national life and the mutually profitable growth of international trade. One of the purposes of this program is to effect the removal of economic and other maladjustments which tend to lead to political conflicts.

As you are also aware, the Government and people of the United States have long had a profound interest in the welfare and progress of China. It goes without saying that the Government of the United States, in continuation of steps already taken toward meeting China's aspirations for readjustment of anomalies in its international relations, expects when conditions of peace again prevail to move rapidly, by processes of orderly negotiation and agreement with the Chinese Government, toward relinquishment of the last of certain rights of a special character which this country, together with other countries, has long possessed in China by virtue of agreements providing for extraterritorial jurisdiction and related practices.

This Government welcomes and encourages every advance made by lawful and orderly processes by any country toward conditions of peace, security, stability, justice and general welfare. The assurances given in Your Excellency's letter under acknowledgment of China's support of the principle of equality of treatment and nondiscrimination in economic relations should have wholesome effect both during the present period of world conflict and when hostilities shall have ceased.

The Government of the United States is dedicated to support of the principles in which the people of this country believe. Without reservation, we are con-

[44] *Ibid.,* p. 929.

fident that the cause to which we are committed along with China and other countries—the cause of national security, of fair dealing among nations and of peace with justice—will prevail.

With kindest regards [etc.]

Sincerely yours,

CORDELL HULL

32

Treaty Between the United States and China for the Relinquishment of Extraterritorial Rights in China and the Regulation of Related Matters, Signed at Washington, January 11, 1943, With Accompanying Exchange of Notes [45]

The United States of America and the Republic of China, desirous of emphasizing the friendly relations which have long prevailed between their two peoples and of manifesting their common desire as equal and sovereign States that the high principles in the regulation of human affairs to which they are committed shall be made broadly effective, have resolved to conclude a treaty for the purpose of adjusting certain matters in the relations of the two countries, and have appointed as their Plenipotentiaries:

The President of the United States of America,

Mr. Cordell Hull, Secretary of State of the United States of America, and

The President of the National Government of the Republic of China,

Dr. Wei Tao-ming, Ambassador Extraordinary and Plenipotentiary of the Republic of China to the United States of America;

Who, having communicated to each other their full powers found to be in due form, have agreed upon the following articles:

ARTICLE I

All those provisions of treaties or agreements in force between the United States of America and the Republic of China which authorize the Government of the United States of America or its representatives to exercise jurisdiction over nationals of the United States of America in the territory of the Republic of China are hereby abrogated. Nationals of the United States of America in such territory shall be subject to the jurisdiction of the Government of the Republic of China in accordance with the principles of international law and practice.

ARTICLE II

The Government of the United States of America considers that the Final Protocol concluded at Peking on September 7, 1901, between the Chinese Government and other governments, including the Government of the United States of America, should be terminated and agrees that the rights accorded to the Government of the United States of America under that Protocol and under agreements supplementary thereto shall cease.

The Government of the United States of America will cooperate with the Government of the Republic of China for the reaching of any necessary agreements with other governments concerned for the transfer to the Government of the Republic of China of the administration and control of the Diplomatic Quarter at Peiping, including the official assets and the official obligations of the Diplomatic Quarter, it being mutually understood that the Government of the Repub-

---

[45] 57 Stat. 767.

lic of China in taking over administration and control of the Diplomatic Quarter will make provision for the assumption and discharge of the official obligations and liabilities of the Diplomatic Quarter and for the recognition and protection of all legitimate rights therein.

The Government of the Republic of China hereby accords to the Government of the United States of America a continued right to use for official purposes the land which has been allocated to the Government of the United States of America in the Diplomatic Quarter in Peiping, on parts of which are located buildings belonging to the Government of the United States of America.

Article III

The Government of the United States of America considers that the International Settlements at Shanghai and Amoy should revert to the administration and control of the Government of the Republic of China and agrees that the rights accorded to the Government of the United States of America in relation to those Settlements shall cease.

The Government of the United States of America will cooperate with the Government of the Republic of China for the reaching of any necessary agreements with other governments concerned for the transfer to the Government of the Republic of China of the administration and control of the International Settlements at Shanghai and Amoy, including the official assets and the official obligations of those Settlements, it being mutually understood that the Government of the Republic of China in taking over administration and control of those Settlements will make provision for the assumption and discharge of the official obligations and liabilities of those Settlements and for the recognition and protection of all legitimate rights therein.

Article IV

In order to obviate any questions as to existing rights in respect of or as to existing titles to real property in territory of the Republic of China possessed by nationals (including corporations or associations), or by the Government, of the United States of America, particularly questions which might arise from the abrogation of the provisions of treaties or agreements as stipulated in Article I, it is agreed that such existing rights or titles shall be indefeasible and shall not be questioned upon any ground except upon proof, established through due process of law, of fraud or of fraudulent or other dishonest practices in the acquisition of such rights or titles, it being understood that no right or title shall be rendered invalid by virtue of any subsequent change in the official procedure through which it was acquired. It is also agreed that these rights or titles shall be subject to the laws and regulations of the Republic of China concerning taxation, national defense, and the right of eminent domain, and that no such rights or titles may be alienated to the government or nationals (including corporations or associations) of any third country without the express consent of the Government of the Republic of China.

It is also agreed that if it should be the desire of the Government of the Republic of China to replace, by new deeds of ownership, existing leases in perpetuity or other documentary evidence relating to real property held by nationals, or by the Government, of the United States of America, the replacement shall be made by the Chinese authorities without charges of any sort and the new deeds of ownership shall fully protect the holders of such leases or other documentary evidence and their legal heirs and assigns without diminution of their prior rights and interests, including the right of alienation.

It is further agreed that nationals or the Government of the United States of America shall not be required or asked by the Chinese authorities to make any payments of fees in connection with land transfers for or with relation to any period prior to the effective date of this treaty.

Article V

The Government of the United States of America having long accorded rights to nationals of the Republic of China within the territory of the United States of America to travel, reside and carry on trade throughout the whole extent of that territory, the Government of the Republic of China agrees to accord similar rights to nationals of the United States of America within the territory of the Republic of China. Each of the two Governments will endeavor to have accorded in territory under its jurisdiction to nationals of the other country, in regard to all legal proceedings, and to matters relating to the administration of justice, and to the levying of taxes or requirements in connection therewith, treatment not less favorable than that accorded to its own nationals.

Article VI

The Government of the United States of America and the Government of the Republic of China mutually agree that the consular officers of each country, duly provided with exequaturs, shall be permitted to reside in such ports, places and cities as may be agreed upon. The consular officers of each country shall have the right to interview, to communicate with, and to advise nationals of their country within their consular districts; they shall be informed immediately whenever nationals of their country are under detention or arrest or in prison or are awaiting trial in their consular districts and they shall, upon notification to the appropriate authorities, be permitted to visit any such nationals; and, in general, the consular officers of each country shall be accorded the rights, privileges, and immunities enjoyed by consular officers under modern international usage.

It is likewise agreed that the nationals of each country, in the territory of the other country, shall have the right at all times to communicate with the consular officers of their country. Communications to their consular officers from nationals of each country who are under detention or arrest or in prison or are awaiting trial in the territory of the other country shall be forwarded to such consular officers by the local authorities.

Article VII

The Government of the United States of America and the Government of the Republic of China mutually agree that they will enter into negotiations for the conclusion of a comprehensive modern treaty of friendship, commerce, navigation and consular rights, upon the request of either Government or in any case within six months after the cessation of the hostilities in the war against the common enemies in which they are now engaged. The treaty to be thus negotiated will be based upon the principles of international law and practice as reflected in modern international procedures and in the modern treaties which the Government of the United States of America and the Government of the Republic of China respectively have in recent years concluded with other governments.

Pending the conclusion of a comprehensive treaty of the character referred to in the preceding paragraph, if any questions affecting the rights in territory of the Republic of China of nationals (including corporations or associations), or of the Government, of the United States of America should arise in future and if these questions are not covered by the present treaty, or by the provisions of existing treaties, conventions, or agreements between the Government of the United States of America and the Government of the Republic of China not abrogated by or inconsistent with this treaty, such questions shall be discussed by representatives of the two Governments and shall be decided in accordance with generally accepted principles of international law and with modern international practice.

ARTICLE VIII

The present treaty shall come into force on the day of the exchange of ratifications.

The present treaty shall be ratified, and the ratifications shall be exchanged at Washington as soon as possible.

Signed and sealed in the English and Chinese languages, both equally authentic, in duplicate, at Washington, this eleventh day of January, one thousand nine hundred forty-three, corresponding to the eleventh day of the first month of the thirty-second year of the Republic of China.

CORDELL HULL
WEI TAO-MING

Secretary Hull to the Chinese Ambassador (Wei Tao-ming)

WASHINGTON, *January 11, 1943.*

EXCELLENCY:

In connection with the treaty signed today between the Government of the United States of America and the Government of the Republic of China in which the Government of the United States of America relinquishes its extraterritorial and related special rights in China, I have the honor to acknowledge the receipt of your note of today's date reading as follows:

"Excellency: Under instruction of my Government, I have the honor to state that in connection with the treaty signed today by the Government of the Republic of China and the Government of the United States of America, in which the Government of the United States of America relinquishes its extraterritorial and related special rights in China, it is the understanding of the Government of the Republic of China that the rights of the Government of the United States of America and of its nationals in regard to the systems of treaty ports and of special courts in the International Settlements at Shanghai and Amoy and in regard to the employment of foreign pilots in the ports of the territory of China are also relinquished. In the light of the abolition of treaty ports as such, it is understood that all coastal ports in the territory of the Republic of China which are normally open to American overseas merchant shipping will remain open to such shipping after the coming into effect of the present treaty and the accompanying exchange of notes.

It is mutually agreed that the merchant vessels of each country shall be permitted freely to come to the ports, places, and waters of the other country which are or may be open to overseas merchant shipping, and that the treatment accorded to such vessels in such ports, places, and waters shall be no less favorable than that accorded to national vessels and shall be as favorable as that accorded to the vessels of any third country.

It is mutually understood that the Government of the United States of America relinquishes the special rights which vessels of the United States of America have been accorded with regard to the coasting trade and inland navigation in the waters of the Republic of China and that the Government of the Republic of China is prepared to take over any American properties that may have been engaged for those purposes and to pay adequate compensation therefor. Should either country accord the rights of inland navigation or coasting trade to vessels of any third country such rights would similarly be accorded to the vessels of the other country. The coasting trade and inland navigation of each country are excepted from the requirement of national treatment and are to be regulated according to the laws of each country in relation thereto. It is agreed, however, that vessels of either country shall enjoy within the territory of the other country with respect to the coasting trade and inland navigation treatment as favorable as that accorded to the vessels of any third country.

It is mutually understood that the Government of the United States of America relinquishes the special rights which naval vessels of the United States of America have been accorded in the waters of the Republic of China and that the Government of the Republic of China and the Government of the United States of America shall extend to each other the mutual courtesy of visits by their warships in accordance with international usage and comity.

It is mutually understood that questions which are not covered by the present treaty and exchange of notes and which may affect the sovereignty of the Republic of China shall be discussed by representatives of the two Governments and shall be decided in accordance with generally accepted principles of international law and with modern international practice.

With reference to Article IV of the treaty, the Government of the Republic of China hereby declares that the restriction on the right of alienation of existing rights or titles to real property referred to in that article will be applied by the Chinese authorities in an equitable manner and that if and when the Chinese Government declines to give assent to a proposed transfer the Chinese Government will, in a spirit of justice and with a view to precluding loss on the part of American nationals whose interests are affected, undertake, if the American party in interest so desires, to take over the right or title in question and to pay adequate compensation therefor.

It is mutually understood that the orders, decrees, judgments, decisions and other acts of the United States Court for China and of the Consular Courts of the United States of America in China shall be considered as *res judicata* and shall, when necessary, be enforced by the Chinese authorities. It is further understood that any cases pending before the United States Court for China and the Consular Courts of the United States of America in China at the time of the coming into effect of this treaty shall, if the plaintiff or petitioner so desires, be remitted to the appropriate courts of the Government of the Republic of China which shall proceed as expeditiously as possible with their disposition and in so doing shall in so far as practicable apply the laws of the United States of America.

It is understood that these agreements and understandings if confirmed by Your Excellency's Government shall be considered as forming an integral part of the treaty signed today and shall be considered as effective upon the date of the entrance into force of that treaty.

I shall be much obliged if Your Excellency will confirm the foregoing.

I avail myself of this opportunity to renew to Your Excellency the assurances of my highest consideration."

I have the honor to confirm that the agreements and understandings which have been reached in connection with the treaty signed today by the Government of the United States of America and the Government of the Republic of China are as set forth in the above note from Your Excellency.

I avail myself [etc.]

CORDELL HULL

33

Statement on Conference of President Roosevelt, Generalissimo Chiang Kai-shek, and Prime Minister Churchill, Cairo, December 1, 1943 [46]

The several military missions have agreed upon future military operations against Japan. The Three Great Allies expressed their resolve to bring unrelenting pressure against their brutal enemies by sea, land, and air. This pressure is already rising.

The Three Great Allies are fighting this war to restrain and punish the aggression of Japan. They covet no gain for themselves and have no thought of territorial expansion. It is their purpose that Japan shall be stripped of all the islands in the Pacific which she has seized or occupied since the beginning of the first World War in 1914, and that all the territories Japan has stolen from the Chinese, such as Manchuria, Formosa, and the Pescadores, shall be restored to the Republic of China. Japan will also be expelled from all other territories which she has taken by violence and greed. The aforesaid three great powers, mindful of the enslavement of the people of Korea, are determined that in due course Korea shall become free and independent.

With these objects in view the three Allies, in harmony with those of the United Nations at war with Japan, will continue to persevere in the serious and prolonged operations necessary to procure the unconditional surrender of Japan.

[46] *Department of State Bulletin*, Dec. 4, 1943, p. 393.

Annexes to Chapter II: A Review of Kuomintang–Chinese Communist Relations, 1921–1944

34

"Telegram to the Nation" (*Manifesto on the Seizure of Chiang Kai-shek*) *December 12, 1936* [1]

Ever since the loss of the North-Eastern Provinces five years ago, our national sovereignty has been steadily weakened, and our territory has dwindled day by day. We suffered national humiliation at the time of the Shanghai Truce, and again with the Tangku Truce and the Ho-Umetsu Agreement. There is not a single citizen who does not feel sick at heart because of this.

Recently there have been startling changes in the international situation. Certain Powers are intriguing with one another, and using our nation and our people as a sacrifice. When hostilities began in East Suiyuan, popular resentment reached its height, and our soldiers everywhere were very indignant.

At this juncture, our Central Leader ought to encourage both military and civilians to organize the whole people in a united war of national defence. But while those soldiers at the front endure death and bloodshed in the defence of our national territories, the diplomatic authorities are still seeking compromises.

Ever since the unjust imprisonment of the patriotic leaders in Shanghai, the whole world has been startled; the whole of our people has been filled with anger and distress. To love one's country is an offence! This is a terrifying prospect.

Generalissimo Chiang Kai-shek, surrounded by a group of unworthy advisers, has forfeited the support of the masses of our people. He is deeply guilty for the harm his policies have done the country. We, Chang Hsueh-liang and the others undersigned, advised him with tears to take another way; but we were repeatedly rejected and rebuked.

Not long ago, the students in Sian were demonstrating in their National Salvation movement, and General Chiang set the police to killing these patriotic children. How could anyone with a human conscience bear to do this? We his colleagues of many years' standing, could not bear to sit still and witness it.

Therefore we have tendered our last advice to Marshal Chiang, while guaranteeing his safety, in order to stimulate his awakening.

The Military and Civilians in the North-West unanimously make the following demands:

1. Reorganize the Nanking Government, and admit all parties to share the joint responsibility of saving the nation.
2. Stop all kinds of civil wars.

---

[1] James Bertram, *First Act in China; the Story of the Sian Mutiny* (New York, The Viking Press, 1938), pp. 126–127.

3. Immediately release the patriotic leaders arrested in Shanghai.
4. Release all political prisoners throughout the country.
5. Emancipate the patriotic movement of the people.
6. Safeguard the political freedom of the people to organize and call meetings.
7. Actually carry out the Will of Dr. Sun Yat-sen.
8. Immediately call a National Salvation Conference.

The eight items above are the points of National Salvation unanimously maintained by us and by all the Military and Civilians throughout the North-West.

We, therefore, hope that you gentlemen will stoop to meet public sentiment and sincerely adopt these demands, so as to open one line of life for the future, and remedy past mistakes that have been the ruin of the country. The great cause is before us: it does not permit glancing backward. We hope to carry out the policies here maintained only for the liberation and benefit of the country. As to our merit or guilt, we leave this to the judgment of our fellow-countrymen.

In sending this telegram, we urgently await your order.

SIANFU, *December 12, 1936.*

35

The Central Committee of the Chinese Communist Party to the Third Plenary Session of the Fifth Central Executive Committee of the Kuomintang, February 10, 1937

[On February 10, 1937 (five days before the Session's opening) the Central Committee of the Chinese Communist Party addressed a telegram to the Third Plenary Session of the Fifth Central Executive Committee of the Kuomintang in which it agreed to make the following alteration in the policies which have characterized the activities of the Communist Party in China:]

"(1) to stop our program of conducting armed uprisings throughout the country for the overthrow of the National Government in Nanking; (2) to change the Soviet Government into the Government of the Special Region of the Republic of China and the Red Army into the National Revolutionary Army under the direct leadership of the Central Government and the Military Affairs Commission in Nanking; (3) to enforce the thorough democratic system of universal suffrage within the special regions under the regime of the Government of the Special Region; and (4) to put an end to the policy of expropriating the land of landlords and to execute persistently the common program of the anti-Japanese united front."

[The telegram then recommended the following five-point program:]

"(1) suspension of civil wars of all sorts and concentration of all the national strength for unanimous resistance to external aggression; (2) freedom of speech, assembly, organization, etc. and release of all political prisoners; (3) convocation of a congress of various parties, factions, military groups and organizations in order to concentrate capable leaders of the country as a whole for the joint salvation of the country; (4) immediate accomplishment of the preparatory work for a war of resistance against Japan; and (5) amelioration of the living conditions of the people at large."

36

Manifesto on Unity by the Central Committee of the Chinese Communist Party, September 22, 1937 [2]

Beloved Compatriots—The Central Executive Committee of the Communist Party of China respectfully and sincerely issues the following Manifesto to all fathers, brothers and sisters throughout the country or:

At the present juncture when the country is facing extreme danger and the fate of the nation is in the balance, in order to save the country from extinction, we have, on the basis of peace and national unity and joint resistance against foreign aggression, reached an understanding with the Kuomintang of China, and are determined to participate in the concerted effort for overcoming the national emergency. This has a profound significance on the future of the great Chinese nation. For we all know that, when the national existence is endangered, only through internal unity can the aggression of imperialistic Japan be overcome. The foundation of national solidarity is now already laid, and the campaign of national emancipation launched. The Central Executive Committee of the Communist Party of China congratulates itself on the brilliant future of the nation. However, in order to transform this future into the realization of a New China, independent, free and happy, all descendants of Huangti (the first Chinese Emperor) must patiently and unceasingly participate in the concerted struggle.

The Central Executive Committee of the Communist Party of China avails itself of this opportunity to propose the following general objectives for the common struggle of the entire people or:

(1) Struggle for the independence, liberty and emancipation of the Chinese nation by promptly and swiftly preparing and launching the national revolutionary campaign of resistance with a view to recovering the lost territories and restoring the integrity of territorial sovereign rights.

(2) Enforce democracy based on the people's rights and convoke the National People's Congress in order to enact the Constitution and decide upon the plans of national salvation.

(3) Improve the well-being and enrich the livelihood of the Chinese people by relieving famines and other calamities, stabilizing the people's livelihood, consolidating national defense and economy, removing the sufferings of the people and bettering their living conditions.

These are the urgent requirements of China, for which the struggle is aimed. We believe that they will receive the whole-hearted support of the entire people. The Communist Party of China is ready to co-operate fully with their compatriots for the attainment of these objectives.

The Communist Party of China fully realizes that this programme is likely to meet with numerous difficulties. The first obstacle will come from Japanese Imperialism. In order to deprive the enemy of all pretext for aggression and dispel doubts on the part of friends, the Central Executive Committee of the Communist Party of China solemnly declares the following in connection with national emancipation:

---

[2] Lawrence K. Rosinger, *China's Wartime Politics, 1937–1944* (Princeton, Princeton University Press, 1944), pp. 96–97.

(1) The San Min Chu-I (Three People's Principles) enunciated by Dr. Sun Yat-sen is the paramount need of China to-day. This Party is ready to strive for its enforcement.

(2) This Party abandons its policy of overthrowing the Kuomintang of China by force and the movement of sovietization and discontinues its policy of forcible confiscation of land from landowners.

(3) This Party abolishes the present Soviet Government and will enforce democracy based on the people's rights in order to unify the national political machinery.

(4) This Party abolishes the Red Army, reorganizes it into the National Revolutionary Army, places it under the direct control of the Military Affairs Commission of the National Government, and awaits orders for mobilization to share the responsibility of resisting foreign invasion at the front.

Beloved compatriots, the sincerity, honesty and faithfulness of the attitude of this Party have already been manifested before the entire people in both words and action, and have received the approval of the people. In order to secure closer unity with the Kuomintang of China, consolidate national peace and unity, and carry out this sacred revolutionary war, we have decided immediately to translate into action those parts of our words which have not yet been enforced, such as the abolition and reorganization of the Red Army in the Soviet Area, in order to facilitate unified command for resisting the enemy.

The enemy have penetrated into our country; the moment is critical. Compatriots, let our 400 million people rise and unite. Our nation, with its long history, cannot be conquered. Rise and struggle for the consolidation of national unity and overthrow of Japanese oppression. Victory will be ours. Long live the victory for resisting Japan. Long live the independence, liberty and welfare of new China.

37

Statement by Generalissimo Chiang Kai-shek on Kuomintang-Communist Unity, September 23, 1937 [3]

The aim of the Nationalist Revolution is to seek freedom and equality for China. Dr. Sun Yat-sen said that the San Min Chu I are fundamental principles of national salvation. He earnestly hoped that all our people would strive with one heart to save the state from its perils. Unfortunately, during the past ten years not all of our countrymen have had a sincere and unwavering faith in the Three Principles of the People, nor have they fully realized the magnitude of the crisis confronting our country. The course of the Revolution in its efforts at national reconstruction has been blocked by many obstacles. The result has been waste in our national resources, widespread suffering among the people, increasing humiliations from outside, and growing dangers to the state.

During the past few years the National Government has been calling ceaselessly upon the nation to achieve genuine internal solidarity, and to face unitedly the national crisis. Those who have in the past doubted the Three Principles of the People have now realized the paramount importance of our national interests, and have buried their differences for the sake of internal unity. The

---

[3] Chiang Kai-shek, *Resistance and Reconstruction; Messages During China's Six Years of War, 1937–1943* (New York and London, Harper & Brothers, 1943), pp. 20–21. In this volume the date is erroneously given as Sept. 24, 1937. (*The Chinese Year Book, 1938–1939*, p. 340.)

Chinese people today fully realize that they must survive together or perish together, and that the interests of the nation must take precedence over the interests of individuals or groups.

The Manifesto recently issued by the Chinese Communist Party is an outstanding instance of the triumph of national sentiment over every other consideration. The various decisions embodied in the Manifesto, such as the abandonment of a policy of violence, the cessation of Communist propaganda, the abolition of the Chinese Soviet Government, and the disbandment of the Red Army are all essential conditions for mobilizing our national strength in order that we may meet the menace from without and guarantee our own national existence.

These decisions agree with the spirit of the Manifesto and resolutions adopted by the Third Plenary Session of the Kuomintang. The Communist Party's Manifesto declares that the Chinese Communists are willing to strive to carry out the Three Principles. This is ample proof that China today has only one objective in its war efforts.

In our revolution we are struggling not for personal ambitions or opinions, but for the realization of the Three Principles of the People. Especially during this period of national crisis, when the fate of China lies in the balance, we ought not to argue over the past, but should try as a nation to make a new start. We should earnestly strive to unite, so that as a united nation we may safeguard the continued existence of the Republic.

If a citizen believes in the Three Principles and works actively for the salvation of the state, the Government should not concern itself with his past, but should give him opportunity to prove his loyalty in service to the Republic. Likewise, the Government will gladly accept the services of any political organization provided it is sincerely working for the nation's salvation, and is willing under the banner of our national revolution to join with us in our struggle against aggression.

The Chinese Communist Party, by surrendering its prejudices, has clearly recognized the vital importance of our national independence and welfare. I sincerely hope that all members of the Communist Party will faithfully and unitedly put into practice the various decisions reached, and under the unified military command that is directing our resistance, will offer their services to the state, fighting shoulder to shoulder with the rest of the nation for the successful completion of the Nationalist Revolution.

In conclusion, I may say that the foundation of the Chinese state rests firmly on the Three Principles first expounded by Dr. Sun Yat-sen. This foundation is one that cannot be shaken or changed. Now that the entire nation is awakened and solidly united, it will boldly follow the unswerving policy of the Government, and will mobilize the entire resources to resist the tyrannical Japanese and save the state from its imminent peril.

Enlightened people the world over now realize that China is fighting not merely for her own survival, but also for world peace and for international faith and justice.

38

Message of Generalissimo Chiang Kai-shek to the People's Political Council, March 6, 1941 [4]

I intend, as a representative of the Government, to explain today its attitude toward the conditions laid down by the Communist members of the Council. Before I make any report I wish to state that the Government did not originally intend to declare publicly its stand on its relations with the Chinese Communist Party. Now that the latter has, however, formally telegraphed these demands to the Council, which is an organ of national opinion, it has acted in a manner quite unlike that usually characterizing its words and deeds. It is, therefore, incumbent upon the Government and the Council to make a formal declaration of their attitude in the interests of the nation, the War of Resistance and the future of national reconstruction. A nation, and more especially when it is engaged in mortal combat with an aggressor, depends for its very life upon the maintenance of discipline, order and the necessity of the Government's writ being obeyed. Given a sound framework of discipline and legality it will be able to overcome whatever perils and difficulties come in its way. If, on the other hand, its military command is not unified and its authority questioned, it will meet with defeat no matter how strong its armed forces may be. We are now pitting the whole strength of the nation against the Japanese militarists in a life-and-death struggle. The fate of our nation is hanging in the balance. It is a time when we must give the most scrupulous attention to the upholding of order and authority in the State. In all matters—whether political, social or party problems—not involving conflict with, or obstruction to national order and authority, there is room for frank and open adjustment of differences in search of rational solutions. This has always been the policy and attitude of the Government in relation to the Chinese Communist Party; the achievement of unity by means of mutual concessions in the face of external aggression and the attainment of success in resistance and reconstruction.

I understand that the Secretariat of the Council has received two sets of demands from the Chinese Communist Party entitled: firstly, "rehabilitation measures;" and secondly, "measures for a provisional settlement"—each set containing twelve points. I can assert that though these demands were received by members of the Council before it assembled, no government institution or individual member of the Government, nor I myself, received them. Now that we have seen them we are, first of all, astonished at the wording of the titles and next, at the formal resemblance of the contents to the demands made by the Japanese prior to the Lukouchiao Incident. One is particularly and painfully reminded of the so-called "Three Principles" announced by the Japanese at that unhappy time. The Chinese Communists are as much citizens of the Chinese Republic as we all are, and yet their presentation of such demands at such a time as this would seem clearly to indicate their intention of taking up a hostile attitude to the National Government and the People's Political Council. We think, therefore, the least said the better, and do not regard it as necessary to rebut each point in detail. It is sufficient to classify the sense of the demands into three main categories of "military," "political," and "party" affairs. The first eight points of the first set of demands regarding "rehabilitation measures" and the first, sixth, seventh, eighth, ninth and tenth points of the second set

---

[4] Chiang Kai-shek, *op. cit.*, pp. 235–241.

regarding "measures for a provisional settlement" belong to the category of military affairs. The ninth and twelfth points of the first set and the third, fourth and fifth points of the second set belong to the category of political affairs, while the tenth and eleventh points of the first set and the eleventh and twelfth points of the second set belong to the category of party affairs. A brief explanation of the bearing of the sense of the demands under each of these three heads upon resistance and reconstruction is indispensable.

Firstly, the demand is, in effect, that the Government should not suppress disobedient and rebellious troops, that government authorities should be punished for so doing and that the losses of the mutineers in such rebellions should be compensated.

Secondly, the implication is that the Government should establish special areas outside the sphere of its authority, recognize the existence of anomalous political organizations and restrict its power to check illegal activities on the part of organizations or individuals. Recognition of a so-called "democratic authority in the enemy's rear" is also demanded. The logical outcome of all this would be disaster—such a disaster as must invariably follow any attempt by a party to take advantage of enemy invasion in order to seize supreme power.

Thirdly, the sense of the demands is that the Communist Party should enjoy a special status and special rights and that the Government should not deal with the Communist members of the Council on the same footing as it deals with all other members belonging to other parties or to none. The Government not being ready to comply, the Communists have refused to attend the present meeting of the People's Political Council. In essence this is really what the demands amount to. I think that when the Communist Party produced them it did not perhaps realize they were of so drastic a nature. But were the Government to accept them without protest, China would scarcely be any longer worthy of being called a nation or the People's Political Council an organ of the national will.

Now I shall further expound the attitude of the Government towards these three categories of demands.

In the category of military affairs the consistent policy of the Government has been to nationalize our armies. That is, under the supreme command of the National Government there is but one system of national armies, and there can be no second system of armies under the control of individual parties or private persons. I can categorically assure the Council that the national revolutionary army is the army of the State and in no way the army of any particular party whatever. It is, therefore, absolutely out of the question to regard a section of it as belonging to the Communist Party. There can be but one source of command. Should a second presume to assert itself, it would be indistinguishable from the "military council" of Wang Ching-wei's puppet regime and accordingly detested and abjured by the whole country. It is inconceivable that the Communists, if devoted to the cause of resistance, should take up such a position.

Next, the political principle of the Government is to democratize the national political system. All citizens, individually or in organized bodies, while they conform to discipline, should shoulder their responsibilities, fulfill their duties and enjoy their rights, possess all due freedom of action, but sovereignty is indivisible. If a second source of political authority were to be allowed to exist outside the Government—such, for example, as might be called by the name of a "democratic authority behind the enemy lines," mentioned in these demands—it would not differ from the traitorous administrations in Nanking and Manchuria. Not only would the Government find it intolerable, but the whole country would see in it an irreconcilable enemy.

Although as a result of the nation's historical development there is now but one party exercising administrative power, while others of varying size and permanency are "in opposition," yet all parties exist in a spirit of equality with one another, this being nowhere more markedly visible than in this democratic institution, the People's Political Council. Here all are equal rather as citizens than as parties. There could be no room for a special status of one party or demands for special rights, such as would vitiate the sprouting of our democratic institutions. I hope that all of you councillors will fully comprehend the nature of this considered and unvarying stand of the Government regarding its relationship with political parties.

Now I would like to elaborate somewhat upon the military aspect of the matter. From the time in 1938 when the 18th Army Corps, in defiance of the orders of the High Command, arbitrarily withdrew to the right bank of the Yellow River and forcibly carried out an illegal occupation of the Sui-Teh district, the Government has been loath to consider this move as instigated solely by the Communist Party, or to hold that party guilty of sabotaging resistance; nor did it think that any such motive was necessarily behind the 18th Army Corps' insubordination. Nevertheless, the effect extended even to the rear where it created general uneasiness on account of the potential dangers it threatened. The result was highly damaging to the whole prosecution of the war, putting a weapon into the hands of the enemy and imperilling the nation in the gravest manner. During the past two years or more the Government has been simultaneously unifying the fighting efforts of the whole army at the front and stabilizing the internal condition of the nation in the southwest and northwest of the rear. It is an exceedingly distressing fact that while all other countries in the world present a united front to external aggression, with us the Government finds added to the task of waging war on an invader that of settling internal troubles. Surely such a state of affairs is not to be paralleled in the history of any other revolutionary country. However, the precautions taken by the Government have been such as to avert any disaster either at the front or in the rear and the country may reckon this as great good fortune. Despite this danger, we find our capacity to withstand the enemy strong enough to ensure our final victory and also a sound and formidable foundation laid for stability in the rear. Had it been otherwise and had timely measures not been taken, by now the provinces of the south and northwest, if not long overrun by the enemy, would have been ruined by the escapades of rebels and antisocial elements; and the people in the rear would be living in such insecurity as those suffer in provinces behind the enemy lines, in Hopei, Chahar, Shantung and Kiangsu where the National Government and its armed forces cannot protect them from the double oppression of the Japanese and the puppets.

However, the fact remains that the forces of resistance are considerably weakened by the enforced retention in the rear of large numbers of troops who might be fighting at the front. This also imposes a grievously depressing weight upon the spirits of the whole army and people. The problem is one that is really not difficult to solve. All that is required is a complete change in the attitude and actions of the Communist Party, in no longer regarding the 18th Army Corps as its peculiar possession or as an instrument for the obstruction of other sections of the national forces to the detriment of resistance. Let the Communists carry out the declaration they themselves made in 1937 wherein they said: (1) Dr. Sun's Three Principles of the People serve the needs of present-day China and the Chinese Communist Party is prepared to strive for their complete fulfillment; (2) they would abandon all violent action and policy aimed at the overthrow of the Kuomintang, the movement for the propagation of communism in China, and the policy of violent confiscation of landowners' holdings; (3) they would abolish the then Chinese Soviet government in the Northwest and work towards a united democratic government for the whole country; (4) they would abolish the name and status of the Red Army and permit its incorporation into the national revolutionary army under the command of the National Military Council of the National Government. If they would now but faithfully carry out their original intention to comply with these conditions and move all the troops connected with their party according to the plans laid down by the National Military Council into the areas appointed for them to defend, the whole country could be united to meet the invader, there would be an end of internal obstacles and anxieties, and it would be possible to deal the exhausted enemy a tremendous blow which I am convinced would bring about within a short time a most sensational victory. At least we could restore the lines held in the autumn of 1938; of this the military authorities are in no doubt. Then lost territory would be recovered and our fellow-countrymen delivered from their sufferings. This would be an immense contribution of the 18th Army Corps to the national cause and the whole country would admire the patriotism of the Communists. Our Government has no other demand to make of the Communist Party and the troops connected with it save this one fervent wish that they will carry out the obligations into which they themselves freely entered and support the Program of Resistance and Reconstruction to which the People's Political Council gave its unanimous endorsement. It merely hopes that the Communists will cast off all party prejudice and put the interests of the nation first by obeying orders, maintaining discipline and working in harmony with all their comrades-in-arms.

There are also two other groups of these demands which have an intimate relation with military affairs: what the Communists call the "prevention of provocation," the "withdrawal of the anti-Communist forces in Central China" and the "immediate cessation of all attacks on us." These three points call for some remark. This sort of senseless, mendacious, misleading and malicious propaganda vilifies our Government and deliberately injures the sacred mission of resistance, but, more than that, it offers insult to the pure spirit of the whole country's united battle against aggression. I need scarcely assert that our Government is solely concerned with leading the nation against the Japanese invaders and extirpating the traitors, and is utterly without any notion of again taking up arms to "suppress the Communists." It desires never again to hear of that ill-omened term which now has a place only in Chinese history. Let them obey orders, give up their attacks on their comrades-in-arms and cease all their provocative acts; the Government will then treat them with all possible consideration. The Government is, moreover, desirous of showing generosity and of letting bygones be bygones. In defense of our national interest it cannot, however, fail to punish and check insubordination, for it would otherwise fail in its duty to the nation. For loyal soldiers it has such a loving solicitude that the charge of provocation and attack is absurd. I can make myself responsible for the statement in your presence that at no future time could there conceivably be another campaign for the suppression of the Communists. I hope that you will address an appeal to Mao Tse-tung, Tung Pi-wu and the other Communist members of this Council to effect a change in the attitude of their party so that we can discuss here all together the questions they have raised and arrive at some reasonable solution of them. You represent the will of the nation and your bounden duty is to strive for the success of resistance and reconstruction and national unity. If the Communist Party will only accept your advice, and say and do nothing in future contrary to the Program of Resistance and Reconstruction and their own manifesto of 1937, the Government will undoubtedly respect whatever resolutions you may adopt for the settlement of the incident and see that they are carried fully into effect without delay.

In conclusion, provided unity can be preserved and resistance carried on to the end, the Government will be ready to follow your directions in the settlement of all outstanding questions. I call upon the Communist members of the Council to realize the national danger at this time of mortal combat with the invader and, acting in the spirit of the saying "brothers quarrel at home but go out together to repel assault from without," to accept the judgment of this Council and make their contribution to national solidarity. This is the fervent prayer of the whole people, and it would moreover deal the enemy a mighty blow. Out of solicitude for the Communist Party and in the desire to see it play its full part in the history of this life-and-death struggle of our country, we beg it to continue in its mission of reconstruction and resistance against aggression.

39

Statement by Generalissimo Chiang Kai-shek to the Fifth Central Executive Committee of the Kuomintang, September 13, 1943 [5]

After hearing the secretariat's report on the question of the Chinese Communist Party and the views expressed by various members of the Central Executive Committee I am of the opinion that first of all we should clearly recognize that the Chinese Communist problem is a purely political problem and should be solved by political means. Such ought to be the guiding principle for the Plenary Session in its effort to settle this matter. If you share my views you should maintain the policy of leniency and forbearance which we have consistently pursued in dealing with our domestic affairs with the expectation that the Chinese Communist Party will be moved by our sincerity and magnanimity no matter in what way they may slander us nor in what manner they may try to create trouble.

In spite of provocations we should abide by the manifesto of the Tenth Plenary Session: "In the case of those who sincerely believe in the Three People's Principles, obey laws and orders, do not hinder prosecution of the war, do not attempt to upset social order and do not seize our national territory in defiance of Government decrees, the Central Government would overlook their past record either in thought or in deed and should respect their opportunities, be they individuals, or political groups, to serve the country." We should, now as ever, continue to be tolerant in strict conformity with the manifesto and earnestly expect the Communist Party eventually to realize and correct their errors. We should make it clear that the Central Government does not have any particular demand to make on the Chinese Communist Party but hopes that it will abandon its policy of forcibly occupying our national territory and give up its past tactics of assaulting National Government troops in various sectors, thus obstructing the prosecution of the war.

We also hope that the Chinese Communist Party will redeem its pledge made in its declaration of 1937 and fulfill the four promises solemnly announced in that

---

[5] *China Handbook, 1937–1945*, pp. 67–68. The Fifth Central Executive Committee was then holding its eleventh plenary session.

document: "(1) To struggle for the realization of the Three People's Principles; (2) To abandon the policy of overthrowing the Kuomintang regime by force, give up the Communist movement and discard the policy of confiscating land by force; (3) To dissolve the present government organization and by carrying into practice the principles of democracy thus held to bring about the political unity of the whole nation; (4) To disband the Red Army by incorporating it into the National Army under the direct command of the Military Council of the National Government. The troops thus reorganized will await orders to move to the front to undertake the tasks of fighting the enemy."

If the Chinese Communist Party can prove its good faith by making good its promises the Central Government, taking note of its sincerity and loyalty in carrying on our war of resistance, will once more treat it with sympathy and consideration so that we may accomplish hand in hand the great task of resistance and reconstruction.

40

Report by the Representative of the National Government [6] to the People's Political Council, September 15, 1944 [7]

Members of the People's Political Council requested a report on the conversations concerning the Chinese communist problem. As a representative of the Government, I shall make a simple and concise statement: On January 17, 1944, Kuo Chung-yung, Liaison Officer of the National Military Council stationed with the 18th Group Army, telegraphed the Board of Military Operations, reporting: "On the 16th of this month, Mao Tse-tung in a talk with me expressed the opinion that the Communist Party would send either Chou En-lai, or Lin Tsu-han, or Commander-in-chief Chu Teh, or all of them, to Chungking to see the Generalissimo for instructions. He asked me to report and seek approval." On February 2, the Board of Military Operations sent a telegram in reply to Liaison Officer Kuo, saying: "Messrs. Chu, Chou, and Lin are welcome. Please telegraph again before their departure." Later, a telegram came from Liaison Officer Kuo stating that, according to Chu Teh, Chou En-lai, and Lin Tsu-han, Lin was scheduled to leave on April 28. The National Government, upon receipt of the information, on May 1 delegated Dr. Wang Shih-chieh and myself to Sian to conduct preliminary conversations with Mr. Lin. We arrived in Sian on May 2 simultaneously with Mr. Lin. Between May 4 and 11, five conversations were held in Sian. The opinions expressed by Mr. Lin during the conversations were all recorded and the minutes were sent to Mr. Lin who, after reading them and making corrections and revisions, handed the minutes back to us in person and signed them. At that time, Mr. Lin inquired whether we could also sign the minutes. In our opinion, these minutes contain the opinions expressed by Mr. Lin or part of our opinions agreed to by Mr. Lin and should be signed by Mr. Lin only. As to the opinions of the National Government, we should formally present them after we returned to Chungking and had consulted with higher authorities. The following is the original text of the minutes signed by Mr. Lin:

---

[6] Gen. Chiang Chih-chung, Minister of Political Training of the National Military Council.
[7] *China Handbook, 1937–1945*, pp. 81–90.

"Points Raised During the Conversations Between May 4 and May 8

"A. *On Military Matters*

"1. The 18th Group Army and troops formerly belonging to the 'New Fourth Army' should obey the orders of the National Military Council.

"2. The Communist troops should be reorganized into at least four armies consisting of 12 divisions, as proposed by General Lin Piao last year.

"3. After reorganization, the troops will take up the defense of their original positions, but they should follow the direction of the commanders of the war zones in which they are stationed. When the war is victoriously concluded, they should abide by orders of transfer issued by the National Government to designated defense areas.

"4. After the reorganization of the troops, their commander, in accordance with the regulations governing personnel promulgated by the National Government, may recommend personnel for appointment.

"5. After its reorganization, the said Army should abide by the rules and regulations governing military supplies, as applied to other armies under the National Government.

"B. *On the Shensi-Kansu-Ningsia Border Area Question*

"1. Its name shall be changed to the Northern Shensi Administrative Area.

"2. This Administrative Area shall be under the direct jurisdiction of the Executive Yuan and shall not be under the Shensi Provincial Government.

"3. The said Administrative Area should embrace the original area (map attached) and its boundaries should be fixed jointly by representatives of the National Government and the Chinese Communist Party.

"4. This Administrative Area should faithfully carry out the Three People's Principles, the *Program of Armed Resistance and National Reconstruction* and the laws and orders of the National Government. Other laws and regulations which are deemed necessary, due to local circumstances, should be submitted to the National Government for approval before promulgation.

"5. The annual budget of the Administrative Area should be submitted to the National Government for approval.

"6. The Administrative Area and the 18th Group Army, after being authorized to receive Government appropriations, should not issue local bank-notes. All the previously issued bank-notes should be properly disposed of by the Ministry of Finance.

"7. The Kuomintang may conduct Party activities and publish newspapers in the Administrative Area and set up a radio station in Yenan. At the same time, the Kuomintang should recognize the legal status of the Communist Party in China and permit the latter to set up a radio station in Chungking to facilitate exchange of opinions between the two Parties and the Government.

"8. The existing organization of the Shensi-Kansu-Ningsia Border Area is not to be changed for the time being.

"C. *On the Party Problem*

"As provided by the *Program of Armed Resistance and National Reconstruction* the Chinese Communist Party should be granted legal status. There should be no more unlawful arrests and no more suppression of books and newspapers, while freedom of speech and democracy should be promoted. Those persons who were arrested on account of the New Fourth Army Incident as well as all imprisoned members of the Chinese Communist Party including Liao Cheng-chih and Chang Wen-ping should be immediately released. Order should be given to protect the families of members of the 18th Group Army and the New Fourth Army.

"D. *On Other Matters*

"1. The Communist Party should express its desire to continue faithfully to keep the four-point pledge and support the war of resistance and the program of national reconstruction under the leadership of Generalissimo Chiang Kai-shek, while the Kuomintang in turn should express its willingness to seek a just and rational readjustment of the relations between the two Parties by political means.

"2. The military blockade on the Shensi-Kansu-Ningsia Border Area should be lifted. As at present, trade and transportation should be given priority.

"3. Military, political and economic problems in guerilla areas behind enemy lines should be solved to the advantage of the war under the direction of the National Government and the National Military Council.—(*Signed*) Lin Tsu-han, May 11, 1944."

"*Appendix: Four Points Proposed by Divisional Commander Lin Piao*

"1. With regard to the Party issue, we wish to obtain a legitimate status under the *Program of Armed Resistance and National Reconstruction* and to enforce the Three People's Principles. The National Government on the other hand may conduct Party activities and run Party papers in the Chinese Communist areas.

"2. With regard to the problem of troops, we desire that our troops should be reorganized into four armies with 12 divisions and be accorded the same treatment as the National Government troops.

"3. The North Shensi Border Area, in its original form, should be turned into an administrative area, while other areas should be reorganized and the laws and decrees of the National Government should be enforced there.

"4. With regard to the area of operations, we accept in principle the National Government's decision that our troops be dispatched to the north of the Yellow River. However, at present we can only make necessary preparations. We guarantee that the decision will be put into effect as soon as the war is terminated. Should war conditions permit (as in the case of a general counter-offensive) arrangements may be made for the transfer of our troops to other areas."

II

Since Lin Tsu-han had expressed concrete opinions, we returned to Chungking on May 17, together with Mr. Lin. At that time, the Central authorities were making preparations for the 12th Plenary Session of the Central Executive Committee of the Kuomintang and the National Administrative Conference. Despite busy preparations, we submitted a report to the National Government on the results of the Sian conversations and the opinions expressed by Lin Tsu-han so as to enable the Government to consider measures for the solution of this problem. On June 5, we met Lin Tsu-han and handed to him the memorandum of the National Government concerning the solution of the Chinese Communist problem through political methods. The original text of the memorandum is as follows:

"Memorandum of the National Government concerning the Solution of the Chinese Communist Problem through Political Means, June 5, 1944."

With the opinions expressed by Representative Lin Tsu-han at Sian as a basis, the following memorandum was drawn up:

"A. *Military Problems*

"1. The 18th Group Army and its units stationed in various localities should be reorganized into four armies consisting of ten divisions with their designations to be decided by order of the National Government.

"2. The said Army must obey the orders of the National Military Council.

"3. The strength of the said Army should be fixed in accordance with the organization of the national armies (orders to be issued by the Ministry of War). The said Army should not form extra echelons, detachments or other units. All such extra units already in existence must be disbanded within a specific date set by the National Government.

"4. In matters pertaining to personnel the said Army may make recommendations to the National Government regarding appointments in accordance with regulations governing personnel.

"5. The said Army should be given military expenses in the same way as other national armies by the National Government, and the independence of the commissariat should be upheld in accordance with the Military Management Act.

"6. The said Army must carry on its training work in accordance with the training program and orders issued by the National Government, which has the right to send men to inspect its training work.

"7. All units of the said Army must be concentrated for service within a certain specified period. Until then the units in the various war zones must be placed under the direction of the war area commanders concerned.

"B. *The Shensi-Kansu-Ningsia Border Area Problem*

"1. The Shensi-Kansu-Ningsia Border Area shall be renamed the North Shensi Adiminstrative Area, and its administrative organ called the North Shensi Administrative Office.

"2. The said Administrative Area should be within the confines of the territory it embraces at present. But its exact territory should be fixed by representatives of the National Government and the Communist Party jointly.

"3. The said Administrative Office should be under the direct control of the Executive Yuan.

"4. The said Administrative Area should carry out the laws and orders of the National Government. Other laws and orders which are deemed necessary because of local peculiar circumstances should be submitted to the National Government for approval before promulgation.

"5. Appointment or removal of the Chairman of the said Administrative Area should be made by the National Government, whereas its commissioners and magistrates may be appointed by the National Government upon the recommendation of the chairman.

"6. The organization of the said Administrative Area should be submitted to the National Government for approval.

"7. The budget of the said Administrative Area should be submitted annually to the National Government for approval.

"8. In the said Administrative Area and the places where the units of the 18th Group Army are stationed, no local bank-notes should be issued. The notes already issued should be disposed of by arrangement with the Ministry of Finance.

"9. All administrative organizations set up by the Chinese Communists themselves in other places should be taken over and dealt with by the provincial governments concerned.

"C. *The Party Problems*

"1. Party affairs for the duration of the war should be conducted in accordance with the *Program of Armed Resistance and National Reconstruction,* while after the conclusion of the war, according to the National Government's decision, a People's Congress should be convened to adopt a constitution and enforce constitutional government. The Chinese Communist Party should obey the laws of the National Government and enjoy the same treatment as other political parties.

"2. The Chinese Communist Party must reaffirm its sincerity to carry out its four pledges."

After handing the National Government's Memorandum to Lin Tsu-han, we stated that, in case the Chinese Communist Party agrees to put the above-mentioned measures into affect, (1) the National Government will consider the withdrawal of the garrison troops in the defense areas and the restoration of the trade communications between these areas and their neighboring districts; and (2) members of the Chinese Communist Party arrested on charges of violating the law will be leniently treated and released on bail by the National Government. Mr. Lin then took a letter from his pocket enclosing a document entitled "Suggestions for the Solution of Some Current Urgent Problems Made by the Central Committee of the Chinese Communist Party to the Central Executive Committee of the Kuomintang." He handed the document to us for reading. Following is the original text:

"Suggestions made by the Central Committee of the Chinese Communist Party to the Central Executive Committee of the Kuomintang concerning the solution of some of the current urgent problems.

"The Kuomintang and the Communist Party have cooperated in the war of resistance already for seven years. That the Chinese Communist Party has been sincere in its effort to promote the welfare of the nation, fought valiantly in the war of resistance, enforced the *San Min Chu I,* fulfilled the four-point pledge and consistently supported the National Government and Mr. Chiang Kai-shek in armed resistance and national reconstruction, must be apparent to all. But at present, when the war situation is becoming very critical and the Japanese invaders are continuing their attacks, the internal political condition and the Kuomintang-Communist relationship have not followed the right track to keep pace with the war requirements.

"With a view to overcoming the present difficulties, repulsing the Japanese invaders and seriously preparing for a counter-offensive, the Chinese Communist Party considers that the only way to achieve these objectives is to adopt democracy and strengthen national unity. For this purpose, the Chinese Communist Party hopes that the Government will solve the following extremely urgent problems. These problems, some of which concern national political affairs and others the outstanding issues between the two Parties, are candidly listed as follows:

"A. *Problems Pertaining to National Political Affairs*

"1. The Government is requested to adopt democracy and safeguard the freedoms of speech, the press, assembly, association and person.

"2. The Government is requested to lift the ban on political parties, recognize the legal status of the Chinese Communist Party and the various anti-Japanese parties and groups, and set free political offenders.

"3. The Government is requested to permit the people to enforce local self-government in name as well as in fact.

"B. *Problems Pertaining to the Outstanding Issues Between the Two Parties*

"1. In consideration of the needs of resistance against Japan, the record of achievements in the war of resistance and the present strength of the troops, the Government is requested to organize the Chinese Communist troops into 16 armies consisting of 47 divisions with 10,000 troops per division. As a compromise, the Government is requested to approve of the organization of at least five armies of 16 divisions.

"2. The Government is requested to recognize the Shensi-Kansu-Ningsia Border Government and the popularly-elected anti-Japanese governments in bases in North China as legally-constituted local governments and to recognize all measures taken to meet war exigencies.

"3. During the period of the war of resistance, the *status quo* be maintained in areas garrisoned by the Communist troops and readjustments be considered after the conclusion of the war.

"4. The Government is requested to give full material aid to the 18th Group Army and the New Fourth Army. Since 1940, the Government has given them not one bullet, not one pill of medicine, not one cent of money or one grain of rice. It is requested that this situation be immediately remedied.

"5. With regard to the weapons, munitions, and medicines furnished China by the Allied countries, the Government is requested to apportion and distribute them equitably among the various armies of China and the 18th Group Army and the New Fourth Army should be given the share due them.

"6. The Government is requested to order its military and political organs to lift the military and economic blockades of the Shensi-Kansu-Ningsia Border Area and the various anti-Japanese bases.

"7. The Government is requested to order its military organs to cease armed attacks on the New Fourth Army in Central China and the guerillas in Kwangtung.

"8. The Government is requested to order the Party and military organs to set free persons arrested in various places, such as Yeh Ting and officers and men of the New Fourth Army in the South Anhwei Incident, Liao Cheng-chih and Chang Wen-ping in Kwangtung, Hsu Chieh, Hsu Min-chiu, Mao Tse-nin, Yang Tse-hua and Pan Chueh in Sinkiang, Lo Shih-wen, Yao Hsien, Li Chun, and Chang Shao-ming in Szechwan, Ho Ping and others in Hupeh, Liu Yin in Chekiang, Hsuan Hsia-fu, Shih Tso-hsiang, Li Yu-hai, Chen Yuan-ying and Chao Hsiang in Sian. These men are all patriots and they should be set free in order to further the interests of war against Japan.

"9. The Government is requested to permit the Chinese Communist Party to conduct party activities and publish party papers in various places in the entire country while the Chinese Communist Party will also permit the Kuomintang to conduct party activities and publish party papers in the Shensi-Kansu-Ningsia Border Area and the various anti-Japanese democratic border areas behind the enemy lines.

"The foregoing concerns only the principal points. The Chinese Communist Party sincerely hopes that the National Government will give them a reasonable and most speedy settlement. As the war against Hitler in the West might be victoriously concluded this year, the counter-offensive against Japan in the East can surely be unfolded next year. Furthermore, the Japanese invaders are now launching large-scale attacks to threaten our anti-Japanese front. If our two parties can not only continue to cooperate but also readjust our internal political affairs and improve the party relationship, not only will the present general situation be greatly improved but we will have bright prospects of victory when our country, in coordination with our Allies, launches a large-scale counter-offensive next year. It is hoped that our Government will give the foregoing its serious and favorable consideration.—Lin Tsu-han, Representative of the Chinese Communist Party."

Then and there we said to Lin Tsu-han: "We did not receive the 20 proposals brought up by you on May 22, and they were withdrawn by you, because there was a wide difference between these proposals and the opinions expressed by you at Sian. Your present 12 proposals, though fewer in number, are similar in content. We ought not to accept this document from you, but as we do not want to disregard your wish we can only agree to keep it. However, we cannot forward it to higher authorities." Mr. Lin said, "Then you may keep it in your place for reference."

III

On June 6, we received a letter from Lin Tsu-han. In this letter two points were raised. First, he thought that the difference between the Government memorandum and the proposals of the Chinese Communist Party of June 4 was too great. Besides reporting the memorandum to the Central Committee of the Chinese Communist Party, he requested us to forward the 12-point proposal of the Chinese Communists to the National Government for a rational solution of the problem. Second, he regarded as contrary to fact the phrase, "based on the opinions expressed by Representative Lin Tsu-han at Sian," appearing in the beginning of the Government memorandum. He regarded the minutes of the Sian conversations as "preliminary opinions, finally reached after joint discussions." He agreed that "each Party should refer to its own central authorities for instructions before making a final decision." So he still hoped the National Government would consider the latest proposals made by the Chinese Communist Party. On June 8, we sent Mr. Lin a letter answering the two points he had brought up. First, we had made it clear that we would not submit Mr. Lin's letter dated June 5 to higher authorities because the difference between the original opinions and the proposals made by Mr. Lin later was too great. Mr. Lin finally said: "You may keep the letter in your place for reference." Therefore, we only consented at that time to keep Mr. Lin's letter and again made it clear that the letter could not be submitted to higher authorities. Second, the opinions recorded in the minutes of the Sian conversations, and corrected and revised by Mr. Lin, who intimated that he would make clean copies and sign again, were duly submitted to the National Government. Therefore the Government memorandum was based on Mr. Lin's opinions and it accepted as many of his opinions as possible. We hoped that he could completely accept the memorandum.

IV

We received another letter from Mr. Lin on June 11. He said that he thought the two points in our reply of June 8 were "quite difficult to comprehend." First, he said that, since we had recognized him as the representative of the Chinese Communist Party, we should not refuse to report to the National Government the opinions formally expressed by the Chinese Communist Party, and yet he was unilaterally asked to accept personally the memorandum of the National Government. How could he make a decision all by himself? Second, he admitted that the 12 points suggested by the Chinese Communist Party and handed to us by him on June 5 are "slightly different" from the opinions obtained during our conversations at Sian, but seeing that the Government memorandum was also different from the Sian conversations, he felt that such divergences of views common to both sides in the conversations were nothing surprising. Now that he had reported the Government memorandum to the Central Committee of the Chinese Communist Party by wire, we should not refuse to forward the opinions formally brought up by the Chinese Communist Party to the National Government for instructions.

In fact, the two points which Mr. Lin said were incomprehensible are very plain. It is because Mr. Lin is the representative of the Chinese Communist Party, that the opinion expressed by him can be counted upon. As to the 12 points raised by the Chinese Communist Party, their contents greatly differ from Mr. Lin's opinions. Moreover, there was no indication of the Chinese Communist Party's intention to carry out the fundamental idea of obeying military command and political orders. What it brought up were one-sided demands. Therefore, it is quite understandable that we declared then that we could not forward the proposal. Nevertheless, hoping to seek an early solution to the problem and especially unwilling to create any misunderstanding, we forwarded the 12 points as handed to us by Mr. Lin to the National Government. Afterwards we received instructions from the National Government stating, "the National Government on June 5 sent its memorandum to Representative Lin for transmission to the Chinese Communist Party. Those of the opinions of the Chinese Communist Party which can be accepted by the National Government have already been embodied in the memorandum to the fullest extent. It is hoped that the Chinese Communist authorities will accept the memorandum."

We informed Mr. Lin by letter on June 15 of the instructions of the National Government. We also explained that the fundamental spirit of the present conversations should follow the principle of the unity of military command and political orders as the prerequisite of improving the current situation and strengthening national unity. But the 12 points raised by the Chinese Communist Party made no mention of how to carry out military and political orders of the National Government, how to improve administrative measures, and how to readjust and reorganize armed units. As to the number of armed units to be reorganized, we said at Sian that the possible number was three armies with eight divisions. Now the Government in the memorandum has decided to increase it to four armies with ten divisions—an increase of two divisions as compared with the figure we mentioned. This shows the readiness of the National Government to compromise as much as possible.

V

After we answered Mr. Lin's letter on June 15, for more than ten days the Chinese Communist Party gave no answer to the Government memorandum. On July 3, Mr. Lin asked us to meet him and verbally raised two points. First, in political affairs he hoped that the National Government would take a broader view of "democracy." Second, concerning the question of troops he hoped that the Communist army could be increased to five armies with 16 divisions. Simultaneously he told us that he had received a wire from Yenan welcoming us to that city for further discussions.

At that time we immediately made an explanation: Regarding the question of democracy, the Government had been adopting various measures to hasten the realization of democratic government. For instance, it had abolished the compulsory system of censoring books and magazines before publication, strictly ordered all the provinces in the rear to complete the establishment of local representative bodies, and was about to promulgate the Regulations for Safe-Guarding the Freedom of the Human Person, and a number of other democratic measures were under consideration, which we need not enumerate. As to the increase of army units, the National Government was now enforcing a policy of emphasizing the quality of soldiers and has been reducing the number of armed units as much as possible. It has gone to the utmost limit to accept the demands of the Chinese Communist Party. Its sympathetic readiness to compromise can be understood if one compares the number of national troops at the beginning of the war with their present total. Finally we believed that if the conversations proceed like this, there appeared to be deliberate intention to protract them. It seemed necessary to give a comprehensive and definite answer to the Government memorandum and then use it as a basis of concrete discussion. It was not advisable to continue empty talks and bargaining lest further complications should arise. We also indicated that if the conversations could come to a conclusion in Chungking, we would consider a visit to Yenan.

VI

Mr. Lin visited us again on July 13. He again requested the National Government to give some instructions in connection with the 12 proposals of the Chinese Communists. He made, however, no mention of how they were going to answer the memorandum given to them by the National Government. As the problems raised by Mr. Lin had been explained in the past and did not need further explanation, we only told him that we understood the purpose of his visit. The meeting was closed after we arranged a date for further conversations.

VII

On July 23, Mr. Lin sent us a letter. He again inquired whether we had asked for instructions for a reply to the 12 proposals brought up by the Chinese Communists. In addition he invited us to go to Yenan.

We met Mr. Lin again on July 25. We gave a comparatively more detailed verbal explanation concerning the problems listed in his 12 proposals. We told him that the memorandum of the National Government represented the National Government's concrete views, and that it was the Chinese Communist Party which had not given an answer after much delay. We also stated that such an attitude on the part of the Chinese Communist Party seemed to indicate its deliberate intention in putting off the matter and its unwillingness to find a solution for the problem.

VIII

During this period, we continued to study the question and considered that, following the previous verbal answer, we should give a written reply so as to put our explanations in more concrete form. We met Mr. Lin again on August 5, telling him that we were going to turn into a written reply our opinions given verbally during the previous meeting. We added, "When you have given a definite answer to the Government memorandum, we shall consider further conversations and the question whether we shall go to Yenan or not."

After this talk, on August 10 we sent Mr. Lin a letter based on our previously expressed opinions. Its gist is as follows:

"Three months have elapsed since we had the honor of consulting with you at Sian. For more than two months we have been waiting for the Chinese Communist Party to give a definite reply to the memorandum of the National Government handed to you on June 5 and this prolonged silence was quite beyond our expectation. Regarding the contents of the memorandum, the National

Government not only accepted almost in total the requests of Divisional Commander Lin Piao but also most of your opinions expressed recently at Sian. Since the Chinese Communist Party supports the unification and solidarity of the nation, please urge it to accept the memorandum.

"In connection with the 12 points raised by the Chinese Communist Party, Articles 1 to 3 of the memorandum pointed out that the Government would carry out during the war the *Program of Armed Resistance and National Reconstruction* as accepted by the Chinese Communist Party and other parties and realize within one year after conclusion of the war constitutional government which will give an equal status to all political parties. This statement is clear and concrete. If vague and empty phrases were employed in addition to this statement, they would only cause further discord in the future. The present fixed policy of the National Government is to enlarge gradually the scope of the people's freedom and to promote local self-government step by step in accord with the progress of the war, the approach of victory, and the stability of society. At the same time the National Government hopes that, after its acceptance of the Government memorandum, the Chinese Communist Party will from time to time express its opinion for the effective enforcement of the *Program of Armed Resistance and National Reconstruction* and actively participate in the work of the People's Political Council and the Commission for the Inauguration of Constitutional Government. It is hoped that the views of both parties will thus be reconciled and true unification and solidarity of the nation brought about. Here lies the true significance of the solution of the problem through political means.

"In the 12-point proposal, there are four articles regarding the organization and stationing of the troops and their food and war supplies. The 18th Group Army originally consisted of three divisions. The National Government now promises to allow it to increase to four armies with ten divisions. In permitting this the National Government has taken a very liberal attitude, for the Government is now adopting the policy of 'quality first' and has ordered the reduction in size of other units. Regarding the stationing of troops, the National Government asserts the principle of concentration for service on the one hand and on the other provides for a system of adjustment, training and command prior to their concentration. The Government has indeed taken into consideration all phases of the problem. Regarding their pay, the National Government promises that the troops will be given the same treatment as the national army. As to the supply of arms, the National Government will from time to time make fair distributions among the armies according to their needs and the duties they perform.

"Another article in the 12-point proposal demands that the National Government recognize the 'Shensi-Kansu-Ningsia Border Area' and the 'Anti-Japanese Governments Elected by the People in Bases in North China.' The National Government in its memorandum has already set forth very liberal measures. Other administrative organs in any other areas should be handed over to the various provincial governments concerned in accordance with the memorandum so as to avoid any discord.

"As for other demands they are either at variance with facts or unreasonable, and we shall not repeat them here since we have given you verbal explanations."

IX

Afterwards we received Mr. Lin Tsu-han's letter of August 30 in which he answered our letter of August 10 under instructions of the Chinese Communist Party. It may be summed up as follows:

"1. The letter of August 10 seems to be written in a reproachful tone blaming the Chinese Communist Party for the unreasonable delay. This is entirely contrary to facts and is a misinterpretation. For, the National Government's memorandum is too far apart in principle from the Chinese Communist Party's 12 written points and eight verbal points. It is pointed out that (a) in the memorandum nothing is mentioned about the establishment of a constitutional Government, recognition of the legal status of various political parties and the setting free of political offenders; (b) The memorandum mentions only the number of reorganized troops, the abolition of units other than the reorganized troops and the concentration of the armies for war service; (c) Only strict observance of laws and orders of the National Government for war purposes is required of the Border Government, making no mention of the realization of the Three People's Principles and giving no recognition to the various existing measures and laws; (d) The democratic governments organized by the people in various anti-Japanese bases are to be abolished. All these are cited as facts showing the vast divergence of the opposing views.

"2. Regarded as the obstacle to the fundamental solution of this problem is the wide gap existing between the viewpoints of the National Government, and the Chinese Communist Party and the 'great masses of the people.' For the Government has been persistently reluctant to realize immediately the Three People's Principles and the democratic system of government.

"3. It is hoped that the National Government will give primary attention to national interests in the solution of the country's political problems and questions regarding the relationship of the Kuomintang and the Chinese Communist Party. It should start from a standpoint that is beneficial to national solidarity in armed resistance and the promotion of democracy." The letter again emphasizes the "political problems," "military problems," and problems concerning "Border area" and "North China, Central China and South China anti-Japanese bases." It reaffirms its attitude toward the various issues mentioned under the first item and simultaneously expands considerably their scopes.

"4. The letter asserts that the Chinese Communist Party is persistent in faithfully carrying out its four pledges, faithfully practising the Three People's Principles, and adhering to the policy of democratic consolidation and political settlement, and does not wish to break off the conversations."

We were greatly surprised to read Mr. Lin's letter of August 30. I believe you gentlemen can all form a very appropriate judgment as to how much truth is in the points listed in that letter and it is not necessary for me to elaborate it. Since we received orders to discuss concrete problems, during the period from our visit to Sian to the present moment, the more we have discussed the problems, the greater the difference of opinions has become. The reason why the divergence of opinions has become greater and greater can be seen from the above-mentioned documents. We cannot help regretting the situation, but do not lose hope. In order to make the Chinese Communist Party really understand our ideas, we sent another reply, the gist of which is as follows:

"The purpose of our conversations with you by order of the National Government is to seek national unification. In other words, to request the Chinese Communist Party to fulfil faithfully its four pledges, and to support faithfully the political unity of the nation. If the Chinese Communist Party had, as you said, faithfully carried out its four pledges, why have there been so many cases of attacks on national troops in different localities by the Chinese Communists? And why is it necessary for the National Government at present to instruct us to discuss with you such questions as the obeying of military command and political orders?

"The National Government, in instructing us to confer with you about unification, aims at laying a solid foundation for the realization of constitutionalism and the Three People's Principles in their entirety. The National Government in its memorandum has made definite statements on the questions of democracy and political parties. In addition, detailed explanations are given in our letter of August 10. How can you say nothing was mentioned? Your letter says that the Chinese Communist Party has thoroughly applied the Three People's Principles in the border area and anti-Japanese bases behind the enemy lines. It also says that the people and anti-Japanese organizations in all the Chinese Communist areas enjoy all forms of freedom and rights. But many facts compel us to deny your statements. Take for instance democracy and freedom. The separation of the five powers as taught by the Father of our Republic is the right way to democracy and is the safeguard for the people's freedom. But is there any factual proof of the independence of judicial power and control power in areas under the Chinese Communist Party? Is there any guarantee of freedom of the press and person for the people in the Communist area, and even for members of the Chinese Communist Party? In our last letter we said that we hoped that no vague and abstract demands in connection with the problems of democracy and freedom would be brought up. Instead, we requested the Chinese Communist Party to discuss thoroughly at any time the means of solving the different problems with the National Government, the People's Political Council and the Commission for the Inauguration of Constitutional Government. Such steps are considered not only appropriate but also necessary.

"We pointed out that answers have already been given one by one to the questions in your letter. It is absolutely true that the National Government's memorandum has accepted most of the opinions put forward by Divisional Commander Lin Piao last year and those raised by you at Sian recently. Yet you still emphatically stated that the divergence of views is too great. But the real reason for the divergence is the steady increase in the number of requests of the Chinese Communist Party. What you asked for at Sian was more than what Divisional Commander Lin asked for last year. The 12 points raised by the Chinese Communist Party outnumber the requests you made at Sian. The present letter adds the eight so-called verbal requests to the 12 points. Since requests increase with time, the divergence of views naturally widens. Take for instance the question of the North Shensi Border Area and other anti-Japanese bases. Divisional Commander Lin requested that the North Shensi Border Area be turned into an administrative area within its original area, and all the other areas be reorganized and obey the laws and orders of the National Government. The document you signed at Sian did not contain other anti-Japanese bases. The 12-point proposal of the Chinese Communist Party asks for the recognition of the Shensi-Kansu-Ningsia Border Area and Anti-Japanese Governments Elected by the People in North China Bases. Your letter now seeks the recognition of Shensi-Kansu-Ningsia Border Area and the Anti-Japanese Governments Elected by the People in Anti-Japanese Bases behind the enemy lines in North, Central, and South China. Under such conditions of steady changes and gradual expansion of requests, which side should be responsible if the conversations cannot be brought to a successful conclusion?

"We have explained that the National Government and the Kuomintang do not place the interest of one single party above the interests of the country and people. It is earnestly hoped that the Chinese Communist Party can share in the observance of this principle.

"Finally we say that we shall be glad to go to Yenan if it would serve any useful purpose. We wish to know whether the Chinese Communist Party can send responsible representatives to Chungking to solve the present problem and who will be appointed to accompany us back to Chungking should we go to Yenan.

"The four pledges made by the Chinese Communist Party in September, 1937:

"(1) The Chinese Communist Party is prepared to fight for the thorough realization of Dr. Sun Yat-sen's Three People's Principles which answer the present-day needs of China.

"(2) The policy of insurrection which aims at the overthrow of the Kuomintang political power shall be abolished. The policy of land-confiscation by force and the policy of Communist propaganda shall be discontinued.

"(3) With the dissolution of the Chinese Soviet Government, a system of political democracy shall be put into practice so that the country may be politically unified.

"(4) The name and designations of the Red Army shall be abolished and the troops shall be reorganized as part of the National Revolutionary Army subject to the control of the National Military Council, and shall be waiting for instructions to take up frontline duties in the war of resistance against Japan."

X

The foregoing is a report on the conversations and the important contents of the related documents. Today the entire nation ardently hopes to arrive at a rational solution of the Chinese Communist problem at an early date in order to achieve national solidarity and unity, the winning of victory, the success of national reconstruction. Entrusted with the mission to carry on the conversations, we naturally have the greatest enthusiasm and hope. What the National Government is seeking is unity of military command and political orders. In this way we can attain real unity and bring about the concerted efforts of the entire army and people of the nation to defeat the enemy. Only thus can our program of resistance and reconstruction be benefited.

In view of this all-important prerequisite, the National Government is always ready to take actual facts into consideration, to arrive at the best possible solution, and to accept the opinions of the Chinese Communist Party as much as possible. This can be clearly seen from the Government memorandum.

As to the problem of democracy and freedom, the National Government has always been realistic and has always tried to do something instead of indulging in empty talks. Under the principles embodied in the *Program of Armed Resistance and National Reconstruction*, it has undertaken to give freedom to the press, to safeguard the people's liberty and to widen the powers of the people's representative organs. It will continue to exert its efforts along this line so that constitutionalism can be successfully adopted after the war. By that time, the question of political parties will be automatically solved. Although the Chinese Communist Party has not yet made any indication of willingness to accept the Government memorandum or to obey the military command and political orders of the Government, we hope the Chinese Communist Party will abide by the principles of solidarity and armed resistance, and realize the true unity of the nation by actual deeds. The National Government will never alter its policy of seeking a political solution. In fact, it is sincerely awaiting an announcement by the Chinese Communist Party that it will revise its standpoint and solve this problem at an early date so as to satisfy the expectations of the entire nation.

Realizing your interest and concern in this problem, I have come here to report on the conversations and to explain the attitude and wishes of the National Government. Your attention to the matter will be appreciated.

41

Report by the Representative of the Central Committee of the Chinese Communist Party [8] *to the People's Political Council, September 15, 1944* [9]

Gentlemen, I have been asked by the Presidium to make a report regarding the conversations which were held during the past four months between Dr. Wang Shih-chieh and General Chang Chih-chung on behalf of the National Government and myself on behalf of the Central Committee of the Chinese Communist Party. I feel greatly honored.

To rectify the relationship between the Kuomintang and the Chinese Communist Party, a just and reasonable readjustment should be made. This is a thing of great political importance. Not only are the members of the People's Political Council concerned over this problem, but it is also receiving the attention of all of our fellow countrymen. What I am going to report at this meeting today concerns what we discussed in the last four months. Connected with my talks with Dr. Wang and General Chang, there were seven documents which are rather important. Copies of these documents have been printed for your information.

Throughout the conversations on this occasion, the Yenan government displayed an attitude of sincerity. We hoped that the National Government would solve all the problems, we also hoped that we would be able to report oftener to the Generalissimo. Although no final decision regarding these problems has been reached, the conversations are being continued with Dr. Wang and General Chang in the most friendly atmosphere. This is because we are all anxious to solve the three main problems.

The first problem relates to military command. Both Dr. Wang and General Chang believe that this problem should be settled by all means. The Chinese Communist Party likewise wished to see a solution. But up to now a solution has not yet been found. Although details cannot be disclosed at the present moment, in general I may say that divergent opinions still exist. But we should frankly tell you gentlemen of the P. P. C. that difference of opinion is the main reason for failing to reach a solution.

There are two points in the documents which, from our viewpoint, are highly important. The first is how to solve these problems fundamentally. That is to say, in the face of the grave national crisis, we should unite under the leadership of Generalissimo Chiang and should exert all our efforts in the prosecution of the war of resistance. Unified, our strength can be increased. I believe that our country has the strength. We have 450,000,000 people and that is strength.

As to how we can bring about unification, the answer is by the ushering in of a democratic form of government even during the war. To have a democratic government certainly can avert national calamity. We have suggested the car-

---
[8] Lin Tsu-han.
[9] *China Handbook, 1937–1945*, pp. 90–94.

rying out of the Three People's Principles, the *Program of Armed Resistance and National Reconstruction*, and the Ten-Point Program of the Chinese Communist Party. If these could be carried out, then the people throughout the country would be unified and the fighting strength would be enhanced.

At the beginning of the war, the Generalissimo declared that "the entire land, irrespective of locality, and the entire people, irrespective of age, must be united and defend the country. Only in this way can we expect to increase our national strength." It is necessary for us to realize that our enemy Japan, well-developed industrially, is strong. It is not that China does not have the strength. Our strength can be secured only by adopting the democratic form of government. Our war is fought for justice and against aggression. We must have a democratic government because our war is an all-out people's war.

The second point involves some military demands which the Chinese Communist Party has put before the Government. Before the outbreak of the war we brought up certain things which we hoped that the Kuomintang would do and certain other things which we hoped that the Chinese Communist Party would do. To mention the more important ones, we hoped that, politically, the National Government would give the people of the entire nation freedom of speech, of the press, and of person; permit the lawful existence of political parties and organizations; and carry out local self-government. Now that the war has entered upon its eighth year, many developments and changes in the military and political situation have taken place. On September 22, 1937, shortly after the war broke out the Chinese Communist Party issued a declaration. Then the Generalissimo issued a statement on September 23. Both declaration and statement aimed at solving all the problems.

Take the army question, for instance. In northern Shensi there were 80,000 men. The National Government gave permission to reorganize them into three divisions with 45,000 men. Soldiers are needed for the prosecution of the war. When the province of Hopei was occupied by the enemy and Taiyuan was lost, the National Government ordered the 18th Group Army to move deep into the area behind the enemy line to destroy the puppet regime and harass the enemy. The 18th Group Army has done all these things, and has done them well.

During that period the 18th Group Army penetrated into Shansi, Hopei and Chahar. It seriously undermined the puppet regimes in various enemy occupied areas and brought these places under the national flag. In the course of more than seven years of war, the Communist military force has developed along the right tracks and consists now of an army of 475,000 men and a people's militia force of 2,200,000 men. Therefore, we hope that the National Government will give us five armies with 16 divisions. This is the demand we have brought up in military affairs.

Second, regarding political administration. The Chinese Communist Party has established in areas behind the enemy line a number of political administrations. There are 15 such units in Hopei, Shantung and Suiyuan, and they serve as bases for the war of resistance. In these places the system of popular election has been adopted. The number of people practicing this kind of civil right is 88,000,000. In some of these places the people have already held two elections, while in other places one election has taken place. We hope that our National Government will administer these political set-ups and direct the exercise of civil rights. This is our demand regarding the people's rights.

Third, we want a lawful existence. In the past the Communist Party hoped that the National Government would give different facilities to different things it undertook. Since other political parties and organizations can lawfully exist, the Chinese Communist Party asks for an open, lawful existence. This point is rather important. The other problems mentioned in our correspondence need not be mentioned here *seriatim*.

Our conversations have centered around two things—one concerns the basic problem of democratic government; the other the solution of some pending questions regarding the Chinese Communist Party. The points which we believe to be important have been brought up in the conversations. The National Government has a memorandum and General Chang Chih-chung told me that we should follow that memorandum.

We feel that there are still differences between our proposal and the Government memorandum, and no solution has yet been made. I shall mention only the more important points here, as all the minor points can be seen from our correspondence.

There are differences in our respective opinions. Where do the differences lie? For instance, I have just said that our aim is to fight the enemy. To fight the enemy we must have troops. At present there are on the guerilla battle fronts behind the enemy lines in North, Central and South China a total of 470,000 regular forces under the leadership of the Chinese Communist Party. In addition there are 2,000,000 men in the people's militia corps. According to these figures, as many as 47 divisions can be organized. At a memorial meeting on March 12, 1944, the death anniversary of Dr. Sun Yat-sen, Chou En-lai said that, in view of the National Government's total planning, we had decided only to ask for the designation of 18 divisions grouped into six armies, although the size of our forces warranted the organization of 47 divisions. In repeated talks afterwards, we were told that there were still difficulties. The Chinese Communist Party then reduced the number to five armies with 16 divisions. But the National Government memorandum calls for only four armies with ten divisions. As most of our armed forces are in war areas behind the enemy line, it would be difficult to direct them if they were divided into too few units. Hence we have asked for an increase in their numerical strength. According to the Government memorandum, these troops after reorganization will be concentrated for war duties, while those which have not been placed under reorganization will be disbanded without delay. We are fighting all the time and it is impossible to cease fighting. It would be very difficult to concentrate the troops.

As to lawful existence of political parties and organizations and other questions in connection with democracy, we believe that there is the necessity of discussing them. For example we have been trying to give freedom of speech and publication, but up to the present session of the People's Political Council this hope has not yet been realized. Another example is found in the case of freedom of person. Although the Regulations for Safe-Guarding the Freedom of the Human Person was promulgated in July, it has not been enforced. For instance, those involved in the New Fourth Army Incident were arrested without a trial. Yeh Ting is not a Communist and at that time he came out at the request of the Chinese Communist authorities. Then there are Liao Cheng-chih, Chang Wen-ping and others who were detained in Kwangtung. We hope that these men as well as many other political offenders will be released simultaneously. Now that the Regulations have been promulgated, we hope that the Central Government will prove its existence by action.

The foregoing is comparatively a basic analysis. Our hope is different from the National Government's memorandum and we hope that the memorandum can be brought nearer to our viewpoint. What I have just mentioned are the more important points. Of course there are things of secondary importance. For instance, when we were at Sian, General Chang and Dr. Wang said that the conversations would be used as preliminary suggestions which, when put in written form, would serve for the reference of the two Parties. But the Central Government's memorandum says that it was the opinion expressed by Representative Lin. This is a misunderstanding on the part of General Chang and Dr. Wang. We discussed this matter only for three hours before a decision was made. Since both General Chang and Dr. Wang have often mentioned this case, I welcome the opportunity to make an explanation here, pointing out the slight discrepancy.

I shall now come to the story of the conversations. Last year a resolution was adopted by the Kuomintang at its 11th Plenary Session to solve the Communist problem by political means. This news was received in Yenan with enthusiasm, and given wholehearted support. Since the New Fourth Army Incident of 1940, the relationship between the two Parties has been a deadlock. Although I am a member of the People's Political Council, I was unable to come out because of the blockade. After the 11th Plenary Session we came out with permission from the National Government. But, owing to the spring sowing movement in the border area, my departure from Yenan was delayed until April 29. Upon my arrival in Sian, I unexpectedly met General Chang and Dr. Wang. As there was then no airplane scheduled to fly to Chungking, we began our conversations in Sian on May 4. We had altogether five talks which served as a preliminary exchange of opinions before reporting to the National Government.

At that time General Chang and Dr. Wang asked me for my opinions. I replied that the National Committee of the Chinese Communist Party likewise discussed the questions related to the conversations. Chou En-lai's speech made in Yenan at the memorial meeting on the anniversary of Dr. Sun Yat-sen's death on March 12, 1944, could serve as the basis of the conversations. This speech dealt with two things—one in connection with democracy and constitutional government; the other about the solution of many impending issues between the Kuomintang and the Chinese Communist Party.

General Chang and Dr. Wang said that these matters would have to be discussed after our arrival in Chungking and that at present emphasis should be laid on military affairs. The military question consists of (1) reduction of the scope of the organization system and (2) reduction of the numerical strength of the forces. I said that we had 470,000 troops and I asked to what size they were to be reorganized with the permission of the National Government. General Chang discussed the matter with me and I said that we should have six armies with 18 divisions. Too many, said General Chang. That question alone we discussed for three days.

Two years ago Divisional Commander Lin Piao proposed that our forces should be reorganized into four armies with 12 divisions. General Chang, who had brought with him the minutes of the talk with Lin Piao, mentioned the old proposal. I told him that I could report that suggestion to the Central Committee of the Chinese Communist Party for consideration. Many other questions discussed concerned political affairs. They are all mentioned in the documents.

Minutes of the last conversation were kept, and the other day Lei Cheng showed me the minutes with the title "Results of the Conversations with Lin Tsu-han," and asked me to sign. I told him that the minutes contained opinions of both parties concerned, and that I would sign after making revisions and would ask both General Chang and Dr. Wang to sign also. They said that it was not necessary to sign because it was not a set of terms and that all they had to do was to forward the minutes to the National Government for instructions. So much for the preliminary conversations.

We flew to Chungking on **May 17**. After receiving our telegram, the Central Committee of the Chinese Communist Party promptly drafted 20 articles on May 20 on the basis of my telegram. The first article dealt with democracy, expressing the hope that the Government would immediately grant the freedom of speech, publication, and person. The second article asked for the recognition of the lawful existence of the Chinese Communist Party and the release of political offenders. The third article dealt with local self-government. The other articles concerned some minor questions.

On May 22 I showed these articles to General Chang and Dr. Wang. After reading the articles, they felt that some of the minor questions were provocative in nature and returned the paper to me. I asked them their opinion, whereupon they replied that the articles had better be changed to 12 articles with the remaining eight articles concerning minor questions to be presented verbally. Although these eight articles on minor questions may not seem of great consequence, they are major issues to Yenan circles.

After receiving my message, the Yenan authorities on June 3 sent me another 12 articles which I delivered to General Chang and Dr. Wang on June 4. Later, I also forwarded to Yenan the 18-point memorandum of the National Government. General Chang and Dr. Wang said that they could not accept my letter. As representative of the Chinese Communist Party I thought that my letter should be sent to Generalissimo Chang. On June 11 I wrote to General Chang and Dr. Wang and received a reply from them saying that my letter had been forwarded to the National Government.

After a long period of time, Minister H. C. Liang declared at a press conference that the Kuomintang-Communist conversations had come to a standstill and the Chinese Communist Party should realize the situation. Several correspondents came to question me and I said that we would do anything that is beneficial to the war of resistance. On July 16 Minister Liang again issued a statement in English. His statement, containing four items, said that some points in the present conversations had been solved while others could not be settled, but there would be no civil war. Several correspondents again came to see me. On August 13, Chou En-lai issued a statement to the effect that the Chinese Communist Party wishes to have the problem solved. In addition he expressed the hope that General Chang and Dr. Wang could go to Yenan to carry on the conversations. I forwarded this message to General Chang and Dr. Wang and, in their opinion, the matter could be given consideration. On August 14 they gave me a reply and on August 30 another reply, making a total of seven documents. Gentlemen, you will understand clearly what has happened during our conversations by referring to the documents.

I have come to Chungking because my comrades in the Chinese Communist Party are anxious to secure a solution of the problem and I am very sincere in purpose. I have been here four months and am still in close touch with General Chang and Dr. Wang, who have exchanged views with me on the matter. But the issue is still pending, even to the present moment. The Chinese Communist Party hopes that the National Government will find a solution. The nation needs unification, especially unification among political parties and organizations. But the fact is quite clear to you, gentlemen: there is still a divergence of opinion between the two Parties after four months of conversations.

ANNEXES

42

Statement by the Chinese Minister of Information (Liang)[10]

May I add a few remarks here concerning Lin Tsu-han's report on the Kuomintang-Communist conversations in the People's Political Council?

In the first place, Mr. Lin said in his report, published in the local newspapers on September 16 and in the *Sin Hua Jih Pao* on September 17, "Minister H. C. Liang once stated in a press conference that conversations between the Kuomintang and Communists have come to a standstill." This is a misrepresentation, as I never said a thing like that. What I did say is "the conversations are still continuing," and "though the conversations are not progressing at a pace as anticipated, it would be incorrect to say that they are running altogether smoothly."

Secondly, Mr. Lin reported, "Minister Liang told the pressmen of Chungking at a press conference held on July 26 that a part of the Kuomintang-Communist problem has been solved but another part is insoluble." Words again differed from my original version which says "Under the present circumstances, a part of the Kuomintang-Communist problem has been solved but it is too much to expect a total solution yet." You may recall that I made these remarks in a statement on the possible trend of the Kuomintang-Communist conversations, and made them on your repeated request.

43

Summary Notes of Conversations Between Vice.President Henry A. Wallace and President Chiang Kai-shek, June 21–24, 1944[11]

CONVERSATION AT PRESIDENT CHIANG'S RESIDENCE, JUNE 21—5 p. m.

Present: President Chiang
        Vice President Wallace
        Dr. T. V. Soong (translating)

President Chiang asked Mr. Wallace whether he had any message from President Roosevelt. Mr. Wallace replied that he had nothing in writing but that he had notes on a conversation with President Roosevelt just prior to his departure from Washington. Mr. Wallace said that President Roosevelt had mentioned the inflationary situation in China but that he (Wallace) did not wish to discuss the subject in Chungking due to the absence in America of the Minister of Finance, Dr. Kung. Mr. Wallace said that President Roosevelt had talked about the Communists in China. President Roosevelt had assumed that, in as much as the Communists and the members of the Kuomintang were all Chinese, they were basically friends and that "nothing should be final between friends". President Roosevelt had cited the Bryan Treaty and had quoted Al Smith and Charles Francis Adams to support his point. President Roosevelt had indicated that if the parties could not get together they might "call in a friend" and had indicated that he might be that friend.

---

[10] Issued at a press conference of Sept. 20, 1944 (*China Handbook, 1937–1945*, p. 94).
[11] By John Carter Vincent, Chief of the Division of Chinese Affairs, who accompanied the Vice President to China. The files of the Department do not contain any indication of the existence of a report in written form made by Mr. Wallace to President Roosevelt or of the nature of any oral report made.

... Mr. Wallace expressed the opinion that there should not be left pending any question which might result in conflict between China and the U.S.S.R. President Chiang suggested that President Roosevelt act as an arbiter or "middleman" between China and the U.S.S.R. (NOTE: President Chiang's suggestion was apparently prompted by Mr. Wallace's earlier statement that President Roosevelt was willing to act as an arbiter between the Communists and the Kuomintang. Mr. Wallace made no comment at the time. However, after discussing the matter with Mr. Vincent that evening, Mr. Wallace made it clear to President Chiang the next morning before breakfast that President Roosevelt had not suggested acting as arbiter between China and the U.S.S.R. and that, whereas he felt that the United States would be quite willing to use its good offices to get the U.S.S.R. and China together, it could not undertake the role of "middleman" in negotiations between the U.S.S.R. and China or become a party or guarantor of any agreement reached between China and the U.S.S.R.)

Mr. Wallace said that he felt that the people of the United States were deeply interested in seeing an increase in Chinese agricultural efficiency which will permit a sound industrialization. The United States desires a strong, democratic China which would make for a healthy political situation in the country. The United States had always had this idea and it felt most strongly in that regard now. Mr. Wallace believed that no matter how dark the present situation was in China, if China exerted herself to the utmost, it could with help from the United States and a kindly attitude on the part of Great Britain, realize its destiny. There would be no time to lose in effecting improvements once the war was over.

President Chiang expressed a desire for friendly understanding with the U.S.S.R. Mr. Wallace mentioned a conversation which he had had in Tashkent with Ambassador Harriman. Ambassador Harriman had told Mr. Wallace of a recent discussion he had had with Mr. Stalin during which China was discussed. President Chiang asked to see a copy of the memorandum which Mr. Wallace had mentioned. Mr. Wallace said he did not have a copy. He recalled that Mr. Stalin had stressed the need for a united China eager to carry on the war against Japan. Mr. Wallace suggested that Dr. Soong discuss the matter with Mr. Vincent, who had probably a better idea of the contents of the memorandum since he had had a number of conversations with Ambassador Harriman. (NOTE: That evening Dr. Soong asked Mr. Vincent about the matter, requesting to see any notes that Mr. Vincent might have made. Mr. Vincent said that he had only his memory to rely upon and informed Dr. Soong of those portions of the memorandum which he thought it appropriate and judicious to give him. Specifically he told Dr. Soong that Mr. Stalin had agreed to President Roosevelt's point that support of President Chiang was advisable during the prosecution of the war; that Mr. Stalin had expressed a keen interest in there being reached a settlement between the Kuomintang and the Chinese Communists, basing his interest on the practical matter of more effective fighting against Japan rather than upon any ideological considerations; that Mr. Stalin had criticized the suspicious attitude of the Chinese regarding the Sakhalin Agreement with Japan; and that Mr. Stalin felt the United States should assume a position of leadership in the Far East.)

Toward the end of the conversation Mr. Wallace described to President Chiang the developments in agriculture which he had observed in Siberia. The discussion ended sometime after 6 p. m.

ANNEXES

Discussion with President Chiang, June 22—4:30 p.m.

Present: President Chiang
Madame Chiang
Vice President Wallace
Dr. T. V. Soong
Dr. Wang Shih-chieh
Messrs. Vincent, Lattimore, and Hazard

Mr. Wallace mentioned the poor showing the Chinese troops had made. He referred specifically to a story he had heard about the Chinese peasants attacking the soldiers in the Honan campaign because they were running away from the Japanese. President Chiang then undertook to explain the situation. He said that Chinese reverses were due to a loss of morale on the part of the soldiers; that this loss of morale was to a large extent due to the economic situation. Mr. Vincent asked President Chiang whether he understood correctly that it was the morale of the troops rather than lack of equipment which had caused the reverses. President Chiang replied, "both". (Note: The next day, at the request of Madame Chiang, President Chiang explained his reference to the effect of the economic situation on the morale of the troops. He said that the soldiers at the front were worried about their families who were suffering at home because of the inflation. He also said that the condition of the troops themselves was adversely affected by inflationary high prices and scarcity of goods. In this latter connection he stated however that the situation was better now than it had been some months ago.)

President Chiang then described what he considered to be basic in the present unfortunate military situation in China. He said that the Chinese people have fought for seven years under conditions of great hardship, and that they had expected help from abroad; that they had expected an all-out Burma campaign early this year and this would have resulted in bringing relief to the Chinese Army; and that the failure to initiate an all-out Burma campaign had had a decidedly adverse effect on Chinese morale. The Chinese people felt that they had been deserted. President Chiang then referred to his conversations with President Roosevelt at Cairo. He said that President Roosevelt had promised an all-out campaign in Burma early in 1944 but that at Tehran President Roosevelt had reversed his decision, indicating that the necessary amphibious landing craft would not be available for such a campaign. President Chiang said that this reversal of decision had had a very unfortunate reaction in China. He referred to his conversation with President Roosevelt, at which time he had told President Roosevelt that, unless very early action were taken to open up Burma he could not count upon a continuance of effective Chinese resistance to the Japanese. Recent developments had proven him correct in his estimate. Mr. Wallace said that he recalled having a conversation with President Roosevelt, either personally or in a Cabinet meeting, regarding this matter but that he did not recall the details. He asked Mr. Vincent regarding the matter but Mr. Vincent said he did not have any detailed information concerning the Cairo conversations. (Note: The day of Mr. Wallace's departure—June 24th—President Chiang asked Mr. Wallace to inform President Roosevelt that he, President Chiang, understood the necessity under which President Roosevelt was working when he reversed his decision regarding the Burma campaign; that he was therefore not criticizing President Roosevelt for his decision; but that he wished to remind President Roosevelt that the prediction which he, President Chiang, had made at the time was sound.)

President Chiang then discussed his relations with the American Army in China. He said that American army officers clearly indicated their lack of confidence in China but that he, President Chiang, "continued to have full confidence in his army". He asked Mr. Wallace to report this to President Roosevelt and to tell him that, in spite of the attitude of the American Army, he would be guided by the advice of President Roosevelt. President Chiang, somewhat apologetically, (but with obvious intent to get across a point) mentioned what he described as a minor incident involving General Stilwell. He said that in the early stages of the Honan campaign he had asked General Stilwell for diversion to his air force of 1,000 tons of gasolene, but that General Stilwell had very abruptly refused the request, saying that the Chinese Army could get the gasolene from its own "over the hump" supplies. President Chiang indicated that it was difficult for him to operate in the face of such an uncooperative attitude. In response to Mr. Wallace's query, President Chiang said that he lacked confidence in General Stilwell's judgment. He went on to say that critical comment in the American press of the Chinese Army and the attitude of the American Army in China had adverse effects on Chinese morale but that he retained the confidence of his army and confidence in his army. Mr. Wallace commented upon the remarkable degree of faith which China had in the Generalissimo. At this point (5 p. m.) President Chiang, Mr. Wallace, Dr. Soong, Dr. Wang Shih-chieh, and Mr. Vincent went into the drawing room to continue the discussion, which lasted until 7:30 p. m.

Mr. Vincent made a brief recapitulation of that portion of the preceding conversation which had dealt with the military situation in China and the question of the present unfavorable position of the Chinese Army and asked President Chiang whether he had any suggestions with regard to measures which might effect an improvement. President Chiang said that he had nothing to suggest at that time. He, President Chiang, went back again to the Cairo Conference decision regarding the Burma campaign, stating that if it could have been carried out the effect on morale in China would have been very great even though the material assistance which might have been afforded China would not have been large, and that the current defeats would have been avoided.

Mr. Wallace asked President Chiang about the "New Life" movement. President Chiang gave a brief description of the movement, stating that its purpose was to train the people in having more disciplined lives and to raise their standards of thinking and conduct.

President Chiang next referred to criticism of China appearing in the American press and said that this criticism should be stopped. He said that the Chinese people were losing hope of receiving aid from abroad.

President Chiang next launched forth into a lengthy complaint against the Chinese Communists. He said that China suffered greatly because of the Communists. He said that the people of the United States did not understand the situation. Although the Communists were not entirely responsible for the situation in China, their subversive actions and propaganda had had a very unfavorable effect on Chinese morale. He referred to the first year of the war when he had received the cooperation of the Communists "within the law", but said that the Communists now were not subject to discipline and refused to obey his orders. He said that the attitude of the Chinese toward the Communists was an important factor in the situation; that the Chinese people did not regard the Communists as Chinese, but regarded them as "internationalists", subject to the orders of the Third International. Mr. Wallace mentioned the fact that the Third International had been dissolved but President Chiang indicated that the situation had not been altered by that fact.

Mr. Wallace mentioned remarks that were made to him by Mr. Martel Hall, Manager of the Peking branch of the National City Bank of New York, who had traveled from Peking through Communist territory to Chungking in 1943. Mr. Hall had spoken in terms of high praise of the Communists, had said that the continued to have confidence in the Generalissimo, but that they felt the Generalissimo was not correctly informed with regard to the situation in Communist areas. President Chiang said that Mr. Hall, like many other Americans, (he mentioned specifically Colonel Carlson) was under the influence of Communist propaganda. President Chiang said that he did not like to use harsh language regarding the Communists; that he would welcome them back into the Government fold; but that the fact was that the low morale of the people and the army was due to Communist propaganda. He said that the Communists desired a breakdown of Chinese resistance against the Japanese because this would strengthen their own position. Mr. Wallace expressed amazement at this statement. President Chiang admitted that the Communists desire the defeat of Japan but that they were now convinced that this defeat could be accomplished without Chinese resistance. They therefore hoped for the collapse of the Kuomintang prior to the end of the war because such a collapse would enable them to seize power, whereas, if the Kuomintang continued in power until peace the Communists would have no opportunity to supplant it. President Chiang referred to the clever Communist propaganda to the effect that they were not tied to the U. S. S. R., that they were in fact nothing more than agrarian democrats. As a matter of fact, the Communists follow the orders of the Third International. The Chinese Government cannot openly criticize the Communists for their connection with the Third International because it is afraid of offending the U. S. S. R. Mr. Wallace referred to the patriotic attitude of the Communists in the United States and said that he could not understand the attitude of the Chinese Communists, as described by President Chiang. President Chiang said that this difference in the attitude of the American and the Chinese Communists might be explained by the fact that there was no possibility of the American Communists seizing power, whereas the Chinese Communists definitely desired to do so in China. He then said that the United States was far removed from the U. S. S. R. but that the U. S. S. R. would not feel safe if the Communists were not in power in China. He then laughingly remarked that the Chinese Communists were more communistic than the Russian Communists.

Mr. Vincent inquired as to the progress of conversations between the Communist representative in Chungking, Lin Tzu-han, and the Kuomintang representatives of which Dr. Wang Shih-chieh was chief. President Chiang said he desired to make the Communists live up to their propaganda in regard to their desire for cooperation and offensive action against the Japanese. He said that there had been Communist proposals for a settlement and Kuomintang counterproposals. The Kuomintang proposal was very simple: support the President, support the Government, and support the war effort. The Chinese Government requires obedience from the Communists and incorporation of the Communist Army within the Chinese Army as its first essential to a settlement. Secondly, the Chinese Government requires that territory now under Communist control become an integral part of China administratively. If the Communists would accede to these two demands they would receive equal treatment with other Chinese in China, they would be guaranteed political amnesty, and given the right to continue as a political party with freedom of assembly and discussion. President Chiang also said that if the Communists would accede to these requirements, the group of American officers would be allowed to proceed to North China as requested. They would not have direct contact with the Communists but would go under the auspices of the Chinese Government to train "converted" Communist troops. Mr. Wallace asked President Chiang whether he was optimistic with regard to a settlement. President Chiang said it was possible if the Communists showed sincerity. If a settlement were reached President Chiang said he could carry out his program for democracy earlier than now expected. He said that he would try his best to reach a settlement.

President Chiang again reverted to the subject of Communist propaganda. He asked Mr. Wallace to inform President Roosevelt that Communist propaganda has his highest respect. President Roosevelt should bear in mind that the Communists could not openly use the U.S.S.R. for support but that they could and did use the U.S.A. (opinion) to force the Kuomintang to accede to their demands. Such tactics make a settlement difficult. The best assistance that the United States could give in this matter would be to display "aloofness" to the Communists. They would then show a greater willingness to reach a settlement with the Kuomintang.

At this juncture, Dr. Wang Shih-chieh said he wished to offer some explanation on the Chinese Government's proposal to the Communists. He said that whereas the Chinese Government required that the Communists submit to its authority it was not the intention to interfere in local administration and that it was not the intention to remove local officials or even army officers who showed themselves cooperative.

Mr. Wallace said that the Generalissimo's description of the situation filled him with "hope and fear". He said that China's relations with the U.S.S.R. were threatened by the attitude demonstrated in conversations which he had had with Mr. Wei and Admiral Shen (Minister of Agriculture) and by President Chiang's remarks. Mr. Wallace did not mention what it was in the situation that filled him with "hope".

Mr. Wallace stated that American Army officers felt that Chinese interpretation of the significance of the transfer of Japanese troops from Manchuria to China was incorrect. Mr. Wallace also pointed out that if, as President Chiang stated, the Chinese Communists were linked with the U.S.S.R., then there was even greater need for settlement. He also expressed his appreciation of the frankness with which President Chiang had spoken.

President Chiang again advised that we adopt an attitude of "coolness" toward the Communists. He said that the United States Army was anxious that all military power in China be utilized against the Japanese but the United States Army did not realize the threat which the Communists constituted to the Chinese Government and overestimated the utility of the Communists against the Japanese. He went on to say that he understood President Roosevelt's policy and asked that President Roosevelt be informed that he, President Chiang, desired a political solution of the problem.

Mr. Wallace asked whether it was not possible to reach an understanding on a "lower level" with a view to maximum use of forces in the north. Mr. Vincent asked what President Chiang thought would be the adverse effects of sending the United States Army intelligence group to Communist areas *now* without awaiting a settlement. President Chiang said that "haste does not make for speed". He said, "please do not press; please understand that the Communists are not good for the war effort against Japan". With this evasive reply the conversation was concluded.

ANNEXES

DISCUSSION WITH PRESIDENT CHIANG, JUNE 23—9 A. M.

Present: President Chiang
Vice President Wallace
Dr. Hollington Tong (translating)
Dr. Wang Shih-chieh
Mr. Lattimore (assisting in translating)
Mr. Vincent

Mr. Wallace reported conversations with General Marshall and with Secretary Stimson before leaving America in regard to China's situation in an endeavor to persuade President Chiang that we are not interested in "Chinese Communists" but are interested in the prosecution of the war. (He and Mr. Vincent had decided upon this line of approach the night before in order to avoid further lengthy discussion of the Communists *per se*.) He spoke of the military situation in East Asia in general terms and of the need for taking all steps that might further hasten the end of the war and reduce the loss of American lives. He felt that the United States Army Intelligence group in North China would be able to gather intelligence which would save the lives of American aviators. Mr. Vincent again stressed the point that whereas he appreciated that President Chiang was faced with a very real problem in handling negotiations for a settlement with the Communists, the American Army was also faced with a very real problem with regard to obtaining intelligence from North China. He mentioned specifically the need for intelligence by the B-29 group at Chengtu. He pointed out that the American Army had no interest whatsoever in Communists but that it had for very urgent reasons an interest in carrying on the war against Japan from China. He urged that President Chiang's problem of reaching a settlement with the Communists and the United States Army problem of obtaining intelligence be treated as separate—as indeed they were.

President Chiang, completely reversing his position of the evening before, said "that can be done". He said that the group could go as soon as it was organized without reference to a settlement with the Communists. He said, however, that they must go under the auspices of the National Military Council rather than under the auspices of the United States Army, and added that Chinese officers must go with them. He then stressed the point that the Communists did not take his orders and gave concrete illustrations. He said with some feeling that the United States Army must realize how essential it is to have a unified command. Much pressure has been brought to bear by the United States Government to have the Chinese Government reach a settlement with the Communists but the United States Government has exerted no pressure upon the Communists. He said that the American Government should issue a statement that the Communists should come to terms with the Chinese Government. He said that the United States Army attitude supported the Communists and requested Mr. Wallace upon his return to America to make it clear that the Communists should come to terms with the Chinese Government. In response to a remark by Mr. Wallace, President Chiang said there were no present questions which would cause conflict with the U.S.S.R. Mr. Vincent again pointed out that solution of President Chiang's important problems of relations with the Communists and the U.S.S.R. need not precede the despatch of military observers to North China. President Chiang said that the military observers would be permitted to go.

President Chiang said, "I am confident that what President Roosevelt stands for is good for China and for the furtherance of the war." "But," he said, "one of the things for which we are fighting this war is the maintenance of order. Please tell President Roosevelt that I will follow his advice but I must insist on the maintenance of law and order and upon the observance of discipline."

Mr. Wallace again stressed the point that there should be no situation in China which might lead to conflict with the U.S.S.R. President Chiang said that the Chinese Government had gone far out of its way to come to an agreement with the Communists in order to avoid conflict with the U.S.S.R. and added that anything not detrimental to the sovereignty of the Chinese Government would be done to avoid conflict with the U.S.S.R. At this point Mr. Wallace again said that the United States could not be expected to be a party to negotiations between China and the U.S.S.R. He also said that President Chiang's formula for settlement with the Communists might prove transitory unless China reached an understanding with the U.S.S.R. He referred again to Ambassador Harriman's discussion with Mr. Stalin as indicating the necessity for an agreement with the U.S.S.R. President Chiang stated that he fully shared Mr. Wallace's views and that the Chinese Government would seek an early opportunity to have discussions with the Government of the U.S.S.R. Although Mr. Wallace had indicated that the United States might not be able to assist in the negotiations he continued to hope that there could be found ways whereby the United States could be of assistance.

Mr. Wallace stated that another reason why a settlement with the Communists might prove temporary was the economic situation in China and expressed a hope that measures could be taken as soon as possible to improve the economic lot of the Chinese people. President Chiang endorsed this view. Mr. Wallace said that in so far as the Communists have power and influence it is due to economic conditions. He said that the Communist revolution in Russia in 1916 was brought about primarily by economic distress. He admitted that it was very difficult to do anything now after seven years of war, but he pointed out how easy it would be to attribute to the Communists social unrest in China when actually this unrest would be due to economic distress.

President Chiang indicated that the making of concessions to the Communists did not matter as long as discipline could be maintained. Mr. Wallace said that unity should express itself in welfare of the people if communism was to be avoided. Mr. Vincent suggested that the best defense against communism in China was agrarian reform. Mr. Wallace said that when the war was over it would take much energy and foresight for the Chinese Government to avoid the fate of the Kerensky government in Russia. President Chiang said that the Chinese Government was proceeding with these considerations in mind.

The conversation ended at 11 a. m. and was resumed at 5 p. m. In the meantime, Mr. Wallace had visited the Embassy in Chungking, had received a message from President Roosevelt advising him to press President Chiang to permit the despatch of the Army observer group, and had arranged that General Ferris join the conversation in the afternoon. Participants were: President Chiang, Mr. Wallace, Dr. Soong (translating), Dr. Wang Shih-chieh, Mr. Lattimore (assisting in translating), Mr. Vincent, General Ferris and Mr. John Service (aide to General Ferris).

Mr. Wallace read to President Chiang President Roosevelt's message. Mr. Vincent made a brief recapitulation of the morning's conversation and asked President Chiang whether his understanding was correct that the observer group might proceed to North China as soon as it was organized. President Chiang replied in the affirmative. Mr. Vincent then asked for an explanation of the conditions under which the group might proceed. There ensued some discussion as to whether the word "auspices" was a correct translation of President Chiang's Chinese term describing the relationship of the National Military Council to the United States Army group. It was decided that whereas "auspices" was not an exact translation, it was about as good as any that could be found and that whatever the translation, President Chiang did not intend that the group would have to operate under orders from the National Military Council.

General Ferris then asked for clarification on a number of points: whether the United States Army group would be allowed direct communication facilities with the American command. President Chiang said they would be. General Ferris said that all information gathered would be made available to the Chinese military authorities. General Ferris asked a number of questions. President Chiang said that he should confer with General Ho Ying-chin in regard to details. General Ferris asked for President Chiang's full support and received the President's assurances in that respect. President Chiang referred to the use of the word "mission" in describing the group and said that he did not believe that it should be so called. At Madame Chiang's suggestion (she had joined the group some minutes before) it was decided to call the group the "United States Army Investigation Section".

President Chiang said that he wanted the American Army authorities to bear in mind that in as much as the Communists did not accept orders from him he could not guarantee the protection of the group while in Communist territory but that he would give all possible aid. General Ferris asked when the group might go. President Chiang said it could go as soon as it was organized. General Ferris said that it would probably comprise 15–20 men. He asked President Chiang whether there would be Chinese officers accompanying the group, and whether the group would be allowed freedom of movement. He pointed out that the members of the group would not of course remain together but would "fan out" on individual assignments. President Chiang said that General Ferris should see General Ho with regard to the composition of the group. General Ferris expressed the hope that General Ho would place no impediments in the way of the group's carrying out its mission. President Chiang said, "See General Ho tomorrow at 4 p. m. He will have my instructions." (NOTE: At this point General Ferris and Mr. Service withdrew.)

Mr. Wallace presented to President Chiang a scroll sent by President Roosevelt to the people of Chungking. President Chiang said, "Representing the people of Chungking, I accept this scroll as a priceless symbol which they will hold forever in gratitude and reverence."

President Chiang then said he had a few questions to raise with Mr. Wallace. He requested Mr. Wallace to mention to President Roosevelt the question of Allied Military Government of Occupied Territories (AMGOT) in the Far East, and suggest to President Roosevelt that there be an agreement between British, American and Chinese authorities on this question. President Chiang said that at Cairo he had raised with President Roosevelt the question of a Chinese-American economic commission to handle projects of post-war reconstruction in China. He hoped that Dr. Kung would have an opportunity to discuss this matter while he was in Washington and requested Mr. Wallace to lend whatever assistance he could. Mr. Wallace expressed approval of the idea and said he would do what he could.

Mr. Wallace referred to a comment he had made to President Chiang soon after his arrival in Chungking regarding the absence of any Russian territorial ambitions in the Far East. Without modifying that statement he wished to add an explanation which had occurred to him since the first conversation. He said that the U.S.S.R. wanted a warm water port in the Far East and that President Roosevelt had suggested that Dairen might be made a free port. Mr. Wallace said that in making this remark he was not acting under instructions from President Roosevelt or speaking officially. President Chiang said that he had discussed the matter with President Roosevelt at Cairo and had indicated his agreement provided the U.S.S.R. cooperated with China in the Far East and provided there was no impairment of Chinese sovereignty.

President Chiang referred to the present economic distress (lack of consumer products) in China and said that Dr. Kung was going to ask for an increase of "over the hump" tonnage to provide for the importation of 2,000 tons of civilian supplies each month. He said that it was very important that this request be granted from the military as well as the economic point of view. In response to Mr. Wallace's question President Chiang said that these civilian supplies would be comprised of cloth, medicines and spare parts. Mr. Wallace mentioned the possibility of using C-54s now that Myitkyina was in Allied hands but he pointed out that it might prove very difficult to persuade the American Army to permit civilian supplies to take up air cargo space. President Chiang asked Mr. Wallace to take a personal interest in the matter.

President Chiang asked Mr. Wallace to inform President Roosevelt as follows: "If the United States can bring about better relations between the U.S.S.R. and China and can bring about a meeting between Chinese and Soviet representatives, President Chiang would very much welcome such friendly assistance." If the United States would "sponsor" such a meeting President Chiang would go more than halfway in reaching an understanding with the U.S.S.R. A conference with regard to Pacific affairs was desirable and the United States would be the logical place for such a conference. Madame Chiang interpolated to suggest that it be called the "North Pacific Conference". Mr. Vincent inquired whether they were not speaking of two related but separate matters, that is, discussions between Chinese and Soviet representatives in regard to their problems, and a conference of nations bordering on the North Pacific to discuss more general problems. He said that it would seem desirable to have the Sino-Soviet discussions prior to any North Pacific conference. Dr. Soong said that a North Pacific conference might be used as a cloak for discussions between Chinese and Soviet representatives. Mr. Wallace said that Dr. Soong would be of value in Washington in laying the foundation for such a conference. President Chiang said that he could not be spared from Chungking and added, laughingly, that with Dr. Kung gone and Madame Chiang planning to go abroad, Dr. Soong was his only mouthpiece in speaking to Americans.

The conversation ended at this point—7 p. m.

June 24th—During the hour's ride from President Chiang's residence to the airport (10 to 11 a. m.) President Chiang made the following comments (Madame Chiang interpreting) which he requested Mr. Wallace to consider as a message from himself to President Roosevelt:

1. The attitude of President Roosevelt at the Cairo Conference, his warmth, etc., has immense historic value to the people and army of China.

2. President Chiang is gratified over the abrogation of the unequal treaties and efforts on behalf of the Exclusion Act.

3. Mr. Wallace's visit to China, as the representative of President Roosevelt, to bring about accord with Russia shows great friendship for China.

4. Mr. Wallace's visit at this dark hour will help the morale of the troops and give hope that America will continue to aid China.

5. Assure the President that President Chiang understands the necessity under which the President acted when he changed plans at Tehran. Nevertheless, President Chiang foresaw what the change meant. When President Chiang sent a strong, frank memorandum to President Roosevelt it was because he foresaw what is now happening. If the Generalissimo sees that China's collapse will come he will tell the President, but China has not yet arrived at the state of collapse which he predicted to the President. Things are not today as bad as he feared.

6. President Chiang greatly respects the President's character, his views, etc.

7. President Chiang was deeply touched when Mr. Wallace told him about how badly the President felt about the Tehran change relating to the Generalissimo personally. Therefore, he again appreciates most deeply that Mr. Wallace should come out on behalf of Russo-Chinese friendship.

8. The Chinese Communist question is an internal political problem but he would nevertheless welcome the President's assistance. He feels that the Chinese Communists are not men of good faith. Their signature is no good. He would not like to see the President blamed for Communist failure to carry out commitments. Just the same he is happy to have the President's help if the President, after mature consideration, decides he would like to give his help. The Generalissimo would not consider the President's participation as meddling in China's internal affairs, but the Generalissimo is a true friend who knows the Chinese Communists through and through and thinks that no matter what the Communists say they will do, it will not be carried out, in which case the President's prestige would suffer a great loss. The Generalissimo wants the President to know that the conflict between the Communists and the Central Government is not like that between capitalism and labor in the United States—the situations are not analogous.

9. The Generalissimo is eager to have closer cooperation and understanding with the President—but how? Too many channels through State Department. Churchill has personal representative in Carton de Wiart who handles both political and military matters. Could President Roosevelt pick someone like this? He could perform an invaluable service. Today military cooperation is very difficult because of personnel. He feels that Chennault is most cooperative. Stilwell has improved, but has no understanding of political matters—he is entirely military in outlook.

10. The Generalissimo has the utmost confidence in Dr. Kung. In helping Dr. Kung the President will be helping the Generalissimo.

11. The Generalissimo is shaping everything toward the democratic path. He wrote *China's Destiny* to get the Communists to fall into line. The Generalissimo wants the Communists to be a political party. He plans such advances in agrarian program that the Communists will have no opportunity to stir up social unrest.

12. He hopes after the war to get the interest rate for farmers down to 10 per cent and hopes to promote land ownership by breaking up large land holdings.

44

President Roosevelt to President Chiang Kai-shek

[WASHINGTON?] *July 14, 1944*

Vice President Wallace has handed me your telegram of July 8 in reply to his letter to you of June 27 [12] I have also received with much interest the Vice President's full report of his conversations with you. Mr. Wallace has told me of the twelve points which you requested that he bring to my attention, and I am grateful for the friendliness and frankness with which your views have been expressed.

With regard to the negotiations now in progress with the Chinese Communists, I have noted with particular satisfaction your assurance that only political means will be employed in seeking a solution. Also I welcome the indication given me by Mr. Wallace of your desire for improved relations between the U.S.S.R. and China, and your suggestion that I use my good offices to arrange for a conference between Chinese and Russian representatives is being given serious thought. It occurs to me that any such conference would be greatly facilitated if a working arrangement had been reached beforehand between the Chinese Government and the Chinese Communists for effective prosecution of the war against the Japanese in North China. The Vice President has also informed me, in this connection, of your encouraging remark that it would be possible to carry out your democratic program earlier than expected if a settlement with the Communists could be secured.

It is with regret that I have received reports of Madame Chiang's ill health and I trust that she will have a speedy recovery.

With warm regards and best wishes,
Sincerely yours,

FRANKLIN D. ROOSEVELT

---

[12] The letter from Vice President Wallace of June 27 and the reply from Generalissimo Chiang Kai-shek of July 8 have not been found.

Annexes to Chapter III: The Ambassadorship of Major General Patrick J. Hurley, 1944–1946

45

The Ambassador in China (Gauss) to Secretary Hull

893.00/8-3144

CHUNGKING, *August 31, 1944*

Yesterday evening President Chiang Kai-shek sent for me. For an hour and a half he talked about the Communist problem, stating that it is not understood in Washington, and it is my duty to be sure the problem is understood. Set forth below are the principal points of the argument which Chiang constantly emphasized and repeated, in addition to the usual charges of bad faith and treachery against the Communists:

In the matter of world problems, China is disposed to follow our lead; and it is not unfriendly for us to suggest that China should improve relations with the Soviet Union. China should receive the entire support and sympathy of the United States Government on the domestic problem of Chinese Communists. Very serious consequences for China may result from our attitude. In urging that China resolve differences with the Communists, our Government's attitude is serving only to intensify the recalcitrance of the Communists. The request that China meet Communist demands is equivalent to asking China's unconditional surrender to a party known to be under a foreign power's influence (the Soviet Union). The Communists are growing arrogant and refuse to continue negotiations since our observer group arrived in Yenan. The United States should tell the Communists to reconcile their differences with and submit to the national government of China.

This could be done by our observer group as well as by the Embassy in any contact we have with representatives of the Communists at this point. In addition, the strength of Communist armies could be determined by observer group. The need of Communist forces to defeat Japan should not be stressed by us. The Chinese Communists are under the influence of a foreign power; neither that power nor the Communists dares condemn it, since to do so would condemn the Communists before the people of China in general. The Communists' expansionist ambitions are what brought about assignment of troops to prevent expansion of this nature; prove all Communists cannot be trusted. Furthermore, Chiang Kai-shek commented that the problem of Communist cooperation would not be solved by introduction of a foreign commander of Chinese armies. Chiang stated that there are persons in Washington who seem to believe that it is merely a matter of issuing military orders to have them obeyed and said that the Communists have not obeyed, although he has ordered them to attack the Japanese.

Since I had been assured that I might speak openly and frankly, it was possible for me to stress that the United States Government is not interested in the Chinese Communists' cause; however, we are interested in seeing a prompt solution of a Chinese internal problem which finds the armed forces of China facing one another instead of facing and making war upon Japan, and, in the present critical period of the war, this is of outstanding importance. My statement to Chiang was that our observation, and reports to Washington, showed a definite breakdown in negotiations between the Kuomintang and the Communists prior to the organization of our army observer group to go to Yenan, that the observer group is in Yenan only for purposes of military intelligence, that the group has no political mission, and what has been described as arrogant refusal to continue negotiations cannot have resulted from their presence.

Answering a question as to whether I believed the people of China favor the Communists, I replied that I did not. However, I remarked that at the present time, the Communist Party is reported not to be practicing or preaching communism, but to be following and supporting the Kuomintang principles of improvement of conditions of the masses and democracy. My statement was that, if I might speak frankly, many believe the Kuomintang Party in power has not in recent years kept their principles first and foremost in mind, and the Embassy has not failed to hear of some of the disaffection, both in military and in other circles, which resulted. The Generalissimo stated that only the Communists obstruct and defy his government, and if reports or suggestions of dissatisfaction exist at other points, it is merely the machination of Communists utilizing stooges removed from themselves to convey propaganda of this nature.

My entire sympathy with the difficult task confronting Chiang Kai-shek in solving the Communist problems was expressed; and I stated we have not suggested that the Chinese Government should yield to the demands of the Communists. The interest of the United States Government is only in dissipation of the existing critical situation and in the unification of China, and it is our hope that a peaceful solution for this situation can be found among themselves by the Chinese.

Having received permission to speak frankly, I continued with the personal observation that although Chiang Kai-shek states that the Communists cannot be trusted, for a long time we have heard equal complaints from the Communists that it is not possible to trust the Kuomintang government. In my opinion, effort should be exerted to clear up this mutual distrust, and it was my own view that a solution might be reached in some measure which would result in sharing of and participation in the responsibilities of the government by competent representatives of other parties and groups. Of course, I was familiar with the contention of the Kuomintang that there can now be only one party government; and I should like to see the difficulty surmounted, but even if it were not possible to overcome it on a broad basis, giving representation in the government to minor parties, it might be that a limited solution could be reached which might provide for able representation of special groups or parties, and these individuals should be invited to come and participate in some form of responsible war council planning and carrying out the plans to meet the serious war crisis by which China is faced at the present time. Perhaps it might be possible to develop, through such a sharing of responsibility, a situation which would overcome existing criticism and mistrust, and a disposition to work together for China's unification, whereupon Chiang Kai-shek commented that the suggestion might be worth studying, at least.

The conversation was an entirely friendly one; most of the talking was done by Chiang Kai-shek, and the conversation ended with Chiang reiterating his arguments as set forth in the opening portion of this message.

GAUSS

46

Secretary Hull to the Ambassador in China (Gauss)

893.00/8-3144

WASHINGTON, *September 9, 1944*

1. Careful consideration has been accorded to your messages by the President and by me, and we are in agreement with you that at the present time, a frank, friendly, and positive approach should be made to Chiang Kai Shek on the matters of governmental and related military conditions in China.

2. The Generalissimo's suggestion that Chinese Communists should be instructed to settle their differences with the government has been noted by us. Chiang Kai Shek made a like suggestion to the Vice President, and Chiang's argumentation in general, as set forth in your previous message, is strikingly like that used with Vice President Wallace; would indicate a discouraging lack of progress in the Generalissimo's thinking, in consideration of dissident developments reported in other areas not under the influence of the Communists, and in the light of Chiang's own professed desire to come to a settlement with the Communists.

3. Unless you regard the step as inadvisable, it is suggested that you inform Chiang if he will arrange for a meeting, you are prepared to talk with the Communist representative in Chungking along the same general lines as you and Vice President Wallace have talked with Chiang; that you will indicate to the Communist representative the urgent need for unity in China in carrying on the war and in making ready for the peace; that to achieve such unity a spirit of good will and tolerance, of give and take, is essential; that at the present time, Chinese of every shade of political thought should cooperate for the defeat of Japan, and that if the principal objective of victory is kept firmly in mind, differences can be settled. The foregoing may be told to Chiang as from the President and from me. You may add that we concur in your comments to Chiang Kai Shek as reported. In addition, please tell Chiang that the observer group in north China is on a military mission and we do not consider it advisable to use it for the purpose which he suggested.

4. Further, we note with approval that you utilized the opportunity afforded by conversation with Chiang to mention your idea of a coalition council as described by you. Please tell Chiang that the President and I feel your suggestion is timely as well as practical, and worthy of careful consideration; that we are concerned not alone with reference to non-settlement with the Chinese Communists but also with regard to reports of dissidence and dissatisfaction among non-Communist Chinese in other areas of the country; that we are not concerned with Chinese Communists or other dissident elements as such, but are anxious, on behalf of the United Nations and on our own behalf, and also on behalf of China, that, under the leadership of a strong but tolerant and representative government, the people of China develop and use the spiritual and physical resources at their command to carry on the war and to establish a lasting democratic peace, and to achieve this, factional differences can, and should be,

settled and merged by intelligent cooperation and conciliation. It is our belief that a most effective means to achieve this end would be a council or some body which represents all influential elements in China, with full powers, under the leadership of Chiang Kai Shek. However, we recognize that Chiang may have in mind some means of achieving the same result which would be equally or more effective.

Further, you may make use as you wish of such portions of the cogent arguments expressed in your telegrams, as coming from us, and also the views which were well expressed by Atcheson on August ninth in his conversation with Sun Fo.

Kindly inform General Hurley, General Stilwell, and Mr. Nelson with regard to the matter. You are authorized to invite one or more of them to go with you to call upon Chiang if you feel that it would serve a useful purpose.

HULL

47

Memoranda by Foreign Service Officers in China, 1943–1945

[Extracts] [1]

1. Soviet intentions with respect to the Far East, including China, are aggressive.

September 17, 1943 (Davies)

"It is perhaps not too early to suggest that Soviet policy will probably be directed initially at establishing frontiers which will insure Russian security and at rehabilitation of the U. S. S. R. There is no reason to cherish optimism regarding a voluntary Soviet contribution to our fight against Japan, whether in the shape of air bases or the early opening of a second front in Northeast Asia. The Russians may be expected to move against the Japanese when it suits their pleasure, which may not be until the final phases of the war—and then only in order to be able to participate in dictating terms to the Japanese and to establish new strategic frontiers."

January 15, 1944 (Davies)

"We need to dispatch immediately, while it is still welcome, a military and political observers' mission to Communist China to collect enemy information, assist in and prepare for certain limited operations from that area, obtain accurate estimates of the strength of Communist armies, report on Russian operations in North China and Manchuria should Russia attack Japan, and assess the possibility of North China and Manchuria developing into a separate Chinese state—perhaps even as a Russian satellite."

April 7, 1944 (Service)

"We must be concerned with Russian plans and policies in Asia because they are bound to affect our own plans in the same area. But our relations with Russia in Asia are at present only a subordinate part of our political and military relations with Russia in Europe in the over-all United Nations war effort and post-war settlement. We should make every effort to learn what the Russian aims in Asia are. A good way of gaining material relevant to this will be a

---

[1] These extracts from reports by John P. Davies, Jr., Raymond P. Ludden and John Stewart Service are grouped in order of the several themes as summarized on pp. 64–65.

careful first-hand study of the strength, attitudes and popular support of the Chinese Communists. . . .

"Chiang unwittingly may be contributing to Russian dominance in Eastern Asia by internal and external policies which, if pursued in their present form, will render China too weak to serve as a possible counter-weight to Russia. By so doing, Chiang may be digging his own grave; not only North China and Manchuria, but also national groups such as Korea and Formosa may be driven into the arms of the Soviets."

2. The Chinese Communists have a background of subservience to the U. S. S. R., but new influences—principally nationalism—have come into play which are modifying their outlook.

June 24, 1943 (Davies)

"Chinese Communist policy appears to have followed the Comintern line. In its initial expression the policy adhered to the program of world revolution. With the Comintern's abandonment of this program, the Chinese Communists embraced in 1935, in compliance with Moscow directives, the policy of the united front.

"The new line, so far as it applied to Asia, was in all probability prompted by the Kremlin's realistic appraisal of the Soviet Union's position in the Far East. Russia was threatened by Japan. The Japanese Army had with its Manchurian adventure apparently decided upon a policy of continental expansion. Confronted by a strong Russian Army in eastern Siberia, the Japanese seemed to be intent upon outflanking the Russians through China. China could not be expected to offer strong resistance to Japanese expansion so long as it was torn by internal dissension. It was therefore evident that China should become unified and actively resist Japanese pressure westward.

"As the Chinese Communists moved away from world revolution to nationalism they also moved in the direction of more moderate internal political and economic policy. Whether these other moves were in compliance with Comintern dictates is less material than that they were historically and evolutionarily sound.

"The trend toward nationalism is believed to be strongest among the troops and guerrillas who have been fighting the national enemy. Although we have no accurate information on the subject, it is suspected that the political leaders of the Party retain their pro-Russian orientation and that they are, notwithstanding the dissolution of the Comintern, likely to be susceptible to Moscow direction. This probable schism within the Party may prove at some later date to be of major importance."

August 3, 1944 (Service)

"The Chinese Communist Party claims that it is Marxist. By this the Communists mean that their ideology, their philosophical approach, and their dialectical method are based on Marxist materialism. Marxism thus becomes to them chiefly an attitude and approach to problems. It is a long-term view of political and economic development to which all short-term considerations of temporary advantage or premature power are ruthlessly subordinated.

"The Communists actively support the war because this gives them an opportunity to mobilize, organize and indoctrinate the people, and to create and train an efficient army.

"They operate by preference in the areas behind the Japanese lines because there they are relatively free from Kuomintang interference.

"Such policies as the abandonment of land confiscation are useful temporary expedients to help them carry on the war and to win unified popular support in the areas of their operations. It also has strong propaganda appeal in other areas.

"Their espousal of democracy appeals to the great majority of the people of China and is a good club for beating the Kuomintang. They realize that popular support must be their principal weapon against the superior arms of the Kuomintang in any contest of strength.

"Their democratic claims, their engagement in guerrilla warfare behind the enemy lines, and their proclamation of liberal economic policies based on private property are also useful in appealing to foreign sympathy and in winning the foreign support which they realize will be necessary, at least for a time, in the economic rehabilitation and development of China following the war."

3. The Chinese Communists have become the most dynamic force in China and are challenging the Kuomintang for control of the country.

October 9, 1944 (Service)

"Reports of two American officers, several correspondents, and twenty-odd foreign travelers regarding conditions in the areas of North China under Communist control are in striking agreement. This unanimity, based on actual observation, is significant. It forces us to accept certain facts, and to draw from those facts an important conclusion.

"*The Japanese are being actively opposed*—in spite of the constant warfare and cruel retaliation this imposes on the population. This opposition is gaining in strength. The Japanese can temporarily crush it in a limited area by the concentration of overwhelming force. But it is impossible for them to do this simultaneously over the huge territory the Communists now influence.

"*This opposition is possible and successful because it is total guerrilla warfare aggressively waged by a totally mobilized population.* In this total mobilization the regular forces of the Communists, though leaders and organizers, have become subordinate to the vastly more numerous forces of the people themselves. They exist because the people permit, support and wholeheartedly fight with them. There is complete solidarity of Army and people.

"*This total mobilization is based upon and has been made possible by what amounts to an economic, political and social revolution.* This revolution has been moderate and democratic. It has improved the economic condition of the peasants by rent and interest reduction, tax reform and good government. It has given them democratic self-government, political consciousness and a sense of their rights. It has freed them from feudalistic bonds and given them self-respect, self-reliance and a strong feeling of cooperative group interest. *The common people, for the first time, have been given something to fight for.*

"The Japanese are being fought now not merely because they are foreign invaders but because they deny this revolution. *The people will continue to fight any government which limits or deprives them of these newly won gains.*"

November 7, 1944 (Davies)

"The Chinese Communists are so strong between the Great Wall and the Yangtze that they can now look forward to the postwar control of at least North China. They may also continue to hold not only those parts of the Yangtze valley which they now dominate but also new areas in Central and South China. The Communists have fallen heir to these new areas by a process, which has been operating for seven years, whereby Chiang Kai-shek loses his cities and principal lines of communication to the Japanese and the countryside to the Communists.

"The Communists have survived ten years of civil war and seven years of Japanese offensives. They have survived not only more sustained enemy pressure than the Chinese Central Government forces have been subjected to, but also a severe blockade imposed by Chiang.

"They have survived and they have grown. Communist growth since 1937 has been almost geometric in progression. From control of some 100,000 square kilometers with a population of one million and a half they have expanded to about 850,000 square kilometers with a population of approximately 90 million. And they will continue to grow.

"The reason for this phenomenal vitality and strength is simple and fundamental. It is mass support, mass participation. The Communist governments and armies are the first governments and armies in modern Chinese history to have positive and widespread popular support. They have this support because the governments and armies are genuinely of the people."

January 4, 1945 (Davies)

"The Current situation in China must afford the Kremlin a certain sardonic satisfaction.

"The Russians see the anti-Soviet Government of Chiang Kai-shek decaying— militarily, politically and economically. They observe the Chinese Communists consolidating in North China, expanding southward in the wake of Chiang's military debacles and now preparing for the formal establishment of a separatist administration.

"It is equally evident to the Russians that the Chinese Communists will not in the meantime be idle. The Communists have amply demonstrated a capacity for independent, dynamic growth. However Marshal Stalin may describe the Chinese Communists to his American visitors, he can scarcely be unaware of the fact that the Communists are a considerably more stalwart and self-sufficient force than any European underground or partisan movement."

4. The Kuomintang and National Government are disintegrating.

June 20, 1944 (Service)

"B. *The position of the Kuomintang and the Generalissimo is weaker than it has been for the past ten years.*

"China faces economic collapse. This is causing disintegration of the army and the government's administrative apparatus. It is one of the chief causes of growing political unrest. The Generalissimo is losing the support of a China which, by unity in the face of violent aggression, found a new and unexpected strength during the first two years of the war with Japan. Internal weaknesses are becoming accentuated and there is taking place a reversal of the process of unification.

"1. Morale is low and discouragement widespread. There is a general feeling of hopelessness.

"2. The authority of the Central Government is weakening in the areas away from the larger cities. Government mandates and measures of control cannot be enforced and remain ineffective. It is becoming difficult for the Government to collect enough food for its huge army and bureaucracy.

"3. The governmental and military structure is being permeated and demoralized from top to bottom by corruption, unprecedented in scale and openness.

"4. The intellectual and salaried classes, who have suffered the most heavily from inflation, are in danger of liquidation. The academic groups suffer not only the attrition and demoralization of economic stress; the weight of years of political control and repression is robbing them of the intellectual vigor and leadership they once had.

"5. Peasant resentment of the abuses of conscription, tax collection and other arbitrary impositions has been widespread and is growing. The danger is ever-increasing that past sporadic outbreaks of banditry and agrarian unrest may increase in scale and find political motivation.

"6. The provincial groups are making common cause with one another and with other dissident groups, and are actively consolidating their positions. Their continuing strength in the face of the growing weakness of the Central Government is forcing new measures of political appeasement in their favor.

"7. Unrest within the Kuomintang armies is increasing, as shown in one important instance by the 'Young Generals conspiracy' late in 1943. On a higher plane, the war zone commanders are building up their own spheres of influence and are thus creating a 'new warlordism.'

"8. The break between the Kuomintang and the Communists not only shows no signs of being closed, but grows more critical with the passage of time: the inevitability of civil war is now generally accepted.

"9. The Kuomintang is losing the respect and support of the people by its selfish policies and its refusal to heed progressive criticism. It seems unable to revivify itself with fresh blood, and its unchanging leadership shows a growing ossification and loss of a sense of reality. To combat the dissensions and cliquism within the Party, which grows more rather than less acute, the leadership is turning toward the reactionary and unpopular Chen brothers clique.

"10. The Generalissimo shows a similar loss of realistic flexibility and a hardening of narrowly conservative views. His growing megalomania and his unfortunate attempts to be 'sage' as well as leader—shown, for instance, by 'China's Destiny' and his book on economics—have forfeited the respect of many intellectuals, who enjoy in China a position of unique influence. Criticism of his dictatorship is becoming outspoken.

"In the face of the grave crisis with which it is confronted, the Kuomintang is ceasing to be the unifying and progressive force in Chinese society, the role in which it made its greatest contribution to modern China.

"C. *The Kuomintang is not only proving itself incapable of averting a debacle by its own initiative: on the contrary, its policies are precipitating the crisis.*

"Some war-weariness in China must be expected. But the policies of the Kuomintang under the impact of hyperinflation and in the presence of obvious signs of internal and external weakness must be described as bankrupt. This truth is emphasized by the failure of the Kuomintang to come to grips with the situation during the recently concluded plenary session of the Central Executive Committee.

"1. *On the internal political front the desire of the Kuomintang leaders to perpetuate their own power overrides all other considerations.* The result is the enthronement of reaction.

"The Kuomintang continues to ignore the great political drive within the country for democratic reform. The writings of the Generalissimo and the Party press show that they have no real understanding of that term. Constitutionalism remains an empty promise for which the only "preparation" is a half-hearted attempt to establish an unpopular and undemocratic system of local self-government based on collective responsibility and given odium by Japanese utilization in Manchuria and other areas under their control.

"Questions basic to the future of democracy such as the form of the Constitution and the composition and election of the National Congress remain the dictation of the Kuomintang. There is no progress toward the fundamental conditions of freedom of expression and recognition of non-Kuomintang groups. Even the educational and political advantages of giving power and democratic character to the existing but impotent Peoples Political Council are ignored.

"The Kuomintang shows no intention of relaxing the authoritarian controls on which its present power depends. Far from discarding or reducing the paraphernalia of a police state—the multiple and omnipresent secret police organizations, the Gendarmerie, and so forth—it continues to strengthen them as its last resort for internal security.

"2. *On the economic front the Kuomintang is unwilling to take any effective steps to check inflation which would injure the landlord-capitalist class.*

"It is directly responsible for the increase of official corruption which is one of the main obstacles to any rational attempt to ameliorate the financial situation. It does nothing to stop large-scale profiteering, hoarding and speculation—all of which are carried on by people either powerful in the Party or with intimate political connections.

"It fails to carry out effective mobilization of resources. Such measures of war-time control as it has promulgated have remained a dead letter or have intensified the problems they were supposedly designed to remedy—as for instance ill-advised and poorly executed attempts at price regulation.

"It passively allows both industrial and the more important handicraft production to run down, as they of course must when it is more profitable for speculators to hold raw materials than to have them go through the normal productive process.

"It fails to carry out rationing except in a very limited way, or to regulate the manufacture and trade of luxury goods, many of which come from areas under Japanese control. It shows little concern that these imports are largely paid for with strategic commodities of value to the enemy.

"It fails to make an effective attempt to reduce the budgetary deficit and increase revenue by tapping such resources as excess profits and incomes of landlords and merchants. It allows its tax-collecting apparatus to bog down in corruption and inefficiency—to the point that possibly not more than one-third of revenues collected reach the government. It continues to spend huge government funds on an idle and useless Party bureaucracy.

"At best, it passively watches inflation gather momentum without even attempting palliative measures available to it, such as the aggressive sale of gold and foreign currency.

"It refuses to attack the fundamental economic problems of China such as the growing concentration of land holdings, extortionate rents and ruinous interest rates, and the impact of inflation.

D. *These apparently suicidal policies of the Kuomintang have their roots in the composition and nature of the Party.*

"In view of the above it becomes pertinent to ask *why* the Kuomintang has lost its power of leadership; *why* it neither wishes actively to wage war against Japan itself nor to cooperate whole-heartedly with the American Army in China; and *why* it has ceased to be capable of unifying the country.

"The answer to all these questions is to be found in the present composition and nature of the Party. Politically, a classical and definitive American description becomes ever more true; the Kuomintang is a congerie of conservative political cliques interested primarily in the preservation of their own power against all outsiders and in jockeying for position among themselves. Economically, the Kuomintang rests on the narrow base of the rural-gentry-landlords and militarists, the higher ranks of the government bureaucracy, and merchant bankers having intimate connections with the government bureaucrats. This base has actually contracted during the war. The Kuomintang no longer commands, as it once did, the unequivocal support of China's industrialists, who as a group have been much weakened economically, and hence politically, by the Japanese seizure of the coastal cities.

"The relations of this description of the Kuomintang to the questions propounded above is clear.

"The Kuomintang has lost its leadership because it has lost touch with and is no longer representative of a nation which, through the practical experience of the war, is becoming both more politically conscious and more aware of the Party's selfish shortcomings.

"It cannot fight an effective war because this is impossible without greater reliance upon and support by the people. There must be a release of the national energy such as occurred during the early period of the war. Under present conditions, this can be brought about only by reform of the Party and greater political democracy. What form this democracy takes is not as important as the genuine adoption of a democratic philosophy and attitude; the threat of foreign invasion is no longer enough to stimulate the Chinese people and only real reform can regain their enthusiasm. But the growth of democracy, though basic to China's continuing war effort, would, to the mind of the Kuomintang's present leaders, imperil the foundations of the Party's power because it would mean that the conservative cliques would have to give up their closely guarded monopoly. Rather than do this, they prefer to see the war remain in its present state of passive inertia. Thus are they sacrificing China's national interests to their own selfish ends.

"For similar reasons, the Kuomintang is unwilling to give whole-hearted cooperation to the American Army's effort in China. Full cooperation necessarily requires the broad Chinese military effort which the Kuomintang is unable to carry out or make possible. In addition, the Kuomintang fears the large scale, widespread and direct contact by Americans with the Chinese war effort will expose its own inactivity and, by example and personal contacts, be a liberalizing influence."

5. The rivalry between these two forces threatens to culminate in a civil war which (a) would hamper the conduct of the war against Japan, (b) would press the Communists back into the arms of the U.S.S.R. and (c) might well lead eventually to American-Soviet involvement and conflict.

January 23, 1943 (Service)

"It is now no longer wondered whether civil war can be avoided, but rather whether it can be delayed at least until after a victory over Japan.

"The dangers and implications of this disunity are obvious and far-reaching. Militarily, the present situation is a great hindrance to any effective war effort by China. Its deterioration into civil war would be disastrous. The situation therefore has direct relationship to our own efforts to defeat Japan.

". . . there can be no denial that civil war in China, or even the continuation after the defeat of Japan of the present deadlock, will greatly impede the return of peaceful conditions. This blocking of the orderly large scale rehabilitation of China will in itself seriously and adversely affect American interests. Even if a conflict is averted, the continuance, or, as is probable in such an event, the worsening of the already serious economic strains within the country may result in economic collapse. If there is civil war the likelihood of such an economic collapse is of course greater.

"There is also the possibility that economic difficulties may make the war-weary, over-conscripted and over-taxed farmers fertile ground for Communist propaganda and thus bring about a revolution going beyond the moderate democracy which the Chinese Communists now claim to be seeking. Such a Communist government would probably not be democratic in the American sense. And it is probable, even if the United States did not incur the enmity of the Communists for alleged material or diplomatic support of the Kuomintang, that this Communist government would be more inclined toward friendship and cooperation with Russia than with Great Britain and America."

June 24, 1943 (Davies)
"Basis for Conflict"

"The Kuomintang and Chiang Kai-shek recognize that the Communists, with the popular support which they enjoy and their reputation for administrative reform and honesty, represent a challenge to the Central Government and its spoils system. The Generalissimo cannot admit the seemingly innocent demands of the Communists that their party be legalized and democratic processes be put into practice. To do so would probably mean the abdication of the Kuomintang and the provincial satraps.

"The Communists, on the other hand, dare not accept the Central Government's invitation that they disband their armies and be absorbed in the national body politic. To do so would be to invite extinction.

"This impasse will probably be resolved, American and other foreign observers in Chungking agree, by an attempt by the Central Government to liquidate the Communists. This action may be expected to precipitate a civil war from which one of the two contending factions will emerge dominant. . . ."

"Chiang Kai-shek and his Kuomintang lieutenants fully realize the risks of an attack on the Communists. This may explain the reported statements of high officials in Chungking that they must prepare not only for the coming civil war but also for the coming war with Russia. Chiang and his Central Government recognize that they cannot defeat the Communists and the Soviet Union without foreign aid. Such aid would naturally be sought from the United States and possibly Great Britain.

". . . we may anticipate that Chiang Kai-shek will exert every effort and resort to every stratagem to involve us in active support of the Central Government. We will probably be told that if fresh American aid is not forthcoming all of China and eventually all of Asia will be swept by communism. It will be difficult for us to resist such appeals, especially in view of our moral commitments to continued assistance to China during the post-war period.

"It is therefore not inconceivable that, should Chiang attempt to liquidate the Communists, we would find ourselves entangled not only in a civil war in China but also drawn into conflict with the Soviet Union."

June 20, 1944 (Service)

"Obsessed by the growing and potential threat of the Communists, who it fears may attract the popular support its own nature makes impossible, the Kuomintang, despite the pretext—to meet foreign and Chinese criticism—of conducting negotiations with the Communists, continues to adhere to policies and plans which can only result in civil war. In so doing it shows itself blind to the facts: that its internal political and military situation is so weak that success without outside assistance is most problematic; that such a civil war would hasten the process of disintegration and the spread of chaos; that it would prevent the prosecution of any effective war against Japan; and that the only parties to benefit would be Japan immediately and Russia eventually."

December 9, 1944 (Davies)

". . . The Generalissimo realizes that if he accedes to the Communist terms for a coalition government, they will sooner or later dispossess him and his Kuomintang of power. He will therefore not, unless driven to an extremity, form a genuine coalition government. He will seek to retain his present government, passively wait out the war and conserve his strength, knowing that the Communist issue must eventually be joined.

"The Communists, on their part, have no interest in reaching an agreement with the Generalissimo short of a genuine coalition government. They recognize that Chiang's position is crumbling, that they may before long receive substantial Russian support and that if they have patience they will succeed to authority in at least North China. . . ."

6. The Communists would, inevitably, win such a war because the foreign powers, including the United States, which would support the Government, could not feasibly supply enough aid to compensate for the organic weaknesses of the Government.

January 23, 1943 (Service)

". . Assuming that open hostilities are for the time being averted, the eventual defeat and withdrawal of the Japanese will leave the Kuomintang still confronted with the Communists solidly entrenched in most of North China (East Kansu, North Shensi, Shansi, South Chahar, Hopei, Shantung, North Kiangsu and North Anhwei). In addition the Communists will be in position to move into the vacuum created by the Japanese withdrawal from Suiyuan, Jehol and Manchuria, in all of which areas there is already some Communist activity. In the rest of China they will have the sympathy of elements among the liberals, intellectuals, and students.

". . . There is undoubtedly a strong revulsion in the mind of the average, nonparty Chinese to the idea of renewed civil war and the Kuomintang may indeed have difficulty with the loyalty and effectiveness of its conscript troops."

October 9, 1944 (Service)

"*Just as the Japanese Army cannot crush these militant people now, so also will Kuomintang force fail in the future.* With their new arms and organization, knowledge of their own strength, and determination to keep what they have been fighting for, these people—now some 90 million and certain to be many more before the Kuomintang can reach them—will resist oppression. They are not Communists. They do not want separation or independence. But at present they regard the Kuomintang—from their own experience—as oppressors; and the Communists as their leaders and benefactors.

"*With this great popular base, the Communists likewise cannot be eliminated.* Kuomintang attempts to do so by force must mean a complete denial of democracy. This will strengthen the ties of the Communists with the people: a Communist victory will be inevitable. . . .

"From the basic fact that the Communists have built up popular support of a magnitude and depth which makes their elimination impossible, *we must draw the conclusion that the Communists will have a certain and important share in China's future* . . . I suggest the future conclusion that unless the Kuomintang goes as far as the Communists in political and economic reform, and otherwise proves itself able to contest this leadership of the people (none of which it yet shows signs of being willing or able to do), the Communists will be the dominant force in China within a comparatively few years."

November 7, 1944 (Davies)

"Only if he is able to enlist foreign intervention on a scale equal to the Japanese invasion of China will Chiang probably be able to crush the Communists. But foreign intervention on such a scale would seem to be unlikely. Relying upon his dispirited shambling legions, his decadent corrupt bureaucracy, his sterile political moralisms and such nervous foreign support as he can muster, the Generalissimo may nevertheless plunge China into civil war. He cannot succeed, however, where the Japanese in more than seven years of determined striving have failed. The Communists are already too strong for him.

"If the Generalissimo neither precipitates a civil war nor reaches an understanding with the Communists, he is still confronted with defeat. Chiang's feudal China can not long coexist alongside a modern dynamic popular government in North China.

"The Communists are in China to stay. And China's destiny is not Chiang's but theirs."

7. In this unhappy dilemma, the United States should attempt to prevent the disaster of a civil war through adjustment of the new alignment of power in China by peaceful processes. The desirable means to this end is to encourage the reform and revitalization of the Kuomintang so that it may survive as a significant force in a coalition government. If this fails, we must limit our involvement with the Kuomintang and must commence some cooperation with the Communists, the force destined to control China, in an effort to influence them further into an independent position friendly to the United States. We are working against time because, if the U.S.S.R. enters the war against Japan and invades China before either of these alternatives succeeds, the Communists will be captured by the U.S.S.R. and become Soviet satellites.

June 20, 1944 (Service)

"We must seek to contribute toward the reversal of the present movement toward collapse and to the rousing of China from its military inactivity. This can be brought about only by an accelerated movement toward democratic political reform within China. Our part must be that of a catalytic agent in this process of China's democratization. It can be carried out by the careful exertion of our influence, which has so far not been consciously and systematically used.

"This democratic reform does not necessarily mean the overthrow of the Generalissimo or the Kuomintang. On the contrary—if they have the vision to see it—their position will be improved and the stability of the Central Government increased. The democratic forces already existing in China will be strengthened, the reactionary authoritarian trends in the Kuomintang will be modified, and a multi-party United Front Government will probably emerge. It is almost certain that the Generalissimo and the Kuomintang would continue to play a dominant part in such a government.

"It goes without saying that this democratization of China must be brought about by, and depend on, forces within the country. It cannot be enforced by us— or by any foreign nation—

". . . If we come to the rescue of the Kuomintang on its own terms we would be buttressing—but only temporarily—a decadent regime which by its existing composition and program is incapable of solving China's problems. Both China and ourselves would be gaining only a brief respite from the ultimate day of reckoning."

October 10, 1944 (Service)

"In the present circumstances, the Kuomintang is dependent on American support for survival. *But we are in no way dependent on the Kuomintang.*

". . . by continued and exclusive support of the Kuomintang, we tend to prevent the reforms and democratic reorganization of the government which are essential for the revitalization of China's war effort. Encouraged by our support the Kuomintang will continue in its present course, progressively losing the confidence of the people and becoming more and more impotent Ignored by us, and excluded from the Government and joint prosecution of the war, the Communists and other groups will be forced to guard their own interests by more direct opposition."

November 15, 1944 (Davies)

"We should not now abandon Chiang Kai-shek. To do so at this juncture would be to lose more than we could gain. We must for the time being continue recognition of Chiang's Government.

"But we must be realistic. We must not indefinitely underwrite a politically bankrupt regime. And, if the Russians are going to enter the Pacific War, we must make a determined effort to capture politically the Chinese Communists rather than allow them to go by default wholly to the Russians. Furthermore, we must fully understand that by reason of our recognition of the Chiang Kai-shek Government as now constituted we are committed to a steadily decaying regime and severely restricted in working out military and political cooperation with the Chinese Communists.

"A coalition Chinese Government in which the Communists find a satisfactory place is the solution of this impasse most desirable to us. It provides our greatest assurance of a strong united, democratic, independent and friendly China— our basic strategic aim in Asia and the Pacific. If Chiang and the Communists reach a mutually satisfactory agreement, there will have been achieved from our point of view the most desirable possible solution. If Chiang and the Communists are irreconcilable, then we shall have to decide which faction we are going to support.

"In seeking to determine which faction we should support we must keep in mind these basic considerations: Power in China is on the verge of shifting from Chiang to the Communists.

"If the Russians enter North China and Manchuria, we obviously cannot hope to win the Communists entirely over to us, but we can through control of supplies and post-war aid expect to exert considerable influence in the direction of Chinese nationalism and independence from Soviet control."

8. A policy of this description would also—and this is a decisive consideration in the war against Japan—measurably aid our war effort.

December 12, 1944 (Davies)

"The negotiations looking to an agreement between the Generalissimo and the Chinese Communists have failed. It is not impossible, however, that one or the other side may in the near future revive the negotiations with a new proposal.

"So long as the deadlock exists, or new negotiations drag on, it is reasonable to assume that the Generalissimo will continue to refuse us permission to exploit militarily the Chinese Communist position extending into the geographical center of Japan's inner zone. With the war against Japan proving so costly to us, we can ill afford to continue denying ourselves positive assistance and strategically valuable positions.

"It is time that we unequivocally told Chiang Kai-shek that we will work with and, within our discretion, supply whatever Chinese forces we believe can contribute most to the war against Japan. We should tell him that we will not work with or supply any Chinese unit, whether Central Government, Provincial or Communist, which shows any inclination toward precipitating civil conflict. We should tell him that we propose to keep him, as head of the recognized government, informed of what supplies we give the various Chinese forces.

"It is time that we make it clear to Chiang-Kai-shek that we expect the Chinese to settle their own political differences; that we refuse to become further involved in and party to Chinese domestic political disputes. We greatly hope and desire that China will emerge from this war unified, democratic, independent and strong. We feel that this goal is to be achieved most expeditiously and with the least possible expenditure of Chinese and American blood and treasure if the United States bends its efforts in China primarily toward working with and assisting whatever elements can contribute most to the speedy defeat of Japan."

February 14, 1945 (Ludden and Service)

"American policy in the Far East can have but one immediate objective: the defeat of Japan in the shortest possible time with the least expenditure of American lives. To the attainment of this objective all other considerations should be subordinate.

"The attainment of this objective demands the effective mobilization of China in the war against Japan. Operating as we are in a land theater at the end of a supply line many thousands of miles in length, the human and economic resources of China increase in importance as we draw closer to Japan's inner zone of defense. Denied the effective use of these resources the attainment of our primary objective will be unnecessarily delayed.

"There is ample evidence to show that to the present Kuomintang Government the war against Japan is secondary in importance to its own preservation in power. China's military failure is due in large part to internal political disunity and the Kuomintang's desire to conserve such military force as it has for utilization in the maintenance of its political power. The intention of the Generalissimo to eliminate all political opposition, by force of arms if necessary, has not been abandoned. In the present situation in China, where power or self-preservation depend upon the possession of military force, neither the Kuomintang nor opposition groups are willing to expend their military resources against the Japanese through fear that it will then *vis-à-vis* other groups.

"The aim of American policy as indicated clearly by official statements in the United States is the establishment of political unity in China as the indispensable preliminary to China's effective military mobilization. The execution of our policy has not contributed to the achievement of this publicly stated aim. On the contrary, it has retarded its effect because our statements and actions in China have convinced the Kuomintang Government that we will continue to support it and it alone. The Kuomintang Government believes that it will receive an increasing flow of American military and related supplies which, if past experience is any guide, it will commit against the enemy only with great reluctance, if at all.

"We cannot hope for any improvement in this situation unless we understand the objectives of the Kuomintang Government and throw our considerable influence upon it in the direction of internal unity. We should be convinced by this time that the effort to solve the Kuomintang-Communist differences by diplomatic means has failed; . . . .

"At present there exists in China a situation closely paralleling that which existed in Yogoslavia prior to Prime Minister Churchill's declaration of support for Marshal Tito. That statement was as follows:

"'The sanest and safest course for us to follow is to judge all parties and factions dispassionately by the test of their readiness to fight the Germans and thus lighten the burden of Allied troops. This is not a time for ideological preferences for one side or the other.'

"A similar public statement issued by the Commander in Chief with regard to China would not mean the withdrawal of recognition or the cessation of military aid to the Central Government; that would be both unnecessary and unwise. It would serve notice, however, of our preparation to make use of all available means to achieve our primary objective. It would supply for all Chinese a firm rallying point which has thus far been lacking. The internal effect in China would be so profound that the Generalissimo would be forced to make concessions of power and permit united-front coalition. The present opposition groups, no longer under the prime necessity of safeguarding themselves, would be won wholeheartedly to our side and we would have in China, for the first time, a united ally."

48 (a)

The Vice Chairman of the Central Committee of the Chinese Communist Party (Chou) to the Ambassador in China (Hurley)

February 18, 1945

DEAR GENERAL HURLEY: I am ever grateful for the kindness extended to me while I was in Chungking. After my return to Yenan I have made a detailed report to the Central Committee of my Party and to Chairman Mao Tze-tung. Since at present the Democratic Coalition Government has not yet come into existence in China and the existing National Government is completely a one-Party dictatorship of the Kuomintang which can represent neither the 10 million people of the Chinese liberated areas nor the common will of the broad masses of people in areas under Kuomintang control; consequently in the United Nations Conference which is to be convened on April 25 in San Francisco, China cannot be represented by a delegation sent by the Kuomintang Government only. While I was in Chungking you told me that the delegation to the San Francisco Conference should consist of the representatives of the Kuomintang, the Communist Party and the Democratic Federation. The Central Committee of our Party and Chairman Mao Tze-tung are in complete agreement with you. We consider furthermore that the representatives of the Kuomintang should be limited to ⅓ of the delegation. The other ⅔ of the delegation should be sent by the Communist Party and the Democratic Federation. Only then can the common will of the Chinese people be fairly represented; otherwise that delegation could never be in a position to settle any problem in the conference on behalf of China. Will you be so kind as to transmit this message to the President of the United States. With my best regards and respects,

CHOU EN-LAI.

48 (b)

The Ambassador in China (Hurley) to the Vice Chairman of the Central Committee of the Chinese Communist Party (Chou)

February 20, 1945

Thanks for your kind telegram. I was happy to hear from you. I did discuss with you the coming conference at San Francisco but I made it clear to you that only the National Government of China has been invited to participate in that conference. I made no attempt to decide how the National Government would be represented in the conference. I had no authority to make a decision on that subject, that is the prerogative of the National Government. It is altogether proper for me to express to you my candid opinion which is that the President and Generalissimo of the National Government of China, known internationally as the Republic of China, will be recognized as the representative of China at the conference and the President alone, in my opinion will select the staff which will accompany him. The conference at San Francisco is to be a conference of nations, not of political parties within nations. The Communist Party of China is not a nation and, as far as I know, no one has recognized it as a nation. It is one of the political parties of China. The only difference from the ordinary political party is that it is armed. I am further of the opinion that recognition by the conference of any armed political party in China other than the National Government would destroy the possibility of unification in China. I urge that Mao Tze-tung, your Chairman, and you, as Vice Chairman and my friends, consider only the methods by which you can unite with, be included in and cooperate under the National Government of China. On my return, I hope to be able to see Chairman Mao, you and General Chu and be in a position to discuss the situation fully with you.

49

Summary of Conversations Between Representatives of the National Government and of the Chinese Communist Party [2]

1. Basic policy on peaceful national reconstruction.—It was agreed that as China's war of resistance against Japanese aggression has been brought to a victorious conclusion, China is now on the threshold of a new era of peaceful national reconstruction, and that peace, democracy, solidarity and unity should form the basis of the nation's concerted efforts. It was likewise agreed that under the leadership of President Chiang, cooperation should be perpetuated and resolute measures taken to avert internal strife so that a new China, independent, free and prosperous, may be built and the Three People's Principles fully implemented. Both parties further agreed that political democratization, nationalization of troops and the recognition of the equal legal status of political parties, as advocated by President Chiang are absolutely essential to achieving peaceful national reconstruction.

---

[2] Issued by the Chinese Ministry of Information on October 11, 1945; *China Handbook, 1937–1945*, pp. 738–740.

2. On political democratization.—It was agreed that the period of political tutelage should be brought to an early conclusion, that constitutional government should be inaugurated and that necessary preliminary measures should be immediately adopted, such as the convocation of the National Assembly (People's Congress) and a Political Consultation Conference, to which all parties and nonpartisan leaders will be invited, to exchange views on national affairs and discuss questions relating to peaceful national reconstruction and the convocation of the National Assembly. Both parties are now conferring with various interested quarters on the membership, organization and function of the proposed council. It was agreed that, as soon as such consultations are completed, the proposed council shall be convened.

3. On the National Assembly.—Three proposals were advanced by the Chinese Communist Party, namely, reelection of all delegates to the National Assembly already held should be valid, but that the number of delegates may be reasonably increased and the increase should be legalized. As regards the May 5 Draft Constitution, the Government representatives reminded the Communists that the Draft Constitution had already been submitted to the public for study and suggestions for its revision were invited. No agreement was reached on those points. But the Communist representatives made it known that they do not wish to permit national unity to be ruptured by the differences. Both parties agreed that the points concerned shall be brought before the proposed Political Consultation Conference for settlement.

4. On the people's freedoms.—It was agreed that the Government should guarantee the freedoms of person, religion, speech, publication and assembly—the rights enjoyed by the people in all democratic nations in normal times. Existing laws and decrees should be either abolished or revised in accordance with this principle.

5. On the legality of political parties.—The Chinese Communists proposed that the Government should recognize the equality and the legal status of the Kuomintang and the Communist Party as well as that of all other parties. The Government stated that a common attribute of constitutional government is that all parties are equal before the law and that this fact will be given immediate recognition.

6. On the special service agencies.—Both parties agreed that the Government should strictly prohibit all offices other than law courts and police to make arrests, conduct trials and impose punishment.

7. On release of political prisoners.—The Chinese Communists proposed that all political prisoners with the exception of those guilty of treason should be released. The Government representatives stated that the Government is prepared to do this of its own accord and that the Chinese Communist Party may submit a list of people who they think should be released.

8. On local self-government.—Both sides agreed that local self-government should be vigorously promoted. General elections should be conducted from the lower level upward. However, the Government expressed the hope that this would not affect the convocation of the National Assembly.

9. On the nationalization of troops.—It was proposed by the Chinese Communists that the Government should effect an equitable and rational reorganization of the entire Chinese Army; decide on the program and different stages of recognition; redemarcate the military zones; and inaugurate a conscription and replenishment system with a view to unifying military command. Under this program, the Chinese Communists finally expressed their readiness to reduce the troops under their command to 24 divisions or to a minimum of 20 divisions.

The Chinese Communists further stated that they would take prompt action to demobilize their anti-Japanese troops now deployed in Kwangtung, Chekiang, southern Kiangsu, southern Anhwei, central Anhwei, Hunan, Hupeh and Honan (not including northern Honan), and that such troops as are to be reorganized will be gradually evacuated from the said areas, to be concentrated in the liberated areas north of the Lunghai Railway and in northern Kiangsu and northern Anhwei. The Government representatives stated that the national troops reorganization program is being carried out, and the Government is willing to reorganize the Communist-led anti-Japanese troops into 20 divisions, if the other issues coming up in the present talks could be satisfactorily settled. Regarding the garrison areas, the Chinese Communists may submit plans for discussion and decision.

The Chinese Communists proposed that the Communist military personnel should participate in the work of the National Military Council and the various departments under the Council, and that the Government should respect the personnel system of the army units and commission the original officers after their units have been reorganized. Discharged officers should be given training in different areas, and the Government should adopt a reasonable and satisfactory system of maintenance and political education.

The Government indicated that it was ready to consider the proposals and discuss details.

In reply to the Chinese Communists' proposal that all the militiamen in the liberated areas should be reorganized into local self-defense corps, the Government expressed the view that this matter will have to be determined in accordance with local conditions and needs. In order to formulate concrete plans in regard to all the questions mentioned in this section, it was agreed that a subcommittee of three, with one representative each from the Board of Military Operations of the National Military Council, the Ministry of War, and the Eighteenth Group Army, be formed.

10. On local governments in the liberated areas.—The Communist representatives proposed that the Government should recognize the popularly elected governments in the liberated areas. The Government representatives pointed out that after the unconditional surrender of Japan the term "liberated area" becomes obsolete and the integrity of the administrative authority of the country should be respected.

The initial formula advanced by the Communist representatives was to redemarcate the provincial and administrative areas according to the conditions that now obtain in the 18 liberated areas. And to preserve administrative integrity, the Communist Party would submit to the Government a list of officials of the popularly elected governments for reappointment.

The Government replied that the redemarcation of provincial boundaries would involve changes of unusual magnitude, and the question should be very carefully and thoroughly considered and could not be resolved in a short time. At the same time the Government representatives reiterated what President Chiang had stated to Mr. Mao Tse-tung, that after the unification of the military command and administrative authority, the National Government would take into consideration administrative personnel nominated by the Communist Party. The Government would consider retaining the services of those functionaries who have served in the recovered areas during the war on the basis of their ability and record without regard to party affiliations.

Upon this, a second formula was proposed by the Communist representatives, asking the National Government to appoint nominees of the Communist Party as chairman and members of the provincial governments of the Shensi-Kansu-Ningsia Border Region, Jehol, Chahar, Hopei, Shantung and Shansi. They further asked that Communist nominees be appointed deputy chairman and members of the provincial governments of Suiyuan, Honan, Kiangsu, Anhwei, Hupeh, and Kwangtung, and deputy mayors of the special municipalities of Peiping, Tientsin, Tsingtao and Shanghai. The Communist representatives also requested participation in the administration of the Northeastern Provinces.

After lengthy discussions on this topic, the Communist representatives modified their proposals by requesting the appointment of their nominees as chairman and members of the provincial governments of the Shensi-Kansu-Ningsia Border Region, Jehol, Chahar, Hopei and Shantung, as deputy chairman and members of the provincial governments of Shansi and Suiyuan, and as deputy mayors of the special municipalities of Peiping, Tientsin and Tsingtao.

The Government representatives replied that the Communist Party might nominate those members of the Communist Party, who possess administrative ability and have rendered commendable service during the war, to the Government for appointment. But if the Communist Party should insist upon nominating chairmen or deputy chairmen or members of the provincial government for specific provinces, this would not be sincerely endeavoring to achieve military and administrative integrity.

The Communist representatives then said they would withdraw their second suggestion and propose a third formula. They suggested that general elections be held in the liberated areas under the existing popularly elected government. Under the supervision of the Political Consultation Council the Communist Party would welcome members of all other political parties as well as members of various professions to return to their native places to participate in the elections. A popular election is to be held in any hsien in which the public officers of more than one-half of its chu or hsiang have been elected by popular vote. Likewise, a popular election is to be held in any province or administrative area in which public functionaries of more than one-half of its hsien have been elected by popular vote. In the interest of administrative integrity, the names of all the provincial, hsien or chu officials thus elected should be submitted to the National Government for appointment.

The Government representatives replied that this formula is not acceptable as such a process is not conducive to real administrative integrity. But the Government might consider the appointment of popularly elected hsien officials. Popular election of provincial government functionaries could only be held after the status of the province has been definitely defined following the promulgation of the constitution. For the time being, only those provincial government officials who have been appointed by the National Government should proceed to take up their posts, so that conditions in the recovered areas may be restored to normalcy at the earliest possible moment.

At this point, a fourth formula was proposed by the Communist representative: that all liberated areas temporarily retain their status quo until the constitutional provision for the popular election of provincial government officials has been adopted and put into effect. For the time being an interim arrangement is to be worked out in order to guarantee the restoration of peace and order.

Finally, the Communist representatives suggested that this particular problem be submitted to the Political Consultation Conference for discussion and settlement. The Government, desirous of the early establishment of administrative integrity so that peaceful reconstruction might not be delayed, hoped that an agreement could soon be worked out on this matter. The Communist representatives concurred. Discussions will continue.

11. On traitors and puppet troops.—The Communist representatives proposed that traitors be severely punished and puppet troops be disbanded. The Government representatives' reply was: in principle there is no question. But traitors should be dealt with according to due process of law and the disbandment of puppet troops should be carried out in such a manner that peace and order in the areas concerned would not be disturbed.

12. On accepting the surrender of Japanese army.—The Communist representatives asked that the Communist troops be allowed to participate in the task of accepting the surrender of Japanese troops and that the areas of surrender should be redefined. The Government representatives answered that the participation of the Communist Party in accepting the surrender of Japanese troops could be considered after the troops of the Communist Party accepted the orders of the National Government.

50

The Ambassador to China (Hurley) to President Truman [3]

[WASHINGTON,] *November 26, 1945*

MY DEAR MR. PRESIDENT: I hereby resign as Ambassador to China.

In tendering my resignation I wish you to know that I am in agreement with the foreign policy outlined by you in your recent Navy Day address.

I am grateful to both you and the Secretary of State for the support you have given me and for your kind offer in requesting me to return to China as Ambassador.

In one capacity or another I have been on the perimeter of America's influence since the beginning of the war. During the war I have served in Java, Australia, New Zealand, and generally in the southwest Pacific, in Egypt, Palestine, The Lebanon, Syria, Trans-Jordan, Iraq, Saudi Arabia, Iran, Russia, Afghanistan, India, Ceylon, Burma and China. Of all of the assignments China was the most intricate and the most difficult. It is a source of gratification to me that in all my missions I had the support of President Roosevelt, Secretary Hull, Secretary Stettinius, yourself, Mr. President, and Secretary Byrnes.

In the higher echelon of our policy-making officials American objectives were nearly always clearly defined. The astonishing feature of our foreign policy is the wide discrepancy between our announced policies and our conduct of international relations. For instance, we began the war with the principles of the Atlantic Charter and democracy as our goal. Our associates in the war at that time gave eloquent lip service to the principles of democracy. We finished the war in the Far East furnishing lend-lease supplies and using all our reputation to undermine democracy and bolster imperialism and Communism. Inasmuch as I am in agreement with you and the Secretary of State on our foreign policy I think I owe it to you as well as to the country to point out the reasons for the failure of the American foreign policy in reaching the objectives for which we said we were fighting the war. I will confine my remarks in this letter to Asia, although I wish to assure you that I will be at your service in discussing frankly other phases of our international relations.

---

[3] Transmitted through the Secretary of State.

I was assigned to China at a time when statesmen were openly predicting the collapse of the National Government of the Republic of China and the disintegration of the Chinese Army. I was directed by President Roosevelt to prevent the collapse of the Government and to keep the Chinese Army in the war. From both a strategical and diplomatic viewpoint the foregoing constituted our chief objective. The next in importance was the directive to harmonize the relations between the Chinese and American military establishments and between the American Embassy in Chungking and the Chinese Government. It will readily appear that the former objective could not be accomplished without the accomplishment of the secondary objective as a condition precedent. Both of these objectives were accomplished. While these objectives had the support of the President and the Secretary of State it is no secret that the American policy in China did not have the support of all the career men in the State Department. The professional foreign service men sided with the Chinese Communist armed party and the imperialist bloc of nations whose policy it was to keep China divided against herself. Our professional diplomats continuously advised the Communists that my efforts in preventing the collapse of the National Government did not represent the policy of the United States. These same professionals openly advised the Communist armed party to decline unification of the Chinese Communist Army with the National Army unless the Chinese Communists were given control.

Despite these handicaps we did make progress toward unification of the armed forces of China. We did prevent civil war between the rival factions, at least until after I had left China. We did bring the leaders of the rival parties together for peaceful discussions. Throughout this period the chief opposition to the accomplishment of our mission came from the American career diplomats in the Embassy at Chungking and in the Chinese and Far Eastern Divisions of the State Department.

I requested the relief of the career men who were opposing the American policy in the Chinese Theater of war. These professional diplomats were returned to Washington and placed in the Chinese and Far Eastern Divisions of the State Department as my supervisors. Some of these same career men whom I relieved have been assigned as advisors to the Supreme Commander in Asia. In such positions most of them have continued to side with the Communist armed party and at times with the imperialist bloc against American policy. This, Mr. President, is an outline of one of the reasons why American foreign policy announced by the highest authority is rendered ineffective by another section of diplomatic officials.

The weakness of American foreign policy has backed us into two world wars. We had no part in shaping the conditions that brought about these two wars. There is a third world war in the making. In diplomacy today we are permitting ourselves to be sucked into a power bloc on the side of colonial imperialism against Communist imperialism. I am opposed to both. I still favor democracy and free enterprise.

Our announced policy in the first world war was to make the world safe for democracy. That slogan was elaborated for the second world war by a definite statement of principles in the Atlantic Charter and the Iran Declaration. We won both wars but in both instances we failed to establish the principles for which we alleged we were fighting. America's foreign policy officials have always been divided against themselves. Consequently, we have always been a prey to the nations that give lip service to our ideals and principles in order to obtain our material support. The war that is now in the making is not even intended to defend or establish democratic ideals. Instead of putting our weight behind the Charter of the United Nations we have been definitely supporting the imperialistic bloc. At the same time a considerable section of our State Department is endeavoring to support Communism generally as well as specifically in China.

The Hydra-headed direction and confusion of our foreign policy in Washington during the late war is chargeable to the weakness of our Foreign Service. If our Foreign Service had been capable of understanding and sympathetic effectuation of our announced war aims it would not have failed so completely to couple our logistical strength with our foreign policy to obtain commitments to the principles for which we claimed to be fighting from the nations to which we gave the strength of our productivity and manpower.

I am purposely omitting from this short paper a discussion of my negotiations with Britain and Russia for the recognition of the territorial integrity and independent sovereignty of China and the procurement from both of these nations of an agreement to support the aspirations of the Chinese people to establish for themselves a free, united, democratic government. These negotiations as you know were successful and so far as Russia is concerned was solemnized in a treaty and exchange of letters.

A democracy must live on its intelligence and its integrity and its courage. The people of a democracy should be given all the facts to enable them to form correct opinions. The discrepancy between American foreign policy as announced in the Atlantic Charter and the Iran Declaration and in your recent Navy Day address and as carried into effect may be attributed in large measure to the secrecy which has shrouded the actions of the State Department. All too frequently information concerning the conduct of our foreign relations "leaks" out to the public in distorted, garbled, or partial form. The result is that the American people have too little basic information to judge the extent to which their State Department correctly interprets and administers the foreign policies of the nation.

During the war we had to maintain secrecy to prevent giving aid to the enemy. I grant that sometimes during the war we had to be expedient. Now we should endeavor to be right. I raise this issue because I am firmly convinced that at this particular juncture in our history an informed public opinion would do much to give intelligent direction and implementation to our international objectives.

With special reference to China and the other nations where I have served in the last four years, the blessings of factual publicity would be manifold. Now that the war is over I am willing that all my reports be made public, together with the reports made by those officials in the foreign service who have differed with the promulgated American policy.

Our true position in China is misunderstood abroad because of this confusion of policy within our own Government. This situation suggests the need for a complete reorganization of our policy-making machinery beginning at the lower official levels. No international policy can succeed without loyal and intelligent implementation. Because of the confusion in our own international policy, make no mistake, Mr. President, America has been excluded economically from every part of the world controlled by colonial imperialism and Communist imperialism. America's economic strength has been used all over the world to defeat American policies and interests. This is chargeable to a weak American Foreign Service.

I wish to absolve from this general indictment some of our career men. Some of them are very admirable and well-equipped public servants who have fought in the State Department and in other countries against overwhelming odds to advance American ideals and interests.

America's economic and diplomatic policies should be coordinated. America's strength should not be allied with any predatory ideology.

America should support the amendment or revision of the San Francisco United Nations Charter to make it democratic. Our strength should be used to uphold the decisions of the United Nations rather than to support conflicting ideologies or war-making power blocs.

Respectfully,

PATRICK J. HURLEY

Annexes to Chapter IV: The Yalta Agreement and the Sino-Soviet Treaty of 1945

51

Treaty of Friendship and Alliance Between the Republic of China and the U.S.S.R., August 14, 1945 [1]

The President of the National Government of the Republic of China, and the Presidium of the Supreme Soviet of the U.S.S.R.,

Desirous of strengthening the friendly relations that have always existed between China and the U.S.S.R., through an alliance and good neighborly postwar collaboration,

Determined to assist each other in the struggle against aggression on the part of enemies of the United Nations in this world war, and to collaborate in the common war against Japan until her unconditional surrender,

Expressing their unswerving aspiration to cooperate in the cause of maintaining peace and security for the benefit of the peoples of both countries and of all the peace-loving nations,

Acting upon the principles enunciated in the joint declaration of the United Nations of January 1, 1942, in the four power Declaration signed in Moscow on October 30, 1943, and in the Charter of the International Organization of the United Nations.

Have decided to conclude the present Treaty to this effect and appointed as their plenipotentiaries:

The President of the National Government of the Republic of China;
His Excellency Dr. Wang Shih-chieh, Minister for Foreign Affairs of the Republic of China,
The Presidium of the Supreme Soviet of the U.S.S.R.;
His Excellency Mr. V. M. Molotov, the People's Commissar of Foreign Affairs of the U.S.S.R.,

Who, after exchanging their Full Powers, found in good and due form, have agreed as follows:

ARTICLE I

The High Contracting Parties undertake in association with the other United Nations to wage war against Japan until final victory is won. The High Contracting Parties undertake mutually to render to one another all necessary military and other assistance and support in this war.

ARTICLE II

The High Contracting Parties undertake not to enter into separate negotiations with Japan and not to conclude, without mutual consent, any armistice or peace

---

[1] *Department of State Bulletin*, Feb. 10, 1946, p. 201.

treaty either with the present Japanese Government or with any other government or authority set up in Japan which do not renounce all aggressive intentions.

ARTICLE III

The High Contracting Parties undertake after the termination of the war against Japan to take jointly all measures in their power to render impossible a repetition of aggression and violation of the peace by Japan.

In the event of one of the High Contracting Parties becoming involved in hostilities with Japan in consequence of an attack by the latter against the said Contracting Party, the other High Contracting Party shall at once give to the Contracting Party so involved in hostilities all the military and other support and assistance with the means in its power.

This article shall remain in force until such time as the organization "The United Nations" may on request of the two High Contracting Parties be charged with the responsibility for preventing further aggression by Japan.

ARTICLE IV

Each High Contracting Party undertakes not to conclude any alliance and not to take any part in any coalition directed against the other High Contracting Party.

ARTICLE V

The High Contracting Parties, having regard to the interests of the security and economic development of each of them, agree to work together in close and friendly collaboration after the coming of peace and to act according to the principles of mutual respect for their sovereignty and territorial integrity and of non-interference in the internal affairs of the other contracting party.

ARTICLE VI

The High Contracting Parties agree to render each other every possible economic assistance in the post-war period with a view to facilitating and accelerating reconstruction in both countries and to contributing to the cause of world prosperity.

ARTICLE VII

Nothing in this treaty shall be so construed as may affect the rights or obligations of the High Contracting Parties as members of the organization "The United Nations".

ARTICLE VIII

The present Treaty shall be ratified in the shortest possible time. The exchange of the instruments of ratification shall take place as soon as possible in Chungking.

The Treaty comes into force immediately upon its ratification and shall remain in force for a term of thirty years.

If neither of the High Contracting Parties has given notice, a year before the expiration of the term, of its desire to terminate the Treaty, it shall remain valid for an unlimited time, each of the High Contracting Parties being able to terminate its operation by giving notice to that effect one year in advance.

In faith whereof the Plenipotentiaries have signed the present Treaty and affixed their seals to it.

Done in Moscow, the Fourteenth August, 1945, corresponding to the Fourteenth day of the Eighth month of the Thirty-fourth year of the Chinese Republic, in two copies, each one in the Russian and Chinese languages, both texts being equally authoritative.

THE PLENIPOTENTIARY OF THE SUPREME SOVIET OF THE U.S.S.R.	THE PLENIPOTENTIARY OF THE PRESIDENT OF THE NATIONAL GOVERNMENT OF THE REPUBLIC OF CHINA.

52

Exchange of Notes Relating to the Treaty of Friendship and Alliance [2]

The People's Commissar for Foreign Affairs (Molotov) to the Chinese Minister for Foreign Affairs (Wang)

August 14, 1945

YOUR EXCELLENCY, With reference to the Treaty of Friendship and Alliance signed today between the Republic of China and the U.S.S.R., I have the honor to put on record the understanding between the High Contracting Parties as follows:

1. In accordance with the spirit of the aforementioned Treaty, and in order to put into effect its aims and purposes, the Government of the U. S. S. R. agrees to render to China moral support and aid in military supplies and other material resources, such support and aid to be entirely given to the National Government as the central government of China.

2. In the course of conversations regarding Dairen and Port Arthur and regarding the joint operation of the Chinese Changchun Railway, the Government of the U.S.S.R. regarded the Three Eastern Provinces as part of China and reaffirmed its respect for China's full sovereignty over the Three Eastern Provinces and recognize their territorial and administrative integrity.

3. As for the recent developments in Sinkiang the Soviet Government confirms that, as stated in Article V of the Treaty of Friendship and Alliance, it has no intention of interfering in the internal affairs of China.

If Your Excellency will be so good as to confirm that the understanding is correct as set forth in the preceding paragraphs, the present note and Your Excellency's reply thereto will constitute a part of the aforementioned Treaty of Friendship and Alliance.

I take [etc.]
V. M. MOLOTOV

The Chinese Minister for Foreign Affairs (Wang) to the People's Commissar for Foreign Affairs (Molotov)

August 14, 1945

YOUR EXCELLENCY: I have the honour to acknowledge receipt of Your Excellency's Note of today's date reading as follows:

"With reference to the Treaty of Friendship and Alliance signed today between the Republic of China and the U. S. S. R., I have the honour to put on record the understanding between the High Contracting Parties as follows:

---
[2] *Ibid.*, p. 204.

"1. In accordance with the spirit of the aforementioned Treaty, and in order to put into effect its aims and purposes, the Government of the U.S.S.R., agrees to render to China moral support and aid in military supplies and other material resources, such support and aid to be entirely given to the National Government as the central Government of China.

"2. In the course of conversations regarding Dairen and Port Arthur and regarding the joint operation of the Chinese Changchun Railway, the Government of the U.S.S.R. regarded the Three Eastern Provinces as part of China and reaffirmed its respect for China's full sovereignty over the Three Eastern Provinces and recognize their territorial and administrative integrity.

"3. As for the recent developments in Sinkiang the Soviet Government confirms that, as stated in Article V of the Treaty of Friendship and Alliance, it has no intention of interfering in the internal affairs of China.

"If Your Excellency will be so good as to confirm that the understanding is correct as set forth in the preceding paragraphs, the present note and Your Excellency's reply thereto will constitute a part of the aforementioned Treaty of Friendship and Alliance."

I have the honour to confirm that the understanding is correct as set forth above.

I avail [etc.]   WANG SHIH-CHIEH

53

Exchange of Notes on Outer Mongolia[3]

The Chinese Minister for Foreign Affairs (Wang) to the People's Commissar for Foreign Affairs (Molotov)

August 14, 1945

YOUR EXCELLENCY: In view of the desire repeatedly expressed by the people of Outer Mongolia for their independence, the Chinese Government declares that after the defeat of Japan should a plebiscite of the Outer Mongolian people confirm this desire, the Chinese Government will recognize the independence of Outer Mongolia with the existing boundary as its boundary.

The above declaration will become binding upon the ratification of the Treaty of Friendship and Alliance between the Republic of China and the U.S.S.R. signed on August 14, 1945.

I avail [etc.]   WANG SHIH-CHIEH

The People's Commissar for Foreign Affairs (Molotov) to the Chinese Minister for Foreign Affairs (Wang)

August 14, 1945

YOUR EXCELLENCY: I have the honour to acknowledge receipt of Your Excellency's Note reading as follows:

"In view of the desire repeatedly expressed by the people of Outer Mongolia for their independence, the Chinese Government declares that after the defeat of Japan should a plebiscite of the Outer Mongolian people confirm this desire, the Chinese Government will recognize the independence of Outer Mongolia with the existing boundary as its boundary.

---

[3] *Ibid.*, p. 204.

"The above declaration will become binding upon the ratification of the Treaty of Friendship and Alliance between the Republic of China and the U.S.S.R. signed on August 14, 1945."

The Soviet Government has duly taken note of the above communication of the Government of the Chinese Republic and hereby expresses its satisfaction therewith, and it further states that the Soviet Government will respect the political independence and territorial integrity of the People's Republic of Mongolia (Outer Mongolia).

I avail [etc.] V. M. MOLOTOV

54

Agreement Concerning Dairen [4]

In view of a Treaty of Friendship and Alliance having been concluded between the Republic of China and the U.S.S.R. and of the pledge by the latter that it will respect Chinese sovereignty in the control of all of Manchuria as an integral part of China; and with the object of ensuring that the U.S.S.R.'s interest in Dairen as a port of entry and exit for its goods shall be safeguarded, the Republic of China agrees:

1. To declare Dairen a free port open to the commerce and shipping of all nations.
2. The Chinese Government agrees to apportion in the mentioned port for lease to U. S. S. R. wharfs and warehouses on the basis of separate agreement.
3. The Administration in Dairen shall belong to China.

The harbor-master and deputy harbor-master will be appointed by the Chinese Eastern Railway and South Manchurian Railway in agreement with the Mayor. The harbor-master shall be a Russian national, and the deputy harbor-master shall be a Chinese national.

4. In peace time Dairen is not included in the sphere of efficacy of the naval base regulations, determined by the Agreement on Port Arthur of August 14, 1945, and shall be subject to the military supervision or control established in this zone only in case of war against Japan.
5. Goods entering the free port from abroad for through transit to Soviet territory on the Chinese Eastern and South Manchurian Railways and goods coming from Soviet territory on the said railways into the free port for export shall be free from customs duties. Such goods shall be transported in sealed cars.

Goods entering China from the free port shall pay the Chinese import duties, and goods going out of other parts of China into the free port shall pay the Chinese export duties as long as they continue to be collected.

6. The term of this Agreement shall be thirty years and this Agreement shall come into force upon its ratification.

55

Protocol to the Agreement on Dairen [5]

1. At the request of the U.S.S.R. the Chinese Government leases to the U.S.S.R. free of charge one half of all port installations and equipment. The term of

---
[4] *Ibid.*, p. 205.
[5] *Ibid.*, p. 205.

lease shall be thirty years. The remaining half of port installations and equipment shall be reserved for the use of China.

The expansion or re-equipment of the port shall be made by agreement between China and U.S.S.R.

2. It is agreed that the sections of the Chinese Changchun Railway running from Dairen to Mukden that lie within the region of the Port Arthur naval base, shall not be subject to any military supervision or control established in this region.

56

Agreement on Port Arthur [6]

In conformity with and for the implementation of the Treaty of Friendship and Alliance between the Republic of China and the U.S.S.R., the High Contracting Parties have agreed as follows:

ARTICLE I

With a view to strengthening the security of China and the U.S.S.R. against further aggression by Japan, the Government of the Republic of China agrees to the joint use by the two countries of Port Arthur as a naval base.

ARTICLE II

The precise boundary of the area provided in Article I is described in the Annex and shown in the map (Annex 1).[7]

ARTICLE III

The High Contracting Parties agree that Port Arthur, as an exclusive naval base, will be used only by Chinese and Soviet military and commercial vessels.

There shall be established a Sino-Soviet Military Commission to handle the matters of joint use of the above-mentioned naval base. The Commission shall consist of two Chinese and three Soviet representatives. The Chairman of the Commission shall be appointed by the Soviet side and the Vice Chairman shall be appointed by the Chinese side.

ARTICLE IV

The Chinese Government entrusts to the Soviet Government the defence of the naval base. The Soviet Government may erect at its own expense such installations as are necessary for the defence of the naval base.

ARTICLE V

The Civil Administration of the whole area will be Chinese. The leading posts of the Civil Administration will be appointed by the Chinese Government taking into account Soviet interests in the area.

The leading posts of the civil administration in the city of Port Arthur are appointed and dismissed by the Chinese Government in agreement with the Soviet military command.

The proposals which the Soviet military commander in that area may address to the Chinese civil administration in order to safeguard security and defence will be fulfilled by the said administration. In cases of disagreement, such cases shall

---

[6] *Ibid.*, p. 205
[7] Map not reproduced. See *ibid.*, pp. 202–203.

be submitted to the Sino-Soviet military commission for consideration and decision.

Article VI

The Government of U.S.S.R. have the right to maintain in region mentioned in Article II, their army, navy and air force and to determine their location.

Article VII

The Government of the U.S.S.R. also undertakes to establish and keep up lighthouses and other installations and signs necessary for the security of navigation of the area.

Article VIII

After the termination of this agreement all the installations and public property installed or constructed by the U.S.S.R. in the area shall revert without compensation to the Chinese Government.

Article IX

The present agreement is concluded for thirty years. It comes into force on the day of its ratification.

In faith whereof the plenipotentiaries of the High Contracting Parties have signed the present agreement and affixed thereto their seals. The present agreement is made in two copies, each in the Russian and Chinese language, both texts being authoritative.

Done in Moscow, August 14, 1945, corresponding to the 14th day of the 8th month of the 34th year of the Chinese Republic.

THE PLENIPOTENTIARY OF THE PRESIDIUM OF THE SUPREME SOVIET OF THE U.S.S.R.	THE PLENIPOTENTIARY OF THE PRESIDENT OF THE NATIONAL GOVERNMENT OF THE REPUBLIC OF CHINA.

57

Appendix to "Agreement on Port Arthur" Signed in Moscow on August 14, 1945 [8]

The territory of the area of the naval base provided for by paragraph II of the Agreement on Port Arthur is situated south of the line which begins on the west coast of Liaotung Peninsula—south of Housantaowan—and follows a general easterly direction across Shihe Station and the point of Tsoukiachutse to the east coast of the same peninsula, excluding the town of Dalny (Dairen).

All the islands situated in the waters adjoining the west side of the area on Liaotung Peninsula established by the Agreement, and south of the line passing through the points 39°00′ North latitude, 120°49′ East longitude; 39°20′ North latitude, 121°31′ East longitude, and beyond in a general northeasterly direction along the axis of the fairway leading to port Pulantien to the initial point on land, are included in the area of the naval base.

All the islands situated within the waters adjoining the eastern part of the area on Liaotung Peninsula and south of the line passing from the terminal point on land in an easterly direction towards the point 39°20′ North latitude, 123°08′ East longitude, and farther southeast through the point 39°00′ North

---

[8] *Ibid.*, p. 206.

latitude, 123°16′ East longitude, are included in the area. (See attached map, scale 1 : 500,000.)[9]

The boundary line of the district will be demarcated on the spot by a mixed Soviet-Chinese Commission. The Commission shall establish the boundary posts and, when need arises, buoys on the water, compile a detailed description of this line, enter it on a topographical map drawn to the scale of 1 : 25,000 and the water boundary on a naval map drawn to the scale of 1 : 300,000.

The time when the Commission shall start its work is subject to special agreement between the parties.

Descriptions of the boundary line of the area and the maps of this line compiled by the above Commission are subject to approval by both Governments.

W. S.   V. M.

58

Agreement Regarding Relations between the Chinese Administration and the Commander-in-Chief of the Soviet Forces After the Entry of Soviet Troops Into the "Three Eastern Provinces" of China During the Present Joint Military Operations Against Japan [10]

The President of the National Government of China and the Presidium of the Supreme Council of the Union of Soviet Socialist Republics, desirous that relations between the Chinese Administration and the Commander-in-Chief of the Soviet forces after the entry of Soviet troops into the "Three Eastern Provinces" of China during the present joint military operations against Japan should be governed by the spirit of friendship and alliance existing between the two countries, have agreed on the following:

1. After the Soviet troops enter the "Three Eastern Provinces" of China as a result of military operations, the supreme authority and responsibility in all matters relating to the prosecution of the war will be vested, in the zone of operations for the time required for the operations, in the Commander-in-Chief of the Soviet forces.

2. A Chinese National Government representative and staff will be appointed for the recovered territory, whose duties will be:

(a) To establish and direct, in accordance with the laws of China, an administration for the territory cleared of the enemy.

(b) To establish the cooperation between the Chinese armed forces, both regular and irregular, and the Soviet forces in recovered territory.

(c) To ensure the active cooperation of the Chinese administration with the Commander-in-Chief of the Soviet forces and, specifically to give the local authorities directions to this effect, being guided by the requirements and wishes of the Commander-in-Chief of the Soviet forces.

3. To ensure contact between the Commander-in-Chief of the Soviet forces and the Chinese National Government representative a Chinese military mission will be appointed to the Commander-in-Chief of the Soviet forces.

4. In the zones under the supreme authority of the Commander-in-Chief of the Soviet forces, the Chinese National Government administration for the recovered

---

[9] Map not reproduced. See *ibid.*, pp. 202–203.
[10] *Ibid.*, p. 206.

territory will maintain contact with the Commander-in-Chief of the Soviet forces through the Chinese National Government representative.

5. As soon as any part of the liberated territory ceases to be a zone of immediate military operations, the Chinese National Government will assume full authority in the direction of public affairs and will render the Commander-in-Chief of the Soviet forces every assistance and support through its civil and military bodies.

6. All persons belonging to the Soviet forces on Chinese territory will be under the jurisdiction of the Commander-in-Chief of the Soviet forces. All Chinese, whether civilian or military, will be under Chinese jurisdiction. This jurisdiction will also extend to the civilian population on Chinese territory even in the case of offenses against the Soviet armed forces, with the exception of offenses committed in the zone of military operations under the jurisdiction of the Commander-in-Chief of the Soviet forces, such cases coming under the jurisdiction of the Commander-in-Chief of the Soviet forces. In disputable cases the question will be settled by mutual agreement between the Chinese National Government representative and the Commander-in-Chief of the Soviet forces.

7. With regard to currency matters after the entry of Soviet troops into the "Three Eastern Provinces" of China, a separate agreement shall be reached.

8. The present Agreement comes into force immediately upon the ratification of the Treaty of Friendship and Alliance between China and the U. S. S. R. signed this day. The Agreement has been done in two copies, each in the Chinese and Russian languages. Both texts are equally valid.

Date_____

ON THE AUTHORIZATION OF THE
NATIONAL GOVERNMENT OF THE
REPUBLIC OF CHINA.

ON THE AUTHORIZATION OF THE GOVERNMENT OF THE UNION OF SOVIET SOCIALIST REPUBLICS.

59

Agreement Between the Republic of China and the U.S.S.R. Concerning the Chinese Changchun Railway [11]

The President of the Republic of China and the Presidium of the Supreme Council of the U.S.S.R., desiring to strengthen the friendly relations and economic bonds between the two countries on the basis of the full observation of the rights and interests of each other, have agreed as follows:

ARTICLE I

After the Japanese armed forces are driven out of the Three Eastern Provinces of China the main trunk line of the Chinese Eastern Railway and the South Manchurian Railway from Manchuli to Suifenho and from Harbin to Dairen and Port Arthur united into one railway under the name "Chinese Changchun Railway" shall be in joint ownership of the U.S.S.R. and the Republic of China and shall be operated by them jointly.

There shall be joint ownership and operation only of those lands acquired and railway auxiliary lines built by the Chinese Eastern Railway during the time of Russian and joint Sino-Soviet administration and by the South Manchurian Railway during the time of Russian administration and which are designed for direct needs of these railways as well as the subsidiary enterprises built during

---
[11] *Ibid.*, p. 207.

the said periods and directly serving these railways. All the other railway branches, subsidiary enterprises and lands shall be in the complete ownership of the Chinese Government.

The joint operation of the aforementioned railway shall be undertaken by a single management under Chinese sovereignty and as a purely commercial transportation enterprise.

Article II

The High Contracting parties agree that their joint ownership of the railway shall be in equal shares and shall not be alienable in whole or in part.

Article III

The High Contracting parties agree that for the joint operation of the said railway the Sino-Soviet Company of the Chinese Changchun Railway shall be formed. The Company shall have a Board of Directors to be composed of ten members of whom five shall be appointed by the Chinese Government and five by the Soviet Government. The Board of Directors shall be in Changchun.

Article IV

The Chinese Government shall appoint one of the Chinese Directors as President of the Board of Directors and one as the Assistant President. The Soviet Government shall appoint one of the Soviet Directors as Vice-President of the Board of Directors, and one as the Assistant Vice-President. Seven persons shall constitute a quorum. When questions are decided by the Board, the vote of the President of the Board of Directors shall be counted as two votes.

Questions on which the Board of Directors cannot reach an agreement shall be submitted to the Governments of the Contracting Parties for consideration and settlement in an equitable and friendly spirit.

Article V

The Company shall establish a Board of Auditors which shall be composed of six members of whom three are appointed by the Chinese Government and three appointed by the Soviet Government. The Chairman of the Board of Auditors shall be elected from among the Soviet Auditors, and Vice-Chairman from among the Chinese auditors. When questions are decided by the Board the vote of the Chairman shall be counted as two votes. Five persons shall constitute a quorum.

Article VI

For the administration of current affairs the Board of Directors shall appoint a manager of the Chinese Changchun Railway from among Soviet citizens and one assistant manager from among Chinese citizens.

Article VII

The Board of Auditors shall appoint a General-Comptroller from among Chinese citizens, and an assistant General Comptroller from among Soviet citizens.

Article VIII

The Chiefs and Assistant Chiefs of the various departments, Chiefs of sections, station masters at important stations of the railway shall be appointed by the Board of Directors. The Manager of the Railway has right to recommend candidates for the above-mentioned posts. Individual members of the Board of Directors may also recommend such candidates in agreement with the Manager. If the Chief of a department is a national of China, the Assistant Chief shall be a national of the Soviet Union, and vice versa. The appointment of the Chiefs and assistant chiefs of departments and Chiefs of sections and station masters shall be made in accordance with the principle of equal representation between the nationals of China and nationals of the Soviet Union.

Article IX

The Chinese Government will bear the responsibility for the protection of the said Railway.

The Chinese Government will also organize and supervise the railway guards who shall protect the railway buildings, installations and other properties and freight from destruction, loss and robbery, and shall maintain the normal order on the railway. As regards the duties of the police in execution of this Article, they will be determined by the Chinese Government in consultation with the Soviet Government.

Article X

Only during the time war against Japan the railway may be used for the transportation of Soviet troops. The Soviet Government has the right to transport by the above-mentioned railway for transit purpose military goods in sealed cars without customs inspection. The guarding of such military goods shall be undertaken by the railroad police and the Soviet Union shall not send any armed escort.

Article XI

Goods for through transit and transported by the Chinese Changchun Railway from Manchuli to Suifenho or vice versa and also from Soviet territory to the ports of Dairen and Port Arthur or vice versa shall be free from Chinese Customs duties or any other taxes and dues, but on entering Chinese territory such goods shall be subject to Chinese Customs inspection and verification.

Article XII

The Chinese Government shall ensure, on the basis of a separate agreement, that the supply of coal for the operation of the railway will be fully secured.

Article XIII

The railway shall pay taxes to the Government of the Republic of China the same as are paid by the Chinese state railways.

Article XIV

Both Contracting Parties agree to provide the Board of Directors of the Chinese Changchun Railway with working capital the amount of which will be determined by the Statute of the Railway.

Profits and losses and exploitation of the railway shall be equally divided between the Parties.

Article XV

For the working out in Chungking of the Statutes of joint operation of the railway the High Contracting Parties undertake within one month of the signing of the present Agreement, to appoint their representatives—three representatives from each Party. The Statute shall be worked out within two months and reported to the two Governments for their approval.

Article XVI

The determination, in accordance with the provisions in Article I, of the properties to be included in the joint ownership and operations of the railway by China and U.S.S.R. shall be made by a Commission to be composed of three representatives each of the two Governments. The Commission shall be constituted in Chungking within one month after the signing of the present Agreement and shall terminate its work within three months after the joint operation of the railway shall have begun.

The decision of the Commission shall be reported to the two Governments for their approval.

Article XVII

The term of this present Agreement shall be thirty years. After the expiration of the term of the present Agreement, the Chinese Changchun Railway with all its properties shall be transferred without compensation to the ownership of the Republic of China.

Article XVIII

The present Agreement shall come into force from the date of its ratification.

Done in Moscow, August 14, 1945, corresponding to the 14th day of the 8th month of the 34th year of the Chinese Republic, in two copies, each in the Russian and Chinese languages, both texts being equally authoritative.

THE PLENIPOTENTIARY OF THE PRESIDIUM OF THE SUPREME SOVIET OF THE U.S.S.R.	THE PLENIPOTENTIARY OF THE PRESIDENT OF THE NATIONAL GOVERNMENT OF THE REPUBLIC OF CHINA.

60[12]

Red Army "War Booty" Removals From Manchuria

60 (a)

State Department notes concerning Soviet removals

Secretary of State James F. Byrnes on February 9, 1946, instructed the American Embassies in Chungking and Moscow to present the following views to the Chinese Government and the Government of the U. S. S. R. respectively:[13]

"Current reports of discussions between officials of the Chinese Government and the Russian Government with regard to the disposition and control of industrial enterprises in Manchuria give concern to this Government.

"The Sino-Soviet Treaty and agreements signed August 14, 1945, provide for joint Sino-Soviet control over certain trunk railways in Manchuria, but these agreements exclude reference to any similar control over industrial enterprise in Manchuria. It is the understanding of the United States Government, which was kept informed of the course of negotiations which led up to the agreements, that exclusive Sino-Soviet governmental control over Manchurian enterprise would be limited to the railways dealt with in the aforesaid agreements. It is

---

[12] Parts A–C of this annex are extracts from a "Report On Japanese Assets in Manchuria to the President of the United States, July, 1946," by Edwin W. Pauley, Personal Representative of the President on Reparations.

[13] See also *Department of State Bulletin* of Mar. 17, 1946, p. 448.

therefore disturbing to this Government to receive reports that discussions are under way which might result in the establishment of exclusive Sino-Soviet control over industrial enterprises in Manchuria. Under present conditions, when free access to Manchuria is not open to nationals of other powers and equality of opporturnity in seeking participation in the economic development of Manchuria is denied Americans and other Allied nationals, it is felt that negotiation of agreements between the Chinese and Russian governments with regard to industries in Manchuria would be contrary to the principle of the Open Door, would constitute clear discrimination against Americans who might wish an opportunity to participate in the development of Manchurian industry and might place American commercial interests at a distinct disadvantage in establishing future trade relations with Manchuria.

"Directly related to this matter of the industries in Manchuria is the matter of reparations policy for Japan because the major portion of the industries of Manchuria were Japanese-owned prior to the defeat of Japan. This Government considers that the ultimate disposition of Japanese external assets, such as the industries in Manchuria, is a matter of common interest and concern to those Allies who bore the major burden in defeating Japan. This Government is now preparing a general policy outline for consideration by the concerned Governments with regard to Japanese reparations. It will be suggested that an inter-Allied Reparations Commission for Japan be established, and that one of the primary functions of this Commission will be the final allocation of Japanese external assets among the various claimant nations. It would seem, therefore, most inappropriate at this juncture for any final disposition to be made of Japanese external assets in Manchuria either by removal from Manchuria of such industrial assets as 'war booty' or by agreement between the Russian and Chinese Governments for the control of ownership of those assets.

"The Government of the United States desires to be cooperative with the Chinese and Soviet Governments in seeking a solution of the problems outlined above and it hopes that the other two Governments are animated by a similarly cooperative spirit. It would therefore appreciate being informed of any discussions which the two Governments may be having or may plan to have or any action they may have taken, in regard to the disposition or control of industrial enterprises in Manchuria and we would welcome full and frank discussion of the general problems."

The Secretary of State today [14] announced that he had received a reply from the Chinese Foreign Office, which reads in part:

"The Soviet Government declared in a memorandum addressed to Chinese Government on January 21, 1946 that all Japanese enterprises in the Chinese northeastern provinces which had rendered services to the Japanese Army were regarded by Soviet Union as war booty of Soviet forces. The Chinese Government considers this claim of Soviet Government as far exceeding the scope of war booty as generally recognized by international law and international usage and for this reason the two governments have not been able to reach a unanimity of views of fundamental principles involved.

"In another memorandum presented to officials of the Generalissimo's Headquarters in Changchun the Soviet Government declared that it proposed to hand over to China a part of the Japanese enterprises which Soviet Union regarded as war booty while remaining enterprises (including specified coal mines, power

---

[14] Mar. 5, 1946; see also *ibid.*

plants, iron and steel industries, chemical industries and cement industries) were to be jointly operated by China and Soviet Union. Chinese Government on its part has found it impossible to agree to this Soviet proposal because it goes beyond provisions of the Sino-Soviet agreements of August 14, 1945 and is contrary to the aforesaid stand of Chinese Government regarding Japanese properties and enterprises in China."

60 (b)

The Personal Representative of the President on Reparations (Pauley) to President Truman

WASHINGTON, NOVEMBER *12, 1946*

DEAR MR. PRESIDENT: Under your instructions to me contained in your letter of April 27, 1945, and subsequent verbal orders you have issued to me, I present to you a report on Japanese assets in Manchuria.

This is a factual report based primarily on the first-hand observations and consultations with informed persons by myself and my Mission in Manchuria in June and July. In addition studies were made and appropriate personnel consulted in Washington and Tokyo prior to the arrival of our Mission in Manchuria.

It would not have been possible to carry through this assignment without the aid and assistance which was received from the Secretary of State and the Secretaries of the War and Navy Departments, and especially from General Douglas MacArthur and General George C. Marshall in the Orient. The Chinese National Government was most helpful in facilitating the activities of my Mission throughout areas under its control. In the Communist-held areas in North Manchuria, Chinese Communist and Soviet Railway officials were also of help.

Sincerely yours,

EDWIN W. PAULEY

60 (c)

General Summary of "Report on Japanese Assets in Manchuria"

A. SCOPE

The objectives of the 1946 Pauley Mission in Manchuria were: to survey Japanese assets subject to reparations; to ascertain the present productive capacity of industry; to estimate what immediate reparations removals from Japan could be utilized to improve or rehabilitate that industry; and to prove or disprove reports that crippling removals had been made from that area.

The Mission was organized in Washington in April 1946 pursuant to instructions from the President. It contained well-known American engineers specializing in various fields of industry. On May 4, 1946, the Mission departed from Washington for the Far East. After a short stay in Tokyo where the Mission was augmented by a number of industrial specialists from General MacArthur's headquarters, the group departed for Seoul for a survey of Korea. A base was established in Mukden, Manchuria, on May 27, 1946 and from there inspection trips were made to the various important industrial and mining centers. Among these were Mukden, Fushun, Liaoyang, Anshan, Penchihu, Kungyuan, Chinchow, Chinhsi, Peipiao, Fouhsin, Hulutao, Kaiyuan, Ssupingchieh, Hsian, Changchun, Kirin, Harbin and Mutanchiang. Dairen, the finest seaport in Manchuria, and an important industrial center, was not reached because authority for the visit could not be secured from the Soviet Government or local authorities. Antung, another important point was not visited because Chinese Communists refused permission. The work of the Mission was greatly facilitated by the wholehearted cooperation of the Chinese National Government and of all United States Agencies in the Far East. Chinese Communists were of assistance in the visits in territory held by them in *Northern* Manchuria. The Mission left China on 15 July 1946 and returned to Washington on 21 July 1946.

The principal sources of data upon which this report is based are the following:

a. In Washington: Conferences with and studies made by appropriate Sections of the State, War, Navy and Commerce Departments, Office of Strategic Services, Foreign Economic Administration and other governmental agencies.

b. In Tokyo: Conferences with and studies made by agencies of Supreme Allied Commander. Interviews with Japanese responsible for the management of Manchurian industry and study of Japanese records.

c. In Manchuria: Inspection of industrial plants in the centers mentioned. On-the-spot interviews with persons who were present before, during and after the Soviet occupation were most fruitful. These included Chinese, Japanese, American and European Nationals. At the time of the survey many Japanese industrial executives had not yet been repatriated, so that many documents such as diaries and production records were available in Manchuria.

It is recognized that in the interviews with individuals, the Mission was dealing with hearsay evidence and that some of the information received was biased and exaggerated. Nevertheless, by comparing data from the different sources and balancing it against observed conditions, it is believed that an accurate picture was evolved and that this report is substantially accurate.

B. BACKGROUND

United States policy in the postwar Far East was predicated upon the establishment of China as a strong, stable, united nation, with a basic economic self-sufficiency, so that nation could take its proper part in the development of a peaceful Asiatic economy. During the years before and after Pearl Harbor the Japanese had created in Manchuria a tremendous industrial structure which was definitely tributary to the economy of Japan. Had this structure remained as intact as it was on the date of Soviet occupancy and had China remained peaceful, the Manchurian industrial complex could have readily been integrated with China's growing economy and so greatly accelerated the overall Chinese industrial development. The large capacities in basic industries in Manchuria would have made possible a rapid absorption by China of further processing equipment removed from Japan as reparations. At the same time this action would have lopped off from Japan one of the most important sources of strength in the Japanese war potential. It was presumed that China could fill at least partially, the economic vacuum resulting from the Japanese defeat and the consequent imposed reduction of Japan's productive capacity to a peacetime level. However, the damage which Manchurian industry has sustained since V-J Day has set back China's industrial progress for a generation and has thus materially delayed the implementation of announced U.S. policy.

Japan's interest in the Asiatic Mainland has been of long standing. The clash of Russian and Japanese interests there, resulted in the Russo-Japanese

War in 1904, and the acquisition by Japan of Russian concessions in South Manchuria. With the establishment of the South Manchurian Railway in 1906, Japan's exploitation of Manchuria took definite form. The railroad expanded into many industrial enterprises which furnished a wedge for further Japanese penetration on the continent. With the seizure of Manchuria from China by the Kwantung Army in 1931 and the creation of the Puppet State of Manchukuo, the exploitation was tremendously accelerated.

Impelling motives in Japan's development of Manchuria stemmed primarily from two sources. One, the ultra patriots including the military clique, the Black Dragon Society, and all dreamers of a Pan-Asiatic hegemony under Japanese domination, found in the conquest and exploitation of Manchuria an essential step in the march to empire. The Japanese Kwantung Army played no small part in advancing the aims of the military clique. The other source, the Zaibatsu (ruling commercial combines) saw in Manchuria an opportunity for an enormous source of profit. The Japanese Government and the puppet Manchukuo Government assisted the Zaibatsu in their exploitation with preferential treatment and subsidies. There was no altruism in these actions. Japan took care that management and technical skills remained in Japanese hands, using the local population primarily as a source of cheap labor.

Manchuria is a relatively rich country. It abounds in many natural resources which exist much more sparsely in the remainder of Asia. It is one of the few areas of great size which has consistently produced agricultural surpluses. Manchuria was fortunate in that the Japanese in their industrial development there provided a far greater capacity in finished products than in any other conquered country. It was Japan's apparent intention to make Manchuria industrially an integral part of the Japanese Empire and a source of economic strength for further military conquest. This is indicated by the fact that a great deal of construction and development of industrial and power facilities were still going on at the end of the war. From 1932 to 1944 coal production was more than doubled and the output of pig iron and iron ore was more than tripled.

The best estimate of the total of Japanese investments in Manchuria as of June 1945 is ¥11,000,000,000. In arriving at this estimate, figures cited by the Chinese Northeast Economic Commission, the British Ministry of Economic Warfare, the U.S. Foreign Economic Administration, and Japanese sources were also consulted.

The defeat of Japan caused the disruption of the production centers and trade channels built up by Japan in its empire-building and conquests, thus upsetting the entire economic structure of the Far East. U.S. policy is now directed toward the establishment of an economy that will promote a lasting peace in the Far East and to prevent the resurgence of Japanese economic domination.

U.S. policy has long held that all Japanese assets whether situated in Japan proper or in other areas were subject to claim as allied reparations. Japanese assets in conquered areas such as the Philippines, China, including Manchuria, and Korea, were to be taken from Japanese ownership and control and were to be operated for the benefit of the countries where the physical assets exist. Under what conditions full and complete title to these assets is to be vested in the local governments and under what conditions the ex-Japanese industrial plants are to be considered as part of the overall reparation allocation, is still under discussion and awaiting allied agreement. It was considered that this primary step was necessary in order to strengthen the economies of the countries which had been victims of Japanese aggression and further to keep the facilities operating in order to prevent loss of needed production and safeguard the livelihood of the local population.

The next step needed is the realignment of production areas and trade channels in the Far East so as to secure a properly balanced regional economy that can be both productive and profitable; an economy that does not have to rely upon subsidies, confiscation, and oppression to maintain itself. The United States reparations plan is aimed at achieving these two important steps: to turn over to local non-enemy governments control of the Japanese assets situated in those countries; and, to transfer surplus capacity from Japan to regions where it can best be used to process the natural resources so as to satisfy the needs of the Far East. In the steel industry, for example, where Japan has a much larger capacity than is needed for her normal peace requirements, the U.S. policy would remove this surplus capacity and place it near sources of iron ore and coking coal. Such areas can be found in **Manchuria, China proper, and the Philippines.**

C. FINDINGS

The difference in condition of the Manchurian industrial plant between Japanese surrender and the dates the Pauley Mission made its survey is appalling, as will be shown in the remainder of this report. How much of the wrecked condition is a direct result of Soviet removals, and how much may be ascribed to pillage, civil war, and other indirect consequences of the Soviet occupation cannot be accurately determined. In any case, the Soviet government must bear the major responsibility.

Soviet forces entered Manchuria on 9 August 1945. Japanese resistance was confined to Northern Manchuria and within a week this ended. Southern Manchuria, which contained over eighty percent of Manchurian industry, was taken practically unopposed and with little if any damage. There was ample opportunity for the orderly occupation of the entire area.

Japan was preparing to surrender prior to the Soviet entry into the Japanese war. The rolling up of the Southwest Pacific front, the rapid penetration of the Pacific defenses, and the powerful blows struck against the Japanese homeland forced Japan to seek means for halting the conflict. A partial chronology of important events from June 15, 1944, taken from General MacArthur's reports and other official sources shows the following:

Landings on Saipan	June 15, 1944
Landings on Guam	July 21
Landings on Leyte	October 20
First B-29 raids on Japan from Saipan	November 24
Landings on Luzon	January 9, 1945
U. S. Navy 3rd Fleet struck Tokyo and Nagoya-Kobe areas	February 16-17
Landings on Okinawa	April 1
Abrogation by Soviets of Treaty of Neutrality with Japan	April 5
Naval operations against Japanese homeland from North Hokkaido to Tokyo	July 14-17
Potsdam Ultimatum issued to the Japanese Government	July 27
First atomic bomb dropped on Hiroshima	August 6
Soviets declare war on Japan and invade Manchuria	*August 9*
World receives news of Japan's acceptance of Potsdam Ultimatum	*August 10*
General MacArthur acknowledges receipt of news of Japanese acceptance	August 11
Sino-Soviet Treaty signed at Moscow	August 14
President Truman announces unconditional surrender of Japan	August 15
Japanese Commander in Manchuria appeals by radio to Soviets to cease attacks	August 16
Unopposed Soviet air landing at Mukden	August 18, 1945
Japanese delegation arrives in Manila to receive orders	August 19
Unopposed Soviet air landings at Kirin and Changchun	August 20
Eighth Army advance party landed at Atsugi Airdrome, Tokyo	August 28
General MacArthur arrives at Atsugi	August 30
Formal signing of surrender terms in Tokyo Bay	September 2

Upon their arrival in the industrial areas of Manchuria, the Soviets began a systematic confiscation of food and other stockpiles and in early September started the selective removal of industrial machinery. It is apparent that they planned to complete these removals by 3 December 1945, the date originally set for the withdrawal of all Soviet military forces from Manchuria.

The term "stripping" as it has been used in the press in connection with removals from Manchuria may be confusing. The Soviets did not take everything. They concentrated on certain categories of supplies, machinery and equipment. In addition to taking stockpiles and certain complete industrial installations, the Soviets took by far the larger part of all functioning power generating and transforming equipment, electric motors, experimental plants, laboratories, and hospitals. In machine tools, they took only the newest and best, leaving antiquated tools behind. In the old Mukden Arsenal, for example, about one-third of the tools were taken, while in the new arsenal, virtually everything was taken or demolished.

Not only were buildings and structures damaged by the removal of the equipment, but the taking of some key equipment, such as generators and pumps from mines resulted in the loss of current production, and in irreparable damage to the mines by flooding. The removal of power facilities not only halted all current industrial production, but also made it impossible to maintain and protect the plants themselves. Water works and sewage facilities in the large cities were made inoperable because of lack of power.

After the removals, the Soviet forces permitted and even encouraged Chinese mobs to pillage, taking official movies of the process in some instances. Apparently the mobs were in search of objects of salable value and of wood for fuel to burn during the bitter Manchurian winter. The fuel problem was, of course, enormously intensified by the stoppage of a large part of coal production because of Soviet removals.

By far the greatest part of the damage to the Manchurian industrial complex occurred during the Soviet occupation and was primarily due to Soviet removals of equipment, and to Soviet failure to preserve order. After the Soviet withdrawal, Chinese Communist action resulted in further damage to some of the installations. It is a sad commentary that the small amount of benefit received by the Soviet Government in its removals from Manchuria could have been readily supplied by reparations removals from Japan proper at a much smaller cost to the world.

The Soviet forces also confiscated approximately three million U. S. dollars worth of gold bullion stocks and over a half billion Manchurian yuan from Manchukuo banks. They also circulated nearly ten billion yuan in occupational currency, almost doubling the total Manchurian note issue. In addition to the removals, mentioned above, occupational currency was used to purchase factories and properties and some privately-owned merchandise and materials.

It is difficult to ascertain in Manchuria the real reasons behind the Soviet actions there. The excuse that the articles removed were in the nature of "war booty" and were desperately needed to replace damage caused by the German invasion at home, does not fully cover the situation. As for reparations, the Soviet military effort in Manchuria which lasted only a few days is minute when compared with the long, tremendous and costly operations in the Pacific. Therefore, the Soviet Government would not be entitled to substantial reparations from Japanese-owned assets merely on the basis of their operations in this area. Obviously Japanese assets in Manchuria did not belong solely to the Soviet Government. Other nations too are logical claimants. In the allied reparations discussions at Moscow, Potsdam and Paris in 1945, the allies expressed as a principle that the greatest economic utility would result if the industrial equipment in Manchuria were left intact there, in the locations for which these items were specifically designed. Moving this equipment has destroyed a large part of its original value and the installations from which this equipment was removed have in many cases become total losses.

It can also be pointed out that there are now in the occupied zones of Germany (other than the Soviet occupied zone) reparations items which under the terms of the Potsdam Agreement were destined to be delivered to the Soviets. The nations occupying these zones are also entitled to Japanese reparations and so have a legitimate claim on the Japanese assets removed from Manchuria by the Soviet Government. Thus Soviet claims on German reparations in occupied zones could be counterbalanced by claims by other nations on the Manchurian removals. However this would require revision of the entire global reparations program.

Soviet actions in Manchuria are high-lighted by the entirely different policy followed in Korea where there were practically no capital removals or destruction of industry. In Manchuria the confiscation and removal of food stocks, the destruction attendant upon and following the removals of machinery, the almost complete halting of productive effort with no regard for the harmful effects upon the Chinese population, all indicate that there were long range strategic reasons behind the Soviet actions. The chaos caused by the Soviets has produced a condition of instability both politically and economically which will take a long time to correct. It left a populace hungry, cold, and full of unrest.

It is generally agreed that China's first economic need is communications, principally railways, transport, and domestic shipping. Less than 10,000 miles of railway is in existence in all of China exclusive of Manchuria and less than half of that is now operable. Manchuria with its abundant natural resources and industrial plant would have been the logical point to begin the rehabilitation of China's transport. If Manchurian industry had been left intact it could also have produced the steel, machinery and consumer goods so badly needed for restoration and for new construction in China.

China's continuing internal strife is a major factor in retarding her economic recovery. But even this cannot minimize the powerful set-back which the destruction of the Manchurian industrial plant has been to Manchuria, to China, and to the Far Eastern World.

D. CONCLUSIONS

The situation in Manchuria today is far from promising. The internal struggle continues intermittently. Dairen, by far the best port, has been practically sealed off by the Soviets for their own exclusive use, despite the fact that under the terms of the Sino-Soviet Treaty of August 14, 1945, Dairen is to be an open port and the Soviets are entitled to use only part of the port facilities. Railway communications to the few remaining secondary ports are under constant harassment by Chinese Communists. Thus, even if Manchurian industry were working full blast, it would be most difficult if not impossible to move any large quantity of finished products to China proper. It would be just as difficult to move into Manchuria the equipment necessary to rehabilitate industry.

Little can be done in the way of rehabilitation in China in the areas where fighting is going on or where the threat of armed action is present. This, however, should not delay the preparation of plans so that when peaceful conditions are resumed and communications restored, a rapid and orderly process of rehabilitation of the plants essential to primary needs of the inhabitants can begin. The natural resources are there. In restoring Manchuria's industrial complex, however, it must be remembered that Manchuria is practically surrounded by territory either wholly or partially under direct Soviet control. Manchuria will thus be vulnerable to further Soviet penetration.

In the meantime no effort should be spared in the industrial strengthening of the peaceful areas of other parts of China. China's urgent needs are manifold, but the prime need is for steel, for railroads, shipping, construction and consumer goods. One important steel producing area lies on the Yangtze River, near Hankow. There are others. These must be surveyed with a view to the immediate transfer to those areas as reparations from Japan, of such equipment as can be efficiently utilized. Similar recommendations have been made with respect to the Philippine Islands. The Chinese Government was urged to take action along these lines during Ambassador Pauley's conferences in Nanking on 25 May 1946. The necessity for immediate transfer of critically needed power equipment for the coal mining areas of Manchuria from Japan was also pointed out in a letter from Mr. Pauley to General MacArthur dated 20 June 1946. Training of additional Chinese personnel in engineering and management of the industrial equipment is also essential.

Manchuria's power installations are first priority in rehabilitation. This includes hydro-electric stations as well as thermal power plants at the coal mines. If sufficient power generating equipment can be quickly transferred from Japan, there is a good chance of salvaging one or two important coal mines that are now flooded or in grave danger of flooding.

Another possible and readily available but limited source of power is what remains of the hydro-electric development now in operation at Tafengmen near Kirin and which is furnishing power to Harbin and Changchun. Transmission lines to the South have been cut by Chinese Communists who will not permit repair. Until peace between the Communists and Chinese Nationalists is restored, this badly needed power is being wasted. Restoration of electric power in Manchuria will go far toward alleviating the immediate needs of the populace.

Given the best of conditions, China's rehabilitation is a matter of many years. In the meantime the stability of the entire Far East is in a large measure dependent upon satisfying the urgent needs of the populations of the various countries lying there. They all need materials and machines for reconstruction. Failure to supply these needs will result in continued unrest and instability.

Annexes to Chapter V: The Mission of General George C. Marshall, 1945–1947

61

President Truman to the Special Representative of the President to China (Marshall)

WASHINGTON, *December 15, 1945*

MY DEAR GENERAL MARSHALL: On the eve of your departure for China I want to repeat to you my appreciation of your willingness to undertake this difficult mission.

I have the utmost confidence in your ability to handle the task before you but, to guide you in so far as you may find it helpful, I will give you some of the thoughts, ideas, and objectives which Secretary Byrnes and I have in mind with regard to your mission.

I attach several documents which I desire should be considered as part of this letter. One is a statement of U. S. policy towards China [1] which was, I understand, prepared after consultation with you and with officials of the Department. The second is a memorandum from the Secretary of State to the War Department in regard to China. And the third is a copy of my press release on policy in China.[2] I understand that these documents have been shown to you and received your approval.

The fact that I have asked you to go to China is the clearest evidence of my very real concern with regard to the situation there. Secretary Byrnes and I are both anxious that the unification of China by peaceful, democratic methods be achieved as soon as possible. It is my desire that you, as my Special Representative, bring to bear in an appropriate and practicable manner the influence of the United States to this end.

Specifically, I desire that you endeavor to persuade the Chinese Government to call a national conference of representatives of the major political elements to bring about the unification of China and, concurrently, to effect a cessation of hostilities, particularly in north China.

It is my understanding that there is now in session in Chungking a Peoples' Consultative Council made up of representatives of the various political elements, including the Chinese Communists. The meeting of this Council should furnish you with a convenient opportunity for discussions with the various political leaders.

---

[1] Not printed; it did not differ substantially from the final text, for which see annex 62.
[2] See annex 62.

Upon the success of your efforts, as outlined above, will depend largely, of course, the success of our plans for evacuating Japanese troops from China, particularly north China, and for the subsequent withdrawal of our own armed forces from China. I am particularly desirous that both be accomplished as soon as possible.

In your conversations with Chiang Kai-shek and other Chinese leaders you are authorized to speak with the utmost frankness. Particularly, you may state, in connection with the Chinese desire for credits, technical assistance in the economic field, and military assistance (I have in mind the proposed U. S. military advisory group which I have approved in principle), that a China disunited and torn by civil strife could not be considered realistically as a proper place for American assistance along the lines enumerated.

I am anxious that you keep Secretary Byrnes and me currently informed of the progress of your negotiations and of obstacles you may encounter. You will have our full support and we shall endeavor at all times to be as helpful to you as possible.

Sincerely yours,

HARRY TRUMAN

[Enclosure]

MEMORANDUM BY SECRETARY BYRNES

[WASHINGTON,] *December 9, 1945*

For the War Department

The President and the Secretary of State are both anxious that the unification of China by peaceful democratic methods be achieved as soon as possible.

At a public hearing before the Foreign Relations Committee of the Senate on December 7, the Secretary of State said:

"During the war the immediate goal of the United States in China was to promote a military union of the several political factions in order to bring their combined power to bear upon our common enemy, Japan. Our longer-range goal, then as now, and a goal of at least equal importance, is the development of a strong, united, and democratic China.

"To achieve this longer-range goal, it is essential that the Central Government of China as well as the various dissident elements approach the settlement of their differences with a genuine willingness to compromise. We believe, as we have long believed and consistently demonstrated, that the government of Generalissimo Chiang Kai-shek affords the most satisfactory base for a developing democracy. But we also believe that it must be broadened to include the representatives of those large and well organized groups who are now without any voice in the government of China.

"This problem is not an easy one. It requires tact and discretion, patience and restraint. It will not be solved by the Chinese leaders themselves. To the extent that our influence is a factor, success will depend upon our capacity to exercise that influence in the light of shifting conditions in such a way as to encourage concessions by the Central Government, by the so-called Communists, and by the other factions."

The President has asked General Marshall to go to China as his Special Representative for the purpose of bringing to bear in an appropriate and practicable manner the influence of the United States for the achievement of the ends set forth above. Specifically, General Marshall will endeavor to influence the Chinese Government to call a national conference of representatives of the major political elements to bring about the unification of China and, concurrently, effect a cessation of hostilities, particularly in north China.

In response to General Wedemeyer's recent messages, the State Department requests the War Department to arrange for directions to him stipulating that:

(1) He may put into effect the arrangements to assist the Chinese National Government in transporting Chinese troops to Manchurian ports, including the logistical support of such troops;

(2) He may also proceed to put into effect the stepped-up arrangements for the evacuation of Japanese troops from the China theater;

(3) Pending the outcome of General Marshall's discussions with Chinese leaders in Chungking for the purpose of arranging a national conference of representatives of the major political elements and for a cessation of hostilities, further transportation of Chinese troops to north China, except as north China ports may be necessary for the movement of troops and supplies into Manchuria, will be held in abeyance;

(4) Arrangements for transportation of Chinese troops into north China may be immediately perfected, but not communicated to the Chinese Government. Such arrangements will be executed when General Marshall determines either (a) that the movement of Chinese troops to north China can be carried out consistently with his negotiations, or (b) that the negotiations between the Chinese groups have failed or show no prospect of success and that the circumstances are such as to make the movement necessary to effectuate the surrender terms and to secure the long-term interests of the United States in the maintenance of international peace.

62

Statement by President Truman on United States Policy Toward China, December 15, 1945 [3]

The Government of the United States holds that peace and prosperity of the world in this new and unexplored era ahead depend upon the ability of the sovereign nations to combine for collective security in the United Nations organization.

It is the firm belief of this Government that a strong, united and democratic China is of the utmost importance to the success of this United Nations organization and for world peace. A China disorganized and divided either by foreign aggression, such as that undertaken by the Japanese, or by violent internal strife, is an undermining influence to world stability and peace, now and in the future. The United States Government has long subscribed to the principle that the management of internal affairs is the responsibility of the peoples of the sovereign nations. Events of this century, however, would indicate that a breach of peace anywhere in the world threatens the peace of the entire world. It is thus in the most vital interest of the United States and all the United Nations that the people of China overlook no opportunity to adjust their internal differences promptly by means of peaceful negotiation.

The Government of the United States believes it essential:

(1) That a cessation of hostilities be arranged between the armies of the National Government and the Chinese Communists and other dissident Chinese

---

[3] *Department of State Bulletin,* Dec. 16, 1945, p. 945.

armed forces for the purpose of completing the return of all China to effective Chinese control, including the immediate evacuation of the Japanese forces.

(2) That a national conference of representatives of major political elements be arranged to develop an early solution to the present internal strife—a solution which will bring about the unification of China.

The United States and the other United Nations have recognized the present National Government of the Republic of China as the only legal government in China. It is the proper instrument to achieve the objective of a unified China.

The United States and the United Kingdom by the Cairo Declaration in 1943 and the Union of Soviet Socialist Republics by adhering to the Potsdam Declaration of last July and by the Sino-Soviet Treaty and Agreements of August 1945, are all committed to the liberation of China, including the return of Manchuria to Chinese control. These agreements were made with the National Government of the Republic of China.

In continuation of the constant and close collaboration with the National Government of the Republic of China in the prosecution of this war, in consonance with the Potsdam Declaration, and to remove possibility of Japanese influence remaining in China, the United States has assumed a definite obligation in the disarmament and evacuation of the Japanese troops. Accordingly the United States has been assisting and will continue to assist the National Government of the Republic of China in effecting the disarmament and evacuation of Japanese troops in the liberated areas. The United States Marines are in North China for that purpose.

The United States recognizes and will continue to recognize the National Government of China and cooperate with it in international affairs and specifically in eliminating Japanese influence from China. The United States is convinced that a prompt arrangement for a cessation of hostilities is essential to the effective achievement of this end. United States support will not extend to United States military intervention to influence the course of any Chinese internal strife.

The United States has already been compelled to pay a great price to restore the peace which was first broken by Japanese aggression in Manchuria. The maintenance of peace in the Pacific may be jeopardized, if not frustrated, unless Japanese influence in China is wholly removed and unless China takes her place as a unified, democratic and peaceful nation. This is the purpose of the maintenance for the time being of United States military and naval forces in China.

The United States is cognizant that the present National Government of China is a "one-party government" and believes that peace, unity and democratic reform in China will be furthered if the basis of this Government is broadened to include other political elements in the country. Hence, the United States strongly advocates that the national conference of representatives of major political elements in the country agree upon arrangements which would give those elements a fair and effective representation in the Chinese National Government. It is recognized that this would require modification of the one-party "political tutelage" established as an interim arrangement in the progress of the nation toward democracy by the father of the Chinese Republic, Doctor Sun Yat-sen.

The existence of autonomous armies such as that of the Communist army is inconsistent with, and actually makes impossible, political unity in China. With the institution of a broadly representative government, autonomous armies should be eliminated as such and all armed forces in China integrated effectively into the Chinese National Army.

In line with its often expressed views regarding self-determination, the United States Government considers that the detailed steps necessary to the achievement of political unity in China must be worked out by the Chinese themselves and that intervention by any foreign government in these matters would be inappropriate. The United States Government feels, however, that China has a clear responsibility to the other United Nations to eliminate armed conflict within its territory as constituting a threat to world stability and peace—a responsibility which is shared by the National Government and all Chinese political and military groups.

As China moves toward peace and unity along the lines described above, the United States would be prepared to assist the National Government in every reasonable way to rehabilitate the country, improve the agrarian and industrial economy, and establish a military organization capable of discharging China's national and international responsibilities for the maintenance of peace and order. In furtherance of such assistance, it would be prepared to give favorable consideration to Chinese requests for credits and loans under reasonable conditions for projects which would contribute toward the development of a healthy economy throughout China and healthy trade relations between China and the United States.

63

Press Release on Order for Cessation of Hostilities, January 10, 1946

We, General Chang Chun, Representative of the National Government, and General Chou En-lai, Representative of the Chinese Communist Party, have recommended to Generalissimo Chiang Kai-shek and Chairman Mao Tse-tung and have been authorized by them to announce that the following order has been issued to all units, regular, militia, irregular and guerrilla, of the National Armies of the Republic of China and of the Communist-led troops of the Republic of China:

"All units, regular, militia, irregular and guerrilla, of the National Armies of the Republic of China and of Communist-led troops of the Republic of China are ordered to carry out the following directive:

a. All hostilities will cease immediately.

b. Except in certain specific cases, all movements of forces in China will cease. There also may be the movements necessary for demobilization, redisposition, supply, administration and local security.

c. Destruction of and interference with all lines of communications will cease and you will clear at once obstructions placed against or interfering with such lines of communications.

d. An Executive Headquarters will be established immediately in Peiping for the purpose of carrying out the agreements for cessation of hostilities. This Headquarters will consist of three Commissioners; one representing the Chinese National Government, one representing the Chinese Communist Party, and one to represent the United States of America. The necessary instructions and orders unanimously agreed upon by the three Commissioners, will be issued in the name of the President of the Republic of China, through the Executive Headquarters."

As a matter of public interest we are further authorized to announce that the following stipulations regarding the above Cessation of Hostilities Order were agreed upon and made a matter of record in the minutes of the conferences.

1. Paragraph *b*, Cessation of Hostilities Order, does not prejudice military movements south of the Yangtze River for the continued execution of the plan of military reorganization of the National Government.

2. Paragraph *b*, Cessation of Hostilities Order, does not prejudice military movements of forces of the National Army into or within Manchuria which are for the purpose of restoring Chinese sovereignty.

3. Lines of communications, mentioned in paragraph *b*, Cessation of Hostilities Order, includes post communications.

4. It is further agreed that movements of the forces of the National Army under the foregoing stipulations shall be reported daily to the Executive Headquarters.

We are also authorized to announce that the agreements, recommendations, and directives of the Executive Headquarters will deal only with the immediate problems raised by the cessation of hostilities.

American participation within the Headquarters will be solely for the purpose of assisting the Chinese members in implementing the Cessation of Hostilities Order.

The Executive Headquarters will include an Operations Section, composed of the number of officers and men required to supervise adequately in the field of the various details.

It is agreed that separate and independent signal communications systems may be established for each Commissioner in order to insure rapid and unhampered communications.

The Headquarters will be located initially at Peiping.

CHANG CHUN
CHOU EN LAI

64

Resolution on Government Organization adopted by the Political Consultative Conference, January 1946 [4]

I. Concerning the State Council: Pending the convocation of the National Assembly, the Kuomintang, as a preliminary measure preparatory to the actual inauguration of constitutionalism, will revise the Organic Law of the National Government in order to expand the State Council. The following are the salient points of the revision under contemplation:

1. There will be forty (40) State Councillors, of whom the Presidents of the Executive, Legislative, Judicial, Examination, and Control Yuan will be ex-officio members.

2. The State Councillors will be chosen by the President of the National Government from among the Kuomintang members as well as non-members of the Kuomintang.

3. The State Council is the supreme organ of the Government in charge of national affairs.

4. The State Council will be competent to discuss and decide on:
A. Legislative principles.
B. Administrative policy.
C. Important military measures.

---

[4] Printed also in *China Handbook, 1937–1945*, pp. 744–745.

D. Financial schemes and the budget.

E. The appointment and dismissal of Ministers of State with or without portfolios, and the appointment of members of the Legislative and Control Yuan.

F. Matters submitted by the President of the National Government for consideration.

G. Proposals submitted by three or more State Councillors.

5. If the President of the National Government is of opinion that any decision of the State Council is difficult to be carried out, he may submit it for reconsideration. In case three-fifths of the State Councillors, upon reconsideration, uphold the original decision, it shall be carried out accordingly.

6. General resolutions before the State Council are to be passed by a majority vote of the State Councillors present. If a resolution before the State Council should involve changes in administrative policy, it must be passed by a two-thirds vote of the State Councillors present. Whether a given resolution involves changes in administrative policy or not is to be decided by a majority vote of the State Councillors present.

7. The State Council meets every two weeks. The President of the National Government may call emergency meetings, if necessary.

II. Concerning the Executive Yuan.

1. All Ministers of the Executive Yuan are ipso facto Ministers of State. There may be three to five Ministers of State without portfolios.

2. Members of all political parties as well as individuals with no party affiliations may become Ministers of State with or without portfolios.

III. Concerning miscellaneous matters.

1. Whether the membership of the People's Political Council should be increased and its powers raised, pending the inauguration of the Constitution, will be left to the Government to decide in the light of the circumstances of the time.

2. All Government employees, whether of the Central Government or of the local Governments, should be selected on the basis of merit. No discriminations on account of party affiliations should be allowed.

NOTE: A. The appointment of State Councillors by the President of the National Government will be made on the nomination of the different parties concerned. In case he does not consent to the candidature of any given individual, the party concerned may nominate another one for the office.

B. When the President of the National Government nominates any individual with no party affiliations as State Councillor whose candidature is opposed by one-third of the other nominees, he must reconsider the matter and make a different nomination.

C. Half of the State Councillors will be Kuomintang members and the other half will be members of other political parties and prominent social leaders. The exact number of members of other political parties and prominent social leaders who are to serve as State Councillors will form the subject of separate discussions.

D. Of the existing Ministers under the Executive Yuan and the proposed Ministers of State without portfolios, seven or eight will be appointed from among non-Kuomintang members.

E. The number of Ministries to be assigned to non-Kuomintang members will form the subject of separate discussions after the PCC has closed.

65

Resolution on Program for Peaceful National Reconstruction Adopted by the Political Consultative Conference, January 1946 [5]

Now that the war of resistance against Japan has ended and peaceful reconstruction should begin, the National Government has invited representatives of the different political parties and prominent social leaders to the Political Consultative Conference to discuss national problems with the double objective of putting an end to the period of political tutelage and inaugurating constitutionalism at an early date. The present program is drawn up to serve as a guide for the Government, pending the actual inauguration of constitutionalism. Representatives of the different political parties and prominent social leaders will be invited to take part in the Government. It is to be hoped that one and all will give first consideration to the needs of the nation and the demands of the people, and that they will cooperate wholeheartedly and work for the realization of the program, whose main features are as follows:

I. GENERAL PRINCIPLES

1. The principles of the San Min Chu I will be regarded as the highest guiding principles for national reconstruction.
2. All forces of the nation will unite under the guidance of President Chiang Kai-shek in order to construct a new China, unified, free, and democratic.
3. It is recognized that the democratization of politics, the nationalization of troops, and the equality and legality of all political parties, as advocated by President Chiang, are necessary paths leading to peaceful national reconstruction.
4. Political disputes must be settled by political means in order to maintain peaceful national development.

II. THE RIGHTS OF THE PEOPLE

1. The freedoms of person, thought, religion, belief, speech, the press, assembly, association, residence, removal, and correspondence should be guaranteed to the people. Any existing laws that contravene these freedoms should be either revised or repealed.
2. Any organization or individual other than judicial organs and the police should be strictly forbidden to arrest, try, and punish the people. Anyone who violates this rule shall be punished. The Habeas Corpus Law which has already been promulgated by the Government should be put into practical operation by Government decree at an early date.
3. The political, social, educational, and economic equality of women should be guaranteed.

III. POLITICAL PROBLEMS

1. All national measures of the moment should take into consideration the proper interests of the people of all localities, classes, and professions, and allow for their equitable development.
2. In order to increase administrative efficiency, the different grades of administrative machinery should be revamped, their rights and duties should be unified and clearly delimited, all unnecessary Governmental agencies should be abolished, the administrative procedure should be simplified, and the principle

---

[5] Printed also in *China Handbook, 1937–1945*, p. 747.

of individual responsibility each for his own section of the work should be introduced.

3. A sound system of civil service should be established: competent individuals should be protected; Government employees should be appointed not on the basis of personal or party allegiance, but on that of ability and past experience; no one should be allowed to hold concurrent jobs or to be drawn into Government service through the exertion of purely personal influence.

4. The unity and independence of the judicial power should be guaranteed, precluding it from political interference. The personnel in the courts of law should be increased, their salaries and positions should be raised, the judicial procedure should be simplified, and prisons should be reformed.

5. The supervisory system should be strictly enforced; corruption should be severely punished; facilities should be given to the people to accuse corrupt officials.

6. Local self-government should be actively pushed forth, and popular elections beginning from the lower administrative units and gradually ascending to the highest unit should be carried out. Provincial, District, and Municipal Councils should be established throughout the country at an early date, and District Magistrates should be elected by the people.

In frontier provinces and districts where minority peoples live, the number of Provincial or District Councillors to be elected by these minority peoples should be fixed according to the proportion they occupy in their respective provinces or districts.

7. All national administrative matters which have to be carried out in the territory of a district which has attained complete self-government must be carried out under the supervision and control of the National Government.

8. The powers of the Central and local Governments should be regulated on the basis of the principle of "a fair distribution of powers". The local Governments may take such measures as are adapted to the special circumstances of the localities concerned, but the regulations issued by the Provincial and District Governments must not contravene the laws and decrees of the Central Government.

IV. MILITARY AFFAIRS

1. The army belongs to the State. It is the duty of the soldier to protect the country and love the people and to insure the unity both of military organization and of military command.

2. All military establishments should be adapted to the needs of national defense. The military system should be reformed in accordance with democratic institutions and the circumstances of the nation. The army and political parties should be separated from each other; military and civil authority should be vested in different hands; military education should be improved; equipment should be adequate; a sound personnel and finance system should be introduced. All these should be done in order to create a modernized national army.

3. The system of conscription should be improved and made to apply fairly and throughout the whole country. Some form of the volunteer system should be maintained and improved upon in order to meet the needs of a fully equipped army.

4. All troops of the country should be reorganized into a lesser number of units in accordance with the provisions of the "Military Reorganization Plan".

5. Preparations for the rehabilitation and employment of disbanded and retired officers and men should be made. The livelihood of disabled officers and men

should be guaranteed. The families of fallen officers and men should be provided for.

6. A time limit should be set for the repatriation of the Japanese troops who have surrendered. Adequate measures should be put into operation at an early date for the disbandment of puppet troops and the liquidation of roving armed bands.

V. FOREIGN RELATIONS

1. The Atlantic Charter, the Cairo Declaration, the Moscow Four-Power Declaration, and the United Nations Organization Charter should be observed. China will take an active part in the UNO in order to preserve world peace.

2. All remnants of Japanese influence in China should be extirpated according to the provisions of the Potsdam Declaration. The problem of Japan should be solved in cooperation with other Allied Nations in order to prevent the resurgence of Japanese Fascist-militarist forces and to guarantee the security of the Far East.

3. Friendly relations with the United States, the Soviet Union, the United Kingdom, France, and other democratic countries should be promoted; treaty obligations should be observed; and economic and cultural cooperation should be undertaken in order to work for the prosperity and progress of the world in conjunction with other countries.

4. Commercial treaties, based on the principles of equality and reciprocity, should be concluded at an early date with other nations when necessary, and the position of Chinese residents overseas should be ameliorated.

VI. ECONOMICS AND FINANCE

1. A plan of economic reconstruction should be formulated in accordance with the teachings of Dr. Sun Yat-sen's "Industrial Planning", and the cooperation of foreign capital and technique should be welcome.

2. Any enterprise which partakes of the nature of a monopoly or which cannot be undertaken by private initiative should be classified as a state enterprise; the people should be encouraged to undertake all other enterprises. Such should be the principles for the first stage of economic reconstruction, which must be effectively carried out. All existing measures should be examined and improved upon in the light of this principle.

3. In order to hasten the process of China's industrialization the Government should convene a National Economic Conference, to which will be invited social leaders interested in the problem of economic reconstruction. In this way the Government will be able to sound out popular opinion and decide upon the measures to be taken.

4. The development of "official capitalism" should be forestalled. Government officials should be strictly forbidden to take advantage of their official position to indulge in speculation and cornering, evade taxes, smuggle, embezzle public funds, and illegally make use of the means of transportation.

5. Active preparations must be made for the construction of additional railroads and highways, harbors and bays, irrigation and other projects. Subsidies should be granted to those who construct houses, schools, hospitals, and other public buildings.

6. Farm rents and interest rates must be effectively reduced. The rights of the lessee must be protected, and the payment of farm rents must be guaranteed. More and larger loans to farmers must be made available, and usury should be strictly prohibited. All these must be done in order to better the peasants' lot.

The land law must be put into operation so as to attain the objective of "He who tills the soil also owns it."

7. Active measures should be taken to help the people increase their productive power by afforestation and the growth of grass, the conservation of water and soil, the development of animal husbandry, the reorganization and further development of agricultural cooperation, the expansion of agricultural experimentation and research, and the utilization of modern equipment and methods to kill locusts and other insects.

8. Labor laws must be put into operation. The conditions of labor must be improved; the bonus system should be put on trial; unemployment and disablement insurances should be started; child and female labor should be given adequate protection; more workers' schools should be established in order to raise the cultural level of the working population.

9. Laws governing industrial association should be made at an early date, so that those engaged in industrial undertakings may form their own associations. Laws concerning factory management should be examined and revised on the assumption that there prevails a spirit of conciliation between capital and labor.

10. Financial accounts should be made public. The budget system and annual accounts system should be strictly adopted. Public expenditure should be curtailed, and revenues and expenditures should be balanced. Central Government finance and local finance should be sharply differentiated. The currency should be deflated and the monetary system should be stabilized. The raising of both domestic and foreign loans and the use to which they will be put should be made public and subject to popular supervision.

11. The system of taxation should be reformed. All illegal taxes and extortions should be completely abolished. The various offices for the collection of taxes should be amalgamated, and the procedure of collection should be simplified. Progressive taxes should be imposed on assets and incomes. National banks should be entrusted with special economic tasks in order to help develop industry and agriculture. Assets which have escaped to foreign countries or have been frozen should be commandeered to be used for the balancing of the budget.

VII. Education and Culture

1. The freedom of learning should be guaranteed. Religious beliefs and political ideologies should not be allowed to interfere with school and college administration.

2. Scientific research and artistic creation should be encouraged in order to raise the national cultural level.

3. Compulsory education and social education should be made nation-wide; illiteracy should be actively wiped out. Professional education should be expanded in order to increase the professional ability of the people; normal education should be further developed in order to educate more qualified teachers for compulsory education. The contents of the teaching material in the various grades of schools should be revised in the light of the democratic and scientific spirit.

4. The proportion of the national budget to be devoted to education and cultural enterprises should be increased. The salaries and retirement annuities of teachers in the various grades of schools should be reasonably increased. Poor students should be subsidized, so that they can go to school and continue their studies. Endowments should be made for scientific research and creative literary and artistic work.

5. Privately endowed schools and cultural work among the people should be encouraged and subsidized.

6. In order to promote national health encouragement and assistance should be given to all forms of child welfare, public health installations should be made nation-wide, and physical exercise should be actively encouraged.

7. The wartime censorships of the press, motion pictures, the drama, letters, and telegrams should be abolished. Assistance should be given to the development of businesses in connection with publications, newspapers, news agencies, the drama, and motion pictures. All news agents and cultural enterprises operated by the Government should serve the interests of the entire nation.

VIII. REHABILITATION AND RELIEF

1. Social order in the liberated areas should be restored at an early date. The people must be relieved of all oppressions and sufferings which were heaped on them in the period of enemy occupation. The tendency for prices to rise in the liberated areas must be curbed. All corrupt practices of officials who were sent to the occupied territories to take over from the enemy should be severely punished.

2. Railroads and highways should be quickly repaired. Inland and coastal shipping should be quickly restored. Those people who have migrated to the interior in wartime must be helped by the government to return to their native districts. Homes and jobs should be found for them, if necessary.

3. Good use must be made of the UNRRA supplies in order to relieve the war refugees; medical supplies must be distributed to them in order to cure and prevent diseases; seeds and fertilizers must be given them in order to restore farming. The authorities in charge of this work will be assisted by popular agencies and organizations in the discharge of their duties.

4. Factories and mines in the liberated areas must be quickly made operative; the property rights of the original owners must be protected; work must be resumed at an early date, so that employment may be found for those without useful occupations. Enemy and puppet property should be properly disposed of in order to enable those factories and individuals who have made significant contributions to the war of resistance in the interior to take part in its exploitation.

5. The Yellow River must be quickly put under control. Other irrigation projects which have been damaged or allowed to lapse in the course of the war must be made good at an early date.

6. The Government's decrees to stop conscription and exempt the people from the payment of agricultural taxes for one year must be carried out to the letter by the different grades of Government. No conscription or agricultural taxes under a different guise should be allowed.

IX. CHINESE RESIDENTS OVERSEAS

1. Chinese residents overseas who have become destitute as a result of enemy oppression will be helped by the Government to reestablish their former business; those members of their families who may be living in China will receive proper relief.

2. Assistance will be given to Chinese residents overseas who have returned to China in the last few years in the course of the war, so that they may go back to their former place of residence. Facilities will be provided for them for the recovery of their property and the reestablishment of their business.

ANNEXES 617

3. All educational and cultural enterprises of Chinese residents overseas will be restored and active assistance will be given them by the Government. Encouragement and assistance will be given to the children of Chinese residents overseas to come back to China for education.

Annex

1. In those recovered areas where the local government is under dispute the status quo shall be maintained until a settlement is made according to Articles 6, 7, and 8 of Chapter III on Political Problems in this program by the National Government after its reorganization.

2. A Committee for the Protection of the People's Liberties will be formed, composed of representatives of the local Council, the Lawyers' Association, and popular organizations. Financial assistance will be given to it by the Government.

3. Revisions will be made, in the light of the usual practices in democratic countries, in the Citizen's Oath-Taking and the examination of candidates for public offices.

4. Membership of the Supreme Economic Council of the Executive Yuan should be increased by the addition of economic experts representing the people at large and of experienced industrialists.

5. It is recommended that the Government put an end to the policy of control over nitrate and sulphur.

6. (a) Those workers originally employed in factories which have been removed to the interior in the course of the war, who now find themselves unemployed due to the closing up of the factories as a result of the war, should be granted a certain amount of financial assistance by the Government.

(b) Those factories which have made significant contributions to the manufacture of military material in the course of the war should continue to receive Government patronage by the latter's purchase of their ready-made articles and as much of their material as possible.

7. The press law should be revised. The Regulations Governing the Registration and Control of Newspapers, Magazines, and News Services in Times of Emergency; Provisional Regulations Governing Newspapers, News Agencies, Magazines, Motion Pictures, and Broadcasts in Liberated Areas; Regulations Governing the Censorship of the Drama and Motion Pictures; Regulations Governing the Censorship of Letters and Telegrams, and other regulations of a similar nature should be repealed. Amusement taxes and stamp taxes on motion pictures, drama, and concert tickets should be lightened.

66

Resolution on Military Problems Adopted by the Political Consultative Conference, January 1946 [6]

I. Fundamental principles for the creation of a national army.

1. The army belongs to the State. It is the duty of the soldier to protect the country and love the people.

---

[6] Printed also in *China Handbook, 1937–1945*, p. 745.

2. The army shall be established in response to the necessities of national defense. Its quality and equipment shall be improved in the light of the progress made in general education, science, and industry.

3. The military system shall be reformed in the light of the democratic institutions and actual conditions prevailing at the time.

4. The system of conscription shall be reformed and applied fairly and universally. Some form of the volunteer system shall be preserved and reforms shall be introduced in order to meet the requirements of a fully equipped army.

5. Military education shall be conducted in the light of the foregoing principles, and shall forever be dissociated from party affiliations and personal allegiance.

II. Fundamental principles for the reorganization of the army.

1. Separation of army and party

A. All political parties shall be forbidden to carry on party activities, whether open or secret, in the army. So shall be all cliques based on personal relations or of a territorial nature.

B. All soldiers on active service who owe allegiance to any political party may not take part in the party activities of the district in which they are stationed, when they are on duty.

C. No party or individual may make use of the army as an instrument of political rivalry.

D. No illegal organizations and activities may be allowed in the army.

2. Separation of civil and military authorities.

A. No soldier on active service in the army may serve concurrently as civil officials.

B. The country shall be divided into military districts, which shall be made not to coincide with administrative districts as far as possible.

C. The army shall be strictly forbidden to interfere in political affairs.

III. Methods aiming at the civilian control of the army.

1. When the preliminary measures for the reorganization of the army have been completed, the National Military Council shall be reorganized into a Ministry of National Defense under the Executive Yuan.

2. The Minister of National Defense shall not necessarily be a soldier.

3. The number of troops and military expenditure shall be decided upon by the Executive Yuan and passed by the Legislative Yuan.

4. All troops shall be under the unified control of the Ministry of National Defense.

5. A Military Committee shall be established within the Ministry of National Defense to be charged with the double duty of drawing up schemes for the creation of a national army and of seeing to it that the schemes are faithfully carried out. Members of the Committee shall be drawn from various circles.

IV. Practical methods for the reorganization of the army.

1. The three-man military commission shall proceed according to schedule and agree upon practical methods for the reorganization of the Communist troops at an early date. The reorganization must be completed as soon as possible.

2. The Government troops should be reorganized, according to the plan laid down by the Ministry of War, into ninety (90) divisions. The reorganization should be completed within six (6) months.

3. When the reorganizations envisaged in paragraphs 1 and 2 have been completed, all troops of the country should be again reorganized into fifty (50) or sixty (60) divisions.

4. A commission for the supervision of the reorganization plan shall be established within the National Military Council. Members of the commission shall be drawn from various circles.

67

Agreement on the National Assembly by Sub-Committee of the Political Consultative Conference

Based on the resolution on this subject introduced by the Government representatives, the following agreement on the National Assembly was reached in the PCC Sub-Committee dealing with this problem by the various delegations:

1. That the National Assembly shall be convened on May 5, 1946.
2. That the power of the National Assembly is to adopt the Constitution.
3. That the Constitution shall be adopted by a vote of three-fourths of the delegates present.
4. That the 1,200 geographical and vocational delegates, who have been or are going to be elected according to the electoral law of the National Assembly, shall be retained.
5. That the geographical and vocational delegates for the Northeast provinces and Taiwan shall be increased by 150.
6. That 700 seats shall be added to the National Assembly and they shall be apportioned among the various parties and social leaders. The ratio of apportionment shall be decided later.
7. That the total number of delegates to the National Assembly shall be 2,050.
8. That the organ to enforce the Constitution shall be elected six months after the Constitution is adopted.

68

Resolution on the Draft Constitution Adopted by the Political Consultative Conference, January 1946 [7]

I. Establishment of a Reviewing Committee.
 1. *Name:* Committee for the Reviewing of the Draft Constitution.
 2. *Organization:* The Committee will have a total membership of twenty-five (25), of whom five (5) will represent each of the five groups composing the Political Consultation Conference. In addition, ten (10) technical experts outside of the PCC will be invited to take part in the work of the Committee. In selecting the technical experts reference should be made to the membership lists of the Association for the Promotion of Constitutionalism and the Association to Assist the Inauguration of Constitutionalism.
 3. *Functions:* The PCC will establish the Committee for the Reviewing of the Draft Constitution, which will draw up a comprehensive scheme for the revision of the 1936 Draft Constitution on the basis of the principles recommended by the PCC and in the light of the recommendations made by the Association for the Promotion of Constitutionalism and the Association to Assist the Inauguration of Constitutionalism and opinions advanced by various other quarters. This

---

[7] Printed also in *China Handbook, 1937–1945,* pp. 746–747.

scheme will be submitted to the National Assembly for adoption. It may also be laid before the PCC for discussion, if necessary.

4. *Duration:* Two months.

II. Principles to be applied in the revision of the Draft Constitution.

1. Concerning the National Assembly.

A. The entire electorate, when they exercise the rights of election, initiative, referendum, and recall, are called the National Assembly.

B. Pending the election of the President by universal suffrage, he shall be elected by an electoral body composed of the District, Provincial, and National Representative Assemblies.

C. The recall of the President is to be effected by the same means as that employed in his election.

D. The exercise of the rights of initiative and referendum will be defined by appropriate laws.

NOTE: The convocation of the first National Assembly will form the subject of discussion by the PCC.

2. Concerning the Legislative Yuan: The Legislative Yuan will be the supreme law-making body of the State and will be elected by the electorate. This function corresponds to those of a Parliament in a democratic country.

3. Concerning the Control Yuan: The Control Yuan will be the supreme organ of control of the State and will be elected by the Provincial Assemblies and the Assemblies of the Self-Governing Areas of Minority Peoples. It will exercise the functions of consent, impeachment, and control.

4. Concerning the Judicial Yuan: The Judicial Yuan will be the Supreme Court of the State, and will not be responsible for judicial administration. It will be composed of a specified number of justices, who will be appointed on the nomination of the President of the National Government and with the consent of the Control Yuan. The different grades of judges shall all be without party affiliations.

5. Concerning the Examination Yuan: The Examination Yuan will be in the form of a committee, whose members will be appointed on the nomination of the President of the National Government and with the consent of the Control Yuan. Its functions will be mainly to examine candidates for civil service and technical experts. Members of the Examination Yuan shall be without party affiliations.

6. Concerning the Executive Yuan.

A. The Executive Yuan is the supreme executive organ of the State. The President of the Executive Yuan is to be appointed on the nomination of the President of the National Government and with the consent of the Legislative Yuan. The Executive Yuan is to be responsible to the Legislative Yuan.

B. If the Legislative Yuan has no confidence in the Executive Yuan as a whole, the latter may either resign or ask the President of the National Government to dissolve the former. But the same President of the Executive Yuan may not ask for the dissolution of the Legislative Yuan for a second time.

7. Concerning the Presidency of the National Government.

A. The President of the National Government may promulgate emergency decrees according to law when the Executive Yuan has so decided. But the action must be reported to the Legislative Yuan within one month.

B. The right of the President of the National Government to call the Presidents of the Executive, Legislative, Judicial, Examination, and Control Yuan into conference need not be written into the Constitution.

8. Concerning the system of local government.

A. The Province is to be regarded as the highest unit of local self-government.

B. The powers of the Province and the Central Government will be divided according to the principle of "a fair distribution of power."

C. The Provincial Governor is to be elected by the people.

D. The Province may have a Provincial Constitution, which, however, must not contravene the provisions of the National Constitution

9. Concerning the rights and duties of the people.

A. All freedoms and rights which are generally enjoyed by the peoples of democratic countries should be protected by the Constitution and should not be illegally encroached upon.

B. If the freedom of the people is to be defined by law, it must be done for its protection and not with a view to restricting it.

C. Labor service should be provided for in the Law on Local Self-Government, and not written into the National Constitution.

D. The right of self-government must be guaranteed to minority peoples who live together in one particular locality.

10. A separate chapter on elections should be provided in the Constitution. Only those twenty-three years of age or over have the right to be elected.

11. Concerning fundamental national policies: A separate chapter in the Constitution should be devoted to fundamental national policies, including items on national defense, foreign relations, national economy, culture, and education.

A. The aim of national defense is to guarantee the safety of the Nation and preserve the peace of the world. All members of the Army, Navy, and Air Forces should be loyal to the State, love the people, and rise above all personal, territorial, and party affiliations.

B. Foreign relations should be carried on in a spirit of independence. Friendly relations with foreign countries should be promoted, treaty obligations carried out, the Charter of the United Nations Organization observed, international cooperation fostered, and world peace guaranteed.

C. Dr. Sun Yat-sen's principle of economic democracy (the Min Sen Chu I) should serve as the basis of the national economy. The State must see to it that he who tills the soil also owns it; that workers have jobs; and that enterprisers have ample opportunities to carry on their business. These things must be done in order to attain the twin objective of fairness and sufficiency in the national economy and the people's livelihood.

D. It should be the aim of culture and education to foster the growth of the national spirit, the democratic attitude of mind, and scientific knowledge and technique. The general cultural level of the people should be universally raised; equality of educational opportunity should be made a reality; freedom of learning should be guaranteed; and scientific development should be pushed forth with vigor.

NOTE: The provisions in the Constitution relative to paragraphs (a), (b), (c), and (d) should not go too much into detail.

12. Concerning amendments to the Constitution: The right to amend the Constitution shall be vested in a joint conference of the Legislative and Control Yuan. The proposed amendments should be passed by that body in which is vested the right to elect the President of the National Government.

69

Press Release by Military Sub-Committee Concerning Agreement on Basis for Military Reorganization and Integration of Communist Forces into National Army, February 25, 1946 [8]

We, General Chang Chih Chung, representative of the Government and General Chou En-lai, representative of the Chinese Communist Party, constituting the Military Sub-Committee of which General Marshall is advisor have been authorized to announce that an agreement has been reached on the basis for military reorganization and for the integration of the Communist forces into the National Army.

The Military Sub-Committee is now preparing the detailed measures to carry the terms of the agreement into execution. The Executive Headquarters at Peiping will be charged with the responsibility of transmitting the necessary orders to the troops in the field and with supervision of their execution.

These measures will be carried out over a period of 18 months so as to insure a minimum of difficulty.

The object of the agreement is to facilitate the economic rehabilitation of China and at the same time to furnish a basis for the development of an effective military force capable of safeguarding the security of the nation, including provisions to safeguard the rights of the people from military interference.

The articles of agreement follow:

BASIS FOR MILITARY REORGANIZATION AND FOR THE INTEGRATION OF THE COMMUNIST FORCES INTO THE NATIONAL ARMY

ARTICLE I—COMMAND

Section 1. The President of the Republic of China being the Commander-in-Chief of the Armed Forces of the Republic of China exercises command through the Ministry of National Defense (or National Military Council). The commanders of the army groups and of the separate armies and the directors of the service areas herein provided for shall report to the Commander-in-Chief through the Ministry of National Defense (or National Military Council).

Section 2. The Commander-in-Chief shall have the power to appoint and relieve all subordinate officers provided, however, that in the event it becomes necessary during the process of the reorganization of the military forces to relieve the commander of any Communist-led unit or any Communist officer holding other position, the Commander-in-Chief shall appoint in the place of the officer relieved an officer nominated by the senior Communist member of the government.

ARTICLE II—FUNCTIONS AND RESTRICTIONS

Section 1. The primary function of the Army shall be to defend the Republic in time of war. In time of peace the principal function of the Army shall be training. It may be employed however, to quell domestic disorders, but only as provided in Section 2 of this article.

Section 2. When, in the event of domestic disorders, the governor of a province shall have certified to the Council of State that the local civil police, and the Peace Preservation Corps have been unable to cope with the situation, the Pres-

---

[8] Printed also in *China Handbook, 1937–1945*, pp. 755–758.

ident, in his capacity as commander-in-chief, shall, with the approval of the Council of State, employ the army to restore order.

Article III—Organization

Section 1. The army shall consist of armies of three divisions each with supporting troops not to exceed 15% of their total strength. At the conclusion of 12 months the armies shall consist of 108 divisions of not to exceed 14,000 men each. Of these, 18 shall be formed from Communist Forces.

Section 2. China shall be divided into 8 service areas under directors responsible to the Minister of National Defense (or National Military Council) for the following functions within their respective areas:

The supply, quartering and pay of all military units located within the areas;

The storage, reconditioning and issue of the weapons and equipment collected from demobilized troops within the area;

The processing of demobilized officers and enlisted personnel within the area and the continued processing of demobilized officers and enlisted personnel passing through the area en route to their homes or other designated destinations;

The processing and elementary training of individual recruits received within the area as replacements for the armies;

The supply of military schools within the area;

The service area directors shall have no authority or control over the armies located within their areas and they are specifically prohibited from interfering with or influencing in any way whatsoever civil administration or affairs;

Each army commander within a particular service area shall maintain in the service area headquarters his own representative to insure that the needs of the forces under his command are fully and expeditiously met;

There shall be a meeting every second month within each service area and presided over by the service area director. These meetings shall be attended by the army and division commanders, or their duly appointed representatives, of each army located within that area. A representative of the Ministry of National Defense (or National Military Council) shall also be present. The instructions of the Ministry of National Defense (or National Military Council) shall be presented, and the state of supply and similar matters of the service area discussed.

Article IV—Demobilization

Section 1. During the 12 months immediately following the promulgation of this agreement the Government shall demobilize all units in excess of 90 divisions and the Communist Party shall demobilize all units in excess of 18 divisions. The demobilization shall start immediately and shall proceed at the rate of approximately one twelfth of the total number to be demobilized during each month.

The Government shall prepare within three weeks of the promulgation of this agreement, a list of the 90 divisions to be retained and the order of demobilization of units during the first two months. The Communist Party shall prepare within three weeks of the promulgation of this agreement, a complete list of its military units stating character, strength, armament, names of brigades and higher commanders and location of units. This report shall include a list of the 18 divisions to be retained and the order of demobilization during the first two months. These lists shall be submitted to the Military Sub-Committee.

Six weeks after the promulgation of this agreement the Communist Party shall submit to the Military Sub-Committee a complete list of the army units to be demobilized and the Government shall submit a similar list.

On receipt of the foregoing lists and documents the Military Sub-Committee shall prepare a detailed plan for the execution of this agreement and submit it for the approval of both parties. After such approval the lists, documents and plan shall be transmitted to the Ministry of National Defense (or National Military Council).

Section 2. The arms and equipment of the army units demobilized may be utilized to complete the arms and equipment of the army units to be retained in service. A detailed statement of such transfers will be submitted to the Ministry of National Defense (or National Military Council) by the Executive Headquarters. The surplus material will be stored as directed by that Ministry (or Council).

Section 3. In order to prevent large scale hardship or lawlessness arising, as a result of the demobilization, the Government and the Communist Party shall initially provide for the supply movement and employment of their respective demobilized personnel. The Government shall take over unified control of these matters as soon as practicable.

Section 4. During the 6 months following the first 12 months the National divisions shall be further reduced to 50 and the Communist divisions shall be further reduced to 10 making a total of 60 divisions to be organized into 20 armies.

Article V—Integration and Deployment

Section 1. During the first 12 months after the promulgation of this agreement there shall be organized 4 army groups each consisting of 1 National and 1 Communist army. Each army shall consist of 3 divisions. The schedule for establishing these army groups shall be as follows: One army group shall be organized during the 7th month; another the 9th month; another the 10th month; and another the 11th month. The staffs of the army groups shall consist of approximately one half National and one half Communist staff officers.

Section 2. The deployment of the armies at the end of the first 12 months shall be as follows:

Northeast China—5 armies each consisting of 3 National divisions, each army with a National commander and 1 army consisting of 3 Communist divisions with a Communist commander—total 6 armies.

Northwest China—5 armies each consisting of 3 National divisions each with a National commander—total 5 armies.

North China—3 armies each consisting of 3 National divisions, each with a National commander; and 4 army groups each consisting of 1 National and 1 Communist army of 3 divisions. 2 army group commanders shall be National officers and 2 army group commanders shall be Communist officers—total 11 armies.

Central China—9 armies each consisting of 3 National divisions, each with a National commander; and 1 army consisting of 3 Communist divisions, with a Communist commander—total 10 armies.

South China (including Formosa)—4 armies each consisting of 3 National divisions, each with a National commander—total 4 armies.

Section 3. During the following 6 months the 4 army groups referred to in Section 2 above shall be reorganized, creating 4 separate armies each consisting of 1

National and 2 Communist divisions and 2 separate armies each consisting of 2 National and 1 Communist divisions. Thereafter, the organization of army groups shall be terminated.

Section 4. The deployment of the armies at the end of the second 6 months (i. e. at the end of a total of 18 months) shall be as follows:

Northeast China—1 army consisting of 2 National and 1 Communist Divisions with a National commander and 4 armies each consisting of 3 National divisions, each with a National commander—total 5 armies.

Northwest China—3 armies each consisting of 3 National Divisions each with a National commander—total 3 armies.

North China—3 armies each consisting of 1 National and 2 Communist divisions, each with a Communist commander; 1 army consisting of 2 National and 1 Communist divisions with a National commander; and 2 armies each consisting of 3 National divisions, each with a National commander—total 6 armies.

Central China—1 army consisting of 1 National and 2 Communist divisions with a Communist commander and 3 armies each consisting of 3 National divisions, each with a National commander—total 4 armies.

South China (including Formosa)—2 armies each consisting of 3 National divisions, each with a National commander—total 2 armies.

ARTICLE VI—PEACE PRESERVATION CORPS

Section 1. Each province shall be authorized to maintain a Peace Preservation Corps in proportion to the population of the province but the strength of the Corps for any one province shall not exceed 15,000 men. After it has become apparent that the civil police of any province have been unable to cope with the situation, the governor of that province is authorized to employ this Corps to quell civil disorders.

Section 2. The armament of the Peace Preservation Corps shall be restricted to the pistol, the rifle and the automatic rifle.

ARTICLE VII—SPECIAL PROVISIONS

Section 1. Executive Headquarters

The Executive Headquarters created in the agreement of the Committee of Three, signed 10 January 1946, shall be the agency through which this agreement shall be implemented.

Section 2. Common Uniform

A common distinctive uniform for the reorganized military forces of China shall be adopted for wear by all officers and enlisted men of the Army of the Republic of China.

Section 3. Personnel System

An adequate personnel system shall be established and the name, grade and assignment of each officer of the Army shall be carried on a single list without political prejudice.

Section 4. Special Armed Forces

Neither the Government nor any political party nor any group or association shall maintain, or in any way support, any secret or independent armed force, after the effective date of this agreement.

Section 5. Puppet and Irregular Troops

All troops which were maintained in China under the sponsorship, directly or indirectly, of Japan and all troops maintained by persons or factions other than the Government or Communist Party shall be disarmed and disbanded as soon as possible. The detailed plan (Article VIII, Section 1) shall provide for the execution of the provisions of this section in a definitely limited period of time.

Article VIII—General

Section 1. Upon approval of this agreement by Generalissimo Chiang Kai-shek and Chinese Communist Party Chairman Mao Tse-tung there shall be prepared and submitted to them for approval by the Military Sub-Committee a detailed plan of the schedules, regulations and specific measures to govern the execution of the provisions of this agreement.

Section 2. It is understood and agreed that the detailed plans above referred to shall provide that the demobilization shall start at the earliest practical date; that the organization of service areas shall be instituted gradually and that the detailed procedure of the integration of armies shall be carried out under the provisions of Article V.

It is further understood and agreed that during the initial period of transition, the Government and the Communist party shall be responsible for the good order, the supply of their respective troops and for their prompt and full compliance with the instructions issued to them by the Executive Headquarters.

General CHANG CHIH CHUNG
Representative of the Government
General CHOU EN-LAI
Representative of the Chinese Communist Party
General GEORGE C. MARSHALL
Advisor

CHUNGKING, CHINA
February 25, 1946

70

Memorandum by the Military Sub-Committee, March 16, 1946

1. The "BASIS FOR MILITARY REORGANIZATION AND FOR THE INTEGRATION OF THE COMMUNIST FORCES INTO THE NATIONAL ARMY," constitutes the general directive to Executive Headquarters covering demobilization, redeployment, and integration.

2. Executive Headquarters will be the medium for the execution of the Basic Plan. The Headquarters will form a Control Group for planning and for supervising the execution of the orders of the Executive Headquarters in these matters. This group will be composed of Government, Communist and U. S. military personnel. Executive Headquarters will utilize combined field teams to supervise on the ground for demobilization, redeployment and integration of the Government and Communist troops.

3. The reports required by the Basic Plan will form the basis for detailed plans and schedules prepared at Executive Headquarters.

4. The demobilization will require the gradual elimination of Military Commands on a higher level than Army headquarters.

5. Puppet units will be disbanded complete by D-Day plus 3 months. Military equipment and munitions in the hands of these units will be turned in to the local Service Area if established, or as directed by Executive Headquarters.

6. Executive Headquarters will direct each division designated to be retained by the Government or the Communist Party to assemble in its general area, and initiate a 12 week's basic training program pending receipt of more detailed instructions.

7. A school of elementary instruction for the 10 Communist Divisions designated for Army integration in the last six months, will be organized under the guidance of the Interim Military Advisory Group of the U. S. Army to conduct a series of basic courses of 3 months duration in organization, training procedure, and administration. Planning for the schools will be coordinated with Executive Headquarters.

8. Movements to effect the necessary redeployment and integration will be ordered by Executive Headquarters in accordance with the general directive of the Ministry of National Defense (or National Military Council). The logistic requirements for the demobilization, redeployment and integration will be coordinated with the Ministry of National Defense (or National Military Council). Executive Headquarters is authorized to deal direct with Directors of the Service Areas regarding logistic problems.

9. Executive Headquarters will prepare the detailed logistic and administrative plans for personnel to be demobilized.

General CHANG CHIH CHUNG
Representative of the National Government
General CHOU EN-LAI
Representative of the Chinese Communist Party
General A. C. GILLEM, Jr.
Representing General G. C. Marshall

CHUNGKING, CHINA
16 March 1946

71 (a)

Agreement on Establishment of the Executive Headquarters, Signed at Chungking, January 10, 1946

PREAMBLE

By joint agreement, we, General Chang Chun, authorized representative of the National Government, and General Chou En-lai, authorized representative of the Chinese Communist Party, do hereby establish, with the approval of the National Government of China, an Executive Headquarters empowered to implement the agreements for the cessation of hostilities.

FUNCTIONS

The Executive Headquarters will implement the agreed policies for the cessation of hostilities. The Headquarters will submit recommendations covering necessary additional subsidiary agreements to insure more effective implementation of the cessation of hostilities orders; such recommendations to include measures for the disarmament of the Japanese forces, restoration of lines of communication and coordination of the movement of Japanese soldiers to the coast for repatriation. The formal instructions unanimously agreed upon by the three Commissioners will be issued in the name of the President of the Republic of China.

ORGANIZATION

The Executive Headquarters will consist of three Commissioners with authority to vote, and to negotiate among themselves; one to represent the Chinese National Government; one to represent the Chinese Communist Party and one to represent the United States of America. The United States Commissioner will be invited to be the chairman.

The Headquarters will have within itself as its implementing agency a group to be called the Operations Section composed of the number of officers and men required to supervise in the field the various agreements, and to render the required reports. The National Government and the Chinese Communist Party will have an equal number of personnel in the Operations Section.

There will be included within the Executive Headquarters the necessary secretarial staff to support the Headquarters.

HOUSING AND SUPPLY

The National Government will furnish adequate living and office accommodations for the Executive Headquarters. The National Government will also furnish the subsistence for this Headquarters. Over all security will be furnished by the local authorities. Immediate security for offices, quarters, and installations will be provided by small units of each Army as required and agreed upon.

LOCATION

The Executive Headquarters will be located initially at Peiping.

PROCEDURE

The Executive Headquarters will operate as the executives of the National Government, the Chinese Communist Party, and the United States respectively.

The three commissioners shall each have one vote. All action must be by unanimous agreement.

The Executive Headquarters will issue the necessary formal orders, directives, and instructions in the name of the President of the Republic of China.

Daily reports will be prepared by the Operations Section to be rendered by the commissioners to their respective chiefs.

The Executive Headquarters will operate through its Operations Section.

The Operations Section will have a United States Army Officer as its director.

The Operations Section will supervise the publication and dissemination of all orders, directives, and instructions to all forces concerned.

The Operations Section may establish sub-stations and will dispatch supervisory and reporting teams as required to implement the policies and agreements.

The National Government, the Chinese Communist Party, and the United States may each maintain independent signal communications at the location of the Executive Headquarters.

DURATION OF AUTHORITY

The Executive Headquarters shall remain in existence and operate until this agreement is rescinded by the President of the Republic of China or the Chairman of the Central Committee of the Chinese Communist Party after due notification to the other party.

CHANG CHUN
CHOU EN-LAI

71 (b)

The Committee of Three to Generalissimo Chiang Kai-shek, Chungking, January 10, 1946

ORGANIZATION OF EXECUTIVE HEADQUARTERS

The approval by Your Excellency and Chairman Mao Tse-tung of the directive to cease hostilities makes it mandatory that the Executive Headquarters become operational at once. The Headquarters should be kept as small as possible for convenience and celerity of operation.

Mr. Walter S. Robertson, who has been nominated as the American Commissioner of the Executive Headquarters, will have initially a staff of not to exceed four persons; a political advisor, an aide, a stenographer, and a translator.

The Operations Section, under Colonel Henry A. Byroade, must contain the necessary personnel to operate various sub-headquarters in critical areas, maintain communications, furnish the required office and housekeeping overhead, etc. The American portion of this Section is initially planned to consist of approximately 26 American officers, 68 enlisted men, and 30 Chinese civilian employees.

Attached is the type of organization Colonel Byroade has planned for the American portion of the Operations Section. Request that you provide, as a matter of urgency, a similar group for the National Government's staff of the Operations Section.

Colonel Byroade will go to Peiping on 11 January 1946 to establish the Executive Headquarters and to assemble the American personnel.

Mr. Robertson will be ready to depart on 13 January 1946. It would be most advantageous if the Commissioner of the National Government, as well as the Communist Commissioner, could be prepared for departure together. General Marshall will provide his personal C-54 aircraft for this purpose.

The staffs for the Executive Headquarters and Operations Section should be organized immediately. The National Government and the Communist Party staffs should each, at least as a beginning, consist of not more than forty officers and ninety enlisted men.

It is very important that adequate facilities be available before arrival of this personnel. It is therefore recommended that the personnel to be assigned to the Operations Section be scheduled to start arrival in Peiping on 15 January. At least half of this personnel should have reported in Peiping by 19 January and the remainder not later than 26 January 1946.

A similar memorandum is being forwarded to Chairman Mao Tse-tung.⁹

CHANG CHUN
CHOU EN-LAI
G. C. MARSHALL

71 (c)

Memorandum on Operations of the Executive Headquarters

The Executive Headquarters was established at Peiping as the agency to implement the cessation of hostilities agreement signed at Chungking on January 10, 1946, and began its official functions on January 14. The functions of the Executive Headquarters were set forth in the document providing for its establishment as follows:

⁹ Not printed.

"The Executive Headquarters will implement the agreed policies for the cessation of hostilities. The Headquarters will submit recommendations covering necessary additional subsidiary agreements to ensure more effective implementation of the cessation of hostilities orders; such recommendations to include measures for the disarmament of the Japanese forces, restoration of lines of communication and coordination of the movement of Japanese soldiers to the coast for repatriation. The formal instructions unanimously agreed upon by the three Commissioners will be issued in the name of the President of the Republic of China."

The Executive Headquarters was headed by three Commissioners: Lieutenant General Cheng Kai-min, representing the National Government, Lieutenant General Yeh Chien-ying, representing the Chinese Communist Party, and Mr. Walter S. Robertson, American Chargé d'Affaires, representing the United States and serving as Chairman. Decisions by the three Commissioners had to be unanimous, as stated in the agreement, and it was envisaged that matters on which they were unable to reach agreement would be referred to the Committee of Three for decision, a procedure which was ultimately followed. Immediately under the three Commissioners and directly responsible to them was a Director of Operations. In accordance with the agreement for the establishment of the Headquarters, a United States Army officer, Brigadier General Henry A. Byroade, was named as the Director of Operations. The Operations Division served as the implementing agency within the Headquarters for the execution of its decisions and directives. Various sections were established under the Operations Division: Plans and Operations Section, Logistics and Supply Section, Conflict Control Group, Communication Group, Army Reorganization Group and Public Relations Group. United States Army planes provided the transportation facilities for the movement of personnel and supplies between Peiping and the various points to which field teams were sent. In the absence of normal communications in China, the only possible means of transportation to the locations of practically all the field teams was by plane.

The key personnel in the functioning of the Executive Headquarters over widespread areas in China were the members of the field teams. They were composed of one representative of each of the three branches of the Headquarters and each branch included in its field team membership communications and interpreting personnel. These teams were sent to areas of conflict or threatened conflict to halt or prevent hostilities. Practical experience in the field revealed that the effectiveness of the field teams could be hampered and necessary investigations actually blocked in cases where one Chinese member of the team vetoed any proposal which might be disadvantageous to his side. When the United States branch of the Headquarters proposed, therefore, a revision of this requirement of unanimity in order to permit the United States team member as chairman to break a deadlock and direct the movement of the team for the purpose of investigating reported violations of the cessation of hostilities agreement—not including the results of the investigation or the action to be taken—the National Government branch approved this proposal but the Communist branch would not agree. At the beginning of May, as the Headquarters was being faced with increased instances of the blocking of team investigations by the refusal of the Communist team members to agree on the movement of the teams, the United States branch proposed that decision for investigation be reached by a majority vote. The National Government branch agreed to this proposal but the Communist branch again refused to assent on the basis that this was contrary to the principle of unanimity under which the Headquarters operated.

Each Chinese side, in approaching problems at issue, both in the Executive Headquarters and in the field, was too often intent upon protracted debate designed to wring the last possible advantage to its cause from the argument, rather than being interested in broad principles and compromise in order to create a spirit conducive to the settlement of differences between the two sides. One side or the other would be willing to block all investigation of reported violations of the cessation of hostilities order unless it received a *quid pro quo* from the rival party, even though there would be no relation between the incidents under discussion. Distrust between the two sides was further heightened by incidents involving field teams. The Communists complained that their team members were on several occasions arrested and beaten and that in some cases their representatives had been kidnapped and had not been heard of since their disappearance. In two cases Communist forces fired on and killed National Government team members and in another incident the United States member of a field team was wounded slightly by a Communist sniper's bullet. Each side apparently organized mass demonstrations in the areas under its control for the purpose of propagandizing the field teams. Such demonstrations sometimes grew out of hand and resulted in incidents leading to near attacks on members of the teams. While these incidents in themselves should not be magnified out of proportion, they were indicative of the bitterness between the two Chinese parties and show some of the difficulties under which the Executive Headquarters and its field teams functioned.

High praise can be given to the United States members of the field teams, who were often stationed in isolated places under primitive and difficult living conditions. The field teams were the key personnel in effecting the cessation of hostilities and it was they who supervised on the spot the carrying out of the directives issued by the Executive Headquarters. United States members of the teams were often under fire, travelled by jeep over near-impassable roads in the performance of their duties and in many ways accomplished miracles in their efforts to bring about cooperation between the two Chinese sides.

Every effort was made to ensure the impartiality of the United States members of the field teams, as their usefulness would have ended if they were felt to be biased. There was inevitably feeling, from time to time, that some United States team members had shown partiality, the majority of such accusations coming from the Communist side. It was believed, however, that this arose chiefly through Communist Party press and radio propaganda directed against United States aid to the Kuomintang, which, not always adhering too closely to the truth, naturally served to arouse bitter feeling among the lower echelons of the Communists forces. It was not believed that any United States member of a field team consciously or intentionally displayed partiality in dealing with problems handled by the teams, and that misunderstanding that arose was due chiefly to the above-described propaganda campaign and perhaps in some cases to honest and unintentional errors of judgment, which were inevitable under the circumstances and which may have been to the advantage of either side.

By September 1946 the total number of Executive Headquarters field teams was 36 and there had been established a wide network of communications facilities to link these outposts with the Executive Headquarters at Peiping. The chief task of the Executive Headquarters at the time of its establishment was that of effecting a cessation of hostilities. Other equally vital functions of the Headquarters, either envisaged in the original agreement for its establishment or in subsequent agreements reached by the Committee of Three (or the

Military Sub-Committee), were the restoration of communications, the repatriation of the Japanese military and civilian personnel and the demobilization and reorganization of the Chinese armies. It is an interesting commentary that the only one of the above-named functions that the Executive Headquarters was able to carry successfully to completion was that of repatriating the Japanese military and civilian personnel. The restoration of communications and the demobilization and reorganization of the Chinese armies were necessarily dependent upon the cessation of hostilities and neither of these two tasks could be carried to completion or even successfully begun so long as armed conflict continued and there was no solution of the political issues involved. The net result was that the Executive Headquarters functioned very successfully within the limits of its possibilities and that its success was governed largely by the over-all political situation. A deterioration in the relations between the National Government and the Chinese Communist Party was soon reflected in the increased difficulties experienced by the Executive Headquarters and among its field teams in effectively preventing violation of the cessation of hostilities order or in carrying out the directives and decisions already agreed upon.

In any event, the Executive Headquarters, as the agency for the implementation of the major non-political agreements reached between the two Chinese parties, played a necessary and vital part in the efforts to bring peace and unity to China and restore the economic life of the country. If its efforts were not completely successful, the responsibility can be charged not to the Executive Headquarters, but rather to those Chinese elements whose bitterness and distrust of each other defeated the peaceful purpose of the field teams.

71(d)

Memorandum Concerning Repatriation of Japanese

One of the objectives set forth in the President's statement of United States policy toward China on December 15, 1945 was that of effecting the repatriation of Japanese troops from China with a view to the elimination of Japanese influence in that country. In this statement it was pointed out that the United States had assumed a definite obligation in the disarmament and evacuation of Japanese troops from China and that the United States was assisting and would continue to assist the Chinese Government to that end.

Although this statement of policy indicated that the elimination of Japanese influence in China was to be achieved through the evacuation of Japanese troops, it was obvious that the elimination of Japanese influence in China also called for the repatriation of Japanese civilians, whose presence in China would permit continued Japanese influence and many of whom, if permitted to remain, would strive secretly for the resurgence of Japanese power and influence on the continent of Asia. It was recognized, however, that the Chinese authorities had expressed a need for the services of Japanese technicians and that the expulsion of all Japanese technicians from China, without an adequate number of trained Chinese to take their places in industry, communications, mining and other fields, would result in injury to the economic life of the country.

In a conference between Chinese Government and United States Armed Forces representatives in October 1945 agreement was reached that the Chinese Government would be responsible for the repatriation of Japanese disarmed military personnel and civilians from China and that, consonant with the terms of the Potsdam Declaration, the United States Government would assist in this repatriation program. The United States Seventh Fleet assumed responsibility for the water lift of Japanese.

The question of the repatriation of Japanese from China was closely related to the cessation of hostilities, as the continued presence of Japanese armed forces in North China represented a very definite threat to peace in that area. This was particularly true because of the continued use by the National Government of armed Japanese units in garrisoning certain points along railway lines in North China and the Communist Party's insistence on the right of its forces to accept the Japanese surrender. With these circumstances in mind, the subject of Japanese repatriation was taken up in the discussions of the Committee of Three regarding the cessation of hostilities and the establishment of the Executive Headquarters. In the agreement for the establishment of the Headquarters, provision was made for the submission by the Headquarters of recommendations for measures for the disarmament of Japanese forces and the coordination of the movement of those forces to the coast for repatriation. It was realized that the dearth of military equipment in China would prevent the carrying out of measures for the destruction of Japanese military equipment and in discussions of the Committee of Three it was agreed that this equipment would be used for units of the 60 divisions to be retained by the National Army.

The scheduled repatriation of all Japanese military and civilian personnel from South China was completed on April 25, from Formosa on April 23, from Central China on July 11 and from North China on August 11. Difficulties were encountered in planning for the repatriation of Japanese from Manchuria owing to the continued occupation of that area by Soviet troops, who did not withdraw from Manchuria until the end of April. A relatively small number of Japanese military personnel was represented in the final repatriation figures for Manchuria and it has been assumed that large numbers of these Japanese troops were removed from Manchuria into Siberia.

The total number of Japanese repatriated under this program at the completion of mass repatriation on December 31, 1946, was as follows: 1,233,244, military personnel; 1,750,306, civilian personnel; total repatriated 2,983,550. The major portion of the task of Japanese repatriation from Chinese territory had been accomplished by September 20, when a total of 2,711,951 Japanese had been evacuated to Japan.

This task was one of great magnitude, involving the movement of Japanese repatriates from various inland points via inadequate lines of communications to the ports of embarkation. It required careful and close coordination between the Executive Headquarters Communication Group (charged with carrying out Executive Headquarters' responsibilities in this program), the field teams, the United States Army repatriation teams at the ports of embarkation, the United States Navy authorities and the Supreme Commander for the Allied Powers, which controlled the bulk of the shipping used for repatriation purposes. It involved the timing and regulation of the flow of repatriates from the interior to the ports of embarkation in such a manner that there would be a minimum of delay in the departure of repatriation vessels without an overloading of the processing and billeting facilities available to the repatriation teams. It required the establishment of food dumps and billets at the necessary points en route. It is a tribute to the effectiveness of the planning and execution of the repatriation program that the evacuation from China of this tremendous number of Japanese was accomplished within a relatively brief period of time.

72

Ratification by Central Executive Committee of the Kuomintang of Resolutions Adopted by Political Consultative Conference, March 16, 1946 [10]

Chungking, March 16 ... The P. C. C. agreements were ratified unanimously by the C. E. C. at this morning's meeting, presided over by President Chiang Kai-shek, Tsungtsai of the Kuomintang. Following the passage of the resolution, Dr. Sun Fo, President of the Legislative Yuan, announced that the Communist Party, the Democratic League and the Young China Party has agreed to certain revisions in the original P. C. C. agreement on the Draft Constitution.

The C. E. C. resolution pledged the Party's all-out observance and support of the P. C. C. agreements.

The resolution's accepting of the P. C. C. agreements expressed three "hopes". The three hopes were:

(1) After the reorganization of the Government, it is hoped that all parties will work sincerely for peace, unity and national reconstruction. It is especially hoped that the Communist Party in its own areas will practice democracy, allowing the freedom of thought, religious belief, expression, publication, assembly, and residence as well as the freedom of organization of other parties and so forth, and that the Communist Party will stop all atrocities against the people in the so-called "liberated areas".

(2) As the nationalization of armies is a prerequisite to national reconstruction, it is hoped the Communist Party will sincerely carry out the military subcommittee's basic agreement for the reorganization of the National Army and the integration of the Communist forces into the National Army and the cessation of hostilities and restoration of communications agreement and that the Communist Party will lift its blockade and siege of Government-held cities and cease drafting young men into its army, so that order will be fully restored in the interests of public welfare.

(3) As the Three People's Principles were accepted by the whole nation and also by the P. C. C. and because the five-power system is indispensable to the realization of the Three People's Principles, meaning that the two are indivisible, it is hoped that any amendments in the Draft Constitution which are contrary to the five-power system should be revised to accord with the plan for national reconstruction and the five-power system.

It is recalled that the P. C. C. agreements caused the longest and the hottest debate in the C. E. C. on March 7 and 8. The members' main objection was directed against the P. C. C. Draft Constitution agreement and they were suspicious of Communist sincerity in carrying out the P. C. C. agreements, especially the agreement on the nationalization of armies.

The chief points of conflict were over the principles of separation powers and the presidential system. The Kuomintang supported them while the other parties opposed them.

The Kuomintang insists that the National Army should be a real existing body, that the American presidential system and the principle of the separation powers be adopted and that federalism should be discarded, that is, provinces should not have their own constitutions.

---

[10] China News Service, Mar. 16, 1946.

The C. E. C. members regard the P. C. C. Draft Constitution agreement as diametrically opposite to Dr. Sun Yat-sen's plan for national reconstruction and the five-power system, which the other parties had agreed to observe.

The members' objection to the agreement was, however, considerably allayed when Dr. Sun Fo announced that at an interparty meeting yesterday the other parties had agreed to make three revisions in the agreement, namely, that the National Assembly should be made a real existing body, that the American presidential system be adopted and that provinces should not have their own constitutions and provincial governments should be provided for in organizational laws.

Dr. Sun said, however, that there are still many technical details to be thrashed out with the other parties.

On the motion of President Chiang Kai-shek, the C. E. C. resolved to give full powers to the C. E. C.'s Standing Committee to make decisions in regard to the Draft Constitution in the course of talks with the other parties.

MANIFESTO OF THE SECOND PLENARY SESSION OF 6TH KUOMINTANG CENTRAL EXECUTIVE COMMITTEE [11]

Following is a translation of the Manifesto issued by the Second Plenary Session of the Sixth Central Executive Committee of the Kuomintang on March 17, 1946:

Our war of resistance was won after the Fifth National Congress of the Kuomintang had met. That brought us into a new era of peaceful national reconstruction.

An opportunity to put Dr. Sun Yat-sen's "Plan for National Reconstruction" into operation presented itself after World War I, but it was lost in the hands of the lingering monarchists and the warlords. Now at the end of World War II we have secured, as a result of eight years of bitter fighting, another rare opportunity for rebuilding our nation. We must not let it pass by again. In order to preserve the fruits of our victory, we must take full advantage of this turning point in history.

To all of our Fellow Countrymen, we of this Plenary Session wish to point out the following:

First, we must achieve social stability, restore peace and order and complete the plan of national rehabilitation in order to inaugurate the task of peaceful national reconstruction. Peace is a requisite for national reconstruction; the two are absolutely indivisible. Confronted with the expensive damages of more than eight years of war, and having encountered numerous obstacles and difficulties in national rehabilitation during the last half year and witnessed the plight of our compatriots in various parts of the country; the suffering awaiting relief; the homeless, repatriation; the unemployed, re-employment; the oppressed, emancipation, we fully realize that no longer should there be turmoil and strife within the country. Nor should the phenomena of local disorder be permitted. We can validate the Party's struggle only by conforming our exertions with the needs of our country and our people. In the past six months the Government made great concessions in the interests of national rehabilitation. This Assembly regards such measures as correct. To bring about a favorable environment for peaceful national reconstruction we, in a spirit of tolerance, invited representatives of the other political parties and prominent social leaders to a Political Consultation Conference before the convocation of the National Assembly. We

---

[11] Special release by China News Service, Mar. 19, 1946.

admit that modifications in the procedure for national reconstruction, as laid down by our Party, might have been made, but our consistent Party spirit of placing the interests of the country and the people above everything else should be plain to all of our fellow countrymen. In conformity with this spirit we will stop at nothing to bring about the speedy completion of national rehabilitation.

Second, we must convene the National Assembly as scheduled to return the Government to the people in order to fulfill our long cherished wish of inaugurating constitutional government.

Our Party has all along advocated political democratization. It was openly declared by the Hsing Chung Hui (organized by Dr. Sun Yat-sen in 1892) as far back as fifty years ago. The revolutionary history of our Party is the history of democracy being fostered in China. Constitutional government would have been inaugurated according to our original program long ago had Japan not launched her campaign of aggression and had there been no military obstacles within the country. Our determination to inaugurate constitutional government at an early date has been made amply manifest by resolutions adopted by the Kuomintang on a number of occasions, as well as by the repeated statements of the Tsungtsai (Director General) of the Party. The Government has never slackened for comparing the way for constitutionalism, even in times of military crises. Our earnest desire has been to return the Government to the people, but we maintain that the convocation of the National Assembly is an essential step towards that end.

Third, we wish to affirm our sincere desire to implement fully the various agreements reached at the Political Consultation Conference and our determination to uphold the "Quintuple-Power Constitution." In view of the need of peace, stability and solidarity in the country and the urgent need of alleviating the people's sufferings, all of us should, after a careful study of the agreements reached at the Political Consultation Conference, very sincerely pledge to exert ourselves in concert with the other parties and prominent social leaders to carry out the agreements. But we maintain that the revision of the Draft Constitution must conform with Dr. Sun Yat-sen's teachings on the "Quintuple-Power Constitution."

The reason for our insistence on the "Quintuple-Power Constitution" is that the Three Principles of the People and the "Quintuple-Power Constitution" are inseparable. Minus the "Quintuple-Power Constitution," the Three Principles of the People cannot be fully carried out. This political system is Dr. Sun's great and profound discovery as a result of his study of the European and American constitutions, of their merits and demerits, as well as of the actual conditions in China, having as his object the laying of an enduring foundation for national peace and security.

A comprehensive and practicable constitution is necessary to insure a sound and firm political structure in our country. If the contents of the constitution should contravene the "Quintuple-Power Constitution", practical difficulties are certain to be encountered in its application, therefore placing the country at a disadvantage. The Kuomintang, therefore, will steadfastly uphold the "Quintuple-Power Constitution". This is indeed taking a long-range view of our national interests. We hope that the other parties and social leaders will appreciate our stand and understand our views.

Fourth, we must lay a foundation for peace and unity by thoroughly carrying out the nationalization of armed forces. The primary requisite of political democratization is the nationalization of armed forces. Only by nationalizing troops can administrative integrity and unity of military command be achieved. Democracy may be truly realized only when there is national unity in deed as well as in name. The existence of a state within a state and regional domination by armed forces are anti-democratic. Such phenomena could not be tolerated in any country. When administrative integrity and unity of military command are wanting and when local peace and order are constantly disturbed, there is no safeguard even for the people's basic need of being able to live and pursue their occupations in peace, let alone carrying out reconstruction measures.

There must be unqualified nationwide observance and thorough execution of the orders issued by the Government a month ago concerning the cessation of hostilities and the restoration of communications. The plans for military reorganization and the integration of the armed forces, recently arrived at at the three-man Military Subcommittee, should be similarly carried out. Only then can we say that the concessions we have made in the interests of national peace and solidarity have not been in vain and our long-harassed people will be given a chance to rest and recuperate. In examining the present situation, this Session feels compelled to demand that a halt be called immediately to the ceaseless military attacks and to acts impeding national unity, so that peaceful national reconstruction may proceed smoothly and the promotion of democracy may not result in empty talk.

Fifth, we must carry out the program bearing upon the people's livelihood as laid down by the Sixth National Congress of the Kuomintang. The fulfillment of the Principle of the People's Livelihood is the ultimate objective of the Three Principles of the People. In promoting the Principle of the People's Livelihood at this stage, efforts may be directed to treat both the symptoms and the causes.

Treatment of the symptoms should begin, first, with the enforcement of peace and order and the relief of the people's distress before embarking on large-scale economic reconstruction projects. Our foremost task now is to alleviate the sufferings of the starving or half-starving like the large farming and laboring classes, civil servants, school teachers, and officers and men who fought to defend the country. Ways and means must be devised to improve their living, and our own work must begin with stabilizing commodity prices and maintaining the value of the currency. The Government should spare no efforts to carry out the required measures.

We should furthermore restore production to increase supplies at home and purchase and transport foodstuffs to give necessary relief. A program of retrenchment should be adopted to curtail unnecessary expenditures. International economic cooperation should be established so that large supplies of goods, particularly production tools, may be imported.

The most urgent task of the moment is the restoration of communications. With communications disrupted at so many places, even the distribution of international relief supplies has not been possible. The destruction of communications, therefore, has not only been of great harm to the people; it is tantamount to condemning the people to death. This Session cannot refrain from frankly pointing this out in the hope that the Executive Headquarters will take effective measures to stop acts of obstructing road repairs and of violating communications administration.

Treatment of causes should stress the equalization of land ownership and regulation of private capital which are fundamental principles of this party which must be fulfilled. Similarly important are the relief of rural districts and the checking of the present trend of land annexation with a view to aiding farmers who till their own soil.

In carrying out our postwar five-year economic reconstruction programs, we have great need of international economic and technical assistance. The economic reconstruction programs adopted by the Fifth National Congress of the Kuomintang are most accurate. It is a matter for regret that they have not been extensively carried out in the past nine months on account of military clashes and rehabilitation work. Henceforth, we must urge the Government departments concerned to execute the measures alluded to so that the people may live and pursue their occupations in peace with eventual raising of the living standard.

Sixth, we must fully realize our primary aim in embarking on the war of resistance, namely, the preservation of our national sovereignty and the consolidation of world peace. Our fundamental foreign policy aims at safeguarding our territorial, sovereign and administrative integrity and at consolidating enduring world peace through faithful adherence to international treaties. This explains why we opposed Japanese coercion, designed to bring us into the anti-comintern pact, and resisted for more than eight years.

With the war of resistance at an end, we desire for our postwar reconstruction not only stability at home but peace all over the world. We do not wish conflicts and misunderstandings between nations which would revive the hope of the defeated aggressors for a resurgence. With utmost sincerity we have supported the United Nations Charter, while at the international conference tables our delegates have taken considerable pains to strengthen the cooperation of the major allies. This is a concrete demonstration of our policy.

In the interests of enduring peace in China and in the world as a whole, we must eliminate completely all chances of Japanese imperialism being revived. This calls for complete understanding and closest cooperation between our country and our allies, particularly the Soviet Union, with which we have the longest continuous border. It is our most sincere desire to further mutual confidence and friendship with the Soviet Union. We firmly believe that strict observance of the Sino-Soviet Treaty of Friendship and Alliance by both parties is the first and foremost prerequisite for the enhancement of mutual trust and friendship.

In the meantime, we welcome, for the completion of our economic reconstruction, financial or technical cooperation from any one of our allies as long as it does not violate Chinese law or contravene China's international commitments. Only when there is an independent, free, united and strong China can the resurgence of Japanese imperialism be effectively eliminated and a durable peace in the Pacific and in the whole world be maintained. We are convinced that with this recognition a reasonable and lawful solution can be found for the present Northeast problem. We will not allow a temporary phenomena to lessen our confidence or slacken our efforts.

At this time when the period of political tutelage is about to be concluded, and our revolutionary work is entering the new phase of national reconstruction, our fellow party members should be aware that, whereas in the past we led the revolution as the only revolutionary political party, we should henceforth work for national reconstruction as the largest political party. We will not evade our responsibility. Let us remember:

First, that the Republic of China was founded by Dr. Sun Yat-sen and the Kuomintang martyrs;

Second, that the task of weeding out the warlords and bringing about national unification was accomplished under the leadership of the Kuomintang;

Third, that the bondage of the century of unequal treaties was removed under the leadership of the Kuomintang; and

Fourth, that, again, it was under the leadership of the Kuomintang that the war of resistance was fought for more than eight years until a magnificent victory was won for the country and the nation.

Inasmuch as we have accomplished these four great missions in modern times, we are the more confident that our Party and our Tsungtsai will lead the entire nation to perform the still greater mission of peaceful national reconstruction.

In the departing period of political tutelage, there have been shortcomings in political and party affairs. We cannot escape responsibility although some mistakes were due to uncontrollable factors. The object of our revolution is precisely what Dr. Sun Yat-sen once said: "To rescue the people from suffering and hardship and lead them to peace and happiness." We are indeed aggrieved that immense difficulties still face the country and that the people are leading such a hard life. We revolutionary workers should bravely assume responsibility for effecting reforms. We should continuously and searchingly examine ourselves, to shoulder the great and difficult responsibility henceforwards, this plenary Session feels that we should consolidate our views, examine and strengthen ourselves, so as to renovate our Party activities; that we should endure hardships and exert our utmost to serve the people in pursuance of our revolutionary aims; and, above all, that we should, in a spirit of frankness and mutual trust, concert our efforts with the other parties and the entire people to insure the success of national reconstruction.

In the past, the Kuomintang, with the support of the entire nation, has accomplished one great mission after another. Now that victory is here, it is our duty to rebuild the Chinese Republic into a modern nation, prosperous, strong, healthy and happy. Let us raise the banner of the Three Principles of the People as we march on toward peaceful national reconstruction.

73

Memorandum by the Chairman of the Committee of Three (Marshall)

January 24, 1946

For General Chang Chun:[12]
General Chou En-lai:[13]

While I do not find reference in the official documents concerning the truce agreements to the effect that the Executive Headquarters has no jurisdiction over hostilities in Manchuria, I am informed by Mr. Robertson, the U. S. Commissioner in Peking that the commissioners are of the opinion and have publicly announced that the Executive Headquarters has no jurisdiction in Manchuria.

In this connection, I have received reports of serious conflicts around Yingkow. I recommend that we here agree to direct Executive Headquarters to dispatch immediately a team to Yingkow.

I propose that further action in Manchuria under the terms of the "cease firing" order be directed by us from Chungking in each instance, but to be carried out by the Executive Headquarters.

If you indicate your agreement, I will dispatch the enclosed message to the Commissioners in Peking.

Faithfully yours,

G. C. MARSHALL

---

[12] Representative of the Chinese National Government.
[13] Representative of the Chinese Communist Party.

74

The Committee of Three to the Executive Headquarters

CHUNGKING, *March 27, 1946*

We, General Chang Chih-chung, authorized representative of the National Government; General Chou En-lai, authorized representative of the Chinese Communist Party and General A. C. Gillem, Jr., acting for General G. C. Marshall; have agreed that Field Teams, with carefully selected personnel, will be sent into Manchuria immediately under the following instructions:

1. The mission of the teams will pertain solely to readjustment of military matters.
2. The teams should operate within the areas of the Government troops as well as the Communist troops, keeping clear of places still under Russian occupation.
3. Teams should proceed to points of conflict or close contact between the Government and Communist troops to bring about a cessation of fighting and to make the necessary and fair readjustments.

It is further agreed that included as a matter of record in the minutes of the Committee of Three conferences will be the following statement:

The Committee of Three will further discuss the military matters pertaining to Manchuria. As to political matters in Manchuria separate discussion will be held with a view to reaching an early settlement.

CHANG CHIH-CHUNG
Representative of the National Government

CHOU EN-LAI
Representative of the Chinese Communist Party

A. C. GILLEM, Jr.
Representing General G. C. Marshall

75

The Committee of Three to the Three Commissioners of Executive Headquarters

NANKING, *May 14, 1946*

This message from the Committee of Three is addressed to the three commissioners of Executive Headquarters. The following agreement has been reached by the Committee of Three and will be placed into effect without delay.

It is agreed that effective implementation of the cessation of hostilities agreements reached by this committee or by the commissioners of Executive Headquarters requires that field teams of Executive Headquarters be permitted to investigate without delay any violation of such agreements as may be reported to them.

To insure prompt investigation of such reported violations, it is agreed that:

1. The military and civil authorities of both the National Government and the Chinese Communist Party shall render all possible assistance to the activities of the field teams, without imposing any delay or restriction.

2. The military and civil authorities of both the National Government and the Chinese Communist Party shall assure the personal freedom and security of the field team members.

3. Equal opportunity for investigation shall be afforded to both the National Government and Communist Party within any team area, but this policy shall not be permitted to delay action or to interfere with the overriding principle that priority of investigation should be based upon the apparent seriousness and urgency of the violations reported to the team.

4. The procedure regarding priority of areas and matters for investigation shall be as worked out by the U. S. representative as the chairman of the team and unanimously agreed upon by the team members for implementation. In case of disagreement the American member will immediately report the disagreement to the commissioners, who will within twenty-four hours either render a unanimous decision or report their disagreement to the Committee of Three.

5. In the event it is established that a false report of violation has been submitted to a team for investigation, a report of the incident will be submitted by the commissioners to the Committee of Three for corrective action.

HSU YUNG-CHANG
Representative of the National Government

CHOU EN-LAI
Representative of the Chinese Communist Party

G. C. MARSHALL
United States Representative

76 (a)

Statement by Generalissimo Chiang Kai-shek on Temporary Truce Period in Manchuria, June 6, 1946

I am issuing orders at noon today to my armies in Manchuria to halt all advances, attacks and pursuits for a period of 15 days commencing noon Friday, June 7th. I am doing this to give the Communist Party an opportunity to demonstrate in good faith their intention to carry out the agreements they had previously signed. In taking this action the Government in no way prejudices its right under the Sino-Soviet Treaty to take over the sovereignty of Manchuria.

The following matters must be satisfactorily settled within the 15 day period:

a. Detailed arrangements to govern a complete termination of hostilities in Manchuria.

b. Detailed arrangements, and time schedules, for the complete restoration of communications in China, and

c. A definite basis for carrying out without further delay the agreement of February 25, 1946, for the demobilization, reorganization and integration of the armed forces in China.

76 (b)

Statement by Vice Chairman of the Central Committee of the Chinese Communist Party (Chou) on Temporary Truce Period in Manchuria, June 6, 1946

The Chinese Communist Party is advocating all the time an unconditional and true termination of civil warfare, which applies to hostilities in China proper and in Manchuria as well. It is due to the persistence of the Chinese Communist Party, the aspiration of the Chinese people, and the efforts exerted by General Marshall, that the Generalissimo's issuance of orders to halt all advances, attacks and pursuits in Manchuria for a period of 15 days and negotiations in the following matters are secured:

    a. Detailed arrangements to govern a complete termination of hostilities in Manchuria.

    b. Detailed arrangements, and time schedules, for the complete restoration of communications in China, and

    c. A definite basis for carrying out without further delay the agreement of February 25, 1946, for the demobilization, reorganization and integration of the armed forces in China.

Though we feel concerned over the shortness of the 15 day period, and that the inevitable involvement of political subjects pertaining to Manchuria, or even China as a whole, into the forthcoming negotiation would call for a longer period for discussion, we concur with the 15 day cease fire arrangement, having in mind that no opportunity for the realization of peace should be skipped over. In doing so, we will exert our best efforts toward bringing the negotiations to a success. We hope that the Kuomintang, in compliance with the desire of the Chinese people as well as nations abroad, would demonstrate in good faith their intention to carry out the agreements they had previously signed, and make the temporary armistice a lasting truce, with advances, attacks and pursuits stopped forever.

77

Directive by the Committee of Three for Reopening of Lines of Communication in North and Central China, June 1946

1. All lines of communications in North and Central China will be opened without delay for free and unrestricted interchange of goods, foodstuffs and ideas, and for free and unrestricted civilian travel.

2. Reconstruction of railways will proceed immediately and will progress as rapidly as is consistent with the time limitations necessarily imposed by labor and matériel requirements. Time estimate for construction of the railroad lines is covered in Appendix A.

3. All local commanders and all team members shall expedite construction by all means within their power. No commander nor team member will permit interference with the construction work or with the work of removal or destruction of fortifications for any reason whatsoever.

4. Construction will start before 30 June 1946 at each of the following points, under supervision of Communications teams and under control of the MOC:

    Team No. 24 or 4—Lunghai RR from Hsuchow to Haichow.
    Team No. 23—   "   "   "   "   Yucheng to Te Hsien.

Team No. 23 or 16—"   "   "   "   Taian to Yenchow.
Team No. 24—   "   "   "   "   Hanchuan to Yenchow.
Team No. 21—Tsinan-Tsingtao RR from Kaomi to Fengtze.
Team No. 23 or 7—"   "   "   "   Chengtien to Fengtze.
Team No. 24 or 4—Lunghai RR from Hsuchow to Haichow.

Construction on other railroad lines will be commenced at the earliest practicable date in conformance with the principles herein contained.

5. All mines, fortifications, blockades, blockhouses, and other military works lying within 1,000 meters on either side of the railroads listed above will be removed or destroyed simultaneously with construction, except those military works constructed for defense of, and lying within 1,000 meters of, vital railroad installations such as 1st or 2nd class railroad stations, tunnels, or bridges of total span of more than 5 meters, and within 200 meters of 3rd class stations. This work of removal or destruction will proceed in the direction of construction within each of the 7 construction areas above listed, at such rate that the removal or demolition will, at all times, be completed for a distance of not less than 1,000 meters in advance of completed construction of the railroad. At the same time, other military works along the operating portions of the above-mentioned lines will be removed or destroyed at a constant rate such that the removal or destruction will have been completed on or before the date of completion of the railroad within the area of control of each of the above 7 listed teams. When work of restoration of the other railroad lines in North and Central China is commenced, this same principle shall apply. However, the Lunghai railroad west of Cheng-hsien and the Peiping-Hankow railroad south of Cheng-hsien are specifically exempted from the program for removal or destruction of military works, and the destruction or removal of military works along the Lunghai railroad between Hsuchow and Cheng-hsien will be deferred until _____. No new fortifications will be erected except to meet attacks against the railroad itself and only after approval by a communications team.

6. Before through traffic is permitted over the reopened sectors of the railroads, qualified railroad personnel of the CCP may be taken into the employ of the MOC in accordance with a plan to be determined. The qualifications of such personnel will be determined by examinations conducted by communications teams or by the Communications Group of the Executive Headquarters.

7. Detailed plans for the restoration of all other lines of communications in accordance with General Directive 4 will be covered by later agreement. This directive shall not prejudice in any way General Directive 4.

Appendix A

Time Schedule

Tientsin Pukow RR from Tsang Hsien to Te-Hsien	75 days
Yucheng to Te-Hsien	60 days
Taian to Yenchow	60 days
Hanchuan to Yenchow	90 days
Tsinan Tsingtao RR	30 days
Lung-Hai RR, Hsuchow to Haichow	30 days
Peiping-Suiyuan RR, Hankow to Paotou	45 days
Peiping-Hankow RR, Yuanshih to Anyang	150 days
Tung-Po RR, Lingfen to Yunchang	50 days
Peiping-Ku Pei Kou RR	30 days
Tatung-Taiyuan RR	30 days

78

Agreement by the Committee of Three on Stipulations for the Resolution of Certain Disagreements Among Field and Communication Teams, and Executive Headquarters in Changchun and Peiping, June 24, 1946

I. FIELD AND COMMUNICATION TEAMS

a. In case of disagreement regarding matters of urgency, the American representative of the field or communication team may render his own report of the situation as he sees it direct to Executive Headquarters in Changchun or Peiping requesting instructions.

b. In case of disagreement, the American representative of the field team is authorized to make decision as to where and when the field team will move within his area to conduct investigations regarding military activities. Regarding the place of investigation, transportation difficulties should not be permitted to prejudice or delay the movement of the teams.

c. In case of disagreement regarding matters relating to cessation of hostilities and separation of forces the American representative of the field team is authorized to issue orders in the name of the Executive Headquarters to the field commanders on both sides to stop fighting at once and to effect the separation of the forces as prescribed in accordance with directives.

d. The area assigned to each field and communication team will be designated by Executive Headquarters.

II. EXECUTIVE HEADQUARTERS IN CHANGCHUN AND PEIPING

a. In case of disagreement the senior American official of Executive Headquarters in Peiping or Changchun may render his own report to Executive Headquarters in Peiping or the Committee of Three based on the situation as he sees it requesting instructions.

b. In case of disagreement regarding the implementation of orders or instructions from the higher level, the senior American official of the Executive Headquarters in Peiping or Changchun is authorized to direct the execution of that order or instruction unless amended or rescinded by the higher level itself.

79

The Committee of Three to the Three Commissioners of Executive Headquarters

[*June 26?*] *1946*

On the basis of the orders of June 6, 1946 halting all advances, attacks and pursuits for a period of 15 days commencing at noon of June 7th, which will be continued in effect, we, the Committee of Three, announce the following instructions to govern a complete termination of hostilities in Manchuria.

a. The terms of 10 January 1946 for the cessation of hostilities will govern except as hereinafter specifically modified, or later directed by the Committee of Three.

b. Commanders of forces in close contact or engaged in actual fighting will immediately direct their troops to cease fighting and will seek to secure a local truce by establishing liaison with the opposing commanders, pending the arrival of a field team. They should both immediately withdraw their respective troops from close contact.

c. The readjustment of troops found to be in close contact or actually engaged in fighting will be directed by the field team on the ground by requiring the withdrawal for specified distances, normally 20 li, of one or both forces according to the circumstances. The local situation believed to have existed at noon of June 7, 1946 will be the basis for determining the readjustment of the troops involved.

d. All movements of Government or Communist troops of a tactical nature will cease. Administrative and supply movements as authorized in the original cease fire order of January 10, 1946 may be carried out within the garrisoned areas if previously approved by a field team.

e. Within fifteen days after the issuance of this agreement, lists showing all units together with commanders of regiments and larger units, strength and locations in Manchuria will be submitted to the advance section of Executive Headquarters in Changchun.

f. The Government will move no additional combat units to Manchuria. However, individual replacements of the Government are authorized for the purpose of bringing up to approved strength those units authorized in the basic plan for the reorganization and integration dated February 25th, 1946, as hereafter amended.

g. Officers failing to carry out the terms of this agreement will be relieved and disciplined by their respective commanders.

80

Preliminary Agreement Proposed by the Chairman of the Committee of Three (Marshall), June 1946

The following conditions are agreed to by the Committee of Three and are to be included in the amendments to the document signed February 25, 1946, "Basis for Military Reorganization and for the Integration of the Communist Forces into the National Army". These conditions are established for the purpose of committing the Government and the Communist Party to certain understandings in order to facilitate the preparation and acceptance of the formal documents required and to permit the immediate issuance of instructions for the final termination of hostilities.

1. The specific disposition of troops in Manchuria and China proper must be finally agreed to at this time for both National and Communist troops. And it is understood that these assignments will refer to definite localities rather than to areas.

2. The ratio previously agreed to between the total strength of the Government and Communist forces will not be altered.

3. The periods previously established for the assignment of the troops into specified localities will be altered for the first phase (originally 12 months) to six months except where specifically stated to the contrary.

4. The Executive Headquarters will immediately determine the localities which have been occupied by the Government or Communist forces in China proper since January 13, 1946 and will require the troops involved to vacate those localities within 20 days after signing this agreement unless specifically directed otherwise.

5. The Executive Headquarters will immediately determine the localities occu-

pied by the Government or Communist forces in Manchuria afternoon of June 7, 1946 and will require the troops involved to vacate those localities within 10 days after the signing of this agreement unless specifically directed otherwise.

6. The Chinese Communist Party agrees to a Government garrison in Harbin of one regiment of not to exceed 5,000 men.

7. The Chinese Communist Party has agreed to concentrate its troops in specified localities, it being understood that the Government troops will not move into the areas thus vacated in China proper and that the present established civil governments and the Peace Preservation Corps for the maintenance of local security, will be continued. It is further agreed that in these areas no restrictions will be imposed on imports or exports, and free communication with adjacent regions will be assured.

8. It is understood and agreed that the formal amendment of the army reorganization plan of February 25, 1946 must be completed and signed within _____ days from the date of this document.

ANNEX PRELIMINARY AGREEMENT OF COMMITTEE OF THREE DATED JUNE 1946 TO GOVERN THE AMENDMENT AND EXECUTION OF THE ARMY REORGANIZATION PLAN OF FEBRUARY 25, 1946

In acordance with paragraph 7 of this agreement the Chinese Communist Party agrees that in implementing the Army Reorganization agreement of February 25, 1946 the following conditions will govern:

a. Communist troops will not be garrisoned or concentrated within any of the following areas:

Anwhei—All of the province after

Kiangsu—South of the latitude of Hwai-an exclusive, after   , and south of the Lunghai RR. after

Shantung—1. Tsaochuang area after
2. Tsingtao-Tsinan R. R. after (including coal mines)
3. Northeast Shantung after
4. Te-Hsien after

Chahar—South of the latitude of Kalgan exclusive, within

Jehol—South of the latitude of Chengte exclusive, within   . Chengte to be evacuated within

Hupeh-Honan Border Area—The Communist troops in that area will be moved to Hopei within

Shansi—Wen-hsi.

Manchuria—All provinces except Hei Lungchiang, Hsing-an, Central and Northern Nun-chiang and Eastern Kirin.

81

Manchuria Annex to Preliminary Agreement Proposed by Chairman of the Committee of Three (Marshall)[14]

The entire demobilization and integration program for Manchuria shall be completed before January 1, 1947. The ultimate strength of military forces in Manchuria shall comprise a total of 6 armies. There shall be 1 army composed of 1 National division and 2 Communist divisions with a Communist Commander, 1

---

[14] Presented to the Representative of the Chinese Communist Party (Chou) on June 17, 1946.

army of 2 National divisions and 1 Communist division with a National Commander and 4 National Armies with National Commanders.

The necessary demobilization or increase in strength to realize the foregoing shall begin on June 22, 1946 and shall be completed before January 1, 1947. Redeployment of divisons to the localities designated hereinafter shall be completed before October 1, 1946. During the month of December 1946 integration of the two armies concerned shall be effected.

The location of armies shall be as follows:

1. One army composed of 1 National and 2 Communist divisions to be located within the three provinces of Hsin Hei Lung Kiang, Hsing-An, and Nun Kiang with one Communist division in Hsin Hei Lung Kiang and North and Central Nun Kiang, one Communist division in Hsung-An and North-Central Nun Kiang, and one National division in Southern Nun Kiang. The division headquarters of the above 3 divisions shall be located at Tsi-tsihar, Hailar and Paicheng respectively. The army headquarters shall be located at Tsitsihar.

2. One army composed of 2 National divisions and 1 Communist division to be located within the Provinces of Kirin and Sung Kiang with one National division in Central Kirin Province, one National division in Eastern Sung Kiang Province and one Communist division in Eastern Kirin Province. The division headquarters of the three divisions shall be located at the cities of Kirin, Mutankiang and Yenki, respectively. The army headquarters shall be located in the city of Kirin.

3. One national army shall be located within the provinces of Sung Kiang and Kirin with one division in Eastern and Central Sung Kiang and two divisions in Central and Eastern Kirin. The division headquarters of the above divisions shall be at Harbin and Changchun respectively. The army headquarters shall be located at Changchun.

4. One National army shall be located within Liao Peh and Liaoning Provinces with one division in Liao Peh Province and 2 divisions in Northern Liaoning Province. The division headquarters of the above divisions shall be located at Ssupingkai and Mukden respectively. The army headquarters shall be located at Mukden.

5. One National army shall be located within Liaoning and Antung Provinces with one division in Western Liaoning Province and two divisions in Antung Province. The division headquarters of the above divisions shall be at Penshi, Antung and Tunghuakai respectively. The army headquarters shall be located at Penshi.

6. One National army shall be located within Southern Liaoning Province. Two of the division headquarters shall be located at Chinchow and one at Yingkou. The army headquarters shall be located at Chinchow.

82

Radio Message by Generalissimo Chiang Kai-shek, July 1, 1946

Priority: Urgent
To: Directors, Generalissimo's Field Headquarters.
    Directors, President's Field Headquarters.
    Directors, Pacification Bureaus.
    Commanding Generals, War Areas.
    Commanding Generals, Pacification Areas.

Commanding Generals, Garrison Commands.
The Commanding General, Nanking Garrison Command.
Commanding Generals, Army Groups.
Commanding Generals, Armies (CG's, Reorganized divisions).
General Cheng Kai-ming, Commissioner, Executive Headquarters, Peiping.

Our Government has been extremely patient, disregarding the great injustice done to itself and conceded time and again, for the purpose of obtaining peace. But up to date, no successful solution is being reached on any problem. Now, for sake of urging the Communist Party to repent itself, so as to reach basis for reaching agreement and establishing peace and unity, the following stipulations are made: If Communist troops do not attack our forces, then our troops will not attack the Communist Forces. Should the Communist troops advance against our forces, then our troops, for sake of self defense, protecting lives and properties of the people, and to keep local law and order will concentrate their strength and counter attack them,—so as to do the duties of us Soldiers. This order is being distributed and strict compliance by all units is requested. Also date of receipt of this order will be reported.

Generalissimo CHIANG KAI-SHEK

83

Joint Statement by Mao Sse Tung [15] and General Chu Teh,[16] July 1, 1946

To: All Communist Field Commanders:

At any place, if the Nationalist troops do not attack our force, our army shall not take the initiative in attacking them. But in case of being attacked, our army shall resolutely take self-defensive measures in order to protect lives and properties of the people and to maintain law and order of the Democratic Governments.

MAO TSE TUNG
CHU TEH

84

Joint Statement by the Special Representative of the President (Marshall) and the Ambassador in China (Stuart), August 10, 1946 [17]

General Marshall and Doctor Stuart have been exploring together every possibility for terminating the present growing conflict in China and for the initiation of the preliminary steps in the development of a truly democratic form of government. The desire for a peaceful solution to the political problems appears practically unanimous on the part of the people. The economic situation demands a prompt solution if a disastrous collapse is to be avoided. The fighting is daily growing more wide spread and threatens to engulf the country and pass beyond the control of those responsible. Both the Government and the Communist leaders are anxious to put an end to the fighting but there are certain issues concerned in the immediate settlements involved regarding which an agreement has not been found. It appears impossible for the two parties to reach a settlement of

---

[15] Chairman of the Central Committee of the Chinese Communist Party.
[16] Commander-in-Chief of the Chinese Communist Armies.
[17] *Department of State Bulletin,* Aug. 25, 1946, p. 384.

these issues which would permit a general order to be issued for the complete cessation of hostilities in all of China. Certain of the unsettled issues relate to the military redispositions of troops. However, these apparently present less difficulty of settlement than a more fundamental issue concerning the character of local or country governments to be maintained in the regions which will be evacuated as a result of the military redisposition pending a basic decision in such matters by the Constitutional Assembly.

85

Statement by President Chiang Kai-shek, August 13, 1946 [18]

My fellow countrymen:

Exactly one year ago today Japan surrendered unconditionally to the Allied Powers.

At the time when the war ended I realized that peace and unity in the country must be established before the people could live and produce, and before reconversion and reconstruction could progress. One year has passed but our national difficulties have not been lessened, nor have the people's sufferings been alleviated. In reviewing the past and looking toward the future, I feel the great responsibilities that fall upon me.

Our principal objective after victory was reconversion to peace. During the past year the government has moved from Chungking to Nanking. Wartime legislation restricting civil liberties has been removed or amended. The National army is being reorganized according to schedule; thousands of officers are being retired from active service. Universities in the interior are moving back to their original campuses. Ruined and broken cities and towns are being repaired, damaged dykes rebuilt.

In areas not occupied or affected by the Communists the main communications systems, such as the Canton-Hankow railway, have been restored. Relief is being given to the famine areas. Systems of election and assembly are being extended in the various provinces and districts. Bumper crops are reported throughout the country this year which give hope of alleviating the famine that followed the war. The taxation system has been improved. Since March the rate of banknote issues has decreased steadily and there was no new issue during July.

This much we have accomplished through hardship and industry during the past year.

However, we have much to regret in the slow progress of our reconversion.

The most critical situation facing the country today is the stoppage of production, economic dislocation, the high cost of commodities and livelihood.

The prime reason for this situation is the disruption of communications. The number of vessels we possess is still inadequate. Our trunk railway lines—the Peiping-Hankow, Tientsin-Pukow, Kiaochow-Tsinan and Lunghai—have been repeatedly destroyed and disrupted. Because of this, our industrial centers lack raw materials, our agricultural and mineral products have no markets. While cargoes clog the commercial ports there is serious shortage of commodities and capital in the interior.

---

[18] English summary of statement on the first anniversary of the Japanese surrender as issued by the International Department of the Chinese Ministry of Information.

Furthermore, there are a number of places now occupied by the Communists who have established their own economic unit enforcing a blockade on foodstuffs, issuing and circulating their own currency, and living off the people in those areas. They have controlled the livelihood of the people in the adjacent areas. This situation has split the national economy and thus has hampered price control, currency stabilization, and reconversion as a whole.

The crux of the difficulties I have just enumerated is the continued disruption of peace and order, and our inability so far to reach a satisfactory settlement of political differences.

When the war ended, the government decided on a policy of "national unity" and "political democracy". It was hoped that through political measures party friction could be eliminated. We knew that the Communist Party was not an ordinary party with a democratic system. It is a party with an independent military force, an independent administrative system. It taxes the people within its areas and remains outside the realm of the National government.

However, the government exerted much effort hoping that the Communists would give up their military occupation of territory and change into a peaceful, law-abiding political party and follow the democratic road to reconstruction. We must not permit another state to exist within a state; nor permit a private army to operate independent of a national army. This is the main obstacle in the settlement of the present situation and is also the minimum demand the government has to put before the Communist party for the interest of the country and the people.

During the past year the government took the first step to open negotiations with the Communist representatives. Then, at the Political Consultative Conference in which all political elements were represented, five agreements were reached. Through the assistance of General Marshall an agreement was signed for ending all hostilities and for the restoration of communications. A plan for reorganization of the National army and integration of the Communist armies into the National army was also reached.

The future of the country and the prosperity of the people largely depended on the execution of these agreements and formulas.

Unfortunately, during the past seven months the Communists have taken advantage of the situation to expand their areas of occupation. They have increased their demands. They have refused to respect the decisions of the Executive Headquarters, in which the government, the Communists, and the Americans are represented and which was created to implement the agreements. They have continued to disrupt peace by their actions.

The people are forced to live in fear and it has increased the difficulties of the government.

Under the present domestic and international situation, China cannot permit another war to break out. However, no government in the world can shirk its responsibility to preserve order and protect the lives of the people.

The government will continue to favor a peaceful settlement of the present differences. Because of long years of war, hardships, sacrifices, and losses, the nation is like a person who has been seriously ill and needs gentle care during his period of recuperation.

The government will always abide by the agreements and formulas to which it is a party. A plan for reorganization of the National army is already being carried out by the government. Even when the Communists have violated the agreements and provoked clashes, the government has accepted the decisions of the Executive Headquarters. The record bears this out.

The government's policy will be:

1. To end the period of political tutelage and institute constitutional government without delay in spite of all obstacles. The National Assembly definitely will be held on schedule November 12.
2. To abide by the agreements reached by the Political Consultative Conference, and to execute them. Sound proposals on principles of constitutional law should be embodied in the draft constitution which will be presented to the National Assembly for adoption.
3. To enlarge the government's political basis by including members of all parties and non-partisans and to put into effect the Program of Peaceful Reconstruction as adopted by the Political Consultative Conference.
4. To abide by the January 10 truce agreement. Our only demand is that the Communists withdraw from areas where they threaten peace and obstruct communications.
5. To continue to use political means to settle political differences; but only if the Communists give assurance and evidence that they will carry out the truce agreement, restore communications, respect decisions of the Executive Headquarters, and integrate the Communist army into the National army, the government will be ready to negotiate all the pending problems.
6. To give protection and security to the people and their properties and to remove any threat to peace so as to enable the people to live in peace and carry on their daily livelihood.

My fellow countrymen:

In looking over the past year, if we had not suffered domestic strife, if a political party with armed forces had not insisted on expanding its territory, our country would be in a high and respected place, our people would have peace and prosperity.

If the Communists had carried out the three agreements reached since last January to cease hostilities, restore communications, and integrate their armies, and if they had, according to schedule, appointed representatives to participate in the National Government and attend the National Assembly, we could by now have instituted constitutional government. We could have completed our transition to political democracy and we would not be misunderstood and criticized by world opinion. The people of Northern Kiangsu, Hopei, and Shantung would not have had to go through again the sufferings of battle and floods.

I earnestly hope that the Communist party, reflecting on these facts, will come to this realization.

Today our one important demand is that the Communist party change its policy of seizing power by military force and transform into a peaceful party. We want them to help us win the peace in China.

We must have a deep understanding of the issues confronting our country and realize our responsibilities. We must put down rebellions, and make China a peaceful, democratic, unified, and strong country. But government officials, also, must review their own mistakes and shortcomings, and exert every effort to fulfill their duties to their country. Furthermore, the people must have faith, patience, and zeal. They must be able to differentiate between right and wrong, true and false, to speak up for justice; to complete the revolutionary work of the nation.

I dedicated myself to the cause of the revolution for the country and the people. I will not let the fruits of victory be lost in a day. I will not change my determination to establish a peaceful, unified, and democratic country. I will assume my responsibilities, and with the help of my fellow countrymen, follow the scheduled course to national reconstruction.

86

President Truman to President Chiang Kai-shek

WASHINGTON, *August 10, 1946*

I have followed closely the situation in China since I sent General Marshall to you as my Special Envoy. It is with profound regret that I am forced to the conclusion that his efforts have seemingly proved unavailing.

In his discussions with you, I am certain that General Marshall has reflected accurately the overall attitude and policy of the American Government and of informed American public opinion also.

The rapidly deteriorating political situation in China, during recent months, has been a cause of grave concern to the American people. While it is the continued hope of the United States that an influential and democratic China can still be achieved under your leadership, I would be less than honest if I did not point out that latest developments have forced me to the conclusion that the selfish interests of extremist elements, both in the Kuomintang and the Communist Party, are obstructing the aspirations of the people of China.

A far sighted step toward the achievement of national unity and democracy was acclaimed in the United States when the agreements were reached on January 31st by the Political Consultative Conference. Disappointment over failure to implement the agreements of the PCC by concrete measures is becoming an important factor in the American outlook with regard to China.

In the United States, there now exists an increasing school of thought which maintains that our whole policy toward China must be re-examined in the light of spreading strife, and notably by evidence of the increasing trend to suppress the expression of liberal views among intellectuals as well as freedom of the press. The assassinations of distinguished Chinese liberals at Kunming recently have not been ignored. Regardless of where responsibility may lie for these cruel murders, the result has been to cause American attention to focus on the China situation, and there is increasing belief that an attempt is being made to resort to force, military or secret police rather than democratic processes to settle major social issues.

American faith in the peaceful and democratic aspirations of the Chinese people has not been destroyed by recent events, but has been shaken. The firm desire of the people of the United States and of the American Government is still to help China achieve lasting peace and a stable economy under a truly democratic government. There is an increasing awareness, however, that the hopes of the people of China are being thwarted by militarists and a small group of political reactionaries who are obstructing the advancement of the general good of the nation by failing to understand the liberal trend of the times. The people of the United States view with violent repugnance this state of affairs.

It cannot be expected that American opinion will continue in its generous attitude towards your nation unless convincing proof is shortly forthcoming that genuine progress is being made toward a peaceful settlement of China's internal problems. Furthermore, it will be necessary for me to redefine and explain the position of the United States to the people of America.

I earnestly hope that in the near future I may receive some encouraging word from you which will facilitate the achievement of our mutually declared aims.

87

The Chinese Ambassador (Koo) to President Truman

WASHINGTON, *August 28, 1946*

MY DEAR MR. PRESIDENT: Referring to my acknowledgement of August 12 of your letter dated August 10 containing a message to President Chiang Kai-shek, I have the honor to transmit to your excellency, in accordance with instructions, the following reply:

"Referring to your message of August 10, I wish to thank you cordially for your expressions of genuine concern for the welfare of my country.

"General Marshall has labored most unsparingly to achieve our common objective; namely, peace and democracy in China, since his arrival. Despite all obstacles, I, too, have done my utmost to cooperate with him in the accomplishment of his task.

"The desire for peace has to be mutual, therefore, it means the Communists must give up their policy to seize political power through the use of armed force, to overthrow the government and to install a totalitarian regime such as those with which Eastern Europe is now being engulfed.

"The minimum requirement for the preservation of peace in our country is the abandonment of such a policy. The Communists attacked and captured Changchun in Manchuria and attacked and captured Tehchow in Shantung after the conclusion of the January agreement. In June, during the cease-fire period, they attacked Tatung and Taiyuan in Shansi and Hsuchow in northern Kiangsu. They have opened a wide offensive on the Lunghai railway in the last few days, with Hsuchow and Kaifeng as their objectives.

"Mistakes have also been made by some subordinates on the government side, of course, but compared to the flagrant violations on the part of the Communists, they are minor in scale. We deal sternly with the offender whenever any mistake occurs on our Government side.

"In my V-J Day message on August 14, I announced the firm policy of the government to broaden speedily the basis of the Government by the inclusion of all parties and non-partisans, amounting to the effectuation of the program of peaceful reconstruction adopted on January 13 by the political consultation conference. It is my sincere hope that our views will be accepted by the Chinese Communist party. On its part, the Government will do the utmost in the shortest possible time to make peace and democracy a reality in this country.

"I am cooperating with General Marshall with all my power in implementing that policy which has as its aim our mutually declared objective. Success must depend upon the sincerity of the Communists in response to our appeals. I am depending on your continued support in the realization of our goal. (Sgd.) Chiang Kai-shek."

I again offer my highest respects.
Yours most sincerely,

V. K. WELLINGTON KOO.

88

President Truman to President Chiang Kai-shek

WASHINGTON, *August 31, 1946*

DEAR PRESIDENT CHIANG: Your message was transmitted to me by letter on August 28 by the Chinese Ambassador Dr. Koo. I note with gratification your references to General Marshall. The strenuous efforts, indicated in the concluding paragraphs of your message, being made to effect the settlement of the internal problems now confronting you are greatly welcomed by me. It is earnestly hoped by me that a satisfactory political solution can soon be reached to bring about a cessation of hostilities, thereby making it possible for the great and urgent task of reconstruction to be continued by you and the Chinese people. With reference to the final paragraph of my policy statement of 15 December 1945, I hope it will be feasible for the United States to plan for assisting China in its industrial economy and the rehabilitation of its agrarian reforms. This can be rendered feasible, I believe, through the prompt removal of the threat of wide spread Civil War in China.

With my best wishes and highest regards.

Sincerely,

HARRY S. TRUMAN

89

The Head of the Chinese Communist Party Delegation (Chou) to the Special Representative of the President (Marshall)

MM 145   SHANGHAI, *September 15, 1946*

DEAR GENERAL MARSHALL: Since the fruitless June armistice, the Committee of Three has been in adjournment up to this moment. At the time when you declared the adjournment, it was presumed that some other means would be sought in order to break the deadlock and bring about the cessation of hostilities. Nevertheless, the Government, taking advantage of this opportunity, played a delaying tactic towards the negotiation and plunged itself headlong into a large-scale civil war. The meeting of the Committee of Five in early July, the entering of Dr. J. L. Stuart into mediation since mid July, the joint statements of yours and Dr. J. L. Stuart's as of 10 August, and Dr. Stuart's proposition advanced about a month ago for an Informal Group of Five, were all exploited by the Government authorities for dovetailing the talks into the fighting with a view to camouflaging the large-scale war which they had waged. Being solicitous for peace, the Chinese Communist Party did not hesitate to recede further ground, and eventually acceeded to the proposition of taking up the issue of government reorganization first in the hope of winning a guarantee for cease-firing. However, the Government authorities countered with dilatory tactics. Instead of giving an assurance for cease-firing, they went so far as to declare that the Chinese Communist Party must designate its representatives for the National Assembly before the promulgation of the order for the cessation of hostilities. At the same time, they intimated that the reorganization of the Executive Yuan would not be undertaken prior to the convening of the National Assembly, and that they had in mind continuing in governmental military occupation of the places recently occupied in Jehol, etc. As the matter now stands, the Kuomintang Government not only has no intention of cease-firing and is designing to realize its 5-point demand through continued military drive towards the areas covered by this demand, but also has thrown overboard one by one the procedures prescribed by the PCC resolutions. The foregoing moves best bear out that the Government authorities did violate the Cease Fire Agreement and overthrow the PCC resolutions, the most striking evidence being the grave fact that a nation-wide civil war is there and is still going on.

From 13 January when the Cease Fire Order came into effect till August, the Government forces in violation of that order have moved as many as 180 divisions (or reorganized brigades), threw 206 regular army divisions (or reorganized brigades) with a strength of 1,740,000 men, i.e. 85 percent of its total strength which is 256 divisions (or reorganized brigades) or about 2,060,000 men, into the offensive against the Communist Liberated Areas; they made 6,000-odd major and minor assaults, conducted over 300 bombing and strafing raids, and had seized and was continuing in occupation by 7 September of 76 cities thus seized. As a matter of fact, the Nationalist troops are everywhere on the offensive, no matter in Manchuria, North China, Central China or South China. Chengteh city has already fallen. Cities like Kalgan, Hwaiyin and Harbin are being made the immediate objectives of the Nationalist drive. Following the seizure of Chinchow-Chengteh Railroad, the fighting along the Chinese Changchun, Peiping-Kupeikow, Peiping-Suiyuan, Tungpu, Taiyuan-Shihchiachwang, Tsingtao-Tsinan, Lunghai, Tientsin-Pukow, and Peiping-Hankow Railroads also became intensified.

Notwithstanding the Kuomintang Government declares that its field forces have been reorganized, the strength of a present-day division in fact surpasses the actual strength of a former army. Now the Government is turning the demobilization back into a new mobilization. As a result of which, over 60 divisional districts originally established for conscription have been restored. This in fact is tantamount to an increase of more than 60 divisions. Furthermore, in order to meet the war requirement, the Government authorities incorporated large numbers of puppets and as in the case of Shantung and Shansi even Japanese war prisoners into the Nationalist army, the latter being recruited under false names.

Up to the present moment, not only the January Cease Fire Agreement has been thoroughly destroyed, but also the war situation has become graver than prior to the signing of that agreement, and from the viewpoint of its scale, it is unparalleled in the twenty years' history of the Chinese civil strife.

On the other hand, the vast assistance received by the Kuomintang Government from the United States for prosecuting the civil war is also unequalled in Chinese History. Since the V-J Day, the quantity of supplies which the Kuomintang Government has received under U. S. Lend-lease Bill, even according to official announcement of the U. S. Government, is equal to the amount delivered during wartime, both being over U. S. $600,000,000 worth. The actual amount presumably would be still more. Whereas during the anti-Japanese war, the American-equipped Chinese divisions had only been used in the India-Burma campaign and later on once in western Hunan; now nearly all of them are thrown into the offensive against the Communist Liberated Areas. Furthermore, the United States Forces also helped to move these troops by air and sea. As this was found still insufficient, the United States Forces further helped the Government by guarding the railroads, cities, towns as well as seaports and by joining its military operations. On the top of that, during the June armistice, the U. S. Government brought before the Congress a bill of 10-year extension of the lend-lease to China, which could serve no other purpose than to bolster up the war spirit of the Kuomintang Government. Later on, the U. S. Government turned over U. S. $825,000,000 worth of surplus properties including naval vessels and other equipment to the Kuomintang Government. It might well be questioned as to what an embarrassed position the large-scale assistance and armed intervention on part of the United States Government have placed you and Dr. J. L. Stuart as its envoys plenipotentiary and mediators into. You, in particular as the Chairman of the Committee of Three which is directing the Executive Headquarters, can well be imagined to be on the worst spot. Unless the U. S. Government has no intention to let its envoys plenipotentiary act as true mediators, and would rather leave them open to public criticism, it should weigh the necessity to change its erroneous policy of assisting the prosecution of the civil war by the Kuomintang, withdraw the American Forces in China, freeze the transfer of the surpluses and withhold all aids, so that you and Dr. J. L. Stuart will be in a position to exercise their fair and equitable mediation. Only under such conditions, peace in China will become highly hopeful, and the Sino-American cooperation will receive high benefit under its influence. It is my sincere hope that you would deeply think the matter over.

Since the June armistice, all intricate ways to solve the issue have proved futile and non-instrumental in breaking the deadlock. Instead they were merely exploited by the bellicose elements to gain time, to befog the public opinion, to enlarge the civil war, and to imperil the people. In view of this, I, as the official representative of the Chinese Communist Party with full authority, wish to advance to you, the Chairman of the Committee of Three, a straightforward proposition for the settlement of the issue, i. e., you would immediately convene a meeting of the Committee to discuss the question of cease-firing.

An immediate termination of the civil strife in China is the aspiration of the people throughout China as well as the call in the world. President Harry Truman's statement and the Moscow Communique of the three Foreign Ministers of last December all pointed towards this end. On this basis you were entrusted with the present mission. And on the invitation of both the Kuomintang and the Communist Parties you took up the role as mediator in the negotiation and became the Chairman of the Committee of Three. And it was on the basis of the Cease Fire Agreement between the two parties that the Peiping Executive Headquarters and the Changchun Advanced Section were established and field teams formed. Now that the situation has become so much worsened, the only hope lies in returning to this sole legal cease-fire agency for seeking a truce arrangement and a direct and simple solution. You as the Chairman of the Committee of Three are hereby requested to transmit our view to the Government and to arrange for the meeting of the Committee at the earliest possible moment in order to discuss the issue.

Your reply is eagerly awaited.

[Signed in Chinese]
CHOU EN-LAI

90

The Head of the Chinese Communist Party Delegation (Chou) to the Special Representative of the President (Marshall)

SM 827 [SHANGHAI,] *September 16, 1946*

MY DEAR GENERAL: Because of some business that requires my attendance, I am called upon to leave for Shanghai to-day. In case there is any matter that you want to communicate to me, please contact my associates Messrs. Liao Cheng-chih and Wang Ping-nan here.

As soon as you have decided to convene the Committee of Three, I will be back on your notice.

Faithfully yours,

[Signed in Chinese]
CHOU EN-LAI

91

The Special Representative of the President (Marshall) to the Head of the Chinese Communist Party Delegation (Chou)

OSE 446 NANKING, *September 19, 1946*

DEAR GENERAL CHOU: Dr. Stuart has informed me that he learns through Dr. Wang Ping Nan that you desire a formal written acknowledgement to your memorandum to me of September 15th in which you request me as Chairman of the Committee of Three to transmit to the National Government the view of the Communist Party of the situation as expressed in this memorandum, and to arrange for a meeting of the Committee of Three at the earliest possible moment.

I have transmitted to the National Government in Nanking a copy of your memorandum. Further when advised at Kuling by radio of your desire regarding Committee of Three meeting I took your proposal to the Generalissimo and was informed by him that he would not authorize the attendance of the Government member of the Committee of Three at such a meeting until there had been a meeting of the informal five man committee headed by Doctor Stuart, and some progress had been made towards an agreement for the organization of the State Council.

Doctor Stuart, I believe, had previously conveyed this information to Mister Wang Ping Nan.

Faithfully yours,

[GEORGE C. MARSHALL]

92

The Head of the Chinese Communist Party Delegation (Chou) to the Special Representative of the President (Marshall)

SHANGHAI, *September 21, 1946*

MY DEAR GENERAL MARSHALL: Your memo OSE 446 dated September 19 has been received.

The extremely serious situation at this moment, as I see, has gone far beyond the scope that it can be resolved by a discussion on government reorganization or any other similar procedure. Instead, the key to it rests with cease firing— a prompt and immediate cease firing. Inasmuch as the sole legal agency handling cease firing matters is the Committee of Three, you as its chairman are therefore called upon to hold joint discussion with the two Chinese parties on this paramount and most urgent problem, no matter what their respective views will be.

I wish to recall that it was largely due to your assuming the chairmanship of the Committee of Three in early January, that the cease fire agreement was concluded, and that the Executive Headquarters in Peiping and the various field teams became established, which in turn secured the implementation of that agreement, and ushered in the incipient rays of peace to China proper. It was due to the same event, that the prospect was opened for the fulfillment of the primary part of your mission in China. Again it was this course of events that entailed the successful conclusion of the PCC and the signing of the Army Reorganization Plan.

As the matter now stands, however, we find ourselves facing a state, which can only find a parallel in days prior to January 10, if not even worse. The only proper approach toward disentangling the many complexities lies therefore in effecting a prompt cessation of hostilities. The function as well as the past record of the Committee of Three further underscore your obligation to call its meeting at once. And the reasons are:

(1) The Committee of Three has been in adjournment for nearly three months, it thus not only bars the prospect for peace, but utterly deprives the Executive Headquarters and the field teams a guiding light amidst this turmoil.

(2) There is no precedent in the record of the Committee of Three that any Chinese party has ever rejected your invitation to its meeting. Nor is it conceivable that anybody would ever boycott such a meeting. In particular the Chinese Communist Party has never undertaken such a step.

I feel therefore all the more justified in requesting a prompt meeting of the Committee of Three at this moment.

As to the rejoinder that the Committee of Three should not be convened until there has been a meeting of the informal five man committee headed by Dr. Stuart, and some progress has been made towards an agreement for the organization of the State Council, it is but a too obvious unwarranted excuse, which I believe you are fully aware. For plainly the informal five man committee would not by itself bring forth a cessation of hostilities. At best, it would only open the way for a discussion on truce,—being still far off from our true objective of cessation of hostilities. Speaking about the reorganization of the State Council itself, it is not a complicated matter at all, unless the Kuomintang government would lavishly play an obstructionist policy. If the Kuomintang would agree to appropriate fourteen seats of the State Council to the Chinese Communist Party and the Democratic League, thus definitely ensuring a one-third vote to safeguard the PCC common program from being infringed upon, the whole issue of the State Council can be settled almost overnight. Would such a course be adopted, I am sure, that Dr. Stuart as the pre-assigned chairman of that committee can very well confer with both sides for a settlement. If a different course be chosen, then even the abandonment by the Kuomintang of its previous claim for a 8-4-4-4 ratio does not rule out the possibility that it may wreck the whole proceeding by substituting that claim with other terms. Facing such a situation, the debate would just go on endlessly without ever resolving the State Council issue, let alone the cessation of hostilities.

Time and again I have explained to Dr. Stuart, that the resolution of the State Council issue does not call for a formal meeting, as it can very well be achieved by informal talks with the two parties, thereby facilitating the discussion on the principal cease-firing issue. Any insistence on placing the informal five man committee before the Committee of Three is not only unwarranted, but merely a pretext for the purpose of obstruction.

In view of the foregoing I earnestly request that you would immediately call the Committee of Three together, and favour me with an early reply.

Should the Committee of Three nevertheless fail to meet, I can hardly convince myself that there is still a second way leading to cessation of hostilities. By reaching such a stage, I would feel myself forced to make public all the important documents since the armistice in June, in order to clarify the responsibility and appeal to the general public for judgement. I wish hereby to serve notice of my contemplated action.

Faithfully yours,

[CHOU EN-LAI]

93

The Special Representative of the President (Marshall) and the Ambassador in China (Stuart) to the Head of the Chinese Communist Party Delegation (Chou)

OSE 446   [NANKING] *September 26, 1946*

DEAR GENERAL CHOU: Since your departure for Shanghai we have been steadily hoping that you would return here and thus make possible a resumption of the efforts to end the spreading civil war. The disastrous consequences to the nation of a continuation of the present situation are apparent to all. We continue in our belief that both the Government and the Communist leaders sincerely desire peace and the establishment of a coalition government and the adoption of a democratic constitution, and that the difficulties are largely questions of procedure.

We desire to help in this to the utmost of our ability. We venture, therefore, on the basis of our past friendly relations and our personal esteem for you, to urge that you return to Nanking without further delay in order that we may together explore all conceivable ways and means for the objective we are seeking to achieve.

We have been informed that the Generalissimo returns to Nanking today or tomorrow, weather permitting.

G. C. MARSHALL
J. L. STUART

94

The Head of the Chinese Communist Party Delegation (Chou) to the Special Representative of the President (Marshall) and the Ambassador in China (Stuart)

NANKING, *September 27, 1946*

DEAR GENERAL MARSHALL AND AMBASSADOR STUART: Thank you for your letter dated 26 September, 1946.

The deterioration and seriousness of the present situation is apparent both to you and to all. I am not unwilling to return to Nanking for a discussion of the ways and means to stop the civil war. The government not only gives no signs for the cessation of hostilities but further is increasing its efforts by many folds in the active offensive upon Kalgan, Harbin, Antung, North Kiangsu, and other areas. A further adventure for negotiation will be nothing helpful to the real peace but a smokescreen for a free hand to make a full scale civil war on part of the government and for the deception of the people. This is why I would rather wait here in Shanghai for the convocation of the Committee of Three.

Your good friendship as expressed in your letter to urge me to return to Nanking is appreciated. However, inasmuch as the actual situation is still unknown, I am requesting Mr. Tung Pi-wu to approach you first on behalf of our side.

Should the government give factual evidence in reply to the demand for cease-fire and prove itself to have sincerity, I shall have no reason not to return to Nanking for a talk.

Sincerely yours,

CHOU EN-LAI

95

Draft of Statement for Generalissimo Chiang Kai-shek [19]

A continuation of the present political and military situation in China will be destructive of the interests of a long suffering people. It will render impossible the unification of our country and will threaten the peace of the world. Therefore, it is necessary that an early solution be found to the present conflict and that peace be restored to the land. But as the responsible head of the Government of China, I must see that the necessary measures are taken to safeguard the security of the nation, since we are dealing with a political party which maintains a large army to support or enforce its political policies.

In the past three months, I have stipulated certain conditions that must be met by the Communist Party before a peaceful accord could be achieved and to which they have thus far refused to agree. They now demand an immediate meeting of the Committee of Three of which General Marshall is the chairman. That committee reached an impasse in its negotiations the latter part of June and unless there are certain preliminary but vital agreements or understandings, a meeting of the committee would not only be ineffective but its future possible usefulness would be fatally impaired. I have insisted that the group of five men selected to reach an understanding between the Government and the Communist Party making possible the establishment of the coalition State Council should first meet under the chairmanship of the United States Ambassador, Doctor Stuart, to give evidence of the good intent of both the Kuomintang Party and the Communist Party towards the reorganization of the government in accordance with the resolutions of the Peoples Consultative Council. With this reassurance of good faith on both sides there would then be a new basis of trust for the termination of the hostilities now disrupting China. I have further stated that concurrent with the termination of hostilities the Communist Party should indicate its honest intention to cooperate in the reorganization of the government by announcing its delegates to the National Assembly to meet on November 12 to determine on a democratic constitution for the Government of China.

In view of the seriousness of the situation, the misunderstandings and public confusion, and the distrust and suspicions unfortunately prevalent, I now make the following public announcement of the conditions under which the Government is prepared to act to secure an immediate cessation of hostilities.

The Five Man Committee under the chairmanship of Doctor Stuart to meet immediately and at the same time the Committee of Three under the chairmanship of General Marshall with the following understandings:

(a) The opposing troops in close contact to be separated in accordance with the terms tentatively agreed to by the Committee of Three in June for the termination of hostilities in Manchuria.

---

[19] Prepared by the Special Representative of the President, (September) 1946.

(b) The restoration of communications to be immediately resumed in accordance with the agreement tentatively reached by the Committee of Three last June.

(c) The method for settling disagreements among the team members of Executive Headquarters and Commissioners at Executive Headquarters to be in accordance with the agreement tentatively reached by the Committee of Three last June.

(d) The implementation of the agreement for the reorganization and unification of the armies of China to be settled by the Committee of Three without delay.

(e) That whatever understanding is reached by the Five Man Committee headed by Doctor Stuart it is to be confirmed by the Steering Committee of the PCC without delay.

(f) All questions of local government to be settled by the newly organized State Council.

(g) Concurrent with the cessation of hostilities, the Communist Party to announce its intention of participating in the National Assembly by publishing its list of delegates to that Assembly.

96

The Head of the Chinese Communist Party Delegation (Chou) to the Special Representative of the President (Marshall)

SHANGHAI, *September 30, 1946*

DEAR GENERAL MARSHALL: Since the interruption of the talks during the June armistice, the Kuomintang Government thenceforth not only went further in ignoring all the previous commitments, but also tore the Cease Fire Agreement of January to pieces, and launched a large-scale drive in China proper. During the last three months they have occupied many cities, destroyed the popularly-elected local administrations of many a place, made ruthless air raids into Liberated Areas, killing and wounding countless civilians. They further advanced the insensible five-point demand setting forth the withdrawal of Communist troops and popularly-elected local administrations from a number of areas. When the Chinese Communists rightfully rejected their proposition on account of its incompatibility with the basic principles of the PCC Joint Platform, they threw their military drive into high gear, in order to achieve this demand by force, and aggrandize their occupation.

Thus, apart from taking away a series of places from the Communist led Liberated areas in Hupeh-Honan, north Anhwei, north Kiangsu, Shantung, Shansi, Hopei and Jehol, the Kuomintang authorities then used the Communist siege over Tatung as an excuse for making the announcement that they would launch ruthless drives for capturing Chengteh, Kalgan and Yenan. What then happened was that Chengteh was soon occupied by them, followed by such key cities like Tsining and Fengchen along the Peiping-Suiyuan rail line. Actually the Communist campaign around Tatung is merely calculated to divert the attacks launched by the Kuomintang troops in Shansi under Yen Hsi-shan and Hu Chung-nan, and as such it is of a besieging nature. Most recently the Communists even announced the formal lifting of the siege, thereby freeing Tatung from any kind of menace.

On the other hand, the Kuomintang troops are still up to the neck engaged in enlarging their occupation in Jehol and east Hopei. Most significantly, at this moment, a three-pronged attack is being formally launched against Kalgan. It thus became obvious that the Kuomintang Government shows even no hesitation to strike against one of the political and military centers of the Communist-led Liberated Areas—Kalgan—, in order to force the Kuomintang-Communist relation into the perilous state of an ultimate break.

Now I am duly instructed to serve the following notice, which I request you would kindly transmit to the Government: If the Kuomintang Government does not instantly cease its military operations against Kalgan and the vicinity areas, the Chinese Communist Party feels itself forced to presume that the Government is thereby giving public announcement of a total national split, and that it has ultimately abandoned its pronounced policy of peaceful settlement. When reaching such a stage, the responsibility of all the serious consequences should as a matter of course solely rest with the Government side.

[CHOU EN-LAI]

97

The Special Representative of the President (Marshall) to President Chiang Kai-shek

OSE 476　　　　　　　　　　　　　　　　　　NANKING, *October 1, 1946*

YOUR EXCELLENCY: Since our conversation of Monday morning, September 30, and General Yu Ta Wei's call on me the same afternoon, I have carefully considered all the factors involved in the present status of negotiations and military operations. I have also taken into consideration the later developments;

(1) The Communist announcement of yesterday stating their refusal to nominate delegates to the National Assembly unless certain PCC conditions are met and the announcement of the governmental Central News Agency regarding the operations against Kalgan;

(2) The informal suggestions (Incl. 1)[20] of Doctor T. V. Soong for a series of actions as conditions precedent to a cessation of hostilities, which he mentioned to Doctor Stuart this morning, and

(3) The memorandum from General Chou En-lai to me (Incl. 2)[21] which was handed to me by Mr. Tung Pi Wu today.

I am not in agreement either with the present course of the Government in regard to this critical situation or with that of the Communist Party. I disagree with the evident Government policy of settling the fundamental differences involved by force, that is by utilizing a general offensive campaign to force compliance with the Government point of view or demands. I recognize the vital necessity of safeguarding the security of the Government, but I think the present procedure has past well beyond that point.

On the part of the Communist Party, I deplore actions and statements which provide a basis for the contention on the part of many in the Government that the Communist's proposals can not be accepted in good faith, that it is not the intention of that Party to cooperate in a genuine manner in a reorganization of the Government, but rather to disrupt the Government and seize power for their own purposes.

I will not refer to the circumstances connected with the ineffective negotiations since last March. I wish merely to state that unless a basis for agreement is

---

[20] Not printed.
[21] See annex 92.

found to terminate the fighting without further delays of proposals and counterproposals, I will recommend to the President that I be recalled and that the United States Government terminate its efforts of mediation.

[GEORGE C. MARSHALL]

AIDE MEMOIRE

Informal suggestion—without commitment

I. Five-men Committee to meet first to discuss Communist participation in State Council.
II. (a) Following this first meeting a 3-man Committee to meet and decide the areas to which Communist troops will be assigned.
  (b) Dates will be set for the movement of Communist troops to designated areas.
  (c) Truce teams will be sent to observe the movement of these troops.
  (d) Upon the acceptance by the Communist delegates of the areas where Communist troops will be stationed and the dates set for their removal to those areas, cease-fire order will forthwith be given.
  (e) When the Communist troops have reached the areas assigned to them, they will be incorporated into the National Army, and trained and equipped like other national divisions.

98

President Chiang Kai-shek to the Special Representative of the President (Marshall)

[Translation]

NANKING, *October 2, 1946*

Your Excellency's letter dated October 1, 1946, which was attached with a letter from General Chou En-lai under date of September 30, 1946 handed to you by Mr. Tung Pi-wu, has been received. The Government is more eager than any other party for an early cessation of hostilities, but past experience shows that the Chinese Communist Party has been in the habit of taking advantage of negotiations to obtain respite and regroup their troops in order to launch fresh attacks on Government troops who have been abiding by truce agreements (attached is a list of important evidences of Communist troops attacking Government troops during the truce periods), and that conflicts only ceased temporarily but flared up again after a short interval. Therefore effective means should be devised to assure that cease fire is permanent and not temporary. The Government, having the responsibility of restoring and maintaining order and security in the country, can not allow the chaotic situation to be prolonged indefinitely.

With a view to saving time and showing its utmost sincerity, the Government hereby, with all frankness, expresses its maximum concessions in regard to the solution of the present problem:

(1) The Chinese Communist Party has been incessantly urging the reorganization of the National Government. This hinges on the distribution of the membership of the State Council. The Government originally agreed that the Chinese Communist Party be allocated eight seats and the Democratic League, four, with a total of twelve. The Chinese Communist Party, on the other hand, requested

ten for themselves and four for the Democratic League with a total of fourteen. Now the Government makes a fresh concession by taking the mean and offering one seat for the independents to be recommended by the Chinese Communist Party and agreed upon by the Government, so that, added to the original twelve, it makes a total of thirteen seats. But the Communist Party should without delay produce the list of their candidates for the State Council as well as the list of their delegates to the National Assembly. This reassignment of seats should be decided by the proposed group of five to be confirmed by the Steering Committee of PCC.

(2) For immediate implementation of the program for reorganization of the army, the location of the eighteen Communist divisions should be immediately determined and the Communist troops should enter those assigned places according to agreed dates. The above should be decided by the Committee of Three and carried out under the supervision of the Executive Headquarters.

If the Communist Party has the sincerity for achieving peace and co-operating with the Government, and is willing to solve immediately the above-mentioned two problems, a cease fire order should be issued by both sides, when agreement has been reached thereon.

Kindly forward the above to the Communist Party and let me know your esteemed opinion about it.

CHIANG KAI-SHEK.

99

The Special Representative of the President (Marshall) to the Ambassador in China (Stuart)

OSE 491

NANKING, *October 6, 1946*

DEAR DOCTOR STUART: I have outlined below my understanding of the arrangement agreed upon this morning between ourselves and the Generalissimo.

You are to notify Wang Ping Nan that we proposed to the Generalissimo a 10-day truce for the operations against Kalgan under the following conditions:

1) The purpose of the truce is to carry out the two proposals of the Generalissimo in his communication to me of October 2. (copy attached)[22]

2) During the period of the truce, Executive Headquarters will check on its observance with teams at all critical points composed and directed as follows:

a. Teams within the Communist lines will not have a National Government member and teams within the Government lines will not have a Communist member.

b. The American member will have the authority to determine where and when the teams shall go and will himself report on any actions which in effect could be considered violations of the truce.

c. Between the two forces a team or teams may be located with both Government and Communist representatives.

3) The public announcement of the truce will be made by you and me, and the Government and the Communists are to refrain from any announcement.

---

[22] See annex 98.

100

Statement by the Chinese Communist Party

YENAN, *October 8, 1946*

1. The truce should be without a time limit because, based on previous experience, it would otherwise be unsatisfactory. The proposal would seem to be a strategy unless the Government troops were withdrawn to their original positions, thus demonstrating the sincerity of the Government.

2. The Communist Party wishes to have the Three- and Five-Man Committees to meet but the discussion should not be limited to the two paragraphs of the October 2nd communication of the Generalissimo. These topics dealt with under truce conditions may be regarded as under military coercion.

3. No reply has been sent to the communication of October 2nd because the Communist Party had been hoping to have some word from General Marshall and Dr. Stuart clarifying the situation for peace. The latest proposal implies that the situation has not changed much. General Chou is therefore preparing to send a formal written reply and sees no need for his returning to Nanking.

101

Joint Statement by the Special Representative of the President (Marshall) and the Ambassador in China (Stuart),[23] *Nanking, October 8, 1946*

On the morning of October 1st General Marshall received through the hands of Mr. Wang Ping-nan, the Communist representative, a memorandum dated September 30th from General Chou En-lai in Shanghai relating to the activities of the Kuomintang Party to which objection was taken and concluding with the following paragraph:

"Now I am duly instructed to serve the following notice, which I request you would kindly transmit to the Government: If the Kuomintang Government does not instantly cease its military operations against Kalgan and the vicinity areas, the Chinese Communist Party feels itself forced to presume that the Government is thereby giving public announcement of a total national split, and that it has ultimately abandoned its pronounced policy of peaceful settlement. When reaching such a stage, the responsibility of all the serious consequences should as a matter of course solely rest with the Government side."

In accordance with the request of General Chou the foregoing memorandum was transmitted to the Generalissimo, and on October 2nd he replied in a memorandum to General Marshall relating certain hostile acts of troops of the Communist Party. In this memorandum the Generalissimo proposed, with a view to saving time and as indicating the sincerity of the Government, the following as the maximum concessions the Government would make in the solution of the present problem:

"1) The Chinese Communist Party has been incessantly urging the reorganization of the National Government. This hinges on the distribution of the

---

[23] *Department of State Bulletin,* Oct. 20, 1946, pp. 723–724.

membership of the State Council. The Government originally agreed that the Chinese Communist Party be allocated eight seats and the Democratic League, four, with a total of twelve. The Chinese Communist Party, on the other hand, requested ten for themselves and four for the Democratic League with a total of fourteen. Now the Government makes a fresh concession by taking the mean and offering one seat for the independents to be recommended by the Chinese Communist Party and agreed upon by the Government, so that, added to the original twelve, it makes a total of thirteen seats. But the Communist Party should without delay produce the list of their candidates for the State Council as well as the list of their delegates to the National Assembly. This reassignment of seats should be decided by the proposed group of five to be confirmed by the Steering Committee of PCC.

"2) For immediate implementation of the program for reorganization of the army, the location of the eighteen Communist divisions should be immediately determined and the Communist troops should enter those assigned places according to agreed dates. The above should be decided by the Committee of Three and carried out under the supervision of the Executive Headquarters."

This communication was immediately transmitted to the Communist representatives and they, later on in the week, called on the American mediators with a request for information as to whether the memorandum of the Generalissimo of October 2nd was a reply to General Chou's memorandum of September 30th, as no mention of Kalgan was made.

There followed a series of discussions between the Generalissimo and General Marshall and Ambassador Stuart which finally resulted in the acquiescence of the Generalissimo that he halt the advance on Kalgan for a period of 10 days during which the Five Man Group and the Committee of Three would meet in order to consider the two proposals of the Generalissimo in his communication of October 2nd. The Generalissimo further agreed that during the period of this truce Executive Headquarters would check on its observance with teams at all critical points and that Government representatives would not accompany teams within the Communist lines while the Communist representatives would not accompany teams within the Government lines. Also that between the two forces, teams will be located with representatives from both sides. Further that the American member would have the authority to determine where and when the teams would go and would himself report on any actions which would, in effect, be considered violations of the truce.

The Generalissimo further agreed to the arrangement that the public announcement of the truce would be made by the American mediators and that the Government and the Communists were to refrain from any announcement.

This information was transmitted immediately at 1:30 on October 6th to the Communist representative, Mr. Wang Ping-nan for transmittal by him to General Chou En-lai in Shanghai.

Today, Tuesday October 8th, Mr. Wang Ping-nan delivered verbally the reply from Yenan through General Chou En-lai, the substance of which was as follows:

"1) The truce should be without a time limit because, based on previous experience, it would otherwise be unsatisfactory. The proposal would seem to be a strategy unless the Government troops were withdrawn to their original positions, thus demonstrating the sincerity of the Government.

"2) The Communist Party wishes to have the Three- and Five-Man Committees to meet, but the discussion should not be limited to the two paragraphs of the

October 2nd communication of the Generalissimo. These topics dealt with under truce conditions may be regarded as under military coercion.

"3) No reply had been sent to the communication of October 2nd because the Communist Party had been hoping to have some word from General Marshall and Dr. Stuart clarifying the situation for peace. The latest proposal implies that the situation has not changed much. General Chou is therefore preparing to send a formal written reply and sees no need for his returning to Nanking."

102

The Head of the Chinese Communist Party Delegation (Chou) to the Special Representative of the President (Marshall)

SHANGHAI, *October 9, 1946*

DEAR GENERAL MARSHALL: Your memo OSE 479 dated October 2, 1946, which you directed Colonel Caughey to send to me and which was attached with a memo from President Chiang under even date, has been duly received.

President Chiang's memo not only refused to reply to my demand expressed in my memo dated 30 September calling for an immediate termination of the military operations against Kalgan, but instead went so far as to raise two claims which directly run counter to the PCC resolutions and the Army Reorganization Plan. For this reason I refrained myself from making an immediate reply, but merely instructing Mr. Wang Ping-nan to deliver verbally my comment to Dr. Stuart, with a view to looking forward that you and Dr. Stuart would further exert fair and impartial efforts for the peace in China.

As was transmitted by Mr. Wang to Dr. Stuart, we could not accept President Chiang's terms for the following reasons:

1) According to the principles of the previous agreement, the Chinese Communist Party and the Democratic League must hold fourteen out of the forty seats in the state council, that is a little over one-third of the total vote, in order to ensure that the Peaceful Reconstruction Program would not be revised unilaterally. However, the Government proposal of thirteen seats could not provide such a safeguard. To regard one of the non-partisan members as belonging to the Chinese Communist Party or the Democratic League is also not in accord with the PCC resolution.

2) The list of National Assembly delegates can be produced only to the reorganized Government, and even so not until the draft constitution has been revised by the PCC, acknowledged as the only draft to be presented to the National Assembly, and the distribution of the membership of the National Assembly has been finally agreed upon. Whereas such is the procedure stipulated by the PCC resolutions, President Chiang demanded that the list of National Assembly delegates be produced to the one-party government, obviously in violation to those resolutions.

3) For an effective implementation of the Army Reorganization Plan, it is essential to determine as to where the troops of both parties will be located during the process of reorganization, and not to determine merely the location of the Communist army, while Government troops are being granted freedom to move around, to menace at any time and to attack at will the Communist troops and the populace in the Liberated Areas.

It was certainly not our expectation that that hope of ours was being misplanted. On 7 October, I received your memorandum to Dr. Stuart under date of 6 October, thereby learning that President Chiang agreed merely under the condition that his two afore-mentioned demands would be carried out to postpone his military drive against Kalgan for ten days. This is obviously an ultimatum to force us to surrender. We feel therefore compelled to reject firmly that proposal.

Now, apart from instructing Messrs. Tung Pi-wu and Wang Ping-nan to transmit my views regarding this matter to you, I wish further to state the following, which I also request to be transmitted to President Chiang Kai-shek:

1. In my memo under date of 30 September, I have already made it clear that the military operations by the Government troops against Kalgan is a demonstration of the Government determination not even to abstain from forcing a national split. At this hour, only an immediate calling-off once for all the drive against Kalgan coupled with a withdrawal of the attacking troops back to their original positions would bear ample evidence to the effect that the Government is willing to break the way for fresh negotiation and to avert a split. Failing which the responsibility for all serious consequences will automatically rest squarely with the Government.

2. With a view to showing its utmost sincerity and concessions, the Communist Party is willing, on Government immediate calling-off once for all its drive against Kalgan, to attend the Committee of Three and the informal five-man committee or the PCC steering committee, to join the simultaneous discussion on the two subjects: cessation of hostilities and implementation of the PCC resolutions. Regarding these the Chinese Communist Party has the following proposals to make:

A. Cessation of Hostilities (to be discussed by the Committee of Three):

a. Both armies shall restore their positions as of January 13 in China proper, and as of June 7 in Manchuria.

b. The location of both armies, instead of that of the Communist army alone, during the reorganization shall be determined.

c. The Government troops having been moved against previous agreements should be ordered to return to their original positions, so as to facilitate reorganization.

B. Implementation of PCC resolutions (to be discussed by the PCC Steering Committee or informal five-man committee):

a. The Chinese Communist Party and the Democratic League shall occupy fourteen seats in the state council, in order to ensure that the Peaceful Reconstruction Program would not be revised unilaterally. The distribution of these fourteen seats will be decided jointly by the Chinese Communist Party and the Democratic League.

b. The reorganization of the Executive Yuan will be taken up along with the reorganization of the state council.

c. The draft constitution, which is being revised by the PCC draft constitution reviewing committee in accordance with the principles and the stipulated procedure of the PCC resolutions, will be presented to the National Assembly as the only basis for discussion. All parties and groups further pledge that they will ensure the adoption of that draft.

d. The final reconvening date of the National Assembly and the distribution of the additional National Assembly membership will be decided by the PCC steering committee.

ANNEXES 669

e. After the government has been reorganized in accordance with paragraph B, items *a.* and *b.*, the various parties will produce to that government lists of their National Assembly membership following the arrangement of paragraph B, item *d.*

f. The local administrations will in accordance with the provisions of the Peaceful Reconstruction Program maintain a status quo, pending the introduction of local self-government after the reorganization of the Central government.

g. In order to ensure that the four promises regarding people's freedom and rights made by President Chiang at the PCC session on January 10 will be carried out first of all and without delay political prisoners should be released, the outrageous incidents occurred since last January should be thoroughly investigated, the culprits punished, the special service organizations should be abolished, and the newspapers, magazines, news agencies, bookstores and people's organizations banned since last January should be restored.

h. The PCC military resolution governing the divorce of military affairs from civil administrative affairs should be carried out, in order to effect demobilization.

All the afore-mentioned proposals in connection with the two big subjects, which originate from the Cease Fire Agreement, Army Reorganization Plan and the five resolutions of the PCC, are indeed the most infallible measures for solving the prevalent crisis. If the government authorities still has sincerity in implementing those agreements, there should be no reason why they do not accept them. If instead, they are but making idle talk about political settlement and implementation of the PCC resolutions, while actually they gear everything to military settlement and overthrow of the PCC resolutions, without even hesitating to force a national split by resorting to civil war and dictatorship, the Chinese Communist Party would feel itself forced to put up stubborn opposition till the very end.

With best regards   Faithfully yours,

CHOU EN-LAI

103

Address Delivered by President Chiang Kai-shek at Nanking, October 10, 1946

Fellow countrymen:

On this 35th anniversary of the birth of the Chinese Republic we commemorate the first October 10th since the return of the Government to Nanking.

To begin with, let us remember the difficulties that faced the Founder of our Republic, Dr. Sun Yat-sen, and of our Revolutionary predecessors in establishing the Republic. Let us review the fruits of sacrifices and struggles of our soldiers in resisting Japanese aggression.

Let us look ahead into the prospects for national unification and peaceful reconstruction in our country.

Let us appreciate fully the precarious nature of the position of our sovereignty and national freedom.

In view of all these we must without exception forge ahead conscientiously and with industry, to implement the teachings of Dr. Sun Yat-sen, to carry forward the task left unfinished by our Martyrs, and build a modern nation according to the Three People's Principles in order to bring about a rich, powerful and prosperous Chinese Republic.

Dr. Sun Yat-sen once said, "Like the building of a house, no rush job can be done of national reconstruction." It requires a spirit of utmost perseverance and a strength of utmost endurance.

Thirty-five years have passed since the Revolution of 1911. A comparison of our revolutionary work throughout this interval of 35 years will show that it has always been making headway. Its consummation, however, remains remote.

Our accumulated exertions from the establishment of the National Government in Nanking and the completion of the Northern Expedition, through the eight years of resistance, culminated in the defeat of Japan's aggressive might, thereby restoring to China the territory of Taiwan (Formosa) and the sovereignty of the Northeast. We have also won the abrogation of the unequal treaties and established the foundation of friendly cooperation with the rest of the world.

All these represent signal achievements of the National Revolution and should be a source of rejoicing to all, even the lost souls of the Revolution.

That our National Government was able to lead the entire nation and people with concentrated will and solidified strength to negotiate difficulty after difficulty, obstacle after obstacle, and to overcome every crisis, internal and external, until the winning of the final victory, is precisely because our program for revolution and national reconstruction corresponds with the wish and desire of the entire nation and people.

As we review our past achievements, we feel impelled to perpetuate and redouble our united efforts to safeguard our sovereignty and national freedom. Above all, we must carry out Dr. Sun Yat-sen's teachings of the Three People's Principles so that China may become unified and powerful enough to uphold peace in the Far East. On this commemorative occasion we must remember Dr. Sun Yat-sen's statement that the "objective in the founding of the Chinese Republic is peace".

A year ago today I pointed out that our future program was "national reconstruction first". Again on New Year's Day I emphasized the necessity of national unification and political democratization.

Unfortunately, as the last 10 months have gone by not one of our programs was implemented as scheduled. Even now disturbances continue unabated. It is painful indeed to see our fellow countrymen suffer directly or indirectly from national disunity, social disorder, and precarious living. I wish to take this occasion to outline for the information of my fellow countrymen just how our national foundation can be stabilized and how the abnormal state of affairs can be set straight.

The National Revolution has been aimed at the implementation of the Three People's Principles and the establishment of an equal, independent and free Chinese Republic. The basic conditions for national reconstruction are national unification and social stability. In the absence of the latter there could be no safeguard for the people's lives and property, still less for peaceful pursuit of happiness and vocations. Furthermore, increased agricultural and industrial production would be out of question and the general living standard could not be elevated.

Likewise, if national unification is not achieved, internal disturbance will multiply, democratic government will have no chance, national reconstruction will stand still, and the realization of the Three People's Principles will be impeded.

Safeguarding national unification, therefore, constitutes the first and foremost consideration of the Government in regard to the current situation in the country. It will seek unification through peaceful channels. We all know that the minimum requirements for national unification are the integration of military command and the unity of administrative decrees. To achieve integration of military command, we must carry out the nationalization of all the troops and thus establish a national army. To attain administrative unity, we must have decrees and regulations enforced throughout the country and eliminate regional domination. If and when in a nation there are two opposing armies and local governments assuming the proportions of regional domination, that nation no longer is a unified nation.

In order to win peace, therefore, we must consolidate our national unification. We may say that without national unification there can be no peace in China. National unification is the absolute condition for peace. Repudiation or violation of this condition would not only lengthen the ordeal of the people but also invite the ruin of the nation. This is a life and death issue for every citizen and also a bounded duty falling on the Government. Under no condition can the Government brook any attempt to prevent national unification or any rebellion aimed at national disintegration. Still less can the entire people and nation look on unconcernedly and allow the country and nation to be plunged headlong into an inextricable abyss. . . .

Today the peaceful avenue to national unification leads also to nationalization of all troops and political democratization. To attain political democratization, we must convoke the National Assembly and broaden the basis of the Government, thereby enabling the Government to return its rein to the people and the citizens to have actual exercise of their political power.

To attain nationalization of troops, we must follow the basis for army reorganization and integration of Communist troops into the National Army, decide where troops are to be located, decide upon the dates and set the time limit for carrying out the measures agreed upon so that no longer any party may fight for political power by force of arms. Only thus will China become a truly unified nation. . . .

Today the Government requests the various parties to participate in the National Government and to attend the National Assembly.

Today the Government asks the Chinese Communist Party to abandon its plot to achieve regional domination and disintegration of the country by military force and to participate along with all other parties in the National Government and National Assembly. Realization of this step will correspond with the agreement reached jointly by the various political parties and groups and the unanimous desire of the entire masses of the people.

It is also the hope of the Government that the various political parties and groups will bring forward according to schedule lists of their candidates to the State Council of the National Government and their delegates to the National Assembly so that reorganization of the National Government may be carried out at an earlier date, and that the National Assembly may satisfactorily convene.

Another thing I wish especially to bring to the attention of my fellow countrymen today is the question of the cessation of armed conflicts. This has been the consistent wish of the Government. What the Government has been wishing for has been a total and permanent cessation of hostilities. The Military Committee of Three met in June this year primarily to seek agreement on restoration of communications and the determination of the location of the Communist troops thereby insuring the cease-fire order. The Committee was deadlocked on account of the obstinacy of the Communist Party.

Seeking permanent peace I, for one, during the last three months, have advanced certain proposals for consideration and acceptance by the Communists, but these were all rejected. The Communists subsequently demanded the immediate convocation of the Military Committee of Three under General George Marshall. . . .

Now the Chinese Communists have rejected the two proposals concerning the reorganization of the National Government and the implementation of the basis for army reorganization and the integration of the Communist troops into the National Army. They have also turned down the truce proposals from General Marshall and Ambassador Stuart, but the Government nevertheless is not going to abandon its policy of a peaceful settlement. It will continue to hope and seek for a settlement by mediation and consultation. The political and military conditions in the country as they are today must not be allowed to continue and thus intensify the ordeal of the people.

In view of the present tense situation and restlessness among some people due to their lack of understanding of the Government's policy, I may take this occasion to assert with all the force of emphasis that in order to break the deadlock in the current situation we must still resort to peaceful consultation in seeking the solution of some of the basic problems.

I wish to propose the convening of the twin committees at the same time. The Five-Man Group should meet to consider mutually acceptable measures for the reorganization of the National Government. The Committee of Three should meet to seek a solution of the problems bearing upon the implementation of the basis for army reorganization and integration of Communist troops into the National Army. As soon as an agreement is reached, the Government will immediately issue a "cease-fire" order provided that the Chinese Communists call a halt to their military operations and cease attacks on National troops.

The Government feels that if these suggestions materialize, the present difficulties will disappear. From the standpoint of the interests and future of the nation and people these are the only sure and passable avenues to peace.

In short, in dealing with the Chinese Communists the Government will under no circumstances whatsoever abandon its expectancy of frank and sincere negotiations if only the Chinese Communist Party will place national interest and the people's welfare above everything else, if only it will give up its prejudiced views, appreciate the Government's difficulties and carry out the aforementioned suggestions, then not merely cessation of hostilities will materialize as a natural consequence, but the mission of peaceful national reconstruction will also be accomplished smoothly.

Fellow countrymen, our undivided unity and hard struggle sustained us through eight years of resistance to foreign aggression and won for us the final victory. To pursue our heavy task of national reconstruction we must all follow with firm faith the prescribed course regardless of the difficulties. We must promote the enforcement of the Quintuple-Power Constitutional System and seek the full implementation of the Three People's Principles.

Above all, we must with concerted purpose and discerning mind consolidate national unification and stabilize social order so as to lay the framework of national reconstruction and accomplish the task of the National Revolution. Thus the nation will ever follow the road to democratic government and the nation will ever retain its glory of independence and freedom, and only thus can the unfinished work of the Founder of our Republic and our Revolutionary Predecessors be fully consummated.

104

Second Draft of Statement for Generalissimo Chiank Kai-shek [24]

A continuation of the present political and military situation in China will be destructive of the interest of a long suffering people. It will render impossible the unification of our country and will threaten the peace of the world. Therefore, it is necessary that an early solution be found to the present conflict and that peace be restored to the land. But as the responsible head of the Government of China, I must see that the necessary measures are taken to safeguard the security of the nation, since we are dealing with a political party which maintains a large army to support its political policies.

In the past three months, I have stipulated certain conditions that must be met by the Communist Party before a peaceful accord could be achieved and to which they have thus far refused to agree. They demanded an immediate meeting of the Committee of Three of which General Marshall is the chairman. That committee reached an impasse in its negotiations the latter part of June and unless there are certain preliminary but vital agreements or understandings, a meeting of the committee would not only be ineffective, but its future usefulness would be fatally impaired. I have insisted that the proposed group of five men under the chairmanship of the United States Ambassador, Dr. Stuart, selected to reach an understanding between the Government and the Communist Party for the establishment of the coalition State Council should first meet as an evidence of the good intent of both the Government and the Communist Party towards the reorganization of the government in accordance with the resolutions of the Peoples Consultative Council. With this reassurance of good faith on both sides, there would be a new basis of trust for the termination of the hostilities now disrupting China. I have further stated that concurrent with the termination of hostilities, the Communist Party should indicate its honest intention to cooperate in the reorganization of the government by announcing its delegates to the National Assembly to meet on November 12 to determine on a democratic constitution for the Government of China.

In view of the seriousness of the situation, the misunderstandings and public confusion, and the distrust and suspicions unfortunately prevalent, I now make the following public announcement of the conditions under which the government is prepared to act to secure an immediate cessation of hostilities.

The Five Man Committee under the chairmanship of Doctor Stuart to meet immediately and at the same time, the Committee of Three under the chairmanship of General Marshall, with the following understandings:

(a) The opposing troops in close contact to be separated in accordance with the procedures tentatively reached by the Committee of Three in June for Manchuria.

(b) The restoration of communications to be immediately resumed in accordance with the agreement tentatively reached by the Committee of Three last June.

(c) The method for settling disagreements among the team members of Executive Headquarters and Commissioners at Executive Headquarters to be in accordance with the agreement tentatively reached by the Committee of Three last June.

---

[24] Prepared by the Special Representative of the President (Marshall) and the Ambassador in China (Stuart), Oct. 14, 1946.

(d) The tentative agreement reached last June by the Committee of Three for the redisposition of troops in Manchuria to be confirmed.

(e) The government troops north of the Yangtze to continue in occupation of localities now under their control until the agreement by the Committee of Three is reached for the redistribution, reorganization and demobilization of troops, Government and Communist alike for the unification of the armed forces in China.

(f) Whatever understanding is reached by the Five Man Committee headed by Doctor Stuart, it is to be confirmed by the Steering Committee of the PCC without delay.

(g) Questions of local government to be settled by the newly organized State Council.

(h) The Constitutional Draft Committee to be convened immediately and the agreed draft to be submitted to the National Assembly as the basis for its action.

(i) Concurrent with the cessation of hostilities which is to be effected immediately following the agreement of the Communist Party to the foregoing procedure, that party is to announce its intention of participating in the National Assembly by publishing its lists of delegates thereto.

105

Statement by Generalissimo Chiang Kai-shek, October 16, 1946

In my October 10th broadcast to the nation, I stated that the Government has always adhered to the political solution of our domestic political problem and would not give up this policy of peaceful settlement under whatever circumstances. I further stated that the cessation of hostilities had also been the consistent policy of the Government.

The Chinese Communists rejected the recent proposal of October 2 by the Government and later also turned down the truce proposals from General Marshall and Ambassador Stuart. The Government, nevertheless, is not going to abandon its policy of "peaceful settlement" and will still seek for a settlement by mediation and consultation. The present political and military situation in the country must not be allowed to continue and thus intensify the suffering of the people. But as the responsible head of the Government of China, I must see that the necessary measures are taken to safeguard the peace and security of the nation, since we are dealing with a political party which maintains a large army to support its political policies.

In view of the new development of the situation, the earnest desire for peace by the whole nation and the hope for an early cessation of hostilities as expressed by the various parties and non-partisans in the last few days, I now reiterate the Government's sincerity in finding a peaceful solution and propose the following concrete and practical procedure, upon the Communist agreement of which, the Government is prepared to act and secure an immediate cessation of hostilities:

The Five Man Committee under the chairmanship of Doctor Stuart to meet immediately to discuss the reorganization of the National Government; and at the same time, the Committee of Three under the chairmanship of General Marshall, with the following understandings:

(1) The restoration of communications to be immediately resumed in accordance with the agreement tentatively reached by the Committee of Three last June.

(2) The method for settling disagreements among the team members of the

Executive Headquarters and commissioners at Executive Headquarters to be in accordance with the agreement tentatively reached by the Committee of Three last June.

(3) The tentative agreement reached last June by the Committee of Three for the redisposition of troops in Manchuria to be carried out according to a fixed schedule without delay.

(4) The Government troops and Communist troops in North China and Central China to continue in occupation of localities now under their control until the agreement by the Committee of Three is reached for the redistribution, reorganization and demobilization of troops, Government and Communist alike, for the unification of the armed forces in China.

(5) Whatever understanding is reached by the Five Man Committee headed by Doctor Stuart, it is to be confirmed by the Steering Committee of the PCC without delay.

(6) Questions of local government, excluding Manchuria, to be settled by the newly organized State Council.

(7) The Constitutional Draft Committee to be convened immediately and the agreed draft to be submitted to the National Assembly, through the National Government, as the basis for its action.

(8) Concurrent with the proclamation of the cessation of hostilities which is to be effected immediately following the agreement of the Communist Party to the foregoing procedure, that party is to announce its intention of participating in the National Assembly by publishing its lists of delegates thereto.

106

Proposals by the Third Party Group, October 1946

Peace is the consistent objective of the Central Government, and the cessation of hostilities has steadily been its hope. We are all moved by the sufferings of the people and realize that a speedy solution should be found. We have therefore proposed three points in the hope that both sides may reach an understanding and very promptly stop the fighting.

1. Both sides at once issue a cease firing order, the troops to remain in their present positions. The procedure for ceasing hostilities and restoring communications will be effected by the Three Man Committee through Executive Headquarters and its field teams. The troops of both sides are to be reorganized according to the previous agreements. Their allocation is to be dealt with by the Three Man Committee. (The location of Communist troops in Manchuria should be determined in advance in Tsitsihar, Peian, Chiang Mu-ssu.)

2. Local administration throughout the nation should be arranged by the reorganized State Council according to the PCC and Peaceful Reconstruction resolutions. Wherever there is dispute the military and civil issues should be separately dealt with without delay. But along the Changchun Railway, except for *hsien* already occupied by the Government, the Government should dispatch railway police to take over.

3. According to the resolutions of the PCC and the adopted procedure, the Steering Committee should be convened in order to plan the reorganization of the Government, in which case all parties will join the Government and discuss the question of calling the National Assembly, thus making it possible for all to

take part in its meetings. At the same time the Constitutional Draft Committee should be convened in order to complete its revision.

Mo Te-hui	Liang Shu-min
Carson Chang	Yu Chia-chu
Li Huang	Chang Po-chun
Huang Yen-pei	Chen Chi-t'ien
Miao Chia-ming	Lo Lung-chi
Tso Shun-sheng	Hsu Fu-liu

107

Initial Draft of Statement for Generalissimo Chiang Kai-shek [25]

On October 16th I made public a statement regarding the policy of the Government, with a series of proposals as a basis for the termination of hostilities. This was formally transmitted to the official representative of the Communist Party, but as yet no formal acknowledgement has been received. Today, on the eve of the meeting of the National Assembly, I wish to reassert the consistent policy of the Government to promote internal peace and national unity and to carry through to consummation the conclusion of the period of political tutelage and the inauguration of constitutional democracy. As a further evidence of the sincere desire of the Government to achieve a lasting peace and political stability for the country, orders have been issued for all Government troops to cease firing except as may be necessary to defend their present positions. Further, I wish to announce that the Government desires to reach an immediate agreement with the Communist Party for the unconditional termination of hostilities.

In accordance with the resolutions of the PCC, the National Assembly was to have been convened on May 5th, 1946. However, the Communist Party and the Democratic League declined to submit the list of their delegates. Later, on July 4th, an announcement was made by the Government to the effect that the National Assembly would be convened on November 12 thus leaving a period of four months for discussions and preparations by all parties concerned. There has been objection to this procedure made by minority parties on the grounds that certain steps in the reorganization of the Government under the PCC agreements had not yet been carried out. To these objections I would say that the general situation had greatly changed since the determination of the agreed procedure for the political development of the Government, serious fighting having developed in Manchuria and spread into North China. In this situation the normal procedure for reaching political agreements was rendered ineffective. However, any further postponement of the National Assembly would only serve to intensify the political and military instability as well as the sufferings of the people. Therefore, it is the decision of the Government that the Assembly be formally convened on November 12th.

The Government is prepared to agree to an immediate but temporary adjournment of the National Assembly after formal convocation until the following conditions shall have been fulfilled:

1. Sufficient time has been allowed to permit the selection and arrival of the delegates who have not yet been selected.

---

[25] Presented on Nov. 7, 1946, by the Special Representative of the President and the Ambassador in China.

2. Reorganization of the State Council has been agreed to by the PCC Steering Committee and the council established.

3. The Draft Constitution Committee shall have completed its work on a basis of the principles set forth in the PCC agreements.

When these conditions have been fulfilled, the National Assembly shall reconvene and proceed to the adoption of the Draft Constitution in the form presented.

As regards the reorganization of the Executive Yuan that, according to the PCC resolutions, is a function of the State Council. Furthermore, it involves a drastic change in the administration of the Government which must be approached with careful deliberation.

The next few weeks are of fateful importance to China. It is within our power to lay the foundations for a strong and prosperous democratic nation. We must overcome natural serious divergence of views as well as deep suspicion and bitterness. The time has come to rise above these difficulties and dedicate ourselves purely to the service of the people.

108

Statement by Generalissimo Chiang Kai-shek, November 8, 1946

On October 16th, I made public a statement regarding the policy of the Government, with a series of proposals as a basis for the termination of hostilities. I had hoped that this would evoke a response from the Communist Party leading to a final and complete cessation of war. Today, on the eve of the meeting of the National Assembly, I wish to reassert the consistent policy of the Government to promote internal peace and national unity and to carry through to consummation the conclusion of the period of political tutelage and the inauguration of constitutional democracy. As a further evidence of the sincere desire of the Government to achieve a lasting peace and political stability for the country, orders have been issued for all Government troops in China proper and the Northeast to cease firing except as may be necessary to defend their present positions.

In accordance with the resolutions of the PCC, the National Assembly was to have been convened on May 5th, 1946. However, the Communist Party and other parties declined to submit the list of their delegates. Later, on July 4th, an announcement was made by the Government to the effect that the National Assembly would be convened on November 12th, thus leaving a period of four months for discussions and preparations by all parties concerned. There has been objection to this procedure made by the minority parties, especially on the ground that certain steps in the reorganization of the Government under the PCC agreements had not been carried out. In this connection, I would say that the general situation changed greatly during the six months after the conclusion of the PCC conferences, serious fighting having developed in Manchuria and spread into the North China area, and the demobilization of Communist forces was not initiated as agreed upon and has not been started. Under these conditions the procedure for reaching political agreements was rendered ineffective. However, legally elected delegates to the National Assembly have already arrived in Nanking and any further postponement of the Assembly would serve not only to intensify political and military instability with the consequent sufferings of the people, but would deny the only legal step by which the Government can return political power to the people. Therefore, it is the decision of the Government that the Assembly be formally convened on November 12th as scheduled.

In my recent statement of October 16th, the Government showed a spirit of conciliation which it was hoped would be reciprocated by the Communists in order that a complete settlement could be reached on all pending problems. The Government stands ready to provide ample opportunity for the Communist Party and other parties to develop along truly democratic lines. Militarily, however, no political party should maintain a private army. All troops should be servants of the State.

In the meeting of the National Assembly, the Government will reserve quotas of the delegates for the Communists as well as for the other parties in the hope that they will participate in the making of the Constitution. The Government also hopes that the Communists will authorize their representatives to participate in meetings of the committees to discuss the immediate implementation of the measures for the cessation of hostilities, the disposition of troops, the restoration of communications and the reorganization and integration of armies as proposed in my statement of October 16.

It is hoped that an agreement for the reorganization of the State Council will be reached and the Council formally established. The reorganization of the Executive Yuan cannot be effected before the adjournment of the present National Assembly. As such reorganization involves a drastic change in the administration of the Government, it must be approached with careful deliberation.

As regards the draft of the Constitution, the Government will submit to the National Assembly the uncompleted draft of the Constitutional Drafting Committee. Within six months after the adjournment of the present National Assembly, a general election will take place according to the adopted Constitution. All parties and all citizens can then freely take part in this election, in order to bring into existence the next National Assembly which will exercise its functions as stipulated by the Constitution. Should any modification be found necessary in the next National Assembly, amendments still could be introduced by all parties.

The next few weeks are of fatal importance to China. It is within our power to lay the foundations for a strong and prosperous democratic nation. We must overcome the serious but natural divergencies of view as well as deep suspicions and much bitterness. The time has come to arise above these difficulties and dedicate ourselves purely to the interests of the people who so urgently need and desire peace and security. I appeal, therefore, to the members of my own and all other parties, to my colleagues in the Government and in the National Army, and to all others concerned to unite in a final effort to reach an agreement by peaceful means for achieving the "democratization of the Government" and "the nationalization of the armed forces".

109

The Head of the Chinese Communist Party Delegation (Chou) to the Special Representative of the President (Marshall)

NANKING, *November 8, 1946*

With reference to my memorandum under date of October 9th which I requested to be transmitted to the Generalissimo, I have not as yet received a reply.

As regards the Generalissimo's statement of October 16th, I have already on October 17th explained the Communist attitude and views to the Government representative, Wu Teh Chen, Shao Li Tze and Lei Cheng in Shanghai. I also explained the same to the Third Party Group on October 18th. On the same day, I received a copy of Generalissimo's memorandum to you under date of October 17th which was forwarded to me from your office. On return to Nanking I thereupon immediately explained our views to you and Dr. Stuart and I presume that you are familiar with those.

Since returning to Nanking all the negotiations were conducted through the Third Party. Through their good offices there is some possibility for the reconvening of the Committee of Three, the PCC Steering Committee and the Draft Reviewing Committee and we are still exerting efforts for this end.

CHOU EN-LAI

110

Address Delivered by President Chiang Kai-shek at Nanking, November 15, 1946 [26]

Fellow Delegates:

The National Assembly is being inaugurated today.

You, ladies and gentlemen, have come from all over China and from overseas to assemble here in the national capital with a vital assignment from the people, namely, to participate in the great task of adopting a Constitution for the Republic of China. The present occasion marks the beginning of China's evolution into the period of constitutional democracy. It is also the most august and grand convention throughout the history of the building of the Chinese Republic.

For this reason, I wish, on behalf of the National Government, to extend to you a warm welcome and to the Assembly sincere greetings.

We should all remember that the late Dr. Sun Yat-sen, in starting the National Revolution and engaging himself in a lifetime struggle, aimed to bring about the revival of China, the establishment of a republic and the implementation of the Three People's Principles, thereby converting China into a nation of, by and for the people, enjoying wealth, power and happiness. The Revolution of 1911 deposed the 4,000-year old monarchy and the Manchu despotism of more than two centuries. The significance of this incident is seen in the remark of Dr. Sun Yat-sen: "Through this revolution, democratic government became nationally acknowledged in China".

Following the founding of the Chinese Republic, however, while its foundation was yet to be strengthened and the Three People's Principles were yet to be implemented, ceaseless disturbances broke out among warlords seeking regional domination. The country was thrown into further chaos by incessant foreign inroads.

Dr. Sun Yat-sen, nevertheless, led and encouraged the revolutionary workers to carry on indomitably the struggle in spite of dangers and hardships. He explicitly made known to the entire nation his firm will and purpose when he said "China is susceptible to democracy" and "We do not concern ourselves with the mere name of republic but with actual sovereignty in the hands of the people".

The quintessence of Dr. Sun's Principle of Nationalism is "the depositing of power in the hands of the people". In other words, it is the form of government which enables the entire people to administer affairs of common concern.

---

[26] At the opening session of the National Assembly.

The formulation of the "Fundamentals of National Reconstruction" by our Republic Founder clearly charted the course of a revolutionary plan, namely, the transition from military and political tutelage to constitutional democracy. The object was to put popular government on a solid basis and to secure a strong safeguard for the republic.

The National Government, with a view to carrying forward the ideals of Dr. Sun, embarked arduously upon political tutelage as soon as it had successfully concluded the Northern Expedition in 1928. Its supreme aim was the inauguration of constitutional government and the consummation of national reconstruction.

I shall leave it to the various offices in charge to render detailed, comprehensive reports regarding preparations for the inauguration of constitutional government and the convocation of the National Assembly.

The election of delegates to the National Assembly took place throughout China shortly after the promulgation by the National Government of the Draft Constitution on May 5, 1936 and, later, of the organizational law and the electoral law of the National Assembly. Even before the war broke out in China, the Chinese Government had already decided to convene, on November 12, 1937, the National Assembly for the institution of a constitution. At that time, the election of delegates in the various localities was about to be completed.

When the war came on July 7, 1937, as a result of intensified Japanese aggression, the Government, however, could not help but pool the whole country's resources to fight for the sheer existence of the nation. The subsequent increased tempo of fighting naturally nullified democratic efforts in areas where the election of delegates was yet to be completed, and the convocation of the National Assembly ran into physical difficulties.

In spite of this, the Fifth Kuomintang Central Executive Committee at its Sixth Plenary Session in 1939 again decided to convene the National Assembly in November, 1940. Once more it was postponed, nevertheless, in view of the further spread of hostilities and the consensus of opinion of many members of the People's Political Council who urged the convocation be delayed.

At the Eleventh Plenary Session of the Kuomintang Central Executive Committee in 1943, it was decided it was necessary to definitely stipulate the date of convocation of the National Assembly. Hence, the resolution was adopted that "the National Assembly shall be convened within one year after the conclusion of the war."

I, for one, considered that the dual program of armed resistance and national reconstruction should be carried through to simultaneous consummation. The early convention of the National Assembly would bring about the early adoption of China's fundamental and vital charter and, in turn, the early realization of the long-cherished wish of the National Government to return political authority of the people. Acting upon this belief, I proposed at the plenary session of the Sixth Kuomintang National Congress in June 1945, that the National Assembly be convoked that year on November 12, the 80th birthday anniversary of Dr. Sun Yat-sen. This proposal was adopted and active preparations to that end began.

My idea at the time was that to inaugurate constitutional democracy was Dr. Sun's greatest wish, for which he had labored selflessly all his life. The temporary retirement of Dr. Sun from his success in the first year of the Republic and his consistent struggle in succeeding years were all in the interests of the welfare and freedom of the country and the people. With this in view, we and all the other people of China could not better remember Dr. Sun, our teacher of national revolution and national reconstruction, than by convening the National Assembly to adopt a constitution.

ANNEXES 681

The National Assembly is meeting today already one year behind its original schedule. Fellow delegates, as we meet before the portrait of the great nation builder and recall the difficult struggle for democratic government, we must be filled with thoughts of reverence and admiration.

The foreign menace to the unification and democracy of our country was removed last year with the capitulation of Japan. But, nevertheless, ponderous difficulties beset the internal situation. The activities of an armed political party affect the nation's peace and stability while political dissensions also impair the nation's strength and power to rebuild after the war.

The National Government, on its part, is intensely aware that, following eight years of extraordinary ravages, the country must head immediately toward extraordinary reconstruction. Also, that the smooth progress of national reconstruction requires the entire nation's concerted efforts of sincerity and unity.

For this reason, the National Government, in January, this year, convoked a Political Consultation Conference wherein the representatives of the various parties and groups as well as social leaders met to discuss the vital problem of peaceful national reconstruction. Twenty days of conference yielded five agreements bearing on political and military matters. Those concerning the National Assembly included the proposal calling for the revision of the principles of the May 5th Draft Constitution, the increase of the number of delegates to the National Assembly, and the fixing of May 5, 1946 as the date of convocation of the Assembly.

As reflected in these agreements, the attitude of the National Government was consistently one of tolerance and conciliation. It approved the conclusion of every one of the agreements, inasmuch as it was guided unswervingly by a spirit to serve the interests of the country and the nation as well as by its consideration of the terrific post-war afflictions of the people and of the urgency of the national reconstruction program.

After the closing of the Political Consultation Conference, the National Government adhered faithfully to all its resolutions and carried them out one by one. The organizational law of the National Assembly was duly revised in accordance with the agreements.

In the meantime, however, numerous new difficulties cropped up and had to be surmounted. Consequently the National Assembly failed to convene on May 5 as scheduled. And until today we have been compelled to hold off the convocation of the long-expected National Assembly. All this I feel called upon to report to you, my fellow delegates, particularly those who have come long distances to the national capital and have been waiting here for so long.

The delegates to the Assembly today have come from various provinces, municipalities and localities. There are also in our midst those who have traveled from far beyond the seas to return to their fatherland for this occasion. Some of you, ladies and gentlemen, are regional delegates and some professional. Some have a vast experience in politics; others are socially preeminent.

However heterogeneous your background and representation, you must all be entertaining the unanimous, fervent hope and wish for the materialization of democracy, unity and progress in our country. Especially those delegates from the Northeast which has been under foreign rule for fourteen years and those from newly recovered Taiwan—their love and admiration for their fatherland, and their willingness and spirit to serve the country must be at an unusually high level.

I trust that you deeply appreciate the two famous sayings of Dr. Sun Yat-sen: "The foundation of a state lies in its people" and "Hundreds of millions of people are linked up to the nation." You will clearly see the relationship between the state and the people as well as the people's responsibility toward the state. You will, according to the law, discharge your respective duties bearing on the adoption of a constitution and thus introduce a good beginning for a constitutionalized China.

As we all know, the constitution of a nation is a fundamental and vital charter, in no way comparable by any ordinary law or regulation. It is an ordinance to be observed by the whole nation. On the one hand, a constitution must embody high and lofty ideals; on the other, the actual and realistic conditions in the country must be taken into consideration.

Our ideals are the Three People's Principles and the Quintuple-Power Constitutional System handed down by Dr. Sun Yat-sen: the reality of our country is that both our nation and society have, since the outbreak of the war of resistance, gone through a long period of evolution and progress. Only a constitution that embodies both ideals and reality will truly answer the needs of the country and be flawless and operative. It will insure for the nation an enduring peace and for the people a genuine well-being.

If we can dedicate ourselves to the institution of a flawless and operative constitution and thus lay down the framework of democracy and government by law, then the will of people in the various places, strata and vocations of the country, and the opinions of the various parties can all be expressed through legally charted channels. Hereafter all problems can be brought before public forums and decided thereby according to the law. Only thus will genuine independence, freedom, unification and democracy take root in our country. And only thus will our people be able to exercise true people's rights and fulfill their obligations as citizens, thereby furthering national prosperity and progress.

From the time I consecrated myself to national revolution under the leadership of Dr. Sun Yat-sen, it has always been my lifelong aim to build China into an independent, free, unified and democratic nation. Our chief war aim during the last eight years of resistance was to eliminate violence and aggression and thus to secure the independence and freedom of China. The victory finally was won through the efforts of all our people, civilian and military alike. Furthermore, along with the conclusion of new treaties with Great Britain, the United States and the Soviet Union during the war, Dr. Sun's wish to abolish all unequal treaties materialized.

Reviewing my life, however, I find my greatest regret in the fact that, from the Mukden Incident till the present moment, no constitution has yet been adopted and inaugurated. In the course of these thirty years, the wish has always been in my thoughts to conclude political tutelage and inaugurate constitutional government in order that the task of national reconstruction might be fully accomplished.

We have been carrying on the struggle of national revolution and reconstruction for the country and the people, for the realization of the Three People's Principles and democratic government based upon the Quintuple-Power Constitutional System. This is the ultimate objective in our revolution. As long as this ultimate objective remains unattained, unfulfilled remains the will of our republic founder. It will also mean that we are yet to fulfill our part towards the country, the people and the revolutionary predecessors of the last fifty years.

I wish especially to point out to you that the exercise of the political powers was delegated to the Chinese Kuomintang in 1931 by the People's Congress while the National Government was authorized to exercise the governing powers in accordance with the provisional constitution for the period of political tutelage.

Throughout these ten years and more, affairs of the state have been administered with utmost conscientiousness and feelings of responsibility.

By fighting the war to a victorious end, the National Government has barely been able to fulfill the trust of the nation. Its one and only wish now is to adopt a constitution and inaugurate constitutionalism at an early date, thus returning political power to all the people of the country and establishing a durable foundation for the Republic. And this sacred and solemn assignment to adopt a constitution is to fall squarely and equally on all of the delegates to the Assembly.

Ladies and gentlemen, after innumerable difficulties, hardships and nightmares, the present National Assembly has at long last become a reality.

In view of the difficulties Dr. Sun Yat-sen encountered in leading the revolution and of the ceaseless and bitter struggle of our revolutionary predecessors, we certainly must exert our utmost to make this Assembly worthy of Dr. Sun and the martyrs.

If only we turn our thoughts back to the Japanese aggression which impeded and delayed our program of national reconstruction, then all of us should, with might and main, accomplish this sacred mission in order that our soldiers and compatriots who gave their lives for the country during the war may not have died in vain.

Meanwhile, if we try to trace the cause for the political turmoil of the present day and also the sufferings of the people, we find that these are all due to the absence of the foundation of the state. And the present adoption of a constitution is a vital step towards stabilizing the foundation of the state and inaugurating constitutional democracy. Such is the solemn and important mission of all of the delegates.

It is indeed an unusual honor for me to attend this great convention. May I, with utmost sincerity, ask all of you to make your best efforts for the country and the success of the Assembly.

111

Statement by the Head of the Chinese Communist Party Delegation (Chou), [Nanking,] November 16, 1946

The National Assembly, a creation of the Kuomintang one-party rule Government, was convened yesterday. The convention, being called by the one-party Government alone, against the PCC decisions and the will of the people, is strongly and firmly opposed by the Communist Party. Not only the date for calling the meeting was not decided through agreement by political consultation, moreover, it is a nation-splitting National Assembly called by the Kuomintang alone, instead of a united one, joined by all political parties and groups.

According to the program and spirit of the PCC, the convention of the National Assembly is only possible, until all those PCC decisions are step by step carried out into working realities and Assembly itself directed by the reorganized Government. The PCC decisions is a temporary political charter agreed by all parties and groups. They are an integral whole which is not to be cut into disintegrating parts.

During the past ten months, all the decisions reached at the PCC have not been carried out to the least extent, furthermore, they have been totally ruined by the Kuomintang authorities. The cease fire agreement is one which has been approved by the PCC. But civil war, began from the Northeast, has extended to areas inside the Great Wall. The Government authorities have thoroughly destroyed the status quo as of Cease Fire Order of January. The four promises pledged by the responsible authority of the Government at the inaugural meeting of the PCC were utterly broken by the Kuomintang Gestapo rule from the time of the Chiaochangkou Incident in Chungking in February this year to the assassination of Li Kung-pu and Wen I-tou, leading members of the Democratic League. Up to the present, no final decision is agreed upon regarding the reorganization of the Government, thus, the peaceful national reconstruction program is also held back from its realization.

As to the local governments in the various Liberated Areas, the Kuomintang authorities in violation of the above-mentioned program, does not allow it to maintain a status quo. Furthermore, attempts have been made for the "taking over" of them. Not allowed, the Kuomintang took steps to capture the places by military occupation.

The underlying principle of the military agreements is the separation of military and civil administrations. Yet it is an obvious fact that at present almost all the provincial governors appointed by the Kuomintang Government are military men in active services.

Regarding the reviewing of the draft constitution, it is a work uncompleted in Chungking, which obliged the Communist Party to announce openly its reservation for its final approval. But this subject has been shelved up till this moment since the Government came back to Nanking.

The decision regarding the National Assembly is the last piece of compromise reached during the PCC sessions. The Kuomintang authorities at that time pledged not to call a National Assembly which is manipulated by one party alone, and which would entail a split. They also pledged to adopt the Constitution which the PCC will bring to completion, whereas all the other parties promised the acknowledgement of the delegates elected ten years ago under the Kuomintang sponsorship to be among the regional and professional delegates on the condition that delegates representing various political parties and the Liberated Areas be added. Moreover, only when the civil war is stopped, the PCC decisions are carried out, the people's freedoms are safeguarded and the reorganization of the Government is achieved, would they attend the convention, and regard the National Assembly as a united National Assembly participated in by all parties.

The National Assembly, being inaugurated now, is called in violation to the above-mentioned decisions and spirit. It is clear enough that even the date for its inauguration or postponement is decided by the one-party Government alone. According to PCC agreement, of the 2,050 delegates, there should be 410 delegates representing the various political parties and non-partisans and 200 representing the Liberated Areas. Yet the list of delegates promulgated by the Government on November 15 published names of 1,580 showing that the Government has illegally annexed 140 more seats. This exposes all the more profoundly that this National Assembly is ruled by one party and spells national split. The so-called reservation of seats for the Communists, itself a violation of the PCC agreement, is only a fraud to seduce all parties other than the Communists to join the meeting and to whitewash the Kuomintang autocracy.

In view of the painstaking efforts made by the third party group, the Chinese Communist Party has during the negotiations of the last month in Nanking made repeated representations to the effect that any form of parley will be agreeable, provided the decisions and program of the PCC are adhered to.

These, however, were again turned down by the Government authorities. And when the inauguration of the one-party National Assembly draws to a close, we firmly urged that this one-party National Assembly should be called off without delay, in order to afford an opportunity for the concurrent meeting of the military Committee of Three, the PCC Steering Committee and the Draft Constitution Reviewing Committee, which will straighten out the various current military and political problems on the basis of the Cease Fire Agreement, the Army Reorganization Agreement and the PCC decisions, and put them into effect. Amidst the peaceful atmosphere thus brought about, it would be feasible for a united National Assembly, participated in by all parties and groups, to take place. But the Government authorities, merely eager to whitewash their own dictatorship, would not pay the slightest thought to that.

The One-Party National Assembly, now being opened, denies the prospect of putting the advocacies of the Communist Party and the third party group put forward during the latest stage of negotiations into materialization. It thus destroyed once for all every resolution since the PCC, as well as the Cease Fire Agreement and the Army Reorganization Agreement, and wrecked the path of peaceful negotiations established since the PCC. At the same time, it unmasked also most drastically the fraudulent nature of the Government's "cease fire order" of November 8.

This unilateral National Assembly is now afoot to adopt a so-called "constitution", in order to "legalize" dictatorship, to "legalize" civil war, to "legalize" split, and to "legalize" the selling-out of the interests of the Nation and the people. Should that come to pass, the Chinese people shall fall headlong into the deep precipice of immense suffering. We, Chinese Communists, therefore adamantly refuse to recognize this National Assembly.

The door of negotiation has by now been slammed by the single hand of the Kuomintang authorities. All the shows that are going to be staged during the National Assembly, even the reorganization of the Government, are not worthy of our slightest attention. To attend such a National Assembly, to recognize all these shows, will constitute the throwing overboard of the PCC decisions, and the destruction of the track laid by PCC leading to peace, democracy, solidarity and unity. Regarding this issue there is no midway.

While the bloody war waged against the Liberated Areas is going on with full vigor, and the policy of the United States Government to assist Chiang in the civil war remains unchanged, a false peace, a false democracy cannot but fail to deceive the people. We, Chinese Communists, are ready to join hands with the Chinese people and all such parties which are truly working for democracy, to struggle for a genuine peace and genuine democracy to the very end.

112

The Representative of the Chinese Communist Party (Tung) to the Special Representative of the President (Marshall)

[NANKING,] December 4, 1946

MY DEAR GENERAL MARSHALL: General Chou En-lai requests the following message to be delivered to your hands:—

"With the inauguration of the one-party-manipulated National Assembly, the PCC agreements have been utterly destroyed by President Chiang Kai-shek, and there is short of a basis for the negotiation between the Kuomintang and the Chinese Communist Party. However, with a view to comply with the aspiration of the entire Chinese people for peace and democracy, our party takes the stand that if the Kuomintang would immediately dissolve the illegal National Assembly now in session, and restore the troop positions as of January 13 in accord with the Cease Fire Order, the negotiation between the two parties may still make a fresh start. Request the foregoing be transmitted to President Chiang."

Yours faithfully

(TUNG PI-WU)

113

Personal Statement by the Special Representative of the President (Marshall), January 7, 1947 [27]

The President has recently given a summary of the developments in China during the past year and the position of the American Government toward China. Circumstances now dictate that I should supplement this with impressions gained at first hand.

In this intricate and confused situation, I shall merely endeavor here to touch on some of the more important considerations—as they appeared to me—during my connection with the negotiations to bring about peace in China and a stable democratic form of government.

In the first place, the greatest obstacle to peace has been the complete, almost overwhelming suspicion with which the Chinese Communist Party and the Kuomintang regard each other.

On the one hand, the leaders of the Government are strongly opposed to a communistic form of government. On the other, the Communists frankly state that they are Marxists and intend to work toward establishing a communistic form of government in China, though first advancing through the medium of a democratic form of government of the American or British type.

The leaders of the Government are convinced in their minds that the Communist-expressed desire to participate in a government of the type endorsed by the Political Consultative Conference last January had for its purpose only a destructive intention. The Communists felt, I believe, that the government was insincere in its apparent acceptance of the PCC resolutions for the formation of the new government and intended by coercion of military force and the action of secret police to obliterate the Communist Party. Combined with this mutual deep distrust was the conspicuous error by both parties of ignoring the effect of the fears and suspicions of the other party in estimating the reason for proposals or opposition regarding the settlement of various matters under negotiation. They each sought only to take counsel of their own fears. They both, therefore, to that extent took a rather lopsided view of each situation and were susceptible to every evil suggestion or possibility. This complication was exaggerated to an explosive degree by the confused reports of fighting on the distant and tremendous fronts of hostile military contact. Patrol clashes were deliberately magnified into large offensive actions. The distortion of the facts was utilized by both sides to heap condemnation on the other. It was only through the reports of American officers in the field teams from Executive Headquarters that I could get even a partial idea of what was actually happening and the incidents were too

---

[27] *Department of State Bulletin*, Jan. 19, 1947, pp. 83–85.

numerous and the distances too great for the American personnel to cover all of the ground. I must comment here on the superb courage of the officers of our Army and Marines in struggling against almost insurmountable and maddening obstacles to bring some measure of peace to China.

I think the most important factors involved in the recent breakdown of negotiations are these: On the side of the National Government, which is in effect the Kuomintang, there is a dominant group of reactionaries who have been opposed, in my opinion, to almost every effort I have made to influence the formation of a genuine coalition government. This has usually been under the cover of political or party action, but since the Party was the Government, this action, though subtle or indirect, has been devastating in its effect. They were quite frank in publicly stating their belief that cooperation by the Chinese Communist Party in the government was inconceivable and that only a policy of force could definitely settle the issue. This group includes military as well as political leaders.

On the side of the Chinese Communist Party there are, I believe, liberals as well as radicals, though this view is vigorously opposed by many who believe that the Chinese Communist Party discipline is too rigidly enforced to admit of such differences of viewpoint. Nevertheless, it has appeared to me that there is a definite liberal group among the Communists, especially of young men who have turned to the Communists in disgust at the corruption evident in the local governments—men who would put the interest of the Chinese people above ruthless measures to establish a Communist ideology in the immediate future. The dyed-in-the-wool Communists do not hesitate at the most drastic measures to gain their end as, for instance, the destruction of communications in order to wreck the economy of China and produce a situation that would facilitate the overthrow or collapse of the Government, without any regard to the immediate suffering of the people involved. They completely distrust the leaders of the Kuomintang and appear convinced that every Government proposal is designed to crush the Chinese Communist Party. I must say that the quite evidently inspired mob actions of last February and March, some within a few blocks of where I was then engaged in completing negotiations, gave the Communists good excuse for such suspicions.

However, a very harmful and immensely provocative phase of the Chinese Communist Party procedure has been in the character of its propaganda. I wish to state to the American people that in the deliberate misrepresentation and abuse of the action, policies and purposes of our Government this propaganda has been without regard for the truth, without any regard whatsoever for the facts, and has given plain evidence of a determined purpose to mislead the Chinese people and the world and to arouse a bitter hatred of Americans. It has been difficult to remain silent in the midst of such public abuse and wholesale disregard of facts, but a denial would merely lead to the necessity of daily denials; an intolerable course of action for an American official. In the interest of fairness, I must state that the Nationalist Government publicity agency has made numerous misrepresentations, though not of the vicious nature of the Communist propaganda. Incidentally, the Communist statements regarding the Anping incident which resulted in the death of three Marines and the wounding of twelve others were almost pure fabrication, deliberately representing a carefully arranged ambuscade of a Marine convoy with supplies for the maintenance of Executive Headquarters and some UNRRA supplies, as a defence against a Marine assault. The investigation of this incident was a tortuous procedure of delays and maneuvers to disguise the true and privately admitted facts of the case.

Sincere efforts to achieve settlement have been frustrated time and again by extremist elements of both sides. The agreements reached by the Political Consultative Conference a year ago were a liberal and forward-looking charter which then offered China a basis for peace and reconstruction. However, irreconcilable groups within the Kuomintang, interested in the preservation of their own feudal control of China, evidently had no real intention of implementing them. Though I speak as a soldier, I must here also deplore the dominating influence of the military. Their dominance accentuates the weakness of civil government in China. At the same time, in pondering the situation in China, one must have clearly in mind not the workings of small Communist groups or committees to which we are accustomed in America, but rather of millions of people and an army of more than a million men.

I have never been in a position to be certain of the development of attitudes in the innermost Chinese Communist circles. Most certainly, the course which the Chinese Communist Party has pursued in recent months indicated an unwillingness to make a fair compromise. It has been impossible even to get them to sit down at a conference table with Government representatives to discuss given issues. Now the Communists have broken off negotiations by their last offer which demanded the dissolution of the National Assembly and a return to the military positions of January 13th which the Government could not be expected to accept.

Between this dominant reactionary group in the Government and the irreconcilable Communists who, I must state, did not so appear last February, lies the problem of how peace and well-being are to be brought to the long-suffering and presently inarticulate mass of the people of China. The reactionaries in the Government have evidently counted on substantial American support regardless of their actions. The Communists by their unwillingness to compromise in the national interest are evidently counting on an economic collapse to bring about the fall of the Government, accelerated by extensive guerrilla action against the long lines of rail communications—regardless of the cost in suffering to the Chinese people.

The salvation of the situation, as I see it, would be the assumption of leadership by the liberals in the Government and in the minority parties, a splendid group of men, but who as yet lack the political power to exercise a controlling influence. Successful action on their part under the leadership of Generalissimo Chiang Kai-shek would, I believe, lead to unity through good government.

In fact, the National Assembly has adopted a democratic constitution which in all major respects is in accordance with the principles laid down by the all-party Political Consultative Conference of last January. It is unfortunate that the Communists did not see fit to participate in the Assembly since the constitution that has been adopted seems to include every major point that they wanted.

Soon the Government in China will undergo major reorganization pending the coming into force of the constitution following elections to be completed before Christmas Day 1947. Now that the form for a democratic China has been laid down by the newly adopted constitution, practical measures will be the test. It remains to be seen to what extent the Government will give substance to the form by a genuine welcome of all groups actively to share in the responsibility of government.

The first step will be the reorganization of the State Council and the executive branch of Government to carry on administration pending the enforcement of the constitution. The manner in which this is done and the amount of representation accorded to liberals and to non-Kuomintang members will be significant.

It is also to be hoped that during this interim period the door will remain open for Communists or other groups to participate if they see fit to assume their share of responsibility for the future of China.

It has been stated officially and categorically that the period of political tutelage under the Kuomintang is at an end. If the termination of one-party rule is to be a reality, the Kuomintang should cease to receive financial support from the Government.

I have spoken very frankly because in no other way can I hope to bring the people of the United States to even a partial understanding of this complex problem. I have expressed all these views privately in the course of negotiations; they are well known, I think, to most of the individuals concerned. I express them now publicly, as it is my duty, to present my estimate of the situation and its possibilities to the American people who have a deep interest in the development of conditions in the Far East promising an enduring peace in the Pacific.

114

Statement by President Truman on United States Policy Toward China, December 18, 1946 [28]

Last December I made a statement of this Government's views regarding China. We believed then and do now that a united and democratic China is of the utmost importance to world peace, that a broadening of the base of the National Government to make it representative of the Chinese people will further China's progress toward this goal, and that China has a clear responsibility to the other United Nations to eliminate armed conflict within its territory as constituting a threat to world stability and peace. It was made clear at Moscow last year that these views are shared by our Allies, Great Britain and the Soviet Union. On December 27th, Mr. Byrnes, Mr. Molotov and Mr. Bevin issued a statement which said, in part:

"The three Foreign Secretaries exchanged views with regard to the situation in China. They were in agreement as to the need for a unified and democratic China under the National Government for broad participation by democratic elements in all branches of the National Government, and for a cessation of civil strife. They affirmed their adherence to the policy of non-interference in the internal affairs of China."

The policies of this Government were also made clear in my statement of last December. We recognized the National Government of the Republic of China as the legal government. We undertook to assist the Chinese Government in reoccupation of the liberated areas and in disarming and repatriating the Japanese invaders. And finally, as China moved toward peace and unity along the lines mentioned, we were prepared to assist the Chinese economically and in other ways.

I asked General Marshall to go to China as my representative. We had agreed upon my statement of the United States Government's views and policies regarding China as his directive. He knew full well in undertaking the mission that halting civil strife, broadening the base of the Chinese Government and bringing about a united, democratic China were tasks for the Chinese themselves. He

---

[28] *Department of State Bulletin*, Dec. 29, 1946, pp. 1179–1183.

went as a great American to make his outstanding abilities available to the Chinese.

During the war, the United States entered into an agreement with the Chinese Government regarding the training and equipment of a special force of 39 divisions. That training ended V-J Day and the transfer of the equipment had been largely completed when General Marshall arrived.

The United States, the United Kingdom and the Union of Soviet Socialist Republics all committed themselves to the liberation of China, including the return of Manchuria to Chinese control. Our Government had agreed to assist the Chinese Government in the reoccupation of areas liberated from the Japanese, including Manchuria, because of China's lack of shipping and transport planes. Three armies were moved by air and eleven by sea, to central China, Formosa, north China and Manchuria. Most of these moves had been made or started when General Marshall arrived.

The disarming and evacuation of Japanese progressed slowly—too slowly. We regarded our commitment to assist the Chinese in this program as of overwhelming importance to the future peace of China and the whole Far East. Surrendered but undefeated Japanese armies and hordes of administrators, technicians, and Japanese merchants, totalling about 3,000,000 persons, had to be removed under the most difficult conditions. At the request of the Chinese Government we had retained a considerable number of American troops in China, and immediately after V-J Day we landed a corps of Marines in north China. The principal task of these forces was to assist in the evacuation of Japanese. Only some 200,000 had been returned to Japan by the time General Marshall arrived.

General Marshall also faced a most unpropitious internal situation on his arrival in China. Communications throughout the country were badly disrupted due to destruction during the war and the civil conflicts which had broken out since. This disruption was preventing the restoration of Chinese economy, the distribution of relief supplies, and was rendering the evacuation of Japanese a slow and difficult process. The wartime destruction of factories and plants, the war-induced inflation in China, the Japanese action in shutting down the economy of occupied China immediately after V-J Day, and finally the destruction of communications combined to paralyze the economic life of the country, spreading untold hardship to millions, robbing the victory over the Japanese of significance to most Chinese and seriously aggravating all the tensions and discontents that existed in China.

Progress toward solution of China's internal difficulties by the Chinese themselves was essential to the rapid and effective completion of most of the programs in which we had already pledged our assistance to the Chinese Government. General Marshall's experience and wisdom were available to the Chinese in their efforts to reach such solutions.

Events moved rapidly upon General Marshall's arrival. With all parties availing themselves of his impartial advice, agreement for a country-wide truce was reached and announced on January 10th. A feature of this agreement was the establishment of a unique organization, the Executive Headquarters in Peiping. It was realized that due to poor communications and the bitter feelings on local fronts, generalized orders to cease fire and withdraw might have little chance of being carried out unless some authoritative executive agency, trusted by both sides, could function in any local situation.

The Headquarters operated under the leaders of three commissioners—one American who served as chairman, one Chinese Government representative, and one representative of the Chinese Communist Party. Mr. Walter S. Robertson, Charge d'Affaires of the American Embassy in China, served as chairman until his return to this country in the fall. In order to carry out its function in the field, Executive Headquarters formed a large number of truce teams, each headed by one American officer, one Chinese Government officer, and one Chinese Communist officer. They proceeded to all danger spots where fighting was going on or seemed impending and saw to the implementation of the truce terms, often under conditions imposing exceptional hardships and requiring courageous action. The degree of cooperation attained between Government and Communist officers in the Headquarters and on the truce teams was a welcome proof that despite two decades of fighting, these two Chinese groups could work together.

Events moved forward with equal promise on the political front. On January 10th, the Political Consultative Conference began its sessions with representatives of the Kuomintang or Government Party, the Communist Party and several minor political parties participating. Within three weeks of direct discussion these groups had come to a series of statesmanlike agreements on outstanding political and military problems. The agreements provided for an interim government of a coalition type with representation of all parties, for revision of the Draft Constitution along democratic lines prior to its discussion and adoption by a National Assembly and for reduction of the Government and Communist armies and their eventual amalgamation into a small modernized truly national army responsible to a civilian government.

In March, General Marshall returned to this country. He reported on the important step the Chinese had made toward peace and unity in arriving at these agreements. He also pointed out that these agreements could not be satisfactorily implemented and given substance unless China's economic disintegration were checked and particularly unless the transportation system could be put in working order. Political unity could not be built on economic chaos. This Government had already authorized certain minor credits to the Chinese Government in an effort to meet emergency rehabilitation needs as it was doing for other war devastated countries throughout the world. A total of approximately $66,000,000 was involved in six specific projects, chiefly for the purchase of raw cotton, and for ships and railroad repair material. But these emergency measures were inadequate. Following the important forward step made by the Chinese in the agreements as reported by General Marshall, the Export-Import Bank earmarked a total of $500,000,000 for possible additional credits on a project by project basis to Chinese Government agencies and private enterprises. Agreement to extend actual credits for such projects would obviously have to be based upon this Government's policy as announced December 15, 1945. So far, this $500,000,000 remains earmarked, but unexpended.

While comprehensive large scale aid has been delayed, this Government has completed its wartime lend-lease commitments to China. Lend-lease assistance was extended to China to assist her in fighting the Japanese, and later to fulfill our promise to assist in re-occupying the country from the Japanese. Assistance took the form of goods and equipment and of services. Almost half the total made available to China consisted of services, such as those involved in air and water transportation of troops. According to the latest figures reported, lend-lease assistance to China up to V-J Day totalled approximately $870,000,000. From V-J Day to the end of February, shortly after General Marshall's arrival, the total was approximately $600,000,000—mostly in transportation costs.

Thereafter, the program was reduced to the fulfillment of outstanding commitments, much of which was later suspended.

A considerable quantity of civilian goods has also been made available by our agreement with China for the disposal of surplus property which enabled us to liquidate a sizable indebtedness and to dispose of large quantities of surplus material. During the war the Chinese Government furnished Chinese currency to the United States Army for use in building its installations, feeding the troops, and other expenses. By the end of the war this indebtedness amounted to something like 150,000,000,000 Chinese dollars. Progressive currency inflation in China rendered it impossible to determine the exact value of the sum in United States currency.

China agreed to buy all surplus property owned by the United States in China and on seventeen Pacific Islands and bases with certain exceptions. Six months of negotiations preceded the agreement finally signed in August. It was imperative that this matter be concluded in the Pacific as had already been done in Europe, especially in view of the rapid deterioration of the material in open storage under tropical conditions and the urgent need for the partial alleviation of the acute economic distress of the Chinese people which it was hoped this transaction would permit. Aircraft, all non-demilitarized combat material, and fixed installations outside of China were excluded. Thus, no weapons which could be used in fighting a civil war were made available through this agreement.

The Chinese Government cancelled all but 30,000,000 United States dollars of our indebtedness for the Chinese currency, and promised to make available the equivalent of 35,000,000 United States dollars for use in paying United States governmental expenses in China and acquiring and improving buildings and properties for our diplomatic and consular establishments. An additional sum of 20,000,000 United States dollars is also designated for the fulfillment of a cultural and educational program.

Before General Marshall arrived in China for the second time, in April, there was evidence that the truce agreement was being disregarded. The sincere and unflagging efforts of Executive Headquarters and its truce teams have succeeded in many instances in preventing or ending local engagements and thus saved thousands of lives. But fresh outbreaks of civil strife continued to occur, reaching a crisis of violence in Manchuria with the capture of Changchun by the Communists and where the presence of truce teams had not been fully agreed to by the National Government.

A change in the course of events in the political field was equally disappointing. Negotiations between the Government and the Communists have been resumed again and again, but they have as often broken down. Although hope for final success has never disappeared completely, the agreements made in January and February have not been implemented, and the various Chinese groups have not since that time been able to achieve the degree of agreement reached at the Political Consultative Conference.

There has been encouraging progress in other fields, particularly the elimination of Japanese from China. The Chinese Government was responsible under an Allied agreement for the disarmament of all Japanese military personnel and for the repatriation of all Japanese civilians and military personnel from China, Formosa and French Indo-China north of the sixteenth degree of latitude. Our Government agreed to assist the Chinese in this task. The scope of the job was tremendous. There were about 3,000,000 Japanese, nearly one-half of them

Army or Navy personnel to be evacuated. Water and rail transportation had been destroyed or was immobilized. Port facilities were badly damaged and overcrowded with relief and other supplies. The Japanese had to be disarmed, concentrated and then transported to the nearest available port. In some instances this involved long distances. At the ports they had to be individually searched and put through a health inspection. All had to be inoculated. Segregation camps had to be established at the ports to cope with the incidence of epidemic diseases such as Asiatic cholera. Finally, 3,000,000 persons had to be moved by ship to Japan.

American forces helped in the disarmament of Japanese units. Executive Headquarters and its truce teams were able to make the complicated arrangements necessary to transfer Japanese across lines and through areas involved in civil conflict on their way to ports of embarkation. American units also participated in the inspections at the port, while American medical units supervised all inoculation and other medical work. Finally, American and Japanese ships under the control of General MacArthur in Japan, and a number of United States Navy ships under the Seventh Fleet transported this enormous number of persons to reception ports in Japan.

At the end of last year, approximately 200,000 Japanese had been repatriated. They were leaving Chinese ports at a rate of about 2,500 a day. By March of this year, rapidly increased efforts on the part of the American forces and the Chinese authorities involved had increased this rate to more than 20,000 a day. By November, 2,986,438 Japanese had been evacuated and the program was considered completed. Except for indeterminate numbers in certain parts of Manchuria, only war criminals and technicians retained on an emergency basis by the Chinese Government remain. That this tremendous undertaking has been accomplished despite conflict, disrupted communications and other difficulties will remain an outstanding example of successful American-Chinese cooperation toward a common goal.

Much has been said of the presence of United States armed forces in China during the past year. Last fall these forces were relatively large. They had to be. No one could prophesy in advance how well the Japanese forces in China would observe the surrender terms. We had to provide forces adequate to assist the Chinese in the event of trouble. When it became obvious that the armed Japanese would not be a problem beyond the capabilities of the Chinese Armies to handle, redeployment was begun at once.

The chief responsibility of our forces was that of assisting in evacuation of Japanese. This task was prolonged by local circumstances. Provision of American personnel for the Executive Headquarters and its truce teams has required a fairly large number of men, particularly since the all important network of radio and other communications was provided entirely by the United States. The Executive Headquarters is located at Peiping, a hundred miles from the sea and in an area where there was the possibility of local fighting. Hence, another responsibility was to protect the line of supply to and from Headquarters. Another duty our forces undertook immediately upon the Japanese surrender was to provide the necessary protection so that coal from the great mines northeast of Tientsin could reach the sea for shipment to supply the cities and railroads of central China. This coal was essential to prevent the collapse of this industrial area. Our Marines were withdrawn from this duty last September. Other units of our forces were engaged in searching for the bodies or graves of American soldiers who had died fighting the Japanese in China. Still others were required to guard United States installations and stores of equipment, and to process these for return to this country or sale as surplus property.

At peak strength a year ago we had some 113,000 soldiers, sailors and marines in China. Today this number is being reduced to less than 12,000, including some 2,000 directly concerned with the operations of Executive Headquarters and will be further reduced to the number required to supply and secure the American personnel of Executive Headquarters and the air field and stores at Tsingtao.

Thus during the past year we have successfully assisted in the repatriation of the Japanese and have subsequently been able to bring most of our own troops home. We have afforded appropriate assistance in the reoccupation of the country from the Japanese. We have undertaken some emergency measures of economic assistance to prevent the collapse of China's economy and have liquidated our own wartime financial account with China.

It is a matter of deep regret that China has not yet been able to achieve unity by peaceful methods. Because he knows how serious the problem is, and how important it is to reach a solution, General Marshall has remained at his post even though active negotiations have been broken off by the Communist Party. We are ready to help China as she moves toward peace and genuine democratic government.

The views expressed a year ago by this Government are valid today. The plan for political unification agreed to last February is sound. The plan for military unification of last February has been made difficult of implementation by the progress of the fighting since last April, but the general principles involved are fundamentally sound.

China is a sovereign nation. We recognize that fact and we recognize the National Government of China. We continue to hope that the Government will find a peaceful solution. We are pledged not to interfere in the internal affairs of China. Our position is clear. While avoiding involvement in their civil strife, we will persevere with our policy of helping the Chinese people to bring about peace and economic recovery in their country.

As ways and means are presented for constructive aid to China, we will give them careful and sympathetic consideration. An example of such aid is the recent agricultural mission to China under Dean Hutchison of the University of California sent at the request of the Chinese Government. A joint Chinese-American Agricultural Collaboration Commission was formed which included the Hutchison mission. It spent over four months studying rural problems. Its recommendations are now available to the Chinese Government, and so also is any feasible aid we can give in implementing those recommendations. When conditions in China improve, we are prepared to consider aid in carrying out other projects, unrelated to civil strife, which would encourage economic reconstruction and reform in China and which, in so doing, would promote a general revival of commercial relations between American and Chinese businessmen.

We believe that our hopes for China are identical with what the Chinese people themselves most earnestly desire. We shall therefore continue our positive and realistic policy toward China which is based on full respect for her national sovereignty and on our traditional friendship for the Chinese people and is designed to promote international peace.

115

Press Release Issued by the Department of State, January 29, 1947

The United States Government has decided to terminate its connection with the Committee of Three which was established in Chungking for the purpose of terminating hostilities in China and of which General Marshall was Chairman. The United States Government also has decided to terminate its connection with Executive Headquarters which was established in Peiping by the Committee of Three for the purpose of supervising, in the field, the execution of the agreements for the cessation of hostilities and the demobilization and reorganization of the Armed Forces in China.

The American personnel involved in Executive Headquarters will be withdrawn as soon as possible.

Annexes to Chapter VI: The Ambassadorship of John Leighton Stuart, 1947–1949

116(a)

Statement Issued January 20, 1947, by the Ministry of Information, Chinese National Government

893.00/1–2147

With a view to establishing constitutional rule and completing national reconstruction, the government has been consistently seeking for peace and unification. As far back as the beginning of the war of resistance, in order to pool together the nation's efforts, the government called the People's Political Council consisting of representatives of all political parties and independents.

From start to finish, the government has regarded the Communist problem as a political problem. The Kuomintang at its tenth CEC plenary session in 1942 and eleventh plenary session the following year persistently advocated an early solution through political means.

After May 1944 the government has been negotiating with the Communist Party without letup in the hope that a peaceful settlement could be reached.

When the Committee for Promotion of Constitutional Rule met on March 1, 1945, President Chiang Kai-shek, being convinced that the Communist problem, if left unsolved, would constitute a serious obstacle in the way of national unification and reconstruction, reiterated his determination of finding a peaceful solution without delay. He also proposed three steps leading toward constitutional government.

After victory, President Chiang Kai-shek invited Communist leader, Mr. Mao Tse Tung, to Chungking for discussions. These discussions resulted in the Double Tenth Agreement with the announcement that negotiations would be continued on the basis of mutual trust and concessions so that satisfactory results will be achieved.

Since the Political Consultative Conference last January, agreements have been reached between the Government and Communists on military and communications problems with the help of United States special envoy General George C. Marshall. These agreements raised hope throughout the world that the Communist problem in China would be solved through political means.

The Government and Kuomintang, especially in the resolution of the party's second plenary session, repeatedly pledged support to the PCC resolutions and expressed their willingness to implement them in cooperation with the other political parties and independents. The failure of realization of the PCC resolution is due to the following factors:

First, according to the Sino-Soviet treaty, the National Government should take over the administration in the nine northeast provinces. When the Soviet troops began withdrawing, Communist troops obstructed in various ways the takeover work of the national army. In the middle of March last year the Communists occupied various places already taken over by the government forces in Liaopei and attacked Szepingkai, Harbin and Tsitsihar. In order to fulfill its treaty obligations and assert its right to recover sovereignty over the northeast, the government on March 27 reached an agreement with the Communists for sending truce field teams to the northeast. Unfortunately nothing was achieved despite the efforts of the field teams under the Executive Headquarters, thus the northeast remains in chaotic conditions. The National Assembly scheduled by PCC to convene on May 5 had to be postponed.

Two. Since the Government returned to Nanking in May 1946, conflicts in the northeast were further intensified and communications in North China continued to be disrupted. The government jointly with the Communists issued a cease fire order for 15 days during which it hoped to put a full stop to the hostilities in the northeast, to restore communications lines throughout the country and to implement the army reorganization plan. On all these three points, the Government and the Communist Party had almost reached agreements. But though the deadline of the truce period was postponed three times, the Communists intensified their attacks during the interval, capturing Tehchow, Taian and attacking Tatung, Tsinan and the outer rim of Tsingtao. Again nothing was achieved.

Three. Before the National Assembly was convoked, in view of the confused domestic conditions and the countrywide demand for peace and especially the sincerity and earnest desire of the various political parties and independents for the early termination of hostilities, the government on October 16 proposed to the Communists an eight point peace program, in the hope that another cease fire order be issued and the National Assembly be called as scheduled to enact a constitution. But despite the strenuous mediatory efforts of the minority parties, and despite the government's intention to make concessions, the Communists stood adamant in its opposition to the compromise suggestion and demanded further postponement of the National Assembly. A deadlock was thus reached.

After the adjournment of the National Assembly, the government, with the date set for the enforcement of the constitution, made further efforts for the resumption of the peace talks. Through Doctor J. Leighton Stuart, United States Ambassador, the government informed the Communist Party of its willingness to send a representative to Yenan to resume the peace negotiations. But the Communists still insisted on the restoration of the troops dispositions extant on January 13 last year, and on the annulment of the constitution adopted by the National Assembly as the sine qua non conditions. But the fact is that great changes have occurred in the troops dispositions during the past year since January 13. It is practically impossible to revert to the original positions. Moreover withdrawal of government troops from recovered areas would surely endanger the peoples lives and property in those areas—a thing most incompatible with the government's obligation to restore order and protect the people and to prevent the recurrence of Communist terrorism.

If the Communists are really sincere to achieve peace, they should implement the army reorganization plan and other programs reached in the committee of three. If so, there should be no need for any dispute over the temporary dispositions of the troops.

As regards the annulment of the constitution, the National Assembly consisted of district, occupational and racial representatives and delegates from various political parties, in accordance with PCC resolution. The Assembly, therefore, was by no means a KMT-dominated Assembly. Moreover, the constitution adopted by the Assembly embodies the very principles laid down by the Communist Party and the other parties represented in the Political Consultative Conference, and in the draft constitution reviewing committee. Therefore, there should not be any reason for the Communists to object to the constitution.

The above stated fact clearly indicated that in order to achieve peace and unity, the government has made the greatest possible concessions to appeal to the reasonable consideration of the Communists. Since political democratization and nationalization of troops were common objectives of the PCC there seems to be no reason why the Communists should cling to their prejudices and suspicions.

Now the war has been over for more than a year, peace and unity must be achieved without delay. It is fervently hoped that the Communists will appreciate the government's earnest efforts to seek a political settlement and agree to resume negotiations. The government is still ready to meet the Communists with tolerance and sincerity.

The government thereby proposes the following four points for the resumption of the peace talks and government reorganization. The four points are:

1. The government is willing to send a representative to Yenan, or to invite Communist delegates to come to Nanking to resume the peace talks, or to call a round-table conference to be attended by representatives of the various parties and independents.

2. The government and the Communists will immediately order their troops to cease hostilities and remain at their present positions and negotiate effective measures to ensure cessation of hostilities.

3. The government is prepared to resume negotiations with the Communists for the enforcement of the army reorganization plan and then restoration of communication agreement in accordance with the principles laid down by the Committee of Three.

4. Before the full operation of the constitution, the government is willing to work out a just and equitable plan for solving the much controverted problem of regional administration.

116(b)

Statement by Lu Ting-yi, Chief of the Department of Information, Central Committee, Chinese Communist Party

893.00/1–2947

[*January 29, 1947.*]

The entire content of the statement by the Kuomintang Ministry of Information is rejection of the two conditions raised by the Chinese Communist Party for restoring peace negotiations—it is rejection of nullification of Chiang Kai-shek's false Constitution and of restoration of military positions of January 13, 1946. Moreover, it raises four points of so-called peace proposal.

These four points have already been transmitted by Chiang Kai-shek to the Chinese Communist Party. It is clear that the so-called peace negotiations are complete fraud and the so-called four points are employed to reject prerequisites for real peace negotiations. Inasmuch as these prerequisites are rejected, what kind of sincerity or peace negotiations remain to be spoken of?

Nullifying Chiang Kai-shek's fake Constitution and restoring the military position of January 13 last year these objectives must and can be attained. If Chiang can utilize every means of fraud and force to transfer 90% of his military strength to attack liberated areas, why then cannot he transfer these armies back to the position of January 13 in pursuance of needs of peace? Already more than 300,000 war prisoners have been captured from Chiang's invading armies by people's liberation armies. From army and division commanders down to rank and file soldiers everyone expresses their unwillingness to fight civil war and everyone yearns to make peace and return to their original positions. Why then must Chiang Kai-shek plunge them into civil war to become cannon fodder? As for so-called "during past year changes in positions of both sides have been extremely great" and therefore restoration of military positions of January 13 last year is impracticable—is this not the clearest deception? Another reason for the statement of the Kuomintang Ministry of Information's rejecting restoration of military positions of January 13 last year is "as soon as the Government withdraws from territories already recovered, people in those areas would have nothing to rely on for their lives and properties" this is utter fabrication. Chiang Kai-shek's armies have occupied over 160 liberated area cities, 179,000 square kilometers of liberated area territory, where dwell over 20,000,000 people of liberated areas—equal to half the population of France. Before invasion and occupation [by] Chiang Kai-shek's troops peasants in these areas had already carried out "land to tillers", democratic governments had already been established, traitors, Japanese, collaborators had already been punished, people of all ranks and classes were living and working in peace and happiness. There were no scourges, no economic crises. After Chiang's troops invaded and occupied these places, the peasant's land was confiscated, Fascist secret police terrorized the populace, traitors, collaborators and local tyrants came back and were made officials by Chiang Kai-shek's Government. Chiang Kai-shek's officials and armies burned, murdered, raped, carried out exorbitant taxation, and conscription of soldiers and grain and corruption pervaded everywhere. Over 20,000,000 people again suffer from the boundless misery of Chiang Kai-shek's dictatorship.

Chiang Kai-shek in truth exhausts his energies in protecting traitors, secret police agents, evil gentry and corrupt officials. Where does he have even one minute in which to protect the lives and properties of people? Precisely for the sake of protecting the lives and properties of people, Chiang Kai-shek's armies should be withdrawn from all of the invaded and occupied territories.

As for the so-called truce at present positions Chiang Kai-shek's "peace proposal", everyone should remember that truce at present positions has taken place three times since the truce order of last January 13. The January truce order was the first time the March 27 cease fire order for Manchuria was the second time and the truce and peace negotiations of last January was the third time. In each case Chinese Communist Party made positive concessions, but the result of these concessions was that Chiang Kai-shek three times in succession broke the agreements. You don't mean to say that the Chinese people are all a bunch of block heads, and after all this must still give Chiang Kai-shek a fourth truce at present positions so that he can break it for the fourth time? So that he can entirely wipe out all liberated areas? Who can guarantee that he will not do this? The present so-called "truce at present positions" of the Kuomintang is truce at "present positions" after Chiang Kai-shek has completely torn up the truce order, PCC resolutions and launched unprecedented large-scale civil war.

This is in order to have the Chinese people recognize the results obtained by his use of military force in faithless betrayal of all agreements and trusts, and thus to encourage warlords to carry out the idle dream of unity through force, and to encourage the reactionaries recklessly to tear up all agreements and wage large-scale civil war. Chiang Kai-shek repeatedly says he believes in "political settlement" but his real activity is "military settlement". If the Chinese people were to agree to this, what hope for peace would there be? If the Chinese Communist Party were to agree to this, what could they say to the people? The Chinese Communist Party for the sake of the people's happiness absolutely cannot recognize the results achieved with military force thus in defiance of law. Therefore, the Chinese Communist Party absolutely cannot agree to so-called "truce in present positions". (which in reality is scheme to wipe *thirteenth* must be completely restored.) The 90% of Chiang Kai-shek's armies which have been illegally transferred must one and all return to their original positions. Otherwise there is absolutely no guarantee of peace.

With regard to the third and fourth points of Chiang Kai-shek's "peace formula"—reorganization of armies, restoration of communications, local governments, et cetera—they have been raised and talked over innumerable times in the past, but either no results were reached or if results were reached they were torn up by Chiang Kai-shek. Before Chiang Kai-shek nullifies the false Constitution and restores positions of January 13, these questions cannot be discussed at all. Hence the first point of Chiang Kai-shek's "peace formula" alleging that the "Government is willing to send a representative to Yenan for talks or even hold a round-table conference, et cetera" is not necessary before the two conditions of the Chinese Communist Party are carried out. Raising of such points by Chiang Kai-shek is but empty stalling to deceive people.

Chiang Kai-shek's fake Constitution must be nullified and can be nullified. This is the third fake Constitution since the country was called the Chinese Republic. Since the two fake Constitutions of Yuan Shih-kai and Tsao Kun were nullified why then cannot Chiang Kai-shek's fake Constitution be nullified since Chiang Kai-shek has treacherously betrayed and violated PCC decisions by unilaterally calling the "National Assembly" and passing the fake Constitution? The people have every reason to order him to nullify his fake Constitution.

The Kuomintang Ministry of Information states that the "Chinese Communist Party has no reason whatsoever to oppose" this Chiang Kai-shek fake Constitution. It can, however, be asked, what reason has Chiang Kai-shek for manufacturing such Constitutions? Did the Chinese people not have reason for nullifying the fake Constitutions of Yuan Shih-kai and Tsao Kun? Since Chiang Kai-shek has manufactured such a fake Constitution, not nullifying it would be tantamount to recognizing Fascist dictatorship, violating of laws and breaking of discipline by warlords; where then can there be talk of political democracy and nationalization of armies? Hence the fake Constitution must be nullified.

The overwhelming bulk of public opinion at home as well as abroad heaped imprecations in concert on the "National Assembly" called by Chiang Kai-shek. The Chinese Communist Party and democrats of all quarters long ago advised Chiang Kai-shek not to convene a one-party illegal National Assembly. But Chiang Kai-shek persisted in ignoring this. When Chiang Kai-shek's National Assembly opened we again advised him to dissolve it but he again refused to listen. Such unbridled lawlessness of Chiang Kai-shek will definitely not be permitted by the Chinese people. The Chinese people and real democrats will absolutely not recognize the validity of such an illegal National Assembly of division.

With regard to representatives of Chiang Kai-shek's "National Assembly" most of them were appointed handpicked and produced through bribed elections. Part of them were provisionally "supplemented" by Chiang Kai-shek and his cronies. Among them are traitors. This National Assembly is worse than the rump assembly of Tsao Kun. Where are the "representatives of all nationalities, all provinces and municipalities and all professions"? When was Chiang Kai-shek's fake Constitution ever finally examined by the Political Consultation Conference? Which of the main question of principles such as people's rights, autonomy of national minorities, relations between legislature and executive, distribution of powers between central and local governments in this fake Constitution accords with PCC principles? Refusal of Chiang Kai-shek to nullify the malodorous Fascist fake Constitution is really a "stubborn clinging to one's opinion," calamity to the entire country, betrayal of the people, betrayal of the nation and determination to be reactionary to the last!

Nullification of the false Constitution and restoration of the military positions of January 13 last year are minimum prerequisites for the restoration of peace negotiations. Reasons these are minimum prerequisites are: Chiang Kai-shek has already completely torn up his four promises, the truce order, the plan for reorganization of armies, the Manchurian cease fire agreement, and the PCC decisions. He has assassinated professors Li Kung-po, Wen I-to and other democratic figures. He has convoked an illegal "National Assembly," concluded the Sino-American commercial treaty of national betrayal, launched large-scale civil war throughout the country, invaded and occupied so much of the liberated areas. After perpetrating all these lawless deeds Chiang Kai-shek still wants to negotiate for peace—of course, this cannot be done without first carrying out a few prerequisites. Otherwise, who can believe he has even a shred of sincerity? If we speak according to law, all bellicose elements of the Kuomintang should be punished as war criminals, all Kuomintang reactionaries and secret police agents who broke PCC decisions should be punished as Fascists, the Kuomintang government officials who signed the Sino-American commercial treaty should be punished as traitors. Furthermore, they should have to compensate to people of liberated areas and of all China for colossal damages suffered from Chiang Kai-shek's launching of civil war. We have not raised all these just and equitable demands, however, but have only demanded nullification of the false Constitution and restoration of the military positions of January 13 last year. What is this if not the most extreme clemency toward Chiang Kai-shek?

To what degree of lawlessness has Chiang Kai-shek reached within the past year? If we do not ask him to carry out our two minimum points, if we "cease fire at present positions," forget all his past crimes and give him time to rest and regroup his troops, consolidate invaded areas, replenish his armies, "reorganize government" to get $500,000,000 or more loans and military aid from the United States Government, then when he has strength to launch a large-scale offensive again, Chiang Kai-shek will certainly be more lawless. What happened last year is a good example.

Therefore, if we still want independence, peace and democracy, we must ask Chiang Kai-shek to nullify his fake Constitution and restore positions of January 13 last year. We will never rest till this goal is attained. All deceptions will be in vain. Now that Chiang Kai-shek has rejected these two points and has brought forward his deceptive "peace proposals" in conflict he will have to bear responsibility for all consequences.

116 (c)

Statement Issued January 29, 1947, by the Ministry of Information, Chinese National Government

893.00/1–3047

It has been more than three months since the government issued a cease-fire order on November 8, 1946. The Communists did not comply with this order, but instead have taken advantage of the opportunity and launched a general offensive on all fronts from the northeast to the eastern section of the Lunghai railway. The Communist offensive has been further intensified recently. For the cause of peace and the interest of the country and the people, the government made one concession after another in the hope that a political solution could be found. It is indeed regrettable that the Communists refused both the government proposal of sending a representative to Yenan for the resumption of negotiations and the four point peace proposal of the government.

Following the adoption, in the National Assembly, of a democratic constitution embodying the principles agreed upon by all parties in the PCC of last January, and having started discussions and preparations for the governmental reorganization plan by inviting all parties and groups to take part in the State Council, the Legislative Yuan, the Executive Yuan and the Control Yuan with a view to broadening the basis of the government, the government on January 24 requested Dr. J. L. Stuart, United States Ambassador to convey to the Communists the following four points:

First, the government is willing to send a representative to Yenan or to invite Communist delegates to come to Nanking to resume the peace talks, or to call a round-table conference to be attended by representatives of the various parties and independents.

Secondly, the government and the Communists will immediately order their troops to cease hostilities and remain at their present positions and negotiate effective measures to insure cessation of hostilities.

Thirdly, the government is prepared to resume negotiations with the Communists for the enforcement of the army reorganization plan and the restoration of communications agreements in accordance with the principles laid down by the Committee of Three.

Fourthly, in the regions where hostilities are now taking place, the government is ready to negotiate with the Communists for a fair and reasonable solution.

Now, the Communists have formally refused all peace negotiations and insisted upon the government's acceptance of their dictates, namely the restoration of the military positions of January 13, 1946 and the abolition of the Constitution. This is equivalent to putting both the National Government and the National Assembly under the yoke of the Communist Party and subjecting them to the orders of the Communists. What would the Chinese Republic be like and what would be left of the rights of the people?

During the one-year period after the PCC and the Committee of Three, the government has spared no effort in inviting the Communist and the minority parties to join the government.

All such endeavors in achieving an understanding with the Communists have been in vain. Since the Communists have taken such an obdurate stand, the only course at present is for the government to carry out its fixed policy of "political democratization".

We hope that all party leaders as well as independents will participate in the government in accordance with their consistent patriotic attitude in order to expedite the preparations and scheduled realization of constitutional rule. We also hope that all parties will cooperate as one man in the gigantic task of national reconstruction, restoration of a balanced economy and improvement of the peoples livelihood.

116 (d)

Statement by Generalissimo Chiang Kai-shek, February 16, 1947

893.00/2–1647

When war ended, our long-tortured country desperately needed relief and rehabilitation, for which peace and unity are prime requisites. The first important postwar problem the Government undertook was to attempt a peaceful settlement with the Communists. With the disinterested mediation of the United States, negotiations were carried on for over a year, now and then glimmering with hopes of success.

However, when the Communists refused to join the National Assembly in November, negotiations came to an end. The people of this country will have decided by now upon whom to lay the blame, and we leave to them and to posterity to render a just verdict. On its part, the Government will confine its military efforts to the protection and restoration of communication systems so necessary for the economic life of the nation, and we shall spare no efforts to continue to seek for a political solution of the Communist problem.

Although settlement with the Communists has failed, at least temporarily, the Kuomintang will go ahead immediately on its historic mission of bringing democracy to the Chinese people. Within a few days we will organize a new State Council charged with the supreme policy making powers of government, and with the task of conducting an election to implement the new Constitution. Membership of the Council will be given to the best men the country could find irrespective of party affiliations. Non-partisans as well as members of all political parties will be given representation.

At the same time, the Executive Yuan and the other Yuans will be immediately reorganized in a similar way, to broaden the basis of government.

Today we are facing not a question of political parties, but the problem of the democratic development, and even the survival of the Chinese nation. I call on all patriots to join with me in working out the salvation of the country and to them I pledge my loyal cooperation.

China is today facing an acute economic crisis. Following the heels of Japanese devastation, internal strife has been raging with the Communist armies even during the period of negotiations. Communist armies have occupied large areas in North China and Manchuria, set up their own separatist Communist administrations, introduced their own currency, and set up economic blockades so that food and produce should not flow into Government-controlled areas. Railways were incessantly attacked and mines and industries were wantonly destroyed because the Communist armies could not hold them. The destructions and dislocation caused by the Communists during the last year exceeded in intensity a similar period of Japanese occupation.

I need only to give a few examples. China is rich in coal deposits and is normally a large exporter, but many of the coal mines and the communications leading to them were systematically destroyed by the Communists so that last year we were even obliged to import some coal from the United States for our industries. Before the war, China was selfsufficient in cotton and tobacco, but this year we have to import over 200 million dollars of foreign cotton and tobacco.

In a word, the economic crisis we are facing today is the cumulative effect of devastation and dislocation of eight years of war and one year of destructive peace.

Our Government last year pursued a liberal foreign exchange policy to enable the country to be supplied with the needs of foreign supplies denied during long years of blockade. However, with the economic situation aggravated by Communist destruction, we have to take new stock of our situation, and meet it realistically and steadfastly by the following emergency measures:

(1) Foreign exchange resources of the Government, including gold, will be conserved for raw material and machinery so that our communications and factories will be kept running, and the basic necessities of our people supplied. We need a new exchange rate bringing our domestic price level attuned to the foreign markets, and which will not be subject to constant fluctuations. After careful consideration, we are fixing the new exchange for both exports and imports at a flat rate of CNC (Chinese National Currency) 12,000 to one US dollar, commencing Monday, February 17. The new rate is much higher than the old rate, but even so it is no higher than the prevailing domestic price level.

(2) The purchase and sale of gold in the market, and circulation of and transaction in foreign currency are prohibited in order to stop speculation. At the same time, the Central Bank will provide sufficient foreign exchange for legitimate purchases.

(3) The Government will relieve the pressure of usurious interests on agricultural and industrial production through loans and other means.

(4) Government expense will be held to the absolute minimum, administration will be streamlined, and all new construction work will be postponed.

(5) The collection of revenues will be conducted with the utmost vigor. Since we have not yet developed a modern accounting system, the collection of income tax and other direct taxes have proved very ineffective. Rough and ready justice will now be applied, and if there are individual cases of suffering, it will have to be remembered by the propertied classes that this Government must be supported at all costs.

(6) In answer to general clamour public services have been kept much below cost, at a tremendous charge on the budget. The Government has decided on an all-out policy to bring about better equilibrium of the budget, and public services, such as the postal system, will have to pay their own way.

(7) During the National Government regime labor wages have been increased manifold, until today they are much higher than the corresponding pay of Government functionaries and the soldiers, and the Government is reserving its foreign exchange resources for the use of industries in which they are employed. We do not intend to take away the just dues of labor, but like all sections of the community, they should demonstrate their patriotic spirit, and there should be a ceiling to wage advances.

(8) All industries owned by the Government except those for national defense and public utilities should be speedily disposed of to private interests. The Government is not in business in competition to private interests.

(9) There will be instituted rigorous control of a few basic commodities such as rice, flour, cloth, food oil and fuel so that prices should not be allowed to run

away. Speculators, hoarders, and profiteers will be punished as severely as the crisis calls for.

(10) Some of the private banks mushroomed during the war have indulged in an orgy of speculation. The Ministry of Finance will inspect their accounts and mete out exemplary punishments.

In spite of the difficulties before us, we have made and are making economic progress. When the Government reoccupied Japanese-controlled areas, there were in running condition only 7,845 kilometers of railways, but today, in spite of Communist attacks, we are operating 11,887 kilometers of railways, an increase by 50 percent. At the end of the war we had only 314,835 tons of shipping, much of which had to be scrapped, today we have a tonnage of 692,071 tons. Last year we produced 960,000 bales of yarn, 8,000 tons of steel, 1,171,155 kilowatts of power, 300,000 tons of cement, and 13 million tons of coal. This year we will produce 2.379 million bales of yarn, 200,000 tons of steel, 1.638 million kilowatts of power, 900,000 tons of cement, and 23 million tons of coal. Compared to industrial nations, our production is still meagre, but it is heartening that we have made this advance during last year in spite of all obstacles.

In agriculture, while we have to import 75 percent of our needs in raw cotton and tobacco in 1947, after this year's crop we will be able to supply 75 percent of cotton and tobacco from our own production. With the 1948 crop we plan to be self-sufficient.

In exports we are rapidly organizing ourselves, and we will presently be able to sell to foreign markets much more yarn and cloth, soya beans, egg products, tea, minerals, essential oils and the varieties that make up Chinese exports. In the recovery of Taiwan with its rich resources of sugar, tea, camphor, and rice, and which in good years under Japanese occupation had a favorable annual balance of trade of over 250 million US dollars, the nation has recovered an asset of the first importance.

There is no reason for us to give way to panic. The basic factors of the agricultural and industrial situation are sound. If we only apply ourselves to our tasks with resolution and energy, we will overcome the immediate difficulties of the Japanese invasion. By so laboring, we are indeed on the way to exercise political freedom and recovery of the free economy that is the distinguishing characteristic of our people. I bespeak the sympathetic understanding of friendly nations as China labors to recover its economy, and equip itself for full participation in world trade and make its contribution to the cause of world peace.

117

Speech by Chou En-lai on January 10, 1947 [1]

893.00/1–1647

This day last year saw the signing of the cease-fire order, and the opening of the political consultative conference. Great were the changes in the situation, and rapid was the growth of the awakening of the people during the past year. Today a year ago, the people throughout the whole country were cheering for peace and cease-fire, but not before long, the nation was again plunged into the abyss of civil strife. All of us have realized that, unless the rule by militarists is put to an end, China can never have peace. The people of the whole nation were celebrating the success of the political consultative conference in January and Febru-

---

[1] Broadcast from Yenan on Jan. 14, 1947.

ary last year; but not before long, the PCC agreements were completely overthrown by the reactionaries in the Kuomintang. All of us have realized that unless the system of individual dictatorship is removed, the democratic PCC line can never be realized. The people of the whole nation were welcoming President Truman's statement on China and General Marshall's mediation efforts in China a year ago, but not before long the true nature of the China policy of the American imperialists was exposed, and the high treason diplomacy of Chiang Kai-shek's regime was also fully unmasked. Since then, from tens of thousands of students to the broad masses of residents in big cities all over China have been shouting these slogans: "US Army quit China," "oppose American intervention in China's internal affairs," "oppose Quisling style diplomacy," "oppose the Sino-American trade treaty," and the like.

In the changes during the past year, not only the KMT reactionaries have started anew the civil war and scrapped the PCC agreements, but also the American witness who affixed his signature on the cease-fire agreement has never again mentioned the January cease-fire order. And the delegates of the Youth Party, the Social Democrats, and a great part of the so-called social leaders who took part in the PCC also participated in the illegal Kuomintang-controlled "National Assembly" which completely destroyed the PCC line, whereby they formulated a dictatorial constitution which runs diametrically counter to the PCC principles, thus deepening the split of the nation. Only the Chinese Communists, genuine democratic parties and groups, genuine civic leaders and the broad masses of the people have never in a moment ceased to uphold the January cease-fire agreement, to fight for the PCC line, and to fight for the realization of the demands that US troops withdraw from China, and the United States stop interfering with China's domestic politics. In looking back over the struggles during the past year, we can't help but think of the martyrs of the April 8 incident who clamored for a cessation of hostilities, and for the implementation of the PCC resolutions, and also of Messrs. Wen, Li and Tao. The spirit with which they fought bitterly against the reactionary bloc which had tried to destroy the cease-fire agreement, and the PCC resolutions has been a constant source of inspiration to us.

Exactly one year after, and on the eve of his departure from China, General Marshall issued a statement summarizing his mediation efforts during the past year. In the light of this statement of his, I will now briefly touch upon a few important points.

General Marshall admitted that there is a reactionary group in the Kuomintang which constitutes a dominant one in the Kuomintang government, and which includes military and political leaders. They oppose a coalition government, have no confidence in internal cooperation, but believe in the settlement of problems by armed force. They have no sincerity in carrying out the PCC resolutions. All these remarks are true. But what is to be regretted is that he did not point out that Chiang Kai-shek is the highest leader of this reactionary group. Chiang Kai-shek said a coalition government is tantamount to overthrowing the government; inter-party conference is a spoils system conference. After the establishment of the executive headquarters in Peiping last year, Chiang Kai-shek and his group opposed the sending of field teams to Manchuria. After the signing of the cease-fire agreement in Manchuria on March 27, Chiang Kai-shek ordered Tu Yu-Ming to launch a big offensive there. That the failure in the truce negotiations in June was caused by Chiang Kai-shek's insistence on the withdrawal of Communist troops from northern Kiangsu, Jehol and two other liberated areas—an act which is a breach of the PCC resolutions. Immediately after that, he conducted a large scale fighting in China proper, and up to now, he continues to act against the PCC agreements in massing 280 brigades (formerly divisions) 90 percent of his total military strength, to attack the communist-held liberated areas. Up to the end of last year, his armies invaded 174,000 square kilometers and took 165 cities in the liberated areas. What are they if these are not armed attacks?

The PCC resolutions were completely violated by members of the one party "National Assembly" and the decision of the constitution was made by Chiang Kai-shek. Therefore, the man who scrapped the cease-fire pact and the PCC resolutions was none other than Chiang Kai-shek himself.

Chiang Kai-shek's reactionary bloc wished by this means to maintain its feudal control. Even General Marshall admits that this further weakens Chiang's government. As to the disruption of economic and communication system, they are attributable to the civil war waged by Chiang Kai-shek. The yearly military expenses constitute 80 percent of the total state expenditures of Chiang's government. Added to these is the exploitation of the people by bureaucratic capital. How can economic ruin be averted?

General Marshall thinks that with the same bad government and still under the leadership of Chiang Kai-shek, but with the participation of a few Kuomintang liberals and minority parties such as the Social Democratic Party and the Youth Party, a good government can ultimately be formed. Will it not be too cheap? Without the participation of the Communists in a coalition government, the dictatorial system instituted by Chiang Kai-shek cannot be abolished, nor can a liberal government be formed.

General Marshall understands full well that the Chiang assembly convened last year is a violation of PCC resolutions and procedures, but he purposely says that the constitution passed by it is a democratic constitution and its main parts are in full agreement with the principles laid down by PCC. Even Communist demands are incorporated in it. This is a big bluff. The main parts of the constitution passed by Chiang's assembly are in direct contravention to the PCC principles. PCC favors the safeguarding the liberties of the people, but Chiang's constitution restricts them. PCC is in support of the granting of the right of self-government to racial minorities, but in Chiang's constitution, such a right is non-existent. PCC wants to make the province the highest unit for regional autonomy, and let it draft its own constitution so that there will be an equal division of power, but Chiang's constitution is pervaded with the idea of centralization of power and the stipulation about the drafting of the provincial constitution is cancelled. PCC desires the cabinet system to be instituted in the coalition government, but Chiang's constitution is all for the President system as contained in the May 5 draft constitution. General Marshall relies on the enforcement of Chiang's constitution and the reorganization of the government for prolonging Chiang's dictatorship, but in this he is mistaken. The consequences will be that Chiang's government will be further discredited and isolated and it will completely fail to gain the support of the people.

That being the case, will the Communists' opposition to Chiang's constitution and the participation in the government under the present circumstances and their demands of a return to the military positions of January 13, the abolition of Chiang's constitution and the convocation of an inter-party conference be considered as a sign of unwillingness to make a fair compromise as the Communists have been so accused by General Marshall? Quite the contrary. These are the most fair compromises and the lowest limit of the Communist demands for peace and democracy. Even General Marshall admitted that during last January and February the Communists were willing to reach a compromise. But, since last

February, the Kuomintang reactionary group has repeatedly violated the PCC resolution and the cease-fire pact. Up to now, the Communists have tried to reach a compromise on the basis of the cease-fire pact signed last January and thru the PCC line. These are really what General Marshall praised as a liberal and forward looking charter.

If we make a comparison, Chiang Kai-shek is violating the cease-fire pact and deviating from the PCC line, whereas the Communists are observing the cease-fire pact and following the PCC line. Is Chiang Kai-chek trying to annihilate the Communists in the liberated areas or are the Communists trying to overthrow the government? Is it fair if Chiang can refuse to accept the two Communist demands while the Communists must accept Chiang's constitution and the positions of the two troops not in accordance with the cease-fire pact?

No Chinese people will believe that the residents of the liberated areas are in the depth of their suffering. This is not an actual fact and is a blasphemy against the Communists. The Communists have worked for the welfare of the people for the last six years and have built up their reputation by their close attachment to the people. If the Communists agree to the occupation of the liberated areas by Chiang's troops and permit Chiang to force the residents to recognize the constitution and to acknowledge his dictatorship, it will be a complete disregard of people's suffering and the interest of the country. Besides, it will not lead to real peace.

There are many naive persons who are too eager to have peace and who are too easily deceived by the apparent peace and do not want to struggle for the minimum safeguards for peace. Chiang Kai-shek has perceived their weaknesses. When it was advantageous for Chiang to launch an attack, he would not hesitate to attack. But when he was defeated and required time to regroup his troops, for instance (he was in such a pass last January and February), he would favor the halting of the war and conducted the so-called peace talks. Let me ask how a fair compromise could be reached. Never. A fair compromise must be built on a basis which is beneficial to the people. That basis is the cease-fire pact signed last January by General Marshall and Chang Chun, Chiang's representative, and the PCC resolutions passed by Chiang Kai-shek. In General Marshall's report, he mentioned the PCC resolutions, but not the cease-fire pact. That was not just a slip of his memory. It was his intention to absolve himself of the responsibility of appending his signature to a pact and try to find a way out for the three man military sub-committee and the Peiping executive headquarters. This further proves that the US Government has been helping Chiang to extend the civil war. It also explains why General Marshall hated very much the propaganda activities carried out by the Communists. Yes, the Communists had since last March repeatedly pointed out the error of the US policy in China, particularly the garrison of the United States forces in this country, their interference in the domestic affairs, and the invasion of the liberated areas. The Anping incident alluded to by General Marshall was one of the thirty-odd incidents.

The Chinese Communists have unremittedly exposed and lodged protests against American aid to Chiang Kai-shek's government troops in the form of transportation, lend-lease materials, surplus property, warships and airplanes, military advisors and technical training, and the colonial policy of the American imperialists (here broadcast was badly garbled). Instead, the Chinese Communists were blamed for their being unable to accept the American mediation, something we must repudiate. General Marshall thought that the above-mentioned kinds of propaganda tend to arouse a bitter hatred of Americans, and are therefore of a vicious nature. The truth is that what aroused people is not abstract propaganda, but living facts. If facts such as those listed above continue to remain, then in the eyes of an independent and freedom loving people they are vicious.

General Marshall has now returned to the United States to take up the post of Secretary of State. I hope that he will, taking the stand of the late President Roosevelt's China policy and for the sake of the traditional friendship between and the interests of the two Chinese and American peoples review again the US China policy during the past year. I hope that the United States will not repeat the past mistakes but stop helping Chiang Kai-shek's government in waging the civil war, evacuate American troops from China, and not intervene again in China internal affairs, but readjust the relations between China and the United States. In so doing, it will be greatly helpful to the efforts of the Chinese people in their striving for peace, democracy, independence and freedom, and will also be beneficial to far faster pace and international cooperation.

We cannot forget this memorable day of the first anniversary of the issuance of the cease-fire order and the meeting of the PCC. We Chinese Communists pledge ourselves to continue to fight, and we believe that democratic people and our fellow countrymen throughout the country will fight for the complete realization of the PCC agreements and the PCC line. We will not cease our efforts until the aims are realized.

118

Memorandum Entitled "Explanation of Several Basic Questions Concerning the Postwar International Situation" by Lu Ting-yi, Chief of the Department of Information of the Chinese Communist Party [2]

893.00/6-2047

It is now the new year—1947. We wish to make an all-sided examination of the whole international situation in order to dispel certain misconceptions in this realm.

During the past year and more and right up to the present time, owing to the complicated changes in the situation and to demagogic propaganda intentionally spread about widely by the Chinese and foreign reactionaries, there are still some people in the camp of democracy in China whose understanding of several basic questions concerning the postwar political situation is not in accord, or not wholly in accord, with the real state of affairs. These people include some Communists, some left-wing critics, some middle of the road critics. The purpose of this article is to offer a general explanation of these several basic questions.

I. Mao Tze-tung's Prediction

16 months have elapsed since the victory in the anti-Fascist war. These 16 months have been a period of extremely complicated changes in the international political situation. The course of changing affairs has taken many twists and turns—one sort of conditions prevailed at the London Foreign Ministers' Conference in September a year before last, there was a change at the time of the Moscow Foreign Ministers' conference in December of the same year, in February and March of last year another change took place, and from September of last year yet another change occurred. After the many changes of the past

---

[2] Printed in Yenan *Emancipation Daily*, Jan. 4 and 5, 1947.

16 months we have ample surety in saying: The development of the international situation is entirely in accord with the prediction of Comrade Mao Tze-tung.

In "On Coalition Government," a political report of Comrade Mao Tze-tung to the 7th National Convention of the Chinese Communist Party, in April, 1945, he made the following prediction of a new world situation following the World War II:

"This new situation differs greatly from that of the first world war and the so-called 'peaceful' period which followed. At that time there was not a Soviet Union like the present one, nor was there such a degree of consciousness as now expressed by the people of Great Britain, America, China, France, and other anti-Fascist Allies, and naturally there could not be such a present world unity headed by three great powers or five great powers. Now we are living in an entirely new situation. There now exist in the world peoples and their organized forces who have been awakened and united, and are in the course of becoming more so. This determines the objective to which the wheels of world history are moving, and the path which should be followed to attain it.

"The defeat of the Fascist aggressor countries and the emergence of a general peace situation do not mean that there will be no more struggle. The widely spread remnant forces of Fascism will certainly continue to make trouble. The anti-democratic forces remaining in the camp of the anti-Fascist war against aggression will continue to oppress the people. Therefore after the realization of international peace, the struggle between the anti-Fascist masses of the people and the remnant forces of the Fascists, and between democracy and anti-democracy will continue to occupy a major part of the world. A most widespread people's victory can only be the outcome of a long period of energetic forces to overcome the remnant Fascist forces and the anti-democratic forces. To attain this is certainly not very quick or very easy, but it will nevertheless certainly come. The victory of the anti-Fascist war—the just World War II— has opened the road to victory for the people's struggle in the post-war period, and it is only after such a victory that a stable and lasting peace can be guaranteed. This is the bright future lying before the people of the world."

I hope all readers will carefully read these words of Comrade Mao Tze-tung several times. This will be helpful to comprehension of basic questions concerning the present international situation.

II. Two Basic Points

These words of Comrade Mao Tze-tung bring out two basic points:

1. The victory in the anti-Fascist war has opened way to progress for democratic forces in all nations. The extent of progress of these democratic forces will be incomparably greater than after the first world war. The attack by the anti-democratic forces on peoples of all nations must of necessity come. But the democratic forces will in necessity of things be able to overcome the anti-democratic forces, secure their own victory and win a firm and lasting international peace. There are the two necessities here: (1) that the anti-democratic forces will of necessity attack and (2) that the democratic forces will of necessity be victorious.

Thus, all erroneous pessimistic contentions are swept clean away. These pessimistic contentions are: alleging that the extent of the progress of the democratic forces after World War II is smaller than that after World War I; allegations about "super colossal" reactionary strength of the American imperialism and Chiang Kai-shek and about how they will oppress the people of China and the whole world till they will be unable to draw a breath; alleging that the World War III is inevitable or will soon arrive; that a firm and lasting peace cannot be attained, etc. All these points of view are obviously erroneous. The reason for committing those errors have been misled by the temporary and outside appearance of might of international and internal reactionary forces or been blinded by reactionary propaganda thereby underestimating the strength of the people.

2. The struggle between the forces of democracy and anti-democracy will cover a greater part of the world. That is to say, in the world there is a socialist Soviet Union in which there has long been no anti-democratic forces and therefore there is no internal struggle between democracy and anti-democracy. Other places in the world besides the Soviet Union—that is the whole of the capitalist world—is filled with struggle between democracy and anti-democracy. Thus, following the World War II, the actual dominant political contradiction in the world between democratic and anti-democratic forces is within the capitalist world and not between the capitalist world and the Soviet Union and also not between the Soviet Union and the United States. Speaking more concretely, the present dominant contradictions in the world are contradictions between the American people and the American reactionaries, the Anglo-American contradictions and the Sino-American contradictions.

Thus, the propaganda of the reactionaries in China and abroad is thoroughly confuted so that all good hearted people will not be misled by such propaganda. Such demagogic propaganda is: that actual dominant political contradiction in the present world is between capitalist and socialist countries, that the Soviet-American contradictions are dominant and the Anglo-American and Sino-American contradictions are secondary; the socialist and capitalist countries cannot peacefully cooperate, the Soviet-American war is inevitable, etc.

We will elucidate below: 1. Who are anti-democratic forces? What is their present and will be their future? 2. Who are democratic forces? What is their present and will be their future?

III. WORLD REACTIONARIES, THEIR SMOKESCREEN AND THEIR REAL ACTIVITIES

After the World War II, the American imperialists took place of the Fascist Germany, Italy and Japan becoming a fortress of the world reactionary forces. So-called reactionary forces are precisely the American imperialists with addition of reactionaries in various countries (China's Chiang Kai-shek, Great Britain's Churchill, France's DeGaulle, etc.) and other Fascist remnants (Spain's Franco Government, Japan's Yoshida cabinet, Germany's von Papen and Schacht, etc.). The reactionaries of all countries and the Fascist remnants have now all become traitors directly or indirectly supported and protected by the American imperialists selling out the people of all countries.

The American wartime industrial production has more than doubled in comparison with prewar figures. During the war, American monopoly capital underwent tremendous development. At the same time, a batch of warlords arose in America. After the conclusion of the war, this batch of monopoly capitalists and militarists, this bloc of extremely small handful of fanatical aggressors, advocated a policy of imperialist aggression to expand markets, wrest away markets, colonies and semi-colonies of other capitalist countries, primarily oppressing the great colonial imperialist countries England and France and oppressing China while at the same time exercising a sole domination over Japan and Latin-America. The American imperialists are carrying out this aggression under slogans of "open door policy and equal opportunity" etc. to be in an overwhelming position to drive others away and monopolize the market. In addition to all this, the American imperialists are undertaking large-scale military preparations against all capitalist countries, colonies, and semi-colonial countries, under all sorts of pretext. Their military bases are spread over many countries, outside the Soviet Union. The American imperialists have through "peaceful" means occupied many "Pearl Harbors" in various countries, saying on the other hand that this is to "prevent another Pearl Harbor."

In February and March of 1946, the world reactionaries schemed to incite a war against the Soviet Union. This was characterized by the reactionary speech of Churchill. This speech has aroused a great vigilance of the people as it should. But Churchill's agitation has met with the opposition of the people of the whole world. The attempt of the reactionaries has suffered a bitter defeat.

The "anti-Soviet war" propaganda launched by Churchill was regarded as a treasure and inherited by the American imperialists. Why the American imperialists love this kind of propaganda? Their purpose is not to launch an anti-Soviet war at present, but to use it as a smokescreen in order to carry out their large-scale aggressive actions abroad and oppression of the American people at home.

What is the meaning of the "anti-Sovietism"? Hitler's "anti-Sovietism" meant enslaving of the German people and invading whole Europe. The Fascist Japan's "anti-Sovietism" meant oppressing the Japanese people and aggressing countries on both sides of the Pacific. The American reactionaries' "anti-Sovietism" at present only means enslaving the American people and world domination.

But the anti-Soviet slogan of the American reactionaries at present differs from that of the former Fascists Germany and Japan. Germany is close to Soviet Union. In addition to other conditions, Fascist Germany was able to attack the latter. Japan is also near the Soviet Union. Owing to the fact that its strength was weaker than Fascist Germany, Fascist Japan could only attack China and the Pacific and was defeated before it had time to invade the Soviet Union. The United States is far away from the Soviet Union with a large area lying between. In this neutral area, there are capitalist countries, colonial and semi-colonial countries of three continents, Europe, Asia, and Africa. In addition to other conditions, it is very difficult for the United States to attack the Soviet Union: therefore the actual meaning of the "anti-Soviet" slogan of America at the post-war period is only to oppress the American people and invade through "peaceful" means all countries besides the Soviet Union.

Certainly there is a contradiction between the American monopoly capital and warlords on the one side and the Socialist Soviet Union on the other. It is a contradiction between the new and old world, is one of the world basic contradictions. The social and political system of the Soviet Union is much stronger than the American capitalism. The Soviet Union is the defender of world peace. Ambition and graft of the American and world reactionaries are impossible to be realized as long as the Soviet Union exists, therefore the American and world reactionaries hate the Soviet Union, and they certainly will persist in an anti-Soviet struggle. But anti-Soviet propaganda is one thing and anti-Soviet war is another. We cannot say that the American imperialists do not want to attack the Soviet Union; but the American imperialists cannot attack the Soviet Union before they have succeeded in suppressing and putting under their control the American people and all capitalist, colonial and semi-colonial countries. To oppress and put under their control these countries is impossible. Therefore, the contradiction between the United States and Soviet Union, though it is one of the basic contradictions, is not an imminent one, not a dominant one in the present political situation. This has been proved by the development of events during the past 16 months. The actual policy of the American imperialists is to attack through "peaceful" means the American people and oppress all capitalist, colonial and semi-colonial countries. However, the American imperialists will keep under cover these activities that they are actually doing. The American imperialists have no way to attack the Soviet Union, yet they are talking loudly about the anti-Soviet war, obviously the slogan is only a smokescreen.

Why do the American imperialists use this smokescreen? Why should we expose this smokescreen? The purpose of the American imperialists in smokescreening is to divert the attention of the American people, the broad masses of all capitalist countries besides America and all colonial and semi-colonial countries so that they will be off guard against attacks of the American imperialists. With the unpreparedness of the American people and the other countries, the American imperialists can more easily fascistize their own country and turn other countries into American colonies and dependencies. If we fail to expose this smokescreen of the American imperialism or we fail to pay due attention to this important work, we will more or less be lured into the trap of the American imperialists or be a mouthpiece speaking for the American imperialists, the common enemy. Therefore, we should not be fooled by the smokescreen of the reactionaries and lose our own judgment, bewildered by such demagogic propaganda as: "The dominant contradiction in the present world is between capitalist and socialist countries", "the World War III is inevitable", etc. The only road to follow and the only duty for each and every one in the democratic camp to fulfill is to expose the reactionaries' smokescreen and to call the people in America, in all capitalist, colonial and semi-colonial countries to fight for their own existence and to resist the attacks and aggressions of the American imperialists, their real enemies.

IV. WORLD DEMOCRATIC STRENGTH

Standing against the world reactionaries—the imperialists of America and their running dogs in various countries—is the world democratic might.

Besides the Soviet Union, which is the main pillar, the world democratic forces are made up of three sections: the broad masses of the American people, the broad masses of the people of all capitalist countries besides America, and the broad masses of the people of all colonial and semi-colonial countries. In terms of class make-up, they include everyone from workers and farmers right up to patriotic elements and advocates of peace among the bourgeoisie.

The American people made heroic contributions during the anti-Fascist war. The object of their self-sacrificing struggle is the winning of world peace and democracy and happy life for themselves. After the conclusion of the war, however, the American people were faced with the following situation: After the defeat of foreign reactionaries loomed domestic reactionaries. They were precisely those monopoly capitalists who fattened on speculation and ill-gotten riches during the war. In the field of domestic policy this batch of monopoly capitalists and their reactionary spokesmen in the government raise prices of goods to press down living standards of the people, crack down on strikes in order to cancel people's liberties, encourage anti-Sovietism to divert attention of the American people so that they will be off guard against attacks of the monopoly capitalists. In the field of foreign policy, the American reactionaries do not call themselves "isolationists", but rather "internationalists". But these "internationalists", however, are international aggressionists and not democratic international cooperationists. These reactionary elements have their men in both American Democratic and Republican parties. The world aggression of these reactionaries has seriously spoiled the reputation of America, ruined the international friendship and is brewing a danger of war.

This is why the American people, including enlightened members of American bourgeoisie represented by Wallace, will certainly rise for a determined struggle with reactionaries.

Capitalist countries outside of America, principally England and France, suffered great wounds from war and compared to America they are second or third class countries. They are objects of the aggression by the American imperialism. The law of uneven development of capitalism forces them resolutely to resist the American oppression.

These capitalist countries are now struggling for economic recovery from wounds of war and are at the same time in the following situation: On the one hand is the democratic movement of the people of their own country, and the demand for independence and autonomy on the part of colonies and semi-colonial countries and on the other is a savage aggression of the American imperialism. The line being taken by the reactionaries like Churchill and de Gaulle within these countries is to rely on America to oppose the democratic movement of the people of their own country and the independence movement of the peoples of colonies and semi-colonies. The price paid for this reactionary line is that it inevitably leads these countries sinking to the position of American dependencies. The people in these capitalist countries have another line: winning the democratic and social reform for their own country and granting colonial and semi-colonial people's independence and autonomy and cooperation with the Soviet-Union, in order to resist the aggression of the American imperialism and maintain the national independence. Beyond all shadow of doubt, the people's line will be victorious. This line will obtain the endorsement of all classes of people including enlightened members of the bourgeoisie. On the other hand, the line of reactionaries must certainly fail, because it will meet with the opposition of the whole nation.

Take the most important among those capitalist countries—Great Britain for instance. In the post-war period, she is exerting her efforts to effect economic recovery. Her exports are gradually rising and this is something about which the American imperialist elements are not happy. The American imperialism schemes to break the sterling bloc by exploiting the need of England for loans and in the name of so-called "defense against Soviet Union's attacks" wants England to enter into a military alliance with her. These are all serious preparatory steps for swallowing up England. England's far-flung dependencies and colonies—Canada, South [Africa], Australia, Atlantic Islands, Middle-east, Palestine and Arabia, Egypt and Mediterranean and finally India, Burma and elsewhere—are all scenes of American imperialistic attacks on England under the American imperialist policy of the world domination. In certain places, these clashes have already become or are brewing up armed struggles. In the future, the possibility exists of America's inciting aggressive wars against other capitalist countries (first of all Great Britain).

The Attlee-Bevin Cabinet which continues the Conservative Party's foreign policy in Great Britain has done many evil deeds in concert with the American imperialism and on many questions has expressed a mutual sympathy and understanding or a common action with the American imperialism. The policy of American imperialism, however, cannot but force the English people gradually into consciousness. The gradual increase of votes in the British Lower House against Bevin's foreign policy is a proof of this. In circumstances of daily growing consciousness of the British people, it will be very difficult for Great Britain to continue her present foreign policy and the time for her to change her foreign policy is already not distant.

Thus it is with England and it will be even more so with France. In circumstances of daily growing consciousness of the French people, France certainly will not follow the road of American imperialists.

The American imperialistic policy of aggression on all capitalist countries must of necessity arouse the opposition of these countries. After the second World War, there are no grounds therefore for the so-called "capitalist encirclements of the Soviet Union". Just the contrary, because of the peaceful democratic international policies and policies of peaceful competition and the friendly commerce with all countries on the part of the Soviet Union and because England, France and other countries must resist the American aggression, escape blows of the economic crisis and furthermore restore their economies, these countries must cooperate and trade with the Soviet Union. So-called capitalist encirclement therefore does not exist.

The American policy with regard to all colonial and semi-colonial nations is to transform them into American colonies or dependencies. The American imperialistic policy towards China is a typical example. There is no difference in nature between the policy of American imperialism towards China and the policy of Japanese Fascists toward China, although there are differences in form. The venomous treachery of means employed by the American imperialism however surpasses that of the Japanese imperialism. After the defeat of the Japanese imperialism, America supports Chiang Kai-shek and other reactionaries in oppressing the Chinese people. In Japan, it supports Yoshida and other reactionaries in oppressing the Japanese people, and helps them to revive the policy of aggression towards China. At the present time the reactionaries of both China and Japan are occupying the same position as running dogs of America, and the peoples of both China and Japan are in the same position bearing oppression of the American imperialism. The self-defense war now being waged by the Chinese people against Chiang Kai-shek and the American imperialists is, in its nature, a war for the motherland. It is an all national war obtaining the full support of the entire nation. This kind of war for the motherland has been taking place in Indo-China, India, Iran, Greece etc. These wars are fought against the American imperialism and its running dogs in various countries. They are directly or indirectly against the American imperialism and for winning a world peace and democracy.

The contradiction between the American imperialism and the democratic forces in the capitalist world is not being slackened, but instead is growing and developing.

When the American economic crisis arrives, the American imperialists, because of this, tighten up their attacks, these contradictions will become sharp. Such a period is not far off because the American economic crisis will arrive this year or next.

V. UNITED FRONT ON WORLD SCALE

The world anti-democratic forces are the American imperialists and reactionaries in various countries. Since the world antidemocratic forces are in unison attacking the American people, the peoples of various capitalist countries, colonies and semi-colonial countries, the peoples of America, various capitalist countries, colonies and semi-colonial countries must also act in unison to form a world-wide united front against the American imperialism and reactionaries in all countries. This world-wide united front, this colossal army comprising well over one billion people is precisely the world democratic might.

This world-wide united front cannot possibly be of any other character than that of a united front hunting for world peace and democracy and independence of all nations against the American imperialism and its running dogs in various countries. This united front will undoubtedly have the sympathy and moral support of the socialist Soviet Union.

This united front on a world scale will characterize a new page in world history: that is the history of world from the end of second world war down to today when the stable and lasting peace of the world is ensured. The Chinese movement for independence, peace and democracy is an important part of this chapter of world history.

Within each capitalist country, colony and semi-colonial country, there will be an extremely broad united front as in China against the American imperialists and the reactionaries within each country.

The immediate cardinal task before the peoples and democratic forces of all countries is a struggle for the realization of this world-wide united front and an united front within each country.

VI. Relative Strength of Forces

Facts in more than one year following the victory in the anti-Fascist war prove that the rate of the world progress is very fast, and some events have developed faster than we had expected. The scope of development of democratic forces in all countries of the world is far greater than that after the world war one.

The progress of people in the capitalist world during the past year and more is manifested in: 1, firm establishment of new democratic regimes in various countries of the eastern and southern Europe; 2, progress by leaps and bounds of the peoples of England and France; 3, the flourishing development of the struggles of the peoples of colonies and semi-colonial countries with China at their head for independence and autonomy; 4, the rapid leftward trend of the peoples of Germany, Italy and Japan; 5, the high tide of American strike movement and the occurrence of Wallace incident (the Wallace incident expresses a split among the American bourgeoisie, just as the British Labour Party's opposition in England expressed a split among the British bourgeoisie); 6, a broad development of democratic forces in all countries of South America.

The scope and speed of the progress of people and the development of democratic forces in the capitalist world is really startling.

The international position of the most progressive country in the world—the socialist Soviet Union—has risen greatly. At present she is devoting all her strength to the peaceful constructive work of a new Five Year Plan. The completion of her first year's industrial production plan one month ahead of its schedule shows that it is entirely possible to complete and overfulfill this new plan for construction. Struggle of the Soviet Union in the realm of small nations achieved great victories in the recent foreign ministers conferences and the United Nations Assembly. A plot of American and British reactionaries to isolate the Soviet Union following Churchill's reactionary utterances of March last year has been smashed. Victories of the Soviet Union in economic construction and in foreign policy will greatly influence the history of world development, and will be beneficial to peoples of all countries.

The world reactionary forces are outwardly strong, but hollow inside. Moreover, they are becoming daily more isolated. The American imperialism reaches the highest peak of the capitalist development, but precisely because of this, it is weaker than the capitalism in any earlier period. The higher they climb, the harder they fall—the American economic crisis which will arrive this year or next cannot but be turbulent in its nature. The reactionary foreign and domestic policies of the American imperialists will necessarily lead, and have led, to the opposition of broadest masses of people both within and without the country. This will daily result in the masses turning against them and their allies deserting them. All running dogs of the American imperialists in various countries, as for example, China's Chiang Kai-shek, cannot but become traitors, and in their countries meet with the opposition of the entire nation. Therefore they cannot but rapidly isolate themselves, turned against by the masses and deserted by their allies. It is thus with China's Chiang Kai-shek and with reactionaries of all countries. The reactionary forces will collapse in the long run. They really appear very ferocious for a time, and can even frighten the feeble-minded people out of their will, so that they express pessimism and disappointment, lose their self-confidence, and even give in and surrender to reactionaries. But the broad masses of people and all men of strong will cannot be frightened away. The people in the course of their own practical experience will recognize not only the reactionary nature of the reactionaries, but also their feebleness. They will recognize that attacks of the reactionaries on the people can be smashed.

To sum up: the world progress, successes of the Soviet Union, and the American crisis are three factors of decisive significance in the history of future development of the world.

VII. Road to Victory

The present time is still a period when the world reaction can be cocky, baring its fangs and extending its talons. This is primarily because struggles of the peoples in the various countries have not entered a higher stage and at the same time this is also because the American economic crisis has not yet arrived. But even in this kind of period, the reactionary forces have already revealed that they are hollow within and outwardly strong. When struggles of the peoples of all countries reach a higher development and the American economic crisis has broken out, that will be the time when the grand arrogance of the reactionaries will collapse. This is already not far distant. Before the arrival of this time, the people of each country will meet with difficulties, and in individual countries and regions, may even meet with very serious difficulties. Difficulties of this kind, however, can and must be conquered. The present task is for every one to exert all efforts and to overcome these difficulties.

Following the development of three factors—world progress, Soviet successes and American crises—the democratic forces will become even stronger and the relative strength of the democratic and anti-democratic forces will become more beneficial to the people. But it is not to be imagined that the reactionary forces will voluntarily abdicate to the democratic forces. Therefore before we have attained what comrade Mao Tze-tung calls "broadest victory of the people" and the "ensurance of stable and enduring peace", there is still a long and tortuous struggle ahead. The Chinese Communists and the Chinese people will fear no difficulties. They will fight on till the complete victory of the democratic cause and winning of the peace and independence of their nation. We have the strongest confidence in this brilliant future, but the world bourgeoisie on the other hand have completely lost confidence in their future. The terrorism whipped up by the anti-democratic forces in various countries after the war against the forces of people, their terror at the strength of the Soviet Union, their fanatical oppression of the peoples, their horror of the truth, their complete reliance on lies for a living—these all are manifestations of their complete loss of confidence. It is certainly not accidental that all newspapers of the Chinese bourgeoisie express an unprecedental pessimism and disappointment with regard to their future.

In general, everything has changed after the second world war, and is still continuing to change. How strong the people have become—how conscious, how organized, determined, and full of confidence! How maniacally savage the reactionaries have become—outwardly strong yet inwardly feeble, turned against by masses and deserted by their allies, devoid of all confidence in their future! It may be forecast categorically that the face of China and the world will be vastly different after three to five more years. All comrades of our party and all people of China must resolutely fight for a new China and a new world.

119

Statement of the Central Committee of the Chinese Communist Party, February 1, 1947

893.00/2-747

The Political Consultative Conference, comprising all major political parties, groups and prominent social figures, convened on January 10, 1946 in accordance with stipulations of the summary of Kuomintang-Communist talks in Chungking on October 10, 1945, is universally recognized by the people of the entire country and world powers as the highest political body in China. Until China has a really democratic national parliament, all important internal and diplomatic affairs which would be passed by a parliament in democratic countries should pass through this Conference or obtain agreement of major political parties and groups before they can be regarded as effective.

Since January 10, 1946, however, Chinese Kuomintang government has not only enacted many arbitrary domestic measures but has also many times singly conducted diplomatic negotiations of a serious nature with certain foreign governments. In the course of understandings both oral and written, secret and open, without these agreements and understandings having been passed by the Political Consultative Conference or consulting opinion of this party and other parties and groups participating in Political Consultative Conference. These diplomatic negotiations include loans from foreign governments, continuation of Lend-Lease, buying and accepting of munitions and surplus war materials, forming of treaties regarding special rights in commerce, navigation, aviation and other economic and legal special rights.

These negotiations and agreements request or permit foreign land, sea and naval forces to be stationed in or operate on the seas, waterways, territories, and in the air of the country, and to enter or occupy and jointly construct or make use of military bases and points strategic to the national defense. They furthermore request or permit foreign military and other personnel to participate in organization, training, transportation and military operations of land, air and naval forces of the country, and to become conversant with military and other state secrets of the country. They also permit such serious matters as foreign intervention in internal affairs.

Those measures of the Chinese Kuomintang government are completely contrary to the will of the Chinese people and they have plunged and will continue to plunge China into civil war, reaction, national disgrace, loss of national rights, colonization and crises of chaos and collapse. In order to rescue the motherland from this calamity, to protect national rights and interests and the dignity of the Political Consultative Conference, the Chinese Communist Party solemnly states: This party will not either now nor in the future recognize any foreign loans, any treaties which disgrace the country and strip away its rights, and any of the above-mentioned agreements and understandings established by the Kuomintang government after January 10, 1946, nor will it recognize any future diplomatic negotiation of the same character which have not been passed by Political Consultative Conference or which have not obtained agreement of this party and other parties and groups participating in the Political Consultative Conference. This party furthermore will absolutely not bear any obligations for the above-mentioned.

120

Article by Mao Tse-tung, Chairman, Commemorating the 28th Anniversary of the Chinese Communist Party [3]

July 1, 1949, means that the Communist Party of China has passed through 28 years. Like a man, it has its childhood, youth, manhood, and old age. The Communist Party of China is no longer a child or a youth in its teens, but is an adult. When a man reaches old age, he dies. It is the same with the party. When classes are eliminated, all the instruments of class struggle, political parties, and the state apparatus, will, as a result, lose their functions, become unnecessary and gradually wither away, end their historical mission, and travel toward the higher plane of the society of mankind.

We are quite different from the political party of the bourgeoisie. They are afraid to talk of abolishing classes, state authority, and the party. But we, however, openly declare that we struggle hard precisely for the creation of conditions to accelerate the elimination of these things. The Communist Party and the state authority of the people's dictatorship constitute such conditions. Anyone who does not recognize this truth is no Communist.

Young comrades who have just joined the party and have not read Marxism-Leninism may not understand this truth. They must understand this truth before they can have a correct world outlook. They must understand that all mankind has to travel along the road of eliminating classes, state authority, and party. The question is only one of time and conditions.

PREPARATION FOR WORLD COMMUNISM

The Communists in the world are more intelligent than the bourgeoisie. They understand the law of the existence and development of things. They understand dialectics and see farther ahead. The bourgeoisie do not welcome this

---

[3] Broadcast by the New China News Agency on June 30, 1949; reprinted from Central Intelligence Agency, Foreign Broadcast Information Branch, *Daily Report of Foreign Radio Broadcasts*, Far East section, July 1, 5, 1949.

truth, because they do not want to be overthrown by the people. To be overthrown—like the Kuomintang reactionaries being overthrown by us at present and like Japanese imperialism having been overthrown by us and peoples of various countries in the past—is painful and is inconceivable to the overthrown.

For the working class, laboring people, and Communists, the question is not one of being overthrown but of working hard and creating conditions for the natural elimination of classes, state authority and the political party, so that mankind will enter the realm of world Communism. We have here touched on the perspective of the progress of mankind to explain the following questions.

Our party has passed through 28 years. Everybody knows that they were passed not peacefully but under difficult surroundings. We had to fight against enemies within the country and abroad and within and outside the party. Thanks to Marx, Engels, Lenin, and Stalin who gave us weapons. These weapons are not machine guns but Marxism-Leninism.

Lenin in his book " 'Left-wing' Communism—An Infantile Disorder," written in 1920, described how the Russians sought for a revolutionary theory. After several decades of hardships and tribulations, they eventually discovered Marxism. Many things were the same or similar in China and Russian before the October revolution. The feudal oppression was the same. The economic and cultural backwardness was similar. Both countries were backward, and China is even more backward. Progressive people struggled hard to seek for revolutionary truth to bring about national recovery. This was the same.

WESTERN TEACHINGS SOUGHT

Since China lost the Opium War in 1840, the advanced Chinese underwent countless tribulations seeking for the truth from the Western countries. Hung Hsu-chuan, Kang Yu-wei, Yen Fu, and Sun Yat-sen represented this group of people who sought for truth from the West before the birth of the Communist Party of China.

At that time, the Chinese who sought for progress read all the books that contained new Western teachings. The students sent to Japan, England, America, France, and Germany reached a surprising number. Efforts were made to learn from the West. The old examination system of officialdom was abolished and schools multiplied.

What I learned in my youth were also such things. They were the culture of Western bourgeois democracy, or the so-called new school of learning which included the sociological doctrines and natural sciences of that time and which were antagonistic to the culture of China's feudalism, or the so-called old school of learning. For quite a long time, people who learned the new knowledge were confident believing that it was sure to save China. Apart from people of the old school, very few of the new school expressed doubt. To save the country, the only way is to enforce reforms, and to enforce reforms, the only way is to learn from foreign countries. Of the foreign countries at that time, only the Western capitalist countries were progressive. They had successfully established the modern bourgeois state.

The Chinese also wanted to learn from the Japanese. To the Chinese of that time, Russia was backward and very few people wanted to learn from her. This was how the Chinese learned from foreign countries during the period from the 40's of the Nineteenth Century.

Imperialist aggression shattered the dream of the Chinese to learn from the West. Really strange, why do teachers always invade students? The Chinese learned much from the West, but what they learned could not be put into effect.

Their ideal could never be realized. The conditions of the country worsened day by day, the environment was such that the people could not live. Doubt sprang up, grew, and developed.

The First World War shook the whole world. The Russians carried out the October Revolution, creating the first socialist country in the world. Under the leadership of Lenin and Stalin, the revolutionary energy of the great Russian proletariat and laboring people, which had lain hidden and could not be seen by foreigners, suddenly erupted like a volcano. The Chinese and all mankind then looked differently at Russians. Then, and only then, the Chinese from the fields of ideology to life entered an entirely new era. The Chinese found the universal truth of Marxism-Leninism which holds good everywhere, and the face of China was changed.

Possibility for World Communism Created

The patterns of the Western bourgeoisie, the bourgeois democracy, and the pattern of the bourgeois republic all went bankrupt in the minds of the Chinese people. The bourgeois democracy gave way to the people's democracy under the leadership of the proletariat, and the bourgeois republic gave way to the people's republic. A possibility has thus been created to reach socialism and Communism through the people's republic, and to attain the elimination of classes and attain world Communism.

Kang Yu-wei wrote a book about world Communism, but he did and could not find the road to it. The bourgeois republic existed in foreign countries but could not exist in China, because China is a country oppressed by imperialism. The only road to the elimination of classes and to world Communism is through the people's republic under the leadership of the working class.

All other things had been tried and had failed. Of those who yearned for something else, some had fallen, some had awakened to their mistake, and some are changing their minds. Events developed so swiftly that many people felt surprised and the need to learn anew. This state of mind of these people is understandable and we welcome such good intentions to learn anew.

The vanguards of the Chinese proletariat learned Marxism-Leninism after the October Revolution and established the Communist Party of China. Following this, it entered into political struggle and traveled a zigzag path for 28 years, before gaining a basic victory.

From the experiences of 28 years, just as from the "experiences of the 40 years" in the will of Sun Yat-sen, a common conclusion has been reached, namely: "The firm belief that to attain victory we must awaken the masses of the people and unite ourselves in a common struggle with those peoples of the world who treat us on the basis of equality."

Sun Yat-sen has a different world outlook from us, and started out from a different . . . standpoint to observe and deal with problems, but on the problem of how to struggle against imperialism in the 20's of the Twentieth Century, he arrived at a conclusion which was in basic agreement with ours.

"Travel the Road of the Russians"

The Chinese found Marxism through the introduction of the Russians. Before the October Revolution, the Chinese not only did not know Lenin and Stalin, but also did not know Marx and Engels. The gunfire of the October Revolution sent us Marxism-Leninism. The October Revolution helped the progressive elements of the world and China to use the world outlook of the proletariat as the instrument for observing the destiny of the country and reconsidering their own problems. Travel the road of the Russians—this was the conclusion.

In 1919 the "May 4" movement occurred in China, and the Communist Party of China was formed in 1921. During his period, Sun Yat-sen came across the October Revolution and the Communist Party of China. He welcomed the October Revolution, welcomed Russian help to Chinese, and welcomed the Communist Party of China to cooperate with him.

Sun Yat-sen died, and Chiang Kai-shek came into power. During the long period of 22 years, Chiang Kai-shek dragged China into hopeless straits. At this period, the antifascist Second World War, with the Soviet Union as its main force, defeated three big imperialist powers, weakened two other big imperialist powers, and only one imperialist country in the world, the United States of America, suffered no loss. However, the domestic crisis of America was very grave. She wanted to enslave the entire world, and she aided Chiang Kai-shek with arms to slaughter several millions of Chinese. Under the leadership of the Communist Party of China, the Chinese people, after having driven away Japanese imperialism, fought the people's war of liberation for 3 years and gained a basic victory.

Two Basic Experiences Gained

Twenty-four years have elapsed since Sun Yat-sen's death, and under the leadership of the Communist Party of China, Chinese revolutionary theory and practice have made big strides forward, fundamentally changing the features of China. Up to the present, the Chinese people have gained the following two basic experiences:

1. To awaken the masses in the country. This is to unite the working class, the peasant class, the petty bourgeoisie, and the national bourgeoisie into a united front under the leadership of the working class and develop into a state of the people's democratic dictatorship, led by the working class, with the alliance of workers and peasants as its basis.

2. To unite in a common struggle with those nations of the world who treat us on the basis of equality and the peoples of all countries. This is to ally with the Soviet Union, to ally with the new democratic countries of Europe, and to ally with the proletariat and masses of the people in other countries to form an international united front.

"You lean to one side." Precisely so. The 40 years' experience of Sun Yat-sen and the 28 years' experience of the Communist Party have made us firmly believe that in order to win victory and to consolidate victory, we must lean to one side. The experiences of 40 years and 28 years show that, without exception, the Chinese people either lean to the side of imperialism or to the side of socialism.

No Third Road Exists

To sit on the fence is impossible. A third road does not exist. We oppose the Chiang Kai-shek reactionary clique who lean to the side of imperialism. We also oppose the illusion of a third road. Not only in China but also in the world, without exception, one either leans to the side of imperialism or to the side of socialism. Neutrality is a camouflage, and a third road does not exist.

"You are too provoking." We are talking of how to deal with domestic and foreign reactionaries, that is, imperialists and their running dogs, and not of any other people.

With regard to foreign and democratic reactionaries, the question of provoking does not arise, for whether there is provoking or not does not make any difference as they are reactionaries.

Only by drawing a clear line between reactionaries and revolutionaries, only by exposing the designs and plots of the reactionaries, arousing vigilance and attention within the revolutionary ranks, and only by raising our own morale and taking down the arrogance of the enemy can the reactionaries be isolated, conquered, or replaced.

In front of a wild beast you cannot show the slightest cowardice. We must learn from Wu Sung, (one of the 108 heroes in the famous historical novel, "All Men Are Brothers") who killed a tiger on the Chingyang Ridge. To Wu Sung, the tiger on the Chingyang Ridge will eat people all the same whether you provoke it or not. You have to choose between the alternatives of either killing the tiger or being eaten by it.

Diplomatic Relations Based on Equality

"We want to do business." Entirely correct. Business has to be done. We only oppose domestic and foreign reactionaries who hamper us from doing business, and do not . . . people. It should be known that it is not any other than imperialists and their lackeys, the Chiang Kai-shek reactionary clique, who hamper us from doing business with foreign countries and even hamper us from establishing diplomatic relations with foreign countries.

Unite all forces at home and abroad to smash domestic and foreign reactionaries and there will be business, and the possibility of establishing diplomatic relations with all foreign countries on the basis of equality, mutual benefits, and mutual respect of territorial sovereignty.

"Victory is also possible without international aid." This is an erroneous thought. In the era when imperialism exists, it is impossible for the true people's revolution of any country to win its own victory without assistance in various forms from international revolutionary forces, and it is also impossible to consolidate the victory even when it is won. The great October Revolution was thus won and consolidated as Stalin had told us long ago. It was also in this way that the three imperialist countries were defeated and the . . . in East Europe liberated. This is and will be the case with the People's China at present and in the future.

Let us think it over. If the Soviet Union did not exist, if there were no victory of the antifascist Second World War, and especially, for us, no defeat of Japanese imperialism, if the various new democratic countries of Europe did not come into being, if there were no rising struggles of the oppressed nations in the east, if there were no struggles of the masses of peoples in the United States, Britain, France, Germany, Italy, Japan, and other capitalist countries against the reactionary clique ruling over them, and if there were no sum total of these things, then the international reactionary forces bearing down on us would surely be far greater than that at present.

Could we have won victory under such circumstances? Obviously not. It would also be impossible to consolidate the victory when it was won. The Chinese people have had much experience about this. The remark made by Sun Yat-sen before his death about joining hands with international revolutionary forces reflected this experience long ago.

No Need for U. S.-British Aid

"We need the aid of the British and American Governments." This is also a childish thought at present. At the present time, rulers in Britain and the United

States are still imperialists. Will they extend their aid to a people's state? If we do business with these countries, or supposing that these countries are willing in the future to lend us money on the condition of mutual benefits, what is the reason for it? This is because the capitalists of these countries want to make money. The bankers want to gain interest in their own crises; there is no aid to the Chinese people.

The Communist parties and progressive parties and groups in these countries are now working to bring about business with us, and even to establish diplomatic relations with us. This is well meant, this is aid, and this cannot be spoken of in the same breath together with the acts of the bourgeoisie in these countries.

During his lifetime, Sun Yat-sen had many times appealed to the imperialist countries for aid. The outcome was futile and instead met with merciless attacks. In his lifetime, Sun Yat-sen received international aid only once and that was from the USSR. The reader can refer to the will of Dr. Sun, in which he did not ask the people to look for aid from imperialist countries, but earnestly bade them "to unite with those peoples of the world who treat us on the basis of equality." Dr. Sun had had the experience; he had been duped. We must remember his words and not be duped again.

Internationally, we belong to the antiimperialist front, headed by the USSR, and we can only look for genuine friendly aid from that front, and not from the imperialist front.

"You are dictatorial." Yes, dear gentlemen, you are right and we are really that way. . . . The experiences of several decades amassed by the Chinese people tell us to carry out the people's democratic dictatorship, that is, the right of reactionaries to voice their opinion must be deprived, and only the people are allowed to have the right of voicing their opinions.

Who are the "people" at the present stage in China? They are the working class, the peasants, the petty bourgeoisie, and the national bourgeoisie. Under the leadership of the working class and the Communist Party, these classes unite together to form their own state and elect their own government to enact dictatorships over the lackeys of imperialism—the landlords, the bureaucratic class, and the Kuomintang reactionaries and their henchmen, representing these classes to oppress them and only allow them to behave properly and not allow them to talk and act wildly. If they talk and act wildly they will be prohibited and punished immediately.

The democratic system is to be carried out within the ranks of the people, giving them freedom of speech, assembly, and association. The right to vote is given only to the people and not to the reactionaries. These two aspects, namely democracy among the people and dictatorships over the reactionaries, combine to form the people's dictatorship.

No Benevolence for Reactionaries

Why should it be done this way? It is very obvious that if this is not done, the revolution will fail, the people will meet with woe and the State will perish. "Do you not want to eliminate State authority?" Yes, but not at present. We cannot eliminate State authority now. Why? Because imperialism still exists, the domestic reactionaries still exist, and classes in the country still exist. Our present task is to strengthen the people's State apparatus, which refers mainly to the People's Army, People's Police, and People's Court, for national defense and protection of the people's interests, and with this as condition, to enable China to advance steadily, under the leadership of the working class and the Communist Party, from an agricultural to an industrial country, and from a new democratic to a socialist and Communist society, to eliminate classes and to realize world Communism. The Army, police and court of the State are instruments for classes to oppress classes. To the hostile classes, the State apparatus is the instrument of oppression. It is violent, and not "benevolent." "You are not benevolent." Just so. We decidedly do not adopt a benevolent rule toward the reactionary acts of the reactionaries and the reactionary classes.

We only adopt a benevolent administration among the people and not toward the reactionary acts of the reactionaries and reactionary classes outside the people.

The People's State protects the people. Only when there is the People's State is it possible for the people to use democratic methods on a Nation-wide and all-round scale to educate and reeducate themselves, to free themselves from the influence of reactionaries at home and abroad (this influence is at present still very great and will exist for a long time and cannot be eliminated quickly— NCNA) to unlearn the bad habits and thoughts acquired from the old society and not let themselves fall on the erroneous path pointed out by the reactionaries, but to continue to advance and develop toward a socialist and a Communist society.

The methods we use in this field are democratic, that is, methods of persuasion and not coercion. When people break the law, they will be punished, imprisoned, or even sentenced to death. But these are some individual cases and are different in principle from the dictatorship over the reactionary class as a class.

REEDUCATION WORK

After their political regime is overthrown, those of the reactionary classes and the reactionary clique will also be given land and work and a means of living to reeducate themselves anew through work, provided they do not rebel, disrupt, or sabotage. If they are unwilling to work, the People's State will compel them to work.

Furthermore, political work, propaganda, and educational work will be carried out among them, and moreover, carefully and adequately, as we did to capture officers. This can also be said to be benevolent administration, but this is what we enact through compulsion to those of a formerly hostile class, and it . . . be mentioned, beside concrete education work among revolutionary people.

Such reeducation of the reactionary classes can only be carried out in the State of the People's democratic dictatorship. If this work is well done, the main exploiting classes of China—the landlord and bureaucratic capitalist classes— will be finally eliminated.

As for the remaining exploiting class, the national bourgeoisie, much appropriate education work can be carried out among many of that class at the present stage. When socialism is realized, that is when the nationalization of private enterprises will be carried out, they can be further educated and reeducated. The people have in their hands a powerful State apparatus and are not afraid of the rebellion of the national bourgeois class.

The grave problem is that of educating peasants. The peasant economy is scattered. According to the experiences of the Soviet Union, it requires a very long time and careful work to attain the socialization of agriculture. Without the socialization of agriculture, there will be no complete and consolidated socialism.

BETRAYAL OF SUN YAT-SEN

And to carry out the socialization of agriculture, a powerful industry with State-owned enterprises as the main component must be developed. The State of the people's democratic dictatorship must step-by-step solve this problem of the industrialization of the country. This article will not go too much into the economic problem, which will not be dealt with here in detail.

In 1924 a well-known manifesto was passed by the Kuomintang First National Congress, which was directed personally by Sun Yat-sen and participated in by Communists. The manifesto stated: "The so-called democratic systems in countries of modern times are often monopolized by the bourgeois class and turned into an instrument for oppressing the common people. But the democracy of the Kuomintang is the common possession of the common people in general, and is not the private possession of a minority."

Except for the question of who is to lead and who is to be led, the democracy mentioned here, when viewed as a general political program, is consistent with the people's democracy or new democracy mentioned by us.

Chiang Kai-shek betrayed Sun Yat-sen and used the dictatorship of the bureaucratic capitalist class and the landlord class as an instrument for oppressing the common people of China. This counterrevolutionary dictatorship remained in force for twenty . . . years and was only overthrown by the Chinese common people under our leadership now.

The foreign reactionaries who vilify us for carrying out a "dictatorship" and "totalitarianism" are in fact the very people who are carrying out dictatorship and totalitarianism. They have been carrying out the dictatorship and totalitarianism of one class, the bourgeoisie, over the proletariat and other people. They are the very people referred to by Sun Yat-sen as the bourgeois class in countries of modern times who oppress the common people. Chiang Kai-shek's counterrevolutionary dictatorship was learned from these reactionary fellows.

Chu Hsi, a philosopher of the Sung Dynasty, wrote many books and made many speeches about which we have forgotten, but there is one sentence we have not forgotten, and this is: "Do to others what others do unto you." This is what we do. That is, do to imperialism and its lackeys, the Chiang Kai-shek reactionary clique, what they do to others. Simply this and nothing more.

Importance of Working Class

The revolutionary dictatorship and the counterrevolutionary dictatorship are opposite in nature. The former learned from the latter. This learning is very important, for if the revolutionary people did not learn the methods of ruling over counterrevolutionaries, they would not be able to maintain their regime, which would be overthrown by the reactionary cliques at home and abroad. The reactionary cliques at home and abroad would then restore their rule in China and bring woe to the revolutionary people.

The basis of the people's democratic dictatorship is the alliance of the working class, the peasant class, and the urban petty-bourgeois class, and is mainly the alliance of the working class and the peasant class because this class constitutes 80 to 90 percent of the Chinese population. It is mainly the strength of these two classes which overthrows imperialism and the Kuomintang reactionary clique. The passing from the new democracy to socialism mainly depends on the alliance of these two classes.

The people's democratic dictatorship needs the leadership of the working class, because only the working class is most far-sighted, just, unselfish, and richly endowed with revolutionary thoroughness. The history of the entire revolution proves that without the leadership of the working class, the revolution is bound to fail, and with the leadership of the working class, the revolution is victorious.

In the era of imperialism, no other class in any country can lead any genuine revolution to victory. This is clearly proved by the fact that the Chinese national bourgeois class led the revolution many times and failed.

The national bourgeois class is of great importance at the present stage. Imperialism is still standing near us, and this enemy is very fierce. A long time is required for China to realize true independence economically. Only when China's industries are developed, and China no longer depends on foreign countries economically, can there be real independence.

The proportion of China's modern industry in the entire national economy is still very small. There are still no reliable figures at present, but according to certain data, it is estimated that modern industry only occupies about 10 percent of the total production output in the national economy of the whole country.

To cope with imperialist oppression, and to raise the backward economic status one step higher, China must utilize all urban and rural capitalist factors which are beneficial and not detrimental to the national economy and the people's livelihood, and unite with the national bourgeoisie in the common struggle.

Capitalism Will Play Minor Part

Our present policy is to restrict capitalism and not to eliminate it. But the national bourgeois class cannot be the leader in the revolutionary united front, and also cannot occupy the main position in the state. The national bourgeoisie class cannot be the leader of the revolution and should not occupy the main position in the institutions of the state, because the social and economic status of the national bourgeois class has determined its feebleness, its lack of foresight, its lacking in boldness, and fear of the masses by many of them.

Sun Yat-sen advocated "awakening the masses" or "helping the peasants and workers." Who is going to awaken and help them? To Sun Yat-sen this meant the petty bourgeoisie and the national bourgeoisie. But this is in fact unfeasible. Sun Yat-sen's 40 years of revolutionary work was a failure. Why? Because in the era of imperialism it is impossible for the petty bourgeoisie and national bourgeoisie to lead any real revolution toward success.

Our 28 years were entirely different. We had plenty of invaluable experiences, and the following were our three main experiences: 1, A party with discipline, armed with the theories of Marx, Engels, Lenin, and Stalin, employing the methods of self-criticism, and linked up closely with the masses; 2, an army led by such a party; 3, a united front of various revolutionary strata and groups led by such a party.

These mark us off from our predecessors . . . on these three things we have won the basic victory. We have traversed tortuous paths and struggled against rightist and leftist and opportunistic tendencies within the party.

Difficult Road Ahead

Whenever serious mistakes were committed in these three things, the revolution suffered setbacks. The mistakes and setbacks taught us, making us wiser. Thus, we were able to do better work. Mistakes are unavoidable for any party or person, but we demand that less mistakes are committed. When a mistake is committed, correction must be made: The quicker and the more thoroughly the better.

Our experiences may be summarized and boiled down into the following single-point—the people's democratic dictatorship based on the workers' and peasants' alliance led by the working class (through the Communist Party—NCNA). This dictatorship must unite in concert with international revolutionary forces. This is our formula, our main experience, our main program.

In the 28 long years of the party we have only done one thing, and that is, we have won the basic victory. This is worth celebrating because it is the people's victory and a victory in a large country like China.

But there is plenty of work before us, and like walking, what has been done in the past is simply the first step in the 10,000-mile-long march. Remnants of the enemy have still to be wiped out, and the grave task of economic construction lies before us.

Some of the things with which we are familiar will soon be laid aside, and we are compelled to tackle things with which we are unfamiliar. This is difficult. The imperialists bank on the belief that we are unable to tackle our economic work. They look on and wait for our failure.

We must overcome difficulties, and master what we do not know. We must learn economic work from all who know the ropes (no matter who they are— NCNA). We must acknowledge them as our teachers, and learn from them respectfully and earnestly. We must not pretend that we know when we do not know. Do not put on bureaucratic airs. Stick to it, and eventually it will be mastered in a few months, one or two years, or three to five years.

At first, many of the Communists in the U.S.S.R. also did not know how to do economic work, and the imperialists also waited for their failure. But the Communist Party of the Soviet Union won. Under the leadership of Lenin and Stalin, they not only could do revolutionary but also reconstruction work. They have already built up a great and brilliant Socialist state.

The Communist Party of the U.S.S.R. is our best teacher, from whom we must learn. We can wholly rely on the weapon of the people's democratic dictatorship to unite all people throughout the country except the reactionaries, and advance steadily toward the goal.

121

The Ambassador in China (Stuart) to Secretary Marshall

893.00/5–2047

NANKING, *May 20, 1947.*

In a move to bring under some semblance of control the 2-weeks-old series of rice and student demonstrations and disorders. the Government on May 18 promulgated a series of decrees forbidding public mass demonstrations and setting up channels for the presentation of grievances. Coincidentally, the Generalissimo issued a statement calling for discipline and the application of the processes of law. The background and development of this mounting crisis appear to be as follows:

As already reported in previous despatches, the first outbreaks were looting of rice shops in areas as widespread as Shanghai and Chengtu, but predominantly in the lower Yangtze Valley. These outbreaks closely followed a spectacular increase in the price of rice, with the merchants refusing to sell accumulated stocks. In self-defense the rice dealers then began to organize themselves. Effective action by the police has reduced the number of rice riots and held them under control.

In the meantime, unrest in the University has increased to such a point that practically every academic center in the country is on strike. The demands in the original University demonstrations were somewhat fanciful in that they comprised such things as protesting the elimination of a course on navigation in the curriculum of the Hangchow Christian College, protests against examinations which are now scheduled, and demands for removal of certain colleges from one city to another. As the demonstrations spread, demands become more basic; now they are principally for an increase of Government subsidies to students and immediate termination of the civil war.

Giving added weight to the current seriousness of student demands is that the majority of sympathy among faculty members is with the students. The highlight in protests by professors came in the form of a manifesto issued by the faculty of the government's National Central University in Nanking which strongly condemns government neglect of education, small appropriations, and attempts to control academic freedom of thought. The manifesto demands higher pay for teachers, larger appropriations for education and purchase of books and scientific instruments. It further warns that unless there is a drastic revision of basic policy, placing education on a more important level, the educational system of China is rapidly heading for disaster.

Demonstrations are estimated at between 3 and 10 thousand students each.

Leadership and motivation of the demonstrations have shown definite signs of changing. Most competent observers believe the original impetus was given by the CC-CC clique which was desirous of inciting a series of disorders which would in time publicly discredit a political science group-dominated government by proving it incapable of maintaining order, and in the long run provide the justification for a strong-arm, right wing government coming into power either through a coup d'etat or through sweeping the elections to be held this fall. All this has coincided with growing public agitations for a new peace movement. Aside from repeated demands for peace in the liberal and independent press, two outstanding examples are the request by three members of the Peoples' Political Council that Communist representatives be invited to attend the session which convenes on May 20, and a petition signed by 13 members of the Legislative Yuan that the government forthwith offer new peace terms. With this kind of public backing it is now apparent that leadership in the disturbances organized by the CC-CC clique is passing into the hands of the Democratic League and the Communists. This development can hardly be displeasing to the CC-CC clique, which can now claim that lack of public order is attributable to their enemies. Just how much of the agitation is now under Communist leadership is debatable, but it must be assumed that the Communists are present and, if not already active, are prepared to exploit the situation should it become necessary or desirable.

Chang Chun's government is facing an important test. Having banned demonstrations on May 18, several thousand Shanghai students on May 19 proceeded to disregard the order and demonstrate for peace. No measures were taken against them. On May 20, students in Nanking organized a demonstration to demand peace at the opening session of the PPC. The government stationed troops around Nanking University to prevent movement in or out. Other university students, under the leadership of the National Central University, organized a movement to "liberate" their fellow students. They marched into the Nanking University, joined forces with students there and marched out. Again no action was taken by either police or soldiers beyond some blank rifle fire. As the students marched on the national assembly hall, where the PPC was meeting, they were confronted by barricades, fire hoses, and blackjacks which resulted in some disorder and a few injuries to students, as the PPC hastily adjourned for the morning.

Large bodies of students are still assembled in the vicinity of the national assembly hall confronting barricades manned by police and gendarmes. It remains to be seen what action the government will take in face of this public flouting of its authority, but it is apparent that there is in train a student movement of considerable proportions which if not halted soon will tend to expand and contribute to further deterioration of the already parlous politico-economic situation.

J. LEIGHTON STUART

122

The Ambassador in China (Stuart) to Secretary Marshall

893.00/6–447

NANKING, *June 4, 1947.*

Wide-spread and comprehensive action by the government was responsible in largely forestalling the projected development of the June 2 general student strike. This action took the form of numerous arrests, the imposition of martial law in many localities and concentration of force in areas where trouble was expected. Symptomatic of government intentions was a meeting between Generalissimo and academic members of the PPC, in which the latter stated that they were doing all they could do to prevent demonstrations but that if they did take place they begged the government to avoid use of violence. The Generalissimo replied that he had personally issued orders against demonstrations and that, therefore, there would be none, but that if there were, any measures necessary would be taken to put them down. The Generalissimo further stated that the student movement was obviously Communist-led and inspired and, therefore, must be dealt with on those terms. The unfortunate coincident, from the student standpoint, that June second was date proclaimed last year by Communists as anti-civil war day was also responsible for causing many students to question advisability of carrying out their original plans on scheduled date. This argument was effectively used, particularly in Nanking, by faculty members in persuading students at least to delay.

Week-end action and developments were in brief as follows: In Shanghai martial law was imposed and student arrests reached the 200 mark. There was a rally on the campus of Chiaotung University but no violence. In Canton there was a fracas between students and unidentified elements resulting in several injuries. Nothing happened June 2. In Nanking there was a large and obvious increase of garrison strength, plans for June 2 were cancelled and *a peaceful rally* was held at the National Central University on June 3. At Hankow, on June 1, students clashed with the police, resulting in three deaths and many injuries among the students. Following this, Hankow faculties went on strike. In Chungking there were some 1,500 arrests, including approximately 20 reporters from independent papers. Tientsin was quiet. In Peiping communications were cut between the city and Yenching and Tsighua universities. Barbed wire barricades were erected around universities within the city confining students to campuses and, as far as is known, one was killed and several were injured trying to break out.

These somewhat anti-climactic developments and superficial success of the government in preventing wide-spread disorders should not be taken as indicating that impetus of student discontent has been diffused or destroyed. Evidence indicates that, if anything, students are more determined than ever to make their views known and to ensure that their rights and security shall in the long run be secured. Educated opinion in Nanking is that the government will continue its repression, mostly through medium of arresting ringleaders, but that this in the end will prove ineffective because too many students are now aroused and in the face of repression are becoming increasingly cohesive in the drive for obtaining their objectives. This opinion believes that something has now been started which cannot be destroyed by force, especially as economic and military position of the government deteriorates during the summer months. There is also evidence that increasingly faculty members sympathize with student aims.

J. LEIGHTON STUART

123

The Ambassador in China (Stuart) to Secretary Marshall

893.00/5–3047

NANKING, *May 30, 1947.*

The Peoples Political Council on May 26 by a large majority passed a resolution inviting Chinese Communist representatives to come to Nanking for discussions on ways and means of bringing about the termination of civil war. The Resolution reads as follows:

"In view of the fact that peace is the unanimous desire of all the Chinese people, and of the delegates to the Peoples Political Council who have decided to do their utmost to solve the present national crisis.

We have therefore resolved to ask the delegates of the Chinese Communists to attend the PPC meeting to discuss national affairs."

It has been broadcast on all government radios.

This resolution points up one phase in the growing agitation, particularly among leftwing and intellectual circles, for a negotiated peace. The first aspect of this movement is that many, perhaps even most, of those involved in the agitation are sincere in their professed belief that the first essential step to the solution of any of China's multitudinous problems is peace. It is perhaps unfortunate that none of the groups or leaders involved have so far brought forth any constructive suggestions as to how this commendable objective is to be accomplished, nor has there been any suggestion that the Communists in their present and relatively favorable position may not be amenable to compromise.

The second aspect is that the government, since the agitation has arisen and presumably having a fairly realistic understanding of what the Communists could or could not be expected to do, may not be altogether displeased that the peace movement has developed as it has. If the words of prominent government spokesmen can be taken at their face value, they must believe that any overtures of peace negotiations would be either ignored or repulsed. Hence it is not unreasonable to assume the probability that the PPC resolution combined with similar agitation in the Legislative Yuan will in the predictable future be followed by a formal government offer to the Communists for negotiations.

J. LEIGHTON STUART

124

The Ambassador in China (Stuart) to Secretary Marshall

893.00/7–147

NANKING, *July 1, 1947.*

Communist military successes, the shrinkage of railway mileage in Nationalist hands, the depreciation and depletion of Nationalist equipment and supplies, the increasing friction between southern military forces and civil administrators on one hand and northern troops and the local civil population on the other, reports of a projected withdrawal of Nationalist forces to intramural China and the abandonment of Manchuria to the Communists, rumors of the early return of Marshal Chang Hsueh-liang to Manchuria, and the expanding economic stagnation suggest the following observations:

The recent Communist drive has met with little Nationalist resistance. Northeast Combat Command sources and military observers admit that many Nationalist withdrawals were premature and without military necessity. The words "strategic retreat" have lost all significance. As a result the Communists possess almost complete initiative and are able to maneuver practically at will. If Ssupingkai with its garrison of 17,000 falls, the Communists should be able to proceed successfully against bypassed Changchun and Kirin and thereupon gain unimpaired control over 90 percent of Manchuria. The fall of Yingkow would leave only ports on the west coast of the Liaotung Gulf in Nationalist hands. The only railway of any appreciable mileage in Nationalist hands is the Peiping-Liaotung main line. The Communist drive eastward through Jehol is threatening even these meager holdings and should this drive be successful and contact be established between these forces and those now in the vicinity of Yingkow, Manchuria will be effectively cut off from land and water communication with China, and Mukden itself will be virtually in a state of siege. Nationalist military intelligence has been outstandingly deficient. The Northeast Combat Command is seemingly in almost complete ignorance of Communist plans and is therefore being constantly outwitted. Northeast Combat Command headquarters officers admit they had no intelligence of the recent Communist drive on Changchun and then southwards, even though it is now known that such plans therefor had been formulated three months prior to the opening of the drive.

Rivalry (if not enmity) between General Hsiung Shih-hui, the Generalissimo's representative, and General Tu Li-ming, commanding the Northeast Combat Command, is openly discussed and the absence of closely integrated military and economic planning in Manchuria is attributed to it.

By holding the initiative, the Communists are able to keep the Nationalists scurrying over the countryside, thereby causing depreciation of Nationalist motorized mobile equipment and depletion of sorely needed supplies. Communist transport on the other hand consists almost wholly of draft animals. Persons in direct contact with the Nationalist troops in rural areas state there are insufficient small arms and ammunition to arm all combatant troops now in the field. These reports are so consistent, some, though not necessarily full, credence must be given them. The Communists also are underarmed, but by guerrilla tactics and surprise night attacks they are able to cause greater loss of weapons and expenditure of ammunition by the Nationalists than by themselves.

Nationalist southern military forces and civil administrators conduct themselves in Manchuria as conquerors, not as fellow countrymen, and have imposed a "carpet-bag" regime of unbridled exploitation upon areas under their control. If military and civil authorities of local origin were in control, they too would probably exploit the populace, but experience has shown that Chinese authorities of local origin, in general, never quite strangle a goose laying golden eggs, and furthermore, it is a human trait to be less resentful toward exploitation by one's own than toward that by outsiders. The result of this is that the countryside is so antagonistic toward outsiders as to affect the morale of non-Manchurian troops and at the same time arouse vindictiveness in southern military officers and civil administrators.

Nationalist withdrawals toward Mukden have progressively cut off Nationalist-held areas from the great food producing regions in Manchuria, thereby causing a potential Nationalist food shortage which was already apparent in extensive grain hoarding and speculation. Puerile efforts have been made toward price control and to combat hoarding, but in general, the results of these efforts have been largely to enforce the requisitioning of grain at bayonet point for controlled prices and to enable the resale of requisitioned grain at black market prices for the benefit of the pockets of rapacious military and civil officials. The common man is being crushed between the rising cost of living and the depreciating currency. (The cost of living index of May, 160 percent compared to 100 percent in April.) Local currency is pegged to Chinese National Currency and has not only fallen with CNC, but also because of the wholesale exodus of families of Nationalist officials and the resulting flight from local currency incidental to frenzied buying of CNC and gold bars. The black market value of the U. S. dollar at Mukden is now TP dollars 3,300 against TP dollars 1,000 March 1.

Little goods move between Mukden and its hinterland. Business is rapidly approaching a standstill, exports from Manchuria have practically disappeared and imports have reduced to a trickle of the normal. Almost all capital has been expended in long-range investment since the Nationalists took over Manchuria and no such capital, government or private, is being invested today. All commodity markets are purely speculative.

The evidence is growing daily that the people of Manchuria not only are prepared for but are keenly desirous of a change in the government. But what change? Most are undecided even though voluble in discontent of the present way of living and the trend of events. It is safe to state that the overwhelming majority in the nation are as dissatisfied with, dislike and would welcome freedom from the present Nationalist regime. A like majority fear and would therefore not welcome the Communist regime. Many talk "revolution" even aloud in public places, but few are able to define their conception of revolution other than as change from the present way of living and even fewer envisage revolution involving armed resistance. There seems no likelihood that an armed uprising would be more than abortive, at least until the national morale and military might has suffered devastating deterioration. One platform on which Manchus seem almost unanimous is "out with Heilien (outsider) Chinese and Manchuria for the Manchus." The return of Ma Chan-shan lent heart to those who look to restoration of Manchu rule under a "native son," but his relegation to figurehead status in a position of impotence has dampened their hopes. Eyes are today turned toward the possibility of the return of the young Marshal to power in Manchuria. His vices, weaknesses and "playboy" tendencies are known but he is nevertheless associated in the minds of the people with prosperity and progress which Manchuria enjoyed under Chang Tso-lin regime. He or some other pre-Manchu leader could serve as a central figure for rallying the Manchu people. Such a change would in all likelihood herald the return of warlordism to Manchuria, but even so Manchuria would remain Chinese with nominal allegiance at least to China and not a "Manchu peoples republic" as it may become if the Communists succeed in sweeping the Nationalists back into intramural China.

There is every reason to believe that punitive military action against the Communists, unless succeeded by overwhelming military occupation will not save Manchuria to China. It is high time for Nanking to be realistic and to replace its present impotent disliked regime in Manchuria with one which will be supported by the local population and would thereby serve to weaken the Communist movement. It may be, and some think that it is, too late to accomplish this purpose. Without some such effective measure there are many indications that it will be only a matter of some months, perhaps six to nine, before Manchuria will be lost.

125

The Ambassador in China (Stuart) to Secretary Marshall

893.00/4–547

NANKING, *April 5, 1947.*

Review of the labors and accomplishments of the Third Plenary Session of the Kuomintang Central Executive Committee reinforces the tentative conclusions which I suggested in my report of March 23. The two principal points of interest were: (1) the efforts of certain factions within the Kuomintang to obstruct reorganization of the government and (2) the struggle for power and position, mainly between the CC–Clique and the Political Science Group.

On the first point, the Generalissimo, supported by the Political Science Group and liberal elements, was successful in blocking the drive to stop reorganization.

In the struggle between factions, the Generalissimo emerged in a stronger position than ever before and higher in the esteem of his party. At the same time the CC-Clique also seems to have emerged in a stronger position, to the detriment of other factions; but full confirmation must await the publication of personnel to the State Council and the Yuan. Evidence of his political astuteness, as well as the strength of his roots in the past, is found in his present trip to his home to sweep the tombs of his ancestors which he can combine with a brief period of "absent treatment" for the third parties. He stopped off for a few hours in Shanghai for business in connection with his position as President of the Executive Yuan.

The CC-Clique (the most fanatically anti-Communist group in China) is far and away the most disciplined Kuomintang faction, and because of its comprehensive organization, reaching into every *hsien* in the country, is able to fulfill the Generalissimo's needs in this phase of his struggle with the Communists.

The tragic paradox of his position, of which he may be unaware, is that he is being compelled by circumstances to utilize the qualifications which the CC-Clique can offer. At the same time this clique exploits its preferred position to render more firm its hold on the Party and the country; and with time the Generalissimo therefore may well become less and less able to dispense with them or to circumscribe their activities, which can only serve to aggravate those social conditions basically giving rise and strength to the Communist movement.

There are many evidences that the Chen brothers are now attempting to insert themselves into the economic field and that Chen Li-fu desires to become Vice-Chairman of the National Economic Council.

It is more difficult to estimate the position now of other groups, such as the Political Science Group, Sun Fo and other liberals. Certainly General Chen Cheng, and probably parts of the military cliques, went along with the CC-Clique and will continue to do so. The Political Science Group was instrumental in helping to unseat T. V. Soong, though in the process it failed in its objectives to consolidate its hold on financial affairs because the CC-Clique was successful in gaining headship of Central Trust. Though having failed to control the

Party, the Political Science Group did block CC attempts to nullify the process of reorganization. In this struggle it was supported by Sun Fo and his followers. The most serious Political Science Group concern now is economic. Wong Wen-hao has said that if Chen Li-fu did become Vice-Chairman of the National Economic Council, it would be impossible for him, and perhaps for others around him, to continue on the Council. Such an eventuality would be somewhat balanced by what now appears to be the certainty that Sun Fo would be Vice President of the reorganized State Council and General Chang Chun President of the Executive Yuan. These factors, of course, must remain to a certain extent speculative until appointments are actually announced since the Generalissimo gives his complete confidence to no one.

On balance, it would appear that the struggle will be continued between the liberals who will control most of the high government positions and have a major interest in the economic world and the CC-Clique largely controlling the Party organization and an influential section of the army, and attempting to inject itself into finance. During the Central Executive Committee the liberals showed their fundamental lack of cohesive organization and their unwillingness or inability to defend each other publicly against the unrelenting CC attack. How far this compromises their standing can only be demonstrated when reorganization has been accomplished.

Recently Chen Li-fu has shown some interest in plans for basic agrarian reform and restriction of corruption within the Party, which are, after all, the two measures which can offer a social as opposed to a military solution of the Communist question. Various liberal elements within the Party who accept the inevitability for the time being of CC-Clique influence are encouraging this interest on his part. It remains to be seen how successful they can be but account must be taken of his past record and the known narrowness of his economic and political views. Those who know him well are by no means sure that he really understands the urgency of the agrarian problem in China or the measures which could reform it.

The economic proposals which Chen Li-fu submitted and which were passed by the Central Executive Committee are being made subject of a dispatch.

The political resolutions are comprehensive, skillful and well designed to secure the avowed intention of tightening Party control and discipline in the face of pressures and disintegration arising from the civil war. It is reported that CC-Clique is putting its main effort in preparing for the elections which will precede implementation of the Constitution on December 25, 1947.

In accordance with the Central Executive Committee resolution, preparations proceed for termination of the period of political tutelage. The Executive Yuan has approved ten basic laws on organization and elections. Negotiations on reorganization are proceeding slowly. In the interim a game of political musical chairs being played by the third parties, the Social Democrats have finally agreed to enter the government, though Carson Chang himself will not; and it is now the turn of the Youth Party to be difficult and increase its demands. Based on the experience of the last few months, it is by no means impossible that the positions of these two minor parties will shortly be reversed. The Foreign Minister remarked the other day on the irony of a situation where the Generalissimo, having been made self-conscious about his ability to dictate political settlement and consequently reluctant to use bludgeoning tactics, finds himself in endless political dickering which only delays that reorganization which his liberal advisors have been urging on him.

126

Summary of the Manifesto Issued by the Kuomintang Central Executive Committee [4]

893.00/3–2547

The present plenary session of our party has taken place just a year after the conclusion of the second plenary session. During the year, the greatest accomplishment in China's political development was the convocation of the National Assembly and the promulgation of the Constitution of the Republic of China.

It is three months since the promulgation of the constitution. We rejoice that the date for the institution of constitutional government is drawing near and that our long-cherished desire of nation building is nearing realization. But as we survey the present situation in our country, we cannot help feeling deeply regretful that our nation is still beset with difficulties and we realize all the more keenly the weightiness of our responsibility for the national revolution.

Now, the plan for broadening the basis of the government is being carried out. Reorganization of the national government will end the political tutelage of the country under our party. Henceforth, the Government of China will no longer be the sole responsibility of one party. And the status of our party and its relations with the government will also differ from those in the past. But the sincere efforts of our party in promoting the welfare of our country and the people must be pushed vigorously forward.

In the light of the internal situation of our country, we wish to enumerate below five important tasks on which we should concentrate our efforts in the future:

1. Complete preparations for the institution of constitutional government and the drafting of a pattern for nation building.

The consistent objective in our party's struggle for the past 50 years has been the destruction of all obstacles standing in the way of democracy and the building of China based on Three People's Principles. After eight years of armed resistance Dr. Sun Yat Sen's Three People's Principles are now subscribed to by the entire nation. During the current interim period preceding constitutional government, the formulation of laws and regulations pertaining to the enforcement of the constitution, the guarantee of liberties and rights of the people, the revision of existing laws and regulations, the establishment of the systems of central and local governments and the holding of elections are all basic measures for laying a sound foundation for constitutional government. Our party should sincerely cooperate with other parties and they should help one another in advancing the welfare of the nation. Meantime, our members should go into and among the masses and help educate them in constitutional government.

2. Remove all obstacles to national unification and consolidate the foundation of the country.

During the past year, the national government issued cease fire orders three times and carried out continuous mediation and negotiations. But the Chinese Communists, pinning their implicit faith in armed force and acting in violation of good faith took advantage of the government's tolerance, and each time when the government made a concession, they carried out general mobilizations in their illegally occupied areas. Now they have launched an all-out offensive and wherever their military force reaches, the people are either displaced from their homes or are plundered and killed. As a consequence, unity of the country

[4] Released by the Central News Agency, Nanking, Mar. 24, 1947.

is undermined and economic reconstruction and rehabilitation are likewise hindered because of the Communists' wanton and systematic destruction of communications. For the sake of preserving the existence of the country and the nation, and for the sake of delivering the people from their present state of distress, this plenary session deems it imperative that the national government should take resolute and speedy measures to suppress the armed rebellion.

3. Carry out the principle of people's livelihood and stabilize national economy.

Another serious obstacle to the development of our nation is economic maladjustment. This plenary session considers that the only way to remedy this situation is to carry into effect the principle of people's livelihood by reforming our economic policies. Thus, all the economic policies of the government must be aimed at promoting the welfare of the masses, including the farmers. Economic rehabilitation and reconstruction must not be confined to large cities but extensively pushed to all rural areas. Further, there should be rational administration of finance, improvement of procedures for extending loans to productive enterprises and extensive establishment of cooperatives. At the same time, the nation as a whole should sincerely observe all the laws and ordinances pertaining to the enforcement of emergency economic measures.

4. Uphold international justice and strive for world peace.

The supreme objective of our foreign policy has always been the maintenance of national independence and equality and the promotion of international justice and peace. The stand we take in our relations with others conforms with our traditional spirit of "not to oppress the weak nor fear the strong."

Our country has never harbored any ambition of dominating the world. Nor will it permit itself to become a pawn in international relations. It is the firm belief of our party that an independent, free and strong China is the *sine qua non* to the maintenance of world peace. As long as world peace is not ensured, China will not be able to pursue her task of national reconstruction unhindered.

At present, the world situation is in a state of confusion and instability, but the wisdom gained by mankind through the tragic sacrifices made in the recent world war should be the main force for establishing world peace and security. We fervently hope that the United Nations Organization will grow quickly and become strong and that through it all international complications may find their satisfactory solution.

5. Vitalize the educational program so as to build up the potential strength for national reconstruction.

What is generally regarded as a matter of great regret in our work of national reconstruction is the inadequacy of our educational measures and the slackening of school discipline.

The youths of our country are dissipating their energy in empty and vague political activities. To build up the nation, it is necessary to have persons specialized in various kinds of technical professions. But many young men today cannot set their mind at peace to receive practical technical training. The government should henceforth lay greater emphasis on education.

Our party, having dedicated itself to the cause of national revolution, thinks only of duty and minds, not power. To whatever is of benefit to the country, we will address ourselves, even at the cost of our lives. It behooves our comrades to resolutely keep faith in their mission, sincerely do their duty, rectify their shortcomings, strive to improve themselves, serve the people and be loyal to the country. Thus, we may not fall short of the expectations of the founder of our Republic, the martyrs of the war of resistance and our distressed fellow countrymen in the postwar period.

127 (a)

Statement by President Chiang Kai-shek Announcing the Reorganization of the State Council [5]

893.00/4–2047

The reorganization of the State Council, which takes effect Monday is another step in the transition from Kuomintang tutelage to constitutional government in China. It gives representation on the nation's highest policy making body to minor parties and to independent.

The composition of the State Council under this reorganization is as follows: The Presidents of the Executive Yuan (ex-officio)—five seats.

Kuomintang 12 seats; Democratic Socialist party—4 seats.

Young China Party—4 seats; independents—4 seats.

At present the Yuan Presidents are all Kuomintang members, so that the total Kuomintang seats number 17. But assumption of these posts by members of other parties or by independents automatically would reduce the Kuomintang representation.

It was originally planned that the membership of the State Council consist of 40, with the Kuomintang members numbering 20. At present 29 seats have been occupied. If the remaining 11 should be filled, the Kuomintang membership will be 17 out of 40, or less than half.

In the case of the Democratic Socialist and Young China Parties, the individuals were selected by the groups themselves. In the case of the independents, I made the selections after consultation with the individuals concerned.

The broadening of political representation on the State Council follows the election of minority party members to the Legislative and Control Yuan and the established multi-party government. The next step is the forthcoming reorganization of the Executive Yuan under the new Premier, with Cabinet ministries assigned to minority parties and independents as well as the Kuomintang.

The effect of the reorganization on the Chinese Government is as follows:

Control of the Government, hitherto exclusively under the Kuomintang, is broadened to control by the KMT, the Democratic Socialist Party, the Young China Party, and Independents. The State Council will direct China's affairs during the transitional period, carry out the mandates of the last National Assembly, and prepare for the inauguration of constitutional government on December 25, 1947.

China's postwar political history has been divided into two phases. First, came an attempt with American mediation to persuade the Communists to join the government and merge their army into the national army.

The second phase began with the National Assembly. The participation by the Democratic Socialists, the Young China Party, and Independents in that body and in the adoption of the constitution meant that they supported the government's effort to bring in the constitutional era.

The world is not static. China's need for peace and reconstruction becomes more urgent every day. China must push vigorously ahead to achieve unity by the quickest means possible. Progress toward democracy and constitutionalism cannot wait indefinitely for the Communists.

---

[5] Released by the Central News Agency, Nanking, Apr. 18, 1947.

If the Chinese Communist Party abandons its policy of seizing power by force and cooperates to achieve the unity of the nation, it still has the opportunity to join the government and participate in the work of national reconstruction. For the sake of China's suffering people, it is hoped that the Communists will change their present attitude of open rebellion.

127 (b)

Text of the Political Program of the National Government of China [6]

893.00/4–1847

The National Government of the Chinese Republic, with a view to establishing constitutional government and promoting democracy has since the political consultation conference (January 1946) decided to reorganize the government and to invite individuals from political parties and groups other than the Kuomintang, as well as independents, to participate. More than one year's persistent efforts have just resulted in a jointly formulated and agreed upon procedure for immediate completion of the government reorganization. Besides, a political program for the National Government after the reorganization, evolving from comprehensive and careful deliberations by all parties concerned, has just been approved, respectively, by the standing committees of the Young China Party, the Democratic Socialist Party and the Chinese Kuomintang; it has also been agreed upon by the Independents who took part in the discussions. The embodiments of the political program, which will be adhered to jointly by the reorganized National Government, are as follows:

One. The program of peaceful national reconstruction shall be the guiding principle of administration for the reorganized National Government, while all participating parties and independents shall be jointly responsible for completing the interim procedure for inauguration of constitutional government.

Two. Cooperation among the various parties and groups shall be based upon the principles of "political democratization" and "nationalization of armed forces" under this common principle, no efforts will be spared toward political progress and national stability.

Three. In order to promote world peace and uphold the United Nations charter, China should pursue a foreign policy of equality and good neighborliness, without discrimination, toward all friendly nations.

Four. Settlement by political means shall remain the basic principle for solution of the Chinese Communist problem. If only the Chinese Communists show willingness for peace and the railway system can be completely restored, the government will seek national peace and unity through political channels.

Five. The responsible Executive Yuan system shall be enforced as an experiment, in accordance with the spirit of the provisions of the constitution. The Executive Yuan should abide by any decisions of the State Council and assume full responsibility for their execution, thus conforming to the principle of "authority and responsibility". Equal respect should be accorded to the functions and powers of the Legislative Yuan. In presenting a bill to the Legislative Yuan, the Executive Yuan authorities shall be present to offer explanations, thereby insuring coordination between the executive and legislative authority.

Six. Pending the inauguration of constitutional government any nomination

---

[6] Published by the Government on Apr. 17, 1947.

to the presidency of the Executive Yuan shall be made by the President (of the Republic) with the previous concurrence of the various parties.

Seven. Provincial administrations shall be governed by principles making a clear distinction between the military and civil authorities and allowing expediencies as local conditions warrant. In matters of personnel, and legislation, a thoroughgoing checkup will be made and reform instituted in order to enable the provincial governments to attain the highest degree of efficiency possible.

Eight. All laws promulgated and all institutions established to meet the needs of political tutelage shall, after reorganization of the National Government, be rescinded and abolished.

Nine. Thorough adjustments shall be made in the tax system and financial setup, the procedure of levying taxes shall be simplified, and the categories of land tax and additional levies shall be reduced, in order to alleviate the burdens of the people.

Ten. Strict guarantee shall be accorded to the people's freedom of person, freedom of speech, freedom of publication and freedom of assembly. Any illegal arrest or interference shall be strictly forbidden. Where restrictions are deemed essential for the maintenance of social order or to avert a crisis, laws governing such restrictions shall be approved by the State Council.

Eleven. Foreign loans henceforth to be contracted shall all be earmarked for purposes of stabilizing and improving the people's livelihood and of production and reconstruction.

Twelve. As far as possible, there should be participation of political parties and independents in the political councils or provisional councils of the provinces, municipalities and hsiens. Local governments in the various provinces should also include representatives of various parties and independents, based on the principle of "selection of the able and efficient."

127 (c)

Statement on April 23, 1947, by the Chinese Minister of Information (Peng)

893.00/4-2347

I am happy to be able to announce that one-party rule in China has come to an end today. The Kuomintang has fulfilled its promise of handing over the political power to the people and carrying out its program for establishing constitutional government after the tutelage period. The formal completion of the process came with the inaugural meeting of the new multiparty State Council, at which the Executive Yuan was reorganized to include representatives of other parties and independents.

This action, following the election of members of different parties to the Legislative and Control Yuan, means that the multiparty transition government has now been fully set up and is ready to govern the country in the spirit of the constitution until the new government provided by that charter is elected.

The composition of the Executive Yuan is as follows: President, Chang Chun; Vice President, Wang Yung-wu; Minister of Interior, Chang Li-sheng; Minister of Foreign Affairs, Wang Shih-chieh; Minister of National Defense, Pai Cheng-hsi; Minister of Finance, O. K. Yui; Minister of Economic Affairs, Li Huang; Minister of Education, Chu Chia-hua; Minister of Communications, Yu Ta-wei; Minister of Agriculture and Forestry, Tso Shun-sheng; Minister of

Social Affairs, Ku Cheng-kang; Minister of Food, Ku Cheng lun; Minister of Water Conservancy, Hsueh Tu-pi; Minister of Justice, Hsieh Kuan-sheng; Minister of Land, Li Ching-chai; Minister of Public Health, Chow I-chun; Chairman of National Resources Commission, Wong Wen-hao; Chairman of Mongolian and Tibetan Affairs Commission, Hsu Shih-ying; Chairman of Overseas Chinese Affairs Commission, Liu Wei-chih; Ministers without Portfolio, Chang Nai-chih, Li Ta-ming, Chiang Yuen-tien, Miao Chia-min, Peng Hsueh-Pei, Lei Chen.

127 (d)

Inaugural Radio Speech by the President of the Executive Yuan (Chang) [7]

893.00/4–2347

My fellow countrymen, four months have passed since the promulgation of the Constitution of the Republic of China. The Kuomintang is now in the process of concluding its political tutelage. It has broadened the basis of the Government. Furthermore, in accordance with the spirit of the Constitution, it has advanced the practice of the responsible Executive Yuan system.

The next eight months will be a period of transition from political tutelage to constitutional democracy. The government must complete preparations for implementation of the Constitution. It must seek to restore national unity and stability. At the same time it must exert its utmost to resolve the serious financial and economic problems of the moment. These tasks are extremely difficult. On their accomplishment depends the fate of the country for generations to come.

It is with much apprehension, and awareness of my own limitations, that I am assuming the premiership at this hour. Fortunately, we have as our highest guiding principles the "fundamentals of nation reconstruction" which were laid down by Dr. Sun Yat-sen, father of the republic. For political and economic reforms during this period, we have also the sound resolutions adopted at the recent Third Plenary Session of the Kuomintang Central Executive Committee. As to the administrative policies to be followed after reorganization of the government there is an agreement reached among the different parties and nonpartisans. These will enable me, under the leadership of the President and in deference to public opinion, to attempt the execution of a difficult task.

We can well anticipate the possible difficulties and obstacles born of long years of war. However, I shall begrudge no effort or labor. Nor shall I be influenced by personal loss or gain. I will give what I have and what I am in the interest of national unity, democracy, peace and reconstruction. On my assumption of office today, I wish to outline a few of my administrative policies and appeal for the solidarity and cooperation of my countrymen.

The first and foremost need for China today is internal stability and unity. This is the prerequisite to national reconstruction. Ever since V–J Day, the Government has, with the greatest zeal and patience, been seeking a political solution of the Chinese Communist problem. During the past year, on instructions of the President, I have time and again participated in the negotiations for peaceful unification. Unfortunately, the situation has deteriorated so that today the Chinese Communists are in an all-out armed rebellion against the state, thus slamming the door for further negotiations and nullifying all past

---

[7] Released at Ministry of Information press conference, Apr. 23, 1947.

efforts toward peace. In order to restore social order and safeguard national unity the Government is constrained to take effective military measures to quell the rebellion. It is the challenge of the time. It is the demand of the people. It is, above all, the duty of any government. In discharging this grave responsibility, however, the Government has not failed to realize the serious consequences or the pains and sufferings necessarily involved. It is my fervent hope that such military measures will quickly bring about a fundamental solution, eventually by political means, of the internal strife and thus successfully restore national unity.

Eight long and difficult years of war have sapped China's economy, and have made life miserable for her people. Another year of internal disturbances has rendered the financial, social and economic crisis of the country more acute than ever before.

As a move to weather the present crisis, the Government has already promulgated a set of emergency economic measures. These will continue to be enforced. In removing the causes of the crisis, the Government will have to carry out step by step the economic program already formulated. In view of the general depression and suffering throughout the country, it is imperative that past mistakes should not be repeated. Special caution must be taken in policy making. Piecemeal action should be avoided, and emphasis must be placed on measures for a fundamental solution. Matters not immediately related to the balancing of the budget, the stabilization of currency, or the requirements of the people's livelihood are not to tax the attention of the Government. Progress should be sought through stability. Above all, no effort should be spared to encourage privately operated economic enterprises in order to divert idle capital to productive channels. And the basis for all progress and reform is the faith and confidence the Government is able to inspire.

As for political reform, the Government will take the responsibility to revitalize the administrative machine. It will uphold strict discipline, eradicate corruption, and break up bad habits of shoddiness and procrastination in order that administrative efficiency may be increased. I appeal to all responsible officials of all levels to carry out Government policies, and to set personal examples of self-discipline, selflessness and fairmindedness. In this way, the rule of law may be secured, and a wholesome political atmosphere created.

The guarantee of civil freedoms and rights is a most essential item in the preparation for constitutional government. The Government will, in accordance with the constitution and the new administrative policies, safeguard all civil freedoms and rights according to law. At the same time, it is my hope that all the people of the country will fully respect the divinity of the law, enhance their law abiding spirit, and realize their responsibility towards the state. In so doing, freedom and law will go hand in hand, thus ensuring the successful development of a constitutional democracy in China.

In the field of foreign relations, what China sincerely hopes to see is a peaceful, righteous, friendly and cooperative world. The Chinese Government therefore reaffirms its consistent stand to live at peace with all friendly nations of the world. Towards her wartime allies such as the United States, the Soviet Union, Great Britain and France, China will spare no effort to perpetuate the friendship and comradeship cemented through a common struggle for a common cause. In the case of any unsettled problem that may adversely affect friendly relations, she is willing and prepared to seeks a reasonable solution through customary diplomatic channels. In the interest of world peace she will also exert her utmost to increase mutual understanding and harmony among her allies.

For the settlement of the various pending postwar issues among nations and the establishment of the peace, order and cooperative relations of the world, China will not fail to contribute her share of the responsibility. Nor will she permit impairment of the standing she has secured in the family of nations. She will support the United Nations Charter, abide faithfully by treaty obligations, and respect the legitimate rights and interests of friendly states. She is equally determined to preserve her own sovereignty and independence as well as her own status among nations.

A most crucial moment has arrived in China's history. On her hands there are a host of practices, either to be initiated or to be reformed. However, China's potential is vast, and her entire populace is enthusiastic for an orderly government. While we should in no wise under-rate our present difficulties and obstacles, I see no ground for pessimism and skepticism about the prospect of China's renaissance if only we can marshal and organize the will and strength of the whole people for developing the potential of the country.

Out of the multifarious tasks pressing for attention and action, the Government will select the most essential ones and tackle them energetically and solidly. Each of us, individually, must shake off his inertia, faithfully observe the laws and regulations and take part in the recovery. Government can lead the way, but there must be patriotic and energetic cooperation by all the people to make leadership successful.

Should it so happen that the laws and decrees of the Government are not faithfully enforced, or should the sufferings or wishes of the people have escaped the attention of the Government, I hope that public opinion will prevail to help repair the shortcomings. The Government will welcome any constructive, helpful and concrete suggestions.

Although I shall make no claim of achievements throughout my thirty years of military and civil service, I find it gratifying that I have never permitted myself to overstep the confines of the law for personal reasons or expediency. Nor has personal gain or loss ever been in my consideration.

As I assume office today, at this time of national distress, I fully realize the grave responsibility on my shoulders. I shall do my duty to my country, faithfully and loyally. I shall try to repay the sympathy and fulfill the aspirations my fellow countrymen and party comrades have shown for me. Animated by a spirit of selflessness and confident of the people's cooperation, I hope this Government will successfully restore national unity, complete the preparations for constitutional government, surmount the economic crisis, and ameliorate the people's livelihood.

128

The Ambassador in China (Stuart) to Secretary Marshall

893.00/4–1947

NANKING, *April 19, 1947*

It is too early to assess with any accuracy the eventual effect of State Council reorganization announced April 17, and any such assessment must be approached with caution in the light of a series of past Chinese Government reorganizations which have been largely for external effect and have brought little effective change to the Chinese domestic scene.

The Embassy's initial impression, however, is that the caliber and standing of Kuomintang appointees indicates real effort to place in positions of power and responsibility the most capable and modern figures of the Party. It is indeed promising that in the case of Kuomintang appointees there is a notable exclusion of persons closely affiliated with the CC-Clique. A possible exception to this is the appointment of Wu Chung-hsin sometime governor of Sinkiang province.

It is also encouraging that the Political Science Group is well represented by its most prominent and ablest members including Chang Chun, Wong Wen-hao, Wang Chung-hui, and Wan Shih-chieh. Chen Pu-lei and Chiang Mon-lin, although not generally considered as members of the Political Science Group, may be expected to support Political Science Group policies.

The appointment of Sun Fo as Vice President of the National Government is no doubt intended to strengthen the progressive or liberal elements and to set the pattern to the Government. The inclusion of Shao Li-tze and T. V. Soong indicates at least a drift away from the traditional aspects of Chinese political conservatism.

Chu Chen, Yu Yu-jen, Tai Chi-tao, Chang Chi, and Chou Lu can be best classified as Party elders, faithful to the Generalissimo and essentially conservative in political outlook, but generally accepted as being in support of high standards of public morality.

A disappointing aspect of the announcement was the failure to change any of the Presidents of the Five Yuan, with the exception of Chang Chun, who replaces T. V. Soong as President of the Executive Yuan and relieves the Generalissimo of his temporary assumption of the office. It had been originally planned that Chang Chun-mai (Carson Chang), leader of the Social Democratic Party, would be appointed President of the Judicial Yuan and that Tseng Chi, leader of the Youth Party, would be given the presidency of one of the other four Yuan. The final refusal of Carson Chang to accept office in the Government, even though sanctioning the participation of his party made it impossible to carry out this plan and for the time being at least all Yuan Presidencies remain in Kuomintang control.

In the case of the Social Democratic Party, even in the final stages of reorganization of the State Council, there was continued reluctance on the part of members of the party to join the government and on the evening of April 17 it was only possible for the Social Democrats to name three members of their allotted four. It has been announced that they will appoint the fourth member as soon as possible.

Youth Party and Social Democratic Party appointees are largely unknown quantities. They represent in the case of the Youth Party a group of Szechuan scholar-landlords who have tended in the past to be affiliated with the right wing of the Kuomintang. The Social Democratic Party appointees are a group of elderly scholars without important political following in the country.

On the other hand, the independent appointees offer considerable promise, particularly in the case of Chen Kwan-pu (K. P. Chan), the most able private banker in China with a high reputation for his statesmanlike judgment and probity in New York and Washington as well as China. Wang Yun-wu, present Minister of Economic Affairs, seems also a satisfactory appointment as an independent. Both K. P. Chen and Wang Yun-wu are sympathetic to the Political Science Group and will tend to strengthen its position in the State Council. Mo Teh-hui has obviously been appointed because of his long affiliation with events in Manchuria. Pao Erh-han (Burkhan), a Turki and present Vice-Chairman of the Sinkiang Provincial Government is no doubt intended as a placatory gesture toward the minorities of the northwest. In this same general connection it will be noted that among the Kuomintang appointees there is included Chang Chia-hutuktu, a Tibetan.

In summary, the composition of the State Council is as regards the Kuomintang and independents as good as could be expected in the circumstances. Whether or not the State Council, which will constitute itself on April 23, if its members can reach Nanking by that date, will assert itself in such a manner as to bring about substantial social and economic reform in China remains, of course, a question depending upon many factors not the least one being the attitude of the Generalissimo toward it and his ability to control the Kuomintang as the still dominant political party in China.

It is interesting to note that at the same time as the appointment of Kuomintang State Councillors, a separate political committee of the Kuomintang was established. The Secretary General of this committee is Chen Li-fu and it is a safe assumption that this committee will have an important role in controlling the Kuomintang political machine and establishing party policies.

Eleven seats in the State Council have been left vacant for the Democratic League and the Communist Party in the event that they wish to join the interim government. On the night of April 17 Lo Lung-chi made known to the Embassy that Democratic League participation was at this time "impossible". Furthermore, it seems extremely unlikely that there will be any Communist participation in the government between now and the end of the year when the new constitution comes into force.

The reorganization of the Executive Yuan which will be carried out by the State Council will offer some indication of how assertive and energetic the Council will be and in what direction the government may be expected to move. Concessions to the CC-Clique, however, because of its control of Kuomintang machinery, may be expected to ensue in this reorganization.

In face of the magnitude of Chinese internal problems, aside from the existence of a state of civil war, to expect too rapid change would be unrealistic, but the calibre of Kuomintang and independent appointees to the State Council offer reasonable ground for hope that there will be an effort made to achieve healthy and substantial change. Such change will come slowly, however, and in the process it must be borne in mind that the CC-Clique, while at the moment not in the forefront, is still substantially in the control of the Kuomintang party machinery. The inclusion of non-Kuomintang groups at least offers promise for the stimulation of political activity and the development of non-Communist opposition, but in the final analysis the major imponderable is whether or not the Generalissimo will be capable of seeking and being guided by the advice of liberal-progressive public servants rather than acceding to the reactionary henchmen personally loyal to him.

STUART

129

The Ambassador in China (Stuart) to Secretary Marshall

893.00/7-547

NANKING, *July 5, 1947*

Following is the text of the resolution on general national mobilization passed by the State Council July 4:

With a view to delivering the people from Communist-held areas, safeguarding the existence of the nation, and consolidating national unity, it is herein proposed that a national general mobilization be enforced to quell the rebellion of the Chinese Communists and remove obstacles to democracy, thereby inaugurating constitutional government according to schedule and implementing thoroughly the program of peaceful national reconstruction:

Following the conclusion of the war, the government immediately embarked upon rehabilitation in order that reconstruction might be launched to resuscitate the people. Admittedly, not all of its administrative measures succeeded as expected.

With regard to the acts of the Chinese Communist Party in carrying out its regional domination through its own army, ravaging towns and cities, and staging armed rebellion against the state, the government consistently and steadfastly held to the policy of political settlement and, to seek its materialization, exercised utmost tolerance and made most liberal concessions.

Since October last year, however, the Chinese Communist Party have renounced the cease-fire orders issued by the Government, boycotted the National Assembly, and furthermore, rejected the Government proposal to send a representative to Yenan for peace negotiations. Lately, the Chinese Communists, through their propaganda organ, flatly turned down the peace proposal initiated by the People's Political Council.

While the Government is concentrating on the reorganization of the army the Chinese Communists are expanding their armed forces to coerce the people. While the Government is engaged in rehabilitation and reconstruction the Communist rebels are everywhere obstructing the work and destroying communications and industrial and mining enterprises. While the Government is devoting itself to the realization of democratic rule and the preparation for inauguration of constitutional government, the Communist rebels are advocating democracy and persecuting people at the same time.

In recent months, the Communist rebels launched large-scale offensives against National troops in North and Northeast China to prevent the Government from taking over national territory and sovereignty. Their intention of destroying the nation is evident and their rebellious actions of instigating riots to disturb social peace and order are obvious.

The Communist rebels, in openly starting their all-out armed rebellion, have practically ostracized themselves from the people of China. In fact, they have long considered themselves as an armed rebellious group rather than a political party. Apparently they are ready to go any length to antagonize the nation. They are so obdurate and incorrigible that the Government's policy to achieve peaceful national reconstruction can no longer be realized through political means.

The suffering of our compatriots in Communist-devastated North China and regions near Communist-held areas is daily aggravating. The Government should no longer fail to redeem its negligence and remain callous to the people's afflictions. The people of the nation, in order to live and work peacefully, must make every effort to remove this greatest obstacle to national reconstruction. Otherwise, they cannot safeguard the foundation of the nation and stabilize social order to ensure security for the country and the people.

It is the duty and responsibility of the Government to achieve unity in the nation and safeguard the survival of its people. If the Communist rebellion is not speedily suppressed, not only constitutional democracy cannot be realized, but unity and security of the nation will not be ensured. It is, therefore, with great reluctance that the Government has determined to quell the Communist rebellion. To remove the obstacles in the way of constitutional democracy, and to attain the final aim of national reconstruction, we must intensify our campaign against the Communists and, at the same time, redouble our efforts in reconstruction, which are to be achieved only through a singleness of purpose and marshalling of national resources.

With this purpose in view, it is proposed that the State Council order a national general mobilization and encourage the people to help in its execution. Plans concerning the acceleration of economic reconstruction, the reform of local governments, the mobilization of manpower and resources, the improvement of food and conscription administrations, the maintenance of social order, the mitigation of the people's sufferings, the protection of their basic rights, the practice of thrift, the increases of agricultural and industrial production, and the amelioration of the treatment of officers and men shall be carefully drafted by the competent authorities and enforced in accordance with law. The competent authorities shall also be instructed to guard against abuses in the execution of those plans.

STUART

130

Central News Agency Bulletin Dated July 5, 1947 [8]

893.00/7-847

General Chang Chun, President of the Executive Yuan, declared in an exclusive interview with Central News this evening that the government is determined to restore national unity through the suppression of the Communist rebellion and to accomplish national reconstruction and rejuvenation by hard self-exertion.

General Chang said that the Executive Yuan received instructions from the National Government yesterday to enforce national general mobilization, to remove obstacles to democracy and to carry out the peaceful reconstruction policy. This is an important step taken by the government for speeding up national reconstruction and it will be put into execution immediately, General Chang added.

Explaining the reason why the government should enforce a national general mobilization to quell the Communist rebellion, General Chang said that the government is deeply concerned over the sufferings of the people and is forced to take military action immediately to quell the Communist rebellion which, otherwise, would probably destroy the whole nation.

China had hoped to embark upon national reconstruction, to democratize her government and to industrialize her economy immediately after the Sino-Japanese war, General Chang recalled, but unfortunately, during the war the Communists took advantage of national grievance, expanded their armed forces which after the war have constituted a serious obstacle to the reconstruction of the country.

The protracted peace negotiations between the government and the Communists, the convocation of the Political Consultation Conference and the mediation of American friends have all failed to stop the Communists' sinister ambition to seize political power by military force, General Chang remarked. During the past two months, the Communists have further intensified their subversive activities, starting open armed rebellion, persecuting the people and destroying whatever construction work the government has done, he added.

The significance of the general mobilization is to rally the national will and strength to speed up political and economic reconstruction by removing all

---

[8] Transmitted by the Ambassador from Nanking, July 8, 1947.

obstacles, General Chang asserted. It is a struggle between the constructive force and destructive force as well as a struggle between the democratic force and the anti-democratic force. It is quite unexpected that China in the course of national reconstruction should have to pass through such a period. Now that it has been forced upon us, we must rally our national strength to overcome all difficulties. We are determined to restore national unity through the suppression of the Communist rebellion and to accomplish national reconstruction through hard self-exertion. The stronger is our will the shorter will be this difficult period, General Chang opined.

The national general mobilization is more positive for national reconstruction than for the suppression of the Communist rebellion, General Chang said. When the nation is striving for peace and unity, the Premier said, all the people should place the interests of the state above their own. The government should respect the rights and freedoms of the people and the people should also respect law and strengthen their sense of responsibility toward the state.

During the period of national general mobilization, the government will see that all orders are faithfully and promptly carried out he said. Government officials should win the confidence and cooperation of the people and coordination among various government departments should be further strengthened. Corruption and delinquency among government officials and armed forces should be wiped out, General Chang emphasized.

Reviewing the history of national revolution, General Chang expressed the belief that China's national reconstruction can never be obstructed by any reactionary force. Now that the government has determined to suppress the Communist rebellion and consolidate national unity, the people all over the country are expected to support the government's policy and contribute their share to bring the task to consummation, General Chang concluded.

131

Radio Broadcast on July 7, 1947, by President Chiang Kai-shek [8a]

893.00/7–1147

My Fellow-countrymen:

On this, the tenth anniversary of the Double Seventh, I feel called upon to earnestly inform you of the following major happenings since the conclusion of the war: the change of our national situation, the crisis confronting our nation as a whole, and the factors that will determine our destiny.

It was primarily to defend her domain, recover the Northeast and preserve her sovereign and territorial integrity that China fought the Japanese aggressor. She will never attain her war aim so long as her sovereignty and territorial administration in the Northeast remain unrestored, nor will the death of millions of Chinese soldiers and civilians be vindicated. The responsibility, therefore, falls equally on the shoulders of the survivors.

In the Northeast, as everybody knows, there were no Chinese Communist rebels prior to the Japanese capitulation. In the one and a half year, however, since National troops entered that part of the country to take over sovereignty there, Communist rebels at different times launched five offensives against Na-

---

[8a] Issued by the National Government Information Office, Nanking, July 7, 1947.

tional troops. They besieged and attacked areas already taken over by the Government, carved up the territory, and slaughtered the populace.

Lately, the Communists' reply to the peace proposal from the People's Political Council was first, a barrage of vituperatives through their propaganda machine, and then a series of fanatical thrusts outside of the Great Wall. The latest Communist offensive in the Northeastern provinces, because of its unprecedented magnitude, is especially significant. Since early May, the Communists, in powerful thrusts, have thrown more than 300,000 men against various strategic bases. Finally, they focussed their attacks on one single locality, Szepingkai, employing a force that outnumbered the defenders ten to one. The battle raged for 18 days and nights.

Thanks to the fighting stamina of our forces developed during the war against Japan, the invading Communists were given a decimating blow. Their plot to encircle Changchun and Kirin and seize Shenyang (Mukden) was crushed, and the tide of war turned in our favor.

Under no circumstances, however, will the Communist rebels abandon their consistent, insidious design of ruining their own fatherland. It cannot be conceded that the Szepingkai victory may have fundamentally removed the crisis facing the Northeast. Everyone knows well just how the Chinese Communist rebels entered the Northeast and how the various rebellious units there were organized.

The Chinese Communists patently are heir to imperialistic Japan and the "Manchoukuo" puppets, and they are now in the process of carrying out the pernicious plot to distintegrate China which was left unfinished by their Japanese predecessors. That plot would not permit restoration of Northeast sovereignty to the Chinese nation nor would it allow the Chinese nation to enjoy territorial and administrative integrity.

Worse still, the Chinese Communists have even made a cat's paw of remnant Japanese troops to ravage our territory and people at their command. In perversion, malignancy and treachery, the Chinese Communists indeed are worse than any bandit, traitor or puppet in Chinese history.

Fellow-countrymen, we must realize that, in thus engaging in armed rebellion, the Communists aim to disintegrate all of China and our whole nation. They seek total elimination of our national spirit and hereditary virtues, eternal enslavement of our race, and the complete deprivation of the basic human attributes of independence and freedom.

Should the Communists, indulging in such bestial acts of destroying human instincts and suppressing human ethical concepts, be allowed to continue to exist, the Chinese nation would in the near future suffer the disaster of national extinction with indiscriminate, wholesale massacre, collective banishment and eternal slavery for all the composite racial groups.

The aim of our National Revolution is to build a new, independent, free China—of the people governed for the people and by the people—on the basis of the Three People's Principles. To build such a nation requires, first of all, national unity and peace. Without national unity, however, there can be no national peace. Nor can there be democracy and liberty. National unity is all the more important for the people's welfare. Therefore, if national unity cannot be achieved, the ideal of national reconstruction will remain illusory and the Principles of Nationalism, Democracy and People's Livelihood can never be realized. The people naturally cannot enjoy normal life when their land is being devastated, their economy monopolized, their production destroyed and their communications disrupted by the Communists.

You may still remember my earnest appeal to the Communist Party after V-J Day: "With the devastating war barely ended, there should not be any civil strife." No responsible government or patriotic individual would let the country and the people fall into another war when they are still suffering from the ravages of a large-scale war.

We have never attempted to castigate communism as a theory or ideal. We continued to hope that the Communists might follow the course of democracy, as the Communists in Great Britain and the United States have done for so many years, by appealing to the electorate for support of their platform. We have been consistent for the past ten years, and even more so in the last year and a half, in our attitude toward the Communists. We have practised extreme tolerance and we have made substantial compromises and concessions, in the hope that the Communists would refrain from disrupting national unity, carrying on military regional domination, and undermining the foundation of the nation, and that they would contribute their share in national reconstruction. The Government was willing to give full consideration to their opinions. But no peace talk, no mediation, has succeeded in dissuading the Communists from staging a rebellion. We had no way of appealing to their conscience to give up their destructive policy in the interest of the nation and the people.

The activities of the Communist rebels in the past year or so were centered in the destruction of communication lines, industrial and mining plants and the already-depleted farms. Every attempt of the Government to appeal for peace and every issuance of a cease-fire order only brought further expansion and attacks of the Communist rebels, which added more difficulties to the National Armies and increased the sufferings and sacrifices of the people, thus creating unparalleled difficulties in our postwar social revival. Now, all fellow countrymen can rest assured that the Communists, whose rebellious character does not seem to change for the better, have no faith in repentance, and apparently are determined to rebel to the last. Their ambition and intrigues will not be halted until the country is ruined and the world as a whole menaced. If we do not discern the treacherous plots of the Communists, and if we are not determined to quell their rebellion, not only will the people's livelihood be impoverished, but the whole country will be disintegrated.

It was the pre-determined policy of the Chinese Communists to rebel against the Government after the conclusion of the war. After V-J Day, they openly launched the so-called "join-the-army movement," "social struggles," and "people's liquidation," in the rebel areas. They looted what food and clothing they could find in order to conserve their rebellious strength. Not even the old men and women or the children are spared from their terrorism and wantoness. Youngsters in rebel areas must either follow their dictates or perish, and burial alive or torture are meted out if the slightest opposition is shown. If a man escapes from rebel control, his whole family is executed. Thousands upon thousands of our compatriots in rebel areas have become sacrifices to the Communists, who have opposed the Government and menaced the people.

In provinces away from the front, especially in large cities of Central and South China, there are still many who do not realize the gravity of our national crisis and the vicious and sinister terrorism of the Communists. They are deluding themselves into false security. They must realize that if it had not been for the struggles of our soldiers to quell the Communist rebellion, they could not maintain their normal living and would be placed in the same tragic conditions as people in North and Northeastern China. Therefore, if we weaken the strength of the National Army, we will deprive the people of their right to exist. Because the people remote from the front are not aware of the realities of the situation, the Communists instigate their reactionary elements everywhere to disseminate anti-civil war and anti-conscription of food and soldiers slogans in an attempt to confuse right and wrong, drug people's minds, bewilder the masses and finally weaken the national foundation. This has been done to prevent us from mustering our man power and resources for suppressing the Communist rebellion and hastening reconstruction.

We can say that our people are being poisoned by Communist propaganda. It is evident that the Communists, in order to implement their plot to betray the country and the people, are trying to blindfold us and deaden our conscience. The aim of the Communists is to confuse the people so they will ignore their national consciousness and the disaster which confronts them and lose their faith in self-improvement and independence, thus falling spiritual captives to the Communists.

The existing confused situation is what the Communists hoped to create. An old saying goes: "A bird nesting on a falling bough is unaware of imminent disaster." As a matter of fact, if the nest eventually falls, none of the eggs will remain unbroken. Fellow-countrymen, procrastination now will bring death in the near future. It will be too late for regret if we fall into the same pit as our compatriots in the rebel areas. Our country and the destiny of all our people face such a serious crisis that I cannot delay calling upon you to be on the alert.

Fellow-countrymen, there are two ways before us and we must immediately choose between them. The first is to vacillate before the ravages and devastation of the Communists and our whole people will perish. The other is to face the facts realistically, put down the rebellious elements and salvage our nation as well as ourselves. Shall we choose to quell the Communist rebellion with concerted efforts, so as to protect our sovereignty, hasten national unity and attain the goal of freedom and democracy? Or, shall we procrastinate before Communist vandalism and see our villages pillaged, our kinsmen humiliated, our children compelled to become instruments of betrayal, and eventually our national life ruined? We must remember how our compatriots are passing their days in North and Northeastern China.

The people in the Northeast underwent more than a decade of Japanese subjugation and enslavement. But since the war ended, Communist terrorism, suppression, looting, and massacring have superseded imperial Japan's despotic rule. During the war, people of North China sustained the greatest losses and underwent the severest tribulations. After the war, instead of having a breathing spell, they were again overrun, this time by the Communists, and thrown into another dark abyss. In their recent offensives the Communists made the "peoples' militia" spearhead the attacks. Wherever the Communists hit, they looted and took prisoners, not sparing even dogs and poultry. Their wantonness surpassed even that of the Japanese. Whenever the Communists occupy a place, tens of thousands of the inhabitants at great risk move into the Government-controlled areas to find shelter, leaving their homes and property behind them. Their lamentations are the most tragic human utterances. How can those of us remote from the front who have the same ancestral origin, remain indifferent to their lot. The aim of the Communist rebels is to exterminate the country and enslave us all. We must suppress the Communist rebels, otherwise we shall undergo the same sufferings in the near future.

With our rehabilitation work yet to be completed, I am fully aware that our people in the recovered areas are leading a hard life. At any rate, they obviously are far better off than their brethren in rebel areas where personal freedom, physical or spiritual, is absolutely forbidden. No whisperings are allowed even between father and son, husband and wife.

Therefore, not only does our suppression of the Communist rebels help to save our compatriots in the rebel areas, but it also helps to save ourselves. If we let the Communist rebellion spread unchecked, we would be inviting ruin. The ambition of the Communists is obvious, and it is our responsibility to quell them.

We suffered cruelly and sacrificed the lives of millions of soldiers and civilians during our war against the Japanese invaders. If we let the Communist rebels attain their goal of destroying the Government and erasing the history of our war of resistance, thus completing the unfinished task of the Japanese to exterminate China, how can the losses we suffered during the war be redeemed?

Suppression of the Communist rebellion, therefore, is aimed at preserving the highest interests of the state and the basic rights of existence, democracy, and liberty of the people. Our struggle against the Communist rebels is as sacred as was our resistance against the Japanese aggressor.

The call to crush the Communist rebels is a continuation of the unfinished task of national reconstruction after our war against Japan. This is necessary, as I have told you, if we are to preserve the fruits of victory. Such a struggle is inevitable if we are to secure national independence and liberty. This being the case, the National troops who have fought and died for the cause should be respected by the people the same as those who fought and died in the Sino-Japanese war. Our 450,000,000 people must not shirk the responsibility of supplying sufficient food and munitions to the National troops at the front. In this task of saving the nation and protecting the people, all persons in areas at the front and in the rear should share their joys and sorrows and decide to live and die together.

Fellow-countrymen, the Communist rebels' ambition has been completely exposed in the recent battles in the Northeast. The national crisis has become more and more serious. Our people should not harbor the illusion that they may avoid participating in the struggle through some lucky occurrence or temporary peace. We must concentrate on our strength and redouble our efforts in suppressing the Communists and reconstructing the nation, so as to eliminate the seeds of misfortune for our future generations. We must achieve national general mobilization with the same spirit as we did during the war of resistance, and we must multiply our efforts in eliminating the deficiencies we had during the war of resistance. We must not hesitate to contribute all our manpower, material strength and lives, if necessary, to the war of suppressing the rebellion in a common effort to save our country and people. Only in this way can we preserve the fruits of our victory over Japan, achieve national independence and liberty and retain the hope of again securing social peace and order.

Fellow-countrymen, the National Government has issued an order for the enforcement of national general mobilization. The purpose of the order is to awaken the people of the whole country to unify their purpose and concentrate their efforts for the struggle. We must call on all patriotic Chinese to rise for the salvation of their country and themselves.

All the measures taken by the Government will be in accordance with law. The Government has implicit faith in the people's patriotic conscience and will let the people themselves serve the country spontaneously on the basis of the principle of nationalism. Every compatriot must love the country and the people, observe national laws and perform his duty. He must make every effort to contribute his part in the suppression of the Communist rebellion and the promotion of national reconstruction.

The nation's social leaders should guide the people in promoting the cause in every possible way. Our youths in particular, upon whom our national existence depends, must discern right from wrong and fair from foul and promote nationalism to safeguard national existence. Unless the youths of China are willing to be Communist instruments and are indifferent about national extinction, they must recognize that they are descendents of Huang Ti and nationals of the Republic of China. If they wish the nation to achieve independence and existence, so that they may have freedom of thought without oppression by the Communists, they must be determined to face the national crisis. Those who go to schools should devote themselves to study, and those who are engaged in agriculture, industry and business must devote themselves to production, so as to increase national strength. Everybody must play his part and do his duty in an effort to stabilize social peace and order in the rear.

Our people must know that the nation-wide Communist rebellion is coordinated and linked up with the Communists' well-planned destruction of social order. Ever since the beginning of our resistance against the Japanese, the Communist Party has consistently disparaged the war efforts of the Government with vituperative propaganda in an effort to undermine the Government. This was done to arouse discord between the Government and the people, weaken our strength in the war, relegate the international position of the nation, erase the history of our war of resistance, minimize the people's faith in winning the war and deaden the people's patriotism.

The Communists not only spread rumors and instigate riots in schools, among the people, in factories and in financial markets, but they also openly declare that such riotous and destructive actions are "the second front" as distinguished from "the first front," military operations. These two fronts are interdependent, so that military operations can disturb the community in the rear and riots in the rear can affect the troops at the front. This is malicious intrigue, and I must call it to your attention so that you may take timely precautions.

I can assure you that the Government's enforcement of national general mobilization will be in accordance with law. All military and administrative organs will respect the basic rights of the people. But anyone who disregards the national crisis and principle of nationalism, and who is willing to take part in the work of "the second front," disturbing social order and jeopardizing public safety under Communist direction, will be punished by the Government according to law, which is responsible for the maintenance of national existence and people's welfare.

At this time, when the war of suppression against the Communist rebels is developing and National troops are fighting at the front, all our patriotic countrymen must struggle with one object in view,—unified strength, definite aim and positive efforts,—so as to solidify our military strength and achieve early suppression of the rebellious forces.

The Government's policy regarding the present situation can be seen in the resolution of the State Council. The national general mobilization has been promulgated not only for the suppression of the Communist rebellion, but also for national reform and reconstruction. Therefore, I wish to point out the following two matters:

First, we must work for national reconstruction. To carry the reconstruction work to completion, we must concentrate today on the suppression of the Communist rebellion by marshalling our spiritual and physical strength, thereby realizing internal unity. We must at the same time intensify our efforts to increase agricultural and industrial production so as to frustrate the Communist intrigue to undermine the national economy by throwing obstacles in the way of reconstruction.

The progress made in the promotion of and the preparation for the inauguration of constitutional democracy will not be impeded by the suppression campaign. The Communists renounced constitutional democracy by boycotting the National Assembly and obstructing the progress of national reconstruction, although they have proclaimed that they are dedicated to democracy. From this, we can see that the Communists are fundamentally opposed to the enforcement of constitutionalism in China and to the accomplishment of national reconstruction. If the Constitution is enforced in China, the Communists will have to relinquish their military forces, and they will be deprived of their chief reliance, rebellion.

If China adopts political democracy, the people will become masters of their own destiny, and dictatorship of the proletarian, advocated by the Communists, can never be realized. Following the institution of constitutional democracy, the Government will embark on the necessary work of economic reconstruction, and the Communists will be unable to create social disturbances and capitalize on them to establish a Soviet regime.

It is on this basis that I want to emphasize to my fellow-countrymen, and especially to those who are actually striving for the realization of freedom in China and the democratization of our Government, that to attain constitutional democracy we must first eliminate the Communist rebels whose principles run counter to constitutional democracy and peaceful reconstruction. To save China from terror and chaos, we are duty bound to expedite the preparations for constitution enforcement, carry out completely the Principle of People's Livelihood and safeguard the people's basic rights. This being our consistent policy, we shall never slacken our efforts toward its realization.

Second, we must exert our utmost to effect administrative reforms. We have committed ourselves to a dual political program: to quell the Communist rebellion and introduce governmental reforms. Admittedly many defects exist in our administration. Weaknesses can also be found in our way of life. Immediately after the conclusion of the eight-year war, the Communist rebellion began, thus, we have been given no time to put our house in order. Our material resources, already drained by the war, are practically exhausted. The defects and weaknesses in the Government and in our way of life, which first made their appearance in the war, have now become more apparent. The sufferings of the people have immeasurably increased. Unless drastic reforms are introduced, China may not be able to exist in the family of nations. Therefore, political, educational, economic and social reforms, which should be made, shall not be delayed until the conclusion of the suppression campaign, but will be initiated right away.

We should seek to increase our national strength, mitigate the people's sufferings, and concentrate our will power to effect a thorough going reform so as to overcome all difficulties confronting us. Constructive criticisms and suggestions from the people on our political and economic policies and especially ways to alleviate the people's afflictions will be sincerely received by the Government, and measures for improvement will be instigated. It is also expected that people will report, with substantial evidence, mistakes made by governments of all levels, so that reforms may be made.

It was for the purpose of concentrating our efforts to effect an over-all reform and remove all obstacles in the way of national reconstruction that national general mobilization was ordered. It is therefore positive rather than negative in nature; it is nation-wide rather than local in scope. It is obligatory not only for the people, but for governments of all levels to seek improvement.

Dedicated to national revolution, I have struggled for the existence of the country and the people, the realization of the Three People's Principles, unity in the nation and the inauguration of constitutional democracy. I have never been mindful of personal gains or losses, glories or eclipses. All I can offer you is my sincerity to save the country and the people. I cannot betray our founding father and our martyrs. I cannot betray the cause of national revolution, for which I have fought so long. I cannot betray the soldiers and the civilians who died in the War of Resistance. I must preserve to the best of my ability the achievements of the eight-year war. I must lead the nation to crush the enemies who are obstructing the realization of our principles, destroying national unity and interfering with our efforts for peaceful reconstruction. I shall not waver till the final aim is achieved.

My fellow-countrymen! On this solemn occasion, I call for a rededication to the unfinished task of national reconstruction and a revival of the same spirit and energy manifested when we fought against the aggressors. At the conclusion of the war I said that the task of national reconstruction would be ten times more difficult than the military victory. In view of the accumulated effects of internal troubles and external aggressions over the last hundred years and the infirm basis on which this Republic was founded, we cannot make a new, indepedent, powerful and prosperous China in a day. But we can count on our long history, large population and the moral strength of our people. I am sure with these assets we shall be able to destroy the force that is hampering our reconstruction.

If only the entire population will rise up against the Communist rebels as they did against the Japanese, if only they will use the same determination and perseverance to deal with the Communist insurgents as they did in the War of Resistance, then the suppression of the Communist rebellion can be effected within a short period of time. Once this great difficulty is overcome, and the final obstacle removed, China will enter upon a glorious stage. We should not be distracted by Communist propaganda or dismayed by present difficulties, but should retain our self-confidence.

I hope we shall always remember our unflinching faith in ultimate victory during the War of Resistance and our strong determination to carry the work of national reconstruction to completion. By quelling the Communist rebellion and overcoming the last obstacle, we can expect to accomplish the important task of national reconstruction, and vindicate the sacrifice of soldiers and civilians who died in the War of Resistance and in the suppression campaign.

132

The Ambassador in China (Stuart) to Secretary Marshall

893.00/7–2147

NANKING, *July 21, 1947*

Following was published in Central News Agency English Service, dated July 19:

"Following is the text of 'The Outline for the Implementation of Mobilization to Suppress Rebellion and Complete Constitutional Government' which was adopted by the State Council today (July 18, 1947), to become effective immediately:

"Article 1. This outline has been formulated in accordance with the stipulations of the program for the enforcement of national general mobilization to suppress the Communist rebellion, remove obstacles to democracy and realize constitutional government as scheduled, which was adopted by the State Council, and the provisions of the National General Mobilization Act (promulgated by the National Government on March 29, 1942, and put into effect on May 5, 1942).

"Article 2. Enforcement of constitutional government and conducting of elections in connection therewith shall all be expedited as stipulated.

"Article 3. Manpower necessary for military, labor and other services required to suppress the rebellion shall be fully mobilized. Any action to evade or obstruct such services shall be punished in accordance with law.

"Article 4. All materials required to suppress the rebellion, including foodstuffs, clothing, medicine, oil, coal, iron and steel, transportation and communication equipment, and other supplies needed by the military, shall be immediately mobilized. Any action to evade or obstruct requisitioning of such supplies, hoard them or profiteer from them shall be punished in accordance with law.

"Article 5. Close cooperation shall be maintained between management and labor in all enterprises. All disputes shall be mediated or arbitrated in accordance with law. Sabotage, tne in-outs or any other actions hampering production or disturbing social order shall be punished in accordance with law.

"Article 6. In order to stabilize the people's livelihood, the government may institute restrictions or controls over market prices of daily necessities, salaries and wages, the flow of materials, use of capital and other financial activities.

"Article 7. The Government shall, in accordance with law, take punitive measures against assemblies where speeches or other actions incite the people to rebellion.

"Article 8. In areas recovered from rebels, authorities concerned shall consolidate security measures and maintain social order. When necessary, loans may be extended, taxes in the areas suspended and social relief and medical aid carried out.

"Article 9. Refugees from rebel-held areas shall be given adequate relief, assistance and accommodation by authorities concerned.

"Article 10. Authorities concerned shall direct needs. In case of a shortage in capital, government banks may grant loans in order to increase supplies. If necessary, the Government may exercise control over finished products.

"Article 11. In areas free from the Communist rebels, local administration shall be revamped and social peace and order safeguarded. To improve the people's livelihood, priority shall be given to urgent projects of production, transportation, irrigation and water conservancy.

"Article 12. Equitable taxation shall be increased and unnecessary expenditure curtailed in order to finance the suppression of the rebellion.

"Article 13. Measures shall be formulated to enforce thrift and increase efficiency, for observance by both the Government and the people.

"Article 14. Basic rights of the people shall be fully respected and adequately safeguarded. Any impingement thereupon shall be strictly prohibited, unless necessitated by laws and decrees required for the implementation of mobilization and the suppression of the rebellion.

"Article 15. Where there is need for separate detailed measures for the implementation of the outline, such measures shall be drawn up by the Ministers and commissions of the Executive Yuan concerned, and, after their approval by the Yuan, promulgated by mandates for enforcement.

"Article 16. Violation of Articles 3 to 7 of the outline or any action that would be outlawed and restrained in accordance with the stipulations of these articles shall be punished in accordance with the provisional penal regulations for obstructors of National General Mobilization Act (promulgated by the National Government on June 29, 1942, and put into force on August 1, 1942).

"Public functionaries who, in the exercise of authority delegated to them under the outline, break the law or neglect their duties shall be punished in accordance with law.

"Article 17. In addition to the stipulations of the outline, the Executive Yuan may, in accordance with the provisions of the National General Mobilization Act, at any time issue mandates to expedite the suppression of the rebellion.

"Article 18. The outline shall be promulgated for enforcement after approval by the State Council."

133

Summary of Remarks Made by Lieutenant General Albert C. Wedemeyer Before Joint Meeting of State Council and All Ministers of the National Government August 22, 1947 [9]

121.893/8–2547

TAXATION:

Approximately 80 percent of the people of China are hard working peasants, their crops are visible and officials can easily appraise the amounts the peasants are able to give toward government. Corrupt officials in many instances take more than the peasants are able to give and this results finally in the peasants leaving the land and forming bandit groups.

In contrast to the taxation of peasants, Chinese businessmen and rich Chinese resort to devious and dishonest methods to avoid payment of proper taxes to their government. It is commonly known that Chinese business firms maintain two sets of books, one showing the true picture of business transactions and the other showing a distorted picture so that they do not pay as much tax as they should.

MILITARY:

For the first year after the war, in my opinion it was possible to stamp out or at least to minimize the effect of Chinese Communists. This capability was predicated upon the assumption that the Central Government disposed its military forces in such a manner as to insure control of all industrial areas, food producing areas, important cities and lines of communication. It was also assumed that the Central Government appointed highly efficient and scrupulously honest officials as provincial governors, district magistrates, mayors, and throughout the political and economic structure. If these assumptions had been accomplished, political and economic stability would have resulted, and the people would not have been receptive, in fact, would have strongly opposed the infiltration or penetration of communistic ideas. It would not have been possible for the Chinese Communists to expand so rapidly and acquire almost undisputed control of such vast areas. I believe that the Chinese Communist movement

[9] Transmitted by the Ambassador in China (Stuart) to Secretary Marshall, Nanking, Aug. 25, 1947.

cannot be defeated by the employment of force. Today China is being invaded by an idea instead of strong military forces from the outside. The only way in my opinion to combat this idea successfully is to do so with another idea that will have stronger appeal and win the support of the people. This means that politically and economically the Central Government will have to remove corruption and incompetence from its ranks in order to provide justice and equality and to protect the personal liberties of the Chinese people, particularly of the peasants. To recapitulate, the Central Government cannot defeat the Chinese Communists by the employment of force, but can only win the loyal, enthusiastic and realistic support of the masses of the people by improving the political and economic situation immediately. The effectiveness and timeliness of these improvements will determine in my opinion whether or not the Central Government will stand or fall before the Communist onslaught.

During the war while serving as the Generalissimo's Chief-of-Staff, I tried to impress upon all Chinese military officials the importance of re-establishing excellent relationships between officers and enlisted men. I explained that officers must show sincere interest in the welfare of their men both in times of war and in peace. Wounded must be evacuated from the battlefield and cared for in hospitals or aid stations. Officers should visit their men in the hospital and find out if they can visit them in any way. Officers should play games with their soldiers such as basketball and soccer. The junior officers should know all of their men in the unit by name. They should talk to them and encourage them to discuss their problems. Explain to them why they are fighting. Explain the objectives of their Government and encourage open discussions. This will create a feeling of mutual respect and genuine affection. Discipline acquired through fear is not as effective as discipline acquired through affection and mutual respect. It would be so easy for the Chinese officers to win the respect and admiration of their men who are simple, kindly and brave and who will gladly endure hardships and dangers if they are properly led and cared for.

Conscription:

I have received many reports that the conscription of men for military service is not being carried out honestly or efficiently. Again, as in taxation peasants are expected to bear the brunt of conscription, although in the cities there are thousands and thousands of able-bodied men, who should be under the conscription laws eligible for military service. Rich men's sons by the payment of money avoid conscription and the sons of rich men are being sent to school abroad instead of remaining here to help their country in a time of great crisis.

Relationship Between Military and Civilians:

I cannot emphasize too strongly the importance of establishing and maintaining good relationship between military forces and the civilian population. Officers and men in the army and air corps should be very careful to be courteous, friendly, cooperative and honest in all of their contacts with civilians. In Manchuria, I was told by many sources that the Central Government armies were welcomed enthusiastically by the people as deliverers from Japanese oppression. Today, after several months of experience with these Central Government armies, the people experience a feeling of hatred and distrust because the officers and enlisted men were arrogant and rude. Also they stole and looted freely; their general attitude was that of conquerors instead of that of deliverers. In Formosa the reports are exactly the same, alienating the Formosans from the

Central Government. All of this is a matter of discipline. Of course if the officers themselves are dishonest or discourteous, one can hardly expect the enlisted men to be otherwise. Good relations between the military forces and the civilians are absolutely essential if the Central Government expects to bring about successful conclusion of operations against the Communists. At first the Communist armies were also crude and destructive and made the people hate even, but in the past few weeks, they have adopted an entirely new approach which requires their officers and men to be very careful in all their relations with civilian communities. You can understand therefore how important it is that your own military forces adopt steps immediately to improve the conditions that I have mentioned.

Promotion in the military service should be by merit and merit alone. Older officers or incompetent ones should be retired and relieved. The retired officers should realize that they must make room for the younger ones and they must accept retirement patriotically and philosophically. There are entirely too many Generals in the Chinese Army. Most of them are not well-educated and are not well versed in modern combat. Generals should never be used in civilian posts of responsibility, for example, as governors, mayors and magistrates, except perhaps as Minister of Defense. Military men should not be permitted to belong to a particular political party. After the constitution goes into effect on December 25, they should be permitted to cast a vote, in other words, exercise the right of suffrage, but no military men should be permitted to hold government office or be active members of a political party.

GOVERNMENT ORGANIZATION:

I have carefully studied the existing organization of the government. In my opinion a definite clear-cut delineation of the authorities and functions of each major division of the government from the State Council on down to subdivisions of the ministries, is urgently required. At present there is an overlapping of responsibilities and authorities causing frictions and inefficiencies. Also a tremendous streamlining program is necessary within each government ministry or bureau. There are entirely too many employees, this would effect economy in manpower and in funds and I am sure would bring about efficiency. In studying your government organization, for example, I could not determine the exact authority and function of the National Assembly and Legislative Yuan with regard to the enactment of legislation. There must be a streamlined organization and clear cut enunciation in the duties of all of the ministries and bureaus of the government. In April a year ago I discovered that there were well over 60 sections in the National Military Council with duplicating functions and conflicting authorities. There was little coordination between the various groups or sections. Actually there were some groups within the National Military Council that were handling matters which had nothing whatsoever to do with national defense matters. Today in the Ministry of Defense we have grouped 60 sections under 6 general heads and reduced the personnel about 50 percent. Actually over 75,000 individuals were eliminated.

CORRUPTION:

One hears reports on all sides concerning corruption among government officials, high and low and also throughout the economic life of the country. With spiralling inflation, the pay of government officials both in civil service and in military service is wholly inadequate. I am sure that persons who are presently practicing dishonest methods would never consider doing so were it not for the fact that they receive insufficient remuneration to meet the bare necessities of life. Many of them are not trying to acquire vast fortunes, but are just trying to provide a standard of living commensurate with their position. On the other hand, certain rich families, some of whom have relatives in high positions of the government, have been greatly increasing their fortunes. Nepotism is rife and in my investigations I have found that sons, nephews and brothers of government officials have been put in positions within the government, sponsored firms, or in private firms to enable them to make huge profits at the expense of their government and their people. It would be interesting and revealing if you would conduct an investigation into various large banking organizations and other newly created business organizations, to ascertain how much money has been made by such organizations and to what individuals or groups of individuals the money has been paid. To reduce corruption, it will be necessary to establish an index of the standard of living and as the exchange rises the pay of civil service and military service must be increased accordingly. I should emphasize that I am sure many patriotic and selfless Chinese are eking out a bare existence under difficult conditions. They are a great credit to China. However, it must be very discouraging to them to realize that many who already had amassed great fortunes have taken advantage of the present unfortunate situation in China to increase their wealth.

NATIONAL ASSETS AND RESOURCES:

I have just completed an extensive tour in England and on Continental Europe. I made a survey of conditions in those areas such as I have just completed in China. The people in Europe are hungry. They have very limited fuel to keep them warm and to run the utilities such as electric power and to provide water. It is difficult for them to obtain as much as 1500 calories a day, which is barely enough to keep a healthy person moving about. Here in China there are untold resources, food, raw materials and manpower. It should be at once apparent that organization and honest, efficient administration will strongly contribute to alleviate your problems.

There are approximately ten million Chinese citizens living abroad. These Chinese in many instances are financially able to help their country in this time of dire necessity. Also there are many Chinese here in China who have vast sums of money invested abroad. They should be required to make a complete report on their holdings in securities and capital goods. It has been conservatively estimated in America that they could raise at least one billion United States dollars from these sources. China is far from bankrupt in a financial sense or with regard to material resources. China is practically bankrupt in spiritual resources. If the people of China really love their country and want it to emerge strong and united, they should be prepared to come forward and make any sacrifice, including their lives if necessary. Again I should like to emphasize that it is predominantly the poor people, the peasants, who are making great sacrifices and predominantly the rich class who are not coming forward to assist their country.

PUNISHMENT AND SECRET POLICE:

I have had reported to me many instances of misdirection and abuse in meting out punishments to offenders political or otherwise. In Formosa there are many so-called political offenders who are still in prison without any charges or sentences. Some have been released but only after paying large sums of money and being required to sign a statement to the effect that they were guilty of an offense against the government. Actually in their hearts and minds they did not feel that they were guilty of such offense. Secret police operate widely, very much as they do in Russia and as they did in Germany. People disappear. Students are thrown into jail. No trials and no sentences. Actions of this nature do not win support for the government. Quite the contrary. Everyone lives with a feeling of fear and loses confidence in the government.

RESTORATION AND REVITALIZING CHINESE ECONOMY

State ownership should be discouraged. Many Japanese Government and private Japanese properties in Formosa, Manchuria and other parts of China have been taken over by the Central Government. This was perfectly normal procedure, but the government should dispose of these properties as quickly as possible to private individuals or groups to encourage free enterprise. It should be a standing rule that persons in government service, civil or military, should not participate in speculative businesses, in banking and commercial enterprises.

FINAL REMARKS

The Government should not be worried about criticism. I think constructive criticism should be encouraged. It makes the people feel that they are participating in government; that they are members of the team. I have mentioned earlier the terrible economic conditions that exist in England. Criticism of the government is expressed freely in meetings on the streets, and in the press, and on the radio. This is in my opinion a healthy condition. The Government should point out that it is made up of human beings who are of course fallible and can make mistakes. The Government should emphasize, however, that once the mistakes are pointed out, effective steps will be taken to remedy them. The Government should publish information freely concerning expenditures, taxation. Let all the people know how much income tax each individual, particularly wealthy people and big business firms are paying. Announce publicly when any official or any individual has been guilty of some crime or offense and also indicate the punishment meted out. By the same token, announce publicly the accomplishment or good work of individual Government activities. All of these matters would contribute to confidence on the part of the people in the Government. They want to know what is going on and they have a right to know. Open and public official announcements on the part of the Government will also serve to stop malicious conjectures and adverse propaganda of opponents of the Government.

I realize that many of the ideas that I have expressed are quite contrary to Chinese tradition. However, I have carefully studied the philosophy of Confucius and I am sure that all of these ideas are in consonance with the fine principles of conduct that he prescribed. I have confidence in the good sound judgment and in the decency of the bulk of the Chinese peoples. I hope sincerely that you will accept my remarks in the same spirit in which they were given, namely, in the interest of China. Anything that I can do to help China become a strong, happy and prosperous nation, I would gladly do. Anything I could do to protect the sovereignty of China and to insure her a place of respect in the eyes of the world in the family of nations, I would gladly do.

ADDITIONAL POINTS:

1. A sign of general frustration on the part of Chinese officialdom.
2. Generalissimo's dabbling in all strata of government.
3. Weak Executive Yuan.
4. Urge closer relationship with the Generalissimo who should encourage criticism.

134

Statement of August 24, 1947, by Lieutenant General Albert C. Wedemeyer on the Conclusion of His Mission in China [10]

As promised in the initial press release, the inquiry into economic, political, military and social conditions has been undertaken without commitment or prejudgment.

All members of the mission have striven for objectivity and impartiality. To that end we have traveled widely to escape influences peculiar to any one area, visiting Mukden and Fusan, Manchuria; Peiping, Tientsin, Tsingtao and Tsinan in North China; Nanking, Shanghai and Hankow in Central China; Canton in South China, and also Taiwan (Formosa).

Successful efforts were made to reach all classes and categories of people as measured by economic position, intellectual attainment and divergent political viewpoints. Foreign business men and officials were interviewed. We have seen officials of national and local governments, members of various political organizations, many of whom were frankly critical of the government and some of whom were far Left in their views.

We have received approximately 2,000 letters, a small proportion of which were anonymous. These letters contained suggestions which we were able to follow up advantageously.

The last week of our stay in China was devoted chiefly to analyzing an enormous mass of data and in relating political, economic and other items together to reach sound judgments and conclusions.

Varied as were the views, there is one point on which all the hearts and minds of China unite: Throughout strife-torn China there is a passionate longing for peace, an early, lasting peace. I wish the means of attaining it were as easily discernible.

After V-J Day the Chinese people rightfully expected to enjoy the fruits of hard-earned victory. They endured hardships and dangers and suffered untold privations in their efforts to expel the ruthless invader.

In China today I find apathy and lethargy in many quarters. Instead of seeking solutions of problems presented, considerable time and effort are spent in blaming outside influences and seeking outside assistance.

It is discouraging to note the abject defeatism of many Chinese, who are normally competent and patriotic, and who instead should be full of hope and determination.

Weakened and disrupted by long years of war and revolution, China still possesses most of the physical resources needed for her own rehabilitation. Recovery awaits inspirational leadership and moral and spiritual resurgence which can only come from within China.

---

[10] Reprinted from the New York *Herald Tribune,* Aug. 25, 1947.

While I am fully aware of the interests and problems of particular individuals or groups within the country, I am profoundly concerned over the welfare of the Chinese people as a whole. It is my conviction that if the Chinese Communists are truly patriotic and interested primarily in the well-being of their country, they will halt the voluntary employment of force in efforts to impose ideologies. If they are sincere in a desire to help the Chinese people, they can better do so by peaceful means, in lieu of the violence and destruction which have marked these tragic months.

Equally important, the existing Central government can win and retain the undivided, enthusiastic support of the bulk of the Chinese people by removing incompetent and/or corrupt people who now occupy many positions of responsibility in the government, not only national but more so in provincial and municipal structures.

There are honorable officials who show high efficiency and devotion to duty, who strive to live within ridiculous salaries and such private means as they possess, just as there are conscientious businessmen who live up to a high code of commercial ethics. But no one will misunderstand my emphasis upon the large number whose conduct is notoriously marked by greed, incompetence or both.

To regain and maintain the confidence of the people, the Central government will have to effect immediately drastic, far-reaching political and economic reforms. Promises will no longer suffice. Performance is absolutely necessary. It should be accepted that military force in itself will not eliminate Communism.

On taking leave, all members of the mission join in expressing sincere gratitude for the assistance uniformly given by the Generalissimo and all patriotic Chinese with whom we had contact. All Americans hope and pray that China will achieve the unity, prosperity and happiness which her people so richly deserve and of which they have been unjustly deprived for so many years.

135

Report to President Truman by Lieutenant General Albert C. Wedemeyer, U. S. Army

19 September 1947.

MEMORANDUM FOR THE PRESIDENT [11]

My dear Mr. President: In compliance with your directive to me of 9 July 1947, the attached "Report on China-Korea" is respectfully submitted.

In consonance with your instructions, advisors from State, Treasury, War and Navy Departments accompanied me on a two months fact-finding mission in the Far East. The principal cities and some rural areas in China and Korea were visited. Successful efforts were made to reach all categories of people as measured by economic position, intellectual attainment and divergent political viewpoints. Conferences were held with public officials and with private citizens in all walks of life. Approximately 1,200 memoranda from individuals and groups were received and considered.

---

[11] All references to Korea have been deleted from General Wedemeyer's report itself as irrelevant to this paper.

ANNEXES 765

The report includes pertinent data in appendices which may be of interest and assistance to appropriate government departments and agencies. The report presents against a global background my estimates of the situations, current and projected, in both China and Korea, and recommends what I deem to be sound courses of action for achievement of United States objectives in the Far East.

Respectfully yours,

A. C. WEDEMEYER,
Lieutenant General, U. S. Army.

MEMBERS OF MISSION
16 July-18 September 1947

Captain James J. Boyle	Aide-de-Camp—Secretary, War Department.
Captain Horace Eng	Aide-de-Camp—Interpreter, War Department.
Lt. Colonel Claire E. Hutchin, Jr	Military Advisor, War Department.
Mr. David R. Jenkins	Fiscal Advisor, Treasury Department.
Mr. Philip D. Sprouse	Political Advisor, State Department.
Rear Admiral Carl A. Trexel	Engineering Advisor, Navy Department.
Mr. Melville H. Walker	Economic Advisor, State Department.
Mr. Mark S. Watson	Press and Public Affairs Advisor, Baltimore Sun, Baltimore, Md.
Lt. General A. C. Wedemeyer	Special Representative of the President of the United States.

INDEX

	Page
Part I General Statement	766
Part II China	769
Part IV Conclusions	773
Part V Recommendations	773

Appendix to Part I—General Statement

Directive to Lieutenant General Wedemeyer	774

Appendices to Part II—China

Appendix A—Political	775
Appendix B—Economic	780
Appendix C—Social-Cultural	806
Appendix D—Military	808

REPORT TO THE PRESIDENT

CHINA

PART I—General Statement

China's history is replete with examples of encroachment, arbitrary action, special privilege, exploitation, and usurpation of territory on the part of foreign powers. Continued foreign infiltration, penetration or efforts to obtain spheres of influence in China, including Manchuria and Taiwan (Formosa), could be interpreted only as a direct infringement and violation of China's sovereignty and a contravention of the principles of the Charter of the United Nations. It is mandatory that the United States and those other nations subscribing to the principles of the Charter of the United Nations should combine their efforts to insure the unimpeded march of all peoples toward goals that recognize the dignity of man and his civil rights and, further, definitely provide the opportunity to express freely how and by whom they will be governed.

Those goals and the lofty aims of freedom-loving peoples are jeopardized today by forces as sinister as those that operated in Europe and Asia during the ten years leading to World War II. The pattern is familiar—employment of subversive agents; infiltration tactics; incitement of disorder and chaos to disrupt normal economy and thereby to undermine popular confidence in government and leaders; seizure of authority without reference to the will of the people—all the techniques skillfully designed and ruthlessly implemented in order to create favorable conditions for the imposition of totalitarian ideologies. This pattern is present in the Far East, particularly in the areas contiguous to Siberia.

If the United Nations is to have real effect in establishing economic stability and in maintaining world peace, these developments merit high priority on the United Nations' agenda for study and action. Events of the past two years demonstrate the futility of appeasement based on the hope that the strongly consolidated forces of the Soviet Union will adopt either a conciliatory or a cooperative attitude, except as tactical expedients. Soviet practice in the countries already occupied or dominated completes the mosaic of aggressive expansion through ruthless secret police methods and through an increasing political and economic enslavement of peoples. Soviet literature, confirmed repeatedly by Communist leaders, reveals a definite plan for expansion far exceeding that of Nazism in its ambitious scope and dangerous implications. Therefore in attempting a solution to the problem presented in the Far East, as well as in other troubled areas of the world, every possible opportunity must be used to seize the initiative in order to create and maintain bulwarks of freedom.

Notwithstanding all the corruption and incompetence that one notes in China, it is a certainty that the bulk of the people are not disposed to a Communist political and economic structure. Some have become affiliated with Communism in indignant protest against oppressive police measures, corrupt practices and mal-administration of National Government officials. Some have lost all hope for China under existing leadership and turn to the Communists in despair. Some accept a new leadership by mere inertia.

Indirectly, the United States facilitated the Soviet program in the Far East by agreeing at the Yalta Conference to Russian re-entry into Manchuria, and later by withholding aid from the National Government. There were justifiable reasons for these policies. In the one case we were concentrating maximum Allied strength against Japanese in order to accelerate crushing defeat and thus save Allied lives. In the other, we were withholding unqualified support from a government within which corruption and incompetence were so prevalent that it was losing the support of its own people. Further, the United States had not yet realized that the Soviet Union would fail to cooperate in the accomplishment of world-wide plans for post-war rehabilitation. Our own participation in those plans has already afforded assistance to other nations and peoples, friends and former foes alike, to a degree unparalleled in humanitarian history.

Gradually it has become apparent that the World War II objectives for which we and others made tremendous sacrifices are not being fully attained, and that there remains in the world a force presenting even greater dangers to world peace than did the Nazi militarists and the Japanese jingoists. Consequently the United States made the decision in the Spring of 1947 to assist Greece and Turkey with a view to protecting their sovereignties, which were threatened by the direct or inspired activities of the Soviet Union. Charges of unilateral action and circumvention of the United Nations were made by members of that organization. In the light of its purposes and principles such criticisms seemed plausible. The United States promptly declared its intention of referring the matter to the United Nations when that organization would be ready to assume responsibility.

It follows that the United Nations should be informed of contemplated action with regard to China. If the recommendations of this report are approved, the United States should suggest to China that she inform the United Nations officially of her request to the United States for material assistance and advisory aid in order to facilitate China's post-war rehabilitation and economic recovery. This will demonstrate that the United Nations is not being circumvented, and that the United States is not infringing upon China's sovereignty, but contrary-wise is cooperating constructively in the interest of peace and stability in the Far East, concomitantly in the world.

The situation in Manchuria has deteriorated to such a degree that prompt action is necessary to prevent that area from becoming a Soviet satellite. The Chinese Communists may soon gain military control of Manchuria and announce the establishment of a government. Outer Mongolia, already a Soviet satellite, may then recognize Manchuria and conclude a "mutual support agreement" with a *de facto* Manchurian government of the Chinese Communists. In that event, the Soviet Union might accomplish a mutual support agreement with Communist-dominated Manchuria, because of her current similar agreement with Outer Mongolia. This would create a difficult situation for China, the United States and the United Nations. Ultimately it could lead to a Communist-dominated China.

The United Nations might take immediate action to bring about cessation of hostilities in Manchuria as a prelude to the establishment of a Guardianship or Trusteeship. The Guardianship might consist of China, Soviet Russia, the United States, Great Britain and France. This should be attempted promptly and could be initiated only by China. Should one of the nations refuse to participate in Manchurian Guardianship, China might then request the General Assembly of the United Nations to establish a Trusteeship, under the provisions of the Charter.

Initially China might interpret Guardianship or Trusteeship as an infringement upon her sovereignty. But the urgency of the matter should encourage a realistic view of the situation. If these steps are not taken by China, Manchuria may be drawn into the Soviet orbit, despite United States aid, and lost, perhaps permanently, to China.

The economic deterioration and the incompetence and corruption in the political and military organizations in China should be considered against an all-inclusive background lest there be disproportionate emphasis upon defects. Comity requires that cognizance be taken of the following:

Unlike other Powers since V-J Day, China has never been free to devote full attention to internal problems that were greatly confounded by eight years of war. The current civil war has imposed an overwhelming financial and economic burden at a time when resources and energies have been dissipated and when, in any event, they would have been strained to the utmost to meet the problems of recovery.

The National Government has consistently, since 1927, opposed Communism. Today the same political leader and same civil and military officials are determined to prevent their country from becoming a Communist-dominated State or Soviet satellite.

Although the Japanese offered increasingly favorable surrender terms during the course of the war, China elected to remain steadfast with her Allies. If China had accepted surrender terms, approximately a million Japanese would have been released for employment against American forces in the Pacific.

I was assured by the Generalissimo that China would support to the limit of her ability an American program for the stabilization of the Far East. He stated categorically that, regardless of moral encouragement or material aid received from the United States, he is determined to oppose Communism and to create a democratic form of government in consonance with Doctor Sun Yat-sen's principles. He stated further that he plans to make sweeping reforms in the government including the removal of incompetent and corrupt officials. He stated that some progress has been made along these lines but, with spiraling inflation, economic distress and civil war, it has been difficult to accomplish fully these objectives. He emphasized that, when the Communist problem is solved, he could drastically reduce the Army and concentrate upon political and economic reforms. I retain the conviction that the Generalissimo is sincere in his desire to attain these objectives. I am not certain that he has today sufficient determination to do so if this requires absolute overruling of the political and military cliques surrounding him. Yet, if realistic United States aid is to prove effective in stabilizing the situation in China and in coping with the dangerous expansion of Communism, that determination must be established.

Adoption by the United States of a policy motivated solely toward stopping the expansion of Communism without regard to the continued existence of an unpopular repressive government would render any aid ineffective. Further, United States prestige in the Far East would suffer heavily, and wavering elements might turn away from the existing government to Communism.

In China [and Korea], the political, economic and psychological problems are inextricably mingled. All of them are complex and are becoming increasingly difficult of solution. Each has been studied assiduously in compliance with your directive. Each will be discussed in the course of this report. However, it is recognized that a continued global appraisal is mandatory in order to preclude disproportionate or untimely assistance to any specific area.

The following three postulates of United States foreign policy are pertinent to indicate the background of my investigations, analyses and report:

The United States will continue support of the United Nations in the attainment of its lofty aims, accepting the possible development that the Soviet Union or other nations may not actively participate.

Moral support will be given to nations and peoples that have established political and economic structures compatible with our own, or that give convincing evidence of their desire to do so.

Material aid may be given to those same nations and peoples in order to accelerate post-war rehabilitation and to develop economic stability, provided: That such aid shall be used for the purposes intended.

That there is continuing evidence that they are taking effective steps to help themselves, or are firmly committed to do so.

That such aid shall not jeopardize American economy and shall conform to an integrated program that involves other international commitments and contributes to the attainment of political, economic and psychological objectives of the United States.

PART II—China

Political

Although the Chinese people are unanimous in their desire for peace at almost any cost, there seems to be no possibility of its realization under existing circumstances. On one side is the Kuomintang, whose reactionary leadership, repression and corruption have caused a loss of popular faith in the Government. On the other side, bound ideologically to the Soviet Union, are the Chinese Communists, whose eventual aim is admittedly a Communist state in China. Some reports indicate that Communist measures of land reform have gained for them the support of the majority of peasants in areas under their control, while others indicate that their ruthless tactics of land distribution and terrorism have alienated the majority of such peasants. They have, however, successfully organized many rural areas against the National Government. Moderate groups are caught between Kuomintang misrule and repression and ruthless Communist totalitarianism. Minority parties lack dynamic leadership and sizable following. Neither the moderates, many of whom are in the Kuomintang, nor the minority parties are able to make their influence felt because of National Government repression. Existing provincial opposition leading to possible separatist movements would probably crystallize only if collapse of the Government were imminent.

Soviet actions, contrary to the letter and spirit of the Sino-Soviet Treaty of 1945 and its related documents, have strengthened the Chinese Communist position in Manchuria, with political, economic and military repercussions on the National Government's position both in Manchuria and in China proper, and have made more difficult peace and stability in China. The present trend points toward a gradual disintegration of the National Government's control, with the ultimate possibility of a Communist-dominated China.

Steps taken by the Chinese Government toward governmental reorganization in mid-April 1947 aroused hopes of improvement in the political situation. However, the reorganization resulted in little change. Reactionary influences continue to mold important policies even though the Generalissimo remains the principal determinative force in the government. Since the April reorganization, the most significant change has been the appointment of General Chen Cheng to head the civil and military administration in Manchuria. Projected steps include elections in the Fall for the formation of a constitutional government, but, under present conditions, they are not expected to result in a government more representative than the present regime.

Economic

Under the impact of civil strife and inflation, the Chinese economy is disintegrating. The most probable outcome of present trends would be, not sudden collapse, but a continued and creeping paralysis and consequent decline in the authority and power of the National Government. The past ten years of war have caused serious deterioration of transportation and communication facilities, mines, utilities and industries. Notwithstanding some commendable efforts and large amounts of economic aid, their overall capabilities are scarcely half those of the pre-war period. With disruption of transportation facilities and the loss of much of North China and Manchuria, important resources of those rich areas are no longer available for the rehabilitation and support of China's economy.

Inflation in China has been diffused slowly through an enormous population without causing the immediate dislocation which would have occurred in a highly industrialized economy. The rural people, 80 per cent of the total Chinese population of 450 million, barter food-stuffs for local handicraft products without suffering a drastic cut in living standards. Thus, local economies exist in many parts of China, largely insulated from the disruption of urban industry. Some local economies are under the control of Communists, and some are loosely under the control of provincial authorities.

The principal cause of the hyper-inflation is the long-continued deficit in the national budget. Present revenue collections, plus the profits of nationalized enterprises, cover only one-third of governmental expenditures, which are approximately 70 per cent military, and an increasing proportion of the budget is financed by the issuance of new currency. In the first six months of 1947 note-issue was tripled but rice prices increased seven-fold. Thus prices and governmental expenditures spiral upwards, with price increases occurring faster than new currency can be printed. With further price increases, budget revisions will undoubtedly be necessary. The most urgent economic need of Nationalist China is a reduction of the military budget.

China's external official assets amounted to $327 million (US) on July 30, 1947. Privately-held foreign exchange assets are at least $600 million and may total $1500 million, but no serious attempt has been made to mobilize these private resources for rehabilitation purposes. Private Chinese assets located in China include probably $200 million in gold, and about $75 million in US currency notes. Although China has not exhausted her foreign official assets, and probably will not do so at the present rates of imports and exports until early 1949, the continuing deficit in her external balance of payments is a serious problem.

Disparity between the prices of export goods in China and in world markets at unrealistic official exchange rates has greatly penalized exports, as have disproportionate increases in wages and other costs. Despite rigorous trade and exchange controls, imports have greatly exceeded exports, and there consistently has been a heavy adverse trade balance.

China's food harvests this year are expected to be significantly larger than last year's fairly good returns. This moderately encouraging situation with regard to crops is among the few favorable factors which can be found in China's current economic situation.

Under inflationary conditions, long-term investment is unattractive for both Chinese and foreign capital. Private Chinese funds tend to go into short-term advances, hoarding of commodities, and capital flight. The entire psychology is speculative and inflationary, preventing ordinary business planning and handicapping industrial recovery.

Foreign business enterprises in China are adversely affected by the inefficient and corrupt administration of exchange and import controls, discriminatory application of tax laws, the increasing role of government trading agencies and the trend towards state ownership of industries. The Chinese Government has taken some steps toward improvement but generally has been apathetic in its efforts. Between 1944 and 1947, the anti-inflationary measure on which the Chinese Government placed most reliance was the public sale of gold borrowed from the United States. The intention was to absorb paper currency, and thus reduce the effective demand for goods. Under the circumstance of continued large deficits, however, the only effect of the gold sales program was to retard slightly the price inflation and dissipate dollar assets.

A program to stabilize the economic situation was undertaken in February 1947. The measures included a wage freeze, a system of limited rationing to essential workers in a few cities, and the sale of government bonds. The effect of this program has been slight, and the wage freeze has been abandoned. In August 1947, the unrealistic official rate of exchange was replaced, for proceeds of exports and remittances, by a free market in foreign exchange. This step is expected to stimulate exports, but it is too early to determine whether it will be effective.

The issuance of a new silver currency has been proposed as a future measure to combat inflation. If the government continued to finance budgetary deficits by unbacked note issue, the silver would probably go into hoards and the price inflation would continue. The effect would be no more than that of the gold sales in 1944–1947, namely, a slight and temporary retardation of the inflationary spiral. The proposal could be carried out, moreover, only through a loan from the United States of at least $200 million in silver.

In the construction field, China has prepared expansive plans for reconstruction of communications, mines and industries. Some progress has been made in implementing them, notably in the partial rehabilitation of certain railroads and in the textile industry. Constructive results have been handicapped by a lack of funds, equipment and experienced management, supervisory and technical personnel.

On August 1, 1947, the State Council approved a "Plan for Economic Reform." This appears to be an omnibus of plans covering all phases of Chinese economic reconstruction but its effectiveness cannot yet be determined.

Social—Cultural

Public education has been one of the chief victims of war and social and economic disruption. Schoolhouses, textbooks and other equipment have been destroyed and the cost of replacing any considerable portion cannot now be met. Teachers, like other public servants, have seen the purchasing power of a month's salary shrink to the market value of a few days' rice ration. This applies to the entire educational system, from primary schools, which provide a medium to combat the nation's grievous illiteracy, to universities, from which must come the nation's professional men, technicians and administrators. The universities have suffered in an additional and no less serious respect—traditional academic freedom. Students participating in protest demonstrations have been severely and at times brutally punished by National Government agents without pretense of trial or public evidence of the sedition charged. Faculty members have often been dismissed or refused employment with no evidence of professional unfitness, patently because they were politically objectionable to government officials. Somewhat similarly, periodicals have been closed down "for reasons of military security" without stated charges, and permitted to reopen only after new managements have been imposed. Resumption of educational and other public welfare activities on anything like the desired scale can be accomplished only by restraint of officialdom's abuses, and when the nation's economy is stabilized sufficiently to defray the cost of such vital activities.

Military

The overall military position of the National Government has deteriorated in the past several months and the current military situation favors Communist forces. The Generalissimo has never wavered in his contention that he is fighting for national independence against forces of an armed rebellion nor has he been completely convinced that the Communist problem can be resolved except by force of arms. Although the Nationalist Army has a preponderance of force, the tactical initiative rests with the Communists. Their hit-and-run tactics, adapted to their mission of destruction at points or in areas of their own selection, give them a decided advantage over Nationalists, who must defend many critical areas including connecting lines of communication. Obviously large numbers of Nationalist troops involved in such defensive roles are immobilized whereas Communist tactics permit almost complete freedom of action. The Nationalists' position is precarious in Manchuria, where they occupy only a slender finger of territory. Their control is strongly disputed in Shantung and Hopei Provinces where the Communists make frequent dislocating attacks against isolated garrisons.

In order to improve materially the current military situation, the Nationalist forces must first stabilize the fronts and then regain the initiative. Further, since the Government is supporting the civil war with approximately seventy per cent of its national budget, it is evident that steps taken to alleviate the situation must point toward an improvement in the effectiveness of the armed forces with a concomitant program of social, political and economic reforms, including a decrease in the size of the military establishment. Whereas some rather ineffective steps have been taken to reorganize and revitalize the command structure, and more sweeping reforms are projected, the effectiveness of the Nationalist Army requires a sound program of equipment and improved logistical support. The present industrial potential of China is inadequate to support military forces effectively. Chinese forces under present conditions cannot cope successfully with internal strife or fulfill China's obligations as a member of the family of nations. Hence outside aid, in the form of munitions (most urgently ammunition) and technical assistance, is essential before any plan of operations can be undertaken with a reasonable prospect of success. Military advice is now available to the Nationalists on a General Staff level through American military advisory groups. The Generalissimo expressed to me repeatedly a strong desire to have this advice and supervision extended in scope to include field forces, training centers and particularly logistical agencies.

Extension of military aid by the United States to the National Government might possibly be followed by similar aid from the Soviet Union to the Chinese Communists, either openly or covertly—the latter course seems more likely. An arena of conflicting ideologies might be created as in 1935 in Spain. There is always the possibility that such developments in this area, as in Europe and in the Middle East, might precipitate a third world war.

Part IV—Conclusions

The peaceful aims of freedom-loving peoples in the world are jeopardized today by developments as portentous as those leading to World War II.

The Soviet Union and her satellites give no evidence of a conciliatory or cooperative attitude in these developments. The United States is compelled, therefore, to initiate realistic lines of action in order to create and maintain bulwarks of freedom, and to protect United States strategic interests.

The bulk of the Chinese are not disposed to Communism and they are not concerned with ideologies. They desire food, shelter and the opportunity to live in peace.

China

The spreading internecine struggle within China threatens world peace. Repeated American efforts to mediate have proved unavailing. It is apparent that positive steps are required to end hostilities immediately. The most logical approach to this very complex and ominous situation would be to refer the matter to the United Nations.

A China dominated by Chinese Communists would be inimical to the interests of the United States, in view of their openly expressed hostility and active opposition to those principles which the United States regards as vital to the peace of the world.

The Communists have the tactical initiative in the overall military situation. The Nationalist position in Manchuria is precarious, and in Shantung and Hopei Provinces strongly disputed. Continued deterioration of the situation may result in the early establishment of a Soviet satellite government in Manchuria and ultimately in the evolution of a Communist-dominated China.

China is suffering increasingly from disintegration. Her requirements for rehabilitation are large. Her most urgent needs include governmental reorganization and reforms, reduction of the military budget and external assistance.

A program of aid, if effectively employed, would bolster opposition to Communist expansion, and would contribute to gradual development of stability in China.

Due to excesses and oppressions by government police agencies basic freedoms of the people are being jeopardized. Maladministration and corruption cause a loss of confidence in the Government. Until drastic political and economic reforms are undertaken United States aid can not accomplish its purpose.

Even so, criticism of results achieved by the National Government in efforts for improvement should be tempered by a recognition of the handicaps imposed on China by eight years of war, the burden of her opposition to Communism, and her sacrifices for the Allied cause.

A United States program of assistance could best be implemented under the supervision of American advisors in specified economic and military fields. Such a program can be undertaken only if China requests advisory aid as well as material assistance.

Part V—Recommendations

It is recommended:

That the United States Government provide as early as practicable moral, advisory, and material support to China in order to contribute to the early establishment of peace in the world in consonance with the enunciated principles of the United Nations, and concomitantly to protect United States strategic interests against militant forces which now threaten them.

That United States policies and actions suggested in this report be thoroughly integrated by appropriate government agencies with other international commitments. It is recognized that any foreign assistance extended must avoid jeopardizing the American economy.

China

That China be advised that the United States is favorably disposed to continue aid designed to protect China's territorial integrity and to facilitate her recovery, under agreements to be negotiated by representatives of the two governments, with the following stipulations:

That China inform the United Nations promptly of her request to the United States for increased material and advisory assistance.

That China request the United Nations to take immediate action to bring about a cessation of hostilities in Manchuria and request that Manchuria be placed under a Five-Power Guardianship or, failing that, under a Trusteeship in accordance with the United Nations Charter.

That China make effective use of her own resources in a program for economic reconstruction and initiate sound fiscal policies leading to reduction of budgetary deficits.

That China give continuing evidence that the urgently required political and military reforms are being implemented.

That China accept American advisors as responsible representatives of the United States Government in specified military and economic fields to assist China in utilizing United States aid in the manner for which it is intended.

APPENDIX TO PART I—GENERAL STATEMENT

Directive to Lieutenant General Wedemeyer

You will proceed to China without delay for the purpose of making an appraisal of the political, economic, psychological and military situations—current and projected. In the course of your survey you will maintain liaison with American diplomatic and military officials in the area. In your discussions with Chinese officials and leaders in positions of responsibility you will make it clear that you are on a fact-finding mission and that the United States Government can consider assistance in a program of rehabilitation only if the Chinese Government presents satisfactory evidence of effective measures looking towards Chinese recovery and provided further that any aid which may be made available shall be subject to the supervision of representatives of the United States Government.

In making your appraisal it is desired that you proceed with detachment from any feeling of prior obligation to support or to further official Chinese programs which do not conform to sound American policy with regard to China. In presenting the findings of your mission you should endeavor to state as concisely as possible your estimate of the character, extent, and probable consequences of assistance which you may recommend, and the probable consequences in the event that assistance is not given.

When your mission in China is completed you will proceed on a brief trip to Korea to make an appraisal of the situation there with particular reference to an economic aid program in Korea and its relation to general political and economic conditions throughout the country. Before going to Korea you will communicate with General MacArthur to ascertain whether he desires you to proceed via Tokyo.

You will take with you such experts, advisers and assistants as you deem necessary to the effectiveness of your mission.

Approved
HARRY S. TRUMAN

July 9, 1947

APPENDIX "A" TO PART II—CHINA

POLITICAL

INDEX

	Pages
Résumé of United States Policy Toward China	771
Current Political Situation	772
Steps Taken and Projected to Improve Internal Political Situation	774
Implications of "No Assistance" to China or Continuation of "Wait and See" Policy	775
Reforms Needed to Improve the Internal Political Situation	775

Résumé of United States Policy Toward China

The fundamental bases of United States policy toward China have remained unchanged since the Open Door notes of Secretary of State John Hay in 1899 and his circular note to the Powers during the Boxer Rebellion: equality of trade and the preservation of China's territorial integrity. Russian and Japanese aggression in Manchuria in the early 1900's and Japanese demands to China during the first world war threatened these principles. During these years the United States protested, often futilely, foreign infringement of the Open Door Policy. In 1921–22 formal international agreement to these principles was expressed in the Nine-Power Treaty. While the United States adopted a non-recognition policy at the time of the Japanese Twenty-one Demands and reiterated this policy at the time of Japanese occupation of Manchuria, the United States was not prepared to take stronger steps to uphold Chinese sovereignty or American trade rights if they involved the risk of war. At the outbreak of Sino-Japanese hostilities in 1937, the United States restated her policy and offered her good offices for mediation, but a meeting of the signatories of the Nine-Power Treaty resulted in no concerted action against Japan. The American neutrality legislation was not invoked since it was felt that enforcement of its provisions would have hurt China more than Japan. Repeated American diplomatic protests proving useless, restrictions were gradually imposed on exports to Japan and material aid to China was progressively expanded. Confronted with the issue of American security in the face of Japanese domination of eastern Asia and possible Japanese and German domination of the world, the United States was for the first time prepared to run the risk of war in upholding her policy. The result was the Japanese attack on Pearl Harbor and United States entry into the world war. Strategic consideration caused concentration of Allied military strength in Europe initially, rather than in Asia, and China received relatively little material aid. This produced some Chinese resentment but the United States attempted to give China various forms of material and moral aid and endeavored to build up China's prestige as one of the major powers. The United States also stressed to China the importance of a strong unified nation and attempted to use influence to that end. Following the Japanese surrender, however, widespread civil war between the National Government and the Chinese Communists threatened. The position of the United States and the Soviet Union was of importance. As a result of the Yalta Agreement, to which the United States was a party, a Sino-Soviet Treaty was signed in August 1945, granting certain rights in Manchuria to the Soviet Union. Although both the United States and the Soviet Union were committed to the return of Chinese territory to Chinese Government control, the Soviet Union utilized its occupation of Manchuria to hamper the Chinese Government and to assist the Chinese Communists. The United States aided the Chinese Government by transporting its troops to former Japanese-occupied areas and thus found itself in the midst of an undeclared civil war. At this juncture President Truman sent General Marshall to China to mediate between the two factions and stated that the United States would be prepared to aid China as it moved toward peace and unity. The early agreement reached by the Chinese factions gradually broke down and civil war was renewed on an increasing scale. Since the end of the American mediation effort in January 1947, the United States has continued to withhold aid to China in the hope that an improvement in the Chinese internal situation would permit the extension of effective aid toward rehabilitation and development of economic stability.

The effect of American policy toward China from the time of the Hay Open Door notes until 1941 was not to preserve China's territorial integrity or provide equality of trade; mutual suspicion among the Powers probably was the only factor that saved China from dismemberment in the early 1900's. When Japanese aggression in 1937 threatened the territorial integrity of China and equality of trade, the United States, as in the past, found diplomatic protests unavailing. It was not until the United States felt her own security and interests seriously endangered that it was finally prepared to accept the risk of war to protect her security and interests. China was thus saved from Japanese domination and control. The American mediation effort, which for the time being stopped the civil war, was accompanied in its later stages by the spread of hostilities in first one and then in another area as the National Government occupied important Communist-held areas. In spite of increased Chinese Government efforts to destroy the Communist forces following the end of the American mediation effort, the civil war has brought no recent major successes to its arms except in Shantung Province. The Communists threaten to occupy all of Manchuria and their strength appears to be increasing in that area. In view of the continued economic deterioration in National Government areas, it may be said that the American mediation effort has been to the advantage of the Chinese Communists and conversely to the disadvantage of the National Government.

Current Political Situation

China is confronted with civil war, a deteriorating economic situation, social unrest and the psychological reactions inevitable under such conditions. Among the people themselves, there is a unanimous desire for peace at almost any cost. There seems, however, to be no possibility of any peaceful settlement in the foreseeable future between the National Government and the Chinese Communist Party, owing to recent Communist military successes in Manchuria, added to Communist awareness of the Government's increasing economic difficulties. The National Government has issued a General Mobilization Order with the object of establishing powers and creating forces in order to destroy the Chinese Communist forces; however, to the detriment of the government it is also being used to suppress opposition which is not Communist at all.

The Chinese Government is headed by Generalissimo Chiang Kai-shek and dominated by the Kuomintang under his leadership. The reactionary character of Kuomintang leadership, the repressive nature of its rule and the widespread corruption among Government officials and military officers have cost the Government heavily in terms of the confidence and support of the people. There is a widespread belief that under present conditions, unless the National Government takes drastic measures of reform, it will, through a slow and gradual process, disintegrate.

The Chinese Communists are self-professed Communists bound ideologically to the Soviet Union. They proclaim as their eventual aim the establishment of a communist state in China. The Chinese Communists constantly foster anti-American feeling in areas under their control, picturing the United States as an imperialistic power which has as its objective the enslavement of the world. Their ruthless tactics of land distribution and oppression of the Christian missionary movement have made for them bitter enemies among many Chinese in the rural areas. Some sources say that Communist land reforms have benefitted the poor peasants who comprise the majority of the rural population and who, therefore, support the Communists, while other sources say that Communist terroristic tactics have alienated the vast majority of peasants. Where local government, regardless of ideology, is competent, honest and humane, there is no local revolt. Whether by suasion or by intimidation, the Communists have in many areas been successful in organizing the countryside against the National Government.

Middle of the road groups in China, desirous of the essentials of democratic government, are caught between the misrule and repression of the Kuomintang and the totalitarian ruthlessness of the Chinese Communists. Yet in the moderate and constructive views of these Chinese, many of them in the Kuomintang, lies one of the greatest possibilities for a governmental program which would be acceptable to the mass of Chinese. The trouble is that these views are not boldly and confidently asserted and cannot be against the present uncompromising power of the extremists. The minority parties, with present leadership and following insufficient to defy intimidation and to assert a vigorous policy, offer little hope in the situation. Existing provincial opposition to the National Government is not yet an important factor, but separatist movements would probably occur in the event of an imminent collapse of the National Government.

The Chinese Government's position in Manchuria has been seriously weakened by Soviet actions. In spite of the Sino-Soviet Treaty of 1945 and its related documents, the Soviet Union has hindered the efforts of the Chinese Government to restore its control over Manchuria, has not given the "moral support and aid in military supplies and other material resources" provided for in these documents and has not permitted the Chinese Government freely to take over the civil administration of Dairen and the Port Arthur area. Rather, the Soviet Union has assisted the Chinese Communists in Manchuria by the timing of the withdrawal of Soviet troops and by making available, either directly or indirectly, large quantities of surrendered Japanese military equipment. Soviet machinations in western Sinkiang and among the Mongols have further embarrassed the Chinese Government. In brief, the Soviet Union has given no indication of any effort to assist the Chinese Government and has, instead, taken action which has aided the Chinese Communists in Manchuria. The result has been to strengthen the Chinese Communist position in Manchuria, with political, economic and military repercussions on the National Government's position both in Manchuria and China proper, and to make more difficult the attainment of peace and stability in China.

Steps Taken and Projected to Improve Internal Political Situation

At the time of General Marshall's departure from China, he stated that while the form for a democratic China had been set forth in the new constitution, practical measures would be the test to see to what extent the Chinese Government would give substance to the form. In mid-April the Chinese Government announced the reorganization of the State Council and shortly thereafter the reorganization of the Executive Yuan. The caliber of the appointees to the State Council indicated that an effort had been made to name some of the most capable, moderate and progressive members of the Kuomintang, qualities which also characterized the non-party appointees to the Council. The only other parties to join the Government were the Youth Party and the Socialist Democratic Party, but their appointees were without particular significance. Seats were also left vacant on the Council for the Communist Party and the Democratic League in the event they wished to participate in the Council at a later date, but this was viewed chiefly as a political gesture. However, the possible effectiveness of the Council was largely nullified by the simultaneous creation of a new Kuomintang Political Committee, the chief figure in which was Chen Li-fu. The important role played by this Committee in controlling the Kuomintang and its policies was seen in the subsequent consolidation of the position and strength of the CC Clique (dominant right wing of the Kuomintang led by Chen Li-fu and Kuo-fu). The reorganized Executive Yuan under General Chang Chun gave similar promise but the political maneuvers of the CC Clique, which was strongly opposed to General Chang and his political colleagues, the pace of military and economic developments, and domination by the Generalissimo tied its hands and neutralized its efforts to take effective action to meet pressing problems. In effect, therefore, there was a limited reorganization of the Government but it was one which failed to bring about any significant changes. Control of the Government and its policies remained, in general, in the same few hands and within this framework the Generalissimo has continued to be the main determinative force in Chinese Government policy.

Since the time of the above-described reorganization, few changes in the Government have occurred. Perhaps the most significant has been the appointment of General Chen Cheng, Chief of Staff, as Director of the President's Office at Mukden to succeed General Hsiung Shih-hui and the consolidation of civil and military administration in Manchuria under his control. This change represents an effort to correct the weaknesses of the National Government position in Manchuria, but it may have come too late and may not be sufficiently far reaching to achieve the desired effect.

Projected steps include elections in areas under National Government control within the next few months in accordance with the new constitution as a prelude to the formation of a constitutional government. However, under conditions of civil war, Kuomintang refusal to permit the minority parties to organize and campaign freely for the elections and control by the Kuomintang CC Clique throughout National Government territory, there is no likelihood that the elections will result in the immediate creation of a government representative of the people's will or the formation of a government any more democratic than the present regime. Even so, the elections should serve as a step forward along the road to representative government.

Implications of "No Assistance" to China or Continuation of "Wait and See" Policy

To advise at this time a policy of "no assistance" to China would suggest the withdrawal of the United States Military and Naval Advisory Groups from China and it would be equivalent to cutting the ground from under the feet of the Chinese Government. Removal of American assistance, without removal of Soviet assistance, would certainly lay the country open to eventual Communist domination. It would have repercussions in other parts of Asia, would lower American prestige in the Far East and would make easier the spread of Soviet influence and Soviet political expansion not only in Asia but in other areas of the world.

It is possible that the adoption of a "wait and see" policy would lead to the Generalissimo's finally carrying out genuine reforms which in turn would enable the United States to extend effective aid and which themselves would furnish the best answer to the challenge of communism. Because of an inevitable time lag in its results, however, such a policy would permit for an appreciable time the continuation of the process of National Government disintegration. At some stage of the disintegration the authority and control of the National Government might become so weak and restricted that separatist movements would occur in various areas now under Government control. At this point, conceivably there might emerge a middle group which would be able to establish a modicum of stability in the areas under its control. It would then be possible for the United States to extend support, both moral and material, to any such group or combination of groups which gave indication of ability to consolidate control over sizable portions of the country and whose policies would be compatible with our own. This, however, represents conjecture regarding a possible future course of events in China. There is the further possibility that such a policy would result at some point in the Generalissimo's seeking a compromise with the Chinese Communists, although it is likely that he would not do so until his position became so weak that the Communists would accept a settlement only on terms assuring them a dominant position in the government. At worst, under a process of continued National Government disintegration, it may be expected that there would be a long period of disturbance verging on chaos, at the end of which the Chinese Communists would emerge as the dominant group oriented toward the Soviet Union.

Reforms Needed to Improve the Internal Political Situation

Reforms to improve the internal political situation should, in general, include measures which would (a) make for efficient government, (b) protect the basic freedoms of the people from arbitrary acts of repression, (c) remove civil administration from military control, and (d) contribute to the welfare of the people. These measures might include, *inter alia*, reforms such as the following: Complete separation of the Kuomintang from the Government and the emergence of the Generalissimo as the leader of the nation rather than of the party; reorganization of the National Government, including both the Executive Yuan and the State Council, to ensure participation by responsible Chinese without regard to party affiliations; a clear-cut delegation of responsibility in the Government to increase efficiency, foster initiative, prevent the domination of governmental affairs and policies by one person and encourage entry into Government service of capable and progressive Chinese now unwilling to serve in the Government; the strengthening of the Control Yuan to ensure the removal and punishment of corrupt officials; the abolition of the existing secret police system; the cessation of arrests of civilians by military organs; the prompt and public trial of persons arrested and the full exercise of the right of *habeas corpus;* the cessation of the use of force and intimidation against teachers and students and the reinstatement of university professors and students dismissed solely for their political views; the carrying out of a land reform program which would lighten the burdens of usury and taxation on the peasant as well as provide him land; decentralization of governmental power to permit more local autonomy and local participation in administration; removal of military officers from posts in civil government while on active status; and publication of complete information regarding fiscal policies and their implementation and of detailed data covering government revenues and expenditures, including National, Provincial and Municipal budgets.

APPENDIX "B" TO PART II—CHINA

ECONOMIC

INDEX

	Page
Financial	777
Disinvestment	777
Fiscal and Monetary Situation	778
Balance of Payments Situation	779
Currency Stabilization	782
Proposed Silver Loan	783
Financial Advisors	784
Industry	784
Coal	785
Electric Power	786
Railways	786
Shipping	787
Harbors	788
Textiles	789
Fertilizer	790
Iron and Steel	791
Cement	792
Crop Conditions	792
Problems Confronting American Business in China	794
Immediate Steps to Strengthen the Economy	796
Considerations on United States Economic Assistance	797
Budgetary Deficits	797
Economic Reconstruction Projects	798
Investment of Private Chinese Funds	798
Export-Import Bank	799
Balance of Payments Assistance	801
Congressional Aid	801

Financial

China has reached a condition of hyper-inflation, and it is difficult to estimate how long the deterioration can continue before the present monetary system ceases to function. During the past six months, two serious upsurges in prices have occurred, each followed by a few weeks of temporary stability and readjustment. The recent history of Chinese inflation, as indicated by the price of rice and by the black market price for U. S. dollars (the two best general indicators of the overall financial situation) has been one of increasingly violent convulsions separated by short intervals of relative stability.

China's hyper-inflation is a classical currency inflation, occurring in a predominantly agrarian country. It requires a longer time to run its course than a comparable inflation would in an urban industrial society. The recurrent price upsurges occur first in the large cities, are diffused gradually through the smaller cities, and finally permeate the countryside. There is some credit inflation through loans by the Government banks for purposes approved by the Government, but this credit inflation is a secondary cause, not to be compared in magnitude or impact with the swelling flood of notes.

A tendency towards panic on the part of the Government officials in the Ministry of Finance and Central Bank very easily develops, since personal responsibility for each crisis is difficult to avoid. It is difficult to explain to the Generalissimo and to such bodies as the People's Political Council and the Legislative Yuan that hyper-inflation results from years of unbalanced budgets and a debilitated economy, and that sudden upsurges in prices are to be expected in a hyper-inflation. Since personal responsibility is frequently assigned and scapegoats found, partly for political reasons, no individual wishes to take remedial action which might result in a price upsurge. Such administrative inertia aggravates the situation, and makes practical measures to forestall or smooth out the fluctuation doubly difficult. Thus, the official rate of CN$12,000 to one U. S. dollar remained in effect from February 11, 1947, until the middle of August, although the black market rate had proceeded by erratic leaps to 40,000. On a number of occasions between February and August it should have been easier than in August to effect a change or abandon the official rate. The weight of administrative inertia, however, was too great. Now that the change has been made, the accumulated maladjustments, the opportunities for market manipulation by exchange speculators who are among the keenest in the world, and the failure to prepare an administrative machine for Central Bank support of the market, will eventually combine to aggravate the crisis, and sooner or later produce another price convulsion which may be more violent than it need have been had the readjustment been made earlier.

Disinvestment—The disorganization in Chinese economy, caused by civil war and hyper-inflation, has resulted in massive disinvestment. This disinvestment has taken principally the forms of living off capital, and capital flight to the United States, Hong Kong, Europe and South America. Disinvestment is also occurring through the deterioration of physical assets, abuse of capital equipment, neglect of maintenance, and overloading of power facilities. In a very real sense, the economy functioned, and is continuing to function, by consuming reserves accumulated by the Japanese, materials purchased with dollars provided by the United States during the war years, and UNRRA and surplus property supplies. The hyper-inflation and the uncertainties of the civil war have further strengthened a traditional Chinese tendency towards the quick exploitation of capital assets, without provision for their maintenance or replacement.

The long-term consequences of disinvestment are very serious for the Chinese economy. The magnitude of this factor is difficult to estimate, because statistics of production and depreciation are not available, but it must be taken into account in any long-term estimate of China's reconstruction needs. Long continuance of the civil war will result in a degree of disinvestment which will make recuperation painfully slow and difficult. The result, a weak and dependent China, promising poor returns on investments for a long period, should be taken into account in planning for the distribution in Asia of United States resources.

Fiscal and Monetary Situation—The expenditures in the budget for the year 1947 were originally estimated at CN$9.4 trillion, against estimated revenues of CN$7.4 trillion. On May 7, a new budget of CN$18 trillion for 1947 was approved. With further increases in prices, new budget revisions will undoubtedly be made to provide for increased governmental expenditures. Receipts from taxes and government-operated enterprises cover approximately one-third of expenditures. The emission of new currency is therefore the principal means of financing the national budget. Increases in the note issue, with static or declining production, bid up prices and in turn require larger government expenditures. This spiralling effect has been evident in China for several years. During the past 18 months it has reached the stage of a hyper-inflation, in which the price increase is proceeding faster than the increase in note issuance. In the first six months of 1947 the note issue increased three times, but cost of living increased five-fold, and rice prices increased seven-fold. Experience in other countries suggests that there is a limit to the process of inflation. In China this limit is more elastic than elsewhere, due to the fact that about 80 per cent of the population live in relatively self-contained village economies. It is obviously unwise to attempt specific or precise predictions of how long the trend of the last six months can continue before there is a disintegration of the authority of the National Government with a possible reversion to regionalism accompanied by a collapse of the urban economies. China might then enter a period of chaos from which it might take as long as a generation to emerge. While the existence of a strong Communist movement makes the recrudescence of a simple pattern of warlordism of the period 1911–27 unlikely, it is doubtful whether the Communists would have the power or the technical skills to unify the country and rapidly bring it under control.

REVENUE OF THE CHINESE GOVERNMENT

Total revenue and expenditures, with percentage breakdown by sources of revenue based on monthly receipts of the Chinese National Treasury.

Month	Receipts and Expenditures (CN Trillions)	Revenue From Taxation (Percent)	Receipts From Public Borrowing (Percent)	Bank Advances (Currency Issuance) (Percent)	Other Receipts (Percent)
1947					
January	1.2	17.9	2.9	70.9	8.3
February	1.0	22.1	7.4	66.2	4.3
March	1.5	19.5	0.6	73.7	6.2
April	2.0	19.9	0.1	53.4	26.6
May	1.9	22.3	4.4	49.8	23.5
June	3.1	18.2	9.5	62.8	9.5

Source: Minister of Finance, O. K. Yui.

CURRENCY NOTES OUTSTANDING IN MANCHURIA, TAIWAN AND SINKIANG
(Billions)

Month	Northeastern Currency Notes (CBC issue for Manchuria)	Taiwan Currency Notes (Bank of Taiwan)	Sinkiang Provincial Bank Notes
1946			
June	4.5	3.7	6.2
July	6.0	4.0	6.6
August	10.1	4.2	7.1
September	15.0	1.2	8.5
October	18.8	2.8	10.0
November	22.9	4.0	11.4
December	27.5	5.0	13.0
1947			
January	36.2	5.7	14.8
February	40.2	6.4	16.6
March	47.5	7.0	18.0
April	55.9	7.5	----
May	64.4	8.9	----
June	74.6	---	----

Source: Minister of Finance, O. K. Yui.

CURRENCY ISSUANCE AND PRICES IN CHINA

Month	Notes Outstanding (Trillions)	Percentage Increase Over Previous Month	Whole Price Index (Shanghai)	Percentage Increase Over Previous Month
1946				
January	1.15	11	92	4
February	1.26	9	175	89
March	1.35	6	255	45
April	1.53	13	258	0
May	1.80	17	380	47
June	2.11	17	372	97
July	2.16	2	407	9
August	2.38	10	428	5
September	2.70	13	509	18
October	2.98	10	536	5
November	3.30	10	531	99
December	3.73	13	571	7
1947				
January	4.51	21	686	20
February	4.84	7	1066	55
March	5.74	18	1120	5
April	6.90	20	1847	64
May	8.38	21	2845	53
June	9.94	16	2993	17
July	11.46	15	3116	5

Source: Minister of Finance, O. K. Yui, "Financial Statistics for Wedemeyer's Mission" August, 1947

Balance of Payments Situation—Official foreign exchange assets of the Chinese Government reached their peak about V–J Day and have since declined. Total gold and short-term dollar assets of the Chinese Government and Chinese nationals were estimated at U. S. $949 million on December 30, 1945, the official portion being $835 million; in addition there were private Chinese long-term assets in the United States amounting to at least $220 million. The official assets held by the Central Bank of China had declined to $327 million on June 30, 1947, and an additional amount of over $123 million was held in other government banks. Private gold and short-term assets have almost certainly increased very substantially from the estimated figure $114 million at the end of 1945. While some private accounts have been drawn down to finance imports, amounts which more than compensate for this decrease have been added through private accumulation of gold and U. S. currency in China, and through flight of capital via Hong Kong, and through other means. Gold sales to the Chinese public out of the 1942 Congressional loan amounted to $150 million, most of which is still in Chinese private hands. There are an estimated $50–75 millions of U. S. currency in private hands in China, a substantial part of which is held by Chinese Nationals; and the flight of capital via underestimation of the value of exports, overestimation of the value of imports, diversion of remittances, etc., has undoubtedly been heavy. A plausible estimate of private Chinese holdings of gold and hard foreign exchange at home and abroad, recently made by the U. S. Treasury Attaché in Nanking, was approximately U.S. $500 million. Estimate of private Chinese foreign exchange assets have gone as high as several billion, but the private assets in the United States which could be identified as Chinese are probably nearer the U.S. $500 million figure.

Chinese Government estimates of the dollar deficit in the international balance of payments for the second half of 1947 are between $106 and $120 million. At the higher rate of usage, the official assets in the Central Bank would be drawn down to $206 million by the end of 1947, and would be exhausted by the end of 1948 or early in 1949. The dollar assets in other government banks would, of course, be intact.

TABLE A

Official Foreign Exchange Assets of China, July 1, 1947, in Deposits, Cash and Investments, Net of Forward Contracts and Margin Deposits

	Millions
U.S. dollars	U.S. $177.3
Pounds sterling	21.9
Hong Kong dollars	12.0
Rupees	0.4
Gold	85.7
Silver	29.4
Total	U.S. $326.6 millions

(Items rounded to nearest U.S. $100,000, therefore slight discrepancy in total.)

TABLE B

U. S. Dollar Holdings of Government Banks, July 1, 1947

	Millions
Bank of China	U.S. $94.8
Bank of Communications	16.6
Farmers Bank of China	2.4
Central Trust of China	4.6
Postal RSB	4.2
Total	U.S. $122.6 millions

Source: Minister of Finance, O. K. Yui.

INTERNATIONAL BALANCE OF PAYMENTS POSITION OF CHINA

(September 1947 to September 1948)

(Official Tentative Estimate by Ministry of Finance in Millions of U.S. Dollars)

EXPENDITURES

	Millions
Imports:	
Raw cotton	U.S. $100
Rice, wheat and flour	40
Coal and Coke	2
Schedule I imports	24
Schedule II and extra quota	215
Schedule III (a)	30
Financed by private exchange holdings	100
Total	511
Approved Financial Services:	55
Government Expenditures:	
Gasoline for military	31
Munitions	10
Debt Services	35
Industrial Supplies, etc.	20
Foreign Services, etc.	25
Total	687

RECEIPTS

Exports	200
Remittances	100
Foreign Expenditures in China	25
Charities, etc.	14
Repatriation of Capital	100
Total	439
Deficit	248

Source: The Minister of Finance, O. K. Yui.

There are several considerations which suggest that China's dollar resources will last at 'least a year and may last longer than 18 months. The most recent Central Bank estimate of China's balance of payments in the next 12 months anticipate in addition to the loss of $120 million of foreign exchange for Government imports and expenditures abroad, a deficit on current account of about the same amount. This estimate is based on fairly realistic assumptions concerning the extent of increase in exports and receipts from overseas remittances as a result of the new foreign exchange policy. Part of this deficit will be met by $30 million from post-UNRRA relief. Therefore, the Central Bank's total net loss of official foreign exchange assets in the next 12 months will be $210 million, leaving $117 million of official foreign exchange assets. This is, of course, a dangerously low figure. Nevertheless, it indicates that China has not yet reached the bottom of her official till, and has not yet tapped the substantial foreign hoards of Chinese nationals.

A complete picture of the balance of payments must also allow for smuggling and flight of capital. If the new regulations, and the recent agreement with Hong Kong, have more than a temporary effect, then smuggling of imports and flight of capital may not amount to more than $110 million, which should be compensated by smuggled exports and diversions of overseas remittances, plus depletion of Chinese private assets.

Private external assets, as indicated above, probably approximate $500 million. The National Government has never made a serious attempt to mobilize these assets for imports, and with a continued deterioration in the financial and economic situation its ability to do so would decrease rather than increase. Any substantial improvement in the general economic situation would undoubtedly begin a reflow of these assets to China and their gradual release for current use. A striking example of the Chinese private holder's unwillingness to invest foreign exchange in the development of China's industry is provided by the Hwainan Coal Mine. This mine is the best mine in Central China in actual operation and thus occupies a crucial position in the event of military failures in or the cutting of communications with the North China coal mining areas. The Hwainan Coal Mine is about 200 miles north of Nanking on a spur of the Tientsin-Pukow railroad, and its production of 90,000 tons a month could be substantially increased with further capital investment. The mine is 80 per cent owned by the China Finance Development Corporation, a Soong-Kung corporation with wide interests and extensive foreign exchange assets. After V–J Day the rehabilitation of the mine was financed by a CN dollar loan from the government and the advance of over U.S. $1 million by the N.R.C. for the purchase of essential transportation equipment. The China Finance Development Corporation did not put up any foreign exchange for this rehabilitation, and will not invest any foreign exchange for its further development. China Finance Development Corporation's attitude can be explained only in terms of short-sighted selfishness and lack of faith in the future of Kuomintang China.

The above calculations indicate that the Chinese Government has sufficient dollars in its official account to maintain the import program for at least one year, more probably for 18 months. The conclusion is that a shortage of official foreign exchange holdings for financing essential imports is not an immediate problem, but it may become acute if there is continued deterioration in China's capacity to produce and export commodities and her ability to prevent excessive diversion of overseas remittances. The essential problem is not one of advancing the foreign exchange required to make up the deficit in China's international balance of payments, as this would be a process which would have to be repeated indefinitely until forces are set in motion to rectify the deficit situation. Rather it is a problem of establishing the conditions which will eliminate the deficit, and of securing the capital for reconstruction and development from Chinese as well as foreign sources.

Currency Stabilization—Since 1942 the Chinese Government has sought to secure financial assistance from the United States for the purpose of stabilizing the Chinese national currency. In 1945 China raised the possibility of a loan of $500 million to be used as a currency reserve fund. This proposal was rejected by the United States on the grounds that China's foreign exchange assets, including the remainder of the 1942 loan, were sufficient to provide a reserve, and that any effort at stabilization would be futile unless the fiscal policy of the Government was changed. Between 1942 and 1946, $400 million was used by the Chinese Government for "economic stabilization purposes." U. S. dollar denominated savings certificates of up to 3-year maturity and bonds redeemable within 10 years were sold for CN currency at the rate of CN $20 to U.S. $1, and $150 million worth of gold was sold to the public by the Central Bank to stabilize prices. The history of these stabilization measures was one of criticism from the United States Government that valuable foreign exchange resources were being dissipated to no avail, and repeated unsubstantiated claims from the Chinese that the anti-inflationary measures would be effective. There were several scandals in connection with the sale of dollar certificates and bonds and gold to insiders and officials on a preferential basis. Notable examples were the gold scandals of March, 1945, in Chungking and February, 1947, in Shanghai.

Since V-J Day there has been continuous discussion of the issuance of a new currency. Recently the principal proposal has been the issuance of a metallic silver currency as an intermediate step in stabilization. The present fiscal situation is inopportune for the introduction of a new currency or the adoption of even an intermediate step towards stabilization. Experience in other countries indicates that after hyper-inflation has reached a certain stage it must run its course before the currency system can be effectively reorganized and stabilized. Mistakes in timing are apt to prove costly and actually serve to delay stabilization.

Proposed Silver Loan—During the past three months proposals have been advanced by the Chinese Government for a silver loan from the United States. It has been proposed to borrow between $200 and $250 million worth of silver from the United States to mint silver coins for circulation in China. Under the proposal it has been suggested that coins would be issued at a fixed rate with CN notes, and would eventually replace the paper currency.

The principal weakness of this proposal is that the Government would presumably continue to finance its budget by the issuance of paper currency. Unless the Government decided to withdraw paper currency from circulation entirely, replace it by silver and thereafter issue no more paper currency, the silver would go into hoards and hyper-inflation would continue. No attempt has been made by the American or Chinese proponents of the silver currency scheme to avoid this dilemma. Their case has been mainly based on four considerations:

(1) China had a relatively stable silver currency in the past, and great psychological importance has been attached to this fact;

(2) The world price of silver has declined from 90¢ to 64¢ during the past year and silver producers in the United States would welcome loans of silver to foreign countries;

(3) The war-time history of the silver lend-lease operations with India set a precedent for lending silver out of U. S. reserves;

(4) U. S. silver stocks are in any case of little use to the United States.

The proposed silver loan for currency stabilization cannot be seriously considered until a real start has been made to solve the Chinese budgetary problem. The issuance of silver coins as a subordinate currency alongside paper currency would have no more effect on the Chinese price level than would the sale to the public of an equivalent amount of metal in silver or gold bars. As the devaluation of the paper currency continued, silver coins would be hoarded for their metal content. On the other hand, if the paper currency were totally withdrawn and permanently replaced by the silver dollars, the Government would have to finance its national budget entirely out of taxation and public borrowing.

A silver loan to China would have many of the features of a budgetary loan. The silver coins would be sold to the public for paper currency and thereafter would be lost to the Government, in the same sense that the gold from the 1942 Congressional loan which was sold to the public in 1945–46, has not been mobilized as a foreign exchange asset for Government use. Therefore, the prospects of repayment would be very slight, and any proposed silver "loan," secured by no physical assets as collateral, might, more properly, be considered as a proposed gift of dollars. The Congress is the only body which can decide to make such a gift. It is suggested that other forms of aid should be considered as having a higher priority, since under existing conditions a gift of silver would have a minimal likelihood of benefit to China, and would carry with it the maximum risk of misuse.

Financial Advisors—The National Government has employed foreign financial advisors for many years, as part of its general policy of using foreign technicians. Most financial advisors have been employed on a personal contract basis. Useful work has been done by American advisors in planning and supervising foreign exchange operations of the Central Bank, but with one or two outstanding exceptions such advisors have usually not had any substantial effect on monetary or fiscal policies. Numerous problems have arisen in private employment of financial technicians, mainly over the difficulties of avoiding involvement in Chinese politics, or avoiding being called upon to exert pressures and exploit their contacts in Washington for specific projects. There have been notable examples of advisors such as Dr. Arthur Young avoiding both these difficulties and performing loyal and useful service to the National Government. The deepening of China's economic crisis, however, and the intensification of the need for foreign financial aid, may make those two difficulties increasingly acute.

One of the major difficulties confronting official American representatives, assigned as advisors to China, would be the increasingly nationalistic trend which is evident in the Chinese Government. Opposition to any policy recommendations from the United States might be based on objection to infringement on Chinese sovereignty. Unless the policy responsibilities of the official advisor were clearly defined by clear-cut agreement between the two governments, it is possible that American financial advisors would be absorbed into the Chinese system and faced with the two problems, indicated above, which have always confronted private American advisors employed by the Chinese Government.

Industry

Chinese vital transportation and communications facilities, mines, utilities and industries have been seriously damaged during 10 years of war. In Manchuria there was considerable stripping of Japanese-developed industrial and power generating equipment by the Russians. Reliable statistics are not available in all cases, but the report of the Working Group on Reconstruction of Devastated Areas for Asia and the Far East, of the United Nations, estimated that 58 per cent of the productive capacity of the cotton textile industry, 90 per cent of the machine and light metal industries, and 70 per cent of the coal, electric power, and iron and steel industry were lost. Chinese Government data indicate that the textile industry has been able to restore 50 per cent of its pre-war capacity, and the machine and light metal industries 25 per cent. The coal industry is up to 53 per cent but is handicapped by loss of mines damaged or held by Communists and by lack of transport. Electric power capacity is 60 per cent restored—in Shanghai nearly 100 per cent—but is in a rundown precarious condition. Since V-J Day, 3,816 km of railways have been restored, using materials and equipment furnished by UNRRA and cannibalized from branch lines and sidings, but on an emergency basis with temporary timber bridges and other substandard materials. Deficiencies in transport are a major obstacle to economic recovery, but until the political situation in North China and Manchuria is resolved, only the lines in Central and South China are available for permanent rehabilitation. Since V-J Day 20,000 km of additional highways have been restored in some measure and added to the 50,000 km regarded in operable condition. Some 20,000 trucks and 60,000 metric tons of highway equipment have been received from UNRRA and the United States.

Ten per cent of the main telecommunication lines have been restored. Some 800,000 tons of shipping have been obtained by the Chinese as compared with a pre-war total of 1,300,000 tons. There is reported an acute shortage on the Yangtze of passenger vessels and cargo vessels with passenger accommodations. Port facilities have deteriorated seriously through the war years and require extensive repairs, but little if any expansion under present conditions. Cement production, an essential element in reconstruction plans is currently 30 per cent of pre-war production. Less than 50,000 tons of steel were produced in pre-war years, though large amounts of ore were mined and shipped to Japan. Accurate figures are not available but iron and steel production appears to be running at less than the pre-war.

It will be noted that, notwithstanding UNRRA and United States assistance, efforts to revive China's communications and industries have not been entirely effective. High labor and raw material costs, shortage of power and fuel, delays in deliveries of vital repair parts from abroad and the critical shortage of qualified supervisors who have the practical "know how," have been deterrents but the major obstacles to recovery are inflation and the lack of capital. A serious threat to China's industrial future and material welfare is imposed at present by the denial to the nation of most North China and Manchurian resources. If this condition were to become complete and final, it would constitute nothing short of a calamity to Chinese prospects for industrialization.

Coal—China's most important natural resource is coal, ranking among the major reserves of the world. The reserves according to National Government data are approximately as follows:

	Million Metric Tons
Coking	2,728
Anthracite	46,001
Bituminous	188,167
Total	236,896

plus 4,738 million metric tons of lignite. The reserves are located mostly in North China, particularly in Shansi Province, and also in Manchuria and Southwestern China.

According to Chinese reports, coal production in 1937 totalled 32 million tons, 12 from Manchuria, 11 from the Northern Provinces and 9 from the remainder of China. During the war, production for all of China reached approximately 72 million tons. Due primarily to disruption of mines and transport by the Communists, production during 1946 was only 15,000,000 tons, and for the first six months of 1947 was 8,577,000 tons.

Since coal is practically the sole source of power except in Manchuria and Taiwan, and of fuel for water transportation, industrial processes, maintenance of essential community services and domestic heating and cooking, this deficit has not only retarded economic recovery but has contributed to discomfort, sickness and unrest among the people. It has also prevented export of coal which would be important to China's exchange position, and to the economic recovery of Japan and other Far Eastern countries.

The complete loss of Manchuria's coal to China would be a crippling blow, and the additional loss of North China sources would be even more serious, for without at least those from the Northern Provinces, China cannot hope to achieve any substantial industrialization, the only hope for a balanced economy and a strong free China.

Lack of transport has played a part in the present coal shortage. At the Kailan Mines in North China, by far the largest remaining producing mine in

China, 500,000 tons of coal have accumulated and been stock-piled for lack of adequate rolling stock to remove all of the daily production for shipment to Chinhuangtao (and Shanghai) and Tientsin. This mine which is currently producing 15,000 tons per day, is frequently in jeopardy from Communist operations. Its loss under present conditions would be disastrous.

Most of the coal mines in China are operated by the National Resources Commission which has had a survey made by foreign consultants and prepared a program of rehabilitation. A loan of $1,500,000, U. S. has been obtained and also considerable quantities of equipment and materials through UNRRA, not much of it yet installed. The mines which are receiving first attention are Yilo near Loyang and Chungfu in Honan Province, Hwantung mines in Kiangsu, Hsiangtan mines in Hunan, Pinghsiang mines in Kiangsi, and those in northern Taiwan, but rehabilitation is going slowly and will require some time to complete. The privately owned Hwainan mines in Anhwei are reported to have uncovered additional deposits and to have plans for expansion as previously mentioned. Other mines proposed for rehabilitation and development are in the politically unsettled North and not available for rehabilitation. The importance under the circumstances of protecting and holding the Kailan Mines is indicated.

Electric Power—There are some 1,350,000 kilowatts of electric power installed in China, with about 900,000 kilowatts actually available, much of it was damaged and deteriorated or obsolete. Since the war, a considerable number of packaged power units, 2,000 kilowatts and smaller, have been obtained through UNRRA, primarily with a view to revival of industry. The principal plants or systems are located in Shanghai, Tientsin-Peiping area, Tsingtao, Canton, Nanking, Hankow, Taiwan, and Manchuria, though the last have largely become unavailable by reason of Communist operations. With the exception of the Shanghai Power Company, Hankow Water Works and Electric Power Company, Nanking Electric Company, and two plants in Tientsin, they are all public owned, and operated by the National Resources Commission, which has prepared a program of rehabilitation and expansion of the North Hopei, Tsingtao, Shanghai, Canton and Taiwan systems. While rehabilitation of plants is undoubtedly needed, any expansion proposed should be carefully coordinated with anticipated industrial expansion and additional power requirements. In Shanghai there is a serious power shortage, and an existing connected load of some 60,000 kilowatts, not in operation and awaiting only the availability of additional power, and this deficit will grow to 100,000 kilowatts or more in the four years required to install additional capacity. A project has been prepared by the Shanghai Power Company to construct a new efficient base load plant to serve, on a wholesale basis, all the power companies in the adjacent area. From an investment standpoint, domestic or foreign, this is a needed and worthy project, provided a franchise be granted and suitable assurances given with respect to servicing and amortization of loans. Taiwan offers many advantages to industrial expansion, a strategic shipping location, appreciable natural resources, adequate transportation, a literate and industrious population and low cost hydro-electric power, and some expansion of power facilities may be indicated, particularly if the fertilizer and other industries are greatly expanded. There is, however, a considerable installed capacity not now available because of damaged transmission lines and sub-stations. In North China, political difficulties will need to be resolved before any permanent improvement or expansion of power systems would be justified.

Railways—The railways of China, operated by the Ministry of Communications as a government monopoly, may be grouped as follows:

ANNEXES

	Kilometers	
	Total	Operable (by Nat'l Gov't)
Manchuria	11336	1647
North China	5749	2362
South and Central China including Lunghai Railroad	8837	6199
Taiwan (Formosa)	3925	3925
Hainan Island	289	....
Totals	30136	4133

From July 1937, when Japan initiated war against China, to October 1938, China lost virtually all railway lines to the enemy or through her own scorched earth policy. On V-J Day 8772 km were in operation in China proper and approximately 11000 km in Manchuria, but since then 3649 km in China proper and 9353 km in Manchuria have been captured or destroyed by the Communists.

With railroad materials and rolling stock furnished by UNRRA, and cannibalized from branch lines and sidings, since V-J Day, 3816 km of railways have been restored in China proper, but largely on an emergency basis with temporary timber bridges and other sub-standard materials.

Deficiencies in transport are a major obstacle to economic recovery but until the political situation is resolved in Manchuria and North China, no rehabilitation of railways in those areas, except on an emergency basis, is feasible. This includes the Lunghai Line which, since the change in course of the Yellow River to the old bed, is now considered in Central rather than North China. Proposed railway rehabilitation programs have therefore been confined to lines south of the Yangtze River, the important North and South artery between Canton (Kowloon) and Hankow, (1242 km main, 106 km branch) and nearly complete rebuilding of the diagonal Chekiang-Kiangsi Railway, from Hangchow to Chuchow (1076 km main, 68 km branch) where it connects with the Canton-Hankow Railway; and the Hunan-Kwangsi-Kweichow line which runs from Hengyang to Kweilin and Tuyun. The latter line could probably be rebuilt at least in part with materials salvaged in rebuilding the other two lines.

Estimates run high, up to $100,000,000 and more, for this program and include such maintenance of way material, rolling stock and railway shop equipment which must be imported. A major obstacle to additional investment in these lines on a loan basis is the heavy and involved capital structure, which is completely out of line with the present deteriorated plant value. Financial reorganization is indicated, with assumption by the National Government of war damage.

Shipping—Inadequacy of coastal and river shipping is a contributing factor to the existing breakdown in trade within China, as well as foreign commerce, upon which national unity and prosperity depend. In this case, however, the situation could be improved, despite the civil war, were it not for the spirit of nationalism and monopoly which characterizes the Chinese government's policy. Foreign flag vessels are no longer allowed to engage in Chinese coastal trade as before the war, and important former ports, such as Hankow, are not open to foreign ships.

In July 1937 when Japan launched an intensified campaign against China, there were 4008 ships of all categories with a gross tonnage of 1,286,000 tons engaged in China's trade. Of these 3457 with a gross tonnage of 576,000 tons were under Chinese registry. As a result of the blockade and seizure of the China Coast and harbor areas by Japanese armed forces, all the sea-going vessels and some of the river steamers together with 7450 junks and 30,000 fishing boats were lost. All ship yards and repair facilities were also lost.

After the war, 60,000 tons of British shipping were leased and numbers of ships obtained, nearly all from the United States. Ships purchased by the National Government and operated by China Merchants total 137 of a gross tonnage of 283,800 tons and those by private (Chinese) firms total 114 of a gross tonnage of 253,400 tons. There is a total, government and private, of 1017 sea going ships of 628,900 gross tons and 1501 river and small craft of 179,893 tons or a total gross tonnage of 808,815. Many of these ships are, however, old and costly to maintain and operate, so that the total falls short of actual needs. There is a reported shortage on the Yangtze of passenger vessels and cargo vessels with passenger accommodations. There is also a serious shortage of ship repair and docking facilities. Rehabilitation of docking and repair facilities at Keelung (Taiwan) will meet a part of this requirement. One major deterrent to resumption of normal shipping traffic is its relatively high cost, due principally to the increased cost of coal and high cost and inefficiency of maritime and cargo-handling labor.

Harbors—All Chinese harbors were occupied by the Japanese after July 1937, and except in North China and Manchuria very little was done to improve or even to maintain them adequately. As a result, at the end of the war, waterfront structures and godowns were in a deteriorated and in some cases damaged condition, and harbors and channels were in some instances, notably in Taiwan, blocked by sunken vessels.

In the early part of 1946, a survey was made by Chinese and American engineers and plans made to rehabilitate and improve a number of the harbors. Some of these plans would appear to be unrealistic and inadvisable, specifically the Whangpoa project at Canton and the Tangku Harbor project in North China. The less ambitious but more realistic Inner Canton Harbor project, and the improvement of the channel and entrance of the Hai Ho River, sponsored by the Hai Ho Conservancy Commission, would seem to be more in consonance with reasonable requirements and funds which can probably be made available. All harbor projects need to be carefully reviewed for economic justification and conformance to the general economic rehabilitation program for China.

Tangku Harbor Project—For more than 40 years, shipping to Tientsin, the commercial and communication center of North China, has been carried on in two types of ships, the majority in small coastwise steamers which crossed the Taku bar at high water, and contingent upon draft proceeded either to Tangku or Taku, or on up the Hai Ho River to Tientsin the remainder in deeper draft ships which anchored outside the bar and were discharged or loaded by special sea-going lighters. Although little cargo was ever lost, there were some delays due to weather, and there was agitation for a deep water port. The Gulf of Chihli contains no natural deep draft harbors nor does it lend itself to their economic construction south of Chinhuangtao because of the shallow water along the coast and the heavy silt content of rivers which discharge into it.

The Japanese undertook the construction of a harbor on the North side of the mouth of the Hai Ho River with a lock connection into the river with a view to shipping coal and salt to Japan. The Tangku Harbor Administration created under the Ministry of Communications has expanded this original Japanese project into a full fledged deep draft harbor. As originally conceived it consisted of a protected dredged harbor with a lock connection into the Hai Ho River and stone jetties extending 16,800 metres (10 miles) over the mud flats to deep water. The approximate estimate at that time was U. S. $30 million. It has already been determined that much more than the originally estimated quantity of stone would be required for the jetties, due to the soft silt bottom, and that even the original quantity of stone was beyond the capacity of the railroad to carry. The Tangku Harbor Commission therefore proposed to substitute cellular construction of steel sheet piling. In view of the soft bottom conditions it is open to question whether this alternative will be satisfactory. The difficulties and high cost of construction under such conditions are well known. In any case, the 80,000 tons of steel required will appreciably increase the cost and the foreign exchange requirements. It is probable that the total cost of the project will exceed U. S. $50 million. Operating difficulties and costs are also likely to be heavy. The mud banks along the harbor and channel will slough indefinitely and require continuous maintenance dredging, and ice conditions inside the harbor and channel, located between the outlets of two fresh water rivers, are likely to be severe, with no appreciable current to facilitate clearance. Difficulties from silting and ice are likely to be encountered in operation of the lock. Since it would be costly and imprudent, if not fatal, to rely solely upon the lock to pass shipping to Taku and Tientsin, it will be necessary to keep open the Hai Ho entrance channel, and since this channel will normally service the bulk of the traffic at nominal cost, the heavy operating and capital costs of the Tangku Harbor project would have to be borne by the deep draft ships. For a fraction of the Harbor cost, worthwhile channel (Koku and Nan Kai cuttings) and entrance (jetty) improvements could be made to the Hai Ho River which would benefit the majority of the vessels normally serving Tangku, Taku and Tientsin. In this connection it is interesting to note as evidence of the need for a coordinating agency, that there are two Government agencies, one under the Ministry of Communications and the other under the Ministry of Water Conservancy, competing, working at cross purposes and devoting their attention and efforts to the same basic problem, namely providing adequate harbor facilities for the Tientsin-Peking area.

Textiles—The textile industry, next to food, is China's largest consumer goods industry and by the same token, the most important toward reviving her economy and meeting her vital clothing need. It was in textiles that China first embarked on her modern industrial development. Before the war there were in China, including Manchuria, 6 million machine spindles and over 50,000 power looms, of which 2.1 million were lost and 1.6 million damaged but susceptible of repair. It is estimated that approximately 3 million spindles are now in operation, and that 4 million may be in operation in another year. These capacities will only partially meet requirements. Cotton production is also below the pre-war, largely because of the disturbed political situation in the North. The cotton summary and outlook for the 1946–1947 and 1947–1948 seasons are shown on the following page. Substantial assistance has been extended to China, largely through UNRRA in the form of clothing, cotton textiles and raw cotton totalling $115 million U. S., and through an Eximbank loan for the purchase of cotton. The former Japanese enterprises which comprised a large part of the pre-war industry have been taken over by a government corporation, the China Textile Industries, Inc., and the earnings of this corporation since V–J Day have provided the government with substantial revenues. It is the intention of the Chinese Government, under the corporation's charter, to sell the mills which it now operates to private enterprise, and appraisals of their worth are currently being made with this object in view. Some inquiries are being made concerning the prospects for investment in these mills by United States textile interests. In view of unsettled political and financial conditions, the latter undoubtedly would require assurances regarding financial control of any enterprise jointly established with Chinese interests, as well as provisions for remission of profits and debt service, fair assessment of taxes, and guarantees of maintaining operations at capacity.

TENTATIVE ESTIMATE CHINA COTTON SUMMARY AND OUTLOOK FOR THE 1946-47 AND 1947-48 SEASONS

	500 lb. Bales, in Thousands
August 1, 1946–July 31, 1947	
Estimated carryover of cotton in warehouses and mills on August 1, 1946	750
Arrivals of UNRRA cotton from August 1, 1946 up to July 31, 1947	258
Arrivals of foreign commercial cotton from August 1, 1946 up to July 31, 1947	568
Total domestic cotton estimated to be available for mills during period ending September 30, 1947, mostly arriving before July 31	800
	2,376
Calculated mill consumption, August 1, 1946–July 31, 1947	1,500
Mill and undistributed stocks	876
TENTATIVE ROUGH FORECAST FOR AUGUST 1, 1947–JULY 31, 1948	
Estimated amounts available to mills from domestic crop to September 30, 1948, mostly arriving before July 31	1,100
Total available supply at manufacturing centers or in the country	1,976
Requirements	
Estimated mill consumption, August 1, 1947–July 31, 1948	1,750
Mill and other visible stocks needed for safe carryover	600
	2,350
Imports needed to July 31, 1948	347
UNRRA cotton to arrive	124
Commercial or other imports scheduled to arrive	150
Further imports needed	100
Third quarter allocation	97

Fertilizer—One of the outstanding needs in China is chemical fertilizer. China is predominantly an agricultural country. More than 80 per cent of her population are farmers, most of them barely able to eke out an existence, with practically no purchasing power or ability to improve their miserable lot. If there is ever to be any real improvement in Chinese economy and standards of living, it must come in large part from increased agricultural production. There is no more effective means of increasing the productivity of land and farmers than by the use of fertilizers. Natural fertilizers traditionally used are inadequate to restore the fertility of the soil, and oil cake wastefully used as fertilizer could more profitably be fed to animals whose by-products—milk, eggs and meat—would greatly improve the diet and health of the people. A good theoretical case can be made for the use of chemical fertilizer, because even at the very high prices to the Chinese farmers, it can produce three to four times its value in crops. A practical problem remains of satisfactory financing arrangements.

In Taiwan 300,000 tons of commercial fertilizer were used annually before the war. In South China about half that amount was used profitably for rice and sugar on the depleted triple-cropped soils of that area, but the bulk of Chinese farmers have no knowledge of its advantages. Merely as a measure of possible requirements, if the same amount were applied as in Japan, Chinese requirements would total 11,000,000 tons annually. Probably only a fraction of that amount will ever be used, primarily because of the prohibitive cost to the farmers, due to the primitive means of transport in the interior of China, and the difficulties of providing any such quantities. It is not feasible for China to import the fertilizers she needs, because of short world supply, and exchange requirements.

The Yungli Chemical Company, privately owned, has a plant near Nanking with a capacity of 30,000 tons per year, of ammonium sulphate, which it is expanding to capacity of 60,000 tons; and has also obtained an Eximbank loan in the sum of $16,000,000 toward the construction of a new plant at Hsiangtan in Hunan Province of a capacity of 90,000 tons of ammonium sulphate per year.

The National Resources Commission has made a survey with the aid of American consultants, and has made plans to develop a production of 705,000 tons of chemical fertilizers annually—481,000 tons of ammonium sulphate and nitrate, 12,000 tons of calcium cyanamid, and 212,000 tons of super-phosphate, and has requested an Eximbank loan in the sum of $50,000,000 to implement them. The projects consist of the rehabilitation and expansion of five existing plants in Taiwan to increase the pre-war capacity of 34,000 tons of both phosphatic and nitrogenous fertilizers to a production of 75,000 tons by 1949; also the construction of two new plants in Taiwan, one an ammonium sulphate plant with a capacity of 181,900 tons annually and the other a super-phosphate plant with a capacity of 170,000 tons annually. The construction of an ammonium sulphate plant at Canton with a capacity of 278,800 tons annually is also proposed. Taiwan is a more favorable location because of the availability of low cost electric power. The proposed construction of the super-phosphate plant may require further consideration because of the present lack of satisfactory phosphate rock. The rock from Haichow is inferior, and the proposal to import from Indo-China and Christmas Island cannot be regarded as a satisfactory solution for a costly permanent installation of this kind. The Japanese are thought to have discovered a large deposit in China, but it has not yet been found. The need to pursue prospecting diligently is evident.

Iron and Steel—The mining and tempering of iron has been practiced in China for several thousand years, but the lack of technical skill has kept the industry at a low level of development. There are few available data on the Chinese pre-war iron industry. There was a rather considerable production of iron ore— perhaps 2 million metric tons annually, largely from the Lungyen Mine in the Liaoning District and the Tayeh Mine in the Yangtze Valley, but most of it went to the Japanese steel industry. Pig iron production in China proper in 1936 was about 155,000 tons, largely from native furnaces, and in Manchuria about 475,000 tons. Less than 50,000 tons of steel were produced. During the war in Free China, iron and steel making facilities were small, primitive and unproductive. In 1944 only 44,000 tons of iron and 13,000 tons of steel were produced. In 1945 steel production was down to 8,000 tons but there has been some revival and the Chinese Government hopes, optimistically, to produce 200,000 tons in 1947.

The National Resources Commission has had a survey made by American consultants, of the iron and steel potential of China. While known iron ore deposits of China are substantial—if all recovered they would produce 300,000,000 tons of steel—they are not impressive for a country as large and populous as China, and in the United States they would suffice for less than six years. The importance of continuing the search for additional high grade deposits, persistently and continuously, is indicated, as well as making a more careful survey and appraisal of the low grade deposits. The latter appear to be considerable and add appreciably to the possibility of creating an iron and steel industry of considerable magnitude in China.

As a result of the survey, the National Resources Commission is proceeding with plans for the construction of a steel plant in the Yangtze Valley, at Tayeh, on the south branch of the Yangtze River about 135 kilometers east of and downstream from Hankow, and is soliciting U. S. funds in the sum of $35,000,000 to undertake this project. The proposed initial capacity of this first plant is 375,000 metric tons per year, of rails, fittings, plates, blooms, billets, structurals, merchant bars, sheets and tin plate. Additional plants are proposed later at Peiping with a capacity of 300,000 tons, at Chungking of 80,000 tons, and at Canton of perhaps 250,000 tons. Neither Manchuria nor Taiwan was considered in this survey. Before final decision is made on the Tayeh site, a further study should be made, and consideration given to a location on Taiwan, inasmuch as the design of the proposed Tayeh plant was predicated on imports of iron ore from Hainan, to the South.

Cement—The development of the cement industry in China has taken place in comparatively recent years. In China proper the production in 1937 was 1,000,000 tons. In 1946, the output was only 300,000 tons and 600,000 tons were imported. Cement is an important element in the reconstruction of industries, harbors, railways, roads and buildings, and plans have been made for the expansion of the industry. Fortunately China has abundant raw material resources. Plans have been made by the National Resources Commission for the rehabilitation and expansion of three plants in Taiwan, at Kao-hsiung, Tsu-Tung and Suao (the latter is poorly located and was badly damaged by bombing); by the Kwa Hsin Cement Company for the development of a new plant at Tayeh, for the rehabilitation and expansion from 200 to 500 tons per day of the North China Cement Company, and the development of the Hunan Cement Company with a capacity of 500 tons per day. The last two projects, both sponsored by the National Resources Commission, should have further study. Funds in the sum of $2,700,000 US have already been obtained for the Taiwan plants, $1,600,000 from UNRRA, $500,000 Eximbank, $260,000 Canadian and $340,000 National Resources Commission, and orders in approximately this amount have been placed for overseas materials and equipment. The present cement output of 150,000 tons per year in Taiwan is adequate for present local requirements. By June 1948, with the increased capacity, it is hoped to produce 600,000 tons per year, 300,000 for local requirements including hydro-electric expansion, and 300,000 tons for export.

The Hwa Hsin Cement Company has undertaken the construction of a modern 1,000 tons per day plant at Tayeh on the site of a pre-war plant of one-fifth that capacity, which was moved to Chengchi in Free China on the approach of the Japanese. The major part of the required machinery has already been ordered from Allis-Chalmers and other U. S. manufacturers and they have received aid from UNRRA in the form of cement mixers, structural steel, earth-moving equipment and miscellaneous items, but they are now seeking a $2,000,000 Eximbank loan to cover the U. S. cost of a 3½ kilometer aerial tramway, conveyors, quarrying equipment, etc., required to complete the project.

Crop Conditions

China's winter and summer food harvests this year, assuming no changes in present summer crop conditions, are expected by the American Agricultural Attaché to be significantly larger than last year's fairly good returns. Poor distribution, however, will result in a serious lack of food in at least five large areas in China which are possible famine districts. It must be emphasized that

China's food stocks since the war have been much lower than normal. Therefore a potentially dangerous situation will continue to exist until food stocks have been built up.

The most important food shortage areas, approximately in order of their importance are:

1) The coastal strip in Kwangtung from Swatow south to the Canton delta country. This area, a large food deficit area in normal times, suffered from the early June floods which occurred in the East, West and North River valleys. The Pearl River estuary and delta and the Han River area around Swatow are expected to be the centers of the shortage. Early reports indicate a good start for the second rice crop.

2) South Hunan in the hsiens around Hengyang. The rest of Hunan expects a good rice crop, but this area, which suffered starvation last year, was damaged again by a flood in the middle of June. It is not clear how badly the June floods damaged south Hunan. Damage may have been overestimated, in which case supplies from within the province will be more than sufficient if properly distributed. However, proper distribution within Hunan is questionable when other areas offer better prices.

3) Northern Kwangsi areas which are part of the extension of the south Hunan shortage area. UNRRA reports state that starvation in this area is partly due to heavy exports of rice to large coastal cities where higher prices for rice are offered.

In early June 100,000 acres of farm land were flooded in Kwangsi along the West River from Nanning to Wuchow. The first rice crop in this area was reported destroyed, but in the rest of Kwangsi crop conditions were reported good.

4) Two areas in Honan, one in the north near the Hopei border, and one in the southeastern reclaimed Yellow River areas. The shortage area in the north, which includes Linhsien, Tangying and Linchang, is apparently suffering from the winter wheat drought as well as fighting. The information on this area is based on reports that have yet to be confirmed.

The southeastern area lacks food since this was in the Yellow River flood area in recent years. In many parts no crops have been harvested since the river was diverted across Shantung. This area also includes parts of the Yellow River flooded areas in North Anhwei.

5) Food shortages are reported by UNRRA in western and northern Shantung, especially in the areas adjacent to the Yellow River. Food is particularly short in the Tehsien area on the Hopei border. There is a definite need for food for the migrants leaving the lowlands and bed of the Yellow River which has been diverted back into northwest Shantung.

6) Recent press reports indicate floods in north Kiangsu both north and south of Hsuchow, with the Peihsien and Suchien areas claimed completely inundated. This area, as well as local areas in southwest Shantung, were the scene of civil war fighting last summer and fall and will undoubtedly require assistance. Actual flood damage to crops in north Kiangsu is still being assessed so that reliable estimates of relief needs are not yet available.

Local areas which are suffering or anticipating food shortages include:
1) the south Jehol mountainous area,
2) some hsiens on the Liaotung Peninsula north of Dairen in Manchuria,
3) scattered areas in Shansi, including the Tatung locality,
4) the Hoo Li area in Chahar will be short until harvest this fall,
5) scattered hsiens in Hopei. Hsiens mentioned by UNRRA as short of are Mancheng, Tingshing, Jungcheng, Chingyuen and Mingho.

6) Famine conditions are expected in Ningteh hsien in north central Fukien. Some of the Fukien coastal hsiens are short of food.

7) UNRRA anticipates famine conditions in the Pescadores Islands.

8) Local flooded areas in south Kweichow, south Kiangsi, southwest Kwangsi and along the rivers in the Chengtu basin in Szechwan.

Shortages may generally develop in north China if summer crops are poor, especially in Shansi, Hopei and Shantung. Crop conditions in north China so far, however, have been reported at least average, except for the flooded areas mentioned above.

During late July and early August an estimated 12 million shih mow (2 million acres) were flooded in the lower Liao River valley south of Mukden. Early reports tentatively indicate that more than a million people in this area were affected by the unusually heavy seasonal flood. Suffering and food shortages in this area are expected as a result of the flood and poor distribution from other parts of Manchuria. However, a surplus production of food is definitely expected for the whole of Manchuria. Nationalist-occupied Manchuria is expected to have a food surplus for the year also, although much smaller than that of the Communist areas.

Taiwan's rice acreage and production appear to have returned to pre-war figures, aided by the use of some land in the southern part of the island that was formerly used for sugar-cane production. As UNRRA Agricultural Rehabilitation men point out, this is significant since this is the first large rice-producing or exporting area in the Far East which apparently has returned to pre-war averages and production.

Problems Confronting American Business in China

In each of the localities visited conferences were held with American businessmen. Much valuable information concerning the situation in China was gained from these sources and from memoranda prepared by the American Chambers of Commerce in Shanghai and Tientsin. American business representatives strongly expressed the view that it would be undesirable for the United States to extend further financial assistance to China, in the present situation, unless strict conditions were attached to assure effective use of the proceeds of any loan for purposes consistent with United States policies. As stated in a Joint Memorandum of the Far East-American Council of Commerce and Industry, Inc., and the National Foreign Trade Council, Inc., submitted to the Department of State June 17, 1947, these two councils are strongly on record in support of a procedure under which, from now on, any public funds which the United States Government may provide or make available to the Government of China, either for relief or general reconstruction purposes, should be only on the basis of strictest control as to handling, end-use, and disposition.

American businessmen stated that the present Chinese Government has been apathetic in its efforts at economic improvement, and has taken refuge in the thought of foreign assistance for solution for China's problems. The American businessmen felt that it would prejudice achievement of necessary reforms in China, if financial assistance were to be provided in any large amount with control of its use to be left in Chinese hands. They regarded this, for example, as a basic defect in the $500 million loan of 1942.

The following are the principal problems which American business is facing in China at the present time. Complaints include the administration of import and exchange controls, particular stress being placed upon the methods used in allocation of import quotas, delays and inefficiency in obtaining import licenses, and the practice on the part of the import licensing board of discriminating against foreign concerns to favor newly established Chinese companies, including those organized by "favored families." It was universally acknowledged that conditions of corruption among lower officials in the import control and customs services were widespread. Legitimate enterprise is restricted under the regulations, but goods which are on the list of prohibited imports can move and do move into China by bribery. Smuggling via Hong Kong is widespread with established fees and procedures.

From the standpoint of China's commercial relations with the rest of the world, as well as of maintaining what historically has been one of the most important sources of revenue to the Chinese Government, great importance attaches to the maintenance of an efficient and honest Chinese Maritime Customs Service. In pre-war years, the reputation of the Chinese Maritime Customs for efficiency and honesty of administration was unexcelled throughout the world. At the present time, in contrast, corruption among the lower officials is widespread, more so it was learned than at any time in the last 94 years. For analogy, comparison would have to be made with the period between 1842 and 1853 when conditions of bribery and corruption were so rampant as to lead to the establishment of the Inspectorate General of Customs. The basic cause for the situation which exists is to be found in the completely inadequate level of wages for customs employees. They are paid a starting wage of around CN $1,500,000 per month and employees who have been employed for six years, now earn around $2 million CN per month (equivalent to U. S. $50.00 at present market rate). These sums are completely inadequate to cover the essentials of life for any man with a family. With opportunity for bribery frequently present, almost the inevitable result is widespread corruption. A similar or worse situation exists in other Chinese tax bureaus. A rise in the wages paid to customs officials would not only do more than any other single factor to restore the integrity of the Maritime Customs but undoubtedly would repay the National Government many fold in terms of receipts acquired.

The most common form of corruption in the customs is understood to be the payment of what is called "convenience money," i. e., a payment made by an importer to expedite action on his case and movement of goods through customs. Much less frequent is an alteration in the amount of custom payment or the sum which goes to the National treasury. In this respect, the record of the Maritime Customs is relatively good. Administrative costs of collecting duties run 9–11 percent. In the Direct Tax Bureau of the Ministry of Finance, it is reported, the "administrative" expense of tax collection runs as high as 60 per cent.

Scarcely any reforms which could be instituted would be more important for China's commercial relations than the taking of measures to restore the efficiency and integrity of its Maritime Customs service.

American business is also concerned with the fact that profits from trade in China cannot be remitted to the States through regular exchange channels. They stress that if China desires the assistance of foreign capital in development of its commerce and industries, provision must be made to permit remission of legitimate profits to the States by American investors. The National Government has recently recognized this fact in principle but stresses the emergency character of the present situation and China's inability with its present small exchange holdings to permit such remission of profit.

Another principal complaint of American business relates to discrimination in the enforcement of various Chinese taxes, particularly the business tax and the income tax. There exists a technical provision in the existing income tax law, and its enforcement regulations, under which many American corporations are required to pay greater income taxes than those paid by Chinese groups; and also for some American corporations to pay an excess profits tax as well, which they would not have had to pay if they had been incorporated under Chinese instead of American law. The principal complaint of American business, however, is that the income tax is collected in practice from only a small proportion of Chinese companies, and, if collected, the sum is a matter of arrangement by payment of a bribe to the local tax official. American companies, on the other hand, are required to pay taxes to the full letter of the law.

American business firms operating in Shanghai are particularly concerned at the operations of the buying and selling agencies of the National Government, and particularly of the developing channel by which China's principal exports, such as bristles and tung oil, have been exported through the Central Trust, a subsidiary of the Central Bank of China, and the Universal Trading Corporation, organized under the State of New York. The Universal Trading Corporation also functions as a purchasing agent on both governmental and private account and forwards its products to China for sale through the Central Trust. During the first six months of 1947, 33 per cent of the exports from Shanghai to the United States were consigned to the Universal Trading Corporation. Development of this channel serves to undermine the position of established American trading firms and agency representatives in China. The recent decision of the Chinese Government to terminate the Chinese Supply Commission in Washington as of 1 August would be welcome were it not for the fact that the Supply Commission functions were announced as being transferred to the Universal Trading Corporation. Recognizing the concern with which American business and government officials may be expected to regard this transfer, it is possible that the National Government will modify the intended functions of the Universal Trading Corporation, as well as of the Central Trust.

Immediate Steps to Strengthen the Economy

The handling of foreign trade through normal private channels with rigorous nondiscriminatory enforcement of import controls is urgently needed. The Central Trust should be taken out of foreign trade and its functions restricted. A free market in foreign exchange, within a system of import controls, and managed by the Central Bank with full cooperation of the Appointed Banks, should provide incentives for private exporters. All ports, including Hankow, should be open to foreign vessels, at least temporarily. A rigid control of smuggling would also be a major step towards the restoration of foreign trade.

China should move towards stabilizing the currency by first attempting to restore a balance between Government receipts and expenditures. Any attempt at currency stabilization through the issuance of a new currency, either paper or silver, will be premature, unless the Government has already taken steps to live within its income. The ultimate objective should be a limit or ceiling on the currency circulation and on borrowing from the Central Bank. Full publicity should be given to the activities of the Central Bank in controlling the issuance of the Chinese National Currency. These measures might help to slow down the rate of price increases, protect the position of the CN dollar as a national currency, and forestall any attempts by provincial authorities to issue separate local currencies.

The economy would be strengthened by disposing of Government-owned industrial concerns and monopolies to private Chinese enterprise, both on the mainland and in Taiwan, through open and honest sales—preferably for foreign exchange or gold—to the highest bidder. This step would increase production by giving an incentive which is at present lacking. The disposal of industrial plants would eliminate expenditures from the national budget to finance Government enterprise, reduce the number of functionaries who are in a position to make private profit at the public expense, bring in large amounts of revenue for the national budget, and assist in retarding the rise in prices. A prohibition against public officials as directors in private corporations would also strengthen the morale of the Government service.

Progress towards a balanced budget should become possible through the foregoing measures, and through increased revenue from taxation and public borrowing. Even under the present tax laws, revenue could probably be increased by strict and punctual enforcement. A tax on profits secured from speculation in commodities would be a useful addition. If there is any prospect of success in stabilizing prices and limiting currency issuance, the public would be encouraged to buy Government bonds and repatriate funds which have been sent abroad, thus materially helping the Government to balance the budget. Improved efficiency in the collection of the land tax in kind would increase the yield and reduce the burden of its incidence. Stability of the Government in the countryside could be rapidly undermined if the incidence of conscription and the land tax in kind becomes too severe. The recrudescence of *likin*—local transit taxes—and military requisitioning at nominal prices should be severely discouraged.

The administrative inefficiency and corruption, which are paralyzing the economy and crippling China as a military power, should be eliminated as rapidly as possible, and the administrative inertia overcome by a delegation of executive power and authority.

Considerations on United States Economic Assistance

Budgetary Deficits—Inflation is China's central economic problem, and the most urgently required assistance is that which can first check the depreciation of the Chinese currency and later permit of its stabilization. The main inflationary pressure comes from budgetary deficits, financed by issuance of paper currency, to cover the increasing burden of military expenditures. Reduction of such deficits requires drastic action by the Chinese government in two principal ways, (1) in reducing military expenditures by setting China's military objectives within the capacities of its economy (with such assistance as the United States can appropriately give), as well as by reforms aimed at eliminating inefficiency and corruption from the Chinese army itself; and (2) by increasing Chinese government revenues, possibly by levying new taxes, but initially by increased efficiency in the collection of existing taxes.

The above reforms are not easy; they call for measures which would alienate many local Army leaders, and require ruthless weeding out of corrupt tax officials and payment of a living wage to tax collection employees. They cannot be accomplished quickly. But unless effective efforts are made in this direction no attack on China's economic problems can hope to succeed.

United States assistance in meeting these problems could best be rendered by making available the services of experienced advisors in the budgetary and taxation fields, and by providing military advisory personnel to assist in developing and supervising an efficient military service of supply. The United States government, in our view, should not extend financial assistance with a view to covering China's budgetary deficit. Nor should financial assistance be extended on any substantial scale for reconstruction projects or to relieve pressure on China's balance of payments unless these basic steps are first taken.

Economic Reconstruction Projects—The Mission has not endeavored to prepare a plan for China's economic reconstruction. It is, however, greatly impressed with the need of a realistic formulation by the National Government of a practical program for economic reconstruction. Most necessary is a greater coordination of effort by military and economic agencies of the National Government, as well as between the National and Provincial governments and private enterprise, both in the formulation and in the implementing of reconstruction projects. China's own resources should be marshalled for solution of her economic problems before there can be assurance that requests for foreign assistance are soundly conceived and can be carried out effectively.

In connection with the Marshall Plan, European nations have been called upon for their plans for economic reconstruction. If the same principle were to apply in the Far East, difficulties would be encountered, because of China's lack of a coordinated program of economic reconstruction and of the personnel and centralized responsibilities for developing one.

The Mission accordingly would recommend, as a prerequisite to United States financial assistance, the establishment by the National Government of a high-level planning and screening agency to review carefully and impartially the projects and programs submitted by various sponsor-Ministries, Commissions, Administrations, provincial, local authorities and by private enterprise, with a view of establishment of an overall priority list of projects on the basis of which China's available resources can be directed towards China's most vital programs and projects. Such a screening and planning agency should assess the economic justification and self-liquidating potentialities of any project submitted; review the technical feasibility and estimated costs; coordinate such project with essential corollary projects of other Ministries, such as power and transportation projects which need to be accomplished prior to or concurrently with a given project; determine the manner of financing and indicate data or revision required to qualify for financing; and finally assign a position on the overall priority list.

Some such agency and procedure are considered essential to a coordinated and effective economic rehabilitation program. Such an agency would be the third place (Ministry of Finance and Ministry of War being the first two) where the services of United States economic advisors could be most effectively employed. They should be assisted also by a staff of qualified technical personnel. Such advisors would not have authority to extend financial assistance. Their job would be to assist in developing a program capable of realistic implementation; to assure that so far as possible China's resources were directed toward most pressing economic reconstruction projects, and to assure, in those cases in which United States financial assistance was required, that the projects were soundly conceived and presented for United States consideration.

Investment of Private Chinese Funds—Under conditions of inflation and financial insecurity Chinese investors are not disposed to place their capital in long term productive enterprises. Short term advances under inflation conditions command interest rates of from 15% to 30% per month. Private capital goes also into hoarding of commodities as a hedge against inflation, and for speculative purposes. The current psychology is entirely an inflationary one, and is not conducive to efforts at longer run economic reconstruction. This is a further compelling reason why the Chinese government must take definite steps toward fiscal reform and a stabilized currency, as a pre-requisite to economic reconstruction, which in large measure requires the investment of private Chinese and foreign capital.

Export-Import Bank—Under date of June 27, 1947, the National Government applied to the Export-Import Bank for loans aggregating almost $270 million to cover the dollar costs of a number of reconstruction projects, and subsequently a $200 million credit for raw cotton. Conclusions with respect to the situation in China as it affects generally the matter of loans from the Export-Import Bank follow:

In framing requests for Export-Import Bank credits the Chinese authorities appear not to have been sufficiently concerned with the requirement of economic and technical justification for individual projects to be considered. They have decided apparently upon a lump sum total of a credit to be requested, and assigned amounts for individual projects to approximate in the aggregate the desired tctal. Although the National Government has employed the services of a number of outstanding American engineering consultant firms to survey its needs in such fields as transportation, mining, electric power and harbor development, the studies made by these firms—submitted by the Chinese in justification for the projects requested of Export-Import Bank—appear to suffer from a basic defect. Under instruction from the National Government they are drawn up to provide China facilities which are comparable to the best in use in the United States, strictly from the engineering standpoint, and are not realistically drawn up in terms of local needs, capacity for repayment of investment, and of utilizing local resources. A case in point is the Canton-Hankow Railroad for which the Chinese made a credit application originally of $42,654,000, subsequently reduced to $37,500,000. The original construction cost of this line was equal approximately only to $20,000,000. The instructions under which the Morrison Knudsen Company undertook this survey reflect an apparent desire on the part of the Chinese Government planners for the best in modern transportation and industrial equipment. Their survey, however, is not an adequate basis for consideration of a loan request. A loan application should provide a realistic appraisal of the traffic potentialities of the road, its contribution to trade and production in the area, how the National Government proposes to meet the local currency costs of its development, the extent to which the necessary development has been met by the bridge materials, track, ties, locomotives, and rolling stock which have been provided by UNRRA, the financial plan according to which the National Government proposes to meet its earlier outstanding indebtedness on the line, the status of its agreement with the Boxer Indemnity Commission under which the British Government financed the construction of the central section of the line and in accordance with which it was agreed that all materials for this section should be purchased in the United Kingdom, etc., etc. None of this data, to our knowledge, has been provided by the Chinese Government in support of any loan application for the Canton-Hankow Railroad.

The mission was impressed with the extent to which Chinese Government requests for Export-Import Bank assistance are being made on behalf of state-owned and operated enterprises. This was particularly apparent in Formosa where the National Resources Commission owns and operates, either itself or in conjunction with the provincial Government, all principal industries on the island except coal, tea and pineapple. The Commission owns and operates, and in most instances has sought Export-Import Bank loans, for such widely diversified industries as electric power, petroleum refining, sugar refining (the Commission owns 250,000 acres of land under sugar cane), cement manufacturing, shipbuilding, machine shops, artificial fertilizer, and paper manufacture. The pattern of development which the National Resources Commission desires is evident. They wish United States financial assistance, but not United States management or control, to provide necessary foreign exchange for materials and equipment to be acquired in the United States, and to hire foreign technicians when necessary to assist in bringing into operation the facilities acquired. In the case of the Takao Refinery now operated by the Chinese Petroleum Corporation, an NRC subsidiary, the National Government refused American oil companies an opportunity to participate in the ownership and operation of the plant, but requested an Export-Import Bank loan to provide foreign exchange financing, and hired foreign technicians to assist in running the plant. On failing to obtain an Export-Import Bank credit the National Government apparently did not find difficulty in providing itself the foreign exchange required to place this refinery in operation. Whatever the statements made by the National Government regarding the extent to which foreign investments in China are to be welcome, the fact remains that at present there exists in China a strong tendency towards state ownership and operation over wide fields of industry. This raises a problem of policy from the standpoint of United States financial assistance, particularly Export-Import Bank financing, since credits from this institution are intended wherever possible to give support to private enterprise. Obviously it would be undesirable from the standpoint of United States policy to be doctrinaire or completely inflexible in granting loans to Government-owned or operated enterprises. A railroad credit, for example, in China would seem a desirable loan to a Government body and there could be other similar examples. In the present situation, however, in which the National Resources Commission is operating in every major field of industry in China except textiles—in which the bulk of Chinese productions by another Government Corporation, the China Textile Industry, Inc.—there is reason to consider carefully every project in its impact on private enterprise, Chinese as well as American.

The fact that individual credit applications for Export-Import Bank funds must be guaranteed by the Central Bank of China places difficulties in the way of giving consideration to what might be worthwhile small projects proposed either by provincial authorities or by private enterprise. In the more effective coordination of reconstruction projects in China, some method must be found to open the way to financing of locally sponsored projects, both provincial, municipal, and private.

As long as present conditions of civil war and inflation continue, and lack of confidence in the situation in China by Chinese investors themselves exists, there is a general difficulty with respect to the possibility for external financing on banking terms. Among the statutory requirements to Export-Import Bank loans is the proviso that there must exist a reasonable assurance of repayment of any loan made. Even though an individual project may be meritorious from the standpoint of meeting China's basic needs, assurances of repayment cannot exist when the value of the Chinese yuan and the general credit or exchange position of the National Government is deteriorating. Until some effective steps are taken towards greater stability in China's public finances and currency, it is difficult to see how ordinary banking loans can be made with adequate assurances for repayment. The Chinese place emphasis upon the desirability of proceeding now with individual projects in areas which are sheltered from the civil war and hence from attacks or destruction by the Communists. There is, however, in China no industrial area which now is sheltered from the effects of currency inflation and depreciation of the National currency.

The credits which China needs for reconstruction projects for the most part will be long term credits for example from 15–20 years. It is doubtful whether the Export-Import Bank desires to undertake such financing over a period that long. Its policies are understood to aim more at shorter term credits, and largely of the exporter-credit type on particular sales of American manufactured materials or equipment. In any event, it is clear that Export-Import Bank loans could not be used to finance local currency expenditures in China for materials and labor required to be purchased there in connection with any project.

Therefore, there are in China now very few projects which can qualify for Export-Import Bank financing. As the situation is improved, particularly in terms of steps towards fiscal and currency stabilization and towards more realistic formulation of economic reconstruction projects, it is possible that increased opportunities will exist for Export-Import Bank financing, particularly of projects sponsored by American and Chinese private enterprises.

Balance of Payments Assistance.—Another necessary approach to the problem of economic stability in China must relate to the exchange value of the Chinese currency, to checking its depreciation and establishment of conditions under which the foreign exchange value of the yuan eventually may be stabilized. Such stabilization may require United States assistance, but in our view is not a practical possibility until definite steps are taken towards fiscal reform and restoring confidence of the Chinese people, and until production in China increases to permit expansion in exports more nearly (with remittances from overseas Chinese) to pay for imports. Again there is need to emphasize the interdependence of China's economic, political, and military problems, and the sequence envisaged for budgetary, reconstruction, and currency stabilization measures of assistance.

Immediately China has the problem of financing its imports, which even on a restricted basis and not counting UNRRA imports, are running at a level several times its exports plus remittances of overseas Chinese, and drawing down external official exchange holdings at the rate of around $200 million per year. It is anticipated that such official assets at the present rate of usage will be drawn down to around $220 million by the end of 1947 and would be exhausted by the end of 1948 or early in 1949. It is hoped that the recently introduced system of partial linking of exports and imports and other measures will result in expansion of exports and improvement of China's foreign exchange position. At best, however, there will be a period of months in which the drain on China's external official holdings of exchange will continue. It may be desirable, therefore, as an interim measure prior to any currency stabilization loan, to give some assistance towards financing a part of China's principal industrial imports, e. g., raw cotton, to prevent too great an impairment of China's official exchange holdings.

Congressional Aid—United States objectives and interests require that positive and constructive aid be rendered to China to arrest the deterioration of economic conditions, and thus to help to develop and maintain a government whose philosophy and aims are compatible with our own. This recommendation is consonant, not only with the present world situation, but with the historical ties—between the United States and China. For reasons stated above, it is not believed feasible that necessary financial assistance can be provided China from the Export-Import Bank. The need in any event is for an integrated program of assistance which would require clarification and authorization by Congress of its intended military, economic and political phases.

Certain major prerequisites to assure effective utilization of any aid extended have been indicated. With concrete evidences of performance in these respects, and with firm commitments for continued progress, it is recommended that the United States government, under Congressional authorization, provide financial assistance to China to assure an early undertaking of projects essential for that country's economic reconstruction, and eventually for stabilization of its currency system. The amount of such aid and specific means of its implementation would be subject to determination by Congress acting upon the recommendations of appropriate agencies of the United States government. However, it would be desirable to inaugurate before July 1, 1948 key reconstruction projects relating to transportation, electric power, coal, and artificial fertilizer, even though more substantial assistance for currency stabilization were to be made available at a later date. This emphasizes that a lump-sum financial grant to be handed over to China is not considered justifiable. It indicates the need for Congressional support for a program of assistance over a period of at least five years in which aid can be made available when, as, and if it can be effectively utilized for the purposes intended.

The priority list for reconstruction projects submitted by the National Government should be prepared by a screening and planning agency in the government assisted by American economic and engineering advisors. In connection with any individual projects so presented, and approved, it is contemplated that suitable provision will be made for financial and technical supervision by United States personnel to assure effective utilization of the aid extended.

APPENDIX "C" TO PART II—CHINA

SOCIAL AND CULTURAL

The unending war has inevitably paralyzed China's ambitious pre-war plans for social and cultural advancement. It has been impossible even to hold such slender gains as were made in the few years between internal revolution and Japanese invasion. The primary schools and the adult education enterprises which in those years had barely started their attack upon the nation's mass illiteracy have lost buildings and textbooks and teachers and even contact with pupils. Today, with depreciated money they are unable to replace their buildings and equipment or to encourage their teachers with adequate pay. The middle schools are no better off. The universities limp along under burdens which almost cause despair even in a nation in which scholarship continues to command universal respect to a degree unknown in the Occident. Most of the universities, being seated in eastern China, were driven out by invasion, thus losing buildings and books and equipment. During the war they kept alive by pooling their scant resources in common properties in interior cities. After the war they rushed back home only to find libraries and laboratories gone and often buildings as well. Endowment and other funds had become so small and so unproductive that teachers' salaries and students' scholarships had vanished: what once would have supported a student for one year now might buy him one notebook. In this situation numerous universities have again pooled their poor resources in an effort to carry on, but with feeble success. That the teaching institution still exists to a respectable degree must be attributed largely to the devotion of the teaching profession whose members, receiving hopelessly insufficient salaries, survive only by selling their possessions item by item or by finding odd jobs to do in spare time. There are fewer nobler examples of patriotism.

Beyond the troubles listed, the universities have lately suffered in another respect. Strong political demonstrations among the students have been sharply punished, in defiance of the students' traditional freedom of expression and, still more seriously, in defiance of the libertarian principle of open trial. Faculty members have been replaced because of their political views. In these cases the National Government defends its suppressive arrests by declaration that the prisoners' actual offense has been sedition rather than merely opposition-thinking, but the fact remains that this sort of suppression does not exist in free lands, and the actual disappearance of victims, untried by any known law process, is itself intolerable. That the universities should be forced to live under this sort of shadow is one of the chief tragedies in China's higher education today.

The professions and technological groups mark time. Not only are individual incomes reduced by inflation, but access to professional magazines and reports, by which under normal conditions proficiency is maintained and increased, remains most difficult (the United States Information Service libraries do what they can toward meeting this acute lack). Newspapers have for the most part become party organs, with a few honorable exceptions. Free expression risks closing down of the newspaper by government order "for reasons of military security" with reorganization under altered direction a requisite to renewed operation. University presses have ceased to operate. Cultural assemblies of every sort, save for political purposes and these thoroughly shepherded, are rare and spasmodic, offering in this field no such continuity of public information as in normal times.

The effects of prolonged social disorder are bad in any land, but a nation which is highly literate can live for a time on the cultural resources of its individuals. In a nation where there already is so wide a gap between a small but select intelligentsia and a mass of mankind largely illiterate, a new blockade in education is far more serious. Public literacy is essential to public readiness for effective self-government.

The steps to revive education which have been taken already are largely local and hence variable. The national program is in existence, but translating it from paper to performance requires, first of all, far more money than China has available for education. In a land at war most revenues are consumed in the insatiable maw of the military, and such funds as do come to civilian departments' hands are likeliest to be diverted to food and other unquestionably urgent necessities, rather than to education. Hence, National Government plans for reopening schools and buying books and desks and granting a somewhat better wage to teachers are not supported by funds. Much the same thing is true of those universities and middle schools which once were generously supported by foreign churches, now grown uncertain about the institutions' future.

There are other uncertainties in education. The very principles of former years are being re-examined—whether to continue sending Chinese students to America (save for training as teachers, committed to prompt return to China's schools) or rather to prevail on Americans who once taught in China to return quickly to China to resume instruction work there. There is a growing feeling that at this stage the cost of sending students to America would more profitably be expended in bringing teachers to China. Not the least consideration for several years to come is the desirability of toning Chinese students to the environment in which they expect to work as adults, rather than to that of the United States.

China's national mechanism for educational direction and supervision has suffered as much as the schools themselves. It will revive best by being put to work, but that, like the restoration of individual schools, must await the provision of funds.

APPENDIX "D" TO PART II—CHINA

THE MILITARY SITUATION IN CHINA AND PROPOSED MILITARY AID

INDEX

	Pages
Military Situation	808
Strategic Importance	809
Military Aid and Assistance	810
Material Aid Programs	811
Motor Vehicle Parts Project	811
Purchase of Additional Military Equipment	811
Ammunition Supply	812
Completion of the 8⅓ Group Program and Possible Augmentation in Military Air Transport	812
China Mapping Program	812
Transfer of Ships	812
Occupation of Japan	812
Military Advice to Chinese Armed Forces	813

Military Situation

Since General Marshall's departure from China, the overall military situation of the Chinese National Government has deteriorated. In March 1947, following the Nationalist capture of Yenan and at the beginning of an all-out Government effort against Communists, the Nationalist Chief of Staff announced that the main Communist armies would be crushed within three months. Like previous predictions of this nature, his statement never came true and fighting between Nationalists and Communists continues, principally in Manchuria, Hopei, and Shantung.

Communist operations in Manchuria have practically rendered Nationalist forces in that area militarily impotent and prompt action is necessary to prevent Manchuria from becoming a Soviet satellite. Continued successful Communist operations could make untenable the entire Nationalist position in Manchuria where they control only a slender finger of territory. Now, with the cessation of rains, it appears that the Chinese Communists will launch an offensive against both flanks of this narrow Nationalist salient. Simultaneously, Communist guerrilla activities and raids in other provinces, such as Hopei, Shantung, and Jehol, will be intensified so as to pin down other Nationalist forces, prevent guerrilla activities and raids in other provinces, such as Hopei, Shantung, reinforcement and interrupt important Nationalist lines of communication. Meanwhile the National Government has done very little to improve its position in the light of these developments. The Generalissimo has designated General Chen Cheng, a capable commander, as the overall commander of Manchurian forces, but it is doubtful that he can weld a strong unified force in view of the continued serious shortages of both supplies and capable subordinates.

Total Nationalist forces of about a million and a half combat troops plus another million service troops are opposing less than a million Communist combat troops and militia supported by an unknown number of service troops. Unfortunately, less is known about Communist forces than ever before, for at the present time there are no competent foreign observers with them. Chinese information on Communist supply, equipment, casualties, and manpower is completely unreliable and inaccurate.

The underlying military reason for Communist success is that they retain the initiative, striking at places of their own selection with local superiority of forces and with a mission of destruction. Nationalist forces, on the other hand, with a mission of protection, are forced to what amounts to a perimeter defense of scattered areas and of long connecting lines of communication. Such widespread defense offers little chance of lateral coordination and mutual support, thus immobilizing forces that would otherwise be available for offensive action. Communist drives appear to meet with little substantial resistance, while Nationalist withdrawals are generally premature and the words "strategic retreat" have lost all signifiance.

The Generalissimo has never waivered in his contention that he is fighting for national independence against forces of an armed rebellion nor has he been completely convinced that the Communist problem in China can be resolved except by force of arms in spite of the fact that his efforts to suppress Communists by military force alone have failed. The present course, unfortunately, functions as a stimulus to the progressive expansion of Communism.

It is essential that the Generalissimo revise his present course, since, particularly in view of the vast areas involved, it is impossible to conceive of complete suppression of Communists by the sole use of any military force which the National Government could foreseeably field and support, even with external aid, in the future. Hand in hand with action to improve the current military situation, social, political and economic reforms must be instituted in order to maintain a happy and satisfied, and therefore loyal, population in Nationalist areas.

All in all, the military situation in China appears to be governed predominantly by Communists enjoying substantial military successes in Manchuria, in Shantung and in Hopei. These successes can be attributed mainly to the lightness and efficacy of their hit-and-run guerrilla type forces, to their mission of destruction as opposed to the Nationalist mission of protection, to the ineptitude and incompetence of Nationalist high command, to the shrinkage of Nationalist communications, to the general depreciation and depletion of Nationalist equipment and supplies, both ground and air, to increased friction between military forces from the south and civil administration in the areas under attack, and to the stigma attached to troops which so often live off the local civil population.

Strategic Importance

Any further spread of Soviet influence and power would be inimical to United States strategic interests. In time of war the existence of an unfriendly China would result in denying us important air bases for use as staging areas for bombing attacks as well as important naval bases along the Asiatic coast. Its control by the Soviet Union or a regime friendly to the Soviet Union would make available for hostile use a number of warm water ports and air bases. Our own air and naval bases in Japan, Ryukyus and the Philippines would be subject to relatively short range neutralizing air attacks. Furthermore, industrial and military development of Siberia east of Lake Baikal would probably make the Manchurian area more or less self-sufficient.

On the other hand, a unified China friendly or allied to the United States would not only provide important air and naval bases, but also from the standpoint of its size and manpower, be an important ally to the United States even though her poor communications and lack of modern industrial development would make her contribution less effective than would otherwise be the case.

An important factor in analyzing the strategic importance of Manchuria and North China is the role of these two areas in the formation of an industrial crescent capable of complementing the economy of either Siberia or China in which the potentiality of these areas for the manufacture of arms and ammunition, for the development of coal and iron resources, and for the operation of arsenals and machine tooling facilities would be possible. This is important in a positive sense in that China requires these areas to complete her economy and it is important in a negative sense in that both these areas must be denied to the Soviet Union.

While Communist success in China would serve Soviet interests through expansion of control of a regime oriented to and sympathetic with the Soviet Union, a continuation of political and economic chaos accentuated by protracted civil war would also produce the same general result. This appears to fit into a pattern of progressively staged Soviet expansion at the expense of China, a pattern which has already resulted in Soviet absorption of Tannu Tuva and Outer Mongolia.

The military problem in China is inextricably involved in psychological, moral, political and economic factors. Moral support of the National Government by the United States will, in bringing about *military* success for the National Government, be of importance in proportion to the degree of actual material assistance, provided there are concurrent drastic political and economic reforms. United States support of a Chinese request to the United Nations for immediate action to bring about a cessation of hostilities would serve as a prelude to further steps which could be taken to prevent the establishment of a Communist Government in Manchuria.

Military Aid and Assistance

In order to improve the current serious military situation, Nationalist forces must first stabilize the fronts and then regain the initiative. Further, since the Government is supporting civil war with approximately seventy percent of its national budget, steps must be taken to decrease the size of the military establishment while increasing its effectiveness and efficiency.

Whereas some rather ineffective steps have been taken to revitalize the command structure, and other more sweeping reforms are projected for the future, the effectiveness of the armed forces requires a sound program of equipment and improved logistical support. The present industrial potential of China is inadequate to support military forces effectively. Hence outside aid in the form of munitions (most urgently ammunition) and technical assistance are essential before any plans of operations can be undertaken with reasonable prospect of success.

The purpose of conditional American military aid to China should be to facilitate reorganization of her armed forces; to regain public confidence in the armed forces; to insure successful resistance of further Communist advances into Nationalist China; to aid in establishing stability. Such aid could be conditioned to foster the emergence of a regime which would develop along lines satisfactory to the United States, at the same time engaging in a holding operation against the progressive spread of militaristic Communism. A program for such military aid to China would necessarily have to be an integrated element of our worldwide policy of military assistance to specified nations.

Extension of military aid by the United States to the National Government might possibly be followed by similar aid from the Soviet Union to the Chinese Communists, either openly or covertly—the latter course seems more likely. Tension between the United States and the Soviet Union might therefore increase, even as it is now in European and Middle East areas.

Military aid and assistance to China could take essentially three forms or a combination thereof: Material, advisory, or active participation in operations by American personnel. This last form is rejected as contrary to current American policy. In all cases, China should take the initial step of requesting United States aid and should inform the United Nations of steps taken.

Consideration has been given to what the Chinese can do themselves to improve their situation as regards military matériel. It is believed that they can do little to help themselves because of their basic deficiency in industrial capacity. However, they can help themselves by implementation of a carefully prepared logistical plan based upon supervised material aid. They can further help themselves by demonstrating a real willingness to achieve stabilization of military fronts, by improving command, by regrouping forces, by reducing the total military force to one which can be supported by the Government with such outside aid as may be furnished, and by implementing necessary social, political and economic reforms.

Material aid programs visualized include:

  Completion of the General Pai Motor Vehicle Parts Project
  Purchase of additional military equipment
  Ammunition Supply
  Completion of the 8⅓ Group Program plus augmentation in military air transport
  China Mapping Program
  Transfer of Ships

Motor Vehicle Parts Project. Sixteen-thousand motor vehicles, chiefly trucks, are inoperative because of lack of parts. It would materially benefit China's military forces and her transportation system to have this program completed by arrangements which would enable the Chinese to purchase these parts on as favorable a basis as possible. The United States is morally obligated to complete this program by virtue of a contract between the National Government and the Foreign Liquidation Commission, which would have made available the required parts from surplus stocks. The United States has unilaterally voided this contract as the required surplus stocks are not available and no legal way for furnishing them exists.

Purchase of Additional Military Equipment. Since completion of the 39 division program nearly two years ago, very little has been supplied. Thus, there are many shortages in military equipment which react to the disadvantage of Nationalist military efforts. Credits should be established for China to purchase the necessary military equipment needed to effect a supervised revitalization of her ground and air forces. Without such aid, American equipment purchased during and subsequent to the war is, or soon will be, valueless since maintenance parts will not be available to continue the equipment in use.

In many cases, reliance upon artillery has been a handicap. Artillery is often a logistic drain, limiting mobility in a fluid situation, and causing the Nationalists to be overly cautious for fear of having it captured; it has, however, been useful in the few instances when Communists have made determined large-scale assaults against Nationalist positions or when they have attempted to hold positions against Nationalist attack. Mortars, automatic weapons and rifles have been the most valuable weapons to either side in the current mobile warfare.

Ammunition Supply. In July, the Navy abandoned 335 tons of ammunition in Tsingtao which was recovered by Nationalists. However, Nationalist armies continue to complain of shortages in ammunition of all types and calibers. There will be severe shortages in the near future unless replenishment from foreign source is accomplished. There is an implied moral obligation to assist the Chinese Government to obtain ammunition.

Completion of the 8⅓ Group Program and Possible Augmentation in Military Air Transport. Major deficiencies which exist in the Chinese Air Force include the lack of an adequate system of logistical support, of a proper maintenance or supply system, of a reclamation system, and of supply and maintenance facilities. All these deficiencies are due to the critical condition of the Chinese economy plus the fact that the 8⅓ group program has not yet been completed. To remedy these deficiencies, the Chinese Air Force would require supplies for first and second echelon maintenance for all types of aircraft, complete fulfillment of the 8⅓ group program which includes equipment for supporting service units; equipment for a complete training program including aircraft spare parts and training aids; and initial TE equipment for two additional air transport groups (C-46). A realistic National Government effort to resolve major logistical problems of its armed forces will necessarily demand the fullest utilization of air transport since in many areas, it is the only remaining means of communication.

China Mapping Program. Because of lack of available United States resources in China, this program, undertaken by special agreement, has been reduced in scale to the mapping of Taiwan only. Such a program is of strategic value to the United States in furnishing up-to-date post-hostilities maps of areas already or potentially involved in conflict. It would also provide China with up-to-date maps of her own territory and thus be of military aid to her. The present program should be expanded to include other areas of vital strategic importance.

Transfer of Ships. Navy Department plants to furnish to China by transfer without compensation, some 137 vessels, craft, and floating dry docks; along with such plans, blueprints, documents, and other information in connection with these vessels and other technical information as is necessary in connection with organization and maintenance of a naval establishment. Cost of repairs, outfit and equipment to these vessels and the transfer of any material will be on the basis of a cash reimbursement by Republic of China. Ninety-three of these vessels are now under lend-lease to the Chinese Government and will be recaptured under terms of the Naval Lease Agreement Charter and retransferred under Public Law Number 512 which authorizes a maximum transfer of 97 similar type vessels through OFLC for use by Chinese Maritime Customs. However, there are still several vessels in the Maritime Customs Program yet to be delivered. As part of a program for aid to China, delivery of vessels under Public Law 512 could be completed.

Occupation of Japan. There is an agreement between United States and China which specifically charges China with logistical support of Chinese Occupation Forces but recognizes that some additional support will be required from the United States. To date, China has taken no action under this agreement and appears to have no inclination to take action in the future. This agreement expires 30 June 1949.

ANNEXES 813

Military Advice to Chinese Armed Forces

Military advice is now available to Nationalist ground, sea and air forces on a General Staff level through American Military and Naval Advisory Groups. The Generalissimo repeatedly expressed to the Head of this Mission a strong desire to have advice and supervision extended in scope to include field forces, training centers and particularly logistical agencies.

Under present instructions, the Advisory Groups have confined their activities to the highest echelons of the Chinese Armed Forces except for assisting in operating schools and for limited technical advice in handling ships and airplanes. They are not allowed to assist directly in actual training of troops which take part in civil war.

Under the basic assumption that the United States "Hands Off" policy is relegated to the past, there remain only two alternatives or lines of action with respect to our present military advisory role: To continue the present scale of advice on a ministry and general staff level or to increase the scope of this advice. Should the latter alternative be adopted, there are several courses of action which could be followed.

A considerable number of forces engaged in combat have lost their effectiveness due to losses in personnel and equipment and in lowered morale. There are now a number of divisions which need to be withdrawn, reorganized and retrained. The scope of the Advisory role could be extended so as to provide assistance in this training.

The United States would be subject to serious charges if it were to become involved in any way in actual combat against Chinese Communists. Although advice indicated above does provide advice *indirectly* to tactical forces, it should be carried on outside operational areas to prevent the criticism that American personnel are actively engaged in fratricidal warfare.

Advice in connection with training technical specialists in the United States and in China should be continued. In addition consideration must be given, not only by the Advisory Groups but also by Chinese industrialists, to preservation of the nuclei of specialists already trained and schooled.

There are two points which should be given consideration by American advisors. First, conscription should be conducted on an equitable basis, to include sons of rich or influential families as well as of the poor. Such is not now the case. Secondly, better relationships and foundations for respect and comradeship between officers and enlisted men should be evolved.

Conclusions

The military situation in China is grave. Communists have the tactical initiative in Manchuria and in North China.

The Nationalist position in Manchuria is precarious, and in Shantung and Hopei provinces strongly disputed. Continued deterioration of the situation may result in establishment of a Soviet satellite government in Manchuria and ultimately in a Communist-dominated China which would be inimical to United States interests.

This spreading internecine struggle within China threatens world peace. Positive steps should be taken to end hostilities immediately.

Soviet aims in the Far East are diametrically opposed to and jeopardize United States interests in China in that their aims envisage progressive expansion of Soviet control and dominant influence. Realization of their aims in

China would threaten United States strategic security. Time works to advantage of the Soviet Union.

The Soviet Union, in achieving her aims, is being actively assisted by the Chinese Communist Party, which by its actions and propaganda is proven to be a tool of Soviet foreign policy.

The only working basis on which national Chinese resistance to Soviet aims can be revitalized is through the presently corrupt, reactionary and inefficient Chinese National Government.

The National Government is incapable of supporting an army of the size it now has in the field.

In order to preclude defeat by Communist forces, it is necessary to give the National Government sufficient and prompt military assistance under the supervision of American advisors in specified military fields.

American military aid to China should be moral, material and advisory. It should be an integrated element of our worldwide policy of military assistance to certain nations. China should take the initial step of inviting the United States to provide such aid.

American military aid to China, ground, sea and air, would if appropriately supervised, contribute to gradual development of stability in the Far East and lessen the possibility of a Communist-dominated China.

Recommendations

It is recommended:

That the United States provide as early as practicable moral, advisory and material support to China in order to prevent Manchuria from becoming a Soviet satellite, to bolster opposition to Communist expansion and to contribute to the gradual development of stability in China.

That China be advised to request the United Nations to take immediate steps to bring about a cessation of hostilities in Manchuria and request that Manchuria be placed under a Five-Power Guardianship or, failing that, under a Trusteeship in accordance with the United Nations Charter.

That China be advised to take steps to reduce its military expenditures in the national budget and at the same time increase the effectiveness and efficiency of the military establishment.

That China give continuing evidence that urgently required military reforms are being implemented.

That China, with the advice and support of the United States, develop and implement a sound program of equipment and improved logistical support.

That arrangements be made whereby China can purchase military equipment and supplies, (particularly motor maintenance parts), from the United States.

That China be assisted in her efforts to obtain ammunition immediately.

That the 8⅓ Air Group Program be completed promptly and that consideration be given to expansion of its air transport.

That the China Mapping Program be extended in scope where practicable.

That the program for transfer of ships to China be completed as rapidly as China is able to utilize them effectively.

That the occupation of Japan program be dropped, but only with the concurrence of the National Government of China.

The military advice and supervision be extended in scope to include field forces, training centers and particularly logistical agencies.

136

The Consul General at Shanghai (Davis) to Secretary Marshall

121.893/9-247

SHANGHAI, *September 2, 1947.*

Premier Chang Chun in an exclusive interview with the United Press today declared there will be no change in either the domestic or foreign policy of the Chinese Government as a result of the Wedemeyer Mission and said "There were many things which Wedemeyer did not know".

The Premier said while he met Lieutenant General Albert C. Wedemeyer several times during the American envoy's visit to China, Wedemeyer did not hold any "serious" discussions with him. "General Wedemeyer paid more attention to people outside the government than in it", Chang said.

The Prime Minister said that many of the reforms suggested in the Wedemeyer farewell statement "were already being carried out before the General visited China. Perhaps General Wedemeyer thought he was not away from China for a long time and still knows China well" Chang said.

"There were many people who wanted to see Wedemeyer and could not. And there were many things not known to the General." Chang said Wedemeyer got lots of help from his advisers "and the General perhaps thought these materials were quite enough."

CRITICIZED BY PEOPLE

The Premier said that he personally was good friends with Wedemeyer and recognized the good intentions of the General "but as a representative of the President of the United States Wedemeyer's statement caused a lot of criticism among the Chinese people."

The Prime Minister said he hopes that in time the critics will understand Wedemeyer's good intention "and Wedemeyer will understand the persons who criticized his statement".

Asked whether his assertion that there would be no change in Chinese domestic policy as the result of the Wedemeyer statement means that he did not agree with Wedemeyer's contention that "drastic and far reaching political and economic reforms" were necessary, Chang replied that such changes were already provided for in the form of the new constitution and forthcoming national election.

QUESTION OF METHOD

Chang said that such changes however must be made "step by step" according to a schedule already decided upon by the Chinese Government. "We are improving", the Premier said. "Minor affairs should not be mixed up with matters of policy. It is a question of method. Chinese policy is fixed and will not change either domestically or foreign.

"Our American friends say the Chinese Government is not efficient. We are studying ways and means and we know we have a lot to learn from the United States and western countries. But changes in China involve many things— old customs, system and procedures. This does not mean we are not trying to improve our present administration and there are many things we can do now. But many must wait.

"We know, for example, that the period of political tutelage is not good and we are trying to conclude it as soon as possible. But it is not feasible to end the tutelage period until the constitution is put into operation. Many similar changes can only be done after the constitution is operative."

The Premier said that even since the government reorganization the national government has heavier responsibility and much more work but nevertheless it is bending all effort to usher in the constitutional period.

GOVERNMENT DETERMINED

"In spite of all obstacles, the government is determined to finish this work this year," Chang asserted.

He said a lot of people had expressed doubts about whether the government really intended to hold the national elections this fall and has suggested that they might be postponed because of the civil war. "The policy is to hold the elections," Chang declared. "And the government is not going to change that policy in spite of obstacles."

The Premier touched on other matters which had been the subject of criticism from "American friends" such as export and import regulations about which business men felt keenly and he said the government was effecting improvements but foreign critics should not expect a change over night.

Chang said the specific reactions of the Chinese Government to the Wedemeyer Mission were contained in a note handed to Wedemeyer a few days prior to the General's departure which he said represented both his views and the views of the Chinese Government.

Chang received me in his spacious office at the Executive Yuan late in the afternoon. He was dressed in a gray civilian suit and spoke Chinese during the formal part of the interview and English during the informal chat. The interview lasted 45 minutes. Samson Shen of the Chinese Information Office acted as the interpreter.

137

The Ambassador in China (Stuart) to Secretary Marshall

121.893/8–3047

NANKING, *August 30, 1947.*

Following is substance of Communist radio comment following departure of Wedemeyer mission.

"North Shensi, August 28th: People here all laugh at Wedemeyer's August 24th departing statement. They say that he is playing another deceptive trick to cover up his imperialistic activities in China by 'criticizing' Chiang's Government, talking of 'peace'.

"However, from Wedemeyer's statement one can clearly see these three points: 1. There is no way to cover up corruption of Chiang Kai-shek's dictatorial rule. 2. There is no way to deny the demand of the Chinese people for ending Chiang's dictatorial rule and U.S. aggression. 3. Even the imperialist Wedemeyer cannot distort the fact that the might of the people of liberated areas, especially that of the people's liberation army, is invincible. The statement shows that even a blood-thirsty butcher like Wedemeyer now sees that to support this evil government of Chiang is difficult under the present circumstances when the peoples of the world including the U.S. are so bitter against Fascists like Chiang. Although Wedemeyer has quit China and has unhappily accepted that 'military force in itself will not eliminate Communism', yet his promise to equip

ANNEXES 817

Chiang's troops and other plots are being put into practice. It is very possible that he will urge Washington for further aid to Chiang to prop up the Kuomintang government from imminent collapse. Chiang Kai-shek will also exert all his effort for a final struggle and American imperialists will rush aid to Chiang.

"People of the liberated areas have known these things too well and they will never be cheated by 'peace' uttered by a hypocrite like Wedemeyer. Real peace can only be attained when Chiang's corrupt rule is thoroughly smashed and American imperialistic force completely driven out of China."

STUART

138

Memorandum from the Chinese Government to Lieutenant General Albert C. Wedemeyer [12]

121.893/9-647

On V-J Day the Chinese Government found itself confronted with the following problems:

1. The question of the Chinese Communists who were maintaining a regular armed force of 310,000 men in addition to a larger number of their so-called "militia". The presence of a large number of yet unsurrendered and undisarmed Japanese and puppet government troops in Manchuria was offering opportunities to the Chinese Communists to acquire more and better equipment.

2. An inflation, which had developed during the long years of war and was threatening the economic life of the nation.

3. The complete standstill of over 90% of China's railways and the acute shortage of inland shipping which made the work of repatriation and of restoring order in areas formerly held by the Japanese or puppet forces extremely difficult and rendered it impossible for many pre-war industries to revive even though the plants were partially recovered.

4. The need for the rehabilitation of rural economy after eight years of neglect and destruction during enemy occupation resulting in widespread shortage of farm labor, livestock and fertilizers and in consequent critical reduction of agricultural production. The total annual production of cotton, for example, was reduced to about 5,320,000 piculs or shih tan, ⅓ of the 1937 level, which was 16,180,000 piculs or shih tan.

5. There were in China proper more than one million Japanese soldiers and approximately an equal number in Manchuria; 600,000 puppet government troops scattered in various parts of China proper and another 330,000 of them in Manchuria; and as a result of Soviet participation in the Far Eastern war, a large Soviet force estimated at 600,000 to 700,000 men deployed in different parts of Manchuria.

6. And at last, but by no means the least, the question of the fulfillment of commitments made by the Government, before and during the war, of the convocation of the National Assembly, the drafting and adoption of a national constitution, the return by the Kuomintang of the responsibility of government to the people, the termination of one-party rule, and the lifting of censorship. These were the most difficult problems that the Government had to deal with all at once on V-J Day. The weight of responsibility that so suddenly fell on the

---

[12] The memorandum handed to Lt. Gen. Albert C. Wedemeyer before his departure and transmitted to Secretary Marshall by Ambassador Stuart Sept. 6, 1947.

Government was far greater than the Government machine then existing could adequately cope with. Not only were the tasks themselves heavy and complicated but they were also in many cases new to the experience of the Government. In the repatriation of Japanese soldiers and civilians and in the timely dispatch of Chinese troops by air and by sea to many areas to take over from the enemy, the Chinese Government was substantially aided by the United States forces in China. Credit must also be given to UNRRA and CNRRA for their contribution toward the solution of many problems in connection with the repatriation of displaced persons and such relief and rehabilitation work as could be undertaken immediately. Meanwhile, the Government itself was tackling all the problems it could in the circumstances. (1) It set about reorganizing the army and reducing the national budget. (2) An immediate attempt was made following V-J Day to restore communications systems, such as railways, highways, waterways, public utility services and conservancy works. (3) Mines and iron works (including a number of those the equipment of which had been largely removed by the Soviet Army from Manchuria or destroyed by the Communists) were reopened and textile and other precarious industries were salvaged. (4) Efforts were made afresh to lay down the foundations for local self-government, such as the reorganizing and re-staffing of municipal and hsien offices, the organization of Pao-Chia system in villages and towns, and the rehabilitation of schools of various grades. (5) Wherever practicable, measures were also taken to revitalize rural economy. In the case of cotton, the extension work carried out by the Government in the past one and one-half years is now expected to result in a production of eleven million piculs or shih tan this year, a 100% increase over the production for the year of the V-J Day. Each of these jobs involved considerable administration, funds and personnel.

When one assesses the work of the Government in this period one should bear in mind the fact that social institutions in China were not yet fully adapted to modern conditions, that a large portion of her territory was under enemy occupation for many years, and that the new economic foundations that had been prepared since 1927 were impaired by the enemy. The immensity and complexity of the task of recovery that followed in the wake of victory must be taken into account.

There can be no doubt that the Government would have achieved greater results and China's politico-economic position would be brighter if the greater part of the Government's constructive effort had not been thwarted at each turn by the non-settlement of the Communist issue and the continuance of the war-time legacy—inflation.

The infiltration of the Chinese Communists into Manchuria during and following the Soviet occupation constituted a new factor in the Communist impasse after V-J Day. The armed opposition of the Communists was the greatest single destructive force against all the effort of the Government in carrying out rehabilitation and in restoring law and order, particularly in areas formerly held by the Japanese. When every possible effort was being made, for instance, to restore the main communication lines, mobile Communist squads were actively engaged in demolition work disrupting newly repaired railways, cutting telegraph and telephone lines, and causing havoc in the countryside.

As a result of the inability on the part of the Chinese Government to disarm and accept surrender from the large number of Japanese and puppet government troops in Manchuria, the attitude of the Communists towards the Government became increasingly challenging and uncompromising. After the meeting of the National Assembly last November and December, the Communists openly denounced the adopted constitution. It was then clear that all hopes of a political settlement had gone. For, by that time the Communists had decided on the immediate launching of a large-scale military offensive. No one could feel more profoundly disappointed than the Government itself at such a turn of events, at a time when so much reconstruction work called for its undivided attention and immediate action.

While the Communist issue remained unsettled, the plan for army reorganization could not materialize owing to Communist obstruction thus hampering the reduction of the armed forces. As a result, a policy of retrenchment in national budget could not be put into effect, and inflation developed to such an extent as to threaten every fabric of our political and economic life. It led to the lowering of the efficiency of the Government administration and the undermining of the morale of the army. The bulk of the civil servants were not paid enough to meet anew the requirements of a bare subsistence. As a result, many Government employees were forced to seek concurrent work in order to maintain their living, while others turned to more lucrative jobs.

To this day there has been no substantial improvement in the treatment of these long-suffering civil servants. However, considering the straitened circumstances of the civil servants in general, it is astonishing to find that the great bulk of them are carrying on without failing in their duties. The loyalty of these people recalls to mind the stolid endurance of the Chinese masses who bore the brunt of the long war against Japanese aggression.

Whatever one may say of the national Government in China, one cannot possibly accuse it of not having steadily pursued the preparatory work for a democratic government as laid down by their leader- Dr. Sun Yat-sen. It has always been the unanimous opinion of the leaders of the Kuomintang that unless it could lead the nation into a multi-party and representative government, it could not be said to be in any way carrying out the principles on which the party was founded. No one of any importance in the party has ever questioned the need to terminate the so-called "period of political tutelage" as soon as the basic conditions stated by Dr. Sun have been fulfilled. In this respect, the party as a whole, never once swerved from its aim.

When Sino-Japanese hostilities broke out in 1937, the momentous decision to resist the enemy was accompanied by a nation-wide effort to preserve, as far as possible, the political and economic foundation that had been laid since 1927. Above all, the general opinion of the party was such that the interlude of war should not nullify the preparatory work for representative government that had already been undertaken.

In 1938, the People's Political Council was founded to provide a broader basis of representative opinion for the guidance of government policy. Except for matters of military strategy and security, the Council served as a war-time organ of public opinion. Here, in the midst of a life-and-death struggle, the national Government decided to invite and accept open questions and criticism and thus to promote representative government. This invaluable tradition has happily continued to this day. Although the 200 members of the first People's Political Council were all elected by the Government from different professions and on the basis of geographical distribution, it was widely acknowledged to be a fairly representative body of the politically conscious sections of the country. Early in 1940, the second People's Political Council met with 240 members, of which 90 were for the first time elected by the various provisional provincial and municipal councils, both on a regional and a professional basis. When the third People's Political Council met in 1942, 164 out of the total 240 members were elected by the provincial and municipal councils. Today, the People's Political Council, in the last phase of its existence, has 362 members, of which 227 were reelected by provincial and municipal councils.

In September, 1938, two months after the first People's Political Council held its inaugural meeting, the national Government promulgated the regulations of the provisional provincial council. Today, such councils have been organized in nearly all the provinces. Here again, the percentage of elected councillors was increased after each meeting, so that in many provinces the members of such councils are now entirely elected representatives. The municipal and hsien councils have also been conducted along the same lines. Thus, while the war was being fought and its priority acknowledged, no effort was spared in preserving the continuity of the effort towards the building up of basic democratic institutions and practices.

Shortly after V–J Day, press censorship was lifted in spite of the existence of a number of factors which might still have argued for its continuance. The National Assembly was convened and the draft constitution adopted in November 1946. The one-party rule had come to an end, although the Kuomintang was still by far the majority party in the Government. The Youth Party and the Demo-Socialist Party are now also represented in the Government.

No observer who is acquainted with Chinese events in the past can possibly fail to notice the existence today of a far greater body of public opinion than had ever existed before. This has come about since V–J Day as a result of the lifting of censorship, the convocation of the National Assembly, the presence of other parties in the Government, the emergence of a responsible Cabinet in the new Executive Yuan and above all, the effect of the periodic open discussions at the People's Political Council. The defense by the Government of its own policy and administration has in turn a stimulating effect on the growth of public opinion. It brings the Government closer to the people.

Since the Kuomintang gained power it may have committed errors in regard to methods for the attainment of its political goal, but never has it for any period deviated from its general political direction. Exigencies of circumstances may at times have retarded the progress of its work, but in the 20-odd years of its government, it has never been known to recede from a step once it has been taken.

China's critics are prone to lose sight of the vastness of the country, the weaknesses of its traditional political, economic and social structures, and the complexity of the problems with which she is confronted. Their views and judgment are apt to be based too much on the situation of a given moment without due regard to the background.

It may be well for us to review briefly the period between 1927 and 1937, a period in which the strength of the Kuomintang was put for the first time to a real test, and in which the Government never had a continued peace for more than a few months. In 1926, when the Government was still in Canton, it launched upon a punitive expedition against the war lords. In 1927, when the national Government was established in Nanking there were still war lords to reckon with; there was internal political opposition to overcome from the Communists as well as remnants of the old regime who were ever ready to lend a hand in any port against the Government; there was no street in Chungking where one could not find public opium dens and such conditions prevailed in many other cities; extraterritorial rights continued and the attitude of the major powers, not excluding the United States, towards the new Government was one of critical skepticism. Since September 18, 1931, when the Japanese started her open aggression, the Government had to resist the enemy on the one hand and on the other to suppress the armed rebellion of the Communists in the south. But in spite of all this, the Government during this hard-pressed period of ten years was able to launch upon a national constructive program.

In 1937, it had completed almost 5,000 kilometers of railways, 100,000 kilometers of highways; had built schools, parks, hospitals and civic centers in many cities, trebled the number of middle schools and doubled that of universities and colleges. The number of middle school and vocational school students totalled nearly 600,000 in 1936. It was estimated that illiteracy decreased by almost 20% in those ten years. Modern ordnance works began in 1926 and at the time of the Lukouchiao incident, China was already able to supply, from her own arsenals, practically all her infantry divisions with rifles, hand grenades, machine guns, trench mortars and various accessories. A national anti-narcotic movement was launched during this period. The number of drug addicts rapidly decreased and by the end of 1938 no public opium den was to be found in areas under the control of the national Government.

When the full-fledged war broke out in 1937, Japanese financial experts predicted that China's finances would collapse within a few months of the war. During the eight years of war China faced financial problems as enormous as they were complicated but as a result of certain vigorous measures taken before the war, such as the adoption of a managed currency, concentration of gold and silver reserves, the reform of the taxation and banking systems, the Chinese Government was able to pass through the early—in fact the most critical—part of the war without any serious financial crisis.

In short the period between the establishment of the national Government in Nanking in 1927 and the beginning of the war with Japan in 1937 was one of severe trial for the Kuomintang. However, the Government concentrated its effort on the two-fold task of suppressing Communist rebellion and resisting the Japanese aggression and this gigantic undertaking received the singleminded support of the entire populace. Moreover, the relations between China and her neighbors were at that time not so complicated as they are. The Government was therefore able to turn this difficult decade into a constructive period. Commerce and industries developed while the people both in rural districts and cities were able to plan and look ahead. Industrial production reached in 1936 a level higher than in any previous year. A general feeling of prosperity and growth prevailed.

The complexity of the problems of today may be greater than those of the prewar years, but the dangers and difficulties which beset the present Government are reminiscent of those that confronted the nation during the early years of war (1937–1942), when China was forced to fight Japan singlehanded. Whether the present Government, for which the Kuomintang is practically still responsible, will be able to overcome these fresh dangers and difficulties as it did in the war and pre-war periods remains to be seen.

It is, however, clear that there is no weakening of determination on the part of the present Government and the Kuomintang to face the new challenge. As to the lines of policy with which the Government will meet the challenge, several things are uppermost in the minds of its leaders. First, the Communists as an armed political party must be suppressed. No half measures should be considered. The Government fully realizes that the success or failure of this fight against the Communist peril will not only decide its own fate but also the life or death of China as a sovereign power. In fact, the outcome of the struggle is bound up with the peace and security of the whole of the Far East. Second, the inflation menace must be brought under control; there should be no further delay in initiating some effective program in this regard because this is the very root of many political, economic and social ills. Third, in the provinces which are free from Communist menace, economic rehabilitation work must be intensified as far as Government resources permit. This must be accompanied by necessary political reform in the local government. Last the Government must pursue its political goal, the building up of a democratic constitutional government, without fear or hesitation. Whatever difficulties the present Communist rebellion and other political factors may cause to the accomplishment of this task, the Government must proceed to give effect to the constitution adopted at the end of last year. No real form of democracy is built in a day and it is the consensus of opinion of the Government that the best way to achieve it is to start it as soon as you can.

139

The Ambassador in China (Stuart) to Secretary Marshall

893.00/8–1147

NANKING, *August 11, 1947*

I have the honor to report a visit with President Chiang last evening.[13] This followed upon the most recent interview General Cheng Kai-min had with him. General Cheng and I have of late been frequently in consultation in our efforts to persuade President Chiang to commit himself wholeheartedly and without further delay to the democratic way. General Cheng had recently submitted to him a memorandum with various concrete suggestions of this nature (a translation of which has been given to General Wedemeyer).

After discussing a brief trip to Tsinan from which I had just returned, he opened the way for me to say what I had in mind. My comments could be summarized as follows:

(1) China should join the democratic group of nations in opposition to aggressive Communism.

(2) The United States has been consistently ready to aid China by such means as are proper and possible, provided only that the present government can give convincing evidence of reforms in this direction and in doing so recover the support of its non-Communist people.

(3) The procedure might well include such measures as these:

(a) The *Kuomintang* should be completely dissociated from the Government and given the status of any other party in a democracy. (President Chiang had already asked General Cheng to secure an outline of the organization of the two principal American parties for him to study.)

(b) *Military Affairs.* The reorganization of the army along the lines of the P. C. C. proposals and with the help of the American Army Advisory Group might be begun on a basis that had due regard for the realities of the civil war. A small army, well-trained and equipped, with adequate physical treatment and a new morale, would be far more effective and less costly than the present one. The problem of deactivating the surplus officers and men could not be neglected.

(c) *Administration.* The rampant venality and similar evils among civil officials could be improved at the outset by enlarging the powers of the Control Yuan and holding it accountable. The civil rights provided for in the Constitution might be declared as taking effect now, in advance of the date set for its

---

[13] Aug. 6, 1947.

enforcement (December 25). But what was more essential than any of these measures was a new revolutionary spirit, with fresh enthusiasm and a dynamic conviction as to the real meaning and value of democracy. This should be incarnated in him. He was too much the head of a Party when he should be the leader of the whole Nation.

There was little new, of course, in any of this, even in previous conversations of mine with him. He made occasional comments as I went along and when I had finished said that he had come to essentially these conclusions.

He said that he had determined to increase the pay alike of civil and military employees of the Government and that this would bring a measure of relief.

As to the military reorganization, he reminded me of his request to you in my presence that you become Supreme Advisor with all the authority that he himself possessed. He said that he was ready to make the same offer to General Wedemeyer and earnestly hoped that this might be accepted.

He claimed that freedom of the press, for instance, was already in existence and cited the unrestrained publicity allowed in discussing the affairs of the two big companies in which members of the Soong and Kung families were involved. I replied that the newspaper editors were by no means aware that such freedom could be relied upon and that it would be in order to issue an unequivocable proclamation supported by a description of means for redress or protection.

He said in conclusion that he was giving this whole subject very careful thought—as is undoubtedly the case—and I remarked that when he was ready to make the rather radical changes involved it might be desirable to issue a very clear announcement.

He left this morning for Kuling where he plans to spend several days alone in order to think over the momentous decisions he must soon be making and some of the detailed issues involved.

140

The Ambassador in China (Stuart) to Secretary Marshall

[Extract]

893.00/8–1947

NANKING, *August 19, 1947.*

The activities of the Wedemeyer Mission have of course aroused a great deal of Chinese comment ranging from vituperative Communist denunciation and the serious misgivings of the liberals who fear that it will play into the hands of reactionaries to the overconfident hopes of many in the Government. The reliance of these latter upon our country to solve their problems for them irritates or angers or at times is merely amusing. But there is a growing number both within the Government and outside of it with whose opinions I must confess to a large measure of sympathy. They admit the logic of all that we argue about what Chinese should do to help themselves, get their own house in order first, etc., but feel utterly impotent in view of the conservatism, feudalistic ideas, selfishness, narrow prejudices and similar limitations prevalent among those who have the power to effect reforms, while the Communists are rapidly making gains. The best among these would not have chosen such a course nor do they intend to stand idly by while we attempt to do it all, but things being as they are in this country, they simply do not see any other way out. Nor do I. Where I perhaps differ from many of them is in being somewhat more hopeful of the moral and psychological influence upon the responsible leaders and the public generally once they all begin to see some hope ahead.

The signs of willingness and ability to institute progressive reforms are still sadly lacking but there are some. President Chiang recently summoned the Provincial Governors for a conference and along with some vehement criticism and pertinent instruction promised certain benefits. From now on provincial revenues should be principally used for provincial needs. Officials from Central Government Ministries and other agencies should be under the provincial authority. He has since then argued with me that, while in theory these governors should be civilians, yet until the Constitution is actually in force and the army reorganized, it would be very difficult for any civilian to hold out against military domination. He added that under existing conditions the best men could not be induced to accept such posts as he had learned from several such efforts. He is making definite plans to dissociate the Kuomintang from the Government at the coming meeting, September 9th, and compel it to accept a status somewhat analogous to our political parties. He has been studying memoranda on this subject. He is also working on the scheme for enlarging the powers of the local police and having them deal with such matters as civil liberties, rather than the military police (practically accountable to him alone), the secret service men, etc. I pointed out that when he is fully prepared to effect this change there should be civilian trials, prompt and public, and authoritative statements explaining the new policy and procedure. The reduplication in Central and local bureaus, in the ordinary officials and those representing him, in unnecessary employees, should be corrected both to reduce expenditure and for greater efficiency. Slight beginnings are being made. Much of this is due to the age-long suspicions by the Central Authority of those away from the Capital and the system of protective devices employed. President Chiang has practiced to the full this method of personalized control. In his case it is acutely aggravated by his fear of ubiquitous Communism which largely explains, if it does not excuse, the terroristic measures against the student strikes last May and similar repressive violations of civilian rights.

141

The Ambassador in China (Stuart) to Secretary Marshall

121.893/8–2647

NANKING, *August 26, 1947*

The Wedemeyer Mission departed August 24 after a busy month at Nanking, Shanghai, Peiping, Tientsin, Mukden, Canton and Hangkow where members of the Mission interviewed Chinese and foreigners and received written communications representing widely differing viewpoints.

The Mission met a few individuals who admitted they were Communists but alleged no direct contact with the Party. In any event these limited contacts had no effect upon Communist Party propaganda which remained vituperative of the Mission throughout its stay, particularly of General Wedemeyer personally, and generally suspicious and critical of the objectives of the Mission. The resumption of Kuomintang-Communist peace talks through American initiative was urged by few individuals, but it was clear that prevailing sentiment was to the effect that such a move was impracticable.

On August 22, General Wedemeyer spoke to the members of the State Council, Cabinet Ministers, and about forty other prominent Chinese including the

President and Madame Chiang. This specific act of General Wedemeyer will continue to have important repercussions as the tenor of his remarks becomes more widely known in Chinese circles (as will certainly result). As the Department is aware, General Wedemeyer made exceedingly frank statements with regard to Government shortcomings, but prefacing and concluding his comments with obviously sincere declarations of his friendship for China and his desire to be helpful. Those present at the gathering were predominately of the old scholar class to whom blunt public statements for a foreign visitor seemed offensive. It has been reported reliably that the president of the Examination Yuan, Tai Chi-tao, actually wept after the meeting adjourned. It was proposed by the State Council that none of the members go to the airfield to bid General Wedemeyer farewell, but President Chiang over-ruled this proposal. The reactions of those present at the meeting resulted partly from regard for "face" but included also the fear that such language from a Presidential envoy might encourage the Communists and arouse more opposition to the Government among non-partisans. There was also the consideration of disturbances in the money market resulting therefrom.

It is interesting to note that prior to General Wedemeyer's talk before the State Council the Generalissimo telephoned the Ambassador and suggested that he might caution General Wedemeyer against being too critical of the Government inasmuch as the State Council and others present represented a very heterogeneous group. The Ambassador informed the Generalissimo that he did not feel in a position to attempt to influence the scope of General Wedemeyer's remarks inasmuch as they were being made at the suggestion of the Generalissimo.

En route to the airfield General Wedemeyer called on President Chiang for an official farewell. The President remonstrated with him over his reported refusal to receive groups of substantial persons in the cities he had visited, such as representatives of Chambers of Commerce and the People's Political Council. General Wedemeyer protested that he had been ready to receive as many of all types as time permitted and that the schedule in each city had been arranged by the local American consuls who were well acquainted with local dignitaries and other persons. General Wedemeyer also stated that some persons who had asked to see him later withdrew their requests without apparent reason and the presumption of intimidation was therefore raised. President Chiang insisted that his orders had been that the Mission should be free to see whomever they wished.' He evidently felt that the groups he had mentioned would have been less critical of the Government than some of the groups with whom the Mission talked.

The Generalissimo also renewed a previous attempt to induce General Wedemeyer to give him a list of names in the General's possession of those Chinese with large financial holdings abroad. The Generalissimo used rather strong language stating that since he wished to force these Chinese to contribute to the national need and General Wedemeyer had advised this course, his unwillingness to facilitate in this respect was an unfriendly act. General Wedemeyer held to his position that since these names had been given him in the strictest confidence he could not do otherwise than refuse. General Wedemeyer parted with the Generalissimo in a friendly if not cordial atmosphere. The leading officials of the Government were at the airfield to wish General Wedemeyer farewell and Wu Ting-chang was present representing the Generalissimo. On the evening of August 25 the Generalissimo called Phillip Fugh, the Ambassador's personal secretary, to his residence and quizzed him at some length with regard to the background of the Wedemeyer Mission. He wished to know whether the Ambassador had had any part in its organization or dispatch, and why it was necessary to send such a mission to China uninvited as long as the Ambassador and his staff were reporting on matters Chinese.

More interesting however, in this unusual procedure was the Generalissimo's apparent preoccupation with whether or not the United States had the intention of forcing his retirement or by any other means wished his removal. The Embassy is not aware in detail of how Fugh handled this conversation except that he has informed the Ambassador that he was "careful" and "non-committal".

The Generalissimo's preoccupation with the possibility that the United States may desire his withdrawal from the scene probably arises from the use of the phrase "inspirational leadership" used by General Wedemeyer as a need in China, and the possibility that Americans felt that he was no longer capable of such leadership. The Ambassador has been informed by sources in which he has confidence that the Generalissimo has personally directed that critical comment of General Wedemeyer's final press release be restricted and that there has also been issued a down-hold order on press speculation with regard to the General's State Council address inasmuch as otherwise comment might be far too critical and vehement against the United States.

Press comment on the Mission in general will be the subject of separate messages.

There can be little question but that General Wedemeyer's talk before the State Council and his final press release have been a rude shock to the Chinese Government, although in the course of the Mission's stay it seemed to have become apparent to many prominent Chinese that they could expect little encouragement from the Mission's visit in the way of unencumbered material aid either economic or military.

The Ambassador has taken occasion to point out to the Generalissimo and to Chang Chun and other prominent Chinese that the State Council speech and all else that has been said by General Wedemeyer on this trip has been with the utmost sincerity and kindest intentions toward China. This as well as facts which brought about such seemingly harsh words, all of these individuals admit, and most politically conscious non-partisan and liberal Chinese undoubtedly largely endorse all that the Mission has said.

142

The Ambassador in China (Stuart) to Secretary Marshall

893.00/9–1747

NANKING, *September 17, 1947.*

The following manifesto was issued by the Fourth Plenary Session of the Sixth Kuomintang Central Executive Committee and published in the Central News Bulletin datelined September 13, 1947:

"Ever since Dr. Sun Yat-Sen led us in our national revolution, our party has undertaken one historical mission after another for the nation. At every such juncture, our party, after reexamining the past, came forth with a new front of solidarity to carry its mission to a successful conclusion.

"Toward the end of the Manchu dynasty, under the leadership of Dr. Sun, the Hsin Chung Hui (China Regeneration Society was reorganized into the Tung Men Hui (Revolutionary League). This subsequently led to the birth of the Republic of China. Then in the third year of the Chinese Republic (1914), the

Kuomintang became the Chung Hua Ke Ming Tang (the Chinese Revolutionary Party). This brought about the downfall of the Yuan Shih-kai monarchy and the reestablishment of the Chinese Republic. In the thirteenth year of the Chinese Republic, the Chung Kuo Kuomintang (Chinese Nationalist Party) came into being as the result of another reorganization. This was soon followed by the Northern Expedition which ended with the elimination of the warlords and the unification of the country. In the twenty-seventh year of the Chinese Republic (1938), important resolutions reached at the extraordinary party congress and the formation of the San Min Chu I Youth Corps, laid the foundation for victory after eight long years of war against Japanese aggression. Now in this post-World War II period, history is again calling upon our party to take up the responsibility of quelling a domestic revolt and carrying on war-delayed reconstruction. Whereupon, our party has reached the momentous decision of combining the party and the San Min Chu I Youth Corps.

"This step is taken, in the light of Dr. Sun's own experience in party reorganization, to rally all party members, and unify our system of command, both for the sake of greater strength. In this way we shall be consolidating the foundation for our revolution, reinforcing our party's leadership in ideology, and enhancing the party's revolutionary spirit. With our forces thus marshalled, we can proceed to tackle the important and difficult tasks at hand, until we attain success in the second phase of our revolution.

"The overthrow of the Manchu dynasty, the founding of the Chinese Republic, the eradication of the warlords, the abolition of unequal treaties, the victorious conclusion of the war of resistance, all these epochal events of the past fifty years have borne witness to our party's important achievements in the cause of the principle of nationalism and that of people's rights. The establishment of representative assemblies at various levels in recent years, the promulgation of a constitution last December, and the forthcoming termination of the period of political tutelage, have given further evidence of our party's determination to persist in its efforts for the realization of democracy. The present military campaign to suppress the Communist rebellion and the general mobilization are for the purpose of unifying China and preserving her sovereignty and territorial integrity. On their outcome will depend China's chance of continued existence as an independent nation and the world's chance of a lasting peace.

"As to the consummation of the principle of people's livelihood, it has been a principal aim of our party all these years. The pressing need of the moment is to relieve the people of their sufferings. In pre-war years, our accomplishments in reconstruction projects with a direct bearing on the people's livelihood were meager, but even this little has been destroyed as a result of the war and postwar spoliation by the Communist rebels. Therefore, no more time must be lost in beginning anew those economic reconstruction projects as directly concern the people's livelihood. In this, as in other types of reconstruction, we should first exert our own utmost. Our party wishes to set this as a goal in our present endeavors.

"We are aware of the difficulties now besetting our efforts, but at the same time we should be equally aware of the fact that our revolutionary strength is really greater than it has been during any previous period in our struggle. Previously with comparatively weak revolutionary strength at our disposal, we managed to overcome such difficulties as arose in various stages of our endeavors. Henceforth, so long as we respect ourselves but not to the extent of egoism, look within ourselves without becoming discouraged, and have confidence in ourselves without feeling self-satisfied, as before, we shall be able to attain our goals.

"We must realize that unless we can continue to gather strength, ours cannot be called a revolutionary party. Those of us who cannot endure injustices and slights, and those who cannot stand trials and tribulations, are not qualified as members of a revolutionary party.

"Our wish is that through unity and struggle, we can create a new life for the party, which will in turn generate a new revolutionary force to effect comprehensive political and economic reforms.

"Bearing in mind the 2,000-year-old Chinese proverb, 'One handling public affairs need not say too much but should try his best under the circumstances,' we are henceforth willing to let deeds speak for themselves and actions bear witness to our determination.

"We must not hesitate to make sacrifices if this is necessary to safeguard our national existence, nor should we hesitate to struggle for the realization of constitutional democracy; nor should we fear to exert our efforts to improve the people's living conditions.

"Our nation is now entering a period of constitutional government. To protect the Chinese Republic and safeguard our nation is a sacred duty, which neither our party as a whole, nor individual party members, can justifiably shirk. We wish to offer this as a common creed of guidance. We are particularly desirous that all our fellow-countrymen, out of our common conceptions of a nation-state, and national consciousness, will, as one man, unite to work for the creation of a new China dedicated to the fulfillment of the Three People's Principles."

STUART

143

The Ambassador in China (Stuart) to Secretary Marshall

893.00/9–2047

NANKING, *September 20, 1947*

There was considerable surprise several weeks ago when the Kuomintang announced that the Fourth Plenary Session of the Central Executive Committee would be held on September 9, since the Third Plenary Session had been held only last spring. The announced purpose of the meeting was to consolidate the San Min Chu I Youth Corps with the Kuomintang. Until ten days prior to the meeting there was little speculation about it but when comment did appear, it was generally assumed there was a more important reason and rumors developed accordingly, mostly along the lines of a drastic reform in the Government and a comprehensive purging of so-called undesirable elements. Despite official denial most sources generally considered the rumors of reform as an aftermath of the Wedemeyer Mission and as a desire to impress the United States with the ability and intention of the Chinese Government to comply with American requirements for substantial assistance. The rumors failed to reveal any particularly clear outlines which this reform might follow.

As for the consolidation of the Youth Corps with the Party, it was apparent there were two main reasons for this step. The first one was the desire to draw into the Party the younger elements in the country and to make use of their youth, energies and ideas. The second one was a desire to eliminate the growing friction between the Kuomintang, now largely dominated by the CC-Clique on a local and organizational basis though with a primarily Political Science Group national administration, and the Youth Corps, largely dominated by the CC-Clique but also resisting that influence through army inspiration. The Youth

Corps had become increasingly noisy in its demands for larger participation in Party affairs but had been resisted in its ambitions by the Party which looked with disfavor on the autonomous features of Corps activities. The CC-Clique favored the consolidation in the hope of continuing its hold, and the Generalissimo hoped to eliminate dissension. Though formally accomplished, the consolidation is reported as so far not having been very successful. As far as can be ascertained, the Central Executive Committee otherwise actually accomplished very little and such political manipulation as did take place was well-concealed from the public view. The first few meetings were devoted to hearing reports from ranking officials in the Government. These were largely routine and devoid of any particular interest except for speeches by the Generalissimo and the Prime Minister.

The main interest in what the Generalissimo had to say was his scathing condemnation of the Party for failure to solve China's problems, his absolution of himself from all responsibility, and his announcement that henceforth China would never again be dependent upon the United States for assistance. The balance of his remarks were devoted to the usual clichés on the extermination of the Communists and the need for rejuvenation in the Party. It should be noted parenthetically that what the Generalissimo said was largely a repeat of a speech he had given to the Standing Committee of the Central Executive Committee last spring.

The main interest in what the Prime Minister said touched on foreign affairs: (1) China was considering the despatch of warships to Indonesia for the protection of Chinese interests; and (2) Chinese policy on Japan generally coincided with that of the Soviet Union and was opposed to 'American policy and that therefore China would be obliged to strengthen its relations with Russia while at the same time preserving its traditional tie of friendship with the United States.

Another salient point of the meeting was the attempt at reform within the Party and the purging of "undesirable" elements. To this end an elaborate if general program of reform was proposed and all indications were it would be adopted. At one of the final sessions the Generalissimo put in a strong demand that the reform program be dropped and that in lieu thereof the Party proceed to carry out unfulfilled promises made during the last two years. As a result of this demand, the final manifesto of the session was couched in most general terms and said nothing that has not already been said innumerable times.

The specific accomplishments of the session, therefore, appear to have been negligible—a preliminary sparring for position prior to the Standing Committee meeting and any reshuffling of the Government would have to come from that present meeting. There may indeed be reform and purge of a kind since the program for consolidation of the Youth Corps provides for a reenlistment of all Party members. It is difficult at this stage to predict what form it will take or what its nature will be, though it can be assumed that it will conform to the desires and ambitions of the dominant clique. In this connection it should be noted that indications are the CC-Clique has emerged in a stronger position than previously because it controls the Youth Corps and because it has been able to exploit current internal and international conditions.

The uncertainties in the Chinese mind concerning the outcome of the Wedemeyer Mission unquestionably played an important role. The Government had assumed—and so advertised it—that the Wedemeyer Mission would bring with it substantial aid or at least specific promises thereof. This would, of course, have greatly strengthened the Political Science Group government which could take credit for the acomplishment. As these hopes have so far failed to materialize, the CC-Clique has been in a position to point an accusing finger thereby weakening the administration in power. This is not to say of course that the CC-Clique basically liked the Wedemeyer statement any more than did the administration, but it was and is able to make political capital of it. That the CC-Clique did not go farther than it did is partly attributable to the continuing uncertainty as to the forthcoming aid and partly to what must be the reluctance of the Generalissimo to take any unduly strong position during the period of uncertainty. His own words were the strongest used by a prominent figure and must have been compounded of anger, disappointment and political maneuvering.

144

The Ambassador in China (Stuart) to Secretary Marshall

893.00/9-2047

NANKING, *September 20, 1947.*

Political, military and economic position of Central Government has continued to deteriorate within recent months in accordance with previous expectations. Currently, the cumulative effect of the absence of substantial, financial and military assistance expected from the Wedemeyer Mission and renewed Communist military activity are intensifying the Chinese tendency to panic in times of crisis.

Department will have noted renewal of Chinese efforts to obtain favorable action on ammunition supplies and despite Embassy's statements that ammunition question is one for decision in Washington, constant inquiries are received with regard to action taken. More recently there has emanated a series of thinly-veiled suggestions from senior officials of the Government obviously intended to convince the Embassy that if aid is not soon forthcoming from the United States, it may become necessary for China to seek assistance from the Soviet Union. It has even been suggested to the Ambassador that the Soviet Ambassador to China, whose return is expected shortly, might be asked to mediate in the civil war and that he would be glad to accept.

Although the Embassy does not overlook the remote possibility of a Sino-Soviet rapprochement and is following the situation closely, it considers that such talk is primarily for effect on the United States and secondarily reflects a feeling of desperation among Chinese leaders. The Department will realize that under present circumstances, and prior to any action as a result of General Wedemeyer's report and recommendation, a Chinese paper flirtation with the Soviet Union by the Vice-President and President of the Executive Yuan is a maneuver reminiscent of similar Chinese tactics in the past, of Dr. Sun Fo's letter to *New York Times* in January 1942. An added element in the over-all situation, of course, is the increasing Chinese fear that the United States is tending more and more to shift the center of gravity of its Far Eastern policy from China to Japan.

At the moment the most serious concern of the Government is the sweeping large-scale raid of Liu Po-cheng into Anhwei and southern Honan which commenced about August 12 and has been increasing in momentum since that time. There is much speculation with regard to Liu's ultimate objective which is variously interpreted to be the crossing of the Yangtze River at some point between Wuhu and Hankow and advancing southward to establish Communist bases in Fukien or Kwangtung or even to make connection with the Communist-led forces of Ho Chi-minh in Indo-China. It is more likely that Liu has no more concrete objective in view than to harass a wide area, further embarrass the Government and cause it to withdraw troops from critical areas in pursuit.

Three divisions have already been withdrawn from southwestern Shantung and despatched in pursuit of Liu. Concurrently Yeh Chien-ying, alleged by the Government to have been contained in Shantung in the Yellow River delta area, has moved his troops southwestward and crossed the Yellow River in the vicinity of Tungo, with a force of approximately 40,000 men. The possibility suggested in my report of August 28 appears now to have become fact and recent Government optimism with regard to Shantung has been proven largely unwarranted.

In Manchuria the military situation remains quiescent. The arrival of Ch'en Ch'eng and the military reforms inaugurated by him have had an excellent effect upon over-all military and civil morale. However, the sixth Communist offensive in Manchuria is imminent and seems to be waiting only upon further drying of the roads which has been delayed this season by unusually heavy rains. It is doubtful that changes made by Ch'en Ch'eng will be in sufficient time to counteract serious decay which set in under Hsiung Shih-hui and Tu Li-ming regime. Furthermore, it is likely that the on-coming Communist offensive will be coordinated with Communist military activity in North China to preclude the despatch of adequate replacements or reinforcements outside the wall. Current activities of Liu Po-cheng in Central China and Yeh Chien-ying in Shantung now tend to confirm this belief. Communist radio broadcasts state that the offensive to "liberate" China north of the Yangtze has been launched, but it is unlikely that the Communists will be successful in attaining this objective within the foreseeable future. Their maneuvers, however, will undoubtedly further shake the economic and political structure of the Central Government throughout China but critically so in the north.

Most disheartening features of present Chinese situation in economic as in other spheres are overt reliance on *deus ex machina* of American aid to extricate China from its pressing problems and corresponding lack of self-reliance and self-help in tackling them. While introduction of the "official" open market rate of exchange on August 17 marked a welcome departure in this respect, toying with a premature and ill-considered project for the introduction of silver coinage, expectation that China's balance of payments deficit will be partly covered in some form or other by the United States, and continued passivity in the face of mounting hyperinflation clearly reflect a dominant trend of dependence on outside assistance. While there is a *prima facie* case for foreign aid, for instance, to cover part of the balance of payments deficit, it would be immeasurably strengthened if there were signs of a concerned and aggressive policy on the part of the Government.

Too early to judge what impact of establishment of "official" open market rate of exchange on China's balance of payments will be, as much depends on whether political pressures will counteract the influence of foreign advisers who rightly wish to hug the black market rate for United States currency. Nevertheless, its establishment is a healthy if belated step in the right direction. The Central Bank had been losing foreign exchange at the rate of $30,000,000 a month, $20,000,000 for financing the gap between commercial imports and receipts from exports, et cetera, and $10,000,000 for Government imports and expenditures abroad. In its first month of operations the Exchange Equalization Committee's receipts have slightly more than covered outgo on commercial imports, but unless this trend can be maintained, China's existing foreign exchange assets of $260,000,000, including 45,000,000 ounces of silver, is barely sufficient to last another nine months.

145

The Ambassador in China (Stuart) to Secretary Marshall

893.00/10-2947

NANKING, *October 29, 1947*

SIR: I have the honor to comment on political trends in China perhaps more as a record of my present impressions than because of any substantial objective changes. Most of this may therefore be mere repetition of what is already familiar.

COMMUNIST PARTY

There is no evidence of any weakening either in fighting power or in morale. Rather the opposite. They seem to be relatively well supplied with ammunition, money and other material necessities, and to be confident of their ability to carry on for the two or three years which they estimate as the time required to get control of the territory north of the Yangtse River. They are steadily improving their organization and discipline. Officers and men share the same hardships and have the enthusiasm of those who are devotedly fighting for a cause which transcends all thought of selfish ambition or enjoyment. There is little if any evidence of material assistance from Moscow but there is undoubtedly very close and conscious affinity in aims, methods and objectives. This will probably become more apparent as the rift widens between the United States and the Soviet Union. The hatred against America is said to be more vocal now than even against Chiang Kai-shek. Reports indicate that the younger student type is more unreservedly pro-Russian or international in its sympathies than the older leaders with whom the nationalistic loyalties aroused by foreign aggression still linger. The younger people argue that if America can help the Kuomintang why should not Russia be allowed to help them. On the other hand the official pronouncements have always been at pains to disavow any such aid or connection realizing the unfavorable effects of this upon the general public. There are numerous and well-authenticated reports of the merciless cruelty of the Communists, especially in newly occupied areas, and of the terrorism this inspires. There is no slightest question but that they intend to carry on their destructive tactics until the present government succumbs. They will then agree to any temporary compromise or coalition that will enable them to extend their control until they achieve their goal of a thoroughly communized China. Nor is there any doubt in my mind but that their control will follow the invariable Communist pattern of a police-state, with no freedom of thought or action and with brutal slaughter or expropriation of all who seem to be in their way.

KUOMINTANG

The corruption and the reactionary forces pervading the Kuomintang are too familiar to call for further emphasis. It should be kept in mind, however, that single-party control always tends to be corrupt, that the period during which this party has been in power has been one of incessant conflict, that the mounting costs of living have greatly aggravated an age-long tradition in China, and that the mood of defeatism in an increasingly hopeless outlook has caused a creeping paralysis upon all creative effort. Even so the men at the very top are of high integrity and continue to struggle bravely against terrific difficulties. There are many more like them within and outside of the Government.

Other Parties

The minority parties are rather disappointing. Those now absorbed into the Government are contributing but little and are busily seeking office for their members. The Democratic League continues to arouse suspicion of its communistic proclivities and offers little prospect of serving as a nucleus for liberal action. My chief concern at present is that the Government through ill-advised persecution will discredit itself further for high-handed oppression thus winning sympathy for the League from those who stand for enlightened constitutional procedure, while the League members will be driven further leftist and to underground activities.

Another factor which is becoming more apparent is the infiltration of Communists not only into bodies like the League but also into the Government itself. The seizures in Peiping following the discovery of a Communist headquarters are grim evidence of this. But of the arrests in other cities because of documents found there all but two have been Government employees. With a revitalized program, supported alike by their colleagues and the public, such men could be largely immunized. Otherwise their members and their sinister influence will tend to increase.

The best hope of the country seems to be in her educated youth. This group should be broadened so as to include those who once were ardently patriotic students, have become more or less cynical or discouraged in their depressing environment, but might be expected under better conditions to recover much of their lost enthusiasm. Assuming American aid of the nature which has in general been under consideration, these young people could be enlisted as "shock troops". If we can manage to sublimate our military and monetary aid into a movement to bring peace, freedom from oppression and economic recovery under democratic principles, including the responsibility of the people to take part in reforming their government, this can win the allegiance of youth and neutralize their suspicions of American imperialism, reliance on force, strengthening an effete regime as an anti-Soviet policy, et cetera. The student class is intensely nationalistic and now thoroughly alarmed. The genius of the Chinese people is naturally democratic rather than communistic. By making our objectives transparently clear we can help toward a resurgent moral awakening aiming at government reform and a better livelihood for all, with students past and present as the animating heart of it. This is what actually happened in the Revolution of 1911 and in the anti-Japanese resistance. It can come again. The convictions of democratic youth will thus match those of communist youth and which of those of the present generation wins will largely determine the destiny of China. Nor need we fear this if we really believe in the democratic way of life and in its ability to win over its greatest rival in our time when the contest is out in the open as this would be. If this process cannot conquer Communist ideology and machinations nothing else will. But a challenge on this high plane ought to have far-reaching consequences in other parts of Asia.

When I stopped off in Nanking in May of last year to pay my respects to the Generalissimo on my return from the United States, he asked me what I thought of the situation. I replied that it was worse than I had reason to expect from press reports in America but that I believed it could be changed if he would lead wholeheartedly in a new revolutionary movement with the adventurous and unselfish zeal of the Kuomintang when he first joined it, rallying present-day youth as it had done when he was one of them. The rallying cry might well be that of patriotic loyalty expressed now in reforming, unifying and constructive effort, and of treason as consisting in all that hinders these. It would be less easy for him now but with our help I still think of this somewhat visionary solution as in the end the most practical one.

Respectfully yours,

J. LEIGHTON STUART

146

Article Published in Central News Agency Bulletin, October 28, 1947 [14]

893.00/11–347

On the charge of complicity with the Chinese Communists in their armed rebellion against the state, the Democratic League has been outlawed, declared a spokesman of the Ministry of Interior, in a statement issued yesterday.

The spokesman said that henceforth all government offices responsible for peace and order will prosecute the activities of the Democratic League and its sympathizers in accordance with the temporary regulations for punishment of saboteurs of the national general mobilization and the regulations for dealing with the Communists in our rear. This puts the Leaguers in the same category as the Communists. The statement asserted that the Ministry was impelled to take this action to stop the activities of the Democratic League which has been playing the part of accomplice to the Communists' boom in the front and the rear against the security of the state. The spokesman cited concrete examples of his charges of the Democratic League's conspiracy with the Communists to overthrow the Central Government. According to the spokesman the League had dispatched Li Ping-chen to take charge of armed activities against the government in the northeast, and Kung Chung-chow, League leader in north eastern China had attempted a revolt in Sian. The League also instigated the student disturbances in May and the recent labor trouble in Shanghai. The statement charged that Li Ying-feng, influential member of the League, has been enlisting brigands for an uprising in Szechuan. Other charges against the League included the open denunciation of the government's general mobilization order by the League's Hong Kong and Singapore branches.

STUART

147

Announcement by the China Democratic League, November 6, 1947 [15]

[Translation]

893.00/11–1347

The China Democratic League has consistently maintained its firm stand for democracy, peace and unity. Unfortunately, the war has become more and more intensified. In the face of this calamity, we, the Leaguers, could only grieve being unable to do anything effective to serve the country. Recently, the Government ordered the outlawing of the League, prohibiting it from engaging in any activities. We, the Leaguers, could no longer be active. So we unanimously elected Huang Yen-Pei, member of the Standing Committee, as our representative, and dispatched him to the Capital from Shanghai to ne-

---

[14] Transmitted to Secretary Marshall by Ambassador Stuart Nov. 3, 1947.
[15] Transmitted by the American Consul General at Shanghai (Davis), Nov. 13, 1947.

gotiate with the Government concerning the problems relating to the dissolution of the League. Following are the measures proposed by the Government:

"(1) The Government has already outlawed the League and hopes that the League will dissolve itself voluntarily, so that the responsible officials of the League can be relieved of their responsibilities.

"(2) Concerning houses and other properties: (a) The properties belonging to the Communist Party, now in the League's custody, should be turned over to the Government; (b) the houses belonging to the League can be retained for the time being; (c) the houses appropriated by the Government for use of the League should be returned to the Government, and if they cannot be vacated immediately, they can be used temporarily; (d) the private residences of League members will not be disturbed and (e) the houses located at Rue Chu Pao San, originally rented by the Communist Party, now in the League's custody, should likewise be handed over to the Government. If the houses are now used for school purposes and can not be vacated, arrangements for the use of the houses by the school should be worked out."

Mr. Huang Yen-Pei gave the following answers to the above proposals:

"(1) Since the League has been outlawed by the Government, its only course it to notify all the Leaguers to cease all party activities, and, following the issue of the notification, the Leaguers themselves will be held personally responsible for their own activities and utterances.

"(2) The various points with respect to houses will be duly observed. However, one further point needs clarification, namely: While it is not known that the League originally had properties of its own, if there should prove to be any such properties, they should be disposed of by the League itself. Furthermore, the League submits the following two requests:

"(3) That the League members in various places be exempted from registering with the Government and enjoy all civil liberties to which they are legally entitled.

"(4) That League members in various places who are considered by the Government as having violated the law, and those who are already under arrest, should be treated by the Government in accordance with the law, and that the Measures for Dealing with the Communists in the Rear should not be applied to League members arrested under alleged but unproven Communist affiliations.

"As to whether or not points (2), (3) and (4) can be carried out, we now await your reply. As for the various documents published in the press critical of the League, they are quite contrary to facts. However, we do not intend to argue or offer refutations now."

Following is the reply made by the Government:

"(1) If the League would obey the order announced by the spokesman of the Ministry of the Interior and formally declare its voluntary dissolution as well as cessation of all activities, then all League members everywhere could be exempted from registering with the Government and would be assured freedom within the law. However, if hereafter some still engage in illegal activities under false pretexts, they will be prosecuted by the security agencies in various places according to law.

"(2) If, after proper investigations by the judicial authorities, League members under arrest for alleged offenses, are found not to be Communist nor working for Communists, then the Measures for Dealing with the Communists in the Rear will not be applied to them.

"Furthermore, all the points relating to houses and other properties will be carried out."

While publishing the foregoing record of the negotiations, we at the same time hereby notify all League members to stop all political activities as from this date. All personnel of the League's General Headquarters will resign en bloc as from this date and the General Headquarters will also dissolve as from this date.

CHANG LAN, Chairman of the China Democratic League

148

The Ambassador in China (Stuart) to Secretary Marshall

893.00/11–547

NANKING, *November 5, 1947.*

SIR: I have the honor to refer to the Embassy's messages concerning the Central Government's declaration outlawing the Democratic League and to set forth in more detail the events immediately prior and subsequent to the Government's action.

Commencing on October 21, 1947 there was published prominently on the front page of the *Chung Yang Jih Pao,* an official Government organ, a public announcement issued jointly by the Nanking Garrison Commander and the Mayor of Nanking that all Communist agents and persons connected with them should register their secession from the Chinese Communist Party prior to October 31, 1947. The announcement stated that those failing to register within the prescribed period would be liable to arrest and punishment according to law. There is enclosed for the information of the Department a copy in translation of the announcement.

The Department will recall that as early as October 14 Democratic League leaders expressed their concern to the Ambassador with regard to the probable outlawing of the League by the Government. It will also be recalled that on October 15, the Ambassador took the occasion of a visit to the Prime Minister to raise the question of repressive measures against the Democratic League, and to suggest that the League request for a conference between Government-appointed representatives and representatives of the League be favorably considered primarily for the sake of the Government itself.

On the morning of October 24 Dr. Lo Lung-chi, a Democratic League leader, called upon an officer of the Embassy to say that commencing on the night of October 23 the Democratic League headquarters had been surrounded by approximately twenty persons. Dr. Lo assumed that these individuals were secret police operatives. He said that residents of the League headquarters had not been molested in any way but that he was being constantly followed by persons in plain-clothes riding in an unmarked jeep. Dr. Lo was in a state of great perturbation and referred to the public announcement by the Nanking Garrison Commander and the Mayor of Nanking which he interpreted as being directed primarily at the League in as much as it was unlikely that there were any actual Communists in Nanking who would appear at the Nanking Garrison Headquarters for registration. Dr. Lo alleged that there was in existence a list containing approximately 600 names who would be arrested following the expiration date for registration mentioned in the Garrison Commander's announcement. On the same morning Dr. Lo also called on the Ambassador to express his growing concern with regard to the Government's attitude.

Dr. Lo's greatest concern stemmed from his conviction that the persons surrounding the League headquarters were members of the military secret police, and that in the event of arrest he anticipated secret action by military tribunals which in many past cases had resulted in the permanent disappearance of persons so arrested.

In passing it is interesting to note that Dr. Lo's fears in this connection are borne out to some extent by checking the registration number of the jeep which followed Dr. Lo to the Ambassador's residence and to the Chancery on October 23 and succeeding days. With the assistance of the Provost Marshal of the Army Advisory Group, the Embassy ascertained that the jeep which followed Dr. Lo was registered with the Secret Affairs Bureau of the Ministry of National Defense and the registration record of the vehicle showed that it had been formerly registered with the office of General Tai Li.

In the early morning of October 28 a spokesman of the Ministry of Interior announced that the Government could no longer tolerate an organization which opposed the national constitution and aimed at the overthrow of the Government and that the Democratic League was therefore pronounced an illegal organization. This announcement was published in the vernacular press on the morning of October 28 and a copy of the announcement in translation is enclosed. At approximately 10:00 a. m. on the morning of October 28 Dr. Lo Lung-chi called an officer of the Embassy by telephone to seek an appointment which was granted. Shortly thereafter Dr. Lo called again to say that he had been refused permission to leave the Democratic League headquarters. Approximately one hour later, however, Dr. Lo was granted permission to leave his place of residence after he expressed to his guards a desire to call upon the American Ambassador and accepted the condition that his car would drive slowly in order that a police vehicle could follow it. Dr. Lo proceeded to the Ambassador's residence and spoke briefly with the Ambassador. It was necessary, however, for the Ambassador to leave to keep an appointment with the Foreign Minister and the Ambassador directed an officer of the Embassy to come to his residence to talk with Dr. Lo. An Embassy officer proceeded to the Ambassador's residence and accompanied Dr. Lo in Dr. Lo's car to the Chancery where Dr. Lo again expressed at considerable length his grave concern at the trend of events. Dr Lo appeared convinced that the announcement by the Ministry of Interior could not have been made without its having been authorized by the highest authority. Dr. Lo believed that instructions had been issued by the Generalissimo, otherwise the Ministry of Interior would not have dared to take responsibility for such action. In this same general connection, an Assistant Naval Attache, while calling on the Municipal Police headquarters with regard to an unrelated matter, was informed by a responsible municipal police official that orders outlawing the Democratic League had been issued personally by the Generalissimo. There is also enclosed a memorandum of conversation between an officer of the Embassy and an American employee of the Government Information Office which also bears on this point.

In the course of conversation with Dr. Lo at the Chancery on October 28, an officer of the Embassy informed Dr. Lo that following the conversation of the League leaders with the Ambassador on October 14 the Ambassador had taken occasion to point out to the Prime Minister, the Ministry of the Interior, and to the Generalissimo's personal secretary the possible adverse effect both abroad and internally of the course of action to which the Government seemed committed. It was also mentioned to Dr. Lo that the Ambassador had in mind mentioning this matter to the Foreign Minister in the course of his conversation on the morning of October 28. It was pointed out to Dr. Lo, however, that the League could not expect the Embassy or the United States Government actively to intervene on its behalf, although he was informed that the Embassy was naturally interested in developments and would appreciate his keeping the Chancery informed.

On October 28 Dr. Lo had lunch with an officer of the Embassy whose residence is in the Chancery compound and while waiting to keep this engagement Dr. Lo had opportunity to speak to a number of foreign correspondents who called at the Chancery during this period and who had previously been refused admission to the League headquarters. Following his luncheon engagement, Dr. Lo proceeded to the Ambassador's residence where he met Hwang Yen-p'ei, another leader of the League, who, in the meantime, had arrived from Shanghai. On October 28, therefore, Dr. Lo was on Embassy property for approximately five hours and this apparently gave rise to the allegation in the headlines of certain minor Shanghai vernacular papers that Dr. Lo was in hiding at the American Embassy. The text of the stories, however, did not bear out the headlines and therefore the Embassy issued no formal denial although the Department was informed that these reports had no foundation in fact.

Since October 28 there has developed a considerable amount of confusion with regard to the current status of the Democratic League. As far as the Embassy can ascertain the action taken by the Ministry of Interior has not been approved by the Executive Yuan, and although the Government continues to regard the League as an illegal organization it has not taken steps to order its dissolution and in fact appears very reluctant to take such action. There have been no important changes in the situation since the Embassy's report of October 31, 1947. There would appear to be little question, however, but that extreme rightist elements in the Government continue convinced of the necessity for complete suppression of the Democratic League. For the time being the indirect action taken by the Embassy and the obvious interest expressed by the foreign correspondents in the Government's move against the League has forestalled a wide scale "witch hunt" and has probably impressed upon the more enlightened elements of the Government the growing need for control of their extremist colleagues. The ability of the former to control the latter, however, is dubious.

The Embassy was gratified to learn from the Department that its action in connection with the Government's move against the League had the full approval of the Department.

For the Ambassador
WILLIAM T. TURNER
First Secretary of Embassy

[Enclosure 1—Translation]

Official Announcement by the Nanking Garrison Headquarters and Nanking Municipal Government

No. 2110   *October 21, 1947*

The resolution concerning the plan for dealing with the Communists in the rear, passed by the 19th Meeting of the Executive Yuan, has been published. Those Communists hiding in Nanking municipality should apply for registration. The measures for the application for registration of secession from the Communist Party drafted in accordance with Article 6 of the plan passed by the Executive Yuan are hereby published. The period from the publication of the measures to October 31 is set for the application for registration and those who fail to register within this period will be liable to arrest, and to be punished according to law. The measures for the application for registration of secession from the Communist Party are hereby publicly announced and it is hoped that registration will be completed within the period established.

MEASURES FOR THE APPLICATION FOR REGISTRATION OF SECESSION FROM THE COMMUNIST PARTY IN NANKING MUNICIPALITY ARE AS FOLLOWS:

(1) These measures are based on Article 6 of the plan for dealing with the Communist rear areas published by the Executive Yuan.

(2) These measures apply to Nanking and its environs.

(3) All Communist agents and persons connected with them, no matter whether they worked for the Communist Party in the past or are working for it at present, should register.

(4) Application for registration should be filed within the period from October 21 to October 31. Those who fail to register within this period will be liable to arrest.

(5) Applications for registration should be filed with the Garrison Command.

(6) Applications for registration should be filed with the Garrison Command during its office hours within the period established.

(7) Application forms may be obtained at the Garrison Command and should be completed there.

(8) These measures will go into effect as of today.

Garrison Commander CHANG CHEN
Mayor SHĘN YI

[Enclosure 2—Translation]

Announcement by the Chinese Government Declaring the Democratic League Illegal

October 28, 1947

The Chinese people have known for a long time that the Democratic League has linked with the Communists and joined the rebellion. According to reports made by various local authorities who are responsible for the preservation of peace and order the following examples are outstanding: Lo Ping-chi, a League member has instigated mutiny among the troops in Manchuria; the responsible League member for the Northwest was responsible for the rebellion of Kung Chung-chou; the student strikes in May and the recent labor strikes in Shanghai were incited by the League. Since the promulgation of the General Mobilization Order by the Government for the suppression of the Communist rebellion the Hongkong and Malaya branches of the League have publicly opposed the Order and indicated clearly that the League action and the action of the Communists are one and the same. Recently, Li Ying-fen, an important League member mustered bandits in Szechuan in order to rise in rebellion and to cooperate with the Communist bandits of Li Hsien-nien. Other plots and underground work carried on by the League of which we have concrete proof are too numerous to mention. In view of the seriousness of the Communist rebellion and the rampant activities carried on by the League, the Government can no longer tolerate an organization which opposes the National Constitution and aims at the overthrow of the Government. For the preservation of peace and order in the rear this Ministry has to take adequate steps to check the activities of the League. The Democratic League is hereby pronounced illegal and local authorities responsible for the preservation of peace and order shall halt the illegal activities of the League and effect punishment according to the measures for the treatment of Communists stated in the General Mobilization Order.

[Enclosure 3]

Memorandum of Conversation [16]

Mr. Votaw, American Adviser, Chinese Government Information Office in discussing the Government order declaring the Democratic League an illegal organization said that a special committee of the Executive Yuan considered the question on October 27 and that Dr. Hollington Tong, Director of the Chinese Government Information Office, was present at the meeting. Dr. Tong vehemently opposed the suppression of the League as an organization and as a result of his recommendation, and that of other members of the Yuan, it was decided to disapprove such action. Although the suppression order was issued by the Minister of Interior at 2:30 AM, October 28, the Ministry steadfastly, until noon of that same day, denied to the CGIO that such action had been taken or was even contemplated. Mr. Votaw maintains that Dr. Tong, up to the present moment, has still been unable to get in touch with the Minister of Interior to ascertain why and how the order was promulgated. Mr. Votaw adds, however, that one of the leading figures in the case was Tao Shih-shen, Vice-Minister of Information of the Kuomintang and a strong supporter of Chen Li-fu. He also adds that Li Wei-kwo, Minister of Information of the Kuomintang, was not privy to the developments.

Mr. Votaw said that the more enlightened elements in Government and party are seriously disturbed at the action against the League; that the action represents another step of the CC Clique in its drive toward the elimination of all opposition and for its own complete and final control of the Kuomintang. He does not believe there is much that moderate elements in the party can do to save the situation unless the Generalissimo himself actively intervenes in favor of the League.

149

The Ambassador in China (Stuart) to Secretary Marshall

[Extract]

893.00/1-948

NANKING, *January 9, 1948*

Full text December 25 statement by Mao Tse-Tung has already been sent airmail to Department. . . . The Embassy gains two dominant impressions: (1) the note of triumphant conviction that the essentials of the Communist struggle for victory in China have been achieved, though Mao is careful to point out that additional great sacrifices will be required, and (2) the continuous and vitriolic attacks on the United States as the great enemy of the world and the agent responsible for the continuing civil war in China. Endlessly Mao reiterates the point that reactionary American imperialism is a major enemy of the people of China. Even though the recent months have witnessed heightening attacks on the United States, this is the first time that one of the top leaders of the party has publicly joined the hue and cry.

[16] Conversation between Maurice Votaw, American Adviser in the Chinese Government Information Office, and John F. Melby, Second Secretary of Embassy at Nanking.

Mao's elaboration of Communist military tactics and strategy is a remarkably candid explanation of how precisely Communist armies operate as far as the Embassy has been able to determine. It is perhaps a mark of Communist contempt for Nationalist military thinking and intelligence that the Communists have so little hesitation in explaining their strategy, which, it must be admitted, has to date not been without success.

Considerable attention in the manifesto is given to explaining the need for relentless pursuit of the land reform program in order to satisfy the aspirations of peasant groups regardless of cost to those who now hold the land. This is in accordance with other scattered and fragmentary reports received by the Embassy in recent months about the stepping up of the land program.

It is interesting to note the appeal for support from the middle group of peasants whom Mao says he believes will be willing to make certain personal sacrifices for the common weal. The threat that any opposition can expect no mercy rather suggests, however, that the Communists are not yet prepared to rely solely upon goodness of heart in securing cooperation. Nor should the gesture of conciliation to the middle groups yet be considered as anything more than a propaganda device which can be reversed at will.

It is significant that this statement moves even farther away than the New Year's message of Lu Ting-I of a year ago, from the lip service to conciliation and moderation which characterized Mao's report to the 7th National Congress of the Chinese Communist Party in April, 1945. It seems to the Embassy there is a striking similarity between the argument and invective advanced by Mao and that of other Communist leaders throughout the world. It also seems to the Embassy that more than at any other time in the past Chinese Communist thinking, with some exceptions made necessary by contemporary conditions, is following the line of reasoning advanced by Lenin in his April theses. All current evidence indicates Communist willingness and intention to adopt and exploit any means possible or necessary to securing the ultimate objective, namely, full power. Not even the obscure vocabulary can obscure the fact that this is precisely what Mao is saying or becloud his conviction that it will work.

150 (a)

The Ambassador in China (Stuart) to Secretary Marshall

893.00/2-548

NANKING, *February 5, 1948.*

Symptomatic, we believe, of the increasing unrest and of disillusionment with the present Chinese Government were the recent disturbances in Shanghai. More than other races, the Chinese are inclined to look for a scape-goat when things go wrong and in this case we have noticed an increasing tendency to blame the Generalissimo and to seek for an alternative to his regime.

Within a five day period, January 29 to February 2, there were three major civil disturbances in Shanghai culminating in outbreaks or mob violence with destruction to property and loss of life and injury to both police and members of the mob. The government's explanation of these events was given in press conference of Shanghai mayor on February 3 in which he stated that disturbances were "Communist stage-managed" and that "Shanghai is main objective of organized red mass uprising headquarters for the Yangtze valley area".

We feel that question of Communist participation in these civil disorders is in large degree academic. While Communists undoubtedly eager exploit events to own ends, these situations are intrinsically manifestations of government's alienation of popular support through administrative ineptitude which has now progressed to a degree endangering government's stability. In each instance of civil unrest, an organized group appeared convinced that government had acted unreasonably and arbitrarily against group's economic or political interests. Government made no adequate arrangements for orderly settlement of points at issue, leaving group no alternatives except to abandon demands or present them through mass action. Government policing of individual situations was inept and exacerbated mass feeling to point where group became mob bent on violent retaliation for real or fancied wrongs. Police unable, or possibly unwilling, to restrain mob until after acts of violence had been committed.

These specific, local situations faithfully mirror government's predicament on national level, which is also largely of government's own making and for which government's sovereign remedy has so far also been force ineptly applied. In most of China north of Yangtze, principal elements opposing government are Communist organized. In remainder of the country still under its control, government's futile attempts to eliminate all opposition and compel support and its failure to devise and implement adequate constructive policies for improvement in its position is rapidly bringing it to the verge of severe crisis which it can hardly hope to survive. Increased urban civil unrest on a large scale may well be the factor precipitating crisis, which the Communists obviously are prepared to exploit.

Growing pessimism and despondency of high Chinese civil and military officials with regard to economic, political and military deterioration has long been apparent. Recently there seems to have developed a sharper awareness of the fact that the government may soon lack the minimum of popular support necessary for its survival. This trend approaches conviction on the part of most that the government lacks capacity to extricate itself from the plight without foreign assistance and fear on the part of many that the government's position is hopeless even though foreign aid is forthcoming.

In this situation several types of response are taking shape. The Generalissimo and those most loyal to him favor strategy of continued resistance to the Communists and repression of other dissident or potentially dissident elements, while effecting such minimum reforms as are possible without antagonizing the most reactionary groups. This group hopes to sustain itself with whatever aid it can get, believing that in the final analysis it will be saved by a Soviet-American war.

Another indefinite grouping responds to the situation with the idea of seeking a negotiated peace with the Communists through the mediation of the Soviet Union, hoping to retain dominant influence and authority in a coalition government which would result from this mediation. Recent reports, unconfirmed but from credible sources, indicate that this group is gaining many adherents among the military and is already exploring means to contact the Soviets to negotiate mediation. While this group may not have yet achieved status of an antigovernment movement, probably because of lack of firm leadership, many factors strongly favor such development. Since the military elements in the group are preponderant, the possibility of defection among the armed forces cannot be overlooked.

The situation is very definitely one to cause pessimism. If American aid should materialize in adequate measure and palatable form, the tide may turn quickly in our favor. On the other hand, when details of American aid are announced, they will be weighed carefully by all factions and if our plans are deemed to be insufficient or unpalatable, or unlikely to be effective, it is more than likely that disaffection of some elements now in the government may ensue. Such disaffection may well result in the replacement of present dominant elements with the group desirous of effecting union with the Communists through the good offices of the Soviet Union. As we have previously reported, the Generalissimo is unalterably opposed to such a move and if those favoring an arrangement with the Communists came into the ascendancy, his retirement from the scene would be inevitable.

STUART.

150 (b)

The Ambassador in China (Stuart) to Secretary Marshall

893.00/2-648

NANKING, *February 6, 1948.*

We are by no means convinced that the general breakdown of law and order in Shanghai is imminent, although we believe further sporadic civil disturbances probable. There is as yet no indication that the Communists are so organized as to be capable of creating and controlling a state of chaos at Shanghai. As we have already reported on February 5, we continue to believe that basic causes of civil disturbances at Shanghai are economic rather than political and must be dealt with by economic measures in conjunction with determined police control. It seems to us that the government is well aware of the need to maintain itself at all costs in the lower Yangtze valley, and at this time we can see no serious threat to its position in this area. However, the fact remains that government control of Shanghai is likely to be endangered by policy of extremist elements in the government in using party secret police to suppress even legitimate dissatisfaction caused by maladministration and thus solidify discontented elements into organized opposition. In such a situation the advantage is thrown to the Communists. Moderate elements who would prefer to deal with the situation by firm but rational methods are handicapped by lack of unified administrative control. For example, the Mayor of Shanghai has no authority over garrison command or over party secret police. Mayor Wu has requested such authority and we are very informally supporting his request with the Generalissimo, pointing out that the deterioration in the Shanghai situation seems to call for firm measures and centralized authority. We consider this feasible because of competence of the Mayor, his loyalty to the Generalissimo and the high regard in which the latter holds him.

In the situation prevailing at Shanghai there is reason for concern but no immediate cause for alarm. In fact, manhandling of Mayor Wu and the apprehension of some leaders may have sobering effect. Shanghai foreign community has long tended to panic over relatively insignificant political developments. This tendency is infectious and inevitably contributes to general unrest and feeling of insecurity.

We do not wish to minimize potentialities of situation at Shanghai but for time being we feel Chinese Government can retain control over situation. Furthermore, there are factors in situation, such as pending American aid, which will undoubtedly have substantial effect on public morale thus tending to stabilize at least temporarily.

151 (a)

The Ambassador in China (Stuart) to Secretary Marshall

893.00/3-1748

NANKING, March 17, 1948.

Political and military disintegration is now rapidly approaching the long expected climax. The most spectacular evidence of this is the breakdown of military morale seen not only in lethargy and passive unconcern, but also in refusal to obey orders or even to act in defiance of orders given. Chinese describe this latter phenomenon as deliberately suicidal in terms of national interest. Civil and military officials, both high and low, are grafting or are planning their escape. In the highest circles, Generalissimo listens only to such civilians as Tai Chi-tao, the Chen brothers, and T. V. Soong, but Chen Kuo-fu is now in disfavor and his brother is less in favor than hitherto. Relations between the Generalissimo and Tai are not cordial, and T. V. Soong is concentrating on his job in south China. Among many of those hitherto most loyal to the Generalissimo, there are definite signs of discontent with his policy. Nor are there any indications of any intention on his part to make the requisite radical changes. In their despair, all groups blame America for urging structural changes, many of which they claim have been undertaken, or reforms which they feel they themselves would carry out if their immediate internal problems were not so acute, while America still delays the long promised aid upon which the survival of democratic institutions depends. At the same time they are proposing that someone be sent to Washington to plead for immediate and adequate assistance. Such names as those of T. V. Soong and Yu Tai-Wei have been mentioned to me of late for this purpose.

There is a growing tendency to postpone the National Assembly due to convene March 29. Tai Chi-tao supports postponement on the ground that in their efforts to settle controversies over the election of delegates they are using authoritarian methods not unlike the Communists whom they are fighting. Others support postponement on the ground of present inexpediency, or because a suitable name for Vice President has not emerged. Vice President candidates being discussed are Yu Yu-jen, Sun Fo, Ho Ying-chin, Cheng Chien, Fu Tso-yi, and Li Tsung-jen. Li is opposed by the inner circles around the Generalissimo because of factional bickering and as being too strong a personality to be willing to leave the Generalissimo in complete power. Some urge that the Vice President should be a civilian. Present indications are that Generalissimo will support Yu Yu-jen with all that implies.

Various rather inconsequential attempts are being made among liberals to organize or to issue appeals, but the controlled press and fear of high-handed repression tend to nullify their efforts. There is, however, a nucleus within the party leadership which is planning something of the sort with some hope of results. I have been asked to advocate their cause with the Generalissimo, but have replied that I have repeatedly suggested to the Generalissimo without success, that he himself lead such a movement, and that while I still think his endorsement is not entirely impossible, I could perhaps be of more influence in supporting the general idea after their movement had attained substantial proportions. I have added that it seemed to me to be of primary importance that the liberals ensure freedom of publication in party papers for their proposed manifesto.

The long expected climax is rapidly approaching, and although we cannot see the Generalissimo voluntarily relinquishing his power almost anything can happen. There is most definitely accelerated demoralization, dismay and frantic search to save something from the wreckage, coupled with a psychopathic inability to do anything.

STUART

151 (b)

The Ambassador in China (Stuart) to Secretary Marshall

893.00/3–3148

NANKING, *March 31, 1948*

Demoralization and deterioration of situation portrayed in our report of March 8, have continued at an accelerated pace. There is an increased feeling of helplessness in government circles as elsewhere and a fervent searching for some means of bringing a stop to civil war and economic and political uncertainties resulting from it. There is an increasing realization, shared even by the Generalissimo, that military victory over Communists is impossible and that some other solution must be reached if Communist-domination of all China is to be avoided. There is a realization that old methods are inadequate and that a new approach is needed. There is, we believe, a sincere search for an effective new approach yet no one has found the formula. No one seems capable of taking positive action towards peace. Each one looks to another for initiative. Those in position to influence the Generalissimo to take positive effective measures fear his anger and are reluctant to put forward their ideas of reform. He has need of more courageous advisers around him and perhaps his reorganized government will supply this need. As straws in the wind and as possible portent of future trends are recent proclamations by intellectual groups advocating reforms. What they are afraid to do individually, they are beginning to do collectively.

The Chinese people do not want to become Communists yet they see the tide of Communism running irresistably onward. In midst of this chaos and inaction the Generalissimo stands out as the only moral force capable of action. We know that he plans to reorganize his Government yet we question a mere shifting of portfolios can result in effective action. Little, if any, new blood seems available. What is needed is inspired leadership, of which so far the Generalissimo seems incapable. Possibly, however, the desperateness of his situation will serve to stimulate him as in the past to leadership required.

In any event, there is ever so slight an indication that the Generalissimo may at last deem the situation so acute that he is prepared to accept and follow sound advice. He is taking measures to improve military situation in Mukden and if he can save Mukden, and it begins to look as though he may do so; if he can bring himself to begin institution of political and economic reforms needed to make his government more acceptable to the people, and there are signs here also that he may have reached that stage; and if we can continue and, if possible, expand our present support, as now seems likely from the Congressional consideration of Aid to China Bill; then the situation may not be entirely beyond redemption.

It is nevertheless desperate and if the Generalissimo does not act and act promptly, there are increasing indications that growing opposition to him within the party may find leadership, possibly under the Political Science Group, and will remove him from the scene, accepting the best possible accommodation with the Communists. Should this stage be reached, we could expect Soviet Ambassador designate, Roschin, to assume his duties at Nanking and could look for acceptance of Soviet offer of mediation. Contrary, however, to belief expressed in our report of March 8 we now incline to the opinion that Soviet mediation would result in a coalition government rather than in territorial arrangement. That road to power is better known to Communists and would, we believe, be more acceptable to dissident elements in government. Under a territorial arrangement the present disposition of Communist forces would likely involve giving them jurisdiction over everything north of Yangtze and east of Sian— a division of territory unlikely of acceptance even by dissident elements of government. On the other hand, we hear expressed on many sides belief that under coalition government fundamental characteristic of Chinese would assure that pattern of Czechoslovakia could be resisted and that democratic government in some form would eventually succeed.

Developments in the National Assembly now in session should throw light on the future. Choice of a vice president will give an indication. China is once more at crossroads. The Generalissimo sees structure he labored so long and so hard to create collapsing about him and he may be expected to fight with his usual courage and ability. Either those of weak heart will prevail and we will find ourselves with a Soviet-sponsored coalition government, or those of stout heart will rally round a Generalissimo in some way reinspired to restore benevolence to his despotism sufficient to attract once more a public following necessary to overcome Communist threat. We hope for the latter but we fear the former.

152 (a)

The Ambassador in China (Stuart) to Secretary Marshall

893.00/4-248

NANKING, *April 2, 1948*

We are informed that the Generalissimo has definitely given consideration to the possibility of accepting the Presidency of Executive Yuan reported on March 18. Dr. Hu Shih, who has been very active in organizing the National Assembly, informs us that this subject is being widely discussed and may have merits. He points out that the office of President, under the Constitution, may become, as in France, largely ceremonial while the President of Executive Yuan will exercise great authority. Also once appointed, the President of Executive Yuan should be secure in office as two-thirds vote of the Legislature Yuan is required to unseat him. Hu Shih also mentioned the fact that the Generalissimo had not announced his candidacy for President. In this connection, Chu Cheng, incumbent President Judicial Yuan and qualified for ceremonial office, has announced his availability for election as President.

Sun Fo is actively campaigning for election as Vice President and as President of the Legislative Yuan as well, maintaining that constitutional prohibition against holding other government office when elected President of Legislative Yuan does not apply to elective offices such as those of President or Vice President of the Republic.

The Vice Presidential campaign has now narrowed to Sun Fo and Li Tsung-jen, but should the Generalissimo decide to seek Executive Yuan Presidency, some arrangement is entirely possible whereby Sun Fo would be elected President of the Republic and would appoint the Generalissimo to the Presidency of Executive Yuan leaving the Vice Presidency free for Li Tsung-jen.

STUART

ANNEXES 847

152⁻(b)

Speech by Generalissimo Chiang Kai-shek Before the Central Executive Committee of the Kuomintang on April 4, 1948 [17]

893.00/4–948

The convocation of the National Asssembly is a great event in the history of China. On the current situation as well as on the course of political development in decades to come it is bound to exercise a most profound and decisive influence. Problems confronting the National Assembly are many. In tackling any one of them, especially that of the presidency and vice-presidency, we must have all the seriousness of mind and a sense of grave responsibility to the nation and posterity. We must carefully study our revolutionary history, analyze the prevailing circumstances, understand the people's psychology and visualize the future of the country. Above all, we must uphold our late leader Dr. Sun's lofty ideal "everything for the people", and make our choice with far sight and circumspection. I, therefore, propose to explain to you with all sincerity the conclusions I have drawn on these questions after careful deliberation.

Before I present to you my views on the question of the presidency and vice-presidency, I wish to make clear three points: First, the ultimate aim of our Party is to save and reconstruct the country. Aside from the paramount interest of the State, the Party has no interest of its own. We have no partisan or personal considerations. Secondly, the only ambition our comrades should have is how to serve the country and the people. We can best render our service only when we perform our duty wholeheartedly, each in his respective post. Thirdly, our late leader Dr. Sun, when leading the revolutionary movement, always took cognizance of the past and gave practical and realistic consideration to existing circumstances. The above three points are what we have to bear in mind when we take decisions on momentous issues. Hence I wish to remind you of a bitter lesson of history and draw a parallel between it and the present situation.

At the beginning of the Republic Dr. Sun Yat-sen was the president of the Provisional Government. Hardly had three months elapsed when the majority of party comrades advocated Dr. Sun's withdrawal from the government in order to make the peace negotiations between the North and South a speedy success. They were mistaken in regarding the provisional constitution, the parliament and the cabinet as constitutional democracy itself. They did not realize that Peiping still was the citadel of reactionary influence with the northern warlords actually in control of everything. In other words, the foundation of the Republic was extremely feeble. At that juncture, our Party, in order to safeguard this foundation, should not have relinquished the presidency. But to Dr. Sun's pleadings our comrades turned a deaf ear. So he failed. And his failure was also that of the Revolution of 1911. The result was the tragic history of the last thirty-odd years and the enormous sufferings of the people. The situation today is, however, fundamentally different from that of 1911. On account of the contributions we made during the Northern Expedition and the War of Resistance the foundation of the Republic has been greatly strengthened. The idea of democracy has become a popular sentiment. In these circumstances, our Party does not need to keep the post and honor of the presidency. On

[17] Transmitted by Ambassador Stuart from Nanking, Apr. 9, 1948.

the contrary, we should develop Dr. Sun's ideal "everything for the people" to the fullest extent. In other words, we can entrust to persons outside the Party the grave responsibility of making the Constitution a living thing. Only in this manner, I believe, shall we rally the support of the people in our common and gigantic task of rebellion, suppression and national reconstruction.

After careful deliberation I consider that the qualifications for the first president should be as follows: First of all, he must be a person who comprehends the essentials of the Constitution. He must have the ability and will to uphold the Constitution, observe it and carry it into practice. To choose the man capable of obeying and enforcing the law is the surest guarantee of the success of constitutional democracy. In the second place, he must be a person inspired by the ideals of democracy and imbued with a democratic spirit. I believe that a true democrat is always a true patriot. I believe that he will, in accordance with the Constitution, carry out the Three People's Principles and build up China as a country by the people, of the people, and for the people. In the third place he must be a person loyal to the basic policy of rebellion, suppression, and national reconstruction. It takes a true democrat to fully comprehend the incompatability between a dictatorship and a constitutional government. In the fourth place, he must be one who has a profound understanding of our history, culture and national traditions. It is evident that the Communists are determined to undermine the very existence of our country. They are equally determined to destroy our history, culture and national traditions. Finally, he must be one who follows world trends and has a rich knowledge of contemporary civilization. He will lead China towards the ideal of universal brotherhood, make China an independent and self-respecting country and guide her to take her rightful place in the family of nations. I sincerely hope that my views will be shared by all of you, especially those who are holding responsible positions. Let a person outside of our Party with such qualifications be nominated as candidate to the presidency. Let all of us support him and help him to be elected. As for myself, being the leader of the Party, I may be the logical candidate for nomination by the Party to the presidency. I believe, however, that since you have been with me for so many years, you must understand that I do not care for high honor and important post. My only concern has always been how to give my best to serve my people. I am ever ready to assist the president in carrying out the democratic principles embodied in the Constitution. I shall contribute what I have and what I am as a soldier to defend the country.

As long as the nation remains disunited, I am determined not to run for the presidency.

This does not mean that I shall shirk the responsibility towards our revolutionary cause and our beloved country. Aside from the presidency and vice-presidency, I shall not fail to answer the call of the new Government. I have been with my people and army throughout these twenty years of great trials and tribulation. Patriotic soldiers and citizens have supported me in uniting and defending the country. They have given their very best. They have sustained great sacrifices. I have the moral obligation to do my utmost so as not to disappoint them and to forfeit the confidence they have placed in me. I shall contribute whatever I can to cooperate with the people, the army and my party comrades towards our common goal. For the good of the country and the good of the people, I am convinced that I should not run for the presidency. This is not mere modesty. It is my sincere conviction. The only hope I cherish is: how to lay a sound and solid foundation for China's constitutional government.

In a word, I propose that our Party will nominate an outstanding non-partisan to be candidate to the presidency.

Comrades: I hope you will appreciate my sincerity, trust my judgment, endorse my opinion and make a decision!

152 (c)

The Ambassador in China (Stuart) to Secretary Marshall

893.00/4-548

NANKING, *April 5, 1948*

During a tense all-day meeting of the Kuomintang's Central Executive Committee on April 4, the Generalissimo affirmed his unwillingness to be a candidate for the presidency and advised both Cheng Chien and Li Tsung-jen not to run for vice president, but to leave both offices open to civilians. Cheng Chien agreed immediately, but Li is reported to have become very angry and to have said it was too late for him to withdraw. After an all night meeting with his associates he has decided to run independently of the Kuomintang, and if he is defeated there may be trouble.

Strong opposition to the Chen brothers is manifest among delegates, and any motion suspected of being sponsored by them is denounced. Also, revolt against party domination is read into the applause which follows reference to such domination.

The Generalissimo today openly advised party members to vote for Hu Shih and Sun Fo for president and vice president respectively, maintaining both are civilians.

STUART

152 (d)

The Ambassador in China (Stuart) to Secretary Marshall

893.00/4-648

NANKING, *April 6, 1948*

The consequence of the Generalissimo's announcement of a desire to withdraw from the presidential race and serve the country in another capacity and his advice to the Kuomintang to select non-party man as its presidential candidate has been to confirm him in a presidential position, rally full support of the party to his leadership and enhance his authority.

Whether wholly calculated or not, the Generalissimo's action was a masterful political maneuver. Original motivation for action was doubtless need more cohesion within the party weakened by factionalism and by mounting discontent with the quality of his leadership. Apprehensive lest the National Assembly serve as a source from which elements within the party could attack his policy and so bring about party split, the Generalissimo apparently decided to risk assuming minor role in new government through quitting presidential race and recommending non-party candidate for party support. Initial reaction of the party to proposal was feeling of vast dismay. Although under the new constitution presidential powers are greatly reduced, the bulk of Kuomintang has long been accustomed to equating party leadership with the presidency and the presidency with control of the government. Thus, the Generalissimo's move encountered violent opposition on the basis that party's control of the government would be weakened and on the basis that the present crisis demands a strong hand at the helm of the ship of state. Following a series of party meetings, CC Clique refused to cooperate with any government not headed by the Generalissimo as president and Whampou group threatened to go over to the Communists rather than serve under any president other than Chiang. The party leaders joined in the refrain that the Generalissimo is indispensable man in presidential role. Thus, bowing to the party mandate the Generalissimo today consented to enter presidential race.

As suggested above this maneuver greatly strengthens Generalissimo's position. He has answered Communist criticism of "personal rule" by attempting to seek less significant position in new government. Thus Communists are now forced to attack "KMT Government" instead of "Chiang Government." Also he has answered other critics at home and abroad by his public advocacy of broadening base of new government by the inclusion of non-party elements in insignficant posts and by his demands that such posts be filled by persons with civil rather than military backgrounds. By facing his critics within the party with unpalatable possibility of their being forced to attempt to dominate the government without him in key position, he has secured from them clear and firm mandate to continue his rule and probable uncritical acceptance of his policies in future. Finally, since under new constitution the president is Commander-in-Chief of the armed forces, he will be able to maintain control over the army.

In the course of discussions the Generalissimo insisted that vice-presidential elections be held on free and competitive basis with party having no candidate of its own. He declined to give personal backing to any candidate. These circumstances will probably improve chances of Li Tsung-jen winning vice-presidential election especially since Sun Fo, having encountered intense opposition to his desire to hold both vice presidency and head Legislative Yuan, now inclines to be content with the latter office only.

STUART

152 (e)

The Ambassador in China (Stuart) to Secretary Marshall

893.00/4–1948

NANKING, *April 19, 1948*

The National Assembly today elected the Generalissimo first constitutional President of China by a vote of 2,430 to 269. The Assembly yesterday passed temporary rebellion suppression authorizing the President to take emergency measures free of restrictions imposed by Articles 39 and 43 of the Constitution but subject to veto of Legislative Yuan under the procedure prescribed in Article 57, Section 2. If the end of the rebellion suppression period is not proclaimed prior to December 25, 1950, a special meeting of the Assembly is to be called to consider extension of the act.

The effect of the act is to permit the President, in conjunction with Executive Yuan, to issue emergency decrees at any time without prior concurrence of legislative Yuan, but subject to revision or revocation by a two-thirds majority vote in Legislative Yuan. From what is known of the composition of the newly-elected Legislative Yuan, it appears very unlikely that a two-thirds majority could ever be mustered against a decree of the executive, so that act, in effect, gives the President practically unlimited power.

STUART

152 (f)

The Ambassador in China (Stuart) to Secretary Marshall

893.00/4–2348

NANKING, *April 23, 1948.*

Someone who has just seen the Generalissimo reports he is still wavering on acceptance of the presidency though it may be assumed he will accept. He had had three long conferences with Hu Shih trying still unsuccessfully to persuade him to be a candidate as he felt the President should be some internationally known figure. He opposed Chu Cheng for this reason, and Chang Po-ling was rejected as too old. He is said to have had more than one stormy argument with his party and with the military over his refusal to run, they insisting that if he would not become President, the elections must be postponed. Finally he had agreed to run as being the only one able and willing to face the responsibility. The Generalissimo is opposed to Li Tsung-jen as Vice President which lessens Li's chances and increases the possibility that Li may make trouble if defeated. The Generalissimo is urging Chang Chun to continue as Premier and intends to have the Executive Yuan function in a more constitutional manner.

It was reported that when the Generalissimo was reminded that he ought to give more authority to others in the Central Government and in the provinces and that under his concept of centralized administration, things had been getting steadily worse, the Generalissimo had replied that others refused to take sufficient responsibility or were unsatisfactory so that he was compelled to act as he did.

Here we have the picture of a strong, resourceful man unquestionably sincere and courageous, yet persisting in a policy which is frustrating his own aims. I am convinced that he does not seek for dictatorial prerogatives from selfish motives, but insists on exercising these to his own detriment and that of the nation. The worse things become under his leadership, the more does he feel impelled to carry the whole burden.

I do not believe he is conceited or intoxicated with power in the usual sense, yet he is dangerously self-opinionated and confident that he understands the situation better and has more experience than anyone else. This is all the more tragic because he is so largely right in these assumptions, and because there really seems to be no one else who could take his place. Yet the election has eliminated Li Tsung-jen in particular and produced in general an unfavorable reaction in China and probably abroad. If the Generalissimo had the vision to take the occasion of becoming President under the constitution to alter radically his procedure, these unfortunate tendencies might be neutralized, but the probabilities, as I see them, are against this.

STUART.

152 (g)

The Ambassador in China (Stuart) to Secretary Marshall

893.00/4–2348

NANKING, *April 23, 1948.*

Persistent reports from informed sources close to Li Tsung-jen state he has made a complete break with the Generalissimo and in event of defeat in vice presidential race plans to take some "action" the type of which is unspecified.

Other less qualified sources feel this may take the form of local military revolt. The bulk of troops in the vicinity of Nanking are Kwangsi and Kwangtung units whose loyalty, whether to Li or to the Generalissimo, is unknown to us. On the basis of present information, we consider armed coup only a remote possibility, though conceivable. Li may act in the heat of anger at what he considers his ill treatment at the hands of the Generalissimo and because of a feeling of frustration over the Kuomintang party machine's rejection of his services to the nation in its present crisis. We believe "action," if any, will take place later; probably in conjunction with Hong Kong and south China dissidents with whom evidence suggests Li is in close contact. Vice Presidential election will probably not be concluded until June 24 or 25.

STUART

152 (h)

The Ambassador in China (Stuart) to Secretary Marshall

893.00/4–2548

NANKING, *April 25, 1948*

In the early morning hours of April 25 Cheng Chien and later Li Tsung-jen announced retirement from the vice presidential race, leaving Sun Fo as the sole remaining candidate. At the Assembly meeting this morning, amidst considerable disorder on the part of delegates, the meeting was adjourned without any action being taken. This morning local vernacular press carried stories of the retirement of both candidates, and Li's supporters issued statement in the form of an advertisement that his withdrawal is in the interest of securing national harmony and to secure vindication from scurrilous rumors being circulated to the effect that he intends to force the Generalissimo to leave the country. At the morning Assembly meeting with Yu Yu-jen acting as chairman, delegates stated that Li's retirement from the race could only be effected with the concurrence of his supporters, and appealed to the chairman for agreement. Yu Yu-jen, weeping copiously, stated that the whole affair was regrettable and that a new set of elections should be held.

As we have previously reported, Li has been under heavy pressure from the Generalissimo to withdraw candidacy and Li has consistently refused. Li's associates say that Li is interested in the vice-presidency as a platform for criticizing shortcomings of the government and suggesting remedial measures, and that he will retire from the army and do so as a private citizen if his campaign fails. Li's supporter, Governor Li Pin-Hsien of Anhwei, has been the target of organized student demonstration and local vernacular paper supporting Li and critical of Sun Fo has been wrecked by a mob, reportedly led by delegates supporting Sun Fo, without interference from the police. Presumably reliable source informs us that the Generalissimo has summoned Pai Chung-hsi and directed him on pain of secret court martial to switch support from Li to Sun Fo.

Our initial reaction to these developments is that Li has been subjected to extremely heavy pressure from party machine and Whampoa army clique. He defies this pressure by resignation of candidacy, thus putting himself in the position of being sought by the office rather than seeking office, in compliance of traditional Chinese practice, and so focusing attention of the general public and all interested parties on opponents' maneuvers to prevent his position. In a free and uninfluenced election Li would almost certainly have majority vote. The bulk of delegates, desirous of effecting efficient government and frustrated by machine control Assembly equate Li's election with satisfaction of their aims. The effect of the latest developments on temper of the delegates may be judged by the remark of one, "this is worse than Tsao Kun's election, at least he paid for his."

We repeat, at this stage tempers on both sides are running high, and eventual course of action adopted by either is unpredictable. However, there is no doubt but what the Kuomintang is severely split over matters of principle, in distinction to ordinary party cleavage on matters of self-interest. The principle at stake is efficacy of present leadership and its policies. It is not difficult to conceive of a situation where attempts would be made to reject this leadership, or where leadership, including the Generalissimo and his closest supporters, would prefer to retire in response to popular demand, since the Generalissimo has not formally accepted the presidency and is understood not yet to have made up his mind to accept.

In the present circumstances the ultimate consequences are difficult to foretell. Reliable sources state resolution of the situation will be forthcoming within the next 24 hours. We will continue to report significant occurrences.

STUART

152 (i)

The Ambassador in China (Stuart) to Secretary Marshall

893.00/4-2648

NANKING, *April 26, 1948*

On the afternoon of April 25 Sun Fo announced his withdrawal from the vice-presidential race, stating that he felt it would be undemocratic to run without opposition. His withdrawal was made at the Generalissimo's direction. In the afternoon the Central Executive Committee of the Kuomintang met and passed a resolution stating candidates withdrawals all invalid. The Assembly did not convene today. Li Tsung-jen's associates state that his withdrawal was a political maneuver designed to focus attention on threats and intimidation directed against his supporters by the Generalissimo, Kuomintang bosses and Whampoa clique. He made the decision when the Generalissimo ordered Pai Chung-hsi to withdraw his support of Li under threat of punitive action and to coordinate his move with Cheng Chien. Pai yesterday issued a statement that Li withdrew because his supporters were continually subjected to intimidation and under those conditions free election was impossible. Cheng's cooperation with Li seems to have begun when the Generalissimo summoned him, asked him to withdraw and throw vote to Sun Fo, and offered to reimburse him for the entire costs of his campaign, which proposition Cheng refused.

Intense political maneuvering by all factions continues today, and even best informed circles are bewildered and uncertain as to outcome. However, it is abundantly clear that recent developments have seriously split the Kuomintang. Rank and file of party and independents, including probably majority of civil servants and army officers, have come to believe that country can survive present crisis only through more liberal effective vigorous leadership than has been evident in past. This group hoped that such leadership might be forthcoming in an orderly manner through implementation of the new constitution. Interference of Generalissimo and party machine with elections to Assembly and the new Yuan, with deliberations of Assembly on constitutional amendment question and flagrant intervention in vice presidential election has thoroughly convinced those desiring effective constitutional government that Generalissimo intends to use new constitution as vehicle for continuation of his personal rule in same close cooperation with CC Clique dominated party machine and Whampoa clique dominated High Military Command as has obtained in past.

There seems little doubt but what vast majority of politically articulate Chinese who are not intimately associated with KMT party machine are aroused over present situation and place blame on Generalissimo. In early stages of vice presidential contest Generalissimo left Sun Fo campaign in hands of Chen Li-fu but intervened personally to influence outcome, despite his pledge of free election, when Sun's defeat appeared likely. The character of Generalissimo's intervention has definitely outraged many of his supporters. Hitherto, respect for Generalissimo's service to nation, tendency to regard him as indispensable man and fear of retaliation have combined to prevent non-Communist elements in Nationalist China from acting or speaking covertly against him. However, action of Cheng and Li and statement of Pai on reasons for Li's withdrawal forces development of political alignments over issue of democratic constitutional government versus personal autocratic rule through entrenched reactionary cliques. Notwithstanding native Chinese genius on techniques of political compromise, the fact that the present issue is clear-cut and open and involves popularly supported challenge to vested authority by groups convinced that continuation of that authority in power must inevitably by reason of its autocratic character and long record of failure and incompetence, involve country in ruin, mitigates strongly against lasting compromise.

The assembly is now slated to reconvene the morning of the 27th with delegates voting on acceptance of the withdrawal of each candidate in turn. Li's managers now claim 1800 votes. The bulk of the Kuomintang is now out of control by party leaders. The Youth party is insisting on free elections and Carson Chang's Democratic Socialists are cautious and irresolute. In this situation it appears entirely possible that democratic, constitutional and anti-Generalissimo propensities of the delegates may result in Li's election. How the Generalissimo would accommodate himself to such defeat involving rejection of his leadership is impossible to foretell. One of the many possibilities is refusal to accept the presidency. Despite the many disturbing features in this situation, we are encouraged by the undeniable fact that democratic forces are now appearing and making themselves felt in protest against autocracy and reaction.

Following the conference, all three contenders have just announced their intention to re-enter race.

152 (j)

The Ambassador in China (Stuart) to Secretary Marshall

893.00/4–2748

NANKING, *April 27, 1948*

The confusion which has characterized political maneuvering in the vice presidential race continued through most of yesterday, but some clarification is apparent this morning. On the morning of the 26th Hu Shih, speaking on behalf of the special committee appointed by the Central Executive Committee of the Kuomintang to deal with impasse in vice presidential elections, stated that all candidates had agreed to reenter race. Shortly thereafter Li's followers began passing out word that Li would not run and was planning to return to Peiping. At this juncture the Generalissimo informed Hu Shih committee of his pleasure at the decision of all the candidates to remain in the race, exhorted the party to act in accordance with his earlier expressed wishes that delegates have freedom of choice in voting, and stated that candidates should not spread slanderous rumors against one another. Adding to the confusion, Li himself then told correspondents of his intention to abandon the race and fly to Peiping today. This statement was immediately denied by Hu Shih. The Generalissimo summoned Li for conference last night and after an hour's discussion persuaded Li to reenter contest. The Assembly will meet tomorrow to proceed with elections.

Li's stand has strengthened his position and gained the sympathy of the delegates who continue to blame the Generalissimo and the party machine for the undemocratic interference in the election procedure. The Youth Party and Democratic Socialists have issued statements calling on the Kuomintang to be "more democratic". On the basis of present information it appears that liberal and independent elements have successfully challenged control of the CC Clique dominated party machine and the election of Li seems likely.

STUART

152 (k)

The Consul General at Shanghai (Cabot) to Secretary Marshall

893.00/4-2748

SHANGHAI, *April 27, 1948*

Reference statement in previous message to effect that, since the Communist supporters believe present regime confirmed and continued in power by recent American aid, more violent anti-American propaganda campaign by the Communists can be anticipated.

Of the politically alert population of nationalist China, there is a very large proportion which is fundamentally anti-Communist and anti-revolutionary; which considers however that Nanking regime as presently constituted must inevitably collapse through incompetence, corruption, and lack of popular support against the Communists; which feels that drastic purge and reform of that regime offers only hope of salvation; and which views American aid prior to revitalization of government with open hostility or grave misgivings as merely serving to confirm rotten regime on its path to disaster. Hopes of these people, who include students, intellectuals, businessmen and many others, have to a significant extent been pinned on National Assembly and especially on Li Tsung-jen's candidacy which, rightly or wrongly, many identify with reform and progress.

If proceedings of National Assembly result in Li's election or other developments involving real change in complexion of government and introduction of new vigorous elements which offer some promise of effecting drastic reform, there is good reason to hope that this important segment of articulate Chinese public will largely swing over to support of liberal forces in government and of American aid.

If, on the contrary, results of the National Assembly are the rejection of Li and other popularly regarded "liberal" forces and the confirmation of stand pat Kuomintang politicians in their domination of government and influence over the Generalissimo, consequent wave of disappointment and revulsion against government, whether or not productive of immediate violence, is bound to be serious. Many of those who have been wavering with respect to support of the government will turn toward Communists and revolution as only alternative.

Their opposition to American aid would be revived and the coincidence of the aid's timing with the National Assembly's confirmation of rightist control of the government would invite a new wave of anti-American feeling.

Despite American aid, or really because of it, if it does in fact assist continuance of CC control, large masses of people will follow exiled liberal leaders in supporting Communists Civil War or at best apathetically regarding Nanking efforts. Either will result in an inevitable extension of Civil War with further destruction and chaos in larger and larger areas where Chinese Communism of a more and more Soviet nature can take root and thrive.

That Communists are preparing to exploit such contingencies would seem to be indicated by report that Chou En-lai is advocating more emphasis on wooing of liberals and by article by Communist "theoretician" Jen Pi-shih published in the April issue of Hong King Communist publication MASSES. While we have not seen this article, we have learned from two good sources that it has caused excitement in local intellectual and liberal circles; and that its main thesis is an admission that Communists have been too severe toward landowners (small, middle and large), industrialists and intellectuals, and will have to treat them more considerately. With respect to intellectuals, the article is said to be aimed directly at those who have lost faith in the government but have hitherto feared persecution by the Communists and to play skillfully on theme of "futility of supporting rotten regime" when good existence under Communists is guaranteed.

In summary, results of unclarified United States aid to China program will be: (1) strengthening of far left groups; (2) indefinite continuation and extension of Civil War; and (3) fostering of anti-Americanism in liberal groups through latter's claim of non-support and in reactionary groups by their claim of inadequate support.

It would seem to us that, while situation now evolving at Nanking thus holds serious potentialities from American standpoint, something can be done toward softening anti-American outburst which may eventuate.

The question has been asked locally why a United States official statement to the press has not been made clarifying our position as one of giving aid to the Chinese people regardless of their government, provided the government is not Communist dominated. and that the United States Government is therefore completely disinterested in the outcome of Nanking political maneuvering. The opportune time for such a statement would be on release of terms of letter of intent. If properly worded, such statement would serve to correct popular misunderstanding that American support of the Generalissimo means underwriting his reactionary coterie, to counteract much Chinese Communist propaganda, and to enhance or help salvage (depending on the National Assembly outcome) American prestige among Chinese liberals.

CABOT

152 (l)

The Ambassador in China (Stuart) to Secretary Marshall

893.00/4–2948

NANKING, *April 29, 1948*

Following the agreement of the three leading contenders to withdraw their withdrawals from the vice presidential race, and vote of the Presidium of the National Assembly to continue with the election, a third ballot was held on April 28 and resulted in 1156 votes for Li Tsung-jen; 1040 for Sun Fo; and 515 for Cheng Chien. The decrease in Li Tsung-jen's support and the general attitude and apathy apparent during the third ballot, led many observers to surmise that possibly sufficient pressure and coercion had been brought to bear to insure that on the fourth and final vote Sun Fo would emerge victorious.

Fourth ballot held on April 29 and resulted in 1438 votes for Li Tsung-jen and 1295 for Sun Fo. The Presidium immediately thereupon proclaimed Li as Vice President. The voting was quiet and orderly until near the end of the counting when it became apparent that Li would win and his supporters became increasingly noisy in expressing their approval of the vote and centered their demonstrations around Madame Li, who was present on the floor of the Assembly.

Public interest in Nanking during fourth ballot was apparent. The proceedings of the Assembly were broadcast and it seemed as though every radio in Nanking was tuned in on it with crowds of people gathered in streets wherever a radio could be heard.

The Embassy will subsequently elaborate its estimate of what this development means. The preliminary appraisal is that it represents a smashing defeat for the CC Clique, a serious setback for the Generalissimo whose determined support of Sun Fo was no secret, and a successful challenge by opposition elements of the party to dictation by party machine centering around CC Clique and Whampoa clique. It remains to be seen how the Generalissimo will accommodate himself to these developments and whether opposition elements can organize effectively to implement a reform program which Li professes. Li appears to have been rallying point for all discontented and opposition elements in Assembly. Question now is whether he can provide effective leadership which can and will coalesce this feeling into an effective and progressive opposition.

STUART

152 (m)

The Ambassador in China (Stuart) to Secretary Marshall

893.00/5–348

NANKING, *May 3. 1948.*

The National Assembly which was convoked solely to elect the president and vice president developed quickly into something far more basic. Success of the Generalissimo's 1948 version of the retreat to Fenghua confirmed him in power personally, but struggle over the vice presidency ended in rejection of his policies. Unquestionably the vice presidential race was the most significant development in the Assembly. There can be no question but the balloting was above the slightest suspicion of fraud. Sun represented the dead reactionary aim of the party machine and his election would have meant the unchallenged continuation of the old political policies, preservation of vested interests, and the elimination of any prospect of that revitalization of the party and government which was necessary to give hope of ultimate success in the face of a dynamic Communist movement. Whatever he may turn out to be in practice, Li Tsung-jen during the campaign became the symbol and the rallying point of discontented and progressive elements who had lost faith in those controlling the government and who demanded new faces and new and more effective policies. Li represented a demand for effective government in contrast to the lack of achievement of the discredited group in power. Lacking experience or organization, his supporters challenged the party machine and won. It now remains to be seen whether Li can provide that kind of dynamic leadership which will coalesce these elements into effective opposition and give substance to the program on which Li based his candidacy. Li's victory was a disastrous blow to the CC clique which not only failed to deliver in one of the most important jobs ever assigned to it but also seriously undermined the position of the Generalissimo himself by misinforming him on what he could expect. Most of the opposition criticism was directed at the person of the Generalissimo for attempting to nullify democratic procedures. Much of the criticism directed at him should more properly have been turned on the CC clique but the adverse effect on his prestige exists nonetheless. The Generalissimo's position is made doubly difficult by the fact that he openly and bitterly opposed the man with whom he must now work. It remains to be seen how he will accommodate himself to this situation. In this sense he continues to be as in the past—the key man. If he attempts to oppose Li and to box him in, he will drive Li to increasingly desperate moves since Li gives all indications of intending to be active in the national life. The Generalissimo on the other hand is a practical man and a politician. If he concludes that Li represents the dominant force in nationalist China and decides that he cannot destroy him, he may well decide to join him, at the same time discarding his previous sources of power. He is reported to have been exceedingly angry over the election of Li. He may indeed now be too old and has been in undisputed power too long to adjust himself, or he may again demonstrate that he is still the master politician in China. The decision is his.

The Kuomintang was originally a revolutionary party and the revolutionary tradition remains strong within it. The party is still committed to the activation of the principles of Sun Yat-sen. Kuomintang dissident groups in Hong Kong and abroad have adopted reform slogans and policies, and in recent months even more conservative groups within the party have been talking in similar terms. The source of this interest in change is the pressure of the success of the Communist revolution. The action of the Assembly confirmed the Generalissimo in power but rejected his anti-reform policies. In his present constitution position he can either accept and implement, or deny the popular demand for change.

However, Li's election also gave this demand a constitutional and legal status, and it may be this circumstance which will constrain the Generalissimo to include new talent in his government and adopt the policies which will represent an attempt to combat revolution by social change. Further proof this is realized is that the two principal defeated candidates, Sun and Cheng Chien, have already started to organize what they call reform groups.

There has yet been no reaction from the Communists. Unless, as is rumored, they have substantial reason to believe that Li is prepared to compromise with them and to take them into a coalition government more or less on their own terms, they must be disappointed, realizing that the election of Sun would have favored continuous growth of a situation calculated to foster Communist causes.

The other group to be considered is the Kuomintang Revolutionary Committee in Hong Kong. This committee claims to have a definite time schedule now for the removal of the Generalissimo. It is known that the committee and T. V. Soong have been making the coyest kind of eyes at each other from afar, just in case such a misalliance might prove convenient. The committee claims that it has maintained closest contact with Li Tsung-jen during recent months. If these allegations are correct, then it may well be that the claimed time-table has foundation and that the struggle in the Assembly was but the first round in a life and death struggle between the Generalissimo, the CC clique and the Whampoa clique on the one hand, and Li and his associates on the other.

If the civil war and economic deterioration continue on their present disastrous course Li and his associates seem assured of eventual success, with increasing probabilities that Li from choice or necessity will be driven into an understanding with the Communists. We shall have to watch developments with extreme care, yet our efforts should, we believe, be directed toward influencing the Generalissimo to accept the situation and support more liberal policies.

STUART

152(n)

Editorial from the New China News Agency Entitled: An Old China is Dying, a New China is Marching Ahead

893.00/5-2748

[PART 1] [18]

The final play which Chiang Kai-shek wanted to enact in his 21 years' rule over China has been performed. From March 29th to May 1st, he convened a gang of henchmen and puppets in Nanking to inaugurate a so-called "National Assembly" which has "elected" him "president". But they have enacted this play so malodorously that people do not know whether they are enacting a jubilant event or a funeral.

All Chinese and foreign papers, periodicals and news agencies in Chiang Kai-shek controlled areas, including those of the various KMT cliques, without exception daily publicised and ridiculed unceasingly all sorts of odious news about the "National Assembly". The "National Assembly" was filled with rifts and divisions, with confusion and despair. Even Chiang Kai-shek blamed his "National Assembly Delegates" as not fit to be "Constitutional Models" while "National Assembly Delegates" counter-blamed Chiang Kai-shek for concealing the real state of the war in his report. They cursed and beat each other, and at the same time opposed the people in concert and made this and that resolution against the people. But as a foreign correspondent puts it, the delegates spoke words of bravado like the frightened child who whistles as he passes a graveyard.

In face of the people's democratic revolutionary upsurge, it is in such panic and despair that they have Chiang Kai-shek make up and appear on the stage. Is it not true that even his masters, the American imperialists, contemplate Chiang Kai-shek's abdication to go abroad at a certain moment after his election as president?

The people of the whole country do not pay the least attention to Chiang Kai-shek's calling of the so-called "National Assembly" and becoming the so-called "president". What the people pay attention to is only how to strike down Chiang Kai-shek swiftly. The people of liberated areas are actively unfolding a victorious people's liberation war. Within the period of the "National Assembly" alone, more than 50 cities and towns including Yenan, Loyang and Weihsien have been liberated. The people in Chiang Kai-shek controlled areas are continuing their movement against hunger and oppression. Since inauguration of the "National Assembly" the student movement has, in particular, begun

---

[18] Broadcast by the North Shensi Radio on May 24, 1948, and transmitted by Ambassador Stuart from Nanking, May 27, 1948, with the following comment: "This editorial presents a fascinating, if completely inaccurate, picture of what took place at the National Assembly, together with a somewhat less fascinating but equally inaccurate picture of what would take place if the Communists were in power."

a new high with Peiping as a starting point, and on May 4th, after Chiang Kai-shek was "elected president", students in Shanghai publicly burned effigies of American aggressors and the dictator of China in "celebration". It can be definitely said that the Chinese people will, in the not distant future, send this "government for implementing the constitution" and its makers into their self-dug graves.

Why does Chiang Kai-shek meet with such a fate? This is because he is the representative of the most corrupt and most reactionary feudal compradore bloc in China. This bloc resolutely carries out an anti-popular policy of national betrayal, civil war and dictatorship and a policy of opposing the vanguard of the people—the Communist Party.

As far back as three years ago, in April 1945, comrade Mao Tze-tung in his book "On Coalition Government" raised the warning: "any government that excludes the Communist Party outside its doors will not be able to achieve any worthy thing. This is the basic characteristic of China in the historical stage of new democracy. In the past eight years of the anti-Japanese war, although the KMT Government has up till now not openly declared general war against the Communist Party because there is a Japanese invader facing them, but is employing measures of localized war, suppression by the secret police, blockades, insults, preparation for civil war and opposition to the organization of a Coalition Government to exclude the Communist Party, it has created for itself such a situation that the more it excludes the Communist Party, the more down slope it goes. If in the future it continues to do this then it is preparing to go down-slope to the bottom".

In January 1946, because of the urging of the people and the Communist Party, the Chiang Kai-shek block convened and participated in the Political Consultation Conference and expressed willingness to cooperate with the Communist Party and other democratic parties and groups. And because of this, they, in a certain sense and to a certain extent, evoked the hope of the Chinese people towards them for the last time. But after facts, democracy was only a piece of deception. Treacherous Chiang Kai-shek tore up the Truce Agreement, and started an all out civil war, tore up the PCC resolutions and convened the fake "National Assembly" of cleavage and dictatorship. Chiang Kai-shek and his backer, American imperialism, entertained the delusion that American aid would enable Chiang Kai-shek to do as he liked, but no quantity of American dollars, airplanes and guns could ultimately change comrade Mao Tze-tung's scientific prediction—the more they exclude the Communist Party, the more downslope they go.

When Chiang Kai-shek excluded the Communist Party in October 1946 and unilaterally issued the order to convene the "National Assembly" he had deceived the people and started on the downslope. But he was then enthralled by his momentary military progress; he still entertained illusions about the rosy prospects before him. But only after a month when he was calling his so-called "National Assembly for framing the constitution", his good but short dream was completely shattered. Up to the present opening of the "National Assembly for implementing the constitution" when the so-called "president" proclaimed the China under his rule a "constitutional", his rule is a symbol of all the confusion and despair of the present odious plan in Nanking, advantageous for the reactionary ruling class.

The new trick that the reactionary clique can now put out is only to use the so-called "anti-Chang" Li Tsung-jen as the "vice president". It is said that the Chinese and American reactionary cliques are preparing to replace Chiang Kai-shek with Li Tsung-jen. The record of his rule over the people and in the eyes of the people is that Li Tsung-jen is not only as counter-revolutionary as Chiang Kai-shek but a partisan in Chiang Kai-shek's long term counter-revolutionary collaboration. Li Tsung-jen's so-called "anti-Chiang" term has nothing in common with the people's anti-Chiang. The people entertain no illusion whatsoever about him. Therefore, even if the Chinese and American reactionary cliques actually use Li Tsung-jen to replace Chiang Kai-shek, it will also be utterly impossible to because of the Chinese people.

Of course, the plot of the Chinese and American reactionary cliques will not succeed at this. When Li Tsung-jen proves incapable of maintaining their support they will also pick out Hu Shih and other figures. Under such circumstances, the sign "liberalism" recently put up by the political science clique paper "Ta Kung Pao", and the Social Economic Research Association organized under the slogan of the "Third Road" by T. V. Soong's subordinates, Chien Chang-chao and company, and other activities of the same kind will still parade about and mislead the masses, adopting new poises to preserve the essence of the reactionary cliques' rule. Especially when Chiang Kai-shek has collapsed and the main forces of his army have exterminated or routed. The reactionary clique will further adopt a certain policy of concealment and will even find certain unsteady figures from among the present anti-Chiang peoples as their protective charm to conceal and rally their force for what they regard as the proper opportunity for the comeback of reactionary forces. Because at that time, Chiang Kai-shek, who is bitterly hated by all, will have fallen from power while the reactionary clique will also adopt a policy of concealment, and it is possible that a part of the people will relay their vigilance. Therefore, today we should tell the people all this beforehand and ceaselessly expose the various plots of the reactionary clique so as to carry out China's new democratic revolution to the very end.

The new democratic revolution is not only to overthrow thoroughly Chiang Kai-shek's personal rule, but also the foundation of Chiang Kai-shek's rule, that is, thoroughly eliminate the imperialism and the system of China's feudalism and bureaucratic capitalism so that any rule of Chiang Kai-shek's pattern will permanently not revive and not reincarnate.

To point out the correct policy of struggle for people throughout the country, the Central Committee of the Chinese Communist Party issued slogans for the current situation on May 1st, the very day the bogus "National Assembly" came to a close. These slogans called for broadening of the united front against imperialism, feudalism and bureaucratic capitalism; swift convening of a new political consultation conference by all liberals, democrats and independent groups and organizations and all social luminaries to discuss and approve the calling of a People's Congress to establish a Democratic Coalition Government. Timed with the advance of the people's war of liberation and the people's democratic movement, these slogans very clearly map out the path for the Chinese people. Without doubt, the Chinese people must resolutely carry the revolutionary war to the end, for the enemy who unleashed the war has not yet been disarmed. Without doubt, the Chinese people must thoroughly eliminate the rule of imperialism, feudalism and bureaucratic capitalism because this is the prerequisite of an era of freedom and peace for the people. Also without doubt, there can be no "third road" in the death struggle between the Chinese people and their enemy. The only path that exists before China today is to continue to preserve the armed forces and prerogatives of the people's enemy. This is the line of semi-feudalism, and semi-colonialism, national betrayal, civil war and dictatorship led by the big landlord bourgeoise class. This is the people's democratic line of the workers, peasants, independent labour, and no matter from what corner they come or what banner they fly, all movements, which in essence preserve the armed forces prerogatives of the people's enemy, show there is no "third road", but only another guise of the counter-revolution army line. This is the path of new democracy; this is the path of the united struggle against imperialism, feudalism, and bureaucratic capitalism; this is the path of the political consultation conference which the present stage of Chinese history determines that China's big landlord, big bourgeoise class cannot join China's democratic ranks and that these ranks can only be led by the working class and its political representative, the Chinese Communist Party. The two years of history since the failure of the political Consultation Conference in 1946, though only a history of two short years, have demonstrated this truth so vividly and fully! Today the people of China, have, through suffering, universally come to know this truth. This insures that the old China of the reactionary clique cannot but wait its doom and the new China of the people cannot but win out.

[PART 2] [19]

When their rule meets with the opposition of the people and there is a crisis, the reactionary ruling class frequently recall and change their representative political figures who have lost prestige and replace them with representative figures whose reactionary face has not yet been completely exposed or with regard to whom the people still entertain illusions, in order to . . . people's opposition, dull the people's vigilance and continue to maintain their rule. The ruling class represented by Chiang Kai-shek today see their rule heading towards doom. They also badly want to do the following: attempt to find a "suitable" figure to replace Chiang Kai-shek who is bitterly hated by all, to carry on their rule. This is why Hu Shih was suggested as a possible "presidential" candidate and Li Tsung-jen has been elected "vice president". This is also why American imperialism and certain reactionary newspapers in the country do their utmost to boost Hu Shih and Li Tsung-jen. It would actually have been a craftier and more advantageous . . . for the reactionary ruling class if they could today find a figure whose reactionary face has not yet been completely unveiled or about whom the people still entertain certain illusions, and who could take the place of Chiang Kai-shek in carrying on their rule. But the Chinese reactionary ruling class is so corrupt and desperate that it is absolutely impossible for them to find out a comparatively "suitable" figure to replace Chiang Kai-shek, and consequently they cannot but put up this Chiang Kai-shek hated by all, to be the "president" and rely on him to maintain their tottering rule.

The new trick that the reactionary clique can now put out is only to use the so-called "anti-Chiang" Li Tsung-jen as the "vice-president". It is said that the Chinese and American reactionary cliques are preparing to replace Chiang Kai-shek with Li Tsung-jen at the proper moment. But of what use is this? In the record of his rule over the people and in the eyes of the people, Li Tsung-jen is not only as counter-revolutionary as Chiang Kai-shek but is also Chiang Kai-shek's long-term counter-revolutionary collaborator. The people entertain

---

[19] Broadcast by the North Shensi Radio on May 30, 1948, and transmitted by the Ambassador from Nanking, June 7, 1948.

no illusion whatsoever about him. Therefore, even if the Chinese and American reactionary cliques actually use Li Tsung-jen to replace Chiang Kai-shek, it will also be utterly impossible to deceive the Chinese people.

Of course, the plot of the Chinese and American reactionary cliques will not stop at this. When Li is also incapable of maintaining their rule, they will also feel out Hu Shih or other figures. Under such circumstances, the signboard of "liberalism" recently put up by the Political Science clique's paper "Ta Kung Pao", and the Social Economic Research Association organized under the slogan of the "third road" by T. V. Soong, Chien Chang-chao and Company, and other activities of the same kind, will still parade about and mislead the masses, adopting new poises to preserve the essence of the reactionary cliques rule. Especially when Chiang Kai-shek has collapsed and the main forces of his army have been exterminated or routed, the reactionary clique will further adopt a certain policy of concealment and will even find certain unsteady figures from among the present Anti-Chiang . . . as their protective charm to conceal and rally their forces to wait for what they regard as the proper opportunity for the comeback of reactionary forces. At that time, Chiang Kai-shek, bitterly hated by all, will have fallen from power and the reactionary clique will also adopt a policy of concealment, and it is possible that a part of the people will relax their vigilance. Therefore, today we should tell the people all this beforehand and ceaselessly expose the various plots of the reactionary cliques so as to carry out China's new democratic revolution to the very end.

The new democratic revolution is not only to overthrow thoroughly Chiang Kai-shek's personal rule, but also to overthrow thoroughly the foundation of Chiang Kai-shek's rule, that is : thoroughly eliminate the prerogatives of imperialism in China and the system of China's feudalism and bureaucratic capitalism so that any rule of Chiang Kai-shek's pattern will not permanently revive nor reincarnate.

To point out the correct policy of struggle for the people throughout the country, the Central Committee of the Chinese Communist Party issued slogans for the current situation on May 1st, the very day the bogus "National Assembly" came to a close. These slogans called for a march on Nanking to take alive the bogus president Chiang Kai-shek; consolidation and broadening of the united front against imperialism, feudalism, and bureaucratic capitalism; swift convening of a New Political Consultation Conference by all democratic parties and groups of all people's organizations and all social luminaries to discuss and realize the calling of a People's Congress to establish a Democratic Coalition Government. Timed with the advance of the people's war of liberation and the people's democratic movement, these slogans very clearly map out the path for the Chinese people. Without doubt, the Chinese people must resolutely carry the revolutionary war to the end, for the enemy who unleashed the war has not yet been disarmed. Without doubt, the Chinese people must thoroughly eliminate the rule of imperialism, feudalism, and bureaucratic capitalism because this is the prerequisite of a life of freedom and peace for the people. Also without doubt there can be no "third road" in the life and death struggle between the Chinese people and their enemy. Only two paths exist before China today: either continue to reserve the armed forces and the prerogatives of the people's enemy—this is the line of semi-feudalism, national betrayal, civl war and dictatorship led by the big landlord, big bourgeoise class—or liquidate the armed forces and prerogatives of the people's enemy—this is the people's democratic line of the workers, peasants, independent labourers, intelligentsia, liberal bourgeoise and other patriots against imperialism, feudalism, and bureaucratic capitalism. No matter from what corner they come or what banner they fly, all movements, which in essence preserve the armed forces and prerogatives of the people's enemy, constitute no "third road" but is only another guise of the counter-revolutionary line at the end of its. . . . All persons advocating the liquidation of the armed forces and prerogatives of the people's enemy have only one . . . differing from the counter-revolutionary one. This is the path of new democracy; this is the path of the united front against imperialism, feudalism, and bureaucratic capitalism; this is the path of the new political consultation conference.

The basic characteristics of the present stage of Chinese history determine that China's big landlord, big bourgeoise class, cannot join China's democratic ranks, and that these ranks can only be led by the working class and its political representative, the Chinese Communist Party. The two years of history since the failure of the Political Consultation Conference in 1946, though only a history of two short years, have demonstrated this truth so vividly and fully! Today the Chinese people have, through their own experience, universally come to know this truth. This insures that the old China of the reactionary clique cannot but meet its doom, and the new China of the people cannot but be victorious.

153 (a)

The Ambassador in China (Stuart) to Secretary Marshall

[*May ?*] *1948*

Our best information at the moment is that the Generalissimo has refused to agree to reforms demanded by Ho Ying-chin and has commanded Chang Chun to remain as Premier and form a new Cabinet.

Nevertheless, when I called on the Generalissimo on May 6 he indicated agreement with various points I felt it desirable to raise with him. In the first place, he promised support for Jimmy Yen's reconstruction plan and agreed with me when I enlarged upon the fact that the Communist issue could not be settled merely by military means; that unless there were drastic reforms in government policy convincing the people that their lot was better than it would be under Communist control, no amount of military effort or American aid could be successful. He continued to agree when I expressed my belief in the extreme gravity of the outlook in the military, financial and economic fields, and particularly in respect of morale among the people as well as with the government. The only hope, it seemed to me, lay in radical reform that would convince the people that the government had stopped merely speaking and intended to act. Now that he had been elected President, I said, the constitution was coming into effect, American aid was beginning to arrive, and he had a superlative opportunity to take the requisite leadership and that if he didn't do so now, it might soon be too late for him to play any part in the steps which must inevitably take place. His expression indicated that he understood I had the revolt surrounding Li Tsung-jen in mind. I went on, with the Generalissimo agreeing, that in my opinion the great majority of Chinese, even the more radical student element, did not want China to be communized, but that they were dissatisfied with the present government. It became, therefore, a question of winning this large majority by demonstrating that the government was more modern, up to date, democratic and liberal than the Communists who, I stressed, represented the last vestige of out-moded, totalitarian and dictatorial political organization. As I saw it, and he seemed to agree, the problem was primarily spiritual rather than military or material and that somehow the spirit of the populace and of the troops would have to be aroused or all his plans and all the American assistance would be useless. Mme. Chiang, who was present, agreed most emphatically with this and I believe will exert her influence toward improving the situation.

In response to his request for specific suggestions, I remarked that the Premier's ten-point program seemed to offer a framework for action and that now was the time to give proof that these points were not just a literary essay, but represented an intention of the government which would be implemented without further delay.

The above doesn't sound too hopeful, yet we are afraid it represents the present attitude of the Generalissimo. He will assent, as he did, but we find it difficult to believe that he is any longer capable of the leadership necessary to instill new spirit into the people or that he has any intention of really instituting necessary reforms.

153 (b)

The Ambassador in China (Stuart) to Secretary Marshall

893.00/5-1948

NANKING, *May 19, 1948.*

The Generalissimo is meeting this afternoon with his top advisers in an attempt to find a workable solution to the present Executive Yuan impasse. Among his most active advisers is Chen Li-fu who, since his election as Vice President of the Executive Yuan, has been extremely vocal in expressing his conviction that the primary need is party unity and that thereafter the government can proceed on questions of reform. Chen's views seem to reinforce the growing conviction of the Generalissimo that Chang Chun is not the man to head the new Cabinet because of his inability to provide forceful leadership. The CC-Clique is urging the Generalissimo to name T. V. Soong as president of the Executive Yuan and the Generalissimo appears inclined to go along with this suggestion. Soong has arrived in Nanking for consultations on this question and will probably accept it if the offer is definitely made. Chen is further urging that Ho Ying-chin be made Vice-Premier and that Pai Chung-hsi be retained as Minister of National Defense in order to heal the rift between the Generalissimo and Li, and to draw the latter into active partnership with government. It is impossible to forecast how this manipulation will turn out. Given past performance, the possibility must not be overlooked that this is another skillful manipulation on the part of the CC-Clique to regain its waning hold on government. On the other hand, the possibility must also be kept in mind that Soong, who has been flirting with the CC-Clique ever since his retirement from the premiership, might be able to provide sufficiently strong leadership to keep CC-Clique activities within bounds. The CC-Clique for some months has been attempting vocally to assume leadership of the reform movement. Only a practical test could determine whether this is merely lip service or honest conviction. Furthermore, there is no indication as to whether Li Tsung-jen would accept the line offered him or would remain wary.

In general the situation remains fluid.

STUART

153 (c)

The Ambassador in China (Stuart) to Secretary Marshall

893.00/5–2248

NANKING, *May 22, 1948.*

The inauguration of the new President was held on the morning of May 20 at a simple but impressive ceremony. The Generalissimo delivered a brief inaugural address in which he said nothing to which anyone could take exception and whose content, if carried out, would go a long way toward solving the internal problems of China. The only flaw in the ceremony was that Li Tsung-jen was largely ignored and was kept in the background at the presentation of the Diplomatic Corps.

Meanwhile, the impasse over the Legislative Yuan is entering a new and more serious phase. Chang Chun abandoned all pretense to the office by departing for Chungking May 21. Chen Li-fu had previously informed the Generalissimo that Chang Chun could have no expectation of securing a vote of confidence in the Legislative Yuan. Two leading contenders now are T. V. Soong and Ho Ying-chin, both of whom are uncertain they can command sufficient majority in the Legislative Yuan to persuade them yet to accept office even though Soong is the CC-Clique candidate.

The struggle now seems to have passed beyond the stage of personalities and into the realm of a major rebellion within interior party circles to the leadership of the Generalissimo. The failure of Soong as the CC-Clique candidate to obtain assurances of a large majority is one indication thereof. Another indication is that on May 20, the Generalissimo ordered a certain motion passed by the Central Executive Committee and lost it. He blames Chen Li-fu for this failure and has ordered him to resign from the Central Executive Committee. The Embassy will attempt to ascertain the nature of the motion. The evening of May 20 the Generalissimo entertained the Central Executive Committee at a tea party. Less than two-thirds of the members showed up. Disobedience of such a request, which normally would have been considered as a royal command, combined with the inability to form a Cabinet, is reported to have the Generalissimo in a highly nervous and irresolute state of mind.

The present course of action devised by the CC-Clique has the Generalissimo's approval:

(1) Ho Ying-chin is to be given a final offer of the Premiership and made to make his position very clear. The greatest possible pressure will be used on Ho.

(2) If Ho refuses it will be offered to Soong. He will accept if he feels he can command sufficient majority of the Legislative Yuan.

(3) If Soong refuses, Ho will be ordered to assume it and take his chances with the legislature, thus attempting to force Central Executive Committee opposition to the Generalissimo into the open. Soong might well then be put in charge of administering the American aid program. In the light of developments during the past week, prognostication of future developments is, of course, open to revision without notice.

This intra-party rebellion is doubtless more serious than that which the Generalissimo faced in the election of Li Tsung-jen because it is a rebellion in the inner circle on which the Generalissimo has for years based his strength. If he fails at this juncture it will be difficult for him to re-establish his control. It must also be admitted that Chen Li-fu has given a good account of himself in the face of enormous odds. Confronted with a major revolt throughout the entire length and breath of the party he still holds a major hand and he plays it well. Unlike many other party leaders he is demonstrating ability to play politics in the open as well as behind the scenes.

The activities of Li Tsung-jen during this period are still obscure. As far as can be ascertained at the moment, he seems to be largely passive. This may be partially due to a nervous let-down after a strenuous campaign. It may be also partially due to a weakness of leadership. He has stated privately that he does not know what to do now because the Generalissimo controls the Army, the government finances and the party machine. For a brief period he even appeared to have given some consideration to going to the United States on the grounds that he could accomplish more there than here.

Another development of some importance is the report, apparently true, that General Wang Yao-wu is being relieved of his military command and his governorship of Shantung. He would be a serious loss to the National Government because he is one of the ablest military commanders in China and has had a highly successful and distinguished record as Governor of Shantung, which is his native province. There is one factor against him. It must be known by the Central Government by this time that Wang, for almost a year now, either directly or through trusted lieutenants, has been considering the establishment of an autonomous regime in Shantung under his own leadership; that he has discussed this question with various Americans, and that in recent months he has approached American officials on the possibility of obtaining American financial and military support for his regime should he feel developments in Nanking warrant such action on his part. The situation in Shantung is hardly improved by the possibility that Wang would be succeeded by General Teng Wen-yi who has never commanded troops and has been a conspicuous failure as military spokesman in Nanking, but is a Whampoa man and completely loyal personally to the Generalissimo. Telegram has just been received from the Shantung Provincial Assembly requesting financial and military aid for Shantung apart from that for the National Government.

STUART

153 (d)

The Ambassador in China (Stuart) to Secretary Marshall

893.00/5-2448

NANKING, *May 24, 1948.*

Prior to my departure for a brief visit to Taiwan, the Generalissimo asked me to call on him. I found him in a calmer frame of mind than he had been reported to be on previous days. Madam Chiang was not present, possibly because of the delicacy of her position in view of the possibility that her brother might be named Premier.

I took advantage of the occasion to express a few of my opinions on the current situation in China and what I believed the general course of action should be. I told the Generalissimo that the American people were gravely disturbed over the friction which had arisen in the Nationalist Assembly and which was now becoming increasingly apparent in the Legislative Yuan. I said that now is the time for strong and decisive action and that someone should be appointed as Premier who could undertake such action. The Generalissimo interposed at this moment that he agreed completely and that he had honestly hoped himself to assume the position of Premier and deeply regretted his plans had gone astray.

I then went on to point out that the reform movement which Li Tsung-jen symbolizes represents a new force in China which cannot be quenched; that now is the time for reforms; and that unless the Generalissimo gives it, some one else will. I suggested that the first step should be the dissolution of the CC-Clique. The Generalissimo expressed his general agreement and said he hoped I would feel free at any time to express to him anything I might have on my mind. He said he realized the criticalness of the present position and that much of the future will depend on what happens now. He then went on to say that Chang Chun is out of the question as Premier because he lacks forcefulness. In answer to my query, he ruled out T. V. Soong on grounds he could not receive a majority in the Legislative Yuan and is so desperately needed in Kwangtung. The Generalissimo said he had every expectation that Ho Ying-chin would accept the position.

I asked the Generalissimo if he had any objections to my trip to Taiwan. He replied at once that he did not; if he needed me, he would ask me to return.

Subsequent to this interview, Philip Fugh called on Ho Ying-chin who expressed great surprise at the Generalissimo's confidence that he would accept the post as Premier. Ho said that whereas he was still considering the matter, the question depended in large measure on who would be Minister of Finance. He did not indicate whom he would like to see as Finance Minister though I do know he would not accept Chang Kia-ngau who at present appears to be a strong possibility since he has resigned as Governor of the Central Bank and has been replaced by O. K. Yui.

With the elimination of Chang Chun and T. V. Soong, both of whom have already left Nanking; and in the event that Ho finally refuses, I would venture to suggest the possibility that the position might be offered to Wang Shih-Chieh who commands general respect for his intelligence, integrity and honesty but who would hardly provide strong leadership and has no substantial following in the party.

STUART

153 (e)

The Ambassador in China (Stuart) to Secretary Marshall

893.00/6–2348

NANKING, *June 23, 1948*

The initial reception of Prime Minister Wong Wen-hao and his Cabinet by the Legislative Yuan and the press is highly critical. Wong's administrative report to the Legislative Yuan on June 12 was vague and full of generalities, as were reports of his Ministerial colleagues. No new policies nor specific panaceas for improvement were offered. Comments of legislators on the Yuan floor were violently critical and caustic. Though the ministers were not personally attacked and though the legislators put forward no specific program of their own, their lack of confidence in the Cabinet was apparent. The vernacular press controlled by the CC-Clique also was censorious, and almost no papers offer the Cabinet any support. This position is a faithful reflection of the general public sentiment of disgust with a government which does not govern.

The Premier and the Cabinet are generally regarded as personal retainers of the Generalissimo and attacks on them are viewed as attacks on the President himself. Up to the present the Generalissimo has failed to defend the Cabinet and apparently is willing to let them receive the blame for the continuing deterioration of the government position. The government's inability to control food prices, which has led to rice riots in Chungking, Ningpo and the Yangtze delta towns, is greatly increasing popular discontent and provides critics with additional ammunition which they use unsparingly.

The present Cabinet was a deliberate creation of the Generalissimo who wanted a compliant group through which he could continue to exercise his personal authority over all aspects of government. Under these conditions we do not expect the Cabinet to come forth with any concrete and specific program of its own, nor do we expect the Premier to provide any dynamic or constructive leadership.

Since the Generalissimo refuses to delegate authority, since he still fails to exercise in any positive or constructive way the authority he has concentrated in his own hands and since the Cabinet is so completely subservient to him, we see few, if any, reasons to believe that more efficient and effective government can be anticipated in the near future. And since the Cabinet is so generally regarded as the Generalissimo's personal machine, criticism of its inevitable shortcomings will be visited equally on the Generalissimo, to the further detriment of his personal prestige.

STUART

154

The Ambassador in China (Stuart) to Secretary Marshall [20]

893.00/6-548

NANKING, *June 5, 1948.*

It is with real regret that I find myself compelled to take cognizance publicly of a growingly dangerous situation which affects not only the interests of the United States, but, I am firmly convinced the vital interests of China as well. I am, of course, referring to the campaign against American policy in Japan. I know you will understand that my sorrow at having to do this is all the greater because most of my life has been spent in Chinese academic circles and because the primary object of my life work has been to assist them in some small measure in increasing the welfare and the mature responsibility of Chinese students to themselves and their country.

It is therefore difficult for me to have to admit that the core of anti-American agitation on the question of Japan is coming from the Chinese student groups. I do not pretend to know who initiated this agitation or for what purpose. I have received varying reports as to its origin and intent. Perhaps all reports are partially valid. What I do know is that it is seriously damaging the traditional cordiality between the United States and China and that if it continues it can have most unfortunate results. It is all the more regrettable that this movement should start at a time when the United States is embarking upon a large-scale and serious program to assist China in its present tragic plight. At a time when the American people are being called upon to assist in the rehabilitation of war-torn areas throughout the world and, I should add, are only too glad to do so, they may well wonder when these efforts are greeted by unreasonable and irresponsible attacks on American policy.

I would be most reluctant to believe that university circles which initiate or follow the anti-American agitation really believe the arguments which they use

[20] Transmitting the Ambassador's statement of June 4, 1948, concerning anti-American student agitation.

against my country. We are charged with fostering the restoration of Japanese military and economic imperialism. These charges are demonstrably false. Immediately after the victorious conclusion of our war against Japan, the United States on behalf of the Allied Powers who destroyed Japanese power, proceeded to disband the Japanese Army, Navy, Air Force and General Staff. I defy anyone to produce a single shred of evidence that any part of Japanese military power is being restored or that there is any intention on the part of the United States other than to assure that it will never rise again. The basis of Japanese aggression was its overseas empire. It has now lost that empire and cannot regain it without military power. You may rest assured the American people and government will make sure it does not do so.

As for Japanese economic and industrial power, the United States again on behalf of the Allied Powers, proceeded to destroy or dismantle all Japanese war industries. We are now faced with a situation where we must restore enough of Japanese economic life to enable the Japanese people to become self-supporting. No one can expect the American taxpayer to continue indefinitely paying the Japanese bills. Japan must be allowed a chance for self-support or it will be a continuing liability not only to the United States but also to China. An indigent country can never become a peace-loving and democratically-minded people. If it be argued that industry can be converted to war-time purposes, I admit the truth of the allegation. In modern warfare, any production is susceptible of war uses. Food is a war product. Textiles are a war product. Any of the articles of consumption are necessary in modern warfare. It will be our responsibility to insure that these products are used for peaceful purposes. This task will be made immeasurably easier if we cooperate thereon. It will be immeasurably more difficult if we squabble among ourselves.

If it be charged that the revival of Japanese economy will be a threat to Chinese economy, then I deny it. Certainly the demands of the peoples of the world for goods and services are far greater than anything all the countries in the world in the predictable future can hope to satisfy. On the contrary, the indefinite continuation of an indigent Japan will continue to lower the standards of living of the world. The world will be deprived of what Japan can produce. It will continue to be a drain on our already depleted resources. As a hungry and restless people, it will continue to be a threat to peace. Such a situation is made to order for Communism. If we are sincere in our profession, that Communism, in the general interest, must be stopped, then we must remove the causes which encourage Communism.

If those of you who agitate or who participate in the agitation against the United States on the question of Japan disagree with what I have said, then you must be prepared to face the consequences of your actions. If in your hearts you know that I am right, and still continue your agitation for other and secret purposes, then I say to you that it is time you examined your consciences. If by dishonest means you are attempting to accomplish some clandestine purpose, you are not only damaging the United States, you are also damaging your own country. You are also damaging your own standing and reputation as students and intellectuals of China whose best and most honest efforts are so desperately needed today by your country. You are the ones who are in the best position in China to know the truth. If you betray it you also betray yourselves. If you are not true to yourselves then most assuredly you cannot be true to any one or any thing else.

I hardly need protest my affection for Chinese student groups. If my life has not proven that, then it has been a total failure. I trust then that you will take the harsh words I have felt compelled to speak in the spirit in which they are intended. My greatest wish is the peace and welfare of all peoples of the world. Unless China and the United States can approach each other with mutual trust and confidence, that peace and welfare are endangered. I have confidence that the students of China will not knowingly lend themselves to evil purposes or betray the trust which has been placed in them by their country.

At the same time I want to assure you that I am fully aware of how much the Chinese people suffered at the hands of the Japanese and how heroically China resisted aggression. I was a prisoner of the Japanese myself and I know what it meant. I also know that the American people are aware of the tremendous Chinese sacrifices and are deeply grateful for that selfless contribution to the defeat of our common enemy. But I would also say that despite the understandable bitterness of China toward Japan, the best guarantee against a recurrence of the tragedy is wisdom, calmness and unity of purpose. In the present distraught situation of the world, misunderstanding among ourselves is the luxury we can least afford.

Your interests in Japan and those of my country are identical. We do not want a Communist Japan, and our surest method of preventing such a calamity is to enable the Japanese people to earn their own living.

155

The Ambassador in China (Stuart) to Secretary Marshall

893.00/8-2048

NANKING, *August 20, 1948*

Local vernacular press carries following text of order issued August 17 by Executive Yuan:

In rebelling against the nation, the Communist bandits are not only engaged in manslaughter, arson, and pillage by force of arms, but also have set spies, circulated rumors and instigated workers' and students' strikes in the rear. The responsible authorities may not have taken strict precautions or handled the situation in earnest. During the bandit suppression period, preservation of social order and elimination of bandit spies are essential to ensuring the safety of the people and guarding the foundation of the state. Attention is hereby called to the following four points:

(1) In accordance with Article 3 of the Prosecution Law of the Criminal Code, in making arrests according to law judicial and police agencies may search residences and other places without a warrant if there is sufficient evidence for establishing the crime of the accused and if the situation is urgent. But places of military secrecy may not be searched without the permisison of the officer-in-charge.

(2) Liaison will be established with responsible administrative agencies in banning bandit-inspired strikes or other activities interfering with production. Those who disobey the ban will be turned over to the special criminal court for punishment according to law.

(3) Student bodies which interfere with the bandit suppression campaign by calling strikes, staging demonstrations, presenting petitions, and making oral or written propaganda on behalf of the bandits are to be dissolved or prohibited from doing so. Chief offenders will be turned over to the special criminal court for treatment according to law.

(4) Those in charge of government agencies, civic bodies, and schools are responsible for ensuring order within their organizations. When they find their fellow members instigating the activities set forth in (2) and (3), they are to report to the local peace preservation agencies and, insofar as possible, help collect evidence. Those who fail to do so will be punished.

STUART

156 (a)

The Consul at Shanghai (Pilcher) to Secretary Marshall

893.00/6-2448

SHANGHAI, *June 24, 1948.*

According to the press, the City Councilor's meeting for the Sixth Plenary Session was explosively attacking the Central Government, particularly its economic policies. The tone of the first three meetings of the Session was unprecedentedly critical of both the Central and local government. Chairman Pan Kung-chan, at the opening meeting on the 21st, is reported to have severely criticized Nanking officials for "blunders, incompetency and apathy" and said they should be held responsible for the economic crises. He is said to have suggested that the Central Government officials refrain from talking before finishing their plans, as senseless talk was causing the recent price upheaval. Pan is also reported to have compared conditions in Shanghai settlement days when residents had more legal protection and self-governing power. Mayor Wu following Pan said he "agreed in principle" with Pan and "agreed 100 percent" with his remarks on economic conditions.

The third day of the meeting of the Council was highlighted with a proposal made by two councillors and supported by one hundred others that application to the Central Government be made to dismiss Finance Minister Wang Yun-wu on the ground of incompetence, as he had made no move to check the steadily deteriorating economic situation. The City police was also under attack for incompetence and corruption. One proposal asked for disbanding of the economic police because it had accomplished nothing towards stabilization of commodity prices and had unjustly harassed the people.

156 (b)

The Ambassador in China (Stuart) to Secretary Marshall

893.00/7-648

NANKING, *July 6, 1948.*

Within the past month the prestige and authority of the Central Government has sunk to an all time low, emphasized by a military debacle on the Kaifeng front and the collapse of the Chinese dollar on the commodity and foreign exchange markets. From information available to us, it appears that, with the exception of Fu Tso-Yi, Nationalist commanders are avoiding combat and are abandoning their positions when combat threatens. The Chinese Supreme Headquarters in Nanking admits that Kaifeng was taken by Communists without resistance from the defending garrison and that the attacking force was even joined by certain Nationalist units. Similar conditions appear to characterize recent military activities in southern Shantung and we are forced to the conclusion that, except in isolated instances, Government armies can no longer be counted on to fight.

Deterioration in the economic sphere is also noteworthy. The new cost of living index, issued just after depreciation in the value of the dollar, is arousing protests of wage earners and salaried groups who argue correctly that their incomes, as based on this index, will be insufficient to permit them to purchase the necessities of life. While their argument is valid, an increase in the index to a point where their basic needs would be satisfied would bankrupt both Government and private enterprise. Commodity prices are stable at the moment but there is little or nothing to prevent other spectacular jumps, with the consequent increase in discontentment and civil unrest.

In this situation, and as has been the case previously, the Government appears to have no remedies. The Military appears unable to stabilize any of the fighting fronts or restore the situation there to the Government's advantage. Civil officials admit frankly that they do not know what to do to curb the present violent inflation.

As we have reported, the Generalissimo is generally and directly blamed for this state of affairs and is criticized for his inability to take any effective action to cope with the situation. He is doubtlessly aware of this criticism and of its implication. He responds to it only by trying to safeguard his own position through placing individuals on whose loyalty he can personally count, in positions of trust, regardless of the fact that these individuals have long records of incompetence or corruption or both.

It is this failure of the Generalissimo to use his authority for the improvement of conditions, that forces provincial military and civil leaders to consider adoption of regional understandings and formation of regional political associations against the day when the government in Nanking either falls or loses the last vestiges of its authority. We have received reports from two independent sources that the purpose of General Li Tsung-jen's present visit to north China is to consult with Fu Tso-yi, Wei Li-haung, Wang Yao-wu, and certain other northern leaders, on the formation of a third government which would control northern China. It has been reported that this government will be independent of both Nationalist and Communist control, that it will reach some sort of an agreement with the Communists and that if necessary, it will include "some Communists." We have reported in the statement of T. V. Soong that he is adopting military measures for the protection of the south and his determination to defend that area should disaster overtake the Generalissimo. Also, there are indications that a provisional government which Marshal Li Chi-sen states he intends forming in the near future, may be essentially regional in character, comprising several provinces in the southwest.

As we noted above, regionalism and particularism is the natural response of those who would preserve, or make a new place for themselves, as the authority and power of the present Government inevitably declines. It is impossible to say what event would precipitate a break between the Generalissimo and any potential regional leader. This could result from an overt move by the Kuomintang Revolutionary Committee or from any comparable occurrence detrimental to the Generalissimo's prestige. In any event, our role in this situation is not a happy one. In the popular mind, we are associated with the Government and are regarded as the principal means by which it keeps itself in power. We are asked with increasing frequency why we adopt the policy of perpetuating in the power a government seemingly bent on its own destruction and facile only in paving the way for the spread of Communism. While we answer such queries by referring to the Generalissimo's adamant stand against Communists, we are forced to admit that it is a stand in name only. A continuation of his regime will almost certainly either plunge the entire country into profound chaos whereupon the Communists will seize power, or result in the seizure of power by local leaders anxious to safeguard themselves.

156(c)

The Consul General at Tientsin (Smyth) to Secretary Marshall

893.00/7-1448

TIENTSIN, *July 14, 1948*

On my recent return to Tientsin after five months' absence, I found the local Chinese military, civil leaders, press, and many civilians increasingly bitter over the National Government's policy of favoring the south against the north. They consider that North China has been deserted by the National Government, and feel that this area has been discriminated against as regards to relief supplies, military supplies, allotment of foreign exchange, and other ways.

Present opinion among the Chinese here is that the National Government is making a deliberate effort to create the impression with American authorities that North China is lost and should not be considered in any American aid plans. The Chinese here do not concur in this defeatist theory. They consider the military situation of North China much better than Honan, Shantung, Hupeh, et cetera. Particularly since the Fu Tso-yi assumption control six months ago, military operations against the Communists have been conducted with more ability and success than in other areas. They state that competent military leaders in North China have been unable to conduct full effort against the Communists, due to lack of cooperation, funds, and military supplies from the Central Government.

Chinese officials here assert that North China can be held against the Communists if given a fair proportion of American economic and military aid before it is too late. They point out that military aid should accompany economic aid to the Kailan mines and it would be more secure if the mines and railways have more adequate military protection. According to these Chinese, Fu Tso-yi has raised and partially trained 100,000 local militia in North China, but they have no arms; they say if arms for this number can be supplied, North China can be held against Communists.

Chinese here mentioned reported plans to use American aid to develop and improve mines, railways in South China, harbors, docks, Canton and Shanghai power plants, water works, industries in South China, and comment on apparent aid to North China not be neglected and be given a fair share. The recent visit of the Stillman group to Tientsin has given some encouragement, but the Chinese here feel that the National Government will block aid to North China unless American pressure is applied. Chinese here consider that if North China is lost, the rest of China will follow sooner or later, also, if North China is lost, due to deliberate refusal, the National Government would meet a bitter resistance in a future effort to recapture that area.

North China people in general, do not want Communism and would prefer to continue allegiance to the National Government if this Government would assist North China and effect some reforms. The Chinese here feel that if the National Government continues to refuse help, North China will have to decide on the future policy, whether to continue to resist or endeavor to make other arrangements. Mere government promises to help will be futile, only concrete action in the form of aid visibly arriving in North China will be effective.

During Stillman's trip to Tientsin, July 7 to 9, he visited the Kailan mines and had discussions with the Mayor of Tientsin and representatives of North China railways, power and other utilities, and Tangku new harbor, also Chinese and American businessmen. His visit and proposed visit of Mr. Lapham, have created a good impression and raised the hopes of North China.

The Tientsin American Chamber of Commerce is sending a memorandum to Lapham, urging strongly aid for North China. Copies are being forwarded to the Department, Embassy, Shanghai, and Peiping.

156(d)

The Ambassador in China (Stuart) to Secretary Marshall

893.00/7-1748

NANKING, *July 17, 1948*

I have the honor to report that on the morning of July 16 I called on President Chiang Kai-shek with the intention of giving him the only advice that seemed to me to have any promise in the present extremely critical situation. He asked me if I had any news and I replied that the news which seemed to me most important was the Communist general meeting to be held next month with the idea of a coalition government on the program, and the news reaching the Embassy from Hong Kong that Li Chi-shen was planning to start his Southwestern Provincial Government in the quite near future with the intention of proposing a coalition with the Communists. These developments taken in connection with the Chinese Communist broadcasts denouncing Tito and others openly committing themselves to world communism under the dictatorship of the Kremlin all supplied the background for the suggestion I had come to make. This was that he summon a small group of leaders who were generally respected and urge them to sink all personal and political differences in view of the real danger China was now facing, which was the loss of her national independence after the Communists triumphed. It had ceased to be merely an issue of Kuomintang factional politics as against Chinese Communists but was also part of a struggle between the fundamental principles of democracy and freedom on the one side and the domination of a minority controlled from Moscow on the other. The revolution and the war against Japan had been fought to win national independence which was now again jeopardized. In such a crisis he and all others ought to put the nation above all minor issues. I mentioned by name Fu Tso-yi, Li Tsung-jen, Pai Chung-hsi, and Li Chi-shen. As to this last, he should be given the opportunity and if he failed to comply on such a basis he should be denounced as preferring Russian communism to national independence. I hoped that this would result in a joint declaration appealing to all who wanted a free nation to face the realities and support the cause. The financial crisis and the economic hardships were very real, but even these were less important than the basic issue. It should be thought of primarily as a war of ideas and he ought to beat the others to it with skillfully prepared publicity. He said that he agreed in principle and would think it over very carefully, and added that he had been planning for a conference to reorganize the Kuomintang. I said that I was quite familiar with this but that my concern was more in personal relationships among the outstanding leaders and that this ought to be as dramatic as possible in order to convince the public.

He then asked about American opinion and I told him that Governor Dewey's announcement about increased aid to China had produced quite a bit of unfavorable editorial and other comment. I had with me the latest USIS bulletin on this subject, which I gave his secretary for reference.[21] I added, however, that if there should be a movement of the kind I was advocating which showed vitality, it would help to neutralize the feeling in the United States that this Government had been too weakened to make any assistance to it of much use. I told him that after all the greatest help that America could give was not money nor military advice but the dynamic force of our ideals which were shared by a great many Chinese but were being misrepresented and replaced by those of the Soviet Union.

He said that Americans tended to overrate the importance of Li Chi-shen, to which I replied that the man himself and his immediate followers need not be taken too seriously but that the whole nation was desperately anxious for peace and that with this popular mood any movement that held out the hope of peace through an understanding with the Communists might find more hearty support than he expected. It seemed to me, therefore, that whatever he did ought to be done with as little delay as possible. He said again that he would think the matter over carefully.

In attempting to draw conclusions from this interview the dominant impression is one of futility. I seriously question whether President Chiang has that quality of greatness which would enable him to assemble those leaders not already completely subservient to him and so to treat them as comrades as to draw out their own ideas in reaching a consensus of opinion and a group decision. The habits of twenty years, reinforced by Chinese traditional concepts, would be hard to alter. If he makes the attempt to cooperate with such a body he probably could not bring himself to do so graciously and with the unreserved sharing of minds which alone would win their confidence and impress the public. Any jointly issued statement would reflect these limitations and be unconvincing. He would also tend to draw in those upon whom he can depend which would further vitiate the effect. But nothing less than such a unified appeal, dramatic in its note of sincerity and urgency, would startle the now apathetic or disillusioned people of the country into realizing that something new and inspiring was actually happening on the highest level of their Government. Any effort to urge him further than I have done would either have to imply much more American aid than is possible or would over-persuade him to relinquish his own judgment. In either case he would cease to be true to himself and the results would almost certainly be unfortunate. It would seem, therefore,

---

[21] The following is the excerpt from the USIS Bulletin of July 17 (Foreign Service Digest—"Not for Publication") referred to by Ambassador Stuart in his conversation with the Generalissimo:

"CHINA: Gov. Dewey's recent criticism of the Truman Administration for its alleged 'Niggardly' aid to China and his assertion that the U. S. should provide 'far greater assistance' to preserve free China against the Communists has been echoed by a number of commentators. Disturbed by reports of increasing Communist activity throughout Southeast Asia, these observers contend China is 'bulwark of stability in the Far East and the only safeguard possible against Soviet expansion' (Manchester, N. H., Union). Criticism of U. S. policy also comes from Far Eastern expert Owen Lattimore and Henry Wallace.

"On other hand, some despair of pouring more American dollars and arms into China, arguing that its economy is 'floundering' and its leaders 'corrupt'. The rat hole in Asia is even more capacious than that in Europe', said the Chicago Tribune. 'Mr. Dewey had better indulge in a little reflection before he starts stuffing dollars into both ends of the hole'. And the Christian Century speculated that while the Republicans 'will undoubtedly have widespread backing in calling for more aid to China, unless their proposals for extending such aid are clearly outlined, they may do harm rather than good'."

that he must be allowed to go his own way, modified to be sure to some extent by suggestions from others, or that sooner or later there will be a movement which will force him out of his present ascendancy. He seems unable to think of Communism as an extreme form of social unrest which cannot be extirpated by the combination of military force and gracious compassion which he thinks to be the method taught by Chinese history. It is tragic that the very qualities of grimly inflexible determination and enduring courage which fitted him preeminently for incarnating the popular will to resist Japan are now in some real sense a hindrance to him in problems calling for very different mental processes.

157 (a)

The Ambassador in China (Stuart) to Secretary Marshall

893.515/8-2348

NANKING, *August 23, 1948*

In summary, we can find no basis for optimism regarding the Gold Yuan's future.

The Cabinet is staking its life on the success of its currency and economic measures. If we assume vigorous, ruthless and effective Government action against hoarders, black marketeers and cheaters (in whose hands control of the wealth of the country largely lies), it would still seem that the most this program can accomplish is three or four month's surcease from the upward flight of prices. In fact, there is surprisingly frank admission in official circles that the Government's eyes are glued to a sympathetic Republican Congress in January and that this program is a plank thrown across the intervening chasm.

The only important, concrete and immediate effect of the currency reform is the invigorating effect on exports which legalizing the black market rate should produce. It is also true that the physical inconvenience of lugging around bales of paper money is removed. Otherwise, the basic factors seem to us to be unchanged. The assets which are announced as backing the present currency are the same assets which, in theory at least, underlay the Chinese National Currency. The Government's budgetary deficit, which is what keeps the printing presses rolling out paper, remains with us, and even given maximum economy where economy is possible, the deficit will of necessity remain unmanageable as long as war goes on.

The measures appear calculated to take advantage of the dramatic effect on the Chinese public of the physically new currency notes. It is probable that this is sufficient temporarily to reduce the velocity in circulation calculated by the Central Bank for early August at a rate approximating 17 times per month. Simultaneously, the Central Bank and Central Trust are reported to be releasing stocks of commodities in Shanghai and Canton, particularly cotton yarn, and restricting bank credit. The combined effect of these measures should at least temporarily stabilize prices and thereby reduce the demand for dollars.

The remainder of the program as it is now constituted consists largely of declarations against: (1) increase in prices of goods and services over the August 19 levels; (2) hoarding of commodities; (3) publication of black market prices of gold and silver foreign exchange or of "daily necessities"; (4) payment of wages and salaries on a cost-of-living index basis; (5) lock-outs of strikes.

Declarations were also made requiring of all natural and juristic persons: (1) surrender of gold, silver and foreign currency held in China to the Central Bank for Gold Yuan notes of, at option of holder, for purchase of Chinese Government

United States dollar gold bonds of 1947, or for dollar deposit with the Central Bank to be drawn for payment of licensed imports, etc.; (2) sale of all gold produced in China to the Central Bank; (3) registration of foreign exchange assets held abroad by Chinese nationals including current and fixed deposits, currencies, gold, stocks, bonds, debentures, land titles, insurance policies, etc.; (4) upon registration of the foregoing, transfer of such assets to the Central Bank. The enforcement of item four aided by the provision of payment of 40 percent in the former's fee.

The announced reserve behind the currency of $200 million is gold, silver and foreign currency does not in fact exist in that amount. Already there is evidence of public skepticism of this part of the program.

As previously reported, the regulation limits the total gold yuan issue to two billion, equivalent approximately to ten times the present note issue. The difference between the amount needed to replace outstanding CNC and NEC will be used by the Central Bank to meet the continuing budget deficit, which there will be, even in the promised increase in tax collections and other revenue, and a reduction of expenditures, are forthcoming. Unless an extremely drastic decrease in the velocity of circulation occurs, there is no possibility apparent that the Chinese economy can absorb such an increase within the next few months without accelerating the inflation. Out payments of additional gold yuan will be largely through wage and salary payments. No significant increase in production is anticipated and imports are to be cut a minimum of 25 percent.

The black market, particularly for gold bars and dollars cannot be eliminated by fiat. Assuming the regulations achieve price stability and a reduction in the demand for dollars for the maintenance of value and liquidity of wealth, there can be only slight weakening of the demand for dollars arising from the flight of capital from areas of military and political insecurity, and for payment of unlicensed imports. This demand alone is sufficient to create black markets for dollars which must be at a premium over official rates and which inevitably will pull prices upward as well.

Against possible deflationary influences arising from the contraction of the money supply and the reduction in velocity, off-setting inflationary factors are reduction of imports, undervaluation of the Gold Yuan in terms of the dollar by 10 to 20 percent, inertia of previously rising prices, reluctance of small entrepreneurs and farmers to accept the psychological effect of the prices of their goods and services amounting to a few Gold Yuan cents when they were previously expressed in millions, and finally, the difficulties of enforcement. A real danger exists that these inflationary forces may go out of control at which time all confidence in the currency would be lost, since the Chinese Government has promised so much in attendant publicity.

157 (b)

Secretary Marshall to the Chinese Minister for Foreign Affairs (Wang) [22]

893.50 Recovery/8–2548

Thank you for your message [23] forwarded to me by Ambassador Stuart. I have just received information regarding the emergency financial and economic measures proclaimed by President Chiang and am now having a careful study

---

[22] Transmitted to Ambassador Stuart on Aug. 28, 1948.
[23] Message of Aug. 25, 1948; not printed.

made of them. I am gratified at your determination, as well as that of your colleagues, to enforce measures designed to help meet China's serious economic problems and view sympathetically the measures of self-help taken by the Chinese Government.

I look forward to seeing you at the United Nations Assembly in Paris and to having the opportunity of discussions on these and several others matters. My warm regards to you.

157 (c)

The Ambassador in China (Stuart) to Secretary Marshall

893.50/10–1548

NANKING, *October 15, 1948*

The China August 19 economic reform appears now to be hastening to its denouement. Efforts and gestures of the last two months may well soon be forgotten and will be back on the basis of the open printing press and all but the open hedging and the speculation in foreign exchanges and commodities. (The black-market trading is now out of hand.) With few exceptions, as public utilities are fixed, the prices are fictions. In Shanghai, where enforcement started off spectacularly and where control has been most stringent, there is now a noticeable lack of zeal and decreasing effectiveness on the part of the police. The several really big names who were early arrested are still in confinement but their trials are dragging on through protracted adjournments and appeals. Chiang Ching-kuo's heralded plans for an industrial resurgence, the "second phase" of the August 19 program, have just been announced; they are uninspiring and follow the same old pattern of "conservation of foreign exchange" and the concentration of authority in the central trust and the trade guilds. The accompanying registration of industrial commodities and the inspection of warehouses are tapering off with no apparent results.

The China note issue is now probably in the neighborhood of Gold Yuan 1.25 billion which represents a quantity of money say five times as great as that in circulation on August 19. This money is not going back to the government in taxes nor into the production enterprise but rather is accumulating and idle in the cities building up the inflationary pressure which has recently been evidenced by:

1. Shanghai's last week retail buying spree which has now spread to other cities stripping shops of their exposed goods;
2. Increasing unavailability in all cities of daily necessities except under the counter and at prices far above the fixed levels;
3. Short-term interest rates are so low as to be practically negligible by Chinese standards (i. e. 4 percent per month);
4. Reestablishment of "organized" black markets in gold bullion and United States currency.

In Peiping and Tientsin where police surveillance has been only nominal, gold is selling for Gold Yuan 1,000 per ounce and United States dollars at Gold Yuan 16 compared to the respective official quotations of Gold Yuan 200 and Gold Yuan 4. In Canton the Hong Kong dollar is up in the past week to Gold Yuan 1.25 as compared to the official .75. In Shanghai where to date the operators have been most circumspect, there is now a good volume of business in currency at Gold Yuan 6 to 7 with TTs bringing about 20 percent premium; the shopkeepers are beginning to again quote and surreptitiously to accept United States dollars; the volume of telephone calls is this week picking up showing the resumption of black-market transactions as pretty much on a "normal" basis.

With the concurrent discouraging military developments, it seems to us impossible that the government much longer can continue to imitate Canute before the economic tide. It appears equally unlikely that it can publicly abandon the program on which so much was staked. What is more likely is that we are seeing the slackening of the pretence of enforcement and a yielding full rein to economic forces which at the moment are so precariously held in check.

158

The Consul General at Shanghai (Cabot) to Secretary Marshall

893.00/11–248

SHANGHAI, *November 2, 1948*

STATEMENT BY CHIANG CHING-KUO NOVEMBER 1, 1948

After past seventy days of my work I feel that I have failed to accomplish the duties which I should have accomplished. Not only did I not consummate my plan and mission but in certain respects I have rather deepened the sufferings of the people which they experienced in course of execution of my task.

I will never shift to others any responsibility which should be borne by me. I will never give up my political platform just because of setbacks I have sustained. I firmly believe that direction I have pointed out as regards "whither Shanghai" is absolutely correct.

Today aside from petitioning to government for punishment so as to clarify my responsibility I wish to take this opportunity of offering my deepest apology to citizens of Shanghai. But in so doing I do not want to be accorded an understanding by them. I only mean to point out to the people here the responsibility which I should bear. I sincerely wish the citizens of Shanghai to use their own strength to prevent unscrupulous merchants, bureaucrats, politicians and racketeers from controlling Shanghai. I firmly believe that a bright future lies ahead for Shanghai.

159

Editorial from the "Chung Yang Jih Pao," November 4, 1948 [24]

893.00/11–548

"LOSE NO TIME IN WINNING THE PEOPLE'S CONFIDENCE"

Recent military reverses in the Northeast are facts which the Government no longer tries to hide and everybody is suffering terribly from the new high prices. The masses of people live under a feeling of fear and are pursued relentlessly by difficult living conditions. Such facts are so undeniably true that they can no longer be ignored just because some people find them unpleasant to the ear, nor can they be white-washed by beautiful words.

At this moment when the nation's fate is flickering, and when the people are suffering terribly, what comfort and hope is there for them? The special privileged classes still enjoy their privileges, and the people can do nothing to them. Those plutocrats who have made their money because of personal or political relations, are either having a nice time abroad, or keeping right on with their

---

[24] Transmitted by Ambassador Stuart from Nanking, Nov. 5, 1948.

activities in fleecing the people. Even now nothing can be done to these public enemies of the people who are able accomplices of the Communists. No one has applied political pressure on them to make them disgorge their money to finance bandit suppression and to relieve the people. Nobody even dares to touch them ever so slightly. Nepotism rides on just as it has always done and the masses of people have no right to say anything. What are we going to do with national affairs like that, with each lao pa hsin with a bellyful of resentment? If nothing is done to release a fraction of that resentment in the bosoms of the 400 million people who are the masters of the country, how can we face the soul of our National Father who devoted his entire life to helping the nation and helping the people? How can we face the souls of our brave warriors who died for the revolution? And how can we face the suffering people who are our brethren?

In the process of bandit suppression, most people pay attention only to equipment and to the methods of combating Communists—in short, to tangible factors only. No emphasis is given to the spiritual factor, particularly political reform. We should all know that "military affairs are only an elongation of political affairs." How can we have satisfactory military conditions if our political affairs are not healthy to begin with? If our politics are not solid and bubbling with life, how can our military affairs be satisfactory? The present state of affairs should be sufficient to make us thoroughly realize that if we want to eradicate the Communists and retrieve the present unfavorable military conditions we should, while it is important to strengthen the tangible equipment of our army, tackle political reform which will give strength to our army. What does this mean exactly?

In the second half of the 19th Century, the Communists enjoyed considerable power in Germany. What did Germany do to cope with the situation? Dr. Sun Yat-sen told us that Bismarck boldly decided to adopt national socialism, and took over from the hands of the Communists their most tantalizing issues. As a result, the Communists could do nothing in Germany. This proves that Bismarck was an able statesman. China today is experiencing troubles unprecedented in seriousness since the Tai Ping Rebellion. Of course our present troubles are enhanced by international intrigue, but we must admit that fundamentally it is because of the many defects that exist in our social system. While the essential purpose of the Communists is to grasp political power, on the surface they capitalize on these social defects in order to attract the people to their banner. This explains why Communist eradication has been such a difficult task. If we want to eliminate the Red menace, we must do what Bismarck did in coping with the German Communists; take over from the hands of the Communists all those tantalizing issues. At present, a handful of people are enjoying all the privileges. They live snobbishly and luxuriously. They do not have to part with one farthing. They will not yield one single man to serve in the army. The entire burden of military service and contribution of food falls on the shoulders of the poverty-stricken masses. How can one feel that it is just? How can we prevent our opposers from using this as an excellent pretext?

With our national affairs as they are at the present, it is imperative that we sacrifice the handful of people to help the masses. Only by doing so can we retrieve the situation. The final test as to whether we are revolutionary or anti-revolutionary lies in our choice of ways: whether we will go along with the masses, or with the handful of people. If we choose to walk with the small minority, then no matter how loudly we shout our revolutionary slogans we are *de facto*, anti-revolutionary. If we choose to walk with the masses, even if we do not speak of being revolutionary the lao pa hsing will know that we are revolutionary. If we can truly rule the country with a heart absolutely free from selfishness, employ officials because of their merits, keep the villains out of our way, remove all officials who do harm to the people, severely punish those who fleece the people by virtue of their power, and transfer the burden now resting on the masses to the shoulders of the plutocrats, we are sure that the people will feel that a new era has indeed dawned—the morale of the troops will bolster like magic. What is this small task of eradicating the Communist bandits?

Giving full allowance for the worst, the area that lies south of the Yangtze River is big enough to contain more than ten European nations and has a population of more than 200 million. There is easy access to the sea, there is an abundance of all kinds of products and adequate transportation facilities. Compared to the time of the Northern Expedition, conditions today are far more favorable. Why then should there be pessimism? This is because something is fundamentally wrong with ourselves. If we can gain full control and make full use of the manpower and material resources within this large tract of land, we have more than the strength we need in eliminating the Communists. However, the key to the full mobilization of this manpower and material resources lies in our winning of the people's confidence and we must realize that the people's confidence cannot be won by the mere issuance of an official order on a sheet of paper. It can only be revived by having the responsible parties of the Government do several things which will remove the feeling of resentment. Facts must be used to prove absence of selfishness and that bandit suppression is not for the purpose of protecting the interests of the privileged classes but for the protection of territorial integrity, freedom and democracy for the people, and our history and culture. If we can accomplish this we are sure to expect a sudden change in the situation.

Waste no time in winning the people's confidence. This is our last chance.

160

The Ambassador in China (Stuart) to Secretary Marshall

893.00/11–148

NANKING, *November 1, 1948*

The following is the full text of two articles twice broadcast by the North Shensi Chinese Communist radio on October 30 and 31:

The American State Department and American espionage organization are jointly undertaking a big plot to destroy national liberation movements of China and various countries of Asia, according to reliable reports obtained by well-informed quarters in Shanghai.

To explain the necessity for this plan, its framers emphasize in their report to Truman the "menace" to America of peoples liberation movements in Asia, especially China. The report holds that "Chinese Communist-controlled areas" are deciding the fate of Communism in Asia. Describing Chinese liberated areas, the report says that for the first time in the history of China, the Chinese people now have a really clean and honest government. Agrarian reform there has not only satisfied the demands of peasants, but has also solved many hitherto unsolved economic problems in "Communist-controlled areas". As a result, the political system there has become a highly effective organization, the report says.

The report admits the complete failure of American economic and military aid to Chinese reactionaries. Economic and military aid to China cannot transform soldiers unwilling to fight into troops with combat power, the report says. In its conclusion the report holds that after the end of World War II, the situation in Asia has become a "powerful and deadly menace" to Western Colonial Powers, first of all to American positions, at a time when America's need for Asia has become more pressing than at any period in the past. The report says that loss of position in Asia will bring with it irreparable and crushing blows to America. It points out that Asia's social life has entered an era of great events and only a carefully thought out plan of action can counteract it.

The report proposes a plan for the setting up of a joint political organization in Washington, especially devoted to opposing the so-called Communistic activities in Asia. The organization is to include departments for work in various parties and groups and trade unions, military work, work among students and women, and espionage and intelligence activities.

The tasks of this joint political organization are stipulated as follows: (1) use all possible means to support "legal government" in various countries; (2) organize and give financial backing to "center parties and groups" to split and destroy national movements; (3) strive to reach understanding with elements with Leftist leanings in Socialist parties; (4) develop anti-Communist activities in trade unions and peasant organizations; (5) stir up discord between Leftist leaders and destroy their prestige; (6) stir up and utilize friction between national groups especially in India, Amman, Burma and Malaya; (7) actively absorb renegades from peoples movements in various countries to do work; (8) gather and study intelligence of peoples government movements.

It is stipulated that the above work is to be under the unified leadership of United States Ambassadors in various countries. The Shanghai report states that this American plot will be linked up with recent American measures in China and Japan. A central espionage organization participated in by American and Japanese spies has recently been set up in MacArthur's staff headquarters in Japan. This organization specifically undertakes disruption of Japan's democratic organizations and opposition to leaders of democratic movement. Many Japanese secret police agents participate in this organization. Among them is the notorious General Arisue. On American instructions, a society of retired Japanese servicemen is still carrying on secret activities, and has established an organization for the specific purpose of disrupting democratic movements.

A China office of U. S. Strategic Services has been set up in Shanghai to collaborate with Kuomintang secret police organizations to destroy any democratic movement in China. This office of U. S. Strategic Services has recently shipped large quantities of radio sets, radio location detectors, and cameras to China to be used for espionage work. American espionage organizations have worked out a specific plan to destroy democratic movements in China. This plan has been approved by Leighton Stuart and Chiang Kai-shek. The organization to execute this plan has decided to set up its headquarters in Nanking, and its local organizations in Manchuria, North China, Central China and Southeast China.

The second article begins: The following is the full text of an important New China News Agency editorial entitled "China and Asia Friends of American People, Bitter Enemies of American Reactionaries."

Today we published a report from Shanghai on the fact that American reactionaries are actively employing every conspiratorial means of disrupting national democratic movements of China and Asia. We have frequently reported facts on oppression, aggression, and armed intervention of American imperialism against peoples of China and Asia.

What is new about this report is:

(1) American reactionaries admit that peoples revolutionary movements of China and Asia have obtained support of broad masses of people. They admit that government, born of the peoples revolution, is truly loyal to the people and very effective.

(2) American reactionaries regard obtaining of due and sacred rights by peoples of China and Asia a "powerful and deadly menace," thus proving how thoroughly the American Government has scrapped its promise of "respecting the right of all peoples to choose their form of government" in Atlantic Charter of August 1941, and also thus proving that American reactionaries are mortal enemies of the people of China and Asia.

(3) American reactionaries admit that the reactionary governments of China and Asia are rotten to the core, so that even such enormous military and economic aid as given by the United States to the Kuomintang Government in China cannot block the victorious development of peoples revolutionary movements.

(4) Under the above conditions, American reactionaries consider that they can now no longer rely on open "legal" methods to save reactionary rule and colonial systems in China and Asia from extinction, but must rely on illegal methods which cannot meet the public eye—methods of secret police organizations. As prescription for prolonging the life of imperialism, American reactionaries have decided to rely on the Gestapo methods of Hitler and Himmler, and to cooperate with the darkest forces of China, Japan and various countries of Asia.

The stupidity of the American Government's reactionary plan is obvious. Himmler could not prolong Hitler's rule. Secret police aid decidedly cannot solve problems that no military or economic aid can solve. Strengthening the activities of American secret police organizations in China and various countries of Asia can only accelerate the fall of ruling blocs in these countries into abysses of isolation and disintegration. However, the peoples of China and Asia should draw important lessons from the vicious schemes of the American Government.

Since the American secret police scheme stresses provocations within the camp of the Left, it behooves the camp of the Left to answer with further consolidation of its own unity.

Since the American secret police scheme stresses buying up "political parties of the center," and developing the "anti-Communist" movement, it behooves those who have illusions about the middle road to abandon their illusions, reject all "anti-Communist" inducements, and to be on guard against the danger of playing into the hands of imperialist conspirators in an off-guard moment. At a time when Chiang Kai-shek, America's number one running dog in China, is bankrupt and useless and it is decided to replace him with the number two running dog, Li Tsung-jen, people self-styled "in the center" should examine their conduct carefully to avoid falling into the trap of American imperialism. This moment is probably very near at hand. Since the American secret police plan stresses utilization of discord among various nationalities, it behooves all oppressed nationalities, and especially various nationalities of multi-national countries, firmly to abandon all kinds of mistaken narrow nationalist thinking for the sake of the common struggle against imperialism. Since the American secret police plan stresses utilization of renegades and spies, of espionage, it behooves all revolutionary organizations to redouble their vigilance and to strengthen the fight against spies, so that all these skulking forces are brought out into the light of day, where they are powerless to realize their schemes.

There will still be difficulties in the way of liberation movements of the peoples of China and Asia. Courage which blasts path through thorny difficulties, and the caution of these who walk on the brink of perilous chasms, are needed to attain our objective; but if only we can act in this manner, we will certainly be able to attain our objective.

American reactionaries in their scheme regard the peoples of China and Asia as their bitter enemies and regard liberation of peoples of China and Asia as a "powerful and deadly menace" to them. This is because American reactionaries wildly think of making the peoples of China and Asia their permanent colonial slaves. But the peoples of China and Asia will never be enemies of American peoples. American reactionaries, Truman, Dewey and their ilk, have received and will continue to receive "irreparable and crushing blows" from the peoples of China and Asia. The America of the people, however, the America of Wallace and the Progressive Party, and the America of laborers and the Communist Party of the United States of America has obtained, and will continue to obtain, the friendship of the peoples of China and Asia. No matter whether American reactionaries like it or not, the peoples of China and Asia will ultimately achieve liberation, while those of American reactionaries in various countries and American reactionaries themselves, will eventually meet their doom. All schemes and conspiracies of American imperialism will, of necessity, crumble to pieces, whereas the friendship of the peoples of China and Asia and America will live forever.

STUART

161

The Ambassador in China (Stuart) to Secretary Marshall

893.00/8–1048

NANKING, *August 10, 1948*

1. Military: The Communists continue to win the civil war. They have retained the initiative with all the advantage given by the offensive and government troops just do not seem to have the will or the ability to fight. There are many reports of defections to the Communists but none from Communist ranks. Occupying as they do most of north China east of Sian and north of the Yangtze River except for a few scattered urban centers such as Peiping and Tientsin and certain lines of communication the Communists now appear intent on removing the last vestiges of government strength from Shantung Province, a prelude possibly to full-scale attack south to Nanking or possibly to an all-out attack on Peiping-Tientsin area. In Central China south of the Yangtze scattered Communist bands operate throughout the countryside creating confusion and disorder with the obvious intent of further weakening the government and preparing the way for some future large-scale operation. In South China though less active Communist guerrilla units operate more or less at will and the government has no forces to employ against them.

It is a gloomy picture and one would expect the government to clutch at any means of improving the situation. Nevertheless it ignores competent military advice and fails to take advantage of military opportunities offered. This is due in large part to the fact that government and military leadership continue to deteriorate as the Generalissimo selects men on the basis of personal reliability rather than military competence. In the distribution of desperately needed military supplies men of proven military competence such as Fu Tso-yi are given low priority and are almost left to fend for themselves. Long contemplated plans for training new armies and replacements are not being implemented or are moving too slowly materially to affect the situation in the coming desperate months.

There is an awareness of the desperateness of the military situation yet no evidence of a will or capability to cope with it.

2. Economic: The inflationary spiral continues at an accelerated pace. Prices have become astronomical and their rise so rapid that the government has been unable to print sufficient money to meet day-by-day needs with the result that barter is becoming more and more the rule. Prices increasingly are quoted either in US dollars, silver or gold. In the interior silver dollars are coming back to use. Thus government has introduced measures to control inflation but the effects have been only temporary and palliative. The fact is that the government in the absence of assured continuing and massive loans from the United States cannot hope to find an answer as long as circumstances require the maintenance of the present military establishment. A renewed and concerted attack on the periphery of the central problem now impends but at best it can only provide a breathing spell.

3. Psychological: After years of war and destruction the all-consuming urge of the people today, and this includes both low and high ranking members of the government and Communist areas as well, is for peace. This urge becomes all the more insistent as most people can see no ray of hope under present conditions. A spirit of defeatism is prevalent throughout the country reaching even men of cabinet rank. Almost without exception there is no longer faith that the present government can bring a return to even a bearable standard of living without some radical reorganization. With this frame of mind a cessation of hostilities is desired at almost any price. There is an overwhelming desire for peace yet the Generalissimo wants only military victory over the Communists and no one has yet found a way to surmount the Generalissimo's objections and win out to peace.

4. The Generalissimo himself: Universally the Generalissimo is criticized for his ineffective leadership and universally no one can suggest any one to take his place. He is the one who holds this vast country together. Without him disintegration seems inevitable yet long experience with him suggests that he is no longer capable of changing and reforming or of discarding inefficient associates in favor of competent ones and unless he can summon the resources to reverse the present trend he will inevitably and in time be discarded. Nevertheless the Generalissimo is a resourceful man and there are signs that he is trying to find a way to continue the fight against the Communists and at the same time prevent a return of the country to regionalism. He has sent former Prime Minister Chang Chun to the north and to the southwest offering regional autonomy in return for continued allegiance to Nanking and there is reason to believe Chang Chun's trip has not been entirely unproductive of results. There is active and violent agitation for reorganization of the Kuomintang which will permit liberal voices greater weight in government circles and there is evidence that under Wong Wen-hao the government is making a valiant effort toward economic and financial reform which may be announced shortly. Unless, however, these drastic measures which are contemplated produce a miracle and result in the retention of the Generalissimo and the Kuomintang in control we may expect to see some kind of an accommodation with the Communists or a regional breakup or a combination of the two. The third possibility seems the most likely.

Even though at present some form of coalition seems most likely we believe that from the standpoint of the United States it would be most undesirable. We say this because the history of coalitions including Communists demonstrates all too clearly Communist ability by political means to take over complete control of the government and in the process to acquire some kind of international recognition. We question whether a Communist government can in the foreseeable future come to full power in all China by means other than coalition. We would recommend therefore that American efforts be designed to prevent the formation of a coalition government and our best means to that end is continued and, if possible, increased support to the present government. Nevertheless deterioration has already progressed to the verge of collapse and it may already be too late for our support to change the course of events. To assure success we should likely have to involve ourselves in great responsibilities, military, economic, political for we should have to undertake the direction of Chinese affairs on a large scale and a scale in fact that would likely involve responsibilities beyond our resources.

162(a)

Secretary Marshall, temporarily in Paris, to Under Secretary Lovett

893.00/11-648

PARIS, *November 6, 1948*

Dr. T. S. Tsiang, Chinese delegate to the United Nations, called on me this morning with a message from Foreign Minister Dr. Wang.

(1) Would the United States agree to the appointment of United States officers in actual command of the Chinese army units under the pretense of acting as advisers?

(2) Would the United States appoint an officer of high rank to head the special mission, primarily for advice and planning on an emergency situation?

(3) Will the United States expedite the supply of munitions?

(4) What was the thought as to the advisability of Chinese appeal to the United Nations because of Soviet training and equipping of Japanese military and also the Koreans?

I explained the efforts regarding the supply of munitions and stated I would request you to press for urgent action. I did not offer encouragement beyond present efforts.

I said I would refer the requests under (2) and (3) to Washington without making any comment to reference (1).

I remarked regarding (2) that the proposition inherently involved great difficulties if favorably considered; that if the individual did not know China it would require months for him to grasp understanding of the possibilities of the situation, and it would therefore be a very serious matter for the United States to send an officer to almost certain failure.

Regarding (4) I said I would have to consult my colleagues of the United States delegation to develop various possibilities; that offhand I thought it an inadvisable procedure and discussed possible Soviet moves to take advantage rather than to counter such a move. Dr. Tsiang told me the proposition had been put to him three times and each time he had recommended against such action.

MARSHALL

162(b)

Secretary Marshall, temporarily in Paris, to Under Secretary Lovett

893.00/11-848

PARIS, *November 8, 1948.*

Your report of November 6 shows why the visit of a high-ranking United States officer to China would be undesirable and unproductive. Even if the record of the repeated failure of the Chinese Government in the past to accept U. S. advice did not exist, it would be foolhardy for the United States, at this stage of disintegration of the Chinese Government authority in civil as well as the military sphere, to embark upon such a quixotic venture. We are doing everything possible to expedite the shipment of military matériel under the $125 million grants. The pattern of defections and other accompaniments of the fall of Tsinan, Chinchow and the Manchurian debacle, although Chinese Government troops had adequate arms, indicate the will to fight is lacking. With respect to the Chinese Government appeal to the United Nations regarding Soviet treaty violations, this is a matter for Chinese decision, but could not be expected to change the internal situation in China.

You are authorized to inform the Foreign Minister that the National Military Establishment is making every effort to expedite the shipments of military matériel under the $125 million grants. You should point out to him the inherent difficulties involved in an attempt on the part of a foreign official to advise the Chinese Government regarding its courses of action even in the unlikely event such official could be completely conversant with all the complexities of the situation, and the even greater difficulties for a foreign official not familiar with China. You should state that it is not believed that the inspection visit of a high-ranking U. S. officer would or could offer the solution to China's problems. With respect to the Chinese Government appeal to the United Nations, you should reply in the sense of the final sentence of the preceding paragraph.

163

President Chiang Kai-shek to President Truman [25]

893.50 Recovery/10–1648

I have the honor to acknowledge receipt of Your Excellency's reply dated October 16, 1948, for which I am deeply grateful.

The Communist forces in Central China are now within striking distance of Shanghai and Nanking. If we fail to stem the tide, China may be lost to the cause of democracy. I am therefore compelled to send to Your Excellency again a direct and urgent appeal.

The general deterioration of the military situation in China may be attributed to a number of factors. But the most fundamental is the non-observance by the Soviet Government of the Sino-Soviet Treaty of Friendship and Alliance, which, as Your Excellency will doubtless recall, the Chinese Government signed as a result of the well-intentioned advice from the United States Government. I need hardly point out that, but for persistent Soviet aid, the Chinese Communists would not have been able to occupy Manchuria and develop into such a menace.

As a co-defender of democracy against the onrush and infiltration of Communism throughout the world, I appeal to you for speedy and increased military assistance and for a firm statement of American policy in support of the cause for which my Government is fighting. Such a statement would serve to bolster up the morale of the armed forces and the civilian population and would strengthen the Government's position in the momentous battle now unfolding in North and Central China.

My Government would be most happy to receive from you as soon as possible a high-ranking military officer who will work out in consultation with my Govern-

---

[25] Delivered to the White House on Nov. 9, 1948, by the Chinese Ambassador. Text as transmitted by the Department to the Embassy in Paris, Nov. 12, 1948.

ment a concrete scheme of military assistance, including the participation of American military advisers in the direction of operations.

As the situation demands your Excellency's full sympathy and quick decision, I shall appreciate an early reply.

CHIANG KAI-SHEK

164

President Truman to President Chiang Kai-shek [26]

893.50 Recovery/11–1248

MY DEAR PRESIDENT CHIANG: This is in acknowledgment of your letter delivered to the White House on November 9 through the good offices of your Ambassador, Dr. V. K. Wellington Koo.

As I stated in my letter of October 16, 1948, everything possible is being done to expedite the procurement and shipment to China of the weapons and ammunition being obtained in this country under the China Aid Program. I am again emphasizing to the appropriate officials the urgency of your needs and the necessity of prompt action. In this connection, I have just been informed that one shipment of arms and ammunition sailed from Guam on November 4 and another from Japan on November 7 en route to China. I have also been informed that a further shipment of ammunition sailed from the West Coast of the United States on November 9 and is scheduled to reach China about November 24.

A message of November 9 from the Secretary of State to Ambassador Stuart, containing Secretary Marshall's reply to a request from the Chinese Foreign Minister for military aid and the visit of a high-ranking United States officer to China, apparently crossed Your Excellency's message in transmission. The Secretary authorized Ambassador Stuart to inform the Foreign Minister that the United States National Military Establishment was making every effort to expedite shipments of military matériel purchased in this country under the China Aid Act. He also authorized Ambassador Stuart to point out the inherent difficulties involved in an attempt on the part of a newly appointed foreign official to advise the Chinese Government regarding its courses of action in the present dilemma, even if such an official would be completely conversant with all the numerous complexities of the situation, and to point out the even greater difficulties for a foreign official not familiar with China.

However, Major General Barr, Director of the Joint United States Military Advisory Group in China, is conversant with the current situation and his advice has always been available to you.

Your attention may have been called to my public statement on March 11, 1948, in which I stated that the United States maintained friendly relations with the Chinese Government and was trying to assist the recognized Government of China maintain peace. I also stated that I did not desire Communists in the Chinese Government. Secretary Marshall stated publicly on March 10, 1948, that the Communists were now in open rebellion against the Chinese Government and that the inclusion of the Communists in the Government was a matter for the Chinese Government to decide, not for the United States Government to dictate. I believe that these statements and the action of my Government in extending assistance to the Chinese Government under the China Aid Act of 1948 have made the position of the United States Government clear.

You will understand the desire of the United States Government to support the cause of peace and democracy throughout the world. It is this desire that has

---

[26] Text as transmitted by the Department to the Embassy in Nanking, Nov. 12, 1948.

led this Government to extend assistance to many countries in their efforts to promote sound economies and stable conditions without which the peoples of the world cannot expect to have peace and the principles of democracy cannot grow. It was with that hope that the United States Government has extended assistance in various forms to the Chinese Government. I am most sympathetic with the difficulties confronting the Chinese Government and people at this time and wish to assure Your Excellency that my Government will continue to exert every effort to expedite the implementation of the program of aid for China which has been authorized by the Congress with my approval.

Very sincerely yours,

HARRY S. TRUMAN

165(a)

The Ambassador in China (Stuart) to Secretary Marshall

893.00/11–548

NANKING, *November 5, 1948*

I have the honor to enclose for the information of the Department the text as released by the Central News Agency in Peiping on October 31, 1948 of a statement made by President Chiang Kai-shek to Mr. Arthur T. Steele of the New York Herald Tribune in reply to a series of ten questions.

The major portion of the President's statement consists of the usual redundancies concerning China's contributions to peace and civilization, a tirade against Communists and the customary assurances that conditions in China are really not as bad as many people think. Some passages are, however, of more than passing interest.

After stating that the Chinese Communists have not the slightest concern for the welfare of the people, the President gives his explanation for the recent Manchurian debacle. It is difficult to deduce from his statement just what he has in mind, but it is apparent that he ignores the real reasons for the defeat and prefers to consider the capture of Mukden by the Communists as being of little significance. He denies any pessimism on his part and states that if the Government should receive moral and financial help from friendly nations the situation could be speedily reversed.

Perhaps the most telling comment he makes, certainly from the standpoint of world opinion, is the parallel he draws between contemporary events in Manchuria and those of 1931. The President says that when Japan invaded Manchuria he pointed out to the world that the Second World War had thereby begun. He says he wishes now to warn that Chinese Communist conquests of the Northeast must be considered the starting point of the Third World War if the Communists are permitted to secure control of the rest of China. He reaches this conclusion because the Soviets' desire to control all Asia and China is the decisive pivot of the area.

The President then makes the interesting statement that the ruthlessness and treachery of Chinese Communists cannot be compared with that of Communists elsewhere. In conclusion he says, "The center of endeavor in Asia must be China. This is the great task unprecedented in human history. I hope that the American people and their statesmen will dedicate their lives to this task."

Shortly thereafter several prominent newspapers echoed the President's sentiments editorially. Typical were the comments of KMT Chung Yang Jih Pao and the Army Ho Ping Jih Pao which pointed out that the problem of China is the problem of the world and that if the United States wishes to avoid a Third World War it had better do something about China soon.

The contents of this statement suggest that it was designed in the main to influence American opinion, particularly because of the emphasis placed on the Japanese invasion of Manchuria and prospects that the Chinese Communists' seizure of the area portends a Third World War. It must be admitted that the President has made an effective point.

For the Ambassador
Lewis Clark
Minister-Counselor

[Enclosure]

Statement by President Chiang Kai-shek to Mr. Arch T. Steele of the New York Herald Tribune

Mr. A. T. Steele, New York Herald Tribune China correspondent, submitted to President Chiang Kai-shek ten questions of which the President made the following observations:

In answer to the question what is the basic reason for the temporary setbacks of Government troops at the present moment, the President said the sole aim of the Government military policy adopted in the war of resistance and in the bandit suppression campaign has always been to preserve China's territorial integrity and sovereignty and also to protect the people's lives and property. This accounts for the fact that no city or place has ever been given up lightly.

The original purpose of fighting the eight long years war of resistance was to recover the Northeast. With the conclusion of the war Government troops took over at great risk important Northeastern regions and consequently could not lightly resort to withdrawal. The traditional ideal and conception of duty of the Chinese soldier decree is that it is imperative for him to die if the city falls or to live if he can hold it and that it is a disgrace for him to withdraw from or give up a city for this reason.

During the past three years, with defense posts scattered all over the areas under Red menace Government forces are availing themselves of this weakness. Communist bandits have employed the tactics of breaking individual posts in isolated areas.

As the Government belongs to the people, the enlistment of men into the army service and the collection of military foodstocks should be done without overburdening the people or violating the law and rulings of the nation. The Communists, however, have not the slightest concern for the people. They issue in different regions, bogus currency notes as they like. They confiscate at any time the people's property, enforce arbitrary conscription and ferret out all foodstuffs they can lay their hands on. Their ways and means cannot be more cruel and inhuman. During the past year, under the pretext of land reform they have resorted to draining the pond in the hope of netting a final catch of the fish. With what they have thus squeezed from the people, they are able to expand their armed forces on a large scale. The scorched earth policy taken on their withdrawals and the human sea tactics in their offensives are certainly not what Government troops should like to follow.

Consequently, while Government troops can surely score victory when they concentrate their forces and engage the main enemy forces in fighting, they would now and then be put into such a position that with troops inferior in number and isolated from main forces they had to suffer setbacks. All this is the fundamental reason for which Government troops for the moment undergo losses. At present, therefore, the Government cannot but subject the strategy and tactics of its Communist suppression campaign to some change. Besides, its military education should undergo thorough reform. The necessity to take the whole situation into consideration so as to ensure ultimate success relieves the Government of contending with feelings of the gain or loss of a city for a moment in isolated areas.

Moreover, I should like to point out that the Communist bandits with whom the Government is engaged in fighting is linked up with Japanese and Korean Communists who in turn receive support of the Communist International.

To the serious nature of this fact, we should be fully awake. A people with long cumulative weakness, we have never been afraid of aggression and violence. We engaged ourselves in eight years of war in resistance against Japanese militarists and we have been fighting for 25 years the Communist bandits fully equipped with arms and brutality from 1924 to 1945.

During the Northern Expedition the Communist bandit suppression campaign and the war of resistance against Japanese aggression, the national revolutionary army in each of the long periods of fighting underwent many setbacks and experienced heavy losses, but eventually in all cases won glorious victories.

Within the two score and five years the Government had more than once encountered situations far more critical than what it is facing at present. But again without any exception it has overcome all the difficulties and the eventual victories were invariably followed immediately after the heaviest losses.

Through our bitter experiences we build up our firm faith with persevering courage. We shall put up a relentless and unflinching struggle. We have a deep faith in the fact that the bandit suppression campaign and national reconstruction will this time also reach the final success.

After this failure, I am not at all pessimistic. Now, instead, I feel confident China expects that its people and soldiers become thoroughly awake to the national crisis and rise to a man for the national salvation.

What we have relied on was the spirit of nationalism and the Three People's Principle and these cannot be destroyed by whatever intrigues and outrages. We do not think lightly of the gravity of the Communist menace, but we are sure the torturous and dastardly extortion the Communists imposed upon the people so that they have been able to launch offensives one after another, will spell their own doom as they are heading for the old rut they had traversed during the period of 1935 and 1936 when they suffered a total defeat in Kiangsi.

Should the Government be able to receive moral as well as material help from the friendly nations and the support of international righteousness ultimate success, it is sure, could be speedily scored.

The President's answer to the question whether or not the Government will hold Mukden with its full strength is as follows:

It has been the invariable decision of the Government to maintain the territory of and sovereignty over the Northeast since September 1931. In view of the fall of Chinchow and Changchun, the situation in the Northeast as a whole has reached an unfavorable stage. Consequently, Mukden as a city in the Northeastern deadlock, is not as vital as it used to be.

The present situation in Mukden is indeed critical. Government troops, however, are still exerting their last strength to fight against the bandits there at any cost. This is being done to discharge their heaviest duty towards both their people and the world. Of the most important international problems, the Northeast is one. It has significant bearings on the world situation particularly on those nations maintaining close relations with the Pacific throughout the past three years.

Such a heavy and hard task has been shouldered by China only. We, being unable to fulfill our part feel quite regretful. Seventeen years ago with the outbreak of the September 18 incident, I signalled to Democratic nations and the League of Nations a warning confirming that the disaster of a world war had since then begun. Although this warning was not considered important by the various countries, history eventually evidenced the truth that the Northeast question was the prelude to World War II.

History is now repeating itself. If international right cannot prevail and extend its influence and if democracies maintain the same stand by watching the fire ablaze across the river, the world is bound to tread the former path of disaster. Should, unfortunately, Communist bandits control China, another world war would surely descend upon this globe. And should the Communists rule over the nine Northeastern provinces, it would mean the virtual beginning of another world catastrophe. What is more obvious, is that without an integral Northeast, there will be no independent Korea, nor will there be a peaceful East Asia. This much I can firmly say the ominous and treacherous clouds will gather with the trouble in the Northeast as their starting point.

The question as to the serious nature of China's role in the world anti-communist struggle, her position in another world war and if the worst should come to the worst, the effect of the Communist control over her on the world situation, the President answered as follows:

China is endeavoring to exterminate the powerful factor threatening the world peace in order to prevent the outbreak of the third world war, consequently I am not inclined to express my views on that position China should hold. In the world war to come of the 2,100,000,000 population, the Asiatics number over 50 percent and of the 1,100,000,000 population of Asia, the Chinese claim one-third.

The importance of Asia's position in the world and of China's in Asia is too obvious to need superfluous remarks. What I should like to point out is (1) In political organization, economic life, social foundation or cultural standard, Asiatic races lag behind the Europeans. In the West, in the prevailing times of poverty and starvation, it is easier for Communist propaganda and organization to achieve effect, (2) The traditional policy of the Communist Internationale in enforcing its world revolution and the present direction of its expansion center upon Asia. And since the future of Asia revolves around China as its decisive pivot, it is the Communist principle that in order to control the world, it is essential to control Asia and in order to control Asia it is essential to control China. I can decidedly affirm that in case China should be subjugated by the Communists, the third world war would surely follow and mankind would once again be precipitated into a tragic disaster.

If the Chinese Government is able to extirpate the Communist today, the factor lurking in Asia and conducive to the next world war will on this account be eliminated. The Chinese Communists hold armed forces, and the ruthlessness and treachery of the Chinese Communists cannot be compared with those of the believers in communism in any other democratic countries. In spite of the difficult circumstances, the Chinese Government has never given up its responsibility towards the nation and the time adhered to international pledges and sense of duty and in addition endeavors to fulfill moral obligations in the past war against aggression. Now it does the same. I deeply believe, that in the anti-communist struggle, the world should present one whole front. There should have been no difference between West Europe and East Asia in significance. However, in West Europe, nations are advanced in industries and enjoy a higher standard of civilization, nationalism and democracy.

Since a history of over one and a half centuries are deeply rooted in the life and thoughts of the people, it is far less urgent for them to rely on the material and moral aid from the United States in their resistance against communism than for Asiatic races. If the American people and their statesmen are sincere in their work for the welfare of mankind they should start to work in the most vast and the most populous area whose people suffer most in their livelihood. There, the former should lift the living as well as cultural standards of the latter and help them to secure their freedom and independence in order to spare mankind the catastrophe of the third world war. It is particularly necessary to come to Asia's rescue. The center of endeavor in the salvation of Asia must be China. This is the great task unprecedented in human history. I hope that the American people and their statesmen will dedicate their lives to this task.

165 (b)

The Ambassador in China (Stuart) to Secretary Marshall

893.00/11–648

NANKING, *November 6, 1948*

We gathered together senior military personnel JUSMAG and Service Attachés, who, after discussing military situation, were unanimous that short of actual employment of U.S. troops no amount of military assistance could save present situation in view of its advanced stage of deterioration. Agreeing that employment U.S. troops impossible, it was conclusion of group that there was no military step China or U.S. could take in sufficient time to retrieve the military situation. It was agreed that Fu Tso-Yi could not resist attack by forces which Communists can mass against him in North China, and that against Nationalist forces known to be of inferior caliber in Hsuchow area, Chen Yi could reach Yangtze River in vicinity Nanking in two weeks.

We reluctantly reach conclusion, therefore, that early fall present Nationalist Government is inevitable. It is too early to say with certainty whether that Government will be replaced by a Communist Government or by a Communist-dominated coalition. In either event, we shall have to make the best of a bad situation and save what we can from the wreckage.

Embassy will remain Nanking unless developments indicate contrary course desirable, in which case Department's instructions will be requested.

STUART

165(c)

The Consul General at Shanghai (Cabot) to Secretary Marshall

893.00/11–2948

SHANGHAI, *November 29, 1948.*

After discussion regarding possibility transfer of power in Shanghai [a high-ranking Chinese Government official] commented extensively on our China policy. He said he felt it was vital to our national security to keep the "flame of democracy" alive in China. When I pointed out many people doubted that present Government could win against Communists regardless of amount of aid we furnished, he said he fully agreed and added that Government was now detested by great majority of people. He said we could be greatly mistaken, however, if we thought we could do business with Communists and mentioned Chinese knew that liquidation had already started in Tsinan. He then suggested 4-point plan and said that in view gravity of situation U.S. should demand its fulfillment threatening aid otherwise. I pointed out gravity of interference in Chinese internal affairs. Program follows:

(1). Generalissimo should remain head of Government but surrender all real power.

(2). Responsible cabinet should be formed representing all non-Communist elements in China and should assume responsibility for war against Communists.

(3). U.S. supreme military adviser should be appointed in effect to run Chinese armies and should be furnished with massive shipment of arms and munitions.

(4). Primarily to stiffen soldiers morale U.S. should lend 250 million ounces of silver to China to pay soldiers.

The official pointed out that such a cabinet could make clear to Chinese people that this was a war against foreign imperialism. I said that deeply moved as I was by plight of China I could only report what he had said to Washington.

CABOT

165(d)

The Ambassador in China (Stuart) to Secretary Marshall

893.00/12–1648

NANKING, *December 16, 1948.*

Chang Chun, acting as Generalissimo's emissary, sent for me morning December 13. He said that Generalissimo was hearing on all sides that he should withdraw from active control of Government and that this view was shared by Americans; that Generalissimo would like my opinion and advice on such step. We talked about two hours and in true Chinese fashion he did not come to point until near end, but that was burden of his mission. He emphasized report that it was Americans who felt Generalissimo should withdraw. I finally replied that it was certainly impression of most of Americans that I had talked to that great mass of Chinese people felt that Generalissimo, as principal obstacle to termination of hostilities, should step down from his position of authority; that what people of China thought and wanted was dominant factor in our policy formation. Chang Chun continued that according to Generalissimo's reports Americans did not believe there was any close connection between Chinese Communists and U.S.S.R., nor that U.S.S.R. was backing CCP. I replied that in my experience Americans were sure there was close connection between aims and methods of CCP and U.S.S.R., and that former represented faithfully policy of U.S.S.R. in China. This did not mean, I added, that in American opinion Soviet soldiers and technicians were actually participating in civil war on Communist side. I continued that what American Government and people wanted were establishment and general application of human liberties and preservation of independence of China. I said that the present Government should make these objectives theirs and should make them known to people of China as its program; that the Kuomintang should stand on these declared principles in any negotiations with other side, and if it were able to inspire people of China with significance of these principles and reenlist their support in sacrifice and suffering and exile against the threat of totalitarian dominion, the National Government could be sure of active sympathy and support of Government of U.S. wherever in free China it might have to move to continue fight. I said that if peace in China could be achieved on basis of human liberties and national independence, well and good, but that there should be no compromise with principles and that if they required continued resistance the Nationalists would have the support and sympathy of entire non-Communist world.

In response to suggestions for outside help on mediation in present stage, I emphasized over and over that present decisions must come from Chinese, that it must be Chinese initiative which either makes peace on honorable terms or inspires people of China to further resistance of totalitarian aggression. I said that we were interested in what Chinese people wanted and were willing to support; that issues must be clarified and confidence of people secured by Chinese leaders themselves and their policies. I continued that these policies should no longer be on a partisan basis of for or against Chiang Kai-shek or his party or his Government, but that they should be lifted to higher non-partisan plane of individual human rights and national independence.

Chang Chun said he thought he understood and would think very seriously about what I had said. I said that he would have to do more than think about it; that he and other Chinese leaders in and out of Government would have to do something constructive and do it fast.

STUART

165 (e)

The Ambassador in China (Stuart) to Secretary Marshall

893.00/12–1948

NANKING, December 19, 1948

On morning December 17 I visited Sun Fo at his request. He was extremely harassed. He at once said he wanted my advice as an old friend of China, should they go on with war or sue for peace. I explained that I could not give such advice without implicitly representing my country and that my instructions on the matter were explicit. He then asked me to help him on personal grounds as far as I felt would be permissible. I described the American dilemma: We are opposed to spread of communism all over world and anxious to assist in preventing this in China, but on other hand, we cannot do this through a Government that has lost the support of its own peoples; to do so would be contrary to those democratic principles, the violation of which is a principal reason for our objection to communism. In reply to further questions or comments, all of which revealed his genuine perplexity, I pointed out that the all but universal desire of the people was for peace, and that, although this could not be registered by any constitutional process, yet it was as evident to everyone as had been the popular will to resist and the consequent support of the Government during the Japanese wars; that President Chiang's determination to resist to the end, then as now, was magnificent in its personal courage and patriotic purpose, but that his own problem as Premier would seem to lie in whether to support the President, in the face of contrary public opinion and the unfavorable military and fiscal trends, or to have the Cabinet discuss and decide the issue for presentation to the President; that, in other words, it might be helpful to the President if he were advised to relinquish his emergency powers and delegate more authority to the Executive Yuan, or if this were too cumbersome, to a small group who had his confidence and could in some real sense represent or at least interpret the people's will; that this did not necessarily involve the President's resignation, but it ought to mean that the delegation of authority was complete and real.

Dr. Sun asked if I had any special information as to results of Madame Chiang's mission and present attitude of General Marshall. I replied that I knew of no changes in American policy resulting from her visit to Washington; that the Secretary of State was still deeply solicitous over Chinese affairs but that he was probably very much perplexed as to what America could do to help; that nothing more was possible until after Congress had assembled; and that I questioned wisdom of Chinese authorities allowing their decisions to be influenced by any expectation of American military aid under existing conditions.

He then put series of questions as to whether Communists wanted peace, or would abide by their promises, or would not continue to use their armies to overrun China since they had the power, et cetera. I replied that these were all pertinent, but that I had no answers that were more than guesses. He asked if I had any direct contact with the CP leaders and when I replied in the negative he remarked that part of the problem was how to reach them and ascertain their views. He wondered if they were in touch with Soviet Embassy and whether he might not undertake to mediate. When I rather discouraged this approach he expressed hope that U. S. and U. S. S. R. might jointly undertake this, to which I replied that such proposal would have to come from the two Chinese parties before it could even be considered seriously, but that I personally inclined to opinion that Chinese had better try to find their own solution despite all the quite obvious difficulties. He remarked that any decision for peace or war by Executive Yuan would be subject to review by Legislative Yuan which, while in a sense representative of people, had about one-third its membership under CC Clique control, and that it would also involve much argument and publicity.

I then tried to sum up my advice to effect that he and his colleagues would have to debate whether in view of all factors they could from now on fight communism more effectively by military or political methods, and that no outside elements could or should decide this for them nor influence their choice; that I was confident that a very large element of the politically conscious people of country were strongly against communism and its ruthless totalitarianism policy; that they should think in terms of preserving individual liberties and national sovereignty as the fundamental issues rather than of the retention of the KMT and its present leadership as against some other procedure; that I could assure them of continuing American sympathy and readiness to help in whatever ways seemed to be beneficial to the Chinese people and their national independence; and I was personally much more sympathetic than my replies to his questions might seem to indicate.

STUART

165 (f)

The Ambassador in China (Stuart) to Secretary Marshall

893.00/12-2148

NANKING, *December 21, 1948*

May I outline below my personal views re political outlook in China and bearing of this on American policy. This is partly for record but chiefly in order to have full benefit of your instructions.

As you are well aware my original hope had been that by military aid to Chiang Government especially in form of advice upon which all else would be conditioned, it might have been possible to keep area south of Yangtse intact and clear coastal region from Nanking northward of militant Communism. It would have been expected that again with American technical advisers and economic aid there would be improvements in local Government and in people's livelihood which would compare favorably with conditions in Communist territory. National Government would guard its frontier but carry on no aggressive warfare against Communists. This would allow public opinion to take form in both sections and be basis for some sort of negotiated settlement. Whether this would have proven practicable and results have justified our efforts now is immaterial.

Dealing with present realities one must begin as always with President Chiang. It is distressing to observe how completely he has lost public confidence in recent months and how widespread is desire he retire. This sentiment is shared by most officials of all ranks in Government and is almost universal among politically conscious citizens. Opposition to him is primarily because of conviction that war as he has been conducting it is hopeless and is bringing upon people almost unendurable economic and other distress. View is not infrequently expressed that he is best asset Communists have. It is ironical therefore that he refuses to turn over active direction of affairs as he has been repeatedly advised to do because this would be in his opinion tantamount to allowing Communists overrun country. Issue is thus confused in his mind as apparently in case of many in U. S. as though American military aid to him were only alternative to complete Communist domination of China. But it would be in violation of basic principle of democracy to maintain in power man who has lost support of his own people. It would arouse greater sympathy for Communist cause and violent anti-American feeling.

In any case our military men all seem to be agreed that such aid would be too late, even under new leadership. It is probable that resistance groups will carry on for some time in south and west and may form a loose federation. But our military aid to these would at this state be in my opinion very unwise and would certainly complicate matters in coastal provinces and central area.

Government leaders are all constantly asking what American policy is going to be or what our advice to them would be or, more insistently whether it would not be in order for us to advise President to retire or go abroad for trip or in some way eliminate himself from absolute control of affairs. He meanwhile is coercing Sun Fo to form new Cabinet without delay but new Premier in addition to having undergone rather painful operation and being met by refusals as he invites one or another of inner circle of party members, is being thwarted by President's interference as he attempts to make up his list. Dr. Sun is therefore in mood of frustration and Government lacks even semblance of functioning Cabinet. President has been advised by various people to organize small emergency group in Cabinet to which he could delegate full administrative authority while he exerted only his constitutional prerogatives. It is generally recognized that this would only be possible if he withdrew to Kuling or elsewhere under some pretext which at present he has no serious thought of doing. However after having repeatedly tried without success to persuade Hu Shih to become Premier he has induced him to come to Nanking for consultation. He is proposing that Hu form a sort of advisory group as "braintrust" but as Hu points out this would be in effect paper-cabinet and would have no more real power than one it would supersede.

On December 17 I had long talks in each case at their request, with Sun Fo and Hu Shih, and these only served to accentuate quandary that Government is in. The conversation with Hu was especially saddening because he represents finest type of patriotic idealism in his attempt to be loyal to Chiang Government. Hu's argument is that Communism is so implacable and intolerant, so diabolically thorough in its indoctrination and so ruthless in enforcing its totalitarian control even in China that Chiang Kai-shek should be supported despite his shortcomings because he alone sees this and has been uncompromising in resisting it, also because he almost alone among KMT leaders has been free from taint of avarice or other typical vices of Chinese officialdom. He believes that if Chiang were forced to retire Central Government would disintegrate and Communists take over virtually on their own terms. He wonders therefore if America could even now be persuaded to recall JUSMAG and assist Chiang in carrying on war rather than allow Communists dominate country and mold it to their own ends. Tears came to his eyes when he asked me, on basis of our long friendship, to tell him what he should say to President Chiang and what else he could do now that he had determined to give up academic career for service to nation. I told him that primary weakness of Chiang Government was moral rather than military, in sense that troops had lost fighting spirit and people had lost confidence in Government's ability to provide for them as well as in cause for which they were being asked to suffer. America was powerless under these conditions. I had repeatedly urged upon President Chiang supreme importance of rallying public opinion behind him but had failed. I wondered if Hu could lead in another "new thought movement" or "literary revolution" on issues of freedom and democracy as he had done with brilliant success thirty odd years ago. He said he bitterly regretted not having used talents in this field since V-J Day rather than selfishly returning, as he had, to more congenial academic activities. This lengthy comment is to prepare way for discussion of our policy if coalition Government will in course of time be formed. Presumably CP will dominate at outset. But whether they continue to do so or will allow their original [position?] to be diluted or modified will depend on number of factors. One of these is extent to which non-Communist elements will participate and exert liberalizing influence. Another is necessity for CP to adopt tolerant course at beginning because of their own limitations. This would doubtless be nothing more than temporary tactics but in that period inter-action between their own ideology and more liberal ideas might have permanent effects. STUART

165 (g)

The Ambassador in China (Stuart) to Secretary Marshall

893.00/12–2948

NANKING, *December 29, 1948*

I called on General Wu Te-chen, new Vice Premier and Acting Foreign Minister yesterday morning. His concern briefly summed up is that Government has failed in its military action against Communists; that for first time new (#) that in announcement of readiness to consider "an honorable peace" there has been no response from Communists. He is, therefore, greatly puzzled as to what Communists want, and what American advice is.

I explained on this last that American hostility to Communism and interest in welfare of China and her people were both unchanged but that it was inherently impossible for U. S. to make any suggestions or promises that might influence solution of their present problems by Chinese themselves. I added that I had greatest admiration for resolute will-power of Generalissimo in fighting Communism by military means, and that, whatever decision responsible leaders should make as to present crisis, I hoped they would all show that same resolute will in resisting the evils of Communism by every available means. They ought not to think of situation as hopeless and irretrievable. They would probably have some very distasteful and even bitter experiences and outlook might seem very depressing, but more thorough cooperation among themselves and grim determination were called for. They should also win support of people in whatever course of action they undertook. I reminded him in leaving that the U. S. was watching with keenly solicitous interest and readiness to help in whatever ways might seem justifiable and effective when time came.

In course of conversation he raised question of the four other members of "Big Five" undertaking to mediate, and I explained difficulties. His mood is one of being quite aware of desperate military failure and on bafflement over unresponsive attitude of Communists.

He apparently is unaware of negotiations in which Vice President has been involved or at least made no reference to them.

STUART

165 (h)

The Ambassador in China (Stuart) to Secretary Marshall

893.00/12–3048

NANKING, December 30, 1948

A successful formation of the Sun Fo Cabinet does not promise to alter prevailing political trends. Agitation for peace both within and without the government is reaching a crescendo, yet nothing can be done without the assent of the Generalissimo. By virtue of action by the National Assembly, the Generalissimo holds emergency powers allowing him to make virtually all policy decisions. The Cabinet can only advise and assist in implementing the Generalissimo's will. Thus as long as the Generalissimo can exercise command over Nanking garrison and police, he has both de facto and de jure authority to continue the war or adopt a peace policy.

Various reports of the impending retirement of the Generalissimo should not be taken as positive indication of the Generalissimo's intentions in spite of the fact that he summarily removed Wu Ting-chang, his faithful Secretary General and replaced him with Wu Chung-hsin solely because of the latter's known ability as a negotiator and for the avowed purpose of arranging the retirement of the Generalissimo. In the present deteriorating military situation it may be assumed that the Generalissimo has given thought to peace as an alternative to continued hostilities. He is under strong pressure to retire and it is conceivable that he may be persuaded to step aside or that Pai Chung-hsi whose troops now garrison Nanking may force his hand by coup d'etat assisted by Chang Chun, Chang Chih-chung and those others demanding peace. His retirement from the scene is prerequisite for any negotiations with the Communists.

The principal motivation of governmental peace advocates appears that if the Generalissimo retires, the government can negotiate with the Communists and a considerable segment of the present Kuomintang can be preserved as a bloc in the coalition government. This view was strengthened by Li Chi-shen on December 20 in the Hong Kong press announcement which indicated that the present government, less the Generalissimo, would be recognized by the Communists as having legal status as a temporary government for the purposes of negotiation. However, in the December 22 Reuter-AP Hong Kong story, "spokesman for one of major groups of 10 anti-Chiang parties exiled Hong Kong" states

Communists not prepared to enter the coalition government which would have representation from the present Nanking regime. We reported December 16 that Li Tsung-jen has a man in Hong Kong negotiating this point and it is possible that Li Chi-shen's statement is a result of these negotiations.

However, that may be, we consider it unlikely that the Communists will permit the Kuomintang to enter the coalition government as a bloc, but will rather permit participation by individual Kuomintang members selected with care. As we see it, should Generalissimo be persuaded to retire or be forced out, Li Tsung-jen as leader of the government would seek through his proclamation to open negotiations with the Communists. He has little with which to bargain, however, and we think it unlikely that the Communists will be willing to treat with him except in terms amounting to unconditional surrender. Their military forces gathered north of Nanking and already moving to encircle the city are overwhelming. Proclamations promising safety and good treatment to technicians both within and without the government and the precedent set in Tsinan and Mukden make it highly likely that sufficient government and public utility officials would remain in their jobs to ease the problem of running the government which will confront the Communists. Even the Kuomintang leadership is offered the opportunity of getting off the blacklist of war criminals or at least being permitted to survive, by proof of acceptable service to the Communist victory.

Therefore, with anticipated refusal of the Communists to negotiate, with the loss of the Generalissimo's leadership should he have retired command, with the deathblow to what remains of military morale in government forces which would result from publicized effort to negotiate, we believe there is little likelihood that the government can continue to rally sufficient support to maintain resistance as a unit. It would be more likely to disintegrate, leaving the autonomous areas in the west and southwest to make their own accommodations with the Communists.

The central point in the present situation remains, however, the fact that the Generalissimo has not yet taken the final step to relinquish his control and that until he has done so, his opposition to Communism will continue as heretofore. He has said that he would remove to Nanchang, then Canton, and Taiwan if necessary and that he would resort to guerrilla tactics if forced into it, but that he would fight the Communists unto death. Those insisting on peace may succeed in persuading him that he is harming the Chinese people by continued resistance, yet his deep conviction in the inhumanity of Communism with the resulting oppression of the Chinese people may lead him to carry out his threat. It would certainly be a more glorious end and more in the traditional pattern than if he were meekly to step aside to spend his dying days in exile.

STUART

166

A Series of Chronicle Summaries by the American Embassy in Nanking to the Department of State during 1948 on the General Situation

NANKING, *February 17, 1948.*

The Chinese lunar New Year celebrations have just come to an end, and we shall take that as a pretext for sending you this second round-up of our thinking on the China scene. As the Chinese arrange matters, or rather try to arrange matters, everyone embarks on the New Year with a clean slate—a new suit of clothes, a full stomach, all debts paid and past sins forgiven. While this may be true for the individual citizen, it is certainly not so for the body politic. Indeed, with the coming of the New Year, we see no reason to believe that it promises anything better for the people of China than the year of the Pig, which has just passed.

Perhaps the most spectacular occurrences in China during the past month were the riots in Canton and Shanghai. The Canton affair, to judge from the way in which the matter was handled by the Government-controlled press, had its beginnings in a calculated attempt by certain elements in Kwangtung to distract public attention from the domestic crisis by an appeal to the xenophobia generally latent in the Chinese intelligentsia and student groups. The appeal was successful, and there is much to suggest that those who roused the feeling of the mob, went on to lead it to acts of vandalism. That the whole affair was a source of considerable embarrassment to Dr. T. V. Soong, could not but be gratifying to its instigators. The Shanghai disorders, except for the demonstration against the British Consulate General, had a totally different character. Here the students of Tungchi University, the taxi dancers and cabaret employees and the cotton mill workers had long standing grievances over what they felt to be the failure of the Government to meet their political and economic requirements. There was, and is, widespread unhappiness with the economic and political outlook, which is so deepseated as to spring into unrest at the slightest provocation. Disgruntled at their lack of success in negotiating their differences with Government representatives, they turned to force, and, in the end, could only be restrained by force. We may expect more of this unless conditions improve sufficiently to inspire hope of a better day.

In recent weeks, besides the disturbances in Shanghai and Canton, we have had reports of unrest in predominantly rural areas of Southern and Southeastern China. The perennial banditry seems to be on the increase and is occasioned we believe by an increasing feeling on the part of the common people that the Government is unwilling or unable to improve conditions. In spite of the increasing tendency on the part of the Government to cry "Communist" at every disturbance, in none of the civil disturbances of which we have heard do we have any credible information that they were instigated by Communist agitation, or that in their totality they form a pattern of Communist subversive activity. This is not to say, of course, that the Communists will refrain from exploiting to the utmost this tendency on the part of the people to solve their economic and political problems by force. In addition, as civil unrest continues, we may expect that the Communists will try to organize and direct it to their own ends. However, for the time being, it appears that the Government police and military can meet force with force, and keep the situation under control.

The lack of confidence in the Government which is becoming general among the common people, and which has occasionally resulted in open opposition, has a parallel development among certain military and civil officials. Here the discontent is founded on the Government's failure in the purely military phases of the civil war, and its general lack of success in dealing with the problems arising therefrom. We have, for some time, been reporting that a deeply pessimistic and defeatist psychology is growing in Government circles, and we have noticed through the past months as the situation has continued to deteriorate, that this feeling is becoming more widespread and more profound. It is easy to understand how officials underpaid as they are and suffering all the ills of inflation (the Vice Minister for Foreign Affairs gets the equivalent of US$35.00 per month) are becoming more and more convinced that the differences between the Government and the Communists cannot be settled by purely military means, or at least cannot be settled in a way that would leave the authority of the Government preponderant and unchallenged. Basically the Chinese are opportunistic, and an increasing number has its finger in the air to make sure which way the wind is blowing.

There are good grounds for pessimism over the Government's ability to force a favorable military decision. In Manchuria, Government armies remain under siege in a few of the principal cities, and a large, well equipped relieving force from Shantung, which was transported by sea to Hulutao, has not been able to open land communications between that port and the Mukden area. Depending entirely on air transport for supply and reenforcement, and with troops and matériel being depleted in defensive engagements, the position of the Government's Manchurian armies is serious, if not critical. As this is being written, we learn of an extraordinary conference of native Manchurian political and military leaders which is to be convened shortly in the capital; extraordinary in the sense that the Government has not, in the past, shown any disposition to forget past differences and consult with Manchurians on Manchurian problems. Despite the Government's announced determination to hold Manchuria at all costs, we feel that even in its highest echelons the Government is coming to regard its Manchurian venture as a very forlorn hope. Thus, if the conference appraises the Manchurian problem realistically, it can hardly do other than recommend the rescue of Government forces now committed there by withdrawal. If this is attempted we are not altogether convinced that the operation would be tactically feasible.

Elsewhere, in China proper, the Government's military position is no brighter. In Hopei, Gen. Fu Tso-yi's forces are mainly engaged in constructing fortified positions in Jehol, roughly parallel to the Great Wall. This is evidently in anticipation of a Government military collapse in Manchuria, which would release Communist armies there for an offensive in China proper. General Fu can scarcely hope to defend this position in strength, and, at the same time, cope with the Communist armies in southern and central Hopei, should they coordinate an offensive with a drive to the south by the Manchurian Communists. The recent reappearance of regular Communist forces in northern Kiangsu has forced the Government to concern itself with the defenses of the northern approaches to Shanghai and of the capital itself. To the west of Hankow, the Communists even have a foothold on or near the north bank of the Yangtze, and will, in all likelihood, soon be able to interdict river shipping unprotected by naval convoy between Szechuan and middle and lower Yangtze ports.

In the sphere of economics, the Government has apparently done better than in its military operations. Vigorous policing of the black market in foreign currency, better smuggling control and a more restricted allotment of foreign exchange for imports has stemmed the advance of the Chinese dollar in terms of foreign currencies. However, this has operated in restraint of export trade and a consequent gain of foreign exchange, since prices of native commodities continue to spiral upwards. Also, recent measures for the centralization of financial controls in the Bank of China, which thereby becomes a national bank in effect, if not in form, provides a more rational banking structure for the country, and brings it under the direction of more responsible political elements than has hitherto been the case. However, the one fact in the economic situation which impresses most Chinese is the upspring in commodity prices unaccompanied by comparable increases in wages and salaries. It is this fact, as much as any other, that is responsible for the growing opposition of the people to their government.

The flow of American relief supplies to China, which is now under way, and the prospect of further aid in the near future has met with a mixed reception. The higher officials of the Government, while expressing suitable gratification, openly say that this aid will be of value only in so far as it may be the forerunner of greater things to come. At least one of the Government's foreign economic advisors has stated that aid as now contemplated will not ameliorate the Government's economic plight to any appreciable degree. Liberal intellectual and even business circles oppose aid on the ground that the Government is certain to misuse it, and that at best it will serve as only a temporary prop for the groups in power and so prolong a civil war which the Government will lose in any event.

Given the conditions we have described above, there is nothing surprising in the fact that many Chinese, both civil and military officials, as well as groups outside the Government, are actively seeking a means to end the civil war. They are aware that this can come only through a negotiated settlement with the Communists, but we doubt that there is any realization that such a settlement would in all likelihood result in either a coalition government in which the Communists would play the dominant role, or in a territorial arrangement which would give the Communists time to consolidate their gains and reform their forces for the next offensive stake. That such an accommodation is likely, is denied by many high government officials, particularly those closest to the Generalissimo. However, we have much information to the effect that even in the Army there is strong sentiment for a negotiated peace.

As we have stated before, the main barrier to a negotiated settlement is the intransigence of the Generalissimo and his closest supporters on one hand, and the Communists on the other. As yet there appears to be no effective, organized opposition to the Generalissimo, yet such opposition seems to be forming. The recently announced candidacy of Gen. Li Tsung-jen for the Vice Presidency may well provide leadership for opposition to the Generalissimo on this matter, and, if General Li should be elected, he would have means for making this opposition effective.

There seems to be some evidence that the Communists would, at this time, view with favor a chance for a negotiated settlement. They are now in a position militarily and politically to demand as much or more than in 1945-1946, and the Government—less the Gimo—might be willing to accede to these demands. Also, the Communists may feel a compulsion to consolidate their political control over the areas they now occupy, or would receive from a negotiated settlement, to train administrative personnel for the government of these areas and to make the necessary preparations for the political penetration of the rest of the country. . . .

Thus, the New Year which confronts the Chinese people presents a picture of little hope, much travail, and small prospect of a solution of their problems. We have noted a tendency to hold everything until the extent and the character of the Aid-to-China program is known. We have endeavored to counteract this tendency by pointing out to all who would listen that the major effort must come from the Chinese themselves and that the best way to insure American aid would be for the Chinese to initiate definite measures for their own economic betterment, but we have encountered expressions of intentions to do just that which were tinged with insincerity.

NANKING, *March 18, 1948.*

At the time our last letter was written, the Generalissimo had secluded himself at Kuling for a winter vacation. His absence from the helm of the ship of state lasted more than three weeks, and through this period he saw no one of consequence in his government. As may be imagined, this excursion in ergophobia gave rise to the wildest rumors, not the least sensational of which was that he had become convinced of his incompetency in governing, and so was selecting his successor. However, better informed and more knowledgeable persons agreed that he had retired to consult with himself as to what measures might be effective in the present exigency, and that on his return to the capital he either would or would not promulgate radical changes in policy. If the latter were true, it was held this could be taken as an indication that the Generalissimo is satisfied that his present policies are adequate to the task at hand.

Over two weeks have elapsed since the Generalissimo's return. In this period he has made no notable policy statements, nor have we any indication that any are contemplated. He has exhorted his officials to improve and purify their administration of public affairs, and he has informed the nation of the government's intention to defend Manchuria come what may, but he has in no wise indicated that he has any new solution for the tasks confronting him. If this be so, and we are of the belief that it is so, we take it as an indication that the Government has no new solution, and so we can see no reason to hope for a halt in the processes of decay and disintegration which have characterized the China scene these past several years.

We have not noted, since our last letter, any particularly spectacular examples of further disintegration in the Government's over-all position. However, the decline continues, and there is little doubt but what the Government will soon be faced with new crises. What is, perhaps, the salient characteristic of the Government's present situation is the fact while certain of its leaders have excellent and feasible plans for solving certain specific problems, there does not exist in the Government a complete and dynamic leadership to integrate such plans, implement them and carry them out. For example, Gen. Wei Li-huang, the Government commander in Manchuria, has an adequate plan for the continued defense of the Mukden area, yet the Government shows no signs of meeting Wei's fairly modest requirements. At the same time, Manchurian leaders have advised the Government that much support could be won from the Communists in the Northeast if the people of Manchuria were given more responsibility and authority in the management of their own affairs, under their own leaders. By way of reply, the Government offered honorary titles to the Manchurian leaders, announced its intention to hold Manchuria at all costs, and seemingly paid no heed to this advice. Similar examples of the attitude of the Government to the problems of China proper could be cited at great length, an attitude expressed in a policy of passive resignation to the many vicissitudes confronting it.

As we have reported before, the people of China, both officials and ordinary citizens regard with increasing disfavor this government which does not govern, or at most governs through inertia. Bitter criticism of its leadership is commonly expressed. The Generalissimo, once regarded as the unfortunate victim of incompetent advisors, is now viewed as personally responsible for his country's ills and feeling runs strong that any great prolongation of his leadership must certainly involve the entire country in ruin. In this situation many officials, particularly those outside the capital, believe that the time has come when they must look to their own interests as a matter of self preservation, and are so proceeding to develop a direct and personal control in the regions where they are assigned. We have been informed that Dr. T. V. Soong now seeks to increase his military resources in Kwangtung, and to integrate Hunan, Kwangsi, Kiangsi and Fukien into his province. In Hopei and Chahar there is some evidence to suggest that Gen. Fu Tso-yi may already have attained some degree of independence from Nanking control in the military sphere. Likewise, the Muhammadan leaders in Ninghsia show signs of questioning the authority of the Central Government, and in Shantung the provincial governor, Gen. Wang Yao-wu, has been openly critical of Government policies and has evinced a desire to seek American aid on a semi-independent basis. From these and similar indications, we conclude that local leaders in several parts of the country are, from lack of faith in the Central Government to continue to perform its functions, beginning to exhibit particularistic tendencies.

Besides this new growth of regionalism, we note, as we have reported, that the Government's ineptitude, particularly as regards the prosecution of the civil war, has brought some officials to consider the advisability of a mediated settlement with the Communists. Despite official Government denials, through its recent military attaché, Gen. Roschin, the Soviet Government informally suggested to certain Government leaders that the good offices of the Soviet Union could be obtained to arrange a mediated end to the present civil strife. The fact that, subsequent to his having made this suggestion, the Government, aware that he had done so, accepted General Roschin as the new Soviet Ambassador to China, leads us to believe that accommodation with the Communists must be favored by many influential persons within the government as preferable to a continuation of the status quo. The Chinese with whom we talk are of the opinion that accommodation means coalition government, and that through participating in a coalition government the Communists might come to control all of China by political means. Yet, faced as they are with mounting defeats in the civil war, and with the most colossal chaos in the administration of the nation's affairs, they cling to a forlorn hope that more can be salvaged from a mediated peace than would be saved if the entire country were to fall into Communist hands as the political disintegration develops.

The fact that at least some members of the Government look with favor on a Soviet offer to mediate an end to the civil war does not, in our opinion, necessarily indicate a firm trend for the Government to orient itself toward the Soviet Union, rather than the United States. Soviet mediation would, we feel, be accepted by non-Communist Chinese only with great reluctance, and only if it were clear that the negotiations with the Communists could come no other way. Except in very limited circles, the U.S.S.R. has no following in non-Communist China, and it is almost universally feared, disliked and mistrusted there. However, the possibility remains that the Soviets may succeed, perhaps through the insistence of their Chinese party, in forcing the Government to accept them as mediators.

In this situation, the slow increase of anti-American sentiment in the country is noteworthy. The origins of this sentiment are complex. In its most vocal expression, as it occurs in the statements of such public personages as Dr. Sun Fo, it is but little more than irresponsible and malicious talk. In other instances it is probably the result, direct or indirect, of Communist propaganda which reiterates the simple, but effective, theme of the Alliance between American imperialism and the rapacious and corrupt reactionary, Chiang Kai-shek. Effective as the Communist propaganda is, it largely serves to reinforce a common conviction, which we have referred to elsewhere, that the Generalissimo is, in fact, leading the country to ruin and chaos, and that he could not do so if it were not for the support which the American government has given him. Regardless of the validity of this idea, it is, as we say, commonly held. Although it is not, of course, found in the Government controlled press, this opinion is held by the intellectuals who staff the press, and so causes them to attack us and our policies for other matters, not directly pertinent to this issue.

As we have suggested above, the main political issue before most non-Communist Chinese today is how a settlement with the Communists can be reached which will leave a maximum of political control with non-Communist elements. It seems clear now that even those Chinese who are most strongly anti-Communist feel that this must be achieved by political means since it cannot be done by military methods. At the moment, the principal barrier to a political settlement is the Generalissimo and some of his closest followers, for, even though they might be inclined to accept such measures, there is no likelihood that the Communists would negotiate with any government led by the Generalissimo and participated in by some of his associates. In these circumstances, the question arises as to whether the Generalissimo would retire so as to make such negotiations possible. We feel sure that he will not do so as long as he has any hope that our military assistance to him will be of a scale and scope sufficient to allow him to gain a military decision or to prolong the civil war until such time as other events may force us to intervene decisively in his favor.

However, regardless of the fact that the Generalissimo may himself decide to depend on a military decision for a settlement of the civil war, there are some strong indications, as we have suggested, that he may not be allowed to do so, for opposition to this course of action continues to mount, and is becoming concrete and organized. It is in this connection that the vice-presidential candidacy of Gen. Li Tsung-jen is significant. General Li's candidacy was announced without reference to the Generalissimo. He has attracted support from Dr. Hu Shih, from other academicians and intellectuals, and, we believe, from many political personages of importance. There is some evidence to suggest that he will have a large amount of support from army circles, and possibly from Marshal Li Chi-shen and his followers. General Li's principal opposition lies in the C. C. Clique, which will support Yu Yu-jen. It is likely that Yu will have the Generalissimo's backing as well. Since the election will be held in the Legislative Yuan, which is almost entirely packed by the C. C. Clique, it is likely that Yu will be elected. However, this cannot be taken as a certainty, for provincial leaders will exercise much influence over provincial delegations, and a real contest may develop. In any event, dissatisfaction with the activities of the Government's leadership will be freely expressed.

As will be noted from the foregoing, we are now entering an era of political change in China. Not all of the forces which make for this change are immediately clear. Though some of the larger outlines are beginning to emerge, any comments as to how current trends will work out must be highly speculative. However, we are on relatively sure ground when we point out, as we have above, that present Government leadership is in the process of being repudiated by those who have formerly supported it; that opposition to this leadership is becoming concrete and organized, and is primarily based on opposition to the Government's policy of settling the Communist question by military means; that the present leadership must almost certainly go unless actively sustained in power by us; and, that if there is a change in leadership, the new leaders will reach a political settlement with the Communists which may very likely result in some form of coalition.

NANKING, *May 1, 1948*

Whatever the ultimate result of the recent session of the National Assembly and the elections of the first President and Vice President under the Constitution, it seems to me that two phenomena were made clear: Firstly, the Gimo, by masterful political strategy, coupled, I believe, with at least a certain amount of sincerity, refused to be a candidate for the Presidency, with the result that he finds himself elected to that office with confirmed authority, albeit somewhat battered by the fray. He succeeded in establishing his indispensability at this stage, even though his policies have been repudiated, and in demonstrating that he, and he alone, can hold together the present governmental structure based, as it is, on the support of more or less independent Generals, with their more or less personal armies, who are restrained from declaring their complete regional autonomy by self-interest, of course, but also largely by their loyalty to the Generalissimo. Should he disappear from the scene at this time, they would inevitably revert, I believe, to the regionalism that existed prior to the march north of the Kuominchun and we would see an era of *sauve qui peut*.

Secondly, the liberals, or the reformers, or whatever you wish to call them—those who were rapidly becoming desperate in their desire to bring new life into a government that was slowly, but surely, committing suicide—were able to demonstrate and make effective their strength by rallying behind Li Tsung-jen, who has emerged, whether he is qualified or not, as the great reformer, and elected him Vice President despite the most violent efforts of an efficient CC Clique machine, supported by an irate, but arrogant and not too adept Generalissimo. The reactionary, who agreed to a secret ballot in that election, will now rue the day he did so. I am told that when Li Tsung-jen's strength became evident, the Generalissimo called Chen Li-fu on the mat and there were heated words as to why Chen had not been able to control the vote as he had promised. Maybe now Chen will once more, as he has in the past, express a desire to visit the U.S. to study "democratic institutions"!

Our interest during the past few weeks, has, of course, been largely centered on these meetings of the National Assembly. Its activities have had pride of place in the press and have formed the topic of conversation everywhere. Even the shopkeeper, avid for his gain, kept one ear on the radio, while the other was listening to his customer. Also, wherever there was a loud-speaker on the streets of Nanking, crowds could be found listening to the results.

Going back a little bit, our information indicates that in the elections to the National Assembly and to the new Legislative Yuan, as well as during the first meetings of the Assembly, it was evident that the party bosses of the KMT regarded the establishment of constitutional government as an exercise in machine politics. It was obviously their intention to use the party machine and the prestige of the Generalissimo to control the new Government as they had the old, and they were prepared to use whatever means were necessary to accomplish this end. They were aghast, therefore, when the Generalissimo, without, I believe, real prior consultation with his supporters, announced his intention not to stand for President. It was the decision he had made in Kuling over the Chinese New Year and which had been long and expectedly awaited although no one, I believe, had previous knowledge of the nature of the decision he had made. To the party machine, the Generalissimo was an indispensable man. He had helped create and had protected the machine and since he ruled through it, it was indispensable to him as well. The Whampoa Generals, the Paoting Generals, and the Generals of no Clique whatsoever, including the Mohammedan Generals of the West, all of whom care little for the Nationalist Government, insisted that if he left the Ship of State, so would they. This situation cannot have been unknown to the Generalissimo, and it is for this reason, even though we do not question his sincerity, that we credit him with a masterful political tactic when he refused to stand for President. Having let himself be persuaded, which, if our assumption is correct, was not a difficult task, that he was indispensable to the country, the circumstances of his past forced him once again to strive to bring the party machine with him in full power into the new Government, to exclude its opponents, and to amend the Constitution so as to make the new Government susceptible to his personal control as had been that Government which was passing. Through an amendment to the Constitution, he obtained the full powers necessary to maintain his personal control and he sought continued power for the party machine through his support of Sun Fo for the Vice Presidency, with every indication that the party machine would find some way to see that Sun Fo remained also as the elected President of the Legislative Yuan.

The machine had rigged the elections to the National Assembly and had thus retained an almost solid bloc of delegates which could be strictly controlled, and which included politically experienced individuals well able to stir the Assembly and to control its deliberations. Also, it had at its disposal a disciplined corps of political workers skilled in such minor political arts as bribery and intimidation. It had a controlled press, which could be counted on not to expose its more flagrant violations of the amenities of democratic procedure and it had at its service, at least so most delegates thought, the secret police. Finally, through its affiliation with the Whampoa Generals, an affiliation so close as to make them, to all intents and purposes, a part of the machine, it had with the bulk of the Army High Command.

Thus, the party machine was an organized political force of no little magnitude. Yet it was committed in support of reactionary principles, which had been implicitly, if not openly and explicitly, rejected by the rank and file of the KMT, and by independent individuals and groups within Nationalist China. These principles involved essentially the perpetuation of the personal autocratic rule of the Generalissimo and his closest followers.

The opponents in the KMT of this reactionary leadership had, and still have, no cohesive organization. Such union as is found among them is based on their common dissatisfaction with the Government's lack of concrete achievement, on their well-grounded fear that the Government, as at present constituted, cannot prevent the further spread of Communism, and on their belief in democracy and in constitutional government. A benevolent despotism had remained despotic while ceasing to be benevolent. The community of interest and views among opponents of the party machine would not, in the ordinary course of events, suffice to move them to united action, yet the flagrant intervention of the machine in the elections and the all too obvious intervention of the machine and of the Generalissimo in the deliberations of the Assembly and in the Assembly's Vice Presidential elections, moved most delegates to consider ways and means of protecting their interest and of representing their constituents.

As a result, revolt against party solidarity developed. The clash came to a head in the Vice Presidential elections. Independent delegates had shown disgruntlement when the party machine, during the meetings of the Assembly, had successfully prevented free debate of the shortcomings of the Government, and they felt further frustration when the Generalissimo and the party machine intervened, all too openly, to prevent the election of Li Tsung-jen. (We are told on good authority that the Generalissimo called in Li Tsung-jen and demanded his withdrawal and that at one stage he offered Ch'eng Ch'ien, who was running third, complete reimbursement for all his campaign expenses if he would withdraw in favor of Sun Fo.) The frustration of these independent delegates and of the disgruntled members of the KMT coalesced in support of Li Tsung-jen as the one who had campaigned for reform.

Aroused by this evidence of mounting dissatisfaction and organized opposition, the KMT machine threw all its resources into the battle, vilifying Li and intimidating his supporters. These tactics aroused violent resentment and Li, in a masterful manoeuvre, announced his withdrawal from the race in order to demonstrate clearly the nature and source of the attacks to which he and his supporters were being subjected. There is evidence that his withdrawal was concerted with that of Ch'eng Ch'ien. As was anticipated, Li's move, supported by that of Ch'eng Ch'ien, gained the sympathy of the general public and of those delegates to the National Assembly not under strict machine control. Blame for the situation was increasingly placed on the Generalissimo, and since Ch'eng Ch'ien, the only other nonmachine candidate remaining in the race, had withdrawn in sympathy with Li, the Generalissimo was forced to direct Sun Fo to withdraw his candidacy as well. Also, in order to persuade Li and Ch'eng to re-enter the race, the Gimo was compelled to give absolute assurances, both private as well as public, that the Vice Presidential race would henceforth be free and without party duress, each member of the National Assembly being allowed to vote as his conscience dictated. Incidentally, to make sure the Generalissimo didn't go back on his promises, the Assembly delegates took elaborate precautions to see that the vote was not only secret, but that the ballots were also accurately counted. The result of all this, as is known to you, was the election of Li Tsung-jen as Vice President by 143 votes (1,438 to 1,295), or, in other words, a photo finish.

It remains to be seen whether the emergence of Li Tsung-jen, as what might be called leader of a reform group, can be confirmed. Those who supported him are of divergent views, and of his qualities as a political leader, we know little, though he shows promise. We can only hope that these stirrings of democracy which were so evident in the Vice Presidential election may grow into legitimate and effective opposition to the reactionary elements in the Government. What existed as opposition to the Generalissimo and to the KMT party machine was, in essence, we believe, a demand for change and reform which had not yet become an organized political force. Having shown sufficient strength to elect Li Tsung-jen as Vice President in spite of the strenuous efforts of the CC Clique, backed by the Generalissimo, the reformers now have a spokesman, and their chosen leader can speak with authority if he plays his cards well. Nevertheless, the Generalissimo and the machine control the key posts in the Government, and how they will accommodate themselves to the pressure for change remains to be seen. We can only hope that the liberal elements which have thus expressed themselves will be able to assert strength toward reform within the Government and within the country sufficient to give some hope that the present onsweep of Communist expansion may be checked and some day reversed.

In the meantime the lull in military activities does not warrant, we believe, any confidence in the ability of the Government at the moment to checkmate any Communist move which Communist strategy may dictate. The Generalissimo announced on New Year's that the Communists would be of no military importance between the Yellow and Yangtze Rivers in six months. Yet months have gone by and we see little sign of action toward accomplishing that end. Weihsien in Shantung, the first walled city to go by frontal attack supported by heavy artillery, is only one more example of the incapability of the National Leadership to direct an offensive. Here, as elsewhere, the Nationalist troops encamp behind walls and wait for the Communists to come pick them off. Present indications are that the Communists may by-pass Mukden, and strike toward Chinhuangtao.

Yet we see no real activity to counter this move. Fu Tso-yi in Peiping, as has Wang Yao-wu in Shantung, is showing increasing tendencies toward independence, and we find it difficult to believe that he will remain in that area under serious Communist threat. We are watching the situation closely in hope that we can give Americans in that area sufficient advance warning should we become convinced that Fu Tso-yi will not fight, but will withdraw toward Chahar and Suiyuan. Wang Yao-wu has already warned Americans in Shantung to seek places of safety, and the situation in Central China looks none too good. There are already creditable rumors that the Communists have penetrated south of the Yangtze and that we will be hearing in due course from new concentrations. Unless some means can be found to revive the spirit of the Nationalist troops and possibly, just barely possibly, Li Tsung-jen and his backers may be able to accomplish this, there seems little hope of effective resistance to continued expansion of the Communists where and when they will.

We have been interested in the failure of Roschin, the former Soviet Military Attaché in Nanking, who has been Soviet Ambassador Designate here, to return to Nanking. We were told the other day that he has asked for a visa and is expected here early in May. We feel that the timing of his arrival has some meaning, but as yet we have no good guess.

One element in the Li Tsung-jen candidacy which has worried us, has been the possibility that he might seek an accommodation with the Communists, and there is recent evidence that he may have had, and may maintain, contact with the KMT Revolutionary Committee in Hong Kong. It is not entirely beyond the realm of possibility, therefore, that Roschin's return to Nanking at this time may in some way be connected with developments in the National Assembly.

NANKING, *June 12, 1948*

Although the military situation has been deteriorating at an alarming rate during the past month, the attention of Government leaders has been directed almost entirely to political maneuvering and the election of a new Government.

With the selection of the Premier and the Cabinet, Government under the new Constitution has finally come into being. The personnel of the new Government is largely recruited from the old, and the new elements present are so dominated by the groups which held power before that no far-reaching changes in policy are likely.

In general, the reaction of the country to the new Government is most unfavorable. We have heard few expressions of faith that it is competent to improve the situation, and there is much talk that it will soon be replaced. When the National Assembly met, it was hoped by many that somehow, through its deliberations, a political renaissance would be effected, which would culminate in the creation of a strong Government capable of halting the spread of Communism. The Generalissimo was given extraordinary powers to achieve this end, and his critics offered their advice and their services to assist him. What was wanted of the Generalissimo was dynamic, effective leadership. The Generalissimo, however, has failed to respond to this demand. While he has retained his almost unlimited authority, he has come forward with no new program. His rejection of the services of Li Tsung-jen as an advisor, and his continued reliance on incompetent men to head the new Ministries combine to convince most people that his leadership will continue to be uninspired and essentially disruptive. Since it has become apparent that he intends to continue his personal rule, and has no intention of responding to the popular demand for change, widespread dissatisfaction develops, and the Generalissimo has become more unpopular than at any time in his career.

In view of this increasing dissatisfaction with the Generalissimo and his Government, it is surprising that there is no apparent popular demand for his removal from office. The opposition elements within the Government talk mainly in terms of supplanting the C. C. Clique and of offering the Generalissimo better and more disinterested advice. If there were open agitation for the Generalissimo's removal, rather than covert dissatisfaction with his rule, Li Tsung-jen and certain groups in the Government would probably respond to it. But there is no popular, open movement in this direction, although the Generalissimo loses in prestige each day he fails to provide that leadership necessary to rally the people in defense against Communism. The prevailing mood is one of despair and resignation to what is regarded as the inevitable victory of Communism. Furthermore, there is a growing belief that Communism would be a not unattractive alternative to the present ineffective regime, particularly since such a change would bring with it an end to civil war.

As an accommodation with the Communists might be expected to include the removal from the scene of the Generalissimo with whom the Communists may be expected to refuse to deal, the question of his successor immediately arises and there is no obvious person available. The Generalissimo has dominated the scene for so long, no one stands out as capable of replacing him. Li Chi-shen of the Kuomintang Revolutionary Committee is, of course, "available" yet we have no way of gauging the strength of his support. It might easily be someone within the Kuomintang itself. Nevertheless, we find it difficult to believe that the Generalissimo can be removed from the scene except at the expense of national unity. It was demonstrated most clearly in the Presidential election that it is the Generalissimo that holds this vast country together and that without him it would likely fall apart. Should he leave the scene and should regionalism result, the Communist task would be made much more easy.

In the military field, it is obvious that the Communists continue to gain and the Government appears incapable of saving that part of China not yet in Communist hands. The military position of the Government is deteriorating rapidly and has become critical in several areas. The Government armies in Manchuria are virtually isolated, must inevitably be contained in their present positions by siege and cannot influence the military decision in China proper, even though their capitulation should be long postponed. The Communist offensive in Jehol is succeeding in reducing the local Nationalist garrisons, and Fu Tso-yi finds himself under heavy attack along the Jehol border. While General Fu should be able to stop the initial assault against his northern defenses, the fact that he has large Communist armies on his flanks and his rear makes his situation dangerous. It is probable that, as the campaign progresses, the Manchurian Communists will be able to secure a foothold on the North China Plain.

Except for a minor Nationalist victory in Northern Kiangsu, there have been no Nationalist successes through the past month. A large Communist concentration has crossed the Yellow River without opposition northwest of the junction of the Lunghai and Tsinpu railroads. The Tsinpu has been cut near Taian, isolating Tsinan. Lin-yi, the last Government garrison in Southern Shantung, is now under attack, and is not expected to offer prolonged resistance. The Communists are in sufficient force just north of the Lunghai to besiege Hsuchou, or to by-pass that point and drive toward the north bank of the Yangtze, near Nanking. While their intentions are not yet clear, the latter move remains a strong possibility.

Observers report no improvement in the morale of the Nationalist forces, now at a dangerously low ebb. Field Commanders and troops are unwilling to fight, except as a last resort, and large-scale defection of combat elements confronted with battle can be expected to continue. While the Government's military situation has probably not yet become critical in the sense that a general military collapse is imminent, only inspired and dynamic military leadership can long postpone, let alone avert, that eventuality, and there are no officers having such qualities in positions of authority.

The general public is well aware of the continuing deterioration in the political, military and economic spheres and is disillusioned and despairing of improvement. In this situation, the notion that stability can come only through the cessation of the civil war has become an *idee fixe*, the currency of which spreads rapidly. Thus, the people of Nationalist China become less and less inclined actively to resist Communism. In this state of mind, our China Aid Program is condemned, even by its direct beneficiaries, as a factor prolonging the civil war. Since the Government prohibits anti-civil war propaganda, this condemnation of our aid is sublimated and transferred into an attack on our policies in Japan by student groups and other elements of the population. This nascent anti-American feeling is, of course, exploited and fanned by Communist propaganda organs, and is further fostered by some elements of the Government-controlled press, which uses this means to distract attention from the Government's own shortcomings. There is inherent in this situation a very grave danger to the American position in China. We still have in this country a large backlog of good-will, particularly among the educated classes. However, in their present suffering the people of China do not discriminate between friend and enemy. Nor do they clearly perceive where their interests lie. In the eyes of many Chinese, we bear the onus for supporting and keeping in power an unpopular regime which does not have the interests of the country at heart. We are blamed for preventing its replacement by a government which promises, as they see it, to be an improvement. And we are further condemned because the regime we support patently fails to meet the minimum requirements that any people asks of those who rule it. This state of mind, we believe, is playing no small part in the present student anti-American campaign.

On the other hand, recent reports from Communist territory indicate that the Communists have difficulties of their own. The principal of these is a shortage of qualified administrative personnel for political posts, and a lack of personnel with the more advanced economic skills. Their revolutionary program and propaganda are now designed to secure the support of potential administrators, but the violence and brutality which has characterized their political activity continue to alienate many. However, in appealing to administrators and to persons possessing knowledge of advanced agricultural, industrial and commercial techniques, the Communist leaders have had to jettison their practice of economic egalitarianism. This costs them at least some of the support of the agrarian and industrial proletariat which forms the mass basis for their revolution. Although the Communists have been spectacularly successful in the military sphere, their victories have been over a most incompetent opponent. Should the efficiency of the Government armies be restored, even to its war-time level, the Communists could no longer hope for cheap victories. Indeed, as the military situation now stands, the Communists may be forced to undertake campaigns involving formal, positional warfare. The Communists have yet to win a battle under such conditions, and should the Government armies dictate the conditions of battle, as they are capable of doing, some large Communist defeats can be anticipated.

It is a black picture, yet in the final analysis, we incline to the belief that the situation of the Government, critical though it is, is not entirely beyond repair. The adoption of only a few positive policies would improve its position immensely. What the Government now suffers from as much as anything is that its own personnel and its own supporters have no confidence in it. To cite a single instance, a high ranking Chinese Government Army officer has told one of the staff officers of AAG that the Executive Yuan is refusing to provide funds for certain military expenditures on grounds that the civil war is already lost.

We are doing what we can to bolster morale in Government circles and we are leaving no stones unturned in our efforts to assure that advantage will be taken of the respite afforded by the Aid to China Program to institute the reforms and find the leadership necessary to rally the people and encourage them to resist Communist expansion. If those vast numbers who do not want to be Communists can be given even one ray of hope it may yet be possible to turn the tide though time is rapidly running out.

NANKING, *August 24, 1948*

In recent weeks the Chinese political scene has been characterized by obscurity. Trends and developments which had been clear and traceable became less evident, and the various definite patterns of political activity which we had been watching became ill-defined and indistinct. It became evident, however, that certain stabilizing factors are beginning to retard the recent rapid decline in the Government's position. We do not feel that these factors will be permanently effective in the sense that they will halt once and for all the general deterioration pervading Nationalist China. Disintegrating forces are still dominant. However, we feel that the Government is in somewhat less danger of collapse than was the case a month or six weeks ago. In fact, the Gimo and his new Cabinet under Wong Wen-hao are showing signs of determination to survive.

The principal dangers to the Government continue to be the progressive deterioration of the military situation, the prospect of a breach in Nationalist ranks through the formation of regional political associations, the crisis in the national economy and the inability of the Government to exercise effective political controls in many spheres of public and private activity. The Government is well aware of the gravity of this situation, and, in its own way, is developing means for meeting it.

The most important recent event, of course, is the series of financial and economic measures promulgated by the Executive Yuan on August 20. A new currency called the Gold Yuan is established, the bank notes themselves being the so-called Sun currency which was actually printed about three years ago. CNC is to be converted to the Gold Yuan at the rate of three million to one, and the Gold Yuan itself has a gold content valuation which works out at four to one U.S. dollar. The Government announced that this currency will be backed by holdings of bullion, specie and foreign exchange amounting to U.S. $200,000,000 and the pledge of securities in Government-owned enterprise, on which latter a valuation of U.S. $300,000,000 has been placed. There is a provision that the Gold Yuan cannot be issued in an amount exceeding the value of this backing. At the moment this is academic since it is calculated that the U. S. dollar value of total CNC and NEC outstanding is only in the neighborhood of U.S. $70,000,000. The difference between that sum and the total "backing" is the authority to the printing presses to meet the deficit in the coming months. So much for the highlights of the currency measures.

The currency reform was accompanied by a series of measures designed to accomplish the near-balancing of the Government's budget, and the reduction of the export-import deficit. Many of these measures involve future executory acts, clarifying regulations, and the establishment of enforcement machinery. Exports are to be stimulated, imports cut, wages and prices frozen as of the August 19 levels, strikes banned, and holdings of gold, silver, and foreign currency, at home and abroad, are to be nationalized. In connection with the latter, there is a whale of an informer's fee; to wit, 40% of the Government's recovery in any individual case.

All of this represents Wong Wen-hao's supreme effort. It has been received so far with complete skepticism by sophisticates and some genuine expressions of hope and relief by rick-shaw boys. Real effort is being made to appeal to the patriotism of all the Chinese people and the Gimo has thrown his full influence behind it. It might work, but if it does it will only be because the Government executes the program with ruthlessness, courage and effectiveness.

So far as the future of the Gold Yuan is concerned, it seems to us the only real change is, first, the acceptance and legalization of the black market rate as the new official exchange rate. If internal prices can be, in fact, frozen as is the intention, this should have a highly beneficial effect on exports. The second accomplishment is nominal. It is the removal of the daily inconvenience which has been entailed in handling bales of CNC for even minor transactions. Otherwise, the basic factors remain just what they were before the measures were promulgated; there is no more backing to the new currency than existed for the old, and the budget of the Government is just as hopelessly out of balance today as it was last week. We don't want to appear unduly pessimistic, but our guess is that we will have a very few weeks of relative stability in prices and then the new Gold Yuan will start sliding in terms of the U.S. gold dollar, picking up where the late, unlamented CNC left off.

In the military field the Government's efforts continue ineffectual. The bulk of its field commanders have proven themselves incompetent in battle, and ignorant or neglectful of the primary objective of military operations—the destruction of the enemy. The Government can still compel and entice its armies to continue resistance, but it does not appear able to mobilize its military and other resources and use them in the offensive effort necessary to restore the military situation to its own advantage. A case in point is now shaping up in the Hsuchow area. The Governor has been anticipating strong Communist attack on Hsuchow and has been concentrating troops in that area. As matters now stand, General Chen-yi, with his strong Communist columns, is maneuvering in the area around Yingchow in Northwest Anhwei. He has gotten himself into such a position that it would be a not too difficult task for the Government troops to encircle him and annihilate his forces. This they plan to do, yet our experience cautions us to anticipate that inability of the Government to compel obedience to its commands, lack of uniform command in the theater, unwillingness of one Government General to cooperate with another or come to the aid of another, and the traditional Chinese inclination to leave an avenue of escape open so as to avoid real battle if possible, will all result in much maneuvering, little actual fighting, and the retirement North of Chen Yi's forces practically intact.

If the Government troops should surprise us and actually encircle and annihilate Chen Yi, which we are informed by competent authority is within their capability, such an action should change the course of military events for some time and might serve as the inspiration needed to spur others on to victory.

Until we are convinced, however, that Government troops are capable of taking strong offensive action, we feel that were it not for the fact that the Communist armies themselves have difficulties, a general military collapse on the part of Government forces would likely occur. It does not appear at the moment, however, that the logistic services of the Communists are such that they can support a massive, protracted assault of sufficient weight and duration to reduce and take any of the more strongly garrisoned Nationalist centers. Under these conditions, the Communists must perforce keep to their strategy of containment, attrition, and limited attack. Changchun is now starving and will fall of its own weight one of these days. This strategy will bring them no quick victory unless there should intervene political and economic factors which contribute to break the will of the Nationalists to continue their resistance; but, as the battle now goes, their victory will be delayed beyond what might have been expected several months ago.

The steps which the Government can take to improve the military picture continue limited. The sheer inertia of a war-weary populace, plus the fact that the Government cannot control many of its own members who place self-interest above the welfare of the nation, militate against the development of an all-out war effort. Given the complex personal and political relationships of the Officer Corps, it is all but impossible to remove incompetent Officers of high rank, or to reward the few men of merit with suitable promotions and authority.

The threat of the formation of independent regional governments appears less imminent than was the case of a month ago, when well-founded reports indicated that the forces of disintegration were actively at work. While there is little doubt that regional leaders, and such dissident organizations as the KMTRC, are still thinking in terms of separatism and still planning to that end, it looks very much as though they have come to think that an overt break with Nanking is not feasible at the present time. This is not to say that the dissidents and potential dissidents have effected any sort of a reconciliation with Nanking, or that they have abandoned the thought that they must prepare to set up their own regime or regimes against the day when the present government disappears. Their liking for the Gimo has not increased, nor has their confidence in his leadership. However, it seems at the moment that they do not intend to influence the course of events by an overt move which would help unseat the Gimo. Rather, it appears that they intend to wait for what they regard as the inevitable collapse of the Nanking Government before venturing on the establishment of their own independent political associations.

If this appraisal is correct, we believe that the reluctance of the dissidents to make an open break very likely stems from a new realization that the present Government still performs for them certain indispensable functions. Principal among these at the moment is Nanking's role in channeling American aid to the Provinces. We have made it abundantly clear that we support the Nanking Government. We have also made it plain that we intend to consult the Nanking Government on the allocation of our economic aid, and it is a well-known fact that the disposition of military aid is Nanking's responsibility. In this situation, the potential dissident, who cannot dispense with American aid, is bound to Nanking by very strong ties. Also, Nanking continues to supply such vital necessities as air and sea transportation, money and civil governmental organization. . . .

Manchurian regionalism also appears quiescent. The Northeastern politicos cannot move without the concurrence of Wei Li-huang, and Wei cannot dispense with the supplies and air transport that he receives from Nanking via Chinchow. Thus, he is even less likely to favor a break with the Gimo than Fu Tso-yi. In this connection, for the past several days the vernacular press has been quoting unidentified "informed sources in Government circles" to the effect that the Young Marshal is soon to be released. Government spokesmen, including Hollington Tong, make no comment on the report. This story appears at irregular intervals, generally when the Northeastern leaders become restive, and is doubtlessly designed to quiet them. We have no reason to believe, however, that the Gimo has changed his hitherto adamant refusal to release the Young Marshal under any circumstances.

The picture remains still black. Yet it is not as black as it has been and there is some evidence that the Government has obtained a new lease on life. If the economic measures can afford the breathing spell required and if the Government succeeds in taking even a part of the drastic action planned for reform, and if, by some miracle, it can bring a real victory in the military field, collapse of the Government may be postponed indefinitely. As we have said so often in the past, the bulk of the Chinese people does not want to be Communist and would cooperate heartily with any regime which gives promise of an efficient alternative. On the other hand, as one Chinese intellectual remarked to us recently: "You can't deny the lessons of history, and history will show that in China, periods of chaos are inevitably followed by periods of tyranny." We are certainly experiencing a period of chaos.

NANKING, *November 8, 1948*

Within the past few weeks, the Government's military power and economic position have so deteriorated that we seriously question its ability to survive for long. There is just no will to fight in Nationalist Government armies and in high official circles there is only befuddlement. We have reported on the various crises that the Government has had to face, and for that matter still faces, and there js no need to recount them here. It will suffice to say that at no time has the Government been able to devise measures adequate and suitable to the tasks confronting it, and that most of the measures adopted have actually operated to the Government's detriment. There is little or no confidence in official Chinese circles that the Gimo has mustered, or can muster, the resources needed to rescue his regime. While there are some in the Government who say that increased American assistance can still save the day, we are inclined to believe that most of those who take this line are not, in fact, convinced that any practicable amount of aid can save them. The departure of the Gimo has been mooted in the Legislative Yuan, and peace has been advocated editorially in the Tientsin vernacular press. These sentiments are widely, if not generally, held, and it cannot be long before further military and economic debacles and their translation into effective political action.

Precisely when and exactly how the present Government will go is impossible to foretell. There are so many imponderables involved that no firm prediction can be made. However, when it goes there must be soonor or later a new government for China, and this must be either wholly Communist in character, or one in which the Communists play a leading role. There will very likely be certain sections of the country that will hold aloof for the time being to see how the wind blows. Nevertheless, it appears at the moment that the new "Central" Government will result from an association of the Communists with the minority parties and a segment of the KMT. In this case the degree of control which the Communists exercise will always be enough to insure that their opponents cannot combine to eliminate them by force. Actually, the extent of this control is virtually at their pleasure, for they can very likely maintain the preponderance of military power which they now hold and so enforce their will against their opponents. Thus, insofar as the opposition cannot, through the foreseeable future, develop the military potential needed for a counter revolution, the new government must be very much what the Communists choose to make it.

If there is one thing certain in this situation, it is that the problems facing the new government will be of an almost indescribable magnitude. The native agrarian economy is in grave crisis, and that segment of the national economy organized along Western lines is in an equally serious plight. At almost all levels political institutions no longer function as they were intended to, so that a state of loosely controlled anarchy obtains. Only a part of the general chaos is directly attributable to the civil war; many of the crises stem from the deeper contradictions of Chinese society. We can assume that the new government will soon succeed in ending civil strife, though conflict may continue briefly in peripheral areas and may flare up anew from time to time. We can also assume that the new government will display more administrative ability and that it will, at least in initial stages, have a higher degree of probity than the present regime. From these assumptions we may expect it to make some substantial progress in solving those problems which are the products of civil war and bad government, and so contribute to its own stability.

We have often pointed out just how the present Government has been wont to do those things it ought not to do, and to leave undone those things it ought to do, and how, in so doing and not doing, it was bringing on its own downfall. The main problem facing the new government is to do those things it ought to do in meeting the minimum requirements any government must provide for those it rules. Here we may fairly question whether the new government has this capacity, and from all indications it would appear that the answer is in the negative. Briefly, the basic problem of the new government will be the ordering of the national economy so as to insure a livelihood to all, and at the same time acquire from the nation's production a surplus for its own support. This involves the rehabilitation of the national economy—not only in terms of repair and replacement to physical plant—but also reconstruction of economic institutions, and it involves the reorganization of the economy in terms of a new economic and social philosophy which is altogether an import and has no real roots in the country. To do these things, the new government will need a feasible program, good administrative personnel, and it will need, above all, matériel. Whether its program is feasible remains to be seen. It is certainly true that it has not worked too well in the agrarian areas which the Communists have held. It may work on a national scale if sufficiently amended, but deep and vital changes will be difficult without doing violence to the Communists' basic, underlying dogma. Good administrative personnel they lack, as do the Nationalists. Indeed, effective, trained administrators are in short supply throughout China. The material most needed are capital goods which cannot be produced within the country and must be imported. There is little prospect in the foreseeable future that, however and by whomever managed, the national economy can produce a surplus, over and above the requirements of the State for its own maintenance, to pay for the imports needed.

The difficulties we mention, while basic, are only a few of the many that will arise. However, on a short term basis the prospects are that a new government will achieve some success, and will gain a considerable measure of popular support. For one thing, it will have brought about an end to the civil war, the consummation devoutly to be wished as far as most Chinese are concerned, regardless of the manner of its coming. Also, it will at the outset likely be able to do certain things of benefit to the masses, which any "good" government could do. Indeed, it may well, over a considerable period of time, be regarded by the body politic as a vast change for the better. But as it must come to grips with its fundamental problems, its chances of giving a satisfactory performance diminish. . . .

Our foregoing comments concern the longer view, rather than the immediate future. As we say, what will come in the next several months, or even weeks, is almost impossible to predict. The fall of Mukden, which occurs as this is written, is likely the beginning of the final series of military debacles for Nationalist arms. At the moment it appears that the isolation of Hsuchou has begun. In this situation, of all the Government there are few, if any, save the Gimo who even profess confidence that the tide may yet be turned. Only a few days before Mukden fell, the Government had five well equipped, supplied and trained armies in the Manchurian field, the most formidable striking force at its command, and within few days these armies were lost. They were lost not from battle casualties, but from defection, although among their commanders were numbered officers long associated with the Gimo, and in whose loyalty he trusted implicitly. The troops at Hsuchou are far inferior to the former Mukden garrison, and their commanders are already resigned to defeat. There is no reason to believe in their will or ability to resist an offensive. And when they are gone, Nanking has no defenses worthy of the name.

It is not difficult to see why the Gimo retains some confidence in his star. His beginnings were modest, and from them, against great odds, he led a revolution and was the principal architect of a new state. For a time his government was successful. More than that he was able to maintain it through the eight years of his war with Japan and in the end to regain the territories that he had lost. His achievements are by no means inconsiderable, and they testify to his qualities. There is a tendency on our part to forget that Chiang succeeded as a revolutionary, and that he still regards his party as a revolutionary party. It was his fate that there should develop in China another revolution in competition with his own, and that, in the broader view, the KMT has become to the Communist revolution what the old, war-lord regimes were to Chiang as he rose to power. The Gimo does not understand this, and so, to some extent, he regards himself as the protagonist of a revolution which must in the end succeed because all men must recognize that it is essentially right. To that extent he must regard his triumph was inevitable and his reverses as but setbacks incidental to the temporary perversion of natural order. These are, in general, the reasons which constrain him to continue the struggle when it has become apparent that it is a lost cause.

There appears no reason to believe that the Gimo has, or will consider, a negotiated peace with the Communists, even should they agree to deal with him. This intransigence will prolong the conflict as long as there are any who will stand by him. It remains to be seen how many of his followers will remain when the news of Mukden becomes generally known. Their members will be appreciably less when the assault on Hsuchou begins. Whether he will have enough of a following to attempt a defense of Nanking is problematical, even doubtful, but it seems clear that once he has left Nanking in flight, he will never again be really effective political force in this country.

167

New Year Message, 1949, of President Chiang Kai-shek [27]

My Fellow Countrymen:

On this thirty-eighth anniversary of the founding of the Republic of China and the first anniversary after the introduction of constitutional Government, I observe with great regret that our national reconstruction efforts have come to a state of suspension and the Three People's Principles still remain to be achieved.

Since the end of the war against Japan, the main object of the Government has been to lay down a firm foundation for peace and reconstruction so as to alleviate the sufferings of the people. The task which the Government considered as of great importance was to recover the Northeast, thereby preserving China's national sovereignty and territorial integrity. But, unfortunately, we have not been able to do this.

On the other hand, Tsinan was lost to the Communists and Chinchow, Changchun, and Mukden fell into their hands in succession. The Mukden tragedy of 1931 has repeated itself. Commercial and industrial cities as well as cultural centers in North and East China are now being menaced by the Communists.

During this national crisis I cannot but blame myself for my inadequate leadership. I am sorry that I have not lived up to the high expectation of the people.

WILL NOT ABANDON LIBERTY

The military situation has entered upon an exceedingly perilous stage. The fate of the nation and the historical and cultural continuity of our people will soon be decided. The issue of this struggle will determine whether the Chinese people will continue to live as free men and women or as slaves, and whether they will live at all or perish.

Everyone is concerned over the policy which the Government has pursued in dealing with the situation. We are convinced that all patriotic citizens will not tolerate the Communist method of "liquidation" and "struggle" and that they are not willing to abandon their liberty and to remain inactive at this critical moment.

But we are also fully aware that military operations have increased the people's burden and that they hope for an early conclusion of the war. Shouldering the responsibility of the conduct of national affairs, I have carefully studied the situation and considered the wishes of the people.

The Father of our Republic once said: "The aim of national reconstruction of the Republic of China is peace." Being a strong believer in the Three People's Principles and abiding by Dr. Sun Yat-sen's bequeathed teachings, I did not have any intention to fight the Communists at the end of the war.

Immediately after V-J Day, the Government declared its principles for peace and reconstruction. Later it went one step further by seeking to solve the Communist question by means of political consultation.

In the subsequent one and a half years, the Communists disregarded every agreement and obstructed every peace effort that was made. As a result, these agreements and the programs which were agreed upon were not implemented.

In the end, the Communists started an all-out rebellion, thereby endangering the very existence of the nation. Unwillingly, the Government was forced to order a general mobilization and to proceed with the anti-Communist campaign. I am sure that these historical facts are still vivid in your minds.

---

[27] Reprinted from *China Information Bulletin* (New York), vol. II, Jan. 7, 1949.

Communism has already had a history of twenty-five years in China. In this period I have never for a moment given up the hope that the Communists would place the national interests above that of their own, would follow the regular courses as befitting a political party, and would join hands with the Government in finding ways to work for peace and national existence.

CHALLENGES REDS' SINCERITY

Such was the purpose of the political consultation which took place shortly after the war, and such remains the objective of the Communist-Suppression Campaign. The key to the problem of peace or war and to the happiness or suffering of the people is not in the hands of the Government, nor can the problem be solved by popular appeal for peace to the Government alone. The problem can be decided only by the Communists. So the sincerity of the Communists for peace must be ascertained before the problem can be solved.

If the Communists are sincerely desirous of peace, and clearly give such indication, the Government will be only too glad to discuss with them the means to end the war.

If a negotiated peace is not detrimental to the national independence and sovereignty, but will contribute to the welfare of the people; if the Constitution is not violated and constitutionalism preserved, the democratic form of government maintained, the entity of the armed forces safeguarded; and if the people's free mode of living and their minimum living standard are protected, then I shall be satisfied.

In my devotion to the cause of the National Revolution, I have known nothing except loyalty to the nation, service to the people and the realization of the Three People's Principles, thereby fulfilling my sacred duties as a Revolutionist. If peace can be secured, I am not at all concerned about my own position. In this I will follow only the consensus of the people.

If, on the other hand, the Communists are not sincerely desirous of peace and will insist on continuing their armed rebellion, the Government, with no other alternative, will fight them to the finish. As the political nerve center of the country, the Nanking-Shanghai area will be held at all costs, and the Government is determined to throw in all available forces for a decisive victory. I firmly believe that the Government will win out in the end, and it also will mark the turning point of the war.

The people of the nation should realize that only by carrying on this war of self-defense can a real peace be secured; and only by making sacrifices can a glorious victory be won. It has been almost forty years since I joined the National Revolution. In every major and prolonged battle, I have suffered many setbacks and have been subjected to vicious propaganda. No matter how serious was the reverse, I never lost confidence in the final victory. And as a rule, victory was obtained in the end.

National spirit, justice, and righteousness, such as they are generally recognized, must constitute our mainstay in this fight. The brutal force of the Communists can wrest from us the Northeast, but it can never subdue our national spirit.

The Communists can penetrate into our heartland, but they can never soil our national character. Righteousness is the strength for victory, and right will always triumph over might. We of this generation have seen the greatest cataclysm in our history; we have on our shoulders an unprecedented mission.

We can, we must, endure temporary afflictions and sacrifices and struggle for the existence of the nation, the continuity of our history and culture, our free way of living, and the prosperity of our offspring.

My countrymen, at this time of national crisis, I feel all the more keenly the weightiness of my responsibilities and the difficulties in fulfilling my mission. It is my hope that all patriotic countrymen will advise me and join hands in the fight for the sanctity of the Constitution, the maintenance of China's territorial and sovereign integrity, the freedoms of the people, and the continuance of our culture.

Dr. Sun said: "Final victory belongs to the one who struggles until victory." I hope that all of us will bear this motto in mind.

168

The Chinese Foreign Minister (Wu) to the Ambassador in China (Stuart)

893.00/1–849

AIDE-MÉMOIRE

NANKING, *January 8, 1949*

The Chinese people, true to their peaceful traditions, have always devoted themselves to the pursuit of international as well as domestic peace. In their long history, it was only when they were in the face of the danger of aggression that they took up arms in self defense. For this reason, the people rose to resist the Japanese invaders, and later, through their close cooperation with their allies, World War II was carried to a successful conclusion. On the eve of victory, China took an active part in organizing and founding the United Nations in the hope that a foundation for world peace might thus be laid and international disputes settled by pacific means. For, it has long been through the maintenance of peace that the continuity and development of human civilization can be ensured.

Following the surrender of Japan, the National Government immediately took steps to initiate and carry on peace negotiations with the Chinese Communist Party. Through the good offices personally offered by General Marshall the Political Consultative Council was set up and a number of meetings took place. Unfortunately, the failure to reach a mutually satisfactory settlement led to a renewal of hostilities. Although these efforts proved abortive at the time, the government and the people have never since abandoned the hope that hostilities may still be brought to an end.

However, in the wake of the long, gruelling struggle against Japan, this renewed conflict has inflicted untold suffering upon the masses and prevented the government from carrying out the plans of reconstruction which it had prepared during the war with Japan. The ravages of war followed by rapid deterioration of the economic life of the nation make it imperative that peace be restored as soon as possible.

As nations today are unavoidably interdependent and international peace and stability depends largely upon degree to which international cooperation can be achieved, it would be difficult for any nation to confine the effect of its own unsettled conditions to itself. The Chinese Government is, therefore, most anxious that her internal situation would not in any way become an impediment to the progress of world peace.

In consideration of the above facts, the President of the Republic of China, in his New Year message on January first, announced without hesitation his determination for the restoration of peace in the country. The decision thus proclaimed by the President has since received the general support of the people, who have through numerous messages and public statements echoed their prompt support for a peaceful settlement of the questions at issue between the government and the Communists.

The United States Government has on many occasions in the past demonstrated its friendly concern over the state of affairs in China and has cooperated with the Chinese Government for the promotion of international peace. The Chinese Government wishes hereby to assure the United States Government of its sincere desire for a peaceful settlement with the Chinese Communist Party and particularly avail itself of this opportunity to ascertain in the views of the United States Government on this subject. The Chinese Government will welcome any suggestion by the United States Government which may lead to an early restoration of peace in China. The Chinese Government further signifies its readiness, through the possible intermediary of the United States Government, to initiate negotiations with the Chinese Communist Party with a view to attaining the end stated above.

Similar notes are being communicated to the French, the Soviet and the British Governments. An early reply from the United States Government will be greatly appreciated.

169

Memorandum on the Situation in Taiwan [28]

Background

The Formosan Chinese greeted the surrender of Japanese authority to the Chinese with immense enthusiasm on October 25, 1945. After fifty years under Japanese control and intensive economic development they welcomed a return to China, which they had idealized as the "Mother Country". The richness of the island and the relatively light population pressure had made rapid economic and social developments possible. Agriculture, food processing and light industry in the best years produced an overseas trade valued at U.S. $225,000,000. To improve Taiwan's economic value the Japanese had raised the general standard of living. Public health standards were high and literacy widely spread among the masses. Formosans had come to place a high value on orderly procedures in the courts and on the orderly enforcement and observance of government regulations, for they found order both profitable and necessary in a complex and semi-industrialized economy.

With the removal of the Japanese the Formosans looked forward to a return to profitable trade and an expansion of their already established industries, with the markets of China ready to receive all that they could produce. The surpluses which had always gone to Japan would now, they thought, go to China. They expected to return to control of the properties taken from them by the Japanese through fifty years and expected a larger share in the management of their own enterprises. Under pressure of the Japanese overlords who were alien to Taiwan, they had developed an island-wide sense of social solidarity. They were free of all internal political strife. The Japanese had rigorously excluded all Communist influence and activity, and had indeed filled the people with fear, dislike and distrust of Communist doctrines. They revered the Generalissimo,

---

[28] Submitted by Ambassador Stuart to President Chiang Kai-shek on Apr. 18, 1947.

believed the Three People's Principles meant new opportunities, and looked forward expectantly to participation in the Central Government. The year 1946 was one of increasing disappointment. Though the majority of petty officials, clerks and office boys of the new Administration were Formosans, they were virtually excluded from all important government offices and from important administrative posts. The legal necessity to place all confiscated Japanese properties and enterprises under Government control led to the creation of syndicates and combines in every field in which the Japanese had had an interest. Though the Government owns (and must heavily subsidize) these companies, the salaried and priviledged administrators are in a position to squeeze freely. It is alleged that raw and finished materials and agricultural products find their way into the hands of unscrupulous officials for their use in private trading and smuggling. Judging from Taiwan's former capacity to produce and the fact that its enterprises continue, qualified Formosans estimate that published records show only one-tenth of actual receipts. As an example, it is alleged by persons formerly connected with the Department of Agriculture and Forestry that fishing boats were withdrawn from their normal bases in 1946 and were used for smuggling in the interests of the authorities concerned.

Formosans have been virtually excluded from the higher levels of economic administration. These persistent allegations of corruption lead them to place responsibility on members of the Government who appear and reappear in lucrative posts as Commissioners, members of Committees, and Directors in a manner which concentrates full control of the total economy in the hands of a clique close to the Governor.

There was a progressive decline in Formosan economic enterprise, especially where there was competition with ex-Japanese interests. Unemployment among Formosans has progressively increased, either through direct discharge (frequently to make room for unqualified newcomers) or by the suspension or abolition of various established enterprises which failed to be profitable under the new management. Whereas about 50,000 Formosans had been employed normally in industrial work, by January 1947 UNRRA officials estimated that less than 5,000 were so employed. Whereas the top government officials created a Taiwan Industrial and Mining Enterprises Syndicate with a capital of two billion Taiwan yen, in which the Commissioners and their associates play leading roles, the Department of Mining and Industry announced an appropriation of only eight million Taiwan yen for loans in aid of private (i. e. Formosan) industrial enterprises after June 1946.

The Quarantine Service broke down and the Public Health Service was badly shattered. Cholera epidemics occurred for the first time in about 30 years; bubonic plague appeared after an even longer absence. Educational standards in the schools were markedly lowered. Friction spread through the schools between Formosans and mainland students and teachers. Trouble between mainland police and local petty officials increased. The press was filled with public charges and counter-charges of corruption and lawless acts among government officers. Formosans claimed that corruption and nepotism among mainland officials increased rather than abated during the year. The cost of living soared. Bank of Taiwan wholesale commodity price indices show advance as follows from November 1945 to January 1947: foodstuffs 3,323 to 21,058; clothing 5,741 to 24,483; fuel 963 to 14,091; fertilizers 139 to 37,559; building materials 949 to 13,612. (Pre-war June 1937 is used as a basis.) Prices shot up most rapidly during February 1947. These figures on the whole reflect the drain of Taiwan wealth from the island, with little or no return to it.

Although the two rice harvests of 1946 were good, a rice shortage grew acute in December 1946 and January 1947. The Government instituted a tax in kind for rice lands, ostensibly to secure an equal distribution, and repeatedly threatened to use military force to punish private hoarders which it blamed for the shortages. In fact there is substantial evidence to support the Formosans in their charges that large quantities of grain were smuggled out or went into private control of officials. It is popularly believed that the army is shipping unpublicised quantities to the northern front on the mainland.

Three governmental acts

Against this background of increasing economic and social dislocation three governmental acts in January and February appear to have crystallized Formosan resentment toward economic policies and toward individuals in the Government.

(1) Throughout 1946 Formosans sought permission to elect city mayors and *hsien* magistrates, in order to ensure themselves of some direct control over local police and over economic functions and public services. The announcement of China's new Constitution was greeted with relief. Prominent Formosan leaders counseled that demands for local elections could wait until the Constitution would become effective at the end of 1947. In early January, however, the Governor General announced that although the Constitution would be effective on the mainland on December 25, 1947, it would be impossible for the Government to allow local elections of mayors and magistrates in Formosa until December 1949. This had an effect which stirred political discussion to a new pitch. Formosans state that until they can elect their own representatives at all levels of local government they will have no security of person; they cannot control the local police, ensure the enforcement of law nor enjoy security of property.

(2) On February 1 the Government announced a new policy for the disposal at auction of certain large categories of Japanese property—principally real estate abandoned by the Japanese and now occupied by Formosans on a low rental basis. The announced procedures were such that it was widely believed that Formosans without great wealth and its influence would be unable to buy real estate which they had believed would be available, especially in view of the fact that it had been taken from them more or less forcefully by the Japanese over the course of fifty years.

This announced procedure was interpreted as a threat to the security of low-income level Formosans who, having lost their former homes during the war, are not anxious to face eviction from houses now occupied if, as they anticipate, new mainland landlords should suddenly greatly increase rentals. (Rental is the one item in living costs which has not risen excessively since 1945, due to the removal of several hundred thousand Japanese.)

(3) The third governmental act was a February 14 announcement of a series of complex financial and trading regulations which Formosans believed effectually concentrated monopoly control in the hands of a small group of officials. It is believed by some observers that these were announced precipitously and rashly in the belief that the crisis in Shanghai was about to provide an opportunity long awaited to establish a semi-autonomous economy for Taiwan, giving into the hands of a few mainland people an absolute control of all external trade and a general control of internal production and business as well.

As an island people, Formosans have been sensitive to overseas trade, and after the Japanese surrender they anticipated the reestablishment and expansion of seaborne commerce. They had proposed to organize their capital for production and individual business, out of which they had expected to be taxed in support of the Central Government and of the local island administration. These new measures seemed to the Formosans not only a threat to return them to the subservient position they had suffered under the Japanese, but to threaten to destroy the very means to create wealth within the island.

The February Incident

Spontaneous protest and unorganized riots

On the evening of February 27 certain armed Monopoly Bureau agents and special police agents set upon and beat a female cigarette vendor, who with her two small children, had protested the seizure of her small cash as well as her allegedly untaxed cigarettes. She is reported to have died soon after as a result of the beating at police hands. An angered crowd set after the agents, who shot at random, killing one person before they escaped into a civil police station. Their Monopoly Bureau truck and its contents were burned in the street, although the agents were allowed to be taken away, on foot and unmolested, from the police station by military police called for that purpose.

On the morning of February 28 a crowd estimated at about 2,000 marched in orderly fashion from the area in which the incident had occurred, past the American Consulate and toward the Monopoly Bureau Headquarters. Placards and banners announced that they intended to protest the action of special armed agents, to demand a death sentence for the responsible man, and to demand the resignation of the Monopoly Bureau Director.

Unfortunately, as they made their way across the city, two Monopoly agents were discovered in a side street molesting a vendor. They were beaten to death by an angry crowd which was not taking part in the initial demonstration. This happened near the Taipei Branch Monopoly Bureau Office buildings which the crowd began to sack. Its contents were burned in the streets. Mainland employees were driven out and if caught were beaten mercilessly. The crowd's anger enlarged to include employees and property of the Trading Bureau, another monopolistic organization greatly disliked. The Consul and the Vice Consul observed the orderly gathering before the Monopoly Bureau Headquarters, where no Monopoly Bureau official would receive the petition which had been brought about noon. Monopoly Bureau police and a few military police were guarding the entrances.

Meanwhile at about one o'clock someone announced to the radio audience that demands were being made on the Government to put an end to its monopolies. All Formosans were urged to support the movement.

The parade, meanwhile, left the Monopoly Bureau for the Governor's office where it was intended to present the petition for reform. At about two o'clock it reached a wide intersection adjacent to the government grounds. Without warning a machine gun mounted somewhere on the government building opened fire, swept and dispersed the crowd and killed at least four. Two consular officers drove through the square immediately after the shots were fired. Two of the dead were picked up a few minutes later by an UNRRA officer.

This shooting was the signal for a citywide outburst of anger against all mainland Chinese, regardless of rank or occupation. Many were beaten, cars were burned and in some few cases offices and houses of minor officials were sacked and the contents burned in the streets. It was observed that the Formosans refrained from looting. One Formosan was found attempting to take cigarettes from a burning heap; he was forced to kneel and beg forgiveness from the crowd and was then driven away. Another was severely beaten. Tires and other equipment were observed to have been left untouched on overturned cars, and remained in evidence until the Formosans lost control of the city March 9. Martial law was invoked in the late afternoon February 28. Armed military patrols began to appear in the city, firing at random wherever they went.

At 10 o'clock a. m., March 1, the Chairman of the Taipei Municipal People's Political Council invited the Council, representatives of)the National and Provincial P.P.C. Councils and the Taiwan representatives to the National Assembly, to form a committee for settling the so-called Monopoly Bureau incident. It was decided to send a delegation to call on the Governor General, requesting, among other things, that a committee be formed to settle the problems jointly by the people and the Government. These men recognized that with the firing on the crowd at the government building, the issues had become much greater than mere punishment of Monopoly Bureau agents and a financial settlement for the injured and dead. They urged the Governor to lift martial law so that the dangers of a clash between the unarmed civil population and the military would be averted. This the Governor agreed to do at midnight, March 1, meanwhile forbidding meetings and parades.

On that day busses and trucks, filled with squads of government troops armed with machine guns and rifles, began to sweep through the streets, firing indiscriminately. Machine guns were set up at important intersections. Shooting grew in volume during the afternoon. At no time were Formosans observed to have arms and no instances of Formosan use of arms were reported in Taipei. Nevertheless, the military were evidently allowed free use in what appeared to be an attempt to frighten the people into obedience.

At approximately 5 o'clock, the Governor General broadcast a message which appears to have increased the anger of the people. He stated that the Monopoly Bureau incident had been settled by a generous payment of money. Without referring to the machine gun fire from his own office he accused the Formosans of increased rioting, but generously promised to lift martial law at midnight.

"There is one more point," the Governor broadcast. "The P.P.C. members wished to send representatives to form a committee jointly with the Government to settle this riot. This I have also granted. If you have any opinion, you can tell me through this Committee." (*Hsin Sheng Pao*, March 2, 1947.)

While he was broadcasting, members of the American Consulate staff witnessed a severe clash between armed government forces and unarmed crowds. Mounted troops had killed two pedestrians near the compound. A crowd gathered. A few hundred yards away Railway Administration special armed police suddenly opened fire from within the Administration building and killed two more pedestrians. The crowd turned on any mainland Railway Bureau employee found nearby. Two more pedestrians who looked like coolies were shot about 300 feet from the Consulate gates. Then as the bodies were carried off the crowd was observed to assemble again some distance from a mounted patrol near an intersection. Suddenly, with no warning, a long burst of machine gun fire swept the area. Some of the wounded and dead were carried past the Consulate gates; it is stated reliably that at least 123 were felled by this burst and that 25 died. How many of the injured walked away is not known.

On this afternoon 25 mainland officials from the neighboring Railway Administration compound took refuge in the Consulate. Although the crowd observed them enter, no attempt was made to pursue them. They were removed eight hours later under police guard.

Organization for settlement recognized by General Chen

The temper of the populace was uncertain. Inflammatory handbills and posters began to appear in increasing numbers. There was a general demand that the Government of Taiwan must be thoroughly reformed.

At 12 noon March 2 the "Untaxed Cigarette Incident Investigation Committee of the Taipei Municipal P.P.C." called on the Governor General, and with this began the attempt to meet and clarify the fundamental political and economic problems which lay back of the uprisings. The Governor had with him the Secretary-General, the Commissioners for Civil Affairs, Communications, and Industry and Mining.

The Governor appears to have been told by the Committee that there could be no peace as long as roving armed patrols were permitted to sweep the streets with gunfire and so paralyze all normal activity.

It is believed that if fully determined the people could have overpowered and ended the patrols which were moving only in the central part of the city.

The Governor therefore agreed to several "temporary demands", i.e., stipulations of conditions to be maintained while the people organized their fundamental demands for reform in government. These included (1) an agreement that a schedule of fundamental reforms should be prepared for discussion by March 10, after representatives of the people throughout the island could be consulted; (2) a promise that the Government would not bring additional troops into the city while these consultations were in progress; (3) a volunteer youth organization under the supervision of the Mayor and the municipal Chief of Police (a mainlander) would maintain law and order temporarily; (4) communications would be restored at once in order to avoid a food shortage.

The Governor agreed to broadcast at 3 o'clock p. m. and agreed to reduce the armed patrols gradually, meanwhile ordering them to patrol with rifles and other arms down on the floor of the trucks and busses, for use only if crowds were found disturbing the peace.

At 2:30 o'clock the first general meeting of the Governor's representatives (the Commissioners of Civil Affairs, Police, and Communications, and the Taipei Mayor) and the Settlement Committee met in the Public Hall, with a capacity audience of spectators. It was announced that as a result of the morning conference the Governor had decided to readjust the Committee to bring into it representatives of the Chamber of Commerce, the Labor Union, student organizations, popular organizations, and the important Taiwan Political Reconstruction Association which has been for many months the most outspoken and emphatically nationalist group urging reform in General Chen's government.

The following temporary demands were formulated:

1. All people arrested in connection with the riots will be released;
2. The Government will pay death gratuities and compensations to the wounded;
3. The Government will not prosecute persons involved;
4. Armed police patrols will be stopped immediately;
5. Communications will be restored immediately.

While in session the meeting was disturbed by volleys of shots outside. When the Governor's promised 3 o'clock broadcast was postponed for almost two hours, it began to be rumored that he was delaying in hope that troops would reach the city from the south and he would not be forced to make public acceptance of the demands.

At approximately 5 o'clock, March 2, the Governor again broadcast, concluding his speech with the statement:

"A committee will be organized to settle the incident. Besides Government officials and members of the P.P.C., representatives from the people of all walks of life will be invited to joint the committee so that it may represent opinions of the majority of the people." (*Hsin Sheng Pao*, March 3, 1947)

On the night of March 2, word reached Taipei that the Governor actually had attempted to get troops to the city. Citizens near Hsinchu city, however, were reported to have halted the troop carriers by removing rails from the main line.

From this time (March 3) the confidence of the people appears to have been undermined. The moderate and conservative element represented by the Committee members were willing to trust the Government's word and to proceed with negotiations. The more skeptical elements agreed to support the Committee in its efforts but at the same time determined to prepare resistance to any military action which might be set against them.

This delegation, received by five Government Commissioners and Chief of Staff Ko, urged that the patrols be withdrawn, for they were still firing wildly in the streets despite the Governor's promises. After long discussion the Government representatives agreed:

1. All troops to be withdrawn by 6 p. m., March 3;
2. Public order to be maintained by a temporary Public Security Service Corps including gendarmes, police, and youths;
3. Communications to be restored at 6 p. m.;
4. Military rice stores to be released to avert crisis;
5. Any military personnel making a disturbance to be sent to General Ko for punishment;
6. Any civilians disturbing the peace to be punished according to law, on the guarantee of the Committee;
7. Troops absolutely would not come from the south to the north. (General Ko is reported to have promised "to commit suicide" if his personal guarantee were broken.)

Meanwhile, a Taipei City Provisional Public Safety Committee was organized by the Settlement Committee. Its members were recommended by the Committee and were to constitute a "Loyal Service Corps." Its effective period was to end on the day normal conditions were restored in Taipei. Meanwhile, events at Taipei were known throughout Taiwan. It appears that Formosans became deeply alarmed at persistent rumors that troops were coming from the mainland, and began to arm themselves to resist a military occupation, insisting, however, that they wanted reform, not civil war. Formosans began to take over local administrative posts everywhere held by mainland Chinese. Government troops offered some resistance but it appears that in many places mainlanders agreed to relinquish their posts peacefully, as at Hualienkang (Karenko). The aborigines are reported to be cooperating fully with the Formosan Chinese. Without prearrangement or preparation, by March 5, Formosan-Chinese were in the ascendency or in control throughout the island.

This called for larger organization in order to prevent ruffians under guise of "local patriotism" from taking advantage of confusion. On March 4, the Settlement Committee enlarged its representative character by creating 17 sub-divisions or local Settlement Committees throughout the island. Circumstances beyond control forced the Committee to so enlarge its duties, and in doing so it announced:

"We should acknowledge the aim of this action, that there is no other desire except to demand a reformation of Government." (*Hsin Sheng Pao*, March 5, 1947)

This was without doubt necessary, for the absence of mainland office-holders from their duties threatened to paralyze the administration.

The Governor and his Commissioners received the Committee's representatives at 3:30 p. m., March 4, and the Governor took occasion to remind them that his duties were related to both national administration and local government and expressed his hope that the people would come forth with more proposals for local administration. He stated that he had ordered the police and gendarmes not to carry weapons.

March 5 was quiet at Taipei. Shops were open and primary schools resumed classwork. The city appeared to be returning to normal while the Settlement Committee worked toward a reform program which would remove the sources of conflict between administration and people.

There was intense popular anxiety, however, for rumors of impending troop movements grew stronger. It was said that the March 10 date set for presentation of the reform proposals would be too late. Each rumor strengthened the arguments of the men who desired to organize resistance and made the task of the officially recognized Settlement Committee more difficult. In an attempt to clarify its own position and to strengthen its influence over dissident elements the Settlement Committee published basic Articles of Organization clearly defining its temporary character.

A Youth League of considerable potential significance came into being, stressing as basic principles a desire to make Taiwan a model province of China and to hasten Dr. Sun Yat-sen's program of National Reconstruction. The founder, former president of the Chamber of Commerce, Chiang Wei-chuan, said:

"We absolutely support the Central Government but will eradicate all corrupt officials in this province. This is our aim which I hope every one of you fully grasp." (*Chung Wei Jih Pao*, March 6, 1947)

Spurred by fears of a military invasion, on March 6 the Settlement Committee completed its draft of items of reform which the Governor had agreed to discuss and to refer to the Central Government wherever necessary. The Committee's executive group acted as sponsors and included four members of the National P.P.C., six members of the Taiwan Provincial P.P.C., five members of the Taipei Municipal P.P.C. and two "reserve members". Everyone of these men had received the approval of the Government as P.P.C. members and represent in fact the most conservative elements in Taiwan. One is a former Consul General at San Francisco, and ex-Mayor of Taipei. The reform proposals, made possible March 7, are set forth on pages 15–18 of this despatch.

The Army's explicit promise that the Central Government would not send troops

On March 8 Major-General Chang Wu-tao, Commander of the Fourth Gendarme Regiment, at 12:00 noon called on the Settlement Committee at its headquarters. According to the press and to witnesses he made the following categorical statement:

"I can guarantee that there will be no social disturbances if the people do not try to disarm the soldiers. I want especially to report to you that the demands for political reforms in this province are very proper. The Central Government will not dispatch troops to Taiwan. I earnestly entreat the people of Taiwan not to irritate the Central Government, but to cooperate to maintain order. I can risk my life to guarantee that the Central Government will not take any military actions against Taiwan. I speak these words out of my sincere attachment to this province and to the nation. I hope Taiwan will become a model province after these political reforms." (*Hsin Sheng Pao*, March 9, 1947.)

The landing of Government troops and subsequent terrorism

Foreign observers who were at Keelung March 8 state that in mid-afternoon the streets of the city were cleared suddenly by machine gun fire directed at no particular objects or persons. After dark ships docked and discharged the troops for which the Governor apparently had been waiting. Fairly reliable sources estimate that about 2,000 police were landed, followed by about 8,000 troops with light equipment including U. S. Army jeeps. Men and equipment were rushed to Taipei. It is reported that about 3,000 men were landed at Takao simultaneously. Troops were reportedly continuing to arrive on March 17.

Beginning March 9, there was widespread and indiscriminate killing. Soldiers were seen bayonetting coolies without apparent provocation in front of a Consulate staff residence. Soldiers were seen to rob passersby. An old man protesting the removal of a woman from his house was seen cut down by two soldiers. The Canadian nurse in charge of an adjacent Mission Hospital was observed bravely to make seven trips under fire into the crowded area across the avenue to treat persons shot down or bayonetted, and once as she supervised the movement of a wounded man into the hospital the bearers with her were fired upon. Some of the patients brought in had been shot and hacked to pieces. Young Formosan men were observed tied together, being prodded at bayonet point toward the city limits. A Formosan woman primary school teacher attempting to reach her home was shot in the back and robbed near the Mission compound. A British business man attempting to rescue an American woman whose house was being riddled with machine gun fire from a nearby emplacement was fired upon and narrowly escaped, one bullet cutting through his clothing and another being deflected from the steering gear of his jeep. Another foreigner saw a youth forced to dismount from his cycle before a military policeman, who thereupon lacerated the man's hands so badly with his bayonet that the man could not pick up his machine.

Anyone thought to be trying to hide or run was shot down. Looting began wherever the soldiers saw something desirable. In the Manka area, near the Consulate, a general sacking by soldiers took place on March 10; many shopkeepers are believed to have been shot.

On March 11 it was reported that a systematic search for middle school students had begun during the night. School enrollment lists were used. A broadcast earlier had ordered all youths who had been members of the Security Patrol or the Youth League to turn in their weapons. Concurrently, all middle school students were ordered to remain at home. If a student was caught on the street while trying to obey the first order he was killed; if the searchers found a weapon in his house, he met a like fate. If a student was not at home his brother or his father was seized as hostage. A reliable estimate was made that about 700 students had been seized in Taipei by March 13. Two hundred are said to have been seized in Keelung. Fifty are reported to have been killed at Matsuyama and thirty at Kokuto (suburbs of Taipei) on the night of March 9.

From March 8 the Government instituted searches for all members of the Settlement Committee and for all editors, lawyers and many prominent businessmen who had in any way been identified with the activities of the Committee between March 1 and 8. Wang Tien-teng, Chairman of the Settlement Committee, was seized and is alleged to have been executed about March 13. Tan Gim, a leading banker, was taken from his sick bed; Lim Mo-sei, editor of the *Min Pao*, was seized in the night and taken without clothing. Gan Kin-en, head of a large private mining interest, was arrested.

Middle school and normal school teachers began to be seized or to disappear March 14. One teacher who had been deprived of his license as a public prosecutor after exposing a case of police corruption in early 1946, was taken on March 15. Another public prosecutor involved in the arrest and punishment of mainland police officers convicted in court of killing an official of the Taichung Court, is said to have been literally dragged out of the Taipei Higher Court by the convicted man who had apparently won release after March 8. A minor accountant in the Taiwan Navigation Company at Keelung was called out and shot, with the explanation that the Manager did not think well of him.

On March 13 a tense crowd was observed near the homes of the Vice Consul and the U.S.I.S. Director; wailing women who came away incoherently said that two students had just been beheaded. UNRRA personnel observed bodies lying along the road between their hostel and the city office. Unclaimed bodies were reliably reported to be lying in the ditches and along an embankment within 2,000 feet of the foreign mission compound. A foreigner reported that on March 10 while at the Army Garrison Headquarters he observed some 15 well-dressed Formosan-Chinese bound and kneeling, with necks bared, apparently awaiting execution. On March 14 and 15 many bodies began to float into the inner harbor at Keelung. Foreigners saw sampans tow them in for possible identification by anxiously waiting people. It is estimated by a reliable Keelung observer that some 300 people had been seized and killed there.

After three days in Taipei streets, government forces began to push out into suburban and rural areas. Mounted machine gun patrols were observed along the highroads 15 to 20 miles from Taipei shooting at random in village streets in what appeared to be an effort to break any spirit of resistance. Manhunts were observed being conducted through the hills near the UNRRA hostel. Foreigners saw bodies in the streets of Tamsui.

By March 17 the order of seizure or execution seemed to have become, successively, all established critics of the government, Settlement Committee members and their aides, men who had taken part in the interim policing of Taipei, middle school students and teachers, lawyers, economic leaders and members of influencial families, and finally, persons who in the past had caused members of the Government or their appointees serious loss of face. On March 16 it was rumored that anyone who spoke English well, or who had close foreign connections was being seized "for examination", and that many Japanese technicians in the employ of the Government were being taken.

On March 9, the Committee began to publish retractions, modifications and denials of acts and proposals made during the preceding ten days. Only the Government's paper, the *Hsin Sheng Pao*, appeared March 9. On that date the Taiwan Garrison Headquarters issued the ambiguous statement that "all illegal organizations must be abolished before March 10 and meeting and parades are prohibited . . ." (Communiqué no. 131, March 9, 1947).

On March 10, General Chen issued the following statement:

"On the afternoon of March 2, I broadcast that members of the national, provincial and municipal P.P.C.s, Taiwan representatives to the National Assembly and representatives from the people may jointly form a committee to receive the people's opinion concerning relief work for the February 28 incident.

"Unexpectedly, since its formation, the committee has given no thought to relief work such as medical care for the wounded and compensation to the killed and so forth. On the contrary, it acted beyond its province and on March 7 went so far as to announce a settlement outline containing rebellious elements. Therefore, this committee (including *hsien* and municipal branch committees) should be abolished. Hereafter, opinions on political reforms concerning the province may be brought up by the Provincial P.P.C., and those concerning the *hsien* and municipalities by their respective *hsien* on municipal P.P.C.s. People who have opinions may bring them up to the P.P.C. or to the Government-General direct by writing." (*Hsin Sheng Pao*, March 11, 1947)

On March 13, it was announced that all but three government-sponsored papers were banned or suspended for having published accounts of the uprising and activities of the Committee. The *Min Pao* press was destroyed effectively on March 10.

By March 17, the Government forces were pushing down the main railway lines toward the center of the island. Martial law was rigorously enforced from 8 o'clock p. m. until 6:30 o'clock a. m.

The Draft Reform Program

Hereafter, events in Formosa and the development of Chinese administration there may be better understood in the light of the draft reform program—the so-called 32 Demands—which are here set forth. Though the rioting after February 27 was spontaneous and the creation of the Settlement Committee an unplanned event, these requests for specific reforms in local government are rooted in fundamental economic and administrative problems which must some day be solved.

It must be pointed out that the Settlement Committee, aware of its responsible official character, was greatly hampered and embarrassed by many impossible demands made on it by individuals and groups who were not authorized to develop a reform program for the Governor's consideration. For example, there were published demands that only Formosans be allowed to hold arms on Taiwan and that all Central Government troops be withdrawn. Some extreme threats to individuals in the Government appeared in handbill and poster form.

Here the Committee's proposals are regrouped as they appear designed to achieve (1) equality in government; (2) security of person and (3) security of means of livelihood. Certain of the measures were clearly open to compromise and negotiation.

Reforms to ensure equality for Formosans in local government

1. A provincial autonomy law shall be enacted and shall become the supreme norm for political affairs in this province so that the ideal of National Reconstruction of Dr. Sun Yat-sen may be here materialized.

2. The appointment of commissioners shall have the approval of the People's Political Council (after new elections have been held.) The People's Political Council shall be newly elected before June 1947. In the meantime such appointments shall be submitted by the Governor General to the Committee for Settling the February Incident for discussion and approval or rejection.

3. More than two-thirds of the Commissioners shall be appointed from those who have lived in this Province for more than ten years. (It is most desirable that such persons only shall be appointed to the Secretariat and to be Commissioners of the Department of Civil Affairs, Finance, Industry and Mining, Agriculture and Forestry, Education, and Police.)

4. Unarmed gatherings and organizations shall enjoy absolute freedom.

5. Complete freedom of speech, of the press and of the right to strike shall be realized. The system requiring registration of newspapers to be published shall be abolished.

6. The Regulations in force covering the formation of popular organizations shall be abolished.

7. The Regulations governing the scrutiny of the capacity of candidates for membership in representative organs of public opinion shall be abolished.

8. Regulations governing the election of members of various grades in representative organs of public opinion shall be revised.

9. A Political Affairs Bureau of the Settlement Committee must be established by March 15. Measures for its organization will be that a candidate be elected by representatives of each village, town and district, and then newly elected by the prefectural or city People's Political Council. The numbers of candidates to be elected in each city or prefecture are as follows:

[Total 30—figures and allocations here omitted]

10. The Office of the Governor General shall be converted into a Provincial Government. Before this reform is approved by the Central Government, the Office of the Governor General shall be reorganized by the Settlement Committee through popular elections so that righteous and able officers can be appointed.

(NOTE: It has been indicated by a Formosan lawyer that the thought behind this was to provide for the interim period leading to the peace treaties and the legal return of sovereignty to China, until which time, it is widely held, a legal Provincial Government cannot be established.)

Reforms to ensure security of person and property

1. Popular election of prefectural magistrates and city mayors shall be held before June of this year and at the same time there shall be new elections of members to all prefectural and municipal political councils.

(NOTE: The reason given for this is the establishment of control over the police systems and to ensure the supremacy of, and respect for the courts.)

2. The posts of the Commissioner of the Department of Police, and of the directors of all prefectural or municipal Police Bureaus ought to be filled by Formosans. The armed Special Police Contingents and the armed police maintained by the Railway Department and the Department of Industry and Mining shall be abolished immediately.

3. No government organs other than the civil police can arrest criminals.

4. Arrest or confinement of a political nature shall be prohibited.

5. All chiefs of local courts of justice and all chief prosecutors in all local courts of justice shall be Formosans.

6. The majority of judges, prosecutors and other court staff membership shall be Formosans.

7. More than half the Committee of Legal Affairs shall be occupied by Formosans and the Chairman of the Committee shall be mutually elected from among its members.

Measures to ensure a revision and liberalization of economic policy and a reform of economic administration

1. A unified Progressive Income Tax shall be levied. No other sundry taxes shall be levied except the Luxury Tax and the Inheritance Tax.

2. Managers in charge of all public enterprises shall be Formosans.

3. A Committee for Inspecting Public Enterprises, elected by the people, shall be established. The disposal of Japanese properties shall be entirely entrusted to the Provincial Government. A Committee for management of industries taken over from the Japanese shall be established. Formosans shall be appointed to more than half the Committee posts.

4. The Monopoly Bureau shall be abolished. A system for rationing daily necessities shall be instituted.
5. The Trading Bureau shall be abolished.
6. The Central Government must be asked to authorize the Provincial Government to dispose of Japanese properties.

Reforms affecting military administration on Formosa

1. The military police shall arrest no one other than military personnel.
2. As many Formosans as possible shall be appointed to Army, Navy and Air Force posts on Taiwan.
3. The Garrison Headquarters must be abolished to avoid the misuse of military privilege.

Reforms affecting social welfare problems

1. The political and economic rights and social position of the aborigines must be guaranteed.
2. Workmen's protection measures must be put into effect from June 1, 1947.
3. Detained war criminals and those suspected of treason must be released unconditionally.
(NOTE: This is stated as designed to secure the release of a number of wealthy and prominent Formosans who have been held for more than a year on general charges of "treason" and "war crimes", who are alleged to be paying continual ransom to ensure the lives of those detained and to ensure the security of their extensive holdings.)

Demands which are subordinate measures or subject to compromise

1. The abolition or unification of the Vocational Guidance Camp and other unnecessary institutions must be determined by the Political Affairs Bureau of the Settlement Committee, after discussion.
(NOTE: An internment camp for persons the Government decides to make into "useful citizens".)
2. The Central Government must be asked to return funds for the sugar exported to the mainland by the Central Government.
3. The Central Government must be asked to pay for 150,000 tons of food exported to the mainland, after estimating the price in accordance with the quotation at the time of export.

In preparing these proposals for reform the Settlement Committee believed that it was preparing a basis for discussion with the Governor and through him with the Central Government. For an examination of public statements by the Governor and his representatives and from the direct testimony of Committee members, it is believed that the Committee was justified in considering itself empowered officially to propose such reforms in administration. These were not put forth as minimum or unalterable demands; they were clearly understood to be intended as a means for reflecting popular opinion. March 10 was mutually agreed upon as a date for presentation in order that people throughout Taiwan could contribute their ideas to the Committee.

AFTERMATH AND SETTLEMENT

Public opinion, Nationalism and Communism

However bitter their criticism of local administrative policy before these uprisings, there can be no question that the Formosan-Chinese have felt loyalty to the Central Government and toward the Generalissimo. Fifty years under Japanese rule had sharpened their sense of Chinese nationality and race and in doing so developed a strong sense of island-wide social unity. Formosans have been ambitious to see Taiwan become a model province of China. From February 28 until March 9, while Formosans were in effective control of the island, the leaders in the Settlement Committee, leaders of the Youth Groups and editors of newspapers which have been most critical of the local government all took great pains to emphasize their fundamental desire to become a model province in China, proud of their race and nationality and proud to be taking part in the National Reconstruction.

(For specific reference, see editorials and speeches quoted in the *Chung Wai Jih Pao*, March 6; *Min Pao*, March 6; *Hsin Sheng Pao*, March 5; and other journals of that week.)

Reference has been made earlier to the intense distrust and fear of communism which was fostered intensively by the Japanese. There are a few Formosans who have been suspected of interest in overseas communism but they have always been counted of little importance. Of direct external influence a few communist pamphlets of mainland origin were found in the autumn of 1946 but they were not especially designed for Taiwan. So long as the living standard remained at a relatively high level there was little danger of communist doctrine finding a reception on Formosa. A large number of Formosans who had been conscripted into Japanese army labor battalions were repatriated from Hainan Island in conditions of extreme poverty in 1946. They had not been treated as "liberated Chinese" but as defeated enemies after the surrender. Failure to find employment on Formosa in the months since has undoubtedly increased their discontent and made them susceptible to the arguments of any confirmed communists who may have come back with them.

It may be therefore said with a high degree of assurance that as of March 1, 1947, communism in any form was of most negligible importance on Taiwan.

However, a local form of communism is not only possible but is believed to be a highly probable development if economic organization collapses under the pressure of continued military occupation.

The military commitment and possible economic consequences

If the Central Government chooses to support a policy of suppression of all criticism of the government and to confirm the authority of present officials by establishment of military garrisons throughout the island, the cost will be very high and will not diminish. Firm control will necessitate the maintenance of troops at all large cities, at all important rail and highway junctions and in the vicinity of the power plants upon which the normal economy depends. The ports and harbors must be garrisoned. Almost 14,000 square miles will have to be policed by military force.

It is not possible before March 17 to assess the truth of some Formosan claims that large supplies of arms had been seized in the central part of the island and transported into hiding. The opportunity presented itself and was probably taken.

It is presumed that the Formosans, if oppression continues, will not attempt a resistance from fixed positions, but will continue to harry Government troops, creating a continuous drain upon men and supplies, and will use the mountainous hinterlands as cover. Perhaps no single province in China involved so little military expenditure as that needed for Formosa before March 1, 1947. It may now well become one of the most costly, if the economic losses in production and hampered transportation are added to outright military costs.

It is significant that throughout the trouble the local government has emphasized the fact that the Army represents the Central Government most directly. Thus, when it began to be clear that the word given by the highest ranking military officers was to be broken, Formosans began to lose faith in the Central Government as well.

With industry in such a precarious condition in February 1947, it must be presumed that the dislocations attendant upon the present trouble and a military occupation will hasten the disintegration of the industrial structure of Taiwan. China loses thereby an asset of immeasurable value. This established industrial structure (including the food processing units which make agriculture so profitable) has a substructure of semi-skilled local labor. UNRRA investigations have shown that young Formosans are no longer able to go into industrial schools or apprenticeships as in the past, but enter the common labor market as they see industry after industry shrivel up as capital investments dwindle and small industries close. Unemployment will increase with acceleration of this trend.

The rice crisis in January indicated that in present circumstances Formosa may have no immediate food surpluses upon which to draw. The addition of large numbers of troops, feeding on the countryside, will further diminish available supplies. Rice and other foods will go into hiding. Sabotage and slow-down tactics may be anticipated.

The total losses of a military occupation are incalculable. Prominent Formosan-Chinese—conservative, liberal and extremists—and many young men have been killed or seized or are driven into hiding. The educational development of the island, especially in the technical schools of middle grade, will be greatly retarded at a time when China needs every trained man. Highly qualified mainland doctors and foreign medical personnel predict that the public health system may break down badly within the year, bringing on a larger scale the cholera epidemics which appeared in 1946.

A state of near anarchy is a distinct possibility for Formosa by the end of 1947 if drastic efforts to revise policy and effect governmental reforms (free of military pressure) are not undertaken speedily. Having known a relatively high standard of living under the Japanese regime, the Formosans are not going to lose what they have without a struggle directed against the forces which they hold responsible. If the Central Government meets increasing difficulties compounded of economics and military struggles of the mainland, the Formosans will be tempted to increase their resistance in proportion.

For eighteen months Formosan-Chinese blamed the provincial administration and at the same time assured themselves that if the Generalissimo were made fully aware of conditons he would reform the system in effect on Taiwan. Later it was assumed that the application of the new Constitution would bring to Taiwan the measure of self-government needed to restore the total economy to its former high level of production, to the permanent benefit of China.

There may be a sullen peace achieved by military action, but it cannot be enforced. Further uprisings of far more serious proportions than these recent spontaneous outbursts may occur at a time when the over-all peace settlement in the Far East is underway, and problems are being reviewed for inclusion or exclusion in the conference agenda. Anyone who wishes to embarrass China will find good material in a revolutionary situation on Taiwan.

Formosa should be put to work earning foreign credit for China. Its peculiar character as an industrialized and technically developed province should be sheltered from the greater economic difficulties found on the mainland. Taiwan was returned to China as an outstanding economic asset, and example of the advanced technological economy toward which all other provinces of China are striving. Two years of concentrated rehabilitation effort in Formosa hereafter will produce permanent assets of two kinds. Raw materials and products such as fertilizers, cement, foodstuffs and industrial chemicals will become permanently available to China in increasing amounts. Others such as tea, camphor, sugar, industrial salt, pineapples and light manufactures can be directed to overseas markets. A moderate share of the foreign credit so created must be returned to Formosa for rehabilitation and expansion of state-owned industries and the expansion of private enterprise. Formosan-Chinese must be admitted to greater participation in all aspects of economic administration and reasonable profit if the island is to prosper and to return to the high and constant level of production achieved in former years. Economic stability and expansion must be founded on a sound political and social administration. Now is the time to act. To encourage and ensure wholehearted effort the Formosan-Chinese must be allowed to take a larger part in government at all levels. Changes in personnel as well as in the structure of the administration must be thoroughgoing; it is felt that halfway measures and palliatives now will only postpone a larger repetition of the current protests against corruption, maladministration and autocracy in the provincial government. Formosa can be restored to its former high level of political allegiance and of economic production by prompt and fundamental reform.

The following developments have been reported as occurring during the end of March and the first part of April:

The continuing presence of fresh bodies in Keelung Harbor and other evidence indicate that the elimination of the informed opposition is continuing. The bodies of at least two men known to neutral sources as having taken no part in any activities during the recent incidents have been identified. It is reported at Taipei that although shots and screams in the night have become less frequent, they continue, and that there is no palpable difference in the tense atmosphere of the city. Mainlanders generally are reported to be apprehensive of further trouble, and many of them are said to feel that Formosan cooperation under present circumstances will be difficult for an indefinite time in the future. Of serious import is the reported continued undermining of Taiwan's advanced economic structure.

Annexes to Chapter VII: The Military Picture, 1945–1949

170

Oral Statement by President Truman to Dr. T. V. Soong Concerning Assistance to China, September 14, 1945

The United States is prepared to assist China in the development of armed forces of moderate size for the maintenance of internal peace and security and the assumption of adequate control over the liberated areas of China, including Manchuria and Formosa. The arrangements for the provision of such assistance should include the method of discharge by the Chinese Government of the financial obligations incurred in connection with the supplies furnished and services rendered by the United States.

Having in mind statements by the Generalissimo that China's internal political difficulties will be settled by political methods, it should be clearly understood that military assistance furnished by the United States would not be diverted for use in fractricidal warfare or to support undemocratic administration.

The exact amount of assistance which can be provided by the United States will need to be agreed between the U.S. and Chinese Governments and will depend on a detailed study by the Chinese and U.S. military authorities. It appears practicable at this time, subject to suitable mutual arrangements concerned with the provision of equipment and supplies to complete the 39-division program, to furnish certain naval craft, particularly those suitable for coastal and river operations, and to equip an air force of commensurate size. After consulting General Wedemeyer further and when the problem has been considered by the Joint Chiefs of Staff and other U.S. agencies concerned and we have completed our determination of availability of equipment, we will be in a position to determine what assistance, if any, beyond the 39-division program will be feasible.

The exact size, composition and functions of an advisory mission will be dependent upon the status and character of the mission and on the size and composition of the Chinese armed forces which may be agreed between the U.S. and Chinese Governments. As to the status and character of the mission, it might be more desirable to relieve officers from active duty for appointment by the Chinese Government than for this Government to organize and appoint such a group.

A U.S. advisory mission composed of officers on active duty can only be established under the emergency powers of the President. Consequently legislation would be required to continue the mission after the expiration of these powers.

It is suggested that Generalissimo Chiang Kai-shek immediately formulate a plan, in collaboration with General Wedemeyer, for the post-war Chinese armed forces and an estimate of U.S. assistance desired and indicate to this Government his views as to the financial and other governmental arrangements which must be made.

171

Study of American Military Matériel and Services Provided to the Chinese Government since V–J Day

I

Sino-American Cooperative Organization Agreement (SACO)

Item	Amount
Payment of lump sum of expenses of training 40 Chinese students as obligated by article 17, SACO agreement	$200,000.00
Equipage, shore bases	585,045.18
Public-works construction and maintenance	79,304.37
Ordnance supplies and equipment	14,284,067.80
Communications	14,746.58
Clothing	2,309.60
Radio equipment and supplies	1,320,664.26
Fiscal codes, aerology	957,782.27
Medical equipment	159,493.57
Aviation supplies and materials	67.25
Furniture and fixtures	63,448.82
Total estimated value of issues, V–J Day to March 2, 1946	$17,666,929.70

Ammunition Dumped and Transferred by the U. S. Marines in North China, April–September 1947

A) The following ammunition was abandoned by the First Marine Division during the months of April–May 1947, in the Peiping-Tientsin Area:

Type	Units
Rockets, HE, AT 2.36 in	3,646
Rockets, HE, AT 4.50 in	300
20 MM	9,493
37 MM	4,993
60 MM Mortar	47,678
80 MM Mortar	20,916
75 MM Gun	5,577
105 MM How	64,538
155 MM How	18,726
155 MM Prop. charge	10,725
Grenades, hand	55,529
Grenades, rifle	23,038
Demolition blocks	47,438
TNT, lbs.	29,787
Charges, M-12, prop	2,420
Bangalore torpedoes	3,020
Mines, anti-personnel	1,014
Mines, anti-tank	2,636
Small arms, .30 cal	2,195,370
.45 cal	94,100
.50 cal	225,515
Grenade adapters	8,592
Flame throwers, portable	35
Flame thrower cylinders	302
Bombs, 500 lbs. GP	62
Demolition charges	3,248
Artillery fuses	16,975
Pyrotechnics	13,174
Blasting caps	32,913

ANNEXES

Type	Units
Blasting, fuse, feet	100, 500
Firing Device	2, 575
Detonators	460
Shaped charges	288
Detonating cord, feet	366, 200
Firecrackers, M-11	1, 200
Ignition cylinder, M-1	3, 000
Napalm, gals.	12, 751
Bomb fuses, AN, M-230	48
Shells, shotgun, 12GA	9, 000
Lighter fuse	72, 581

B) The following ammunition was transferred to the Chinese Navy:
   (1) Ammunition charged to Lend Lease Account, transferred from storage at Tsingtao airfield (previously removed from magazines of vessels transferred):

Type	Units
3″/50	1, 246
40 MM	6, 592
20 MM	169, 560
50 cal.	38, 150
45 cal.	250
30 cal.	99, 000

   (2) Ammunition charged to Lend Lease Account transferred in ships' magazines:

Type	Units
3″/50	1, 781
40 MM	37, 767
20 MM	208, 835
50 cal.	80, 255
45 cal.	29, 520
30 cal.	157, 414
22 cal.	55, 560

   (3) Ammunition charged to Lend Lease Account, transferred at Shanghai after special shipment from U. S. as training allowance:

Type	Units
3″/50	250
40 MM	100, 000
20 MM	150, 000
30 cal.	20, 000

C) Unserviceable ammunition in the hands of the Fleet Marine Force, Western Pacific, was abandoned by dumping small quantities at a time in revetments near Tsangkou Airfield, Tsingtao. The Chinese National Army Garrison Commander, was informed of the intention to abandon this ammunition. Dumping operations began on 19 May 1947, and were completed on 13 September 1947. During this period, the following ammunition was dumped:

Type	Units
105 MM Howitzer	24, 665
81 MM Mortar	30, 903
60 MM Mortar	28, 042
75 MM Howitzer	9, 337
155 MM Prop charge	6, 485
155 MM Prop charge	929
Grenade, hand, fragmentation	27, 575
Grenade, hand, all others	13, 640
Grenades, rifle, all types	9, 650
Bangalore torpedoes	1, 810
Small arms, cal. .30, carbine & rifle	1, 488, 490
Mines, anti-tank	372
Mines, anti-personnel	686

Type	Units
Shaped charges 40#	634
Shaped charges 10#	200
Grenade adapters, all types	4,272
Shell, 37 MM, all types & shot	1,035
Rocket, HE, AT	321
Flares, trip, all types	911
Device, firing, pressure type	980
Device, firing, pull type	1,410
Device, firing, push type	340
Device, firing, release type	1,040
Lighter, fuse, waterproof	102,000
Lighter, fuse, friction type	55,000
Pyrotechnic signals, ground	1,010
Fuse, igniting, hand grenade	7,725
Shells, shotgun # OOB	720
Cord, detonating, (Prima) 500 ft. Spools	280

TRANSFER OF U. S. NAVAL VESSELS UNDER PUBLIC LAW 512 (GRANT)

PR 4	LST 755
DE 6	LST 1030
DE 47	LST 993
PCE 867	LST 716
PCE 869	LST 717
AM 257	LST 1017
AM 258	LST 1050
AM 259	LST 1075
LST 537	LCI (L) 514
LSM 155	LCI (L) 517
LSM 157	AG 124
LSM 285	LCT 512
LSM 457	LCT 515
LSM 431	LCT 849
AM 260	LCT 892
AM 266	LCT 1143
AM 273	LCT 1145
AM 276	LCT 1171
AM 246	LCT 1213
AM 274	AOG 42
AM 286	AFDL 34
PC 1247	25 LCM
PC 1549	25 LCVP
PGM 20	AM 287
PGM 26	AM 216
PGM 12	YMS 339
PGM 13	PC 490
PGM 14	PC 492
PGM 15	PC 593
SC 648	PC 595
SC 698	SC 704
LSM 433	SC 708
LSM 442	SC 722
LSM 456	SC 723
LCI (L) 233	SC 735
LCI (L) 631	AOG 22
LCI (L) 417	AFDL (c) 36
LCI (L) 418	ARL 41
LCI (L) 630	DE 102
LCI (L) 632	DE 103
LST 557	DE 104
	DE 112

Total procurement cost of above 131 vessels: $141,315,000.

II

Public Law 512—79th Congress
Chapter 580—2d Session
H. R. 5356

AN ACT

To provide assistance to the Republic of China in augmenting and maintaining A Naval Establishment, and for other purposes.

Be it enacted by the Senate and House of Representatives of the United States of America in Congress assembled, That notwithstanding the provisions of any other law, the President is authorized, whenever in his discretion the public interests render such a course advisable, or will assist in relieving United State forces of duty in China or putting the Government of the Republic of China in a better position to protect or improve the safety of navigation in its waters, to provide to the Republic of China such naval services, training, plans, and technical advice as he may deem proper; and to dispose of naval vessels and craft, not to exceed two hundred and seventy-one vessels and craft under authority of this Act, which are in excess of the naval needs of the United States, floating drydocks of capacity sufficient to accommodate any vessel or craft disposed of under authority of this Act, and material necessary for the operation and maintenance of the vessels and craft disposed of under authority of this Act and for the training of the crews of such vessels and craft, to the Republic of China by sale, exchange, lease, gift, or transfer for cash, credit, or other property, with or without warranty, or upon such other terms and conditions as he may deem proper: *Provided*, That prior to the disposition under the authority of this Act of any battleship, aircraft carrier of any type, cruiser, destroyer (but not destroyer escort), or submarine the President shall first obtain the authority of Congress in each instance: *Provided further*, That no information, plans, advice, material, documents, blueprints, or other papers, bearing a secret or top-secret classification shall be disposed of or transferred under authority of this Act.

Sec. 2. The President is authorized, upon application from the Republic of China, and whenever in his discretion the public interests render such a course advisable, to detail not to exceed one hundred officers and two hundred enlisted men of the United States Navy and Marine Corps to assist the Republic of China in naval matters: *Provided*, That United States naval or Marine Corps personnel shall not accompany Chinese troops, aircraft, or ships on other than training maneuvers or cruises: *Provided further*, That the Secretary of the Navy is authorized to pay to such persons such additional compensation as may be necessary to make appropriate adjustment for increased cost of living occassioned by reason of detail to such duty: *And provided further*, That while so detailed such officers and enlisted men shall receive the pay and allowances thereunto entitled in the United States Navy or Marine Corps and shall be allowed the same credit for longevity, retirement, and for all other purposes that they would receive if they were serving with the forces of the United States.

Sec. 3. The provisions of this Act shall terminate five years after the date of its enactment.

Approved July 16, 1948.

III

EXECUTIVE ORDER

Authorizing the Secretary of the Navy to Transfer Certain Vessels and Material and to Furnish Certain Assistance to the Republic of China

Whereas the act of July 16, 1946, Public Law 512, Seventy-ninth Congress, provides, in part:

"That notwithstanding the provisions of any other law, the President is authorized, whenever in his discretion the public interests render such a course advisable, or will assist in relieving United States forces of duty in China or putting the Government of the Republic of China in better position to protect or improve the safety of navigation in its waters, to provide to the Republic of China such naval services, training, plans, and technical advice as he may deem proper; and to dispose of naval vessels and craft, not to exceed two hundred and seventy-one vessels and craft under authority of this Act, which are in excess of the naval needs of the United States, floating drydocks of capacity sufficient to accommodate any vessel or craft disposed of under authority of this Act, and material necessary for the operation and maintenance of the vessels and craft disposed of under authority of this Act and for the training of the crews of such vessels and craft, to the Republic of China by sale, exchange, lease, gift, or transfer for cash, credit, or other property, with or without warranty, or upon such other terms and conditions as he may deem proper: *Provided*, That prior to the disposition under the authority of this Act of any battleship, aircraft carrier of any type, cruiser, destroyer (but not destroyer escort), or submarine the President shall first obtain the authority of the Congress in each instance: *Provided further*, That no information, plans, advice, material, documents, blueprints, or other papers, bearing a secret or top-secret classification shall be disposed of or transferred under authority of this Act.

"Sec. 2. The President is authorized, upon application from the Republic of China, and whenever in his discretion the public interests render such a course advisable, to detail not to exceed one hundred officers and two hundred enlisted men of the United States Navy and Marine Corps to assist the Republic of China in naval matters: *Provided*, That United States naval or Marine Corps personnel shall not accompany Chinese troops, aircraft, or ships on other than training maneuvers or cruises. . . ."

Whereas the Republic of China has requested the United States to transfer to it certain specified naval vessels, craft, and floating drydocks, and to furnish it certain technical advice and assistance in connection with the organization and maintenance by it of a naval establishment; and

Whereas such vessels and craft are in excess of the naval needs of the United States; and

Whereas it appears that the transfer of such vessels, craft, and floating drydocks, and the furnishing of such advice and assistance to the Republic of China would be in accordance with the conditions and limitations of the said act of July 16, 1946, and would be in the public interest:

Now, therefore, by virtue of the authority vested in me by the said act of July 16, 1946, and as President of the United States and as Commander-in-Chief of the Army and Navy of the United States, it is hereby ordered as follows:

Section 1. Subject to the conditions and limitations contained in the said act of July 16, 1946, the Secretary of the Navy is authorized:

(a) To transfer to the Republic of China without compensation the said vessels, craft, and floating drydocks.

ANNEXES 945

(b) To repair, outfit, and equip the vessels, craft, and floating drydocks which are to be transferred under paragraph (a) of this section, and to transfer material deemed by the Secretary of the Navy to be necessary for the operation and maintenance of the vessels and craft so transferred, all on the basis of cash reimbursement of the cost thereof by the Republic of China.

(c) To furnish to the Republic of China such plans, blueprints, documents, and other information in connection with such vessels, craft, and floating drydocks, and such technical information and advice in connection with the organization and maintenance of a naval establishment by the Republic of China which has not been classified as secret or top-secret as the Secretary of the Navy may deem proper.

(d) To train personnel for the operation of such vessels, craft, and floating drydocks, and for such other naval purposes as the Secretary of the Navy may deem proper.

(e) To detail not more than one hundred officers and two hundred enlisted men of the United States Navy or Marine Corps to assist the Republic of China in naval matters under such conditions and subject to such rules and regulations as the Secretary of the Navy may prescribe.

Section 2. The authority hereby granted shall be exercised by the Secretary of the Navy subject to concurrence by the Secretary of State; and if at any time the Secretary of State shall determine that the transfer of further vessels and craft or material would not be in the public interest, such transfers shall be discontinued.

HARRY S. TRUMAN.

THE WHITE HOUSE,
April 25, 1947.

IV

OFLC SHIPMENTS OF ARMS AND AMMUNITION TO CHINA

ACCUMULATED FIGURES—JANUARY 1, 1948 TO MARCH 31, 1949

Item	Quantity shipped	Procurement cost	Sales price
Air Force			
Aircraft P47-D	42	$3,999,534.00	$147,000.00
Aircraft P47-D	70 [1]	5,771,220.00	350,000.00
Aircraft C46-F	13 [2]	3,292,991.00	292,500.00
Aircraft P51-D	53	2,781,917.00	397,500.00
Aircraft Engines	683	8,729,563.50	1,210,077.00
Aircraft Spares	Mixed-bulk		
Parts and Tools	Shipments	11,729,011.45	2,023,745.32
20mm Guns	200	332,827.36	33,282.74
TOTALS		36,637,064.31	4,454,105.06
Other equipment			
Chemical	M/T 273.92	29,992.28	3,749.04
Engineer	M/T 439.91	77,037.09	9,629.64
Medical	M/T 77.05	42,500.28	5,312.54
Ordnance	" 7,072.63	1,590,699.39	198,837.43
Quartermaster	" 1,011.14	309,224.55	38,653.07
Signal	M/T 182.42	214,443.58	26,805.45
TOTALS	M/T 9,057.07	2,263,897.17	282,987.17

U. S. RELATIONS WITH CHINA

Accumulated Figures—January 1, 1948 to March 31, 1949—Continued

Item	Quantity shipped	Procurement cost	Sales price
Ammunition			
Cal. 30	37,972,793 rnds	$1,865,421.86	$24,621.46
Cal. 50	18,571,550 rnds	2,540,350.79	41,913.07
Cal. 45	1,836,600 rnds	71,878.38	4,259.50
20mm	138,696 rnds	42,977.50	4,708.26
37mm	346,874 rnds	848,689.56	42,989.04
60mm	152,411 rnds	452,660.67	4,526.62
81mm	83,475 rnds	432,546.24	4,325.44
4.2 m	36,918 rnds	415,327.50	41,717.34
75mm	151,933 rnds	1,499,335.68	61,070.58
105mm	354,780 rnds	5,484,691.89	155,800.95
155mm	287,732 rnds	1,293,128.48	64,805.22
155mm (propelling charge)	8,889 rnds	63,310.65	3,150.69
Grenades	216,668	317,665.76	32,062.24
Mines	52,133	208,532.00	20,853.20
Bombs, grenades and L/T mines (mixed)	5,666	2,691,336.23	26,913.36
Bombs (photoflash)	200	6,200.00	620.00
Ammunition—(mixed, bulk)	4,125	2,989,866.52	29,898.67
Metallic Links	Mixed-Bulk	15,169.01	620.00
Boosters, Flares, Fuses, etc.	L/T 696	330,495.03	3,304.95
Clusters	M/T 506	137,952.35	1,379.52
TOTALS		21,707,536.10	569,071.80
GRAND TOTALS		60,608,497.58	5,306,164.03

[1] Delivered to Taiwan in September and December of 1948 in combat operational condition.
[2] Delivered to airfields in China in mid-1948 in operational condition.

V

PUBLIC LAW 472—80TH CONGRESS

"CHINA AID ACT" [Excerpt]

Sec. 404. (a) In order to carry out the purposes of this title, there is hereby authorized to be appropriated to the President for aid to China a sum not to exceed $338,000,000 to remain available for obligation for the period of one year following the date of enactment of this Act.

(b) There is also hereby authorized to be appropriated to the President a sum not to exceed $125,000,000 for additional aid to China through grants, on such terms as the President may determine and without regard to the provisions of the Economic Cooperation Act of 1948, to remain available for obligation for the period of one year following the date of enactment of this Act.

VI

THE PRESIDENT'S LETTER TO THE SECRETARY OF STATE, JUNE 2, 1948

THE WHITE HOUSE
WASHINGTON

June 2, 1948

MY DEAR MR. SECRETARY: I am in general in accord with the position expressed in your memorandum to me of May 14, 1948, regarding the provision of additional aid to China as authorized by Section 404 (b) of the China Aid Act of 1948. It is my desire that the grants to China under this section of the Act be made under the following procedures:

1. The Chinese Government will, from time to time, submit to the Department of State requests for payment with respect to commodities or services procured by it, supported by invoices or other appropriate documentation evidencing the transactions.

2. The Department of State will examine the documentation submitted by the Chinese Government to determine that the request is not in excess of the total represented by the invoices or other supporting data, and will authorize the Treasury to make the appropriate payments to the Chinese Government.

3. The Secretary of State will request from the Chinese Government monthly reports showing in as much detail as possible the purposes for which expenditures have been made out of the funds provided to it under the authority of Section 404 (b) of the Act.

Attached is a copy of my letter to the Secretary of the Treasury informing him of this procedure and making an allocation of $13,500,000 to carry out the provisions of Section 404 (b) of the China Aid Act of 1948.

Sincerely yours,

HARRY S. TRUMAN.

Attachment.

VII

THE PRESIDENT'S LETTER TO THE SECRETARY OF THE TREASURY, TYPED JUNE 2, 1948

THE WHITE HOUSE
WASHINGTON

June 2, 1948

MY DEAR MR. SECRETARY: Pursuant to the authority of Section 404 (b) and Section 406 of the China Aid Act of 1948 (Title IV, Public Law 472, 80th Congress), I hereby allocate to you the sum of $13,500,000 out of the funds advanced by the Reconstruction Finance Corporation to carry out the provisions of the said China Aid Act of 1948. Please take the necessary steps to effect this allocation.

Out of the funds allocated hereunder disbursements are to be made by you to the Chinese Government upon certification by the Department of State that the amounts requested are supported by invoices submitted by the Chinese Government, which the Department has examined to determine that the request is not in excess of the total represented by these invoices. A record of these disbursements should be forwarded monthly to the Department of State.

The Secretary of State will further advise the Chinese Government to furnish him monthly reports showing in as much detail as practicable the purposes for which expenditures have been made out of the funds made available under the authority of Section 404 (b) of the China Aid Act of 1948.

At such time as appropriations may become available for the purpose of carrying out Section 404 (b) of the China Aid Act of 1948, further allocations will be made out of such appropriations, to be disbursed in accordance with the terms of this letter.

Sincerely yours,

HARRY S. TRUMAN

VIII

NOTE FROM THE UNDER SECRETARY OF STATE TO THE CHINESE AMBASSADOR, JUNE 28, 1948

June 28, 1948

EXCELLENCY: I have the honor to inform you that, in accordance with the authorization contained in Section 404 (b) of the China Aid Act of 1948 (Title IV of the Foreign Assistance Act of 1948) and subject to the provisions of the Act appropriating funds thereunder, the Government of the United States is prepared, for the period of one year following the date of the enactment of the Act, to extend to the Government of the Republic of China additional aid through grants in the amount of $125,000,000 which have been appropriated for this purpose by the Congress in the Foreign Aid Appropriation Act of 1949. As stated in Section 404 (b) of the China Aid Act of 1948, this aid is to be extended on such terms as the President of the United States may determine and without regard to the provisions of the Economic Cooperation Act of 1948.

Pursuant to the authorization under the Act, the President of the United States has determined that the extension of additional aid under these grants shall be governed by the following terms:

1. The Government of the Republic of China shall, through its authorized representatives in Washington, present from time to time to the Secretary of State formal written requests for payment with respect to commodities or services procured or to be procured by it, supported by invoices, contracts or other appropriate documentation evidencing the transactions.

2. The Secretary of State shall upon the receipt of such requests, supported by invoices, contracts or other appropriate documentation evidencing the transactions, authorize the Secretary of the Treasury to make the appropriate payments to the Government of the Republic of China.

3. The Government of the Republic of China shall furnish the Secretary of State monthly reports showing in as much detail as practicable the purposes for which expenditures have been made out of funds provided to it under the authority of Section 404 (b) of the China Aid Act of 1948.

I should appreciate receiving notification of your Government's agreement to the terms set forth above for the extension of this additional aid under Section 404 (b) of the China Aid Act of 1948. Upon the receipt of a note indicating your Government's acceptance of these terms, the implementation of this Section of the Act may be promptly undertaken.

Accept [etc.]

For the Secretary of State:
ROBERT A. LOVETT
Under Secretary

IX

NOTE FROM THE CHINESE AMBASSADOR TO THE SECRETARY OF STATE, JULY 1, 1948

July 1, 1948

SIR: I have the honor to acknowledge the receipt of your note dated June 28, 1948, stating that, in accordance with the authorization contained in Section 404 (b) of the China Aid Act of 1948 (Title IV of the Foreign Assistance Act of 1948) and subject to the provisions of the Act appropriating funds thereunder, the Government of the United States is prepared, for the period of one year following the date of enactment of the China Aid Act of 1948, to extend to the Government of the Republic of China additional aid through grants in the amount of $125,000,000 which have been appropriated for this purpose by the Congress in the Foreign Aid Appropriation Act of 1949. It is understood that this aid is to be extended on such terms as the President of the United States may determine and without regard to the provisions of the Economic Cooperation Act of 1948.

My Government has authorized me to inform you of its agreement to the terms determined by the President of the United States to govern the extension of additional aid under these grants as set forth in your note under acknowledgement.

It is understood that the Government of the Republic of China shall, through its authorized representative in Washington, present from time to time to the Secretary of State formal written requests for payment with respect to commodities or services procured or to be procured by it, supported by invoices, contracts or other appropriate documentation evidencing the transactions. It is understood that the Secretary of State shall upon the receipt of such requests, supported by invoices, contracts or other appropriate documentation evidencing the transactions, authorize the Secretary of the Treasury to make appropriate payments to the Government of the Republic of China. It is also understood that the Government of the Republic of China shall furnish the Secretary of State monthly reports showing in as much detail as practicable the purposes for which expenditures have been made out of funds provided to it under the authority of Section 404 (b) of the China Aid Act of 1948.

My Government concurs in the understanding expressed above.

Accept [etc.] V. K. WELLINGTON KOO

X

THE PRESIDENT'S LETTER TO THE SECRETARY OF STATE JULY 28, 1948

THE WHITE HOUSE
WASHINGTON

July 28, 1948

MY DEAR MR. SECRETARY: My letter of June 2, 1948, addressed to you concerning the provision of additional aid to China as authorized by Section 404 (b) of the China Aid Act of 1948 is amended to read in pertinent part as follows:

"It is my desire that the grants to China under this Section of the Act, which grants are hereby made, shall be paid under the following procedures:

1. The Chinese Government will from time to time submit to the Department of State requests for payment with respect to commodities or services procured or ordered by it, supported by purchase orders, contracts, invoices, or other appropriate documentation evidencing the transactions.

2. The Department of State will examine the documentation submitted by the Chinese Government to determine that the request is not in excess of the total represented by the supporting data and will authorize the Treasury to make the appropriate payments to the Chinese Government. The Treasury Department shall make the payments in accordance with such authorization.

3. In those cases in which the Chinese Government wishes to arrange for the procurement or furnishing of supplies or services by any department, agency, or establishment of the United States Government, subject to the approval

of the Secretary of State as to the availability of funds prior to the procurement or furnishing of such supplies or services and pursuant to Sections 403 and 113 (a) of the Foreign Assistance Act of 1948, such department, agency, or establishment is authorized to submit to the Department of State requests for reimbursement of appropriations or for advance payments. On the basis of such requests, the Department of State will authorize the Treasury Department to make reimbursements or advance payments to such department, agency, or establishment.

4. The Secretary of State will request from the Chinese Government monthly reports showing in as much detail as possible the purposes for which expenditures have been made out of the funds provided to it under the authority of Section 404 (b) of the Act."

Attached is a copy of my letter to the Secretary of the Treasury advising him of this decision.

Sincerely yours,

HARRY S. TRUMAN

Attachment.

XI

THE PRESIDENT'S LETTER TO THE SECRETARY OF DEFENSE JULY 28, 1948

THE WHITE HOUSE
WASHINGTON

July 28, 1948

MY DEAR MR. SECRETARY: I enclose copies of letters addressed by me to the Secretary of State and to the Secretary of the Treasury setting forth the procedures to be applied to the additional aid to China authorized by Section 404 (b) of the China Aid Act of 1948. I also enclose a copy of a memorandum addressed to me by the Secretary of State with reference to facilitating the procurement of military supplies by the Chinese Government. There are further enclosed copies of an exchange of letters on the same subject with Chairmen Bridges and Taber of the Senate and House Appropriations Committees.

Will you please take such action as may be appropriate in the circumstances to facilitate the acquisition by the Chinese Government of such military supplies as the Chinese Government may request, either by making available existing stocks of the National Defense Establishment or by arranging for the procurement of such supplies on behalf of that Government.

Sincerely yours,

HARRY S. TRUMAN

Enclosures

XII

THE PRESIDENT'S LETTER TO THE SECRETARY OF THE TREASURY JULY 28, 1948

THE WHITE HOUSE
WASHINGTON

July 28, 1948

MY DEAR MR. SECRETARY: My letters of allocation under Section 404 (b) of the China Aid Act of 1948 (Title IV, Public Law 472, 80th Congress), dated June 2 and July 16, 1948 are hereby amended in pertinent part to conform with the attached letter addressed to the Secretary of State establishing procedures under which payments under that Act shall be made.

Sincerely yours,

HARRY S. TRUMAN

Attachment.

ANNEXES

XIII

Note From the Under Secretary of State to the Chinese Ambassador, July 30, 1948

Department of State, Washington
July 30, 1948.

Excellency: I have the honor to refer to my note of June 28, 1948 in which were set forth the terms decided upon by the President of the United States to govern the extension of additional aid to the Government of the Republic of China through grants authorized under Section 404 (b) of the China Aid Act of 1948 and to your note of July 1, 1948 indicating your Government's acceptance of those terms.

I am now authorized to inform you of the following procedure established by the President by which United States Government departments, agencies or establishments may assist the Chinese Government in arranging for the procurement or furnishing of supplies or services under Section 404 (b) of the China Aid Act of 1948:

In those cases in which the Chinese Government wishes to arrange for the procurement or furnishing of supplies or services by any department, agency or establishment of the United States Government, subject to the approval of the Secretary of State as to the availability of funds prior to the procurement or furnishing of such supplies or services and pursuant to Sections 403 and 113 (a) of the Foreign Assistance Act of 1948, such department, agency or establishment is authorized to submit to the Department of State requests for reimbursement of appropriations or for advance payments. On the basis of such requests, the Department of State will authorize the Treasury Department to make reimbursements or advance payments to such department, agency or establishment.

Accept [etc.]

For the Secretary of State:
Robert A. Lovett
Under Secretary

XIV

Note from the Chinese Ambassador to the Secretary of State August 6, 1948

Chinese Embassy, Washington
August 6, 1948

Sir: I have the honor to refer to your note of July 30th, 1948, stating that, pursuant to the following procedure established by the President, departments, agencies or establishments of the United States Government may assist my Government in arranging for the procurement or furnishing of supplies or services under Section 404 (b) of the China Aid Act of 1948:

"In those cases in which the Chinese Government wishes to arrange for the procurement or furnishing of supplies or services by any department, agency or establishment of the United States Government, subject to the approval of the Secretary of State as to the availability of funds prior to the procurement or furnishing of such supplies or services and pursuant to Sections 403 and 113 (a) of the Foreign Assistance Act of 1948, such department, agency or establishment is authorized to submit to the Department of State requests for reimbursement of appropriations or for advance payments. On the basis of such requests, the

Department of State will authorize the Treasury Department to make reimbursements or advance payments to such department, agency or establishment."

I am authorized to inform you in reply that my Government accepts the procedure set forth above, which, together with the terms communicated to me by your note of June 28th, 1948, and accepted by my Government in my note to you of July 1st, 1948, no doubt will greatly facilitate the procurement programs of my Government.

Accepted [etc.]

V. K. WELLINGTON KOO

XV

REPORT RECEIVED FROM THE CHINESE EMBASSY ON THE USE OF FUNDS OBTAINED UNDER THE $125 MILLION GRANTS

Summary of the Use of Funds Received—Total Accumulative

Category	Amounts ($)
(a) Chinese Air Force	
1. Aircraft	$2,867,700.00
2. Aircraft Parts	8,088,203.38
3. Aircraft Engines	2,690,895.78
4. Aircraft Accessories & Parts	520,796.71
5. Casing, Tube, Rubber Materials	310,267.87
6. Fuel & Lubricant	7,528,903.83
7. Electrical Supplies & Accessories	8,247.16
8. Gunnery Equipment	21,947.50
9. Flying Shoes	112,500.00
10. Radio Equipment	28,901.00
11. Tools & Equipment	223,882.72
12. Field & Hangar Equipment	459,473.64
13. Armament & Ammunition	90,282.25
14. Raw Materials & Hardware	4,034.60
15. Photographic Supplies	6,831.28
16. Chemicals, Gas & Oil	4,604.38
17. Rubber & Hose	273,570.24
18. Medicine	42,566.96
19. Critical Items	129,868.08
20. Shipping Charges	534,253.07
21. Insurance & Handling	58,986.50
22. Services	3,984,283.05
SUBTOTAL	28,000,000.00
(b) Chinese Army	
1. Ordnance, Weapons & Ammunition	42,604,465.47
2. Ordnance, Materials for Arsenals	12,512,779.61
3. Transportation, Trucks	359,987.64
4. Transportation, Vehicle Spare Parts	9,706,094.39
5. Transportation, Tools & Equipment	375,646.33
6. Transportation, Materials	124,020.57
7. Signal, Field Communication Equipment	4,133,465.87
8. Signal, Equipment & Supplies	332,763.76
9. Signal, Miscellaneous	1,038.00
10. Engineer, Supplies & Equipment	397,114.51
11. Armored Force, Equipment & Supplies	1,000,033.43
12. Intelligence, Equipment	90,000.00
13. Intelligence, Miscellaneous	702.09
14. Medical Supplies	7,000,000.00
15. Petroleum Products	8,375,000.00
16. Shipping Charges	483,274.85
17. Insurance Premiums	3,373.88
18. Miscellaneous Charges	239.60
SUBTOTAL	87,500,000.00

Category	(c) Chinese Navy	Amounts ($)
1. Vessels, Guns & Ammunition, Equipment & Supplies		$6,557,020.00
2. Petroleum Products		2,942,980.00
SUBTOTAL		9,500,000.00
TOTAL		125,000,000.00

XVI

Monthly Shipments Under China Aid Program, Authorized by Sec. 404 (b), China Aid Act of 1948, June Through December 1948

June—Miscellaneous aircraft spare parts purchased from private companies in the U. S.	19,197.74
July—Approximately 10,000 tons of small arms and artillery ammunition (procurement cost $8 million) and miscellaneous aircraft spare parts	344,869.09
August—Aviation gasoline, aircraft spare parts, and communications equipment	1,043,026.74
September—P-47 fighter aircraft (procurement cost $4 million) Aviation gasoline and other petroleum products, aircraft spare parts, communications equipment, reconditioning naval vessels	1,913,942.17
October—Ammunition, aircraft spare parts, ordnance supplies, naval supplies and services, aviation gasoline and other petroleum products	7,006,893.91
November—Small arms and ammunition, naval supplies and services, aircraft parts, aviation gasoline and other petroleum products	20,644,970.71
December—Small arms and ammunition, fighter aircraft, tanks, medical supplies, naval supplies and services, aviation gasoline and other petroleum products	28,219,461.65
Undistributed [1]	1,766,429.37
TOTAL AS OF DECEMBER 31, 1948	60,958,791.38

[1] Records not yet available showing exact month in which shipment was made. This figure reflects miscellaneous shipments of aviation supplies known to have been made on a countinuing basis beginning in August 1948 and deliveries of petroleum products transferred primarily from bonded stocks in China which were available to the Chinese Government in August 1948.

XVII

Shipments Under China Aid Program by Agencies of U. S. Government and by Chinese Agencies, Authorized by Sec. 404 (b), China Aid Act of 1948, as of December 31, 1948

A. *Items Procured through U. S. Government Agencies*

(1) Department of the Army

  a) U. S. S. *Algol*—Sailed from the U. S. Nov. 9; arrived Shanghai Dec. 1, 1948.
    Small arms and ammunition ... $16,127,081.91

  b) U. S. S. *Washburn*—Sailed from the U. S. Nov 29; arrived Taiwan Jan. 4, 1949.

Rifles .30 cal.	$4,491,621.00	
Auto. rifles and sub-MGs	360,970.00	
Johnson rifles and Johnson MGs	315,151.06	
Bayonets	423,034.80	
Grenades and rockets	408,471.50	
Small arms ammunition	5,457,394.83	
		11,456,643.19

  c) U. S. S. *Yancey*—Sailed from the U. S. Dec. 16; arrived Taiwan, Jan 4, 1949.

Rifles .30 cal.	1,632,000.00
Auto. rifles and sub-MGs	657,806.00
4.2″ Chemical mortars	199,500.00
75 mm. Pack howitzers w/fire control equip	1,400,416.00
Powder and propellants	558,816.25
.30 cal. ammunition	388,552.50
Quonset huts	48,420.00

(1) Department of the Army—Continued
   c) U. S. S. *Yancey*—Continued
      Blankets.................................... $31,726.12
      Dry cell batteries 22,206.29
      Medical supplies............................. 2,353,727.19
      Miscellaneous ordnance material................. 456,913.82
      Spare parts for weapons and vehicles............. 1,250,000.00
      Transportation, packing and handling of above-listed supplies... 918,541.12
                                                                                                                                $9,918,625.29
   d) Arms and ammunition from Far East Command—shipments completed, 16 November 1948.. 2,225,102.62
   e) Explosives and demolition equipment from Hawaii—arrived Shanghai, 3 December 1948.. 218,382.75
   f) Surplus ordnance material from Shanghai..................... 72,364.33

      TOTAL, DEPARTMENT OF THE ARMY 40,018,200.09

(2) Department of the Navy
   a) Fuel, lubricants and petroleum products..................... 19,000.00
   b) Military vessels and watercraft........................... 746,000.00
   c) Technical navy equipment.............................. 315,000.00
   d) Ordnance and ordnance stores........................... 2,768,000.00

      TOTAL, DEPARTMENT OF THE NAVY 3,848,000.00

(3) Department of the Air Force
   a) Ammunition and armaments............................. 73,676.00
   b) Aviation fuel and lubricants—shipped in October 1948........... 1,387,781.14
   c) Miscellaneous supplies and equipment...................... 160.50
   d) Miscellaneous administrative expenses, applicable to above...... $41,633.43
   e) Ocean transportation.................................. 232,388.49

      TOTAL, DEPARTMENT OF THE AIR FORCE............... 1,735,639.56

(4) Bureau of Federal Supply, Treasury Department
   a) Motor gasoline, from off-shore sources..................... 526,785.00
   b) Kerosene, from off-shore sources.......................... 5,150.26
   c) Diesel oil, from off-shore sources.......................... 115,136.00
   d) Fuel oil, from off-shore sources........................... 134,145.71

      TOTAL, BUREAU OF FEDERAL SUPPLY 781,216.97

(5) Office of the Foreign Liquidation Commissioner
   a) Ammunition (10,000 tons), the bulk of which was shipped on July 3 and 16, 1948................................ 336,916.05
   b) Aircraft—delivered in September and December 1948 .... 582,250.00
   c) Aircraft spare parts and armament parts 296,568.60
      TOTAL, OFFICE OF THE FOREIGN LIQUIDATION COMMISSIONER 1,215,734.65
      TOTAL U. S. GOVERNMENT AGENCIES $47,598,791.27

B. *Items Procured Directly by Chinese Government*

(1) Chinese Air Force
   a) Aircraft.. $260,000.00
   b) Aircraft engines..................................... 205,780.00
   c) Aviation gasoline and motor oil......................... 4,701,626.31
   d) Tires and tubes...................................... 126,008.52
   e) Flying boats.. 110,830.00
   f) Snow plows and trucks................................ 112,466.70
   g) Portable heaters..................................... 110,776.26
   h) Aircraft parts and miscellaneous air force equipment 1,511,179.55
   i) Shipping charges, including insurance.................... 361,852.62
   j) Miscellaneous services rendered........................ 25,062.78

      TOTAL, CHINESE AIR FORCE 7,525,632.74

ANNEXES 955

B. *Items Procured Directly by Chinese Government*—Continued

(2) Chinese Military Procurement Technical Group
    a) Signal equipment and supplies $671,027.50
    b) Ordnance material 590,702.09
    c) Transportation equipment 148,000.00
    d) Armored Force equipment 285,531.17
    e) Gasoline, fuel oil and other petroleum products 3,652,457.88
    f) Shipping charges 486,648.73

    TOTAL, CHINESE MILITARY PROCUREMENT TECHNICAL GROUP 5,834,367.37
    TOTAL, ITEMS PROCURED DIRECTLY BY CHINESE GOVERNMENT $13,360,000.11
    GRAND TOTAL 60,958,791.3

XVIII

REPORT RECEIVED FROM THE CHINESE EMBASSY ON SHIPMENTS UNDER THE $125 MILLION GRANTS

Period of Report: January 1–January 31, 1949

Part I—Chinese Air Force

Description	Value ($)	Weight	Name of vessel	Date of sailing	Port of embarkation
(1) ITEMS PROCURED BY CHINESE AIR FORCE					
Aircraft Engines	$132,500.00	82,500 lbs	Belleville	Dec. 19, 1948	Miami.
Mechanics Tools	149.44	38¼ lbs	Manderville . . .	. . do	New York.
Flying Boots	1,620.00	766 lbs	Pioneer Cove . .	Dec. 29, 1948	Do.
Portable Ground Heaters.	191.42	385 lbs	. . do	. . do	Do.
Fuses for Aircraft . . .	111.86	60 lbs.	Mount Davis .	Dec. 31, 1948	Do.
Jeep Replacement Parts .	4,765.00	3,509 lbs.	. . do	. . do	Do.
Regulators	2,324.92	809 lbs	. . do	. . do	Do.
Radio Compass . . .	4,037.60	5,739 lbs	. . do	. . do	Do.
Power Unit Canopy Actuator.	2,575.59	96 lbs	. . do	. . do	Do.
Valve-Oil dil.	3,202.70	1,230 lbs	. . do	. . do	Do.
Diaphragm	446.26	183 lbs	. . do	. . do	Do.
Airplane Parts	726.85	187 lbs	. . do	. . do	Do.
Generator	330.75	150 lbs	. . do	. . do	Do.
Accumulator	2,307.64	311 lbs	. . do	. . do	Do.
Airplane Part	19,417.24	4,192 lbs	. . do	. . do	Do.
Aircraft (P-51) (Machine Guns) (20).	260,000.00	320,700 lbs . . .	Colorado	. . do	Houston.
Merlin Aircraft Engines.	73,280.00	169,700 lbs	. . do	. . do	Do.
Brake Assemblies . . .	5,715.00	1,978 lbs	. . do	. . do	Do.
Strut Assemblies	420.00	100 lbs	. . do	. . do	Do.
Aircraft Parts & Bomb Sight and Isopropanol.	896,767.35	150,834 lbs	. . do	. . do	Do.
Pump and Refueling Unit Ass'y.	17,170.00	16,600 lbs	Transocean A. L.	Jan. 7, 1949	Oakland.
16 P-51 D Airplane . . .	208,000.00	251,600 lbs . . .	Ferndale	Jan. 15, 1949	Houston.
Total	1,636,059.62	1,011,667¼ lbs.			

U. S. RELATIONS WITH CHINA

Part II—Chinese Army and Navy

Description	Value ($)	Weight	Name of vessel	Date of sailing	Port of embarkation
(1) ITEMS PROCURED BY CHINESE MILITARY PROCUREMENT TECHNICAL GROUP					
Armored Force					
Periscopes, Head Assemblies & Tank Tracks 469 Cs.	$18,843.17	73,301 lbs	S. S. Courser	Dec. 1, 1948	Honolulu.
Ordnance					
Calculating Machine, 1 Pc.	702.09	94 lbs	C. N. A. C.	Dec. 16, 1948	San Francisco.
Telescopes 350 Pcs.	3,535.34	814 lbs.	Mt. Mansfield	Jan. 22, 1949	New York.
Signal					
Calculating Machine, 1 Pc.	702.09	94 lbs.	C. N. A. C.	Dec. 16, 1948	San Francisco.
Typewriters, 2 Pcs.	335.91	252 lbs.	Philippine Bear.	Jan. 18, 1949	Do.
Paraffin Wax 98 Cs.	2,184.16	20,249 lbs.	Philippine Transport.	Dec. 28, 1948	Do.
Zinc Chloride, 82 Dms.	6,515.84	52,172 lbs.	Grete Maersk.	Jan. 18, 1949	New York.
Graphite Powder 66,000	4,290.00	67,652 lbs.	Mt. Davis	Dec. 31, 1948	Do.
Switchboard BD-72 620 Pcs.	7,440.00	87,200 lbs.	..do.	Dec. 31, 1948	Do.
Field Telephone EE8 4000 Pcs.	30,004.92	54,910 lbs.	..do.	Dec. 31, 1948	Do.
Field Tel. EE8, 1530 Pcs	13,064.90	21,349 lbs.	President Fillmore.	Jan. 7, 1949	Do.
Field Telephone EE8 900 Pcs.	8,569.92	12,412 lbs.	Mt. Mansfield	Jan. 22, 1949	Do.
Switchboard BD-72, 180 Pcs.	3,083.92	20,250 lbs.	..do.	..do.	Do.
Switchboard BD-71 250 Pcs.	4,060.31	27,982 lbs.	..do.	..do.	Do.
Radio Tubes 20 Cs.	20,179.82	6,681 lbs.	..do.	..do.	Do.
Zinc Sheet 100 Cs.	15,015.21	61,605 lbs.	..do.	..do.	Do.
Ammonium Chloride 582 bbls.	12,815.26	174,600 lbs.	..do.	..do.	Do.
Transportation					
Retreading & Recapping Stock, T2.	38,253.06	167,610 lbs.	Philippine Bear.	Jan. 18, 1949	San Francisco.
Retreading & Recapping Stock, T2.	38,938.55	166,352 lbs.	Lakeland Victory.	Jan. 29, 1949	Los Angeles.
Spare Parts for Motor Vehicles T3.	531,964.81	631,026 lbs.	Philippine Bear.	Jan. 18, 1949	San Francisco.
Do.	16,314.86	7,496 lbs.	Lakeland Victory.	Jan. 29, 1949	Los Angeles.
GMC 2.5T 6x6 Army Truck 38 Cs.	134,099.06	394,900 lbs.	Philippine Bear.	Jan. 18, 1949	San Francisco.
Auto Spark-Plugs 46 Cs.	22,562.78	12,532 lbs	Mt. Mansfield	Jan. 22, 1949	New York.
Rubber Compd. & Tire Patches 56 Cs.	25,650.63	27,526 lbs	..do	Feb. 5, 1949	Los Angeles.
Testing Apparatus Electric 46 Cs.	46,018.32	15,565 lbs	..do	Feb. 10, 1949	San Francisco.
SUBTOTAL (items on 1)	1,005,148.93	2,104,624 lbs.			

Part II—*Chinese Army and Navy*—Continued

Description	Value ($)	Weight	Name of vessel	Date of sailing	Port of embarkation
(2) Items Supplied by U. S. Army and Navy					
SCR 522 Radio Sets 150 Pcs.	43,534.16	150,867 lbs	U. S. S. Washburn.	Dec. 16, 1948	Bangor.
Signal Equipment Parts 246 Bxs.	78,285.20	42,000 lbs	Philippine Transport.	Dec. 28, 1948	San Francisco.
Navy Jackets & Coats 1,500 Pcs.	18,250.00	8,800 lbs	R. C. S. Tai-Ho.	Jan. 11, 1949	Norfolk.
Subtotal (items on 2)	$140,069.36	201,667 lbs			
(3) Items Supplied by U. S. Bureau of Federal Supply					
Navy Lubricating Oil 587 x 55 Gals.	16,759.59	257,400 lbs	M. S. Belleville.	Jan. 12, 1949	New Orleans.
Navy Lubricating Oil 3857 x 54 Gals.	61,959.59	1,697,520 lbs	S. S. City of Alabama.	Jan. 25, 1949	Do.
Auto-Gasoline 10,000 x 53 Gals.	217,300.00	3,800,000 lbs	Philippine Bear	Jan. 18, 1949	San Francisco.
Auto-Gasoline 9,943 x 53 Gals.	216,061.39	3,778,340 lbs	Lakeland Victory.	Jan. 29, 1949	Los Angeles.
Subtotal	$512,080.57	9,533,260 lbs			
Total (Army and Navy)	1,657,298.86	11,839,551 lbs (5,381.6 long tons)			

Part III—*Summary*

	Approximate total value ($)	Approximate total weight (long tons)
Chinese Air Force	1,636,059.62	459.9
Chinese Army and Navy	1,657,298.86	5,381.6
Grand Total	3,293,358.48	5,841.5

958 U. S. RELATIONS WITH CHINA

XIX

REPORT RECEIVED FROM THE CHINESE EMBASSY ON SHIPMENTS UNDER THE $125 MILLION GRANTS

Period of Report: February 1–February 28, 1949

Part I—Chinese Air Force

Description	Values ($)	Weight	Name of vessel	Date of sailing	Port of embarkation
(1) ITEMS PROCURED BY CHINESE AIR FORCE					
Aircraft Parts	7,542.18	5,860 lbs	Luxembourg V.	Jan. 19, 1949	Los Angeles.
Static Dischargers	414.00	50 lbs	..do	..do	Do.
Aircraft Parts	1,935.00	426 lbs	..do	..do	Do.
Do	5,546.85	2,578 lbs	..do	..do	Do.
Do	1,513.75	508 lbs	..do	..do	Do.
Do	8,950.00	4,600 lbs	..do	..do	Do.
Transport Tires & Tubes.	79,204.10	159,057 lbs	..do	..do	Do.
AT-6 Aircraft	330,000.00	179,520 lbs	..do	..do	Do.
Truck Tires & Tubes	34,408.29	62,598 lbs	..do	..do	Do.
Attachment Screw	154.00	54 lbs	..do	..do	Do.
R-100—Hose	806.74	869 lbs	..do	..do	Do.
Expander Tubes	2,278.19	744 lbs	..do	..do	Do.
Airplane Tires	1,527.90	972 lbs	..do	..do	Do.
Hose	1,214.51	1,195 lbs	..do	..do	Do.
Airplane Tubes	750.00	1,802 lbs	..do	..do	Do.
Airplane Engines	64,000.00	103,800 lbs	Fernfield	..do	New York.
Do	78,200.00	47,650 lbs	..do	..do	Do.
Generators	1,560.00	340 lbs	..do	..do	Do.
Airplane Parts	6,103.65	395 lbs	..do	..do	Do.
Radio Tubes	1,236.00	636 lbs	..do	..do	Do.
Disc. Etc	1,825.40	113 lbs	..do	..do	Do.
P-47 Tires & Tubes	11,168.88	6,899 lbs	..do	..do	Do.
Radio Compasses	4,851.00	2,233 lbs	..do	..do	Do.
Coil Assembly	2,544.00	154 lbs	..do	..do	Do.
Protectors	31.75	7 lbs	..do	..do	Do.
Relays, Reg.	1,295.94	761 lbs	..do	..do	Do.
Airplane Parts	68,531.00	59,634 lbs	..do	..do	Do.
Aircraft Parts	349.35	140 lbs	Lakeland, Vic.	Jan. 29, 1949	Long Beach.
AT-6 Aircraft	20,185.00	89,760 lbs	..do	..do	Do.
Propeller Ass'y for C-46	5,445.00	12,100 lbs	..do	..do	Do.
Do	1,485.00	3,300 lbs	..do	..do	Do.
AT-6 Aircraft	20,185.00	89,760 lbs	Mt. Mansfield	Feb. 6, 1949	Los Angeles.
Aircraft Parts	1,500.00	230 lbs	..do	..do	Do.
Do	4,025.00	6,752 lbs	..do	..do	Do.
Truck Tires & Tubes	11,528.72	24,952 lbs	..do	..do	Do.
P-47 Tires & Tubes	692.12	631 lbs	..do	..do	Do.
P-47 Airplanes K/D with Machine Guns.	35,000.00	118,525 lbs	..do	Feb. 14, 1949	Houston.
Merlin, V-1650-7 New Engines, Aircraft.	18,320.00	41,600 lbs	..do	..do	Do.
Internal Combustion Eng.	31,900.00	85,550 lbs	..do	..do	Do.
P-51 Airplanes K/D with Machine Guns.	127,500.00	268,744 lbs	..do	..do	Do.
Aircraft Engines (Pratt & Whitney).	212,000.00	13,200 lbs	..do	..do	Do.
24 cc Pertussis Endotoxid Vaccine.	13,527.00	1,475 lbs	Airlines	Feb. 16, 1949	Washington, DC.

Part I—Chinese Air Force—Continued

Description	Value ($)	Weight	Name of vessel	Date of sailing	Port of embarkation
(1) ITEMS PROCURED BY CHINESE AIR FORCE—Continued					
100's Penioral Tablets, Buffered Penicillin.	$9,020.00	466 lbs	Airlines	Feb. 16, 1949	Washington, D.C.
Aircraft Clock A-11	195.00	20 lbs	Titania	Feb. 18, 1949	New York.
Airplane Engine Parts	125.50	56 lbs	..do	..do	Do.
Airplane Engines	115,920.00	140,700 lbs	..do	..do	Do.
Snow Plow Parts Auto	17,039.52	11,690 lbs	..do	..do	Do.
Aircraft Engine Parts	1,676.40	405 lbs	..do	..do	Do.
Pumps & Refueling Unit	1,875.00	1,900 lbs	..do	..do	Do.
Aircraft Engine Electric Relay Assembly.	4,721.76	1,983 lbs	..do	..do	Do.
R378-1 Spark Plugs	67,103.02	66 lbs	..do	..do	Do.
Lead Assemblies	4,832.40	486 lbs	..do	..do	Do.
Bolts	97.85	225 lbs	..do	..do	Do.
Aircraft Magneto	437.75	35 lbs	..do	..do	Do.
Leather Packing	1,566.72	69 lbs	..do	..do	Do.
Contact Springs and Lead Assembly.	5,207.26	563 lbs	..do	..do	Do.
Aircraft Material	1,125.60	348 lbs	..do	.do	Do.
Carburetor Air Filters	8,401.00	4,733 lbs	..do	..do	Do.
Gun, Automatic 20mm M2 & parts.	33,134.00	48,664 lbs	..do	do	Do.
Aluminum Sheets	1,498.00	3,373 lbs	..do	..do	Do.
Aircraft Batteries	1,473.00	1,432 lbs	Axel Salen	..do	Do.
Spark Plugs	1,152.00	282 lbs	..do	..do	Do.
Engine Rad	9,970.64	3,708 lbs	..do	..do	Do.
Motor Assembly	370.80	128 lbs	..do	..do	Do.
Aircraft Parts	2,278.85	770 lbs	..do	..do	Do.
Dic. Ass'y Snubbing Super-Vision.	582.12	1,280 lbs	..do	..do	Do.
Engine Parts Misc	8,116.63	2,326 lbs	..do	..do	Do.
100/130 Octane Aviation Gas.	970,127.54	15,819,174 lbs	General Guisan	Feb. 19, 1949	St. Rose, La.
AT-6 Airplanes	20,185.00	89,760 lbs	Chas. E. Dant	Feb. 21, 1949	Long Beach.
Carburetors	2,700.00	1,245 lbs	Tantara	do	Los Angeles.
Aircraft Parts	7,977.60	1,625 lbs	..do	do	Do.
Do	2,150.00	1,140 lbs	..do	do	Do.
Auto Tires with Tubes Ins.	51,586.40	101,672 lbs	..do	do	Do.
Aircraft Parts	84.00	38 lbs	..do	do	Do.
Do	980.70	917 lbs	..do	do	Do.
Propeller Assembly	12,720.00	16,080 lbs	..do	do	Do.
Aircraft Parts	3,031.00	897 lbs	.do	do	Do.
Auto Cleaning Equip. and Supplies.	18,259.30	12,810 lbs	..do	do	Do.
Airplanes	20,185.00	89,760 lbs	..do	..do	Do.
Propeller Assemblies	2,176.02	3,025 lbs	Jesse Lykes	Feb. 23, 1949	Houston.
R-2600-29 Wright Engines.	46,440.00	53,100 lbs	..do	..do	Do.
(9) R-2600-29 Wright Engines.	17,550.00	26,550 lbs	..do	..do	Do.
(13) Airplanes P-47 K/D Links	136,500.00 19,644.11	308,165 lbs 76,300 lbs	..do Chas. E. Dant	do Feb. 27, 1949	Do. San Francisco.
TOTAL	2,851,452.89	18,228,140 lbs			

Part II—Chinese Army and Navy

Description	Value ($)	Weight	Name of vessel	Date of sailing	Port of embarkation
(1) Items Procured by Chinese Military Procurement Technical Group					
Armored Force					
Spare Parts for Truck, GMC 176 Items.	217,701.68	84,915 lbs.	Mt. Mansfield	Feb. 11, 1949	San Francisco.
Engines & Spare Parts for Tank 876 cs.	170,184.18	405,718 lbs.	..do.	Feb. 18, 1949	Honolulu.
Tank Tracks 589 Pks	9,358.84	562,500 lbs.	President Buchanan.	Feb. 19, 1949	New York.
Auto Mechanics Tool Set 100 Cs.	29,087.20	25,142 lbs.	..do.	..do.	Do.
LVT Gun Shields etc. 400 Pcs.	26,475.07	155,930 lbs.	Gen. Meigs	Feb. 2, 1949	Honolulu.
Ordnance					
Cartridges Balls 2800 Cs ORD-6.	262,005.65	177,200 lbs.	President Buchanan.	Feb. 19, 1949	New York.
Signal					
Field Telephones EE-8 1,550 Pcs.	14,015.15	21,037 lbs.	..do.	..do.	Do.
Transportation					
GMC 2.5T Army Truck 22Cs TRANS-1.	77,628.49	250,800 lbs.	China Victory	Feb. 18, 1949	Los Angeles.
Dry Storage Batteries 185 Cs T-10.	9,845.83	36,515 lbs.	..do.	..do.	San Francisco.
Machinery & Parts 3 Plants T-4.	82,131.03	130,164 lbs.	President Buchanan.	Feb. 19, 1949	New York.
Tire Repair Equipment 45 Cs T-5.	11,692.53	15,060 lbs.	..do.	..do.	Do.
Auto Carburetors & Parts 23 Cs T-8.	24,965.77	11,926 lbs.	..do.	..do.	Do.
Auto Storage Batteries 821 Cs T-9.	36,953.21	93,378 lbs.	..do.	..do.	Do.
Subtotal (items on 1).	972,044.63	1,960,285 lbs.			
(2) Items Supplied by U. S. Army and Navy					
Navy Ships Spare Parts & Communication Equipment.	607,000.00	330,000 lbs.	U.S.S. Warrick	Feb. 2, 1949	San Francisco.
Army Tubes & Tires & Medicals.		725,139 lbs.	Mt. Mansfield	Jan. 23, 1949	New Jersey.
Items for Ord, Trans, Med, Sig.		5,594,398 lbs.	Seminole	Feb. 19, 1949	Bangor.
Items for Trans, Sig, Ord, 661 MT.		336,600 lbs.	President Buchanan.	..do.	New York.
Items for Trans etc. 655 T.		552,200 lbs.	Pacific Transport	Feb. 24, 1949	San Francisco.
Subtotal:					
(Items on 2 Navy).	607,000.00	7,538,337 lbs.			
(Items on 2 Army).	3,000,000.00				
	3,607,000.00				

Part II—Chinese Army and Navy—Continued

Description	Value ($)	Weight	Name of vessel	Date of sailing	Port of embarkation
(3) ITEMS CONTRACTED BY U. S. BUREAU OF FEDERAL SUPPLY					
Chinese Army					
Hydraulic Brake Fluid 105 x 54 gals	15,309.00	52,290 lbs	China Victory	Feb. 11, 1949	Los Angeles.
Motor Gasoline 4,636,000 AG	1,344,400.00	12,980 tons	Ex-ware-Shanghai by Texas Co.		
Fuel Oil A-3	435,150.00	15,000 tons	..do		
Lubricating Oil 59,000 AG	22,597.00	195 tons	..do		
Grease [Grease]	4,719.00	33,000 lbs	..do		
Motor Gasoline 2,452,500 AG	846,855.00	6,867 tons	Ex-ware-Canton by Texas Co.		
Chinese Navy					
Hydraulic Brake Fluid 43 x 54 gals	6,153.30	18,700 lbs	China Victory	Feb. 11, 1949	Los Angeles.
Hydraulic Brake Fluid 45 x 54 gals	5,346.00	19,800 lbs	..do	Feb. 4, 1949	New York.
Motor Gasoline 527,900 AG	160,490.00	1,478 tons	Ex-ware-Shanghai by Texas Co.		
Kerosene 26,593 AG	7,646.26	80 tons	..do		
Diesel Oil	705,856.00	15,470 tons	..do		
Fuel Oil	560,190.00	19,000 tons	..do		
Lubricating Oil 177,882 AG	71,466.79	586 tons	..do		
Motor Gasoline 66,000 AG	20,460.00	185 tons	Ex-ware-Canton by Texas Co.		
Kerosene 5,000 AG	1,635.00	15 tons	..do		
Diesel Oil	140,400.00	3,000 tons	..do		
SUBTOTAL:					
(items on 3 Army)	2,669,030.00	85,290 lbs & 35,042 long tons			
(items on 3 Navy)	1,679,643.35	38,500 lbs & 39,814 long tons			
	4,348,673.35	123,790 lbs & 74,856 long tons			
TOTAL (Army and Navy)	8,927,717.98	79,230 long tons on wt. basis as last month.			

Part III—Summary

	Approximate total value ($)	Approximate total weight (long tons)
Chinese Air Force	2,851,452.89	8,285.5
Chinese Army and Navy	8,927,717.98	79,230.0
GRAND TOTAL	11,779,170.87	87,515.5

XX

REPORT RECEIVED FROM THE CHINESE EMBASSY ON SHIPMENTS UNDER THE $125 MILLION GRANTS

Period of Report: March 1–March 31, 1949

Part I—Chinese Air Force

Description	Values ($)	Weight	Name of vessel	Date of sailing	Port of embarkation
(1) ITEMS PROCURED BY CHINESE AIR FORCE					
C-46 Tires	4,750.75	5,980 lbs	Chas. E. Dant	Feb. 26, 1949	San Francisco.
Truck Tires and Tubes	14,349.55	28,391 lbs	..do	..do	Do.
Truck Tires	12,986.96	23,986 lbs	..do	..do	Do.
AT-11 Tires and Tubes	485.75	323 lbs	..do	..do	Do.
Fuel Hose	3,358.09	3,588 lbs	..do	..do	Do.
Discs and Gaskets	408.23	150 lbs	..do	..do	Do.
11 AT-6 Airplanes	165,000.00	89,760 lbs	Phil. Transport	Feb. 25, 1949	Los Angeles.
Truck Tires and Tubes	19,317.50	36,928 lbs	..do	Feb. 28, 1949	San Francisco.
C-6 Tools and Spare Parts	6,783.77	1,611 lbs	Axel Salen	Mar. 2, 1949	Los Angeles.
Airplanes P-47 K/D (3)	27,000.00	72,000 lbs	Almeria Lykes	..do	Houston.
Internal Combustion Engines	21,000.00	15,600 lbs	..do	..do	Do.
Aircraft Parts	670.00	989 lbs	Mongabarra	Mar. 10, 1949	Los Angeles.
Do	152.00	105 lbs	..do	..do	Do.
Do	900.00	172 lbs	..do	..do	Do.
Do	2,079.00	164 lbs	..do	..do	Do.
Do	4,210.60	1,211 lbs	..do	..do	Do.
Do	391.50	114 lbs	..do	..do	Do.
Aircraft Equipment	6,463.19	500 lbs	..do	..do	Do.
C-46 Aircraft Parts	25,681.80	16,532 lbs	..do	..do	Do.
Aircraft Parts	4,422.00	4,604 lbs	..do	..do	Do.
13 AT-6 Aircraft	195,000.00	106,080 lbs	..do	..do	Do.
Aircraft Parts	3,632.90	708 lbs	..do	..do	Do.
Paint Thinner	1.00	38 lbs	..do	..do	Do.
35 R-1340 Aircraft Engines	80,500.00	57,950 lbs	..do	..do	Do.
17 R-2800-75 Converted to R-2800-59 Airc. Engines	21,436.01	55,250 lbs	..do	..do	Do.
1 Pratt & Whitney Engine	1,000.00	3,100 lbs	..do	..do	Do.
T11BK Ctg. .50 Cal. M2	3,805.53	8,176 lbs	..do	Mar. 13, 1949	San Francisco.
T11CN Ctg. Cal. .50 Belted	716.89	1,638 lbs	..do	..do	Do.
Aircraft Parts	502.50	252 lbs	..do	..do	Do.
AT-6 Aircraft (11)	165,000.00	89,760 lbs	Indian Bear	..do	Long Beach.
Air Brake Assembly	3,750.00	1,390 lbs	..do	..do	Do.
Truck Tires and Tubes	29,980.50	61,782 lbs	..do	Mar. 18, 1949	San Francisco.
C-46 Tires and Tubes	15,048.19	17,314 lbs	..do	..do	Do.
C-46 De-Icer Parts	295.96	14 lbs	..do	..do	Do.
Aluminum Rivnuts	17.70	11 lbs	..do	..do	Do.
Aircraft Repl. Parts	20,961.31	21,250 lbs	Howell Lykes	Mar. 15, 1949	Houston.

ANNEXES

Part I—*Chinese Air Force*—Continued

Description	Values ($)	Weight	Name of vessel	Date of sailing	Port of embarkation
(1) ITEMS PROCURED BY CHINESE AIR FORCE—Con.					
P-51 Airplane Parts	3,118.20				
Do	4,367.80	2,367 lbs.	Howell Lykes	Mar. 15, 1949	Houston.
Do	318.97				
Gauge Fuel Level	112.50	65 lbs.	.. do	.. do	Do.
P-47 Airplanes with Machine Guns.	180,000.00	480,000 lbs.	.. do	.. do	Do.
Glass Assy for P-51, incl. Canopy	1,754.53	8,111 lbs.	.. do	.. do	Do.
B-24 Spare Parts					
Aircraft Parts	2,152.50	898 lbs	Ivarah	Mar. 18, 1949	New York
Aluminum Sheets	1,619.50	5,740 lbs	.. do	.. do	Do.
Do	654.25	1,629 lbs	.. do	.. do	Do.
Airplane Prop. Assembly.	8,095.80	10,275 lbs	.. do	.. do	Do.
Aircraft Material	1,152.27	675 lbs	.. do	.. do	Do.
Vix Syn-Packing	618.62	45 lbs	.. do	.. do	Do.
Carburetors and Parts	1,786.50	869 lbs	.. do	.. do	Do.
Aircraft Accessories	853.98	260 lbs	.. do	.. do	Do.
Emulsion Spray Outfit	872.50	1,688 lbs	.. do	.. do	Do.
Oil Pressure Gages	290.00	85 lbs	.. do	.. do	Do.
Harness Assy—Ignition Comp.	1,200.00	2,215 lbs	.. do	.. do	Do.
Military Windlasses	867.00	1,167 lbs	.. do	.. do	Do.
LE45 Spark Plugs	11,256.00	2,061 lbs	.. do	.. do	Do.
Internal Comb. Engines	6,250.00	7,000 lbs	.. do	.. do	Do.
Spare Parts	4,809.26	214 lbs	.. do	.. do	Do.
Chamois Leather	690.00	108 lbs	.. do	.. do	Do.
Cylinder and Valve Assy.	2,292.87	1,168 lbs	.. do	.. do	Do.
P-47N Repl. Parts	11,496.32	8,335 lbs	.. do	.. do	Do.
Airplane Parts	1,230.00	325 lbs	.. do	.. do	Do.
Aircraft Repl. Parts	842.44	831 lbs	.. do	.. do	Do.
W-670-24 Aircraft Engines.	53,900.00	39,600 lbs	.. do	.. do	Do.
Aircraft Engines	21,887.37	140,700 lbs	.. do	.. do	Do.
O-435-11 Aircraft Engines.	60,000.00	27,400 lbs	.. do	.. do	Do.
Tank Units; Electric Fuel.	1,329.50	188 lbs	.. do	.. do	Do.
Plug Valves	280.28	14 lbs	.. do	.. do	Do.
Aircraft Tools	11,001.64	1,890 lbs	.. do	.. do	Do.
11 AT-6 Aircraft	165,000.00	89,760 lbs	Lakeland Victory.	Mar. 26, 1949	Long Beach.
T11 BK Ctg. Armor Piercing Cal. .50 M2 Grade MG.	4,724.95	100,000 lbs	Arizona	Mar. 27, 1949	San Francisco.
Do	4,174.57	88,440 lbs	.. do	.. do	Do.
Do	4,049.96	85,890 lbs	.. do	.. do	Do.
Do	2,513.05	53,240 lbs	.. do	.. do	Do.
TOTAL	1,438,623.02	1,890,674 lbs.			

Part II—Chinese Army and Navy

Description	Values ($)	Weight	Name of vessel	Date of sailing	Port of embarkation
(1) ITEMS PROCURED BY CHINESE MILITARY PROCUREMENT TECHNICAL GROUP					
Armored Force					
Spare Parts for Truck 2½ T 150 cs A-3.	$1,355.86	88,530 lbs	President Buchanan.	Mar. 8, 1949	San Francisco.
Spare Parts for Tank 1,363 cs A-5.	4,000.00	315,728 lbs ...	Pioneer Mail ..	Mar. 21, 1949	Honolulu.
Army Engineer					
Barbed Wire Machine 4 pcs E-11.	16,798.66	23,680 lbs	President Van Buren.	Mar. 19, 1949	New York.
Testing Apparatus & Magnetos 5 cs E-5, 14.	1,580.33	546 lbs	.. do	.. do	Do.
Road Grader Parts etc. E-9.	4,844.73	10,756 lbs	.. do	.. do	Do.
Crates Pneumatic Chain Saw 5 cs E-21.	3,000.34	825 lbs	.. do	.. do	Do.
Boring Bars & Parts 10 cs E-15.	4,692.00	2,050 lbs	.. do	.. do	Do.
Ordnance					
Brass Plate 652 Cs O-9, 10.	31,474.28	285,665 lbs ...	.. do	.. do	Do.
Cartridges Balls 3750 Cs O-6.	357,722.72	239,250 lbs ...	.. do	.. do	Do.
Transportation					
Machinery & Parts 2 plants T-4.	54,754.02	86,776 lbs	.. do	.. do	Do.
Auto Accessories 59 Cs T11.	8,931.71	15,403 lbs	.. do	.. do	Do.
Machinery & Parts 4 Sets T13.	33,409.20	48,992 lbs	.. do	.. do	Do.
SUBTOTAL (items on 1).	$572,563.85	1,118,201 lbs or 500.00 long tons.	....	....	
(2) ITEMS SUPPLIED BY U. S. ARMY					
Army Tubes and Tires .	60,000.00	96,687 lbs	Pioneer Mail ..	Mar. 4, 1949	Do.
Items for Ordnance ...	10,000.00	285,409 lbs ...	.. do	.. do	Do.
SUBTOTAL (items on 2)	70,000.00	382,096 lbs or 170.50 long tons.	....	....	

Part II—Chinese Army and Navy—Continued

Description	Values ($)	Weight	Name of vessel	Date of sailing	Port of embarkation
(3) ITEMS CONTRACTED BY U. S. BUREAU OF FEDERAL SUPPLY					
Chinese Army					
Motor Gasoline 70 Octane 899,993 AG.	332,997.41	2,520.00	Ex-ware-China by Standard Oil Co.	. . . .	. . . . .
Commercial St. Fuel Oil A-3.	184,453.12	5,902.50	. . do	. . . .	. . . . .
Industrial St. Diesel Oil A-4.	69,012.50	1,290.00	. . do	. . . .	. . . . .
Motor Oil SAE 30 & 40 174,996 AG.	72,338.40	532.00	. . do	. . . .	. . . . .
Chinese Navy					
Lubricating Oil N-8, 9, 10, 89,557 AG.	37,412.29	271.00	. . do	. . . .	. . . . .
Red Engine N-16 17,606 AG.	6,778.31	53.50	. . do	. . . .	. . . . .
SUBTOTAL					
(items on 3 Army).	658,801.43	10,244.50 long tons.	. . . .		
(items on 3 Navy).	44,190.60	324.50 long tons	. . . .		
	702,992.03	10,569.00 long tons.	. . .		
TOTAL (Army and Navy).	1,345,555.88	11,239.50 long tons on wt. basis as last month.			

Part III—Summary

	Approximate total value ($)	Approximate total weight (long tons)
Chinese Air Force	1,438,623.02	859.4
Chinese Army and Navy	1,345,555.88	11,239.5
TOTAL	2,784,178.90	12,098.9

XXI

REPORT RECEIVED FROM THE CHINESE EMBASSY ON SHIPMENTS UNDER THE $125 MILLION GRANTS

Period of Report: April 1–April 30, 1949

Part I—Chinese Air Force

Description	Values ($)	Weight	Name of vessel	Date of sailing	Port of embarkation
(1) ITEMS PROCURED BY CHINESE AIR FORCE					
Aircraft Engine Parts	27,596.88	8,670 lbs	Tarifa	Mar. 31, 1949	New York.
Clocks	97.50	9 lbs	.. do	.. do	Do.
Seal Disc Assy	670.65	16 lbs	.. do	.. do	Do.
Aircraft Repl. Parts	457.69	95 lbs	.. do	.. do	Do.
Magneto Repair Parts	873.00	70 lbs	.. do	.. do	Do.
Shaft and Casings	326.16	63 lbs	.. do	.. do	Do.
Stromberg Carburetor Tools	11,473.82	2,660 lbs	.. do	.. do	Do.
Aircraft Engines	29,900.00	20,500 lbs	.. do	.. do	Do.
Breaker, Slip Ring	1,083.00	94 lbs	.. do	.. do	Do.
Airplane Parts	657.11	193 lbs	.. do	.. do	Do.
Aircraft Engines	18,023.10	117,250 lbs	.. do	.. do	Do.
Airplane Parts	2,284.00	271 lbs	.. do	.. do	Do.
Aircraft Engine Parts	53,900.00	39,600 lbs	.. do	.. do	Do.
Aircraft Engines	16,616.77	46,800 lbs	.. do	.. do	Do.
Propeller Assy	3,000.00	5,400 lbs	President McKinley.	Apr. 4, 1949	Los Angeles.
11 AT-6 Aircraft	165,000.00	89,760 lbs	.. do	.. do	Do.
Do	165,000.00	89,760 lbs	Philippine Bear	Apr. 8, 1949	Long Beach.
AT-6 Tools and Spare Parts.	174.30	85 lbs	.. do	.. do	Do.
AT-11 Aircraft (5)	437,500.00	90,400 lbs	China Victory	Apr. 22, 1949	Do.
C-46 Tires and Tubes	5,199.73	7,020 lbs	Philippine Bear	Apr. 27, 1949	San Francisco.
Aircraft Hose	321.18	316 lbs	.. do	.. do	Do.
De-Icer Parts	1,057.50	340 lbs	.. do	.. do	Do.
Aircraft Parts	31.50	12 lbs	Vingnes	Apr. 21, 1949	Los Angeles.
Do	6,598.00	1,757 lbs	.. do	.. do	Do.
11 AT-6 Aircraft	165,000.00	89,760 lbs	.. do	.. do	Do.
Aircraft Parts	11,202.67	18,643 lbs	.. do	.. do	Do.
Do	1,168.02	1,893 lbs	.. do	.. do	Do.
Do	2,303.50	2,504 lbs	.. do	.. do	Do.
Do	13,182.30	10,424 lbs	.. do	Apr. 25, 1949	San Francisco.
5 AT-11 Aircraft	437,500.00	90,400 lbs	Pacific Trans.	Apr. 27, 1949	Los Angeles.
Aircraft Parts	537.60	35 lbs	.. do	.. do	Do.
Do	4,391.70	1,408 lbs	.. do	.. do	Do.
Do	23,376.00	3,008 lbs	Lisholt	Apr. 25, 1949	New York.
Ring Leather Packing	1,684.23	67 lbs	.. do	.. do	Do.
Aircraft Engines	22,050.00	16,200 lbs	.. do	.. do	Do.
Brush Assy Slip Ring	3,900.00	50 lbs	.. do	.. do	Do.
Disc. Assy for Fuel Seles.	43.35	6 lbs	.. do	.. do	Do.
Automotive Carb. & Parts.	1,080.00	658 lbs	.. do	.. do	Do.
58289 Diaphragm	248.75	90 lbs	Pan American A. L.	Apr. 27, 1949	San Francisco.
Oxygen Regulators	550.00	1,122 lbs	S. S. Fernbay	Apr. 16, 1949	New York.
Airplane Spare Parts	222.20	68 lbs	.. do	Apr. 16, 1949	Do.
Do	1,236.75	17 lbs	.. do	Apr. 16, 1949	Do.
Carburetor Tools	3,853.05	304 lbs	.. do	Apr. 16, 1949	Do.

ANNEXES 967

Part I—*Chinese Air Force*—Continued

Description	Values ($)	Weight	Name of vessel	Date of sailing	Port of embarkation
(1) Items Procured by Chinese Air Force—Continued					
Airplane Spare Parts	$298.60	25 lbs	S. S. Fernbay	Apr. 16, 1949	New York.
Do	218.85	34 lbs	..do	Apr. 16, 1949	Do.
Do	8,856.00	754 lbs	..do	Apr. 16, 1949	Do.
Do	336.00	86 lbs	..do	Apr. 16, 1949	Do.
Leather "V"	372.06	22 lbs	..do	Apr. 16, 1949	Do.
Carburetor Overhaul Tools.	1,376.67	263 lbs	..do	Apr. 16, 1949	Do.
Aircraft Engines	53,900.00	39,600 lbs	..do	Apr. 16, 1949	Do.
Replacement Parts	11,292.01	7,837 lbs	..do	Apr. 16, 1949	Do.
Auto Parts	74,004.27	137,493 lbs	..do	Apr. 16, 1949	Do.
R-2800 Aircraft Engines.	15,750.00	20,100 lbs	..do	Apr. 16, 1949	Do.
Mobile Grease Aero	2,482.88	10,440 lbs	..do	Apr. 16, 1949	Do.
Total	1,810,159.35	964,452 lbs (438.4 long tons).			

Part II—*Chinese Army and Navy*

Description	Values ($)	Weight	Name of vessel	Date of sailing	Port of embarkation
(1) Items Procured by Chinese Military Procurement Technical Group					
Army Engineer					
Parts for H. Machine & Tools E13, E27.	$16,935.00	6,982 pounds	President Jefferson.	Apr. 2, 1949	New York.
Parts for H. Machine E-2, E-10.	6,260.00	2,727 pounds	Marine Snapper	Apr. 13, 1949	Do.
Misc. Tools E-22, E-26, E-28.	8,295.00	3,853 pounds	..do	..do	Do.
Blasting Machine, Galvanometers E12.	10,282.00	1,804 pounds	China Victory	Apr. 29, 1949	San Francisco.
Cylinder Reconditioning Outfit E17.	1,956.50	1,153 pounds	..do	..do	Do.
Ordnance					
Cartridges Ball 1,750 Cs	156,596.69	109,250 pounds	President Jefferson.	Apr. 2, 1949	New York.
Cartridges Balls 2,000 Cs.	173,946.66	124,000 pounds	Marine Snapper.	Apr. 13, 1949	Do.
Brass Plates 68 Cs Ord-10.	8,171.35	27,242 pounds	..do	..do	Do.
Signal					
Radio Tubes for 2nd Div. 7,820 Pcs.	4,445.70	723 pounds	..do	do	Do.
Transportation					
Dry Storage Batteries T10 412 Cs.	21,546.80	79,298 pounds	President Van Buren.	Apr. 7, 1949	San Francisco.
Auto Accessories T11 8 Cs.	714.98	1,040 pounds	President Jefferson.	Apr. 2, 1949	New York.
Auto Accessories T11 85 Cs.	20,694.56	19,223 pounds	Marine Snapper.	Apr. 13, 1949	Do.
Lubrication Equipments T7 307 Cs.	56,618.86	99,539 pounds	..do	..do	Do.
Spare Parts for Trucks T3 196 Cs.	85,699.90	82,100 pounds	China Victory	Apr. 29, 1949	San Francisco.
Sub-total (Items on 1).	572,164.00	558,934 pounds or 250 long tons.			

844538—49——64

Part II—Chinese Army and Navy—Continued

Description	Values ($)	Weight	Name of vessel	Date of sailing	Port of embarkation
(2) ITEMS SUPPLIED BY U. S. ARMY					
Ord. Misc. Surplus Items.	$122,039	526 long tons	LST No. 799	Apr. 4, 1949	Manila.
Med. Misc. Tools & Parts.	10,000	4 metric tons	President Jefferson.	Apr. 2, 1949	New York.
Ord. Maintenance Materials.	10,000	83 metric tons	.. do	.. do	Do.
Sig. Radio Sets	230,000	112 metric tons	.. do	.. do	Do.
Sig. Intelligence		0.2 pound	.. do	.. do	Do.
Trans. Tires & Parts	869,097	4,160 metric tons	.. do	.. do	Do.
SUB-TOTAL (Jefferson).	$1,119,097	4,359.2 metric tons or 1,000 long tons approx.			
AFC Guns	1,540	8 metric tons	John Towle	Apr. 24, 1949	San Francisco.
Med. Medicines & Misc.	300,000	108 metric tons	.. do	.. do	Do.
Ord. Maintenance Materials.	30,000	471 metric tons	.. do	.. do	Do.
Sig. Batteries	48,000	67 metric tons	.. do	.. do	Do.
Trans. Tires & Parts	354,325	1,396 metric tons	.. do	.. do	Do.
SUB-TOTAL (John Towle).	733,865	2,050 metric tons or 800 long tons approx.			
Med. Instruments & Drugs.	$30,000	31 metric tons	China Victory	Apr. 29, 1949	San Francisco.
Ord. Maintenance Materials.	2,000	5 metric tons	.. do	.. do	do.
Trans. Tire & Tubes	136,400	551 metric tons	.. do	.. do	do.
SUB-TOTAL (China Victory).	$168,400	587 metric tons or 160 L/T approx.			
Med. Drugs & Misc	$500,000	295 metric tons	Explorer	.. do	New York.
Ord. Maintenance Materials.	200,000	203 metric tons	.. do	.. do	do.
Sig. Radio Sets	380,000	180 metric tons	.. do	.. do	do.
Sig. Intelligence		0.4 metric ton	.. do	.. do	do.
Trans. Tires & Parts	604,261	2,640 metric tons	.. do	.. do	do.
SUB-TOTAL (Explorer).	$1,684,261	3,318.4 metric tons or 1000 L/T approx.			
Ord. Pig Lead	$1,343,865	2,525 long tons	Cotton State	Apr. 30, 1949	Tampico, Mexico.
SUB-TOTAL (Items on 2).	5,171,527	6,011 long tons			
TOTAL (Items 1 and 2).	$5,743,691	6,261 long tons on wt. basis as last month.			

Part III—Summary

	Approximate total value ($)	Approximate total weight (long tons)
Chinese Air Force	1,810,159.35	438.4
Chinese Army and Navy	5,743,691.00	6,261.0
GRAND TOTAL	7,553,850.35	6,699.4

172

Categories of American Military Aid Extended to China Since V-J Day

The following table outlines briefly the categories and totals of military aid extended since V-J Day, figures being in millions of United States dollars:

Military Aid	Grants	Credits	Sales of U. S. Government Excess and Surplus Property		
			Procurement Value	Realization by U. S.	
				Init.	Ult.
1. Lend-Lease ($694.7 million)	$513.7	$181.0			
2. Military Aid Under SACO	17.7				
3. Sale of excess stocks of U. S. Army in West China		20	(¹)	(²)	² $20
4. Ammunition Abandoned and transferred by U. S. Marines in North China (over 6500 tons)	(³)				
5. Transfer of U. S. Navy Vessels (PL 512)	141.3	(⁴)			
6. Sales of surplus Military equipment (total shipped)			102.0	6.7	6.7
7. $125 Million Grant Under China Aid Act of 1948	125				
TOTAL MILITARY AID	$797.7	$201.0	$102.0	$6.7	$26.7

¹ No information regarding procurement value available.
² Down payment covered under Bulk Sale Agreement of August 30, 1946.
³ No estimate of total value available.
⁴ Vessels valued at procurement cost.

LEND-LEASE

Though lend-lease terminated for most countries on June 30, 1946, in order to continue assistance to the National Government lend-lease to China was extended on a reimbursable basis under terms of a military aid agreement of June 28, 1946. As of June 30, 1948, a grand total of $781.0 million in post V-J Day lend-lease transfers had been reported to the Treasury Department by United States Government agencies. Of this amount, $50.3 million represented deliveries on 3(c) credit terms under the lend-lease "pipeline" agreement, and $36 million covered United States Navy vessels originally lend-leased to China but subsequently transferred under the terms of PL 512 to which consideration is given later in this paper.

Of the balance of $694.7 million, $181.0 million is considered subject to payment. Settlement of this amount is now under negotiation.

Listed below are the major categories of Post V-J Day lend-lease supplies:

Ordnance and Ordnance Stores	$117,869,076.94
Aircraft and Aeronautical Material	43,683,604.63
Tanks and other Vehicles	96,009,610.08
Vessels and other Watercraft	49,940,642.57
Miscellaneous Military Equipment	99,762,611.71
Facilities and Equipment	36,198.74
Agricultural, Industrial and other Commodities	37,918,928.21
Testing and Reconditioning of Defense Articles	2,338.88
Services and Expenses	335,817,910.56
Total	$781,040,922.32

These transfers included by tonnage equipment sufficient to complete the war-time program to equip 39 Chinese divisions which as of V-J Day was approximately 50 per cent complete. The transfer also included the bulk of the 936 planes and other equipment provided under lend-lease for the 8⅓ group program for the Chinese Air Force.

Also included in the lend-lease transfers were many thousands of military vehicles, of great importance in giving the Government's forces mobility. As of V-J Day the Government had an overwhelming superiority over the Communists in combat equipped troops conservatively estimated at 5-1 and a virtual monopoly of all heavy equipment. This already existing superiority in men and arms reveals the significance of American aid in transporting Government troops to north China and in furnishing transport equipment, which properly employed would have enabled the Government to bring to bear its superior forces.

SINO-AMERICAN COOPERATIVE ORGANIZATION AGREEMENT

The military transfers under the Sino-American Cooperative Organization Agreement (SACO) consisted primarily of ordnance supplies furnished the Chinese between September 2, 1945 and March 2, 1946 by the United States Navy. These transfers were accomplished in fulfillment of a wartime agreement calling for the furnishing of equipment in exchange for certain services provided by the Chinese Government. A detailed breakdown of the figures is provided in Annex I, part 1.[5]

WEST CHINA SALE

The sale of a broad assortment of military supplies in west China was made on the departure of United States forces from that area. This property was transferred for a sales price of $25 million (U. S.) plus $5.16 billion (Chinese). Down payments of $5.16 billion (Chinese) and $5 million (U. S.) were made in the form of offsets against the United States indebtedness to China. (The $5 million (U. S.) down payment was incorporated in the realized return to the United States under the surplus property sales agreement of August 30, 1946). It was agreed that $20 million (U. S.) would be paid over a period of time by China. The terms of repayment are subject to negotiation.

AMMUNITION ABANDONED BY UNITED STATES MARINES

Between April and September 1947 the United States Marines abandoned or transferred to the Chinese Government approximately 6,500 tons of ammunition in connection with their withdrawal from north China. Included was a wide variety of small arms and artillery ammunition, grenades, mines, bombs, and

---
[5] See annex 171, section I.

miscellaneous explosives. No estimate of the total value of this material transferred is provided in Annex I, Part 2,[6] which includes figures on certain naval ammunition transferred in the same operation but charged against lend-lease.

TRANSFER OF UNITED STATES NAVY VESSELS

Public Law 512 of the 79th Congress authorized the President to transfer 271 naval vessels to the Chinese Government on such terms as he might prescribe. On December 8, 1947 an agreement was signed between the United States Government and the Republic of China relative to the implementation of this act. The text of this agreement was published by the Department of State in the Treaties and Other International Acts Series 1691. A total of 131 vessels with a procurement cost of $141.3 million had been transferred to the Chinese Navy under PL 512 as of December 31, 1948 on a grant basis. This figure includes approximately $36 million representing vessels originally lend-leased to China but subsequently transferred under PL 512.

The naval vessels transferred included destroyer escorts, patrol ships, landing craft and many other types of vessels, which, after conferences between appropriate American and Chinese naval Personnel, were selected for their suitability in meeting Chinese naval requirements. Of the 131 vessels transferred under PL 512, the 96 which had originally been lend-leased had all their combat equipment. Of the remainder some were still combat equipped. Ammunition for these was made available during the summer of 1947 when the 6,500 tons of ammunition were transferred in north China, and in the fall of 1948 under the $125 million grants. A list of the vessels transferred is attached as Annex I, Part 3,[7] together with copies of Public Law 512 and as Executive Order authorizing its implementation.

SALE OF SURPLUS MILITARY EQUIPMENT

The United States continues to make military equipment available to the Chinese Government following the termination of lend-lease, through the transfer of surplus United States equipment at a small fraction of its original procurement cost. The following is a listing, in summary form, of military surplus shipments:

Commodity and Source	Procurement Cost	Sales Price
1) 130 million rounds of 7.92 ammunition (sold by Office of the Foreign Liquidation Commission under contract dated June 25, 1947).	$6,564,992.58	$656,499.27
2) 150 C–46 airplanes (sold by War Assets Administration under contract dated December 22, 1947).	34,800,000.00	750,000.00
3) Additional Office of the Foreign Liquidation Commission transfers:		
Ammunition, Cal. 30 to 155 Howitzer	21,707,536.10	569,071.80
Air Force material and equipment, including 178 aircraft and 683 engines	36,637,064.31	4,454,105.06
Ordnance, Signal, and other military equipment (over 9,000 tons)	2,263,897.17	282,987.17
TOTAL	$101,973,490.16	$6,712,663.30

[6] See annex 171, section I (B).
[7] See annex 171.

A portion of the total military surplus shipments was financed by the Chinese Government from the $125 million grants authorized under the China Aid Act of 1948. A detailed breakdown of Office of the Foreign Liquidation Commission transfers from January 1, 1948 to March 31, 1949 is included in Annex I, part 4.[8]

$125 MILLION GRANTS

Section 404 (b) of the China Aid Act of 1948 (Title IV of Foreign Assistance Act of 1948) authorized to be appropriated to the President a sum not to exceed $125,000,000 for additional aid to China through grants on such terms as the President might determine.

It was evident from Congressional debate on Section 404 (b) of the China Aid Act of 1948 that the grants were to be expended by the Chinese Government for whatever purpose it desired, though it was expected that the funds would be used for the purchase of military equipment. It was likewise evident that the funds were to be expended by the Chinese Government on its own option and responsibility. Under terms decided upon by the President the Chinese Government was required to submit to the Department of State requests for payment with regard to goods or services procured, with supporting documentation evidencing the transaction. The terms also stated: "The Department of State will examine the documentation submitted by the Chinese Government to determine that the request is not in excess of the total represented by the invoices or other supporting data, and will authorize the Treasury to make the appropriate payments to the Chinese Government." The initiative in the expenditure of the funds lay wholly with the Chinese Government and no payments were made unless that Government submitted a request for disbursement.

The Chinese Government did not submit its first request for withdrawals from the funds until July 23, 1948 although the Department had transmitted the President's terms to the Chinese Ambassador on June 29, 1948, in a note dated June 28, and the Chinese had accepted the terms in a note dated July 1, 1948. The Chinese Government however utilized approximately $10 million from the grants to pay for military material purchased under contracts made during the late spring and early summer of 1948 prior to the submission of the first request on July 23.

As a means of assisting the Chinese Government in purchasing desired material the Department took the initiative in arranging a procedure whereby American Government departments, establishments, and agencies were authorized to transfer equipment from their own stocks or to procure for the Chinese material to be paid for from the grants. Such a procedure had not been specifically provided for in the legislation on the grants. The President's directive authorizing such action was issued on July 28, 1948.[9]

The grants have been used by the Chinese for the most part to purchase items of a military nature. As of April 1, 1949 the Department of Treasury had disbursed the total $125 million appropriated. Disbursements were made to the Chinese Government direct or to American Government agencies requested by the Chinese Government to engage in procurement activities as follows:

---

[8] See annex 171, section IV.
[9] The text of Section 404 (b) of the China Aid Act of 1948, copies of directives from the President, to various agencies of the Government, appropriate communications among agencies of the Government, and communications between the Department of State and the Chinese Embassy with respect to the grants are attached as annex 171, section V.

Agent	Item	Disbursement
Department of the Army	Arms, ammunition, medical supplies, motor vehicles, spare parts, etc.	$64,595,178.25
Department of the Navy	Naval vessels, reconditioning of naval vessels, ammunition	6,892,020.00
Department of the Air Force	Miscellaneous air force equipment and aviation gasoline	7,750,000.00
Bureau of Federal Supply	Petroleum products, ordnance raw materials	13,765,522.12
Office of Foreign Liquidation Commissioner	Surplus aircraft, aircraft spares, ammunition, etc.	[10] 2,690,910.88
Republic of China	Miscellaneous supplies and equipment, from commercial sources	29,306,368.75
TOTAL		$125,000,000.00

[10] In addition, OFLC has received by direct payment from the Chinese Government $1,045,693.80 of the $29,306,368.75 paid to the Chinese Government by the Treasury Department.

The first significant shipments of military material paid for out of the $125 million grants consisted of approximately 10,000 tons of small arms and artillery ammunition purchased by the Chinese Government from the Office of the Foreign Liquidation Commissioner at a fraction of the procurement cost and shipped to China in two ships which left Hawaii on July 3 and July 16, 1948. Fifty-one fighter aircraft purchased from the same agency with funds from the grants were delivered to China in September, 1948 in combat operational condition, and aviation gasoline, aircraft spare parts, and communications equipment were shipped to China during the above period.

The most significant Chinese purchases under the grants were made through the Department of the Army and covered equipment for 7 Armies and 3 Divisions. The Chinese request for disbursement of funds to cover this purchase was received in the Department of State on September 27, 1948 and payment by the Treasury was authorized on October 1, 1948. The requests at the program for small arms and small-arms ammunition were placed ahead of those for the United States Army. The first shipment of military materiel purchased under this requisition arrived in China on November 11, 1948 and subsequent major shipments reached Chinese ports on November 29, 1948 and January 4, 1949 (two shipments on this date). An additional shipment of Army-supplied cargo procured under the above and allied purchases reached China and in mid-March, four full cargoes being shipped without charge to the Chinese in United States Navy owned vessels. Following are figures showing certain Chinese requests under this program and the amount of material delivered according to the latest figures available:

Item	Number Requested	Number Delivered
U. S. Rifles, Cal. 30	124,383	132,851
Browning Automatic Rifles, Cal. 30	8,104	8,793
Heavy Machine Guns, Cal. 30	1,566	1,707
Sub. Machine Guns, Cal. 45	8,920	12,975
Rocket Launcher	1,134	1,196
Grenade Launcher	5,592	5,758
30 Cal. Ammunition	291,104,500	231,221,082
45 Cal. Ammunition	26,760,000	26,577,498
Rocket Ammunition	90,720	66,380
Grenades	559,200	280,560

In certain categories as revealed above, more than the originally specified amount of equipment was provided, following discussions between American and Chinese military officers in which the desire of the Chinese representatives to obtain the additional amount of equipment was expressed. Chinese requests for mortars and mortar and artillery ammunition were for the most part unfulfilled since funds transferred to the Department of the Army were inadequate to pay for these. Decision concerning use of the grants rested solely with the Chinese Government and if that Government had desired, funds used for purchasing other items of less immediate military value, such as raw materials for arsenals, could have been made available to the Department of the Army for further purchases under the 7 Army, 3 Division program. It should be noted, however, that shipments of surplus ammunition from the Pacific during 1948 contained large quantities of mortar and artillery ammunition.

The pricing formula adapted in mid-1947 during implementation of the aid programs for Greece and Turkey was applied to Chinese requests under the $125 million grants. Since most of the items desired were not surplus but had to be replaced in Army stocks, the Chinese were charged replacement costs.

At the time the first of the above shipments of arms was arriving in China, United States Army forces in Shanghai transferred (abandoned) without cost to the Chinese approximately $500,000 worth of small arms and ammunition.

There are attached in annex 167, section XV, tables showing:

a) Summary of the use of funds received—a report submitted to the Department by the Chinese Embassy;
b) Reports on monthly shipments to China of goods purchased under the grants (the reports covering 1949 were prepared by the Chinese Embassy);
c) Report on major shipments of material by agencies of this Government, and by Chinese procurement agencies.
d) Department of the Army report on the China Aid Program.

Following the rapid deterioration of the military situation in north and central China and in view of the danger that stocks delivered to China proper might eventually fall into the hands of the Communists, the Chinese Government late in December 1948 requested that shipments of material purchased under the grants be delivered to Taiwan. Pursuant to this request, subsequent shipments have been made to Taiwan. At the end of February 1949 the Acting President requested that shipments of munitions be stopped pending reorganization of the Executive Yuan. In accordance with a later request from him they were again renewed during the latter half of March.

173

Transfer and Sale of Ammunition and Matériel to the Chinese Government during 1947 and 1948

On the same date (May 26, 1947) the Chinese were informed that the Department would approve the sale to China of 130 million rounds of surplus 7.92 rifle ammunition, and would approve applications for export licenses for transport planes and for spare parts for all equipment, including combat items previously transferred under the 8⅓ Group Program.

Subsequent to this date the Chinese on June 25, 1947 purchased the 130 million rounds of 7.92 rifle ammunition for $656,499.27 or 10 per cent of procurement cost.

Shipment of this ammunition was made from Seattle on July 14 and August 11, 1947.

In July 1947, the Chinese expressed a desire to purchase 43 C-47 aircraft but wanted these considered part of the 8⅓ Group Program. Since the quota of C-47's under the Program had been fulfilled, the Chinese were informed that transport planes would be made available through normal surplus channels. The Chinese signed a contract with the War Assets Administration for the purchase of 150 C-46's on December 22, 1947, purchasing for $5,000 each planes which had a procurement cost of $232,000 each.

The contract covering civilian end-use items in the Pacific for the 8⅓ Group Program was concluded on November 6, 1947 at 12½ cents on the dollar.

On December 9, 1947, the Chinese Government signed a commercial contract for 6,500,000 rounds of .50 caliber ammunition.

On December 16, 1947, the Chinese were informed of the availability of surplus ammunition and explosives and combat matériel including combat planes for the 8⅓ Group Program. In March and April of 1948 the Department of the Army provided the Department of State for transmission to the Chinese certain information on the quantity and type of surplus ammunition available in Hawaii and the Pacific. Prior to this, however, the Chinese, following negotiations with the CFIC, concluded on January 7, 1948, an open-end contract for the purchase of all surplus ammunition in the Marianas at the nominal cost of one cent on the dollar. As the result of further negotiations, a contract was signed on January 30, 1948, for the purchase at 17½ cents on the dollar of all surplus stocks in the United States, including Hawaii, available for the 8⅓ Group Program, except combat aircraft, which were available and were separately negotiated. (This contract was revised on March 16, 1948.)

On January 31, 1948, a contract supplementing that of November 6, 1947, was signed covering the sale of surplus combat equipment in the Pacific applicable to the 8⅓ Group Program, the ammunition component being sold at the nominal cost of one cent on the dollar.

On April 29 and June 11, 1948, contracts were signed covering the sale of surplus ammunition located on Hawaii.

On May 22, 1948, a contract was concluded for the sale of the surplus ammunition remaining in the Pacific and not included in previous contracts. The bulk of the ammunition covered by this contract was located at Okinawa.

174

Statement Submitted by Brigadier General T. S. Timberman to the Committee on Foreign Affairs of the House of Representatives, June 21, 1949

HISTORY OF THE CHINA AID PROGRAM

Public Law 472, 3 April 1948, and Public Law 793, 28 June 1948, authorized an Aid Program to China involving a grant of $125,000,000.

The terms of Public Laws 472 and 793 did not provide specifically for participation of the U.S. military establishment in the program, nor for the transfer of funds to its Departments to permit the necessary replacement of those items withdrawn from military stocks to meet the requirements of the Chinese military program.

On the 28th of July 1948 Presidential letters to the Secretaries of State, of Defense, and of the Treasury authorized not only assistance to the Chinese Government by the National Military Establishment, but also the transfer of funds allocated to the China Aid Program to United States governmental agencies participating in the supply program. The Secretary of Defense, by memorandum to the three Service Secretaries dated 29 July 1948 forwarded copies of the Presidential letters of 28 July 1948 and requested the implementation of the China Aid Program by the Army, Navy and Air Force.

On 2 August 1948 the Department of the Army established a procedure for fulfilling the Army requirements of the Chinese Government.

By August 1948 the Department of the Army had disposed, in the main of all surplus supplies of World War II procurement, and particularly of those items which the Chinese listed as their priority requirements.

Nevertheless, availability studies based upon Chinese requirements were initiated by the Department of the Army on 3 August 1948. Paralleling the availability studies was the computation of the prices which the Department of the Army would have to charge in order that those supplies issued directly from stock could be replaced.

The Chinese representatives in Washington, in the hope of obtaining supplies at the lowest possible price, canvassed a number of possible commercial sources. The Chinese representatives were reluctant to place orders with the Department of the Army until they had completed the canvassing of all possible commercial sources and the Department of the Army had completed computation of prices. The Chinese wanted to compare prices before making a definite commitment for purchases.

The Department of the Army gave highest priority to the study of availability and computation of prices of caliber .30 rifles and ammunition. On 19 August the Chinese representatives were informed that the Department of the Army could supply, if the Chinese so desired, caliber .30 rifles and ammunition in sufficient quantities to meet the total requirements. On 31 August the Chinese were further informed that the Department of the Army could supply caliber .30 carbines and caliber .45 ammunition. They delayed placing their order for small arms and accessories for about a month.

The Department of the Army completed and delivered to the Chinese representatives data as to availability and pricing for Signal, Quartermaster, and Medical supplies in the period 7–9 September and that for Engineer supplies and the remaining Ordnance supplies on 19 September.

On 10 September the Department of the Treasury transferred to the Department of the Army as the result of a Chinese request, the sum of $25,130,431.55 for payment in connection with firm requests which the Chinese were concurrently preparing. The items requested by the Chinese for purchase with this sum were raw materials, such as metals and powder base for the Chinese arsenal program; radios for Chinese signal communications; tires and tubes; spare parts for motor transportation and demolition supplies. Demolition materials were immediately available from surplus stocks still existing in Hawaii. They were ordered shipped without delay; transportation was arranged and, approximately 1,000,000 pounds of TNT, sold at surplus prices were moved in November via commercial shipping from Hawaii. The Department of the Army had available from stock approximately 65% of the motor vehicle spare parts requested. These supplies were likewise moved immediately to a port for shipment. The remaining items, however, of the specific types required by the Chinese in this request, are not carried in stock by the Department of the Army and consequently must be manufactured expressly to fill the Chinese requirements. Contracts were negotiated in accordance with statutory requirements. Delivery of some of these types of items will not be completed (as the Chinese were fully aware when their request was submitted) until the Fall of 1949.

The Chinese Ambassador, Dr. Koo, delivered to the Secretary of Defense on 20 September 1948, a revised list of requirements for the Military Aid Program. This list included primarily weapons and ammunition. It voided all previous Chinese requests and action by the Department of the Army with respect to these particular items. The Department of the Army on 21 September initiated new availability studies and computation of prices, considering them in the light of possible free transportation and 1945 list prices. It was immediately apparent that this revised list of requirements for weapons and ammunition, at the lowest possible price which the Department of the Army could arrange, would amount to more than $50,000,000. In a meeting with the Chinese representatives it was learned that approximately $40,000,000 remained available in the China Aid Fund with which to purchase the supplies of this new list. The Chinese were thereupon advised to show the requirements in the order of the most urgent priority. The priorities were submitted to the Department of the Army on 24 September and on 4 October the Chinese specified destinations in China for shipment of these supplies. These destinations and the approximate percentages of the supplies to be delivered thereto follows:

Shanghai	60%
Tsingtao	10%
Tientsin via Tsingtao	30%

Also on 4 October 1948 the Department of the Army received from the Treasury Department $37,783,386.68, transferred from the China Aid Fund at the request of the Chinese representatives in Washington in payment for the arms and ammunition of the revised list. Upon receipt of these funds, and without awaiting the completion of the availability study or the computation of prices, the Department of the Army ordered the preparation for shipment of weapons and ammunition in fulfillment of the requirements contained in Priority I of the revised program. Based upon informal information received from the Navy Department on 9 October and later confirmed in a letter from the Secretary of the Navy to the Secretary of the Army, ports were selected for handling and loading these supplies, utilizing U.S. Navy vessels for transportation free of charge to the Chinese. In an effort to transport the maximum quantity of urgently needed supplies in the shortest possible time, the Department of the Army ordered the shipment, in first priority, of ammunition from depots throughout the U. S. to the selected port on the West Coast. Following inspection, preparation of packages and marking with shipping instructions, the actual movement of this ammunition to port commenced early in the week of 25 October. The first Navy vessel, of 5,000 ton capacity, reached the port on 1 November and commenced loading immediately. This vessel departed 9 November for the port of Shanghai. Approximately 2500 tons of ammunition remaining at the port following departure of the first vessel, together with such weapons as had arrived at the port by that time, were loaded on a second naval vessel of 5000 tons capacity which reached the port about 21 November. This second vessel completed its loading and departed for the same destination on 1 December. A third shipment, comprised of the remaining weapons, and miscellaneous supplies departed from the port on 16 December. It should be noted that in order to meet this schedule it was necessary to place the inspection, necessary repair and preparation for shipment of the rifles of this program ahead of a similar program in connection with the expansion of our own armed forces.

In a further effort to ship weapons and ammunition to China in the shortest possible time, the Department of the Army on 5 October transmitted the entire list of Chinese requirements to General MacArthur and requested that he make a survey of his entire Command and report those items which he could supply immediately. The Department of the Army in making this request offered to replace in his stocks any supplies which he could make available for the Chinese. Subsequently it was determined that the Commander of the Naval Forces Western Pacific could provide transportation for shipment of these supplies free of charge. After coordinating his report with the action underway in the U.S., General MacArthur was ordered on 27 October to prepare and deliver to the port of Yokohama those supplies which he had reported available. These supplies, amounting to approximately 1200 tons of small arms and ammunition, actually reached China by mid-November.

The first vessel with Army supplied cargo which departed from a U.S. West Coast port on 9 November, reached Shanghai on 29 November, discharged 60% of its cargo for Shanghai, an additional 30% for onward shipment to Tientsin because of better facilities available in Shanghai for transferring the cargo to smaller vessels, and then proceeded to Tsingtao where discharge of the remaining 10% was completed on 7 December. Meanwhile on 6 December 1948 the Department of the Army was notified that the Chinese Government desired all future shipments of the Aid Cargo then en route and to be shipped to Shanghai be diverted to Keelung, Taiwan (Formosa). The subsequent shipments via U.S. Navy vessels and commercial vessels alike have been routed to Taiwan in accordance with this request. In all, four full shiploads of Army supplied cargo were transported to Chinese ports free of charge in U.S. Navy owned vessels. The last of these departed from the West Coast of the U.S. on 19 February.

Although some supplies which were procured from commercial concerns expressly for the China Aid Program were shipped free of charge on board the four U.S. Navy vessels, these vessels carried mainly the items which were immediately available from Army stocks. Since the readily available items were thereby virtually exhausted, shipments thereafter depended upon the rate of completion of manufacture by the commercial sources from which the supplies were being procured. In addition there were small amounts of supplies being requested by the Chinese for purchase with the residue of funds remaining after computation of the cost of the large purchases made earlier. Nevertheless, supplies becoming available would arrive at the port in less than shipload lots. To permit accumulation would have delayed the program. It was decided thereupon to contract with commercial shippers to move the cargo as it reached the ports. This procedure will be followed until completion of the program which it is estimated will continue with small shipments until the Fall of 1949.

Sale of Military Supplies by the Department of Army in Accordance With China Aid Act of 1948

In accordance with the China Aid Act of April 3, 1948, and the July 28, 1948, implementing directives of the President, the Department of the Army has furnished and is continuing to furnish military supplies as they are requested by the Chinese Government. These supplies, when available, are furnished direct from existing stocks or, if unavailable in stock, are procured from commercial sources normally used by the Department of the Army.

The prices charged by the Department of the Army for supplies furnished the Chinese Government are in accord with pricing formula adopted in mid-1947 during the implementation of the aid program for Greece and Turkey as authorized by Public Law 75, Eightieth Congress. Briefly stated, the pricing formula is as follows:

(a) Items entirely surplus to the needs of the United States armed forces are sold at surplus prices, averaging 10 percent of 1945 procurement cost price.

(b) Items stored as war reserve, i. e., needed to equip units in event of a mobilization, are sold at 1945 procurement cost price.

(c) Items needed for current use of the United States armed forces and which if disposed of must be replaced immediately are sold at current replacement costs.

Of course, items which are not available in stock must be procured and are charged to the foreign government at the exact price charged by the manufacturer, plus any costs involved for handling and shipping.

All appreciable quantities of surplus items had been disposed of prior to the implementation of the China Aid Act. They had been previously applied to the foreign military assistance programs, including Greece and Turkey, and in addition virtually all surplus items in the Pacific and Far East areas, except in the Philippines, had been sold to China as surplus under the Soong-McCabe agreement (bulk sales). Moreover, aside from the exhaustion of stocks of surplus supplies, the Surplus Property Act after June 30, 1948, could no longer be used for disposition of surplus supplies in the continental United States, and, therefore, was no longer a valid instrument for possible implementation of the China Aid Act had there in fact been a surplus. Overseas, surplus supplies that did exist were already committed, much of them to China in bulk sales arrangements.

The Military Establishment was first authorized to furnish supplies and service to the Chinese Government in connection with the China Aid Act of 1948, as a result of a Presidential directive of July 28, 1948. Implementation of a definite program commenced on August 3, 1948. As stated above virtually no surplus stocks remained at this time, consequently, relatively few items requested by the Chinese Government could be made available at the surplus prices. Regardless of the priority given the China aid program we proceeded to its immediate implementation. In fact for delivery of some items, notably small arms and small arms ammunition, the China aid program was placed ahead of the supply of the United States Army. It was by such a priority that the first shipload of United States Army procured supplies for China departed from the west coast on November 9 or little more than a month after the Chinese had placed a firm request for their needs on the Department of the Army.

It should be noted that of the $125,000,000 appropriated, the Chinese Government has placed orders with the Department of the Army for an amount approximately only $64,500,000. The remainder of the funds have been allotted for purchases from the United States Air Force, United States Navy, and purchases by the Chinese themselves direct from commercial sources. The Department of the Army has furnished supplies to the Chinese in all categories of prices—a small quantity at surplus prices, considerably more at 1945 procurement cost prices, but the majority at either replacement cost prices or at the price actually charged by the majority at either replacement cost prices or at the price actually charged by the manufacturer, where the supplies were procured expressly for the Chinese. Through the use of Army channels for procurement, the Chinese Government has been given the advantage of any special considerations provided by commercial enterprises to the United States Government.

Of the $64,500,000 authorized for purchases from or through the United States Army, supplies valued at $47,081,500 have been shipped from the west coast to date. Delivery of supplies available direct from Army stocks has been completed except for new requisitions recently received from Chinese. However, shipments are continuing at a normal rate paced by the rate of deliveries from the commercial sources of procured supplies that were not available in Army stocks. One exception is a small quantity of ammunition in Hawaii which has been blocked from shipment by the longshoremen's strike. The Department of the Army has attempted to offset this delay by making available additional ammunition of the same type for immediate shipment from the west coast of the United States. Two new requisitions were received from the Chinese during the past week. One for tool sets for fifth echelon repair of tanks, the other for 37 twin Diesel engines for M-5 tanks. Incidentally, the latter item will be furnished at the surplus price as were the tanks for which they are intended.

To relate the China aid program to the aid programs for Greece and Turkey, it must be recalled that the latter were initiated by Public Law 75 passed May 22, 1947. Hence supplies were furnished to Greece a full year before the implementation of the China aid program. In the main, the requirements for Greece and Turkey were fulfilled from military surplus stocks. All surplus items were sold at surplus prices. During the same period surplus supplies also were sold to other foreign governments, notably to China. The items sold to China likewise were sold at surplus prices. As a result of all these sales the surplus stocks of the Army were largely depleted when the China aid program was initiated. It might be noted that the aid programs for Greece and Turkey were continued by Public Law 472, the same law which initiated the China aid program. The provisions of law for continuation of the programs for Greece and Turkey, unlike the China aid program, were such as to permit continued implementation by the National Military Establishment. Hence it was possible to supply to Greece and Turkey such surplus items as existed so long as those items lasted. Because of these factors, including the previous sale of surplus supplies to the Chinese at surplus prices as well as to Greece and Turkey, there simply was little available when the China aid program commenced. The pricing formula has been applied alike in the furnishing of supplies in the fulfillment of all programs. When surplus stocks became exhausted subsequent sales to Greece and Turkey were at the higher prices depending upon the category of the item in accordance with the formula.

In the handling within the Department of the Army of requests from the Chinese Government in comparison with the handling of those from Greece and Turkey, there has been no difference except that at the outset of the China aid program the programs for Greece and Turkey were already operating smoothly as the result of a year's experience. All of this experience which was applicable was adapted immediately to the program for China and served to reduce considerably the time that normally would have elapsed in the solving of new problems.

Annexes to Chapter VIII: The Program of American Economic Aid, 1947-1949

175 (a)

Message From President Truman Transmitting Recommendation That the Congress Authorize a Program for Aid to China in the Amount of $570,000,000 to Provide Assistance Until June 30, 1949

To the Congress of the United States:
   On several occasions I have stated that a primary objective of the United States is to bring about, throughout the world, the conditions of a just and lasting peace. This is a cause to which the American people are deeply devoted.
   Since V-J Day we have expended great effort and large sums of money on the relief and rehabilitation of war-torn countries to aid in restoring workable economic systems which are essential to the maintenance of peace. A principle which has guided our efforts to assist these war-torn countries has been that of helping their peoples to help themselves. The Congress is now giving careful consideration to a most vital and far-reaching proposal to further this purpose—the program for aid to European recovery.
   I now request the Congress to consider the type of further assistance which this country should provide to China.
   A genuine friendship has existed between the American people and the people of China over many years. This friendship has been accompanied by a long record of commercial and cultural association and close cooperation between our two countries. Americans have developed a deep respect for the Chinese people and sympathy for the many trials and difficulties which they have endured.
   The United States has long recognized the importance of a stable Chinese nation to lasting peace in the Pacific and the entire world. The vast size and population of China make her an important factor in world affairs. China is a land which has a rich tradition and culture and a large and energetic population. It has always been our desire to see a strong, progressive China making a full contribution to the strength of the family of nations.
   With this end in view, we have supported the National Government of China since it first came to power 20 years ago. China and the United States were allies in the war against Japan, and as an ally we supported China's valiant war efforts against the Japanese. Since the Japanese surrender we have provided a great deal of additional assistance. Military aid was given the Chinese Government, not only to help defeat the Japanese invaders but also to assist in reoccupying Japanese-held areas. The United States contributed the major share of the extensive aid received by China under the program of the United Nations Relief and Rehabilitation Administration. We made available to the Chinese Government at minimum cost large quantities of surplus goods and

equipment of value to China's economy. We are currently extending further aid to China under our foreign-relief program.

Nevertheless, the Chinese Government and people are still laboring under the double and interrelated burden of civil war and a rapidly deteriorating economy. The strains placed upon the country by 8 years of war and the Japanese occupation and blockade have been increased by internal strife at the very time that reconstruction efforts should be under way. The wartime damage to transport and productive facilities has been greatly accentuated by the continued obstruction and destruction of vital communications by the Communist forces.

The civil warfare has further impeded recovery by forcing upon the Government heavy expenditures which greatly exceed revenues. Continual issuances of currency to meet these expenditures have produced drastic inflation, with its attendant disruption of normal commercial operations. Under these circumstances, China's foreign-exchange holdings have been so reduced that it will soon be impossible for China to meet the cost of essential imports. Without such imports, industrial activity would diminish and the rate of economic deterioration would be sharply increased.

The continued deterioration of the Chinese economy is a source of deep concern to the United States. Ever since the return of General Marshall from China, the problem of assistance to the Chinese has been under continuous study. We have hoped for conditions in China that would make possible the effective and constructive use of American assistance in reconstruction and rehabilitation. Conditions have not developed as we had hoped, and we can only do what is feasible under circumstances as they exist.

We can assist in retarding the current economic deterioration and thus give the Chinese Government a further opportunity to initiate the measures necessary to the establishment of more stable economic conditions. But it is, and has been, clear that only the Chinese Government itself can undertake the vital measures necessary to provide the framework within which efforts toward peace and true economic recovery may be effective.

In determining the character and dimensions of the program which might be suited to this purpose, we have had to take into account a number of diverse and conflicting factors, including the other demands on our national resources at this time, the availability of specific commodities, the dimensions and complexities of the problems facing the Chinese Government, and the extent to which these problems could be promptly and effectively alleviated by foreign aid. United States assistance to China, like that provided to any other nation, must be adapted to its particular requirements and capacities.

In the light of these factors, I recommend that the Congress authorize a program for aid to China in the amount of $570,000,000 to provide assistance until June 30, 1949.

The program should make provision for the financing, through loans or grants, of essential imports into China in the amount of $510,000,000. This estimate is based upon prices as of January 1, 1948, since it is impossible at present to predict what effect current price changes may have on the program. Revised dollar estimates can be presented in connection with the request for appropriations if necessary. The essential imports include cereals, cotton, petroleum, fertilizer, tobacco, pharmaceuticals, coal, and repair parts for existing capital equipment. The quantities provided for under this program are within the limits of available supplies. The financing of these essential commodity imports by the United States would permit the Chinese Government to devote its limited dollar resources to the most urgent of its other needs.

ANNEXES 983

The program should also provide $60,000,000 for a few selected reconstruction projects to be initiated prior to June 30, 1949. There is an urgent need for the restoration of essential transportation facilities, fuel and power operations, and export industries. This work could be undertaken in areas sheltered from military operations and could help in improving the supply and distribution of essential commodities.

As in the case of aid to European recovery, the conduct of this program of aid should be made subject to an agreement between China and the United States setting forth the conditions and procedures for administering the aid. The agreement should include assurances that the Chinese Government will take such economic, financial, and other measures as are practicable, looking toward the ultimate goal of economic stability and recovery. The United States would, of course, reserve the right to terminate aid if it is determined that the assistance provided is not being handled in accordance with the agreement or that the policies of the Chinese Government are inconsistent with the objective of using the aid to help achieve a self-supporting economy.

Pending establishment of the agency which is to be set up for the administration of the European recovery program, the assistance to China should be carried forward under the existing machinery now administering the foreign-relief programs. Legislation authorizing the Chinese program should make possible transfer of the administration of the Chinese program to the agency administering our aid to European recovery. The need for authority in the administering agency to make adjustments in the program from time to time will be as great here as in the European recovery program.

The proposed program of aid to China represents what I believe to be the best course this Government can follow, in the light of all the circumstances. Nothing which this country provides by way of assistance can, even in a small measure, be a substitute for the necessary action that can be taken only by the Chinese Government. Yet this program can accomplish the important purpose of giving the Chinese Government a respite from rapid economic deterioration, during which it can move to establish more stable economic conditions. Without this respite the ability of the Chinese Government to establish such conditions at all, would be doubtful. The achievement of even this limited objective is of such importance as to justify the proposed program of aid.

I recommend, therefore, that this program be given prompt and favorable consideration by the Congress.

HARRY S. TRUMAN.

THE WHITE HOUSE, *February 18, 1948.*

175 (b)

Statement by Secretary of State Marshall regarding the China Aid Program, February 20, 1948

In consideration of a program of assistance to China, it should be recognized that for the main part the solution of China's problems is largely one for the Chinese themselves. The great difficulty in determining a basis and procedure to justify a program of assistance lies in the conditions which exist in China, military as well as economic.

Thus far, the principal deterrent to the solution of Chinese economic problems is the civil war which has drained the Chinese Government's internal and foreign-exchange resources, continued the destruction of property and the constant disruption of economic life, and has prevented recovery. The Communist forces have brought about the terrible destruction to wreck the economy of China. This is their announced purpose—to force an economic collapse.

The Chinese Government is in dire need of assistance in its present serious economic difficulties. However, the political, economic, and financial conditions in China are so unstable and so uncertain that it is impossible to develop a practical, effective, long-term over-all program for economic recovery. Nevertheless, it is desirable that the United States Government render assistance to China in her present critical situation in order to help retard the present rapid rate of economic deterioration and thus provide a breathing space in which the Chinese Government could initiate important steps toward more stable economic conditions.

While there are a multitude of factors in China that are involved in the consideration of such a program, the following appear of first importance:

China is a country of vast area and population. Through communications north of the Yangtze River are almost nonexistent except by coastal shipping. Local governments are often so corrupt that they are undependable for assistance in the administration of relief measures. The political control by long-entrenched groups is a great difficulty to be overcome in the restoration of China to economic stability. The conduct by the Government of the civil war now in progress, particularly in view of the geographic disadvantages—exposed and lengthy communications, and the inherent difficulties in dealing with guerrilla warfare—demands a high order of aggressive leadership in all major echelons of command, which is lacking. The civil war imposes a burden on the national budget of 70 percent or more and the financing is now carried on by means of issuance of paper money. Industrial production is low and transportation facilities are poor, the lack of adequate transportation affecting particularly the movement of foodstuffs. The results are an extreme, really a fantastic, inflation of currency, and the inevitable speculation in commodities as well as hoarding.

In considering the measures to be taken by the United States to assist China, it is very necessary, I think, to have in mind that a proposal at the present time cannot be predicated upon a definite termination for the necessity of such assistance as in the case of the European-recovery program. Provision of a currency stabilization fund would, in the opinion of our monetary experts, require large sums which would be largely dissipated under the present conditions of war financing and civil disruption. In view of this situation, the program should not involve the virtual underwriting of the future of the Chinese economy. The United States should not by its actions be put in the position of being charged with a direct responsibility for the conduct of the Chinese Government and its political, economic, and military affairs.

The proposed program of aid for China would provide economic assistance in the amount of $570,000,000 for the period ending June 30, 1949. Of this amount, $510,000,000 would cover minimum imports of essential civilian type of commodities, chiefly foodstuffs and raw materials, and $60,000,000 would be for key reconstruction projects. The program concentrates on those commodities believed to be of maximum aid to Chinese civilian economy and those which will insure the greatest aid per dollar spent.

While the total import needs of China cannot be accurately estimated, in view of the generally disturbed and, in certain regions, chaotic conditions of production and trade, the need for the commodities listed can be demonstrated, we feel, with reasonable assurance. The program will therefore meet the most essential commodity requirements. China will need other imports, of course, including civilian-type commodities not included in the program, and military supplies. In addition, China has certain international financial obligations.

To meet these additional needs for foreign exchange, China will have available certain financial resources of her own. These include proceeds from exports, miscellaneous receipts from such sources as overseas remittances, the sale of surplus property, and foreign government and philanthropic expenditures in China; and finally, to be called upon if necessary China's reserves of gold and foreign exchange which were estimated as totaling the equivalent of $274,000,000 as of January 1, 1948. This amount would be increased to the extent the Chinese are able to bring about an improvement in their net foreign exchange receipts. On the other hand, the amount will be reduced to the extent that reserves must be used, for lack of other available funds, to make necessary payments after January 1, 1948.

It is proposed, in the program submitted, that it would be administered by the agency or establishment of the Government created by law for the purpose of administering programs of assistance to foreign countries or, pending the establishment of such agency, temporarily by the Department of State in cooperation with the other agencies of the Government directly concerned. The conditions under which assistance is to be extended should be spelled out in an agreement with the Chinese Government, which would be based on the same considerations underlying the conditions for assistance to European countries but of necessity adjusted to the different conditions in China.

176

Statement Issued by the Ambassador in China (Stuart) upon the Presentation to Congress of the China Aid Bill [1]

893.00/12-2247

A personal message to the people of China.

From President Truman's statement to Congress you know something of the proposed efforts of the United States to assist the people of China. May I, therefore, take this opportunity to attempt to interpret to you the purposes controlling American policy toward China, and the problems involved. I do this from the standpoint of one who was born and has spent most of his life in your country and who is as deeply concerned over its welfare as any of you.

Fortunately the government and the people of the United States desire for China precisely what all truly patriotic Chinese themselves are struggling to achieve; its freedom and independence, internal peace and prosperity, the establishment of a genuinely modernized and democratic government. We Americans earnestly desire all of this but nothing more.

Our problem has been how to help the common people who have been the chief sufferers from the devastating internal conflict which has continued since V–J Day. What the common people need is peace and productive activity under a government that cares for their welfare.

More specifically the problem is how to benefit the common people and to protect them alike from the extreme reactionary or selfish elements and from the extreme radicals with their brutally destructive revolutionary tactics. Both of

---
[1] Issued on Feb. 20, 1948.

these groups are highly organized. Both place their partisan or their individual interests far above those of the suffering people.

We Americans believe thoroughly in democracy and we are convinced it will work in China if given a fair chance and sufficient time. Negatively, a democratic government guarantees freedom from forcible interference in the daily pursuits of the people and freedom from fear. Positively, it fosters conditions under which the more intelligent and progressive leaders can educate and in other ways assist the ordinary people to appreciate the duties and the rights of citizens in the democratic way of life and to apply constitutional procedures in exercising these under rule of law rather than under caprice of individuals.

As has always been true in Chinese history, the masses will follow educated leaders in whose moral character they have confidence. By adapting this ancient democratic Chinese process to modern constitutional procedures, the corrupt or incompetent elements in the present regional, provincial and local governments can be gradually eliminated and replaced by those whom the people freely choose to administer public affairs for the public good.

Personally from my long association with Chinese students I have confidence in their patriotic idealism. They, whether having already graduated and occupying responsible positions in government, in education, in business, or any other walks of life, or whether still in school, should be the ones to lead in this latest form of patriotic, public-spirited effort. By their public-spirited and unselfish example, they should be able to surmount those at the other extreme who are so fanatically devoted to their party, so intolerant of all other political faiths, so utterly ruthless in the methods they employ, that they are willing to destroy public and private property and inflict upon the helpless people all the horrors of rapine and war in the attainment of their own arbitrary objectives.

We Americans, under the leadership of Mr. Marshall, did our utmost to prevent the development of the situation which now exists and all the suffering it entails for the Chinese people. Nevertheless, with the traditional friendship between the American and Chinese peoples, and given our belief that the economic well-being of the Chinese people will redound to the benefit of the world, we are proposing, through a program of economic assistance to China, to provide a further opportunity to the Chinese Government and people to take the initial steps toward laying a solid foundation for economic recovery and stability in China.

The real task, the responsibility, however, rests with the Chinese people themselves. No amount of American material assistance nor any number of skilled American technical advisers can accomplish what is required to bring political stability and economic recovery to China. The major effort must be Chinese and there must be a sincere and deep-seated determination to put selfishness aside and strive unceasingly for the common good.

The meanings of freedom and democracy have been confused by the wholly different interpretations being put upon these terms today. There should be no misunderstanding of these issues. Under a totalitarian system there can be no intellectual freedom—those who attempt to think for themselves either succumb to regimentation or are promptly liquidated. Democracy is government not only for the people, but also by the people. In this truly democratic sense the people must, however, continuously bring the weight of enlightened public opinion to bear upon the conduct of government to prevent misuse of power by those in office. This requires, therefore, freedom of debate and publication and free access to news objectively reported. In a totalitarian system these freedoms cannot exist. Instead, news becomes propaganda scientifically developed. It depends for its effects upon unrestrained vituperation and incessant repetition without regard for the truth.

China today is faced with insidious dangers which will require the united effort of all public spirited citizens to overcome. This calls for clear-sighted vision, a high degree of courage and grim determination. It is hoped that the freedom-loving patriots of China, together with all elements of the population, will join in a constructive evolutionary process that will bring unity and peaceful progress to the entire nation.

177

Statement by the Department of State, the Department of the Treasury, and the Federal Reserve Board on Possible Use of Silver for Monetary Stabilization in China in Connection With China Aid Program

[February 1948]

The China Aid Program does not provide for the use of silver to bring about monetary stability in China. It does not do so for three main reasons: *one*, because conditions in China do not now furnish a basis for any lasting currency stabilization; *two*, because even if basic conditions now favored stabilization of the currency and price level it would not be practical to restore the silver standard in China; and *three*, because the introduction of silver as an emergency measure at this time would involve such technical difficulties as to make it a costly and uncertain venture.

I

No provision was made for a fund for currency stabilization because under present conditions of civil war and economic disruption, such provision would result in the inevitable dissipation of large sums of money.

The basic cause of inflation in China is the massive budgetary deficit of the Chinese Government. This deficit is, of course, immediately occasioned by military expenditures and therefore depends on the exigencies of civil war. Overall military expenditures are estimated to have accounted for not less than 65 to 70 percent of total government expenditures in 1947. Instead of being financed by taxes and loans these expenditures are financed by expanding the note issue. As long as the expenditures of the Chinese Government continue vastly to exceed its revenues, and as long as the deficit continues to be financed by increasing the money supply, inflation will persist in China. When the total amount of spending is, by reason of this deficit, greatly in excess of the available supply of goods at any given price level, prices will continue to rise regardless of the kind or kinds of monetary units employed. It is therefore not feasible to contribute effectively to monetary stabilization in China until this deficit is reduced to manageable dimensions.

Since inflation in China is essentially an internal problem, the basis for a permanent solution will ultimately have to be provided primarily by the Chinese themselves. Funds are, therefore, not provided for currency stabilization in the proposed China Aid program. The program does, however, assure a continued supply from abroad of commodities and raw materials essential to the prevention of starvation and the maintenance of industrial output, and in this sense is anti-inflationary.

II

Even if basic conditions in China favored measures to restore monetary stability, there would be serious disadvantages in any attempt to restore the silver standard in China.² While the eventual reform of the currency in China might provide for the use of subsidiary metallic coins, including silver coin in reasonable amounts, silver is too bulky for efficient handling and shipment of large sums of money, especially in a country like China where transportation is so costly. Moreover, the progressive demonetization of silver throughout the world has brought about very unstable prices and market conditions for silver. The result is that the external value (foreign exchange rate) of a Chinese currency based on silver would be exposed to the risks of radical fluctuations in the price of silver unrelated to economic conditions in China. These fluctuations would in turn have disturbing repercussions on the Chinese economy and would inhibit the freedom of the Chinese authorities in pursuing desirable fiscal and monetary policies at home.

Finally, it must be pointed out that China, a member of the International Monetary Fund, has committed herself in principle to stability of exchange rates in terms of gold. When conditions permit, it is presumed that China will take steps to establish a stable monetary system and a stable exchange value for the Chinese currency in terms of gold. To assist China to establish a silver standard currency would appear to be inconsistent with the principles of the Fund Agreement, and consequently with established United States international financial and monetary policy.

III

To try to mitigate monetary instability in China now by injecting silver into her currency system would be a hazardous as well as a costly undertaking.

The mechanics of putting silver into circulation in China would be highly complex and technical even if the operation were handled most efficiently and without abuses. The Chinese Government would probably use silver coins for its expenditures and make a standing offer to redeem paper currency with silver coins. Overnight conversion would be impossible in China and a short-period redemption offer would amount to a repudiation of a large part of the currency. On the other hand, to make expenditures in silver without standing ready to redeem outstanding notes would accelerate the flight from the paper currency. While acceptance of notes in payment of taxes might tend to retard their depreciation,

---

² It has been suggested that China successfully employed a silver monetary system for hundreds of years, that China would still be on the silver standard if the United States' silver purchase policy in 1934 and 1935 had not forced its abandonment, and that the historical silver base should be re-established. Actually China has only had a modern national monetary system since 1933 when the old silver *tael* (not a coin but a unit of weight in silver) and various circulating silver coins were abandoned as legal tender, and the Sun Yat Sen dollar was first minted by the new National Mint in Shanghai. From 1933 until November 1935 China was on a unified silver standard system. On November 4, 1935 this system was abandoned as a result of high and unstable silver prices. A managed paper currency system backed by adequate gold and dollar reserves was substituted. The Government undertook to maintain the stability of the yuan by buying and selling foreign exchange at fixed rates in unlimited quantities. These reforms of 1935 were successfully carried through, and China enjoyed markedly stable prices and exchange rates for at least two years until after the outbreak of hostilities with Japan in 1937.

While fluctuating silver prices precipitated the abandonment of the silver standard in China, the announced tendency of Chinese monetary policy was already in the direction of a monetary system based on reserves of gold and foreign exchange, and the Chinese people quickly and easily adapted themselves to the use of paper currency. Without such a system China would have found it impossible to finance the war against Japan.

the Government, in the absence of unlimited convertibility of paper currency into silver, would probably recognize this depreciation by continually altering its official "conversion" rate between silver and paper; such action would itself tend to accelerate the depreciation.

Since the Government could not afford to have the existing currency collapse, for reasons of prestige and because it would wish to make some expenditures in paper currency (at times and places that silver was not on hand), both spending in silver and redemption of paper on demand would be necessary. The Government would therefore require to have on hand very large physical stocks of silver in order to maintain unlimited convertibility. Estimates of the amount of silver that would be required for such an operation range from 500 million to over one billion ounces.

If China is not able concomitantly to take the measures required to re-establish fiscal equilibrium, further large amounts of silver would be required to meet the continuing budgetary deficits. As pointed out above, as long as deficit spending continues on a large scale and the deficit is financed by increasing the money supply, inflation will continue regardless of the kind of monetary units employed. Even if silver coins are introduced and used in considerable quantities, the continuing increase in their supply will result both in increased prices of commodities in terms of silver and in a continued drain of silver into hoards or into black market channels for export. The leakage of silver into foreign markets through such channels would provide a means for financing unauthorized and luxury imports and further flight of capital abroad and thus would not reduce the deficit in the balance of payments which must be met out of official foreign exchange holdings and foreign aid. Moreover, it would disrupt the New York silver market unless the United States Treasury spent large sums in order to support this market. Such an operation would not give China a permanently stable monetary system, and would be a purely palliative measure.

Thus the use of silver as a temporary monetary expedient would be an extremely expensive as well as hazardous means for the possible attainment of a limited objective.

Any silver provided for Chinese domestic monetary purposes would thus have to be *in addition* to the aid already proposed, for it would not obviate or lessen the necessity for providing assistance in the form of supplies of badly needed imports as is proposed in the recommendations now before Congress.

178(a)

Secretary Marshall to the Ambassador in China (Stuart)

893.00/1-1248

WASHINGTON, *January 12, 1948.*

For your confidential information the final decisions regarding the China aid program have not yet been made by the Secretary, and thereafter proposed legislation will have to be reviewed by the National Advisory Council and submitted to the Bureau of the Budget before it is presented to Congress. Accordingly it is not possible to send authoritative information to the Embassy at this stage. It is suggested that pressure on the part of the Chinese for details of the program can be met by indicating Congress' prior rights in receiving such a message from the President. A report containing sufficient data will of course be sent you for communication personally to the Generalissimo and the Foreign Minister a day or so before public presentation.

The question of the appointment of technicians in connection with implementing the aid program will form part of the proposed legislation and no definitive action can be taken until at least the attitude of Congress manifests itself. Incidentally it is not clear how the Generalissimo's request for a "supreme economic adviser" and his suggestion of Blandford for that position jibes with his memorandum in which it is stated that the Chinese Government wishes to employ its own American or foreign technicians. No doubt the United States will have to send to China additional personnel to act in a supervisory and advisory capacity in connection with the aid program, but these may well be very limited in number due to the unavailability of experienced personnel. There are, however, two obvious and serious disadvantages to appointment of a "supreme economic adviser": First, there is the basic question of how effective under present circumstances in China he can be and secondly, and more important, the strong implication that his presence would carry of continuing United States responsibility for economic, financial and governmental situation in China, a responsibility which the United States cannot assume and which China and other countries must not be misled to believe has been or is going to be assumed.

This is no less applicable to the civil war. Consequently, the activities of the Military Advisory Group must be carefully delimited and they are not regarded as constituting an integral part of the aid program, which is essentially economic in character. It is expected that decisions regarding certain changes in the Military Advisory Group's directives and what additional military training center can be appropriately authorized will be made before General Barr's departure.

The importance of the considerations set forth above is reinforced by certain current indications that elements in the Chinese Government are looking more to external assistance than to their own exertions in meeting China's problems and seem to be directing their efforts towards shifting to the United States the responsibility for the conduct and the course of the civil war, the welfare of the Chinese people and the efficacy of the regime.

178(b)

Secretary Marshall to the Ambassador in China (Stuart)

893.50 Recovery/4–1448　　　　　　　　　　　Washington, *May 7, 1948*

The Department is studying United States policy aspects of the problem of furnishing qualified advisers to the Chinese Government and agrees that some advisory assistance is necessary in connection with the aid program. With regard to top level advisers for functions involving policy, the Department is of the opinion that if provided by the United States, they should be limited to a small number for highly select fields. Account must be taken not only of the limited number of competent advisers available, but also of the significance of their proposed fields of action from the standpoint of the objectives of the aid program and the extent to which reasonable prospects exist for implementation of recommendations made. The fields of advice and the relationship of the advisers to the Chinese Government and the aid Mission should minimize the possibility for undesirable involvement of the United States Government in the course of developments in China and its implied responsibility therefor. This is particularly true for certain aspects of fiscal policy and operations where the fundamental solution cannot be reached under present civil war conditions and where the United States effort to exert pressure, control, and the reduction of military expenditures might imply United States responsibility for the Chinese Government military effort and be exploited to obtain commitment in that regard. This would be contrary to the intent of Congress as described earlier.

The Department believes certain basic fiscal and other policy problems, such as those above, cannot be solved through technical advice, but that continuous effort can and should be made in the direction of improvements by well-timed informal pressure at top levels, e. g., by the Chief of the ECA Mission and top Embassy officials.

The assignment of United States technical personnel as advisers at the operational level should also be highly selective and primarily for functions directly related to implementation of the aid program, such as reconstruction projects financed by United States appropriation and/or the Chinese currency account. In exceptional cases, technical personnel might be assigned to advise operations indirectly related to the aid program which involve a minimum of policy issues, such as certain aspects of the foreign exchange operations of the Central Bank. The largest number of technical personnel in an advisory capacity probably should be provided for reconstruction. United States technical assistance to Chinese Government agencies responsible for control or operations of the distribution of expendable U. S. aid commodities should be rendered by members of the aid Mission in the course of the performance of the normal functions of observation and reporting, and not by United States personnel in the capacity of advisers assigned to the Chinese Government agencies concerned.

Departmental thinking now is that specific recommendations on types of advisers should be deferred until the Chief of the ECA China Mission has had opportunity to study the question in China and is able to determine the exact needs of the Chinese Government and their abilities to use advisers in terms of the China Aid Program. In the meantime the Department is studying the best methods to correlate the provision of technical assistance under the Smith-Mundt Act with the China Aid Program.

179

China Aid Act of 1948

(TITLE IV OF PUBLIC LAW 472)

Sec. 401. This title may be cited as the "China Aid Act of 1948".

Sec. 402. Recognizing the intimate economic and other relationships between the United States and China, and recognizing that disruption following in the wake of war is not contained by national frontiers, the Congress finds that the existing situation in China endangers the establishment of a lasting peace, the general welfare and national interest of the United States, and the attainment of the objectives of the United Nations. It is the sense of the Congress that the further evolution in China of Principles of individual liberty, free institutions, and genuine independence rests largely upon the continuing development of a strong and democratic national government as the basis for the establishment of sound economic conditions and for stable international economic relationships. Mindful of the advantages which the United States has enjoyed through the existence of a large domestic market with no internal trade barriers, and believing that similar advantages can accrue to China, it is declared to be the policy of the people of the United States to encourage the Republic of China and its people to exert sustained common efforts which will speedily achieve the internal peace and economic stability in China which are essential for lasting peace and prosperity in the world. It is further declared to be the policy of the people of the United States to encourage the Republic of China in its efforts to maintain the genuine independence and the administrative integrity of China, and to sustain and strengthen principles of individual liberty and free institutions in China through a program of assistance based on self-help and cooperation : *Provided*, That no assistance to China herein contemplated shall seriously impair the economic stability of the United States. It is further declared to be the policy of the United States that assistance provided by the United States under this title should at all times be dependent upon cooperation by the Republic of China and its people in furthering the program : *Provided further*, That assistance furnished under this title shall not be construed as an express or implied assumption by the United States of any responsibility for policies, acts, or undertakings of the Republic of China or for conditions which may prevail in China at any time.

Sec. 403. Aid provided under this title shall be provided under the applicable provisions of the Economic Cooperation Act of 1948 which are consistent with the purposes of this title. It is not the purpose of this title that China, in order to receive aid hereunder, shall adhere to a joint program for European recovery.

Sec. 404. (a) In order to carry out the purposes of this title, there is hereby authorized to be appropriated to the President for aid to China a sum not to exceed $338,000,000 to remain available for obligation for the period of one year following the date of enactment of this Act.

(b) There is also hereby authorized to be appropriated to the President a sum not to exceed $125,000,000 for additional aid to China through grants, on such terms as the President may determine and without regard to the provisions of the Economic Cooperation Act of 1948, to remain available for obligation for the period of one year following the date of enactment of this Act.

Sec. 405. An agreement shall be entered into between China and the United States containing those undertakings by China which the Secretary of State, after consultation with the Administrator for Economic Cooperation, may deem necessary to carry out the purposes of this title and to improve commercial relations with China.

Sec. 406. Notwithstanding the provisions of any other law, the Reconstruction Finance Corporation is authorized and directed, until such time as an appropriation is made pursuant to section 404, to make advances, not to exceed in the aggregate $50,000,000, to carry out the provisions of this title in such manner and in such amounts as the President shall determine. From appropriations authorized under section 404, there shall be repaid without interest to the Reconstruction Finance Corporation the advances made by it under the authority contained herein. No interest shall be charged on advances made by the Treasury to the Reconstruction Finance Corporation in implementation of this section.

Sec. 407. (a) The Secretary of State, after consultation with the Administrator, is hereby authorized to conclude an agreement with China establishing a Joint Commission on Rural Reconstruction in China, to be composed of two citizens of the United States appointed by the President of the United States and three citizens of China appointed by the President of China. Such Commission shall, subject to the direction and control of the Administrator, formulate and carry out a program for reconstruction in rural areas of China, which shall include such research and training activities as may be necessary or appropriate for such reconstruction : *Provided*, That assistance furnished under this section shall not be construed as an express or implied assumption by the United States of any responsibility for making any further contributions to carry out the purposes of this section.

(b) Insofar as practicable, an amount equal to not more than 10 per centum of the funds made available under subsection (a) of section 404 shall be used to carry out the purposes of subsection (a) of this section. Such amount may be in United States dollars, proceeds in Chinese currency from the sale of commodities made available to China with funds authorized under subsection (a) of section 404, or both.

Approved April 3, 1948.

180

The Ambassador in China (Stuart) to Secretary Marshall

893.50 Recovery/5–1048

NANKING, *May 10, 1948*

The Embassy agrees that a bilateral aid agreement should be negotiated in Nanking and that the period of its negotiations presents time and opportunity to continue to press the Chinese Government for undertakings regarding self-help and tangible acts in the execution of the Premier's January 28 statement. Pressures in these directions have been applied by the Embassy whenever and wherever the occasion was offered. The Embassy agrees that they should be intensified now and during the period of bilateral negotiation with implicit but not an explicit link.

Two important factors, however, must be borne in mind in any advance estimate of progress which may be made with the Chinese Government. In the first place, any broad or powerful bargaining position vis-a-vis the Chinese Government disappeared on the date Congress passed the China Aid Act of 1948. Our position rests basically now on the more tenuous ground of Chinese hopes for the continuation and expansion of aid beyond the time period covered by the present Act. It is true, however, that we retain and should make full use of our bargaining position in the bilateral negotiations with respect to (1) methods of procurement for aid commodities, (2) methods of distribution of aid commodities in China and (3) utilization of Chinese National Currency proceeds from the sale of aid commodities provided under the grant. On the broad front of governmental reform and positive, self-generated fiscal and economic action, we rely for all practical purposes today, in the Embassy's opinion, on the effectiveness of moral pressure and not on a trading position.

The second element to be considered is the limitation on the Chinese Government's ability as opposed to its willingness to take bold constructive and effective action. The economic and financial status is deteriorating with increased momentum, as witnessed by the doubling within the past week of the black market CNC rate for the United States dollar. The military situation shows no improvement nor signs of any in prospect. Politically, there is a paralysis of leadership at the top which has permitted, for example, the tangle over the membership of the Legislative Yuan to make it impossible, until a settlement has been reached, for the Generalissimo to appoint his new Cabinet.

Under these circumstances, the Embassy strongly recommends that we display no haste in the negotiation or conclusion of the bilateral agreement. The exchange of interim letters provides an entirely satisfactory basis on which to operate in the coming weeks. Moreover, working out in practical terms with the Chinese officials the procedures and operational methods under which the new aid program is to be handled will make more meaningful the language finally agreed upon and imbedded in the bilateral agreement. Delay will give time, presumably, to learn at least what individuals will head the Ministries directly concerned. Finally, it will extend the period in which our pressures can be applied.

In the Embassy's opinion, the Generalissimo, under the emergency powers granted him by the National Assembly, can sign a bilateral agreement without the necessity of ratification by the Legislative Yuan. We believe it safe to proceed on this assumption, though we are checking in various governmental quarters, recognizing, however, that no one is in a position to give an authoritative answer in advance of an announcement of the Cabinet and the membership of the Judicial Yuan. The Embassy, accordingly, recommends that the opening of negotiations be deferred until June 1. Meanwhile, pressure for reform will be continued and discussions with the Chinese operating officials of procedures, drawing on experience, should be pushed.

With respect to topics to be covered in corollary discussions, the Embassy believes the Premier's Ten Points of January 28 provide comprehensive agenda with desirable emphasis to be placed on implementation of land reform, on extension of rationing and on fiscal and economic measures to maximize exports. It is presumed that protection of private trade channels can be achieved in the course of specific bilateral negotiations on methods of procurement and distribution of aid commodities.

181

Economic Aid Agreement between the United States of America and the Republic of China, July 3, 1948 [3]

PREAMBLE.

The Government of the United States of America and the Government of the Republic of China:

Considering that it is the policy of the Government of the United States of America to extend economic assistance to the people and the Government of China in accordance with the provisions of the China Aid Act of 1948; and

Considering that it is the policy of the Government of China to undertake a vigorous program of self help in order to create more stable economic conditions in China, and to improve commercial relations with other countries;

Have agreed as follows:

ARTICLE I.

The Government of the United States of America undertakes to assist China, by making available to the Government of China or to any person, agency or

---

[3] Treaties and Other International Acts Series 1837. Printed also in Economic Cooperation Administration, *Economic Aid to China under the China Aid Act of 1948* (Washington, Feb. 1949), pp. 113–122.

organization designated by the latter Government such assistance as may be requested by it and approved by the Government of the United States of America. The Government of the United States of America will furnish this assistance under the provisions, and subject to all of the terms, limitations and conditions, of the China Aid Act of 1948 (other than Section 404 (b) thereof), acts amendatory and supplementary thereto and appropriation acts thereunder, and will make available to the Government of China only such commodities, services and other assistance as are authorized to be made available by such acts. The Government of the United States of America may suspend or terminate at any time the assistance under this Article.

Article II.

1. In order to achieve the maximum improvement of economic conditions through the employment of assistance received from the Government of the United States of America, the Government of China undertakes

(a) to adopt or maintain the measures necessary to ensure efficient and practical use of economic resources available to it, including

(1) such measures as may be necessary to ensure that the commodities and services obtained with assistance furnished under this Agreement are used for purposes consistent with this Agreement;

(2) to the extent practicable, measures to locate, identify and put into appropriate use in furtherance of its efforts to improve economic conditions, in China, assets, and earnings therefrom which belong to nationals of China and which are situated within the United States of America, its territories or possessions. Nothing in this clause imposes any obligation on the Government of the United States of America to assist in carrying out such measures or on the Government of China to dispose of such assets;

(b) to promote the development of industrial and agricultural production on a sound economic basis;

(c) to initiate and maintain financial, monetary, budgetary and administrative measures necessary for the creation of more stable currency conditions and for the promotion of production and marketing of goods for domestic consumption and export; and

(d) to cooperate with other countries in facilitating and stimulating an increasing interchange of goods and services with other countries and in reducing public and private barriers to trade with other countries.

2. The Government of China will take the measures which it deems appropriate to prevent, on the part of private or public commercial enterprises, business practices or business arrangements affecting international trade which have the effect of interfering with the purposes and policies of this Agreement.

Article III.

1. The Government of China undertakes to make all practicable efforts to improve commercial relations with other countries, including measures to improve the conditions affecting the carrying on of foreign trade by private enterprises in China.

2. The Government of China, in carrying out the provisions of paragraph 1 of this Article, will, among other measures, administer such import and exchange controls as are, or may be, made necessary by the exigencies of China's international balance of payments and the foreign exchange resources available to the Government of China, in a uniform, fair and equitable manner.

3. The Government of the United States of America and the Government of China will consult, upon the request of either, regarding any matter relating to the application of the provisions of this Article.

ARTICLE IV.

1. All commodities provided by the Government of the United States of America pursuant to this Agreement shall be processed and distributed by commercial enterprises or by private or Chinese Government agencies, and in accordance with terms and conditions, agreed upon from time to time between the Government of the United States of America and the Government of China.

2. The Government of China, in consultation with representatives of the United States of America, will take all appropriate steps designed to achieve fair and equitable distribution within the areas under its control of commodities provided by the Government of the United States of America pursuant to this Agreement and of similar commodities imported into China with other funds or produced locally. To the extent that circumstances and supply availabilities permit, a distribution and price control system shall be inaugurated or maintained in urban centers of China with the intent of insuring that all classes of the population shall receive a fair share of imported or indigenously produced essential civilian supplies. In permitting expendable commodities made available under this Agreement to be utilized in support of the Chinese efforts to improve consumption and price controls, it is understood that the Government of the United States of America takes no responsibility for the success of these urban programs.

3. The prices at which supplies furnished by the United States of America pursuant to this Agreement will be sold in China shall be agreed upon between the Government of the United States of America and the Government of China.

ARTICLE V.

1. The provisions of this Article shall apply only with respect to assistance which may be furnished by the Government of the United States of America on a grant basis pursuant to this Agreement.

2. The Government of China agrees to establish a special account in the Central Bank of China in the name of the Government of China (hereinafter called the special account) and to make deposits in Chinese currency to this account as follows:

(a) The unencumbered balance at the close of business on the day of the signature of this Agreement in that special account in the Central Bank of China in the name of the Government of China established pursuant to the Agreement between the Government of the United States of America and the Government of China made on October 27, 1947, and any further sums which may from time to time be required by such Agreement to be deposited in that special account. It is understood that subsection (E) of Section 114 of the Foreign Assistance Act of 1948 constitutes the approval and determination of the Government of the United States of America with respect to the disposition of such balance referred to in that Agreement, and

(b) The unencumbered balances of the deposits made by the Government of China pursuant to the exchange of notes between the two Governments dated April 30, 1948.

(c) Amounts commensurate with the indicated dollar cost to the Government of the United States of America of commodities, services and technical information (including any costs of processing, storing, transporting, repairing or other services incident thereto) made available to China on a grant basis pursuant to this Agreement less, however, the amount of deposits made pursuant to the exchange of notes referred to in sub-paragraph (b). The Government of the United States of America shall from time to time notify the Government of China of the indicated dollar cost of any such commodities, services and technical information and the Government of China will deposit in the special account at such times as may be specified by the Government of the United States of America a commensurate amount of Chinese currency computed at a rate of exchange to be agreed upon between the Government of the United States of America and the Government of China. The Government of China will upon the request of the Government of the United States of America make advance deposits in the special account which shall be credited against subsequent notifications pursuant to this paragraph.

3. The Government of the United States of America will from time to time notify the Government of China of its requirements for administrative expenditures in Chinese currency within China incident to operations under the China Aid Act of 1948 and the Government of China will thereupon make such sums available out of any balances in the special account in the manner requested by the Government of the United States of America in the notification.

4. The Government of China will further make such sums of Chinese currency available out of any balances in the special account as may be required to cover: A. Expenditures required to carry out the purposes of the Joint Commission on Rural Reconstruction in China as provided for by Section 407 of the China Aid Act of 1948; and B. Costs (including port, storage, handling and similar charges) of transportation from any point of entry in China to the consignee's designated point of delivery in China of such relief supplies and packages as are referred to in Article VII.

5. The Government of China shall dispose of any remaining balance in the special account only for such purposes as may be agreed from time to time with the Government of the United States of America including in particular: A. Sterilization as a measure of monetary and financial stabilization; B. Expenditures incident to the stimulation of productive activity and the development of new sources of wealth including materials which may be required in the United States of America because of deficiencies or potential deficiencies in the resources of the United States of America; C. Expenditures upon projects or programs the external costs of which are being covered in whole or in part by assistance rendered by the Government of the United States of America or by loans from the International Bank for Reconstruction and Development; or D. Expenditures upon uncompleted relief or work relief projects undertaken pursuant to the Agreement between the Governments of the United States of America and of China of October 27, 1947.

6. The Government of China will maintain the value in terms of United States dollar equivalent of such amount of the special account as is: A. Indicated by the Government of the United States of America as necessary for administrative expenditures referred to in paragraph 3 of this Article; B. Required for the purposes of paragraph 4 of this Article; and C. Agreed between the two Governments to be necessary to defray the expenses in Chinese currency associated with reconstruction projects or programs the external costs of which are met in whole or in part by assistance rendered by the Government of the United States of America pursuant to the Agreement. The Government

of China will carry out this provision by depositing such additional amounts of Chinese currency as the Government of the United States of America may from time to time determine after consultation with the Government of China.

7. Any unencumbered balance remaining in the special account on April 3, 1949, shall be disposed of within China for such purposes as may hereafter be agreed between the Governments of the United States of America and of China, it being understood that the agreement of the United States of America shall be subject to approval by act or joint resolution of the Congress of the United States of America.

ARTICLE VI.

1. The Government of China will facilitate the transfer to the United States of America for stockpiling or other purposes of materials originating in China which are required by the United States of America as a result of deficiencies or potential deficiencies in its own resources upon such reasonable terms of sale, exchange, barter or otherwise and in such quantities and for such period of time as may be agreed to between the Governments of the United States of America and of China after due regard for the reasonable requirements of China for domestic use and commercial export of such materials. The Government of China will take such specific measures as may be necessary to carry out the provisions of this paragraph. The Government of China will, when so requested by the Government of the United States of America, enter into negotiations for detailed arrangements necessary to carry out the provisions of this paragraph.

2. The Government of China will, when so requested by the Government of the United States of America, negotiate such arrangements as are appropriate to carry out the provisions of paragraph (9) of subsection 115 (b) of the Foreign Assistance Act of 1948 which relates to the development and transfer of materials required by the United States of America.

3. The Government of China, when so requested by the Government of the United States of America, will cooperate, wherever appropriate, to further the objectives of paragraphs 1 and 2 of this Article in respect of materials originating outside of China.

ARTICLE VII.

The Government of China will, when so requested by the Government of the United States of America, enter into negotiations for agreements (including the provisions of duty free treatment under appropriate safeguards) to facilitate the entry into China of supplies of relief goods donated to or purchased by United States voluntary non-profit relief agencies and of relief packages originating in the United States of America and consigned to individuals residing in China.

ARTICLE VIII.

1. The two Governments will, upon the request of either of them, consult regarding any matter relating to the application of this Agreement or to operations or arrangements carried out pursuant to this Agreement.

2. The Government of China will communicate to the Government of the United States of America in a form and at intervals to be indicated by the latter after consultation with the Government of China:

(a) detailed information regarding projects, programs and measures proposed or adopted by the Government of China to carry out the provisions of this Agreement;

ANNEXES 999

(b) full statements of operations under this Agreement, including a statement of the use of funds, commodities and services received thereunder, such statements to be made in each calendar quarter;

(c) information regarding its economy and any other relevant information which the Government of the United States of America may need to determine the nature and scope of operations, and to evaluate the effectiveness of assistance furnished or contemplated under this Agreement.

3. The Government of China will assist the Government of the United States of America to obtain information relating to the materials originating in China referred to in Article VI which is necessary to the formulation and execution of the arrangements provided for in that Article.

ARTICLE IX.

1. The Government of China will keep the people of China fully informed of the progress achieved by the Government of China in implementing the undertakings contained in this Agreement designed to achieve more stable economic conditions in China, and it will provide continuously information to the people of China regarding the nature and extent of assistance furnished pursuant to this Agreement. It will make such information available to the media of public information and will take practicable steps to ensure that appropriate facilities are provided for the dissemination of such information.

2. The Government of the United States of America will encourage the dissemination of such information and will make it available to the media of public information.

3. The Government of China will make public in China in each calendar quarter full statements of operations under this Agreement, including information as to the uses of funds, commodities and services received.

ARTICLE X.

1. The Government of China agrees to receive a Special Mission for Economic Cooperation which will discharge the responsibilities of the Government of the United States of America in China under this Agreement.

2. The Government of China will, upon appropriate notification from the Ambassador of the United States of America in China, consider the Special Mission and its personnel as part of the Embassy of the United States of America in China for the purposes of enjoying the privileges and immunities accorded to that Embassy and its personnel of comparable rank. The Government of China will further accord appropriate courtesies to the members and staff of the Joint Committee on Foreign Economic Cooperation of the Congress of the United States of America and will grant them the facilities and assistance necessary to the effective performance of their responsibilities.

3. The Government of China will extend full cooperation to the Special Mission and to the members and staff of the Joint Committee. Such cooperation shall include the provision of all information and facilities necessary to the observation and review of the carrying out of this Agreement, including the use of assistance furnished under it.

ARTICLE XI.

1. The Governments of the United States of America and of China agree to submit to the decision of the International Court of Justice any claim espoused by either Government on behalf of one of its nationals against the other Govern-

ment for compensation for damage arising as a consequence of governmental measures (other than measures concerning enemy property or interests) taken after April 3, 1948 by the other Government and affecting property or interests of such national including contracts with or concessions granted by duly authorized authorities of such other Government. It is understood that the undertaking of each Government in respect of claims espoused by the other Government pursuant to this paragraph is made in the case of each Government under the authority of and is limited by the terms and conditions of such effective recognition as it has heretofore given to the compulsory jurisdiction of the International Court of Justice under Article 36 of the Statute of the Court. The provisions of this paragraph shall be in all respects without prejudice to other rights of access, if any, of either Government to the International Court of Justice or to the espousal and presentation of claims based upon alleged violations by either Government of rights and duties arising under treaties, agreements or principles of international law.

2. The Governments of the United States of America and of China further agree that such claims may be referred in lieu of the Court to any arbitral tribunal mutually agreed upon.

3. It is further understood that neither Government will espouse a claim pursuant to this Article unless the national concerned has exhausted the remedies available to him in the administrative and judicial tribunals of the country in which the claim exists.

Article XII.

1. This Agreement shall become effective on this day's date. It shall remain in force until June 30, 1950, and, unless at least six months before June 30, 1950, either Government shall have given the other notice in writing of intention to terminate the Agreement on that date, it shall remain in force thereafter until the expiration of six months from the date on which such notice shall have been given. Article V shall remain in effect until all the sums in the currency of China required to be disposed of in accordance with its own terms have been disposed of as provided in such Article.

2. This Agreement may be amended at any time by agreement between the two Governments.

3. The Annex to this Agreement forms an integral part thereof.

4. This Agreement shall be registered with the Secretary-General of the United Nations.

In witness whereof the respective representatives duly authorized for the purpose have signed the present Agreement.

Done at Nanking in duplicate in the English and Chinese languages, both texts authentic, this third day of July 1948, corresponding to the third day of the seventh month of the thirty-seventh year of the Republic of China.

J. LEIGHTON STUART,
*For the Government of the
United States of America.*

WANG SHIH-CHIEH,
*For the Government of
The Republic of China.*

Annex.

1. It is understood that the requirements of paragraph 1 (a) of Article II, relating to the adoption of measures for the efficient use of resources would

include, with respect to commodities furnished under the Agreement, effective measures for safeguarding such commodities and for preventing their diversion to illegal or irregular markets or channels of trade.

2. It is understood that the Government of China will not be requested, under paragraph 2 (a) of Article VIII to furnish detailed information about minor projects or confidential commercial or technical information the disclosure of which would injure legitimate commercial interests.

3. It is understood that the Government of the United States of America in making the notifications referred to in paragraph 2 of Article X would bear in mind the desirability of restricting, so far as practicable, the number of officials for whom full diplomatic privileges would be requested. It is also understood that the detailed application of Article X would, when necessary, be the subject of intergovernmental discussion.

NANKING, *July 3, 1948*

J. LEIGHTON STUART
WANG SHIH-CHIEH

182

Informal Memorandum Regarding Basic Reforms, Handed by Ambassador Stuart to President Chiang Kai-shek on May 22, 1948

The American people noted with deep interest the statement issued on January 28, 1948, by the President of the Executive Yuan which comprised ten financial and economic reform measures which the Chinese Government intended to undertake. The United States Government, including the Congress during its debate of the Aid to China Act, accepted this statement as a program which the Chinese Government would vigorously pursue in order to insure by its own actions that financial assistance from the United States Government would provide the maximum results for the Chinese people.

The Premier's statement represented a coherent and promising framework for individual measures and actions of the Chinese Government. A number of measures in execution of this program have been taken with respect to these objectives but they have often appeared as isolated acts, unnoted and even unrelated to the program as a whole. And in some important areas it has seemed that no appreciable progress can be measured in the past four months. Some of these areas, apparently vacant insofar as effective action and visible results are concerned, are noted below. The numbering of the paragraphs below follows the numbering of the Premier's ten points.

1. On control of Government expenditures, even granting all the difficulties, little seems to have been accomplished. The first steps would appear to be to establish standardized accounting with firm budgetary controls in the hands of a central fiscal authority possessing the power to determine allocations for all expenditures whether military or civil. Needless to say, this authority would require the unremitting personal support of the President. Another step would be the ruthless elimination of all non-productive expenditures. In both the civilian and military establishments there would appear to be room for the removal of duplicatory or unnecessary services and individuals.

2. With respect to securing an increase in tax yields and distributing the tax burden more equitably, it is recognized that the severity of the inflation of the

currency accentuates the Government's difficulties. It is a truism, however, that public confidence in the currency can only be recaptured if a drastic reduction in curtailable expenses is accompanied by a massive increase in tax collections. Even to the casual observer the administration of existing tax collection measures can be greatly improved. It is my impression, for instance, that urban real estate taxes are low compared to tax rates in the country districts. Increased reliance on ad valorem taxes and taxes collected at the source should help to compensate for loss of real revenues due to currency depreciation. The projected sale of certain Government assets is surely another step in the right direction which could be effectively followed by further acts of the same sort.

3. Although superficially increases in wages of civil servants and soldiers will add to the budgetary difficulty, it would seem essential that equitable adjustments must be made if loyalty and efficiency are to be retained. The weeding out of unnecessary personnel should be tied directly to the program of upward salary adjustments.

4. The rice and flour rationing program seems by general agreement to have been a substantial success, particularly in Shanghai, Canton, Peiping and Tientsin, and to lesser degree in Nanking. It would seem that this experience urgently justifies increasing the number of urban centers in which a rationing system is installed and, equally important, increasing the number of commodities covered. I have particularly in mind the addition of edible oils, cotton cloth, kerosene and automotive gasoline. Accompanying this would be the institution of practical measures to get commodities such as kerosene and cotton yarn flowing into the agricultural areas to provide the incentive for increased production and collection of foodstuffs.

5. It would appear that the fifth objective of the Prime Minister can only approach achievement if reduction of expenditures and increase in tax collections are vigorously and successfully pursued as a first step.

6. It would seem that the Central Bank has made some progress in its efforts to check speculation and pursue a deflationary credit policy. Loopholes, however, obviously continue to exist through which capital finds refuge in foreign currency and transfers abroad. The loss, both of Government customs revenues and foreign exchange, appears to be substantial in the two-way smuggling operations which by common report are widespread. The intensification of the present campaign against smuggling would yield returns to the Government on both scores. The Maritime Customs will need support and re-equipping to play their part.

7. Internal measures can reduce Chinese dependence upon the large imports now needed but only if such measures are accompanied by successful efforts to increase exports from China can the foreign exchange crisis be surmounted. There are many measures which the business community has repeatedly pointed out would contribute to an increase in exports. One such measure would be the directing of incentive goods referred to above into the interior areas of production. Another would be the establishment of realistic exchange rates for foreign currencies. Another would be the reduction in red tape now involved in arranging exports. Finally, the Government could do much by concentrating its encouragments on exporting industries which could increase their exportable surplus if for example, they were given priorities for securing spare parts and raw materials which must be imported.

8. On import controls, a clear policy of encouraging private enterprise by simplification of procedures would seem to promise the best results. Such acts

as the recent issuance of regulation No. 131 by the Central Bank should be considered in these terms in advance of promulgation. The result of this particular regulation has been to bring the import trade to a complete standstill and to deepen the already deep discouragement.

9. The recommendations of the joint Sino-American Agricultural Mission, many of which have been only partially acted upon, seem to provide a comprehensive framework for action in this important field. If there is any single area where reform in deeds and not words is most necessary and most sought by the people, it is land reform. The Land Law of April 29, 1946 contains a carefully considered program regarding limitations on land ownership, land redistribution, and of utmost importance, control and reduction of rents and taxes. Subsequent regulations dealing with particular aspects of land reform have been contained in such measures as the Principles Governing the Administration of Areas Aimed at Achieving Social Stability and Relieving the People, passed by the Supreme National Defense Council on October 23, 1946 and the "Measures for Dispostion of Land Ownership in Pacification Areas," promulgated by the Executive Yuan on October 26, 1946. One hears on all sides that reforms have not yet been carried out, and the special investigators of the Executive Yuan have reported on various occasions regarding the non-implementation of these measures. Carefully prepared measures extending land reform to wider areas were strongly recommended by the Ministry of Land Administration to the Conference of Pacification Areas Commanders held in Nanking in March 1948. Successful policies which have related land and agrarian reform to the problem of defense seem to have been applied in the 10th Adminstrative Area of Hopei Province, which might merit extension to other areas.

10. Under the difficulties imposed by internal strife and shortage of materials, the restoration of the Chinese railroads has been inspiring. In the broad field of communications and reconstruction of industry important steps have been achieved. There are some related areas where it would seem China's self-interest would dictate action. For example, the closure of the River ports to foreign flag ocean shipping is contrary to the policy of great nations. This situation damages China's own interests in that transportation costs are heavily increased on American Aid oil shipments to Hankow, to take one case. The delay in reaching agreement in the long drawn out negotiations on the restoration of pre-war cable facilities is another case in point. Meanwhile certain difficulties which have arisen in connection with the Sino-U. S. Bilateral Air Transport Agreement remain unresolved.

In conclusion, the Premier's statement seems as cogent and comprehensive today as on the date when it was issued. There would seem to be nothing to add to this statement of objectives but there would seem much still to be done in attaining them. China does not seek a subsidy but it has looked to the United States for help in this difficult period in order that it might the better help itself. It was in this spirit that the United States Government has responded and it is in these terms that the American people and the American Congress in the coming months will follow with acute interest the progress that the Chinese Government makes in solving the broad and pressing problems of economic and financial reform.

183

Exchange of Notes between the United States Government and the Republic of China, Signed in Nanking on August 5, 1948, Providing for the Establishment of a Sino-American Joint Commission on Rural Reconstruction [4]

The Ambassador in China (Stuart) to the Chinese Minister for Foreign Affairs (Wang)

EXCELLENCY: I have the honor to refer to Section 407 of the China Aid Act of 1948 enacted by the Government of the United States of America (hereinafter referred to as the Act), which provides, among other things, for the conclusion of an agreement between China and the United States of America establishing a Joint Commission on Rural Reconstruction in China. In pursuance of the general principles laid down in the Act, and in particular section 407 thereof, I have the honor to bring forward the following proposals regarding the organization of the Joint Commission and related matters:

1. There shall be established a Joint Commission on Rural Reconstruction in China (hereinafter referred to as the Commission) to be composed of two citizens of the United States of America appointed by the President of the United States of America and three citizens of the Republic of China to be appointed by the President of China. The Commission shall elect one of the Chinese members as chairman.

2. The functions and authority of the Commission shall, subject to the provisions of the above-mentioned section of the Act, be as follows: (a) to formulate and carry out through appropriate Chinese Government agencies and international or private agencies in China a coordinated program for reconstruction in rural areas of China (hereinafter referred to as the program); (b) to conclude arrangements with the agencies referred to in the preceding paragraph establishing a basis for their cooperation; (c) to recommend to the Governments of the United States of America and of China within the limits prescribed by the Act the allocation of funds and other assistance to the program, and to recommend to the Government of China the allocation of such other funds and assistance as are deemed essential to the success of the program; (d) to establish standards of performance for implementation of the program, including the qualifications, type and number of personnel to be used by cooperating agencies in the program, and to maintain a constant supervision of all phases of the program with authority to recommend changes in or stoppage of any phase of the program; (e) to appoint such executive officers and administrative staff as the Commission deems necessary to carry out the program, it being understood that the chief executive officer shall be a citizen of China. Salaries, expenses of travel, and other expenses incident to the administrative functions of the Commission itself shall be paid from funds made available under Section 407 (B) of the Act.

3. In its program the Commission may include the following types of activity to be carried out in agreement with the agencies referred to in paragraph 2 (a): (a) A coordinated extension-type program in agriculture, home demonstration, health and education for initiation in a selected group of Hsien in several

---

[4] Printed in Economic Cooperation Administration, *Economic Aid to China under the China Aid Act of 1948* (Washington, Feb. 1949), pp. 126–129.

provinces to include a limited number of subsidiary projects suited to conditions in the areas where the program is developed, in such fields as agricultural production, marketing, credit, irrigation, home and community industries, nutrition, sanitation, and education of a nature which will facilitate the promotion of all projects being undertaken; (b) Consultation with the Chinese Government concerning ways and means of progressively carrying out land reform measures; (c) Subsidiary projects in research training and manufacturing to be carried out in suitable locations to provide information, personnel and materials required by the program; (d) Projects to put into effect over a wider area than provided for in the coordinated extension-type program specified in (a) any of the above lines of activity which can be developed soundly on a larger scale, of which examples might be the multiplication and distribution of improved seeds, the control of rinderpest of cattle, the construction of irrigation and drainage facilities and the introduction of health and sanitation measures; (e) Related measures in line with the general objectives of this program; (f) The distribution of the assistance in this program on the principle of giving due attention to strengthening rural improvement in areas where selected projects can be progressively developed and where their development will contribute most effectively to the achievement of purposes for which this program is undertaken but that the principle of distributing aid will not be controlled by proportionate or geographical consideration *per se*.

4. In respect of any decision of the Commission, the approval of the Government of China shall be obtained prior to its execution if the Commission or its chairman, with the concurrence of the Chinese members, deems it necessary.

5. The Commission shall publish in China and transmit to the Government of the United States of America and the Government of China, in such form and at such times as may be requested by either of the two governments, full statements of operations, including a statement on the use of funds, supplies and services received, and will transmit to the two governments any other matter pertinent to operations as requested by either of the two governments. The Government of China will keep the people of China fully informed of the intended purpose and scope of the program and of the progress achieved by the Commission in implementing the program, including the nature and extent of the assistance furnished by the Government of the United States of America.

6. The Government of China will, upon appropriate notification of the Ambassador of the United States of America in China, consider the United States members and personnel of the Commission as part of the Embassy of the United States of America in China for the purpose of enjoying the privileges and immunities accorded to that Embassy and its personnel of comparable rank. It is understood that the Ambassador of the United States of America in China in making the notification will bear in mind the desirability of restricting so far as practicable the number of officials for whom full diplomatic privileges and immunities would be requested. It is also understood that the detailed application of this paragraph would, when necessary, be a subject of inter-governmental discussion.

7. All supplies imported into China for use in the program shall be free of customs duties, conservancy dues, and other charges imposed by the Government of China on similar supplies which are imported through regular commercial channels.

8. The Government of the United States of America and the Government of China will consult with respect to problems incident to the interpretation, implementation and possible amendment of the terms of the agreement embodied in

this exchange of notes whenever either of the two governments considers such action appropriate.

9. The Government of the United States of America reserves the right at any time to terminate or suspend its assistance or any part thereof provided under this exchange of notes. Assistance furnished by the Government of the United States of America under Section 407 of the Act and pursuant to this exchange of notes shall not be construed as an express or implied assumption by the Government of the United States of America of any responsibility for making any further contributions to carry out the purpose of Section 407 of the Act or of this exchange of notes.

10. This note and Your Excellency's reply accepting the above proposals on behalf of the Government of China will constitute an agreement between the two governments in the sense of Section 407 of the Act. Subject to the provisions of paragraphs 8 and 9, this exchange of notes will remain in force until June 30, 1949, or, upon the request of either government transmitted to the other government at least two months before June 30, 1949, until the date of termination of the Economic Aid Agreement between the two governments concluded on July 3, 1948.

I avail myself [etc.]

J. LEIGHTON STUART

The Chinese Minister for Foreign Affairs (Wang) to the Ambassador in China (Stuart)

EXCELLENCY: I have the honor to acknowledge receipt of your note of today's date which reads as follows:

[Here follows text of preceding note.]

On behalf of the Government of China I have the honor to accept the proposals contained in the note quoted above.

In recognition of the importance of the program as one of the essential means of achieving the objectives in which the Governments of China and of the United States of America unite in seeking under the Economic Aid Agreement between the two governments concluded on July 3, 1948 the Government of China undertakes to afford to the execution of the program the full weight of its support and to direct cooperating agencies of the Government of China including the local officials concerned to give such assistance and facilities as are essential to the success of their undertakings under the program.

I avail myself of this opportunity to renew to your Excellency the assurances of my highest consideration.

WANG SHIH-CHIEH

184

Economic Aid to China under the China Aid Act of 1948 [5]

PART I—INTRODUCTION

At the time the China Aid Act was passed, China was in the grip of the longest sustained inflation in modern history. Her external resources had dwindled from approximately a billion dollars on V-J Day to less than one-quarter of that

---

[5] Excerpts from document published by the Economic Cooperation Administration Washington, February 1949.

sum at the beginning of 1948. Foreign trade was at a low ebb. Continuation of deficit financing to support the civil war against the Communists kept the fires of inflation burning; the currency inflation in turn caused production and other constructive business activity to stagnate and contributed greatly to a popular loss of confidence in the National Government. While the military strength of the Communists was increasing, Nationalist strength was being sapped by military defeats, sinking morale among the troops, and a crumbling economic front in the rear of the Government's armies.

Character of the 1948 Economic Aid Program for China

The China Aid Program was not originally conceived as something that could by itself turn back or even arrest these trends. It was described as an effort to "assist in retarding the current economic deterioration and thus give the Chinese Government further opportunity to initiate the measures necessary to the establishment of more stable economic conditions."

The program of economic aid was organized and carried on against a background of continuing civil war and progressive contraction of the area and resources under the control of the National Government. It has been directed toward bringing economic assistance as directly as possible to areas and people who have needed the type of assistance which could be supplied by the use of U.S. dollars.

Food has been provided through a controlled ration system to nearly 13,000,000 inhabitants of seven major Chinese cities. Cotton financed under the program has kept the mills operating in China's largest industry, providing cloth for direct consumption, for barter to encourage the bringing of indigenous food into the cities, and for export to earn foreign exchange that can be used to pay for more imports. Petroleum has kept in operation basic utilities, transport facilities and industries, and also provided goods for which the farmers in the countryside are prepared to exchange their produce. Fertilizer imports have been planned for use in the production of spring crops in 1949. A Joint Commission on Rural Reconstruction has been established, and has formulated principles and a program for attacking some of the root causes of poverty and unrest among China's vast rural population. An industrial program of replacement machinery and reconstruction projects has been initiated with the participation of private American engineering firms; although actual procurement and construction had to be suspended for the most part due to uncertainties connected with the civil war, much useful engineering survey work has been done. A "counterpart" fund in local currency, established by agreement with the Chinese Government and managed jointly by Chinese and Americans, has been used to maintain many hospitals, welfare programs, and dike-building projects.

In spite of the growing chaos around them, these activities, by and large, have been managed with care and have been carried out successfully within their own limited terms of reference. In the case of the commodity program particularly, the supplies provided have been an important and at times crucial factor in keeping unrest to a minimum in the main cities of the coastal areas controlled by the Nationalist Government. In this narrow but significant sense, therefore, the efforts of ECA in China have been constructive and useful. Supplies financed by the U.S. have been and are being effectively distributed to the people intended to receive them.

Economic Aid in a Setting of General Deterioration

But the atmosphere surrounding these efforts has been one of continuing discouragement and defeat for those who had hoped the Chinese National Government, after a decade of upheaval and in face of all difficulties, could and would do the things that needed to be done if it were to provide an adequate counterforce to the Communists in China. The incapacity of the Government to put into effect the reforms which it had in January announced its intention of initiating; the inability of the Nationalist commanders to lead and inspire an effective military effort against the growing Communist threat; a series of ill-conceived economic and financial measures which made the situation behind the lines even worse than it needed to be; the widening breach between the people and their Government—all these were factors so demoralizing in their effect that it became only a matter of time until the Government would reach the brink of disaster.

Chinese economic problems cannot be separated from problems which are ordinarily termed political and military. The inflation itself, dramatic as it has been, is only a symptom of broader and deeper problems. The prodigious increase in the issue of currency has been a devastating economic fact, but the reason for it is to be sought in the military fact that more than two-thirds of all currency issued has been used directly to support the Government's military efforts. Sudden increases in the velocity of circulation can be related directly to sudden drops in public confidence due to military defeats.

On August 19, 1948, the Chinese Government published a series of apparently sweeping financial reforms, in an attempt to arrest the runaway inflation of the Chinese National Currency (CN), and draw in for public use the large private holdings of foreign exchange. The drastic and dramatic reforms, including the introduction of a new Gold Yuan (GY) currency, seemed to hold the inflation in suspense for more than a month. But they did nothing to increase revenues or to reduce expenditures; thus they failed to attack the basic cause of the inflation, which is the gross imbalance of the Government's budget. Internal contradictions in the new regulations soon appeared. A new commodity tax was not put into effect because it would have meant breaking the price ceilings set forth in the same regulations. Although the Government reported collection of more than US$150 million worth of foreign exchange, it had to pay out in return so large an amount of the new Gold Yuan currency, without any compensating increase in supplies or production, that the new currency rapidly depreciated further both in real value and in the esteem of the Chinese people.

With these economic influences at work, the resumption of the inflationary spiral and a breakdown of the attempt to maintain August 19 ceiling prices was inevitable. Attempts to enforce arbitrary price ceilings in Shanghai, and to a less extent in other cities, brought about an almost complete stagnation of economic activity. The more strictly the regulations were enforced, the less food came into the cities, and the worse the situation became. Finally, in November, the regulations became so ineffective and disruptive of economic activity that they were officially revoked in the face of a downward slide of the Gold Yuan which has continued thereafter.

Internal financial deterioration and the maintenance of artificial exchange rates have held down official receipts by the Chinese Government from exports and inward remittances. Although China has had to draw down also some $100 million from her contracted dollar assets, official holdings of foreign exchange may have exceeded slightly, at the end of 1948, the balance existing when the China Aid Act was passed. This has been due in part to the existence of the China Aid Program itself, which has paid for most of China's basic commodity imports since June 1948. But it has been due also to two factors unfavorable to China: first, the fact that imports outside the ECA program were held to a level so low as to impair seriously production and trade; and second, the fact that private exchange holdings were called in under the August 19 regulations in such a way as to heighten the inflation and at the same time to wipe out extensively, middle class savings. Thus the balancing for a time of China's official international payments accounts was achieved at a prohibitive internal cost.

China's drawings upon restricted foreign exchange resources were largely for current requirements, not for importations of capital equipment. The Government even sold valuable productive properties in order to meet current outlays.

A further debilitating effect of the civil war was to be found in the phenomenon of "disinvestment" within China, which contrasted with the process of expanding investment in the ECA-aided countries of Europe. In a setting of spiralling inflation and universal uncertainty as to the future, private capital was almost wholly directed into non-productive channels of financial speculation and hoarding of goods for sale at higher prices; banks demonstrated an increasing reluctance to extend long-term credit for industrial investment. As a result, not only did China's productive plant fail to expand, but existing productive facilities deteriorated. The lack of repairs and rehabilitation of productive capacity has lowered output.

These facts, taken together, point to a steady decline in the overall productive capacity of the Chinese economy during 1948.

The relationship between military defeat and economic deterioration has been further demonstrated in the case of coal and food supplies.

Coal production in China during 1948 was at about the same level as 1947. Supplies reaching consuming areas, however, were sharply reduced, particularly during the latter half of the year, as mining centers were cut off or fell into Communist hands. An especially serious loss, toward the end of the year, was that of the output from the Kailan Mines north of Tientsin, which were supplying more than half of the coal produced in the whole of Nationalist China.

The output of foodstuffs in 1948 reached a postwar peak at a level roughly equal to that of prewar years. In spite of this recovery in the agricultural regions, China's urban centers were able to meet their food requirements only with the continuing assistance afforded by substantial shipments from abroad. Factors contributing to this situation were Communist occupations of producing areas in Manchuria and much of north China and the consequent disruption of distribution patterns; and, in accessible areas—particularly, during the autumn months—an increasing unwillingness on the part of farmers to market their crops in view of rigid price controls and continuing currency depreciation.

Similar trends could be noted in every other sector of the economy. Mill output of cotton textiles held up during the first half of the year at 1947 levels and then began to drop sharply. Operable rail mileage in Nationalist hands was reduced by 2,500 kilometers despite the rehabilitation of lines in the south. Shipping capacity was maintained but the pressure of military needs reduced the amount available for commercial requirements. Costly air traffic increased under the necessity of supplying cities besieged by Communist armies. During the last few months of the year, important cities in north and central China were virtually cut off from major supply sources and economic activity became thoroughly demoralized. ECA imports, in the latter part of the year, played an increasingly large role in supplying urban areas with essential food and raw materials.

Preliminary Review of the ECA China Aid Program

Within a few weeks after the Economic Cooperation Administration came into being, economic aid to China was an operating reality. Initial funds from the

Reconstruction Finance Corporation were advanced to ECA, a "Program No. 1" for using these funds was approved by the Administrator, and the first procurement authorization was issued. An exchange of notes between the Secretary of State and the Chinese Ambassador in Washington set up interim arrangements for providing assistance pending conclusion of a formal bilateral agreement. Mr. Roger D. Lapham was appointed Chief of the ECA Mission to China, arriving at his post in Shanghai the first week of June. The Chinese Government created a Council for U.S. Aid, a cabinet level committee to deal with the ECA Program. To "backstop" the Mission, a China Program Division was created in the ECA Headquarters office. And on July 3, three months after the Foreign Assistance Act was approved, the formal Economic Aid Agreement between China and the United States was signed by the Chinese Foreign Minister and the U.S. Ambassador to China.

The ECA Mission to China was faced with the problem of getting itself organized quickly for the job ahead. To speed up the process, it took over and adapted to the new purpose the China Relief Mission which had been responsible in China for the U.S. Foreign Relief Program under Public Law 84 (Eightieth Congress). ECA also inherited some continuing functions of a relief character, including the distribution of P. L. 84 supplies which had not reached end-users by the time that law expired, on June 30, 1948. ECA likewise continued support to a number of special projects started by the China Relief Mission and financed from a local currency "Special Account."

Operating under a strict limitation on dollar administrative expenses, the Mission has made a maximum use of alien staff, paid in local currency. ECA has arranged for a part of the work of supervising and controlling portions of the program to be done by private firms and voluntary relief agencies.

The program itself has consisted of three parts: the provision of a limited number of basic commodities (food, fuel, cotton, fertilizer and coal); the initiation of an industrial replacement and reconstruction program; the formation and support of a Joint Commission on Rural Reconstruction in China. In addition, ECA has participated in the management and use of a Special Account, or "counterpart" fund, in Chinese currency provided by the Chinese Government. Of the total $275 million appropriation for the ECA China Program, $203.8 million was earmarked for commodities, $67.5 million for the industrial program, $2.5 million for dollar expenditures on the rural reconstruction program, and $1.2 million for administration.

The commodity program called for average ECA imports into China of supplies costing roughly $20 million a month. As of December 31, $194 million of the commodity funds had been authorized for procurement, and about $112 million worth of these supplies had arrived in China. The commodity program was, therefore, well up to schedule. But obligations against the industrial program had been limited to allotments of money for "preproject" engineering survey work. Toward the end of the year, some of the projects were about ready to start actual procurement and construction work; but in December, it was necessary to suspend allocations for such work pending clarification of the political and military situation in China. Similarly, the Rural Reconstruction Commission was only emerging from the planning stage at the end of 1948, and had tapped only a small part of the $2.5 million set aside for its U.S. dollar expenses.

In all phases of the program, as much emphasis as practicable has been placed on the use of commercial channels of supply and distribution. The food program is the sole exception as regards supply; rice from southeast Asia and wheat and flour from the U.S. have been bought and shipped by the Commodity Credit Corporation, an agency of the U.S. Department of Agriculture. The major portion of the petroleum products, most of which originate in the Persian Gulf, have been procured and shipped by private oil companies. American cotton has been shipped by American firms and received in China by American cotton importers. Fertilizer, coming from a variety of sources under allocations by the International Emergency Food Committee, has likewise been supplied through private commercial channels.

After each commodity shipment arrives in China, the ECA Mission keeps track of its receipt, processing, distribution, and end use. Food is distributed through the first general civilian rationing system ever developed in China's urban areas, with the Chinese Government and ECA each providing a part of the total ration requirements. Cotton becomes yarn, yarn becomes cloth, and the end-products are used for export, for barter and for domestic sale—all under the watchful observation of a Joint Management Board in which ECA participates. Petroleum products are distributed by the importing companies, who themselves assist in end-use control and reporting, and provide detailed sales records for each product to the ECA Mission. As of December 31, 1948, fertilizer had not been distributed since it was for use in 1949 spring production; a part, it was planned, would be handled in direct exchange with farmers for rice, a part sold through commercial channels and a part used by the Rural Reconstruction Commission. The small amount of coal imported before the end of the year went directly to utilities and other users under the supervision of the ECA China Mission. Medical supplies imported by ECA's predecessor in China, the U.S. China Relief Mission, are distributed by a special group set up by agreement between the Ministry of Health and voluntary agencies. Pesticides, also inherited from the China Relief Mission, have been distributed largely through commercial channels, the remainder being earmarked for agricultural demonstration purposes.

The industrial program started with an intensive investigation of proposed replacement and reconstruction projects conducted by a special Reconstruction Survey Group. This group faced a double problem—an extensive need for replacement and reconstruction equipment, and a serious lack of the engineering and management skills needed in China to make certain that such equipment would be effectively absorbed into the economy. The group prepared tentative recommendations for allocation among approved projects from the $67.5 million set aside for this purpose. The projects thus recommended were largely limited to the field of basic industry and transportation—the largest provisional allotments proposed being for power plants, coal mines, the rehabilitation of railroads, and the manufacture of fertilizer. The Survey Group also developed procedures for making maximum use of private American engineering firms as "project engineers" to help individual projects in drawing up plans, procuring the right equipment, and making sure that equipment is correctly installed and effectively operated. To manage the whole scheme, ECA and the Chinese Government agreed to retain a high-grade American firm of management engineers.

The uncertainties in the China situation had in December caused the suspension of all but survey work under this program, leaving open the possibility of selected projects being carried forward as circumstances permit. The technique adopted for administering this program may prove to be of significance in relation to future programs involving industrial projects in underdeveloped countries.

The Joint Commission on Rural Reconstruction in China was established in accordance with Section 407 of the China Aid Act to "formulate and carry out a program for reconstruction in rural areas of China." Initiated on August 5 by an exchange of notes between the Chinese and U.S. Governments, the Joint

Commission consisted of three Chinese and two American members, appointed in September by the Presidents of China and of the United States.

Intensive planning and survey work were undertaken by the Commission after the members had agreed on the general statement of objectives and principles. In general, the Commission has been moving in the direction of: assisting people in rural areas to improve their living conditions, increase food production, and develop local self-government; strengthening and improving the operations of government agencies concerned with rural problems; stimulating local movements and private agencies in efforts on behalf of the rural people; and affording to progressive elements in the population real opportunities to participate in the program. The Joint Commission operates under the supervision of the Administrator, who has delegated his authority in this field to the Chief of the ECA Mission to China. The American members and staff of the Commission are ECA staff members engaged in full-time work with the Commission.

A special concern of the ECA in connection with the China Program has been the development of sources of strategic materials required by the U.S. Although China is a major producer of three such materials—tin, tungsten, and antimony—the limitations upon funds for stockpiling purposes have made it impracticable to pick up antimony and tungsten which are available for purchase in China. Extensive investigations on the development and supply of tin concentrates and tin metal, however, had resulted before the end of December 1948, in a tentative arrangement for tin purchasing as part of a general scheme for rationalizing the supply of metal and the development of processing facilities in Yunnan Province.

The special local currency account, or counterpart fund, provided for in the Economic Aid Agreement with China, differed from corresponding accounts in Europe, two of its features being unique. The first is an arrangement for deposits of local currency, which leaves the timing of deposits in the discretion of the U.S. Government; this discretion is used to relate deposits to actual needs for the local currency, without large surpluses which would rapidly shrink in value. The second unique feature is a "maintenance of value" clause which provides that for certain important uses the Chinese Government would protect appropriations made from the special account against currency depreciation, by expressing the appropriation in terms of some more stable unit, such as U.S. dollars or a basic commodity like rice or cotton yarn.

Since it was clear from the outset that the sterilization of the entire special account would not by itself be an important influence toward control of the inflation, the Chinese Government and the ECA, after consultation with the National Advisory Council in Washington, followed a policy of making expenditures from the account for important public purposes which might not otherwise be provided for, if such expenditures were of demonstrated urgency. The main categories of expenditures have been for administrative costs, the expenses of delivering relief packages and supplies in China, local currency costs of projects sponsored by the Joint Commission on Rural Reconstruction, expenditures on special projects in the field of water conservancy, health and welfare, and the internal costs to date of the replacement and reconstruction program, in cases where money could not be raised from other sources. It was estimated, according to the plans envisaged during 1948, that the total of these expenditures would amount to less than half of the total potential account.

By the end of December 1948, notifications of U.S. grant aid had been given to the Chinese Government to the amount of $94,470,926. According to preliminary and tentative estimates, pending final determination upon a formula for computing exchange rates, Gold Yuan equivalent to approximately $9,543,000 had been requested for deposits, and the equivalent of approximately $5,839,000 had been spent.

PART II—Economic Aid Program for China to December 31, 1948

Scope and Rationale

The President, in his message of February 18, 1948, to Congress on aid to China recommended authorization of an economic aid program in the amount of $570 million, to provide assistance over a fifteen-month period extending to June 30, 1949. Of this amount, $510 million was estimated as required for financing essential commodity imports into China, "which would permit the Chinese Government to devote its limited dollar resources to the most urgent of its other needs," and $60 million was recommended for "a few selected reconstruction projects to be initiated prior to June 30, 1949." "Essential imports" cited included cereals, cotton, petroleum, fertilizer, tobacco, pharmaceuticals, coal and repair parts for existing capital equipment. Reduced to a twelve-month basis, the program of economic assistance proposed by the President would have called for approximately $403 million for commodity shipments to China and an additional $60 million for aid to selected reconstruction projects.

The China Aid Act of 1948 authorized for expenditure during the ensuing twelve-month period (April 3, 1948, to April 2, 1949) $338 million for economic assistance to China, of which $275 million has been appropriated, and an additional $125 million for aid to China through grants "on such terms as the President may determine and without regard to the provisions of the Economic Cooperation Act of 1948."

The program of economic aid to China administered by the ECA during 1948 has been limited to expenditures within the $275 million appropriated by the Congress.

In Section 407 of the China Aid Act of 1948 (Public Law 472, Title IV), the Congress authorized for "a program for reconstruction in rural areas in China," an amount "equal to not more than 10 per centum" of the funds made available for economic assistance under the Act, which amount could be "in United States dollars, proceeds in Chinese currency from the sale of commodities made available . . . or both." Thus a third category of assistance was specified. The China Aid Act did not further stipulate the relative magnitude of expenditures to be incurred in behalf of the three general types of limited assistance contemplated, namely: a commodities program, an industrial reconstruction program, and a rural reconstruction program.

Related to these three types of aid within China and available for helping to carry them out was a special local currency or "counterpart" fund, established by the Chinese Government pursuant to the terms of an "Economic Cooperation Agreement between the United States of America and the Republic of China." (The text of this bilateral Agreement is quoted below, under the heading, "Documents.")

In administering economic aid to China, as approved by Congress, the ECA has faced the obligation to ensure as efficient use as possible, under prevailing conditions, of the $275 million appropriation provided by Congress, recognizing that the assistance thus furnished would, to be fully effective, have to be supplementary to, and not a substitute for, vigorous efforts on the part of the Chinese Government and people.

With limited resources and under prevailing conditions in China, it has not been possible for the ECA to undertake a comprehensive approach to China's broad problems of budgetary and financial stabilization and economic recovery. It has been necessary, instead, to concentrate upon a few restricted activities designed to furnish some assistance at critical points in the Chinese economy; to maximize in the aid program, where possible, the use of private trade channels as one means of sustaining a degree of normal economic activity; and to devise effective end-use controls designed to ensure efficient utilization of all the economic aid provided.

Initiation of the Program

On April 30, 1948, notes were exchanged between the Secretary of State and the Chinese Ambassador in Washington, setting up interim arrangements for the initiation of the China Aid Program, pending the negotiation of a bilateral economic aid agreement. These notes (a) confirmed the Chinese Government's adherence to the purposes and policies set forth in Section 2 of the China Aid Act of 1948; (b) specified that prior to the conclusion of an agreement under Section 405 of the China Aid Act and until July 3, 1948, the extension of aid to China as authorized by Section 404 (a) of the Act, would be provisionally governed, subject to agreed modifications, by the Agreement negotiated in connection with the United States Foreign Relief Program, dated October 27, 1947; and (c) recorded an understanding relating to the establishment of special mission for economic cooperation to China, together with an assurance that the Chinese Government would extend the fullest cooperation to representatives of the United States Government concerned with operations in implementation of the China Aid Act.

Bilateral Agreement

Section 405 of the China Aid Act provided that an agreement should be "entered into between China and the United States containing these undertakings by China which the Secretary of State, after consultation with the Administrator for Economic Cooperation, may deem necessary to carry out the purposes of this title and to improve commercial relations with China." Consequently, negotiations were begun in early June between the United States Embassy in Nanking and the Chinese Ministry of Foreign Affairs regarding the terms of a bilateral economic cooperation agreement between the two countries. These negotiations were concluded satisfactorily and the Agreement was signed on July 3, 1948 by Ambassador J. Leighton Stuart and the Chinese Minister of Foreign Affairs, Wang Shih-chieh. (The full text of the Agreement is quoted below in the section entitled "Documents.")[6]

In general, the Agreement with China followed the pattern of the bilateral agreements being negotiated simultaneously between the United States and those European countries which participated in the Organization for European Economic Cooperation. The language of certain articles was made almost identical for those undertakings specified by Title I of the Foreign Assistance Act which applied in principle to the Chinese as well as to the European situation. Because of certain basically different aspects of the Chinese situation, however, some standard articles were modified considerably in the China Agreement, or unique provisions were added. In view of conditions prevailing in China, the scope of joint control, particularly with respect to prices and allocations, was broader under the terms of the China Agreement than under the European bilateral agree-

---

[6] See annex 181.

ments. One unique article in the China Agreement, that calling for improvement of commercial relations, was required specifically by Section 405 of the China Aid Act.

The Agreement with China set forth a number of undertakings by the Chinese and/or the U. S. Government relating to the following:

provision of aid to the Chinese Government in accordance with the terms of the China Aid Act of 1948 (other than Section 404 (b) thereof); measures for improvement of general economic conditions including effective use of aid goods, appropriate use of private Chinese assets in the U. S., development of industrial and agricultural production, creation of more stable currency conditions, cooperation with other countries to increase international trade, and prevention of commercial arrangements which interfere with the purposes of the Agreement;

improvement of commercial relations with other countries, with particular reference to the conditions affecting foreign trade by private enterprises in China;

fair and equitable distribution of aid goods, and of similar goods produced locally or imported with other funds, and the method of determining terms, conditions and prices for distribution of aid goods;

deposits of Chinese currency in value commensurate with the value of U. S. aid provided on a grant basis, and the principles governing disposal of such deposits;

facilitating the acquisition by the U. S. from China of materials in short supply in the U. S.;

negotiation of duty-free treatment for imports into China of relief goods by private agencies or individuals;

joint consultation, and provision of information by the Chinese Government, regarding matters relevant to the Agreement;

publicity within China regarding provision of aid under the Agreement;

establishment in China of, and treatment to be accorded to, a U. S. Special Mission for Economic Cooperation;

settlement, by reference to an agreed upon international tribunal, of claims espoused by either government on behalf of its nationals against the other government for compensation for damage arising as a consequence of governmental measures taken after April 3, 1948;

entry into force, amendment and duration of the Agreement.

Advisory Bodies

Two advisory bodies have on request furnished helpful counsel and guidance on broad questions relating to the planning and conduct of the ECA China Aid Program: The National Advisory Council on International Monetary and Financial Problems, established by Congress, and the Public Advisory Committee for the China Program, appointed by the Administrator under authority granted in Public Law 472, Section 107 (b).

Members of the National Advisory Committee for the China Program have been: Isaiah Bowman, president-emeritus of Johns Hopkins University and a member since 1940 of the Permanent International Commission for China and the United States; Arthur B. Foye, senior partner of the international public accountant firm of Haskins and Sells and, since 1945, president of the Far East-America Council of Commerce and Industry; Paul V. McNutt, former ambassador and United States high commissioner to the Philippines, and president and chairman of the Board of United Service to China; Elizabeth Luce Moore, former chairman of the USO Council, one of the founders in 1940 of United China Relief, and a trustee of Wellesley College, of the China Institute in America, and of the United Board for Christian Colleges in China; and Walter S. Robertson, former minister-counselor for economic affairs at the United States Embassy in Chungking, and a principal assistant to General George C. Marshall during his special mission to China in 1945–1946.

ECA Mission to China

Authority for the establishment of a special ECA Mission to China is contained in Public Law 472, Sections 109 and 403.

The organization of the China Mission began with the appointment of Roger D. Lapham, former mayor of San Francisco, as Chief of the Mission. The appointment was made on May 5, 1948, and Mr. Lapham arrived in China on June 7, accompanied by initial members of a Reconstruction Survey Group. Staffing of the Mission has been kept at a minimum consistent with the efficient performance of ECA economic aid functions in China. As of December 31, 1948, 89 Americans and 355 non-Americans were on duty with the Mission.

Clearances between ECA Headquarters and the China Mission are conducted through a China Program Division in Washington. This is a staff office of 20 persons which facilitates the integration, without needless duplication, of China operations within the general framework of ECA financing and supply operations.

RELATIONS WITH THE CHINESE GOVERNMENT

To provide for an orderly conduct of relations between the Chinese Government and the ECA China Mission, the Government appointed a Council for United States Aid (CUSA), with the Prime Minister as Chairman, which includes in its membership the Ministers of Foreign Affairs, Finance, and Communications, the Governor of the Central Bank, the Chairman of the National Resources Commission, the Mayor of Shanghai and the Chairman of the Chinese Technical Mission to the United States.

The Economic Cooperation Agreement between the United States and the Chinese Governments, signed at Nanking on July 3, 1948, by the United States Ambassador and the Chinese Minister for Foreign Affairs, provided the framework of understanding and agreements on the basis of which ECA operations in China have been conducted. The text of the Agreement appears in the final section of this paper.

TAKEOVER FROM U. S. CHINA RELIEF MISSION

The first organizational problem faced by the Chief of the ECA Mission to China was the need to make provision for the orderly transition from the work of the U. S. China Relief Mission, which had been responsible for the $45,000,000 interim relief program in China, previously provided under Public Law 84, to the new program under ECA direction. Arrangements were made for the temporary transfer of considerable numbers of the personnel in the China Relief Mission, in order to ensure the orderly liquidation of that Mission's ressponsibilities under the supervision of ECA, and at the same time to utilize, for the benefit of the ECA program, the experience of personnel already available in China, who had been working with a program similar in certain respects to the China Aid Program.

ANNEXES 1017

Takeover responsibilities included principally the receipt and distribution of residual China Relief Mission supplies, responsibility for residual proceeds from the sale of such supplies, and the carrying on or liquidation of various local currency projects agreed to by the China Relief Mission.

Approximately 25,000 tons of CRM rice and flour valued at about $3.8 million were on hand on June 30, 1948, which were taken over and distributed under the supervision of the ECA Mission through the rationing system. Approximately $5.2 million worth of medical supplies and $670,000 worth of pesticides were on order in the United States, to be delivered during the early months of the ECA program. The general policy governing distribution of medical supplies has been to distribute them for the greater part free of charge and in large part in outlying areas where it has not been feasible to ship ECA bulk supplies. About a third of the pesticides has been reserved for the use of the Rural Reconstruction Commission, the remainder being sold through normal commercial channels or distributed free by the Ministry of Agriculture through agricultural demonstration centers.

There was virtually no cash balance in the CRM local currency account at the time of the ECA takeover. However, commitments had been entered into for over 260 projects predicated on anticipated proceeds from the sale of undistributed rice and flour. The ECA, accordingly, assumed responsibility for the orderly completion or liquidation of these projects. In July and August, the equivalent of US $197,600 was disbursed from the local currency Special Account for these purposes, about 55 percent for public works, 43 percent for medical purposes, and 2 percent for miscellaneous projects. After August, considerable weeding out was done in order to reduce the number of projects to a number which would permit adequate supervision and these have been included in the overall ECA-CUSA program for the Special Account.

ORGANIZATION

Headquarters of the ECA Mission to China were established in Shanghai, and regional offices in Nanking, Peiping, Tientsin, Tsingtao, Canton and Taipeh (on Taiwan or Formosa).

The approved pattern of the Mission as of December 31, 1948, is reflected in the accompanying organizational chart. The principal functions of each organizational unit within the Mission are set forth in the Appendix.

Assistance has been given to the Mission by ECA Headquarters in the recruitment of American personnel and the coordination of personnel procedures, fiscal activities, and administrative management in accordance with Headquarters procedures and in compliance with foreign service requirements of the State Department.

ADMINISTRATIVE EXPENSES

The ECA China Program has operated under a limitation, for administrative expenses incurred in U. S. dollars, of $1.2 million—less than one-half of one percent of the amount appropriated for the current China program. This necessitated rigid economies in the planning of staff requirements, and a maximum use of other agencies and means in order to develop an effective field organization. The $1.2 million ceiling did not apply to administrative costs provided from counterpart local currency funds in China, from which source approximately three-fifths of the administrative costs of the Mission are being met.

Administrative expenses, with the benefit of special arrangements referred to below, were held, up to the end of December 1948, within an amount provisionally estimated at approximately $560,000. However, a large percentage of these expenses were incurred during the last quarter of the calendar year 1948. This was attributable chiefly to two factors: (a) the fact that the ECA China Mission was not fully staffed, and operations in China were not in full swing, until the October–December quarter; and (b) the necessity of incurring increased expenses (nottably for extensive transfers of supplies and personnel, including the removal of some dependents) as a result of unsettled and uncertain conditions in north and central China. A third factor contributing to higher costs was beginning to appear at the end of the year, namely, the necessity, with the excessive rate of depreciation of Chinese currency, of meeting certain administrative expenses out of U.S. dollars instead of local currency.

Payment for expenses incurred on behalf of American members of the Mission, including travel for members and dependents, is governed by U. S. Foreign Service regulations which are mandatory with respect to ECA employees.

Military developments in China have made necessary budgetary provisions for the voluntary removal of certain dependents and household effects from threatened areas. As of December 31, 1948, some dependents and women employees with children were being evacuated, and some members of the Mission had been reassigned in accordance with changing program plans.

The use of consulting engineers or engineering firms on a contract basis, in connection with the development of surveys and plans for reconstruction projects in the industrial field, has made it possible to have competent engineering surveys and to prepare for supervising this part of the program without incurring direct administrative expenditures in excess of the ceiling on administrative costs.

A similar saving has been effected in the case of the rural reconstruction program. As indicated above, the Congressional appropriation for this program, to be supervised by a Joint Commission on Rural Reconstruction, was "an amount equal to not more than 10 per centum" of the appropriation for economic aid to China, which amount could be in U.S. dollars, proceeds in Chinese currency from the sale of commodities made available to China, or both. From the ceiling of $27.5 million thus established for the rural reconstruction program, $2.5 million was tentatively earmarked for availability in U.S. dollars, to be used principally for salaries, dollar administrative requirements and essential procurement of agricultural supplies and educational media. The Joint Commission's allotments for both program and administration represent a program cost and are thus not chargeable to the limitation on administrative funds for the China Mission.

To avoid needless administrative duplication and expense, administrative arrrangements were entered into between the State Department and the China Program of ECA, in which the State Department agreed to provide communication facilities and to assume disbursing functions with respect to U.S. dollars and to perform such minor services, in return for which ECA would reimburse the State Department, either through direct payment or through the provision of agreed services as needed by American or alien personnel.

Economies in time and space facilities were effected by the takeover of office and warehouse space and equipment previously utilized by the China Relief Mission operating under P.L. 84. Effective coordination with the Chinese Government Council for U.S. Aid (CUSA) was facilitated by a provision for CUSA offices in the same location as those of the ECA China Mission.

The civil war, with its attendant disruption of rail services, has made necessary an almost exclusive use of air travel on the part of the members of the

Mission in China, including chartered flights when necessary. Telegraph workloads in excess of available capacities through diplomatic or military channels have necessitated a considerable use of commercial telegraph facilities for unclassified operational messages.

Through the economies and special arrangements outlined above, direct administrative expenses charged against the ECA program in China were, as of December 31, 1948, within an administrative budget based upon the $1.2 million limitation for the one-year period of the authorizing legislation. And it was expected that administrative expenses incurred in the course of operations through April 2, 1949, would, despite the rising costs referred to above, be kept within this limitation.

COMMODITIES PROGRAM

The commodities program has had as its aim the provision of a continued flow to China of certain key commodities essential to the maintenance of minimum economic activity and subsistence in the urban centers of China. As indicated above, resources available for ECA commodity imports into China were not of a sufficient order of magnitude to reduce substantially the great imbalance in the Chinese national budget or to solve the nation's balance of payments problem by providing all essential imports which could not be financed by the Chinese themselves. It was essential, therefore, to concentrate upon the commodities which were of most strategic importance in helping to bolster China's internal economy. Commodities procured under the ECA program have included food, cotton, petroleum, fertilizer, and coal. In addition, as mentioned above, some residual medical supplies and pesticides were taken over by the ECA, from the earlier U.S. Foreign Relief Program, for distribution. The scope and character of each of these commodity programs are discussed below.

Procurement and Shipment

Following consultation with the National Advisory Council, ECA decided to finance commodities for China entirely on a basis of grants, not loans. The reason for this action lay in the state of the Chinese Government's external finances, as described in an earlier section of this paper.

Commodity procurement has been conducted by two methods—through private trade channels for cotton, fertilizer, petroleum and coal, and through the U.S. Department of Agriculture for rice, wheat and flour.

Cotton has been purchased through ECA financing by the Chinese Textile Industries, Inc., a quasi-government corporation, from U.S. cotton brokers submitting bids through agents in Shanghai. Fertilizer has been purchased by the Central Trust of China from suppliers presenting bids, over-all quantities purchased being governed by the size of International Emergency Food Committee allocations to China. Petroleum products have been purchased from suppliers on the basis of recommendations submitted by a joint Chinese-American subcommittee of CUSA, these recommendations being based on the prewar supply pattern; although this method of selecting suppliers has to some extent reduced the scope of price competition, prices paid for petroleum have been carefully scrutinized in the light of Section 202 of Public Law 793.

Procurement of wheat and flour has been from United States surpluses, purchases being made by the Commodity Credit Corporation of the U.S. Department of Agriculture from private suppliers on the basis of competitive bidding. These purchases have been against U.S. Department of Commerce allocations, determining the total quantity of U.S. wheat exportable to China. Rice has also been procured by the Commodity Credit Corporation, pursuant to Section 121, Public Law 472, chiefly in Siam and Burma, purchases being made against IEFC allocations.

Up to December 31, 1948, more than 99 percent of the ECA-financed cargo tonnage originating in the United States and delivered to China had been shipped in U.S.-flag vessels; this was far in excess of the over-all requirement for ECA (in section 111 (a) (2) of Public Law 472) "that at least 50 per centum of the gross tonnage of commodities, procured within the United States out of funds made available under this title and transported abroad on ocean vessels, is so transported on United States-flag vessels to the extent such vessels are available at market rates."

Procurement and Pricing of Commodities in China

Aid in providing essential commodities has been regarded by the ECA as a supplement to, and not a substitute for, production and supply efforts by the Chinese Government. This has been especially true with regard to the food program, in connection with which the ECA China Mission has undertaken to secure as effective performance as possible by the Government in providing from indigenous sources a substantial share of the food supplies required for the cities receiving ECA food shipments. In order to minimize the degree of subsidy to private consumers at the expense of government income, the China Mission has undertaken, with varying results, to exert its influence in favor of the selling of rationed food at, or near to, actual market prices; the same is true with respect to cotton goods and petroleum products. Similar influence has been exerted, as far as practicable, with regard to prices for coal, rates for electric power, or levels at which any enterprise, directly or indirectly assisted by ECA, sells its products.

End-Use Control

Measures essential to effective end-use control have been carefully developed for each of the commodity programs, in order to assure that supplies provided through ECA would go to the recipients for which they were intended, to furnish maximum assistance to people and institutions within China, to support efforts of the Government to increase production and stabilize economic conditions, and generally to secure the best results attainable through the expenditure of ECA dollars.

Food has been distributed through controlled rationing systems in major cities of China, and a detailed record has been kept of individual recipients of this aid; ECA representatives attend as observers the meetings of City Food Committees, and ECA investigators inspect and report on all phases of operations under the rationing program. The cotton aid program is directed in China by a Joint Management Board whose decisions require CUSA and ECA concurrence; a system has been established for following cotton through conversion into yarn, the conversion of yarn into cloth, and the subsequent domestic use or export of the resulting textiles. Petroleum has been distributed primarily by major oil companies which themselves help to make sure that ECA-financed oil goes only to the uses for which it is allocated; a joint CUSA-ECA Petroleum Committee estimates requirements and supervises distribution. Control arrangements are being developed to insure that fertilizer will be distributed in a way that will achieve maximum effect in increasing food production.

Further details with respect to end-use controls are contained in the description below of the several commodity programs, and in the Appendix.

Food

The interior of China—including countryside, towns and cities—has normally been relatively self-sufficient in foodstuffs, but the larger coastal cities have in recent decades become increasingly dependent, for part of their food supply, on imports from abroad. As previously indicated, the problem of food supplies for these cities became acute in the spring of 1948 due to the disruption of communications and trade by the civil war, spiralling inflation, and increasing strains upon the Government's foreign exchange resources.

INCEPTION OF FOOD RATIONING IN POSTWAR CHINA

Food rationing in postwar China was first developed in the program of the United States China Relief Mission. Under this program the U. S. Government provided—for the five major coastal cities of Shanghai, Nanking, Canton, Peiping and Tientsin—approximately 200,000 tons of rice, wheat and flour, of which more than 150,000 tons was distributed before the end of June 1948. Contributions from the Chinese Government approximately matched this tonnage, with the result that between March and the close of June about 300,000 tons of food was sold at prices considerably lower than those prevailing on the open market to between 11 and 12 million inhabitants of these cities.

Each individual, under the rationing program, was limited to a monthly purchase of 16.5 pounds of rice or flour, although no one was limited in the amount that might, if available, be purchased at inflated prices on the open market.

This program was an innovation in China. Food rationing on a major scale had not previously been practiced there as it has in most other countries of the world where shortages posed a problem of equitable distribution of available supply. Chinese officials considered the matter long and carefully before undertaking the responsibility for a program which depended for its success upon the development and maintenance of relatively complicated administrative machinery. However, once started, the administration of the program was carried out with a record of competence, precision and honesty that became a source of gratification to all parties concerned, including the Chinese officials responsible for the operation.

SEVEN-CITY RATIONING PROGRAM

Following the first arrival of ECA food supplies in China, it was decided that the rationing program should be continued as the best means of applying U.S. aid in an equitable manner, of retarding somewhat the rapid rate of price increase, and of providing an added source of revenue to the Government. Under the ECA program, the number of cities participating in rationing was extended to include Swatow and Tsingtao. In the latter city, the U. S. Navy maintained a base in an area which was surrounded by Communists and cut off from local sources of food supply.

The somewhat fluctuating population of the seven cities participating in the rationing program ranged, in total, between 12.7 and 13 million during 1948.

Under arrangements agreed upon between the ECA China Mission and the Chinese Government Council for U. S. Aid (CUSA), agreement was reached on the setting up, within the Chinese Government's Ministry of Food, of an Office of Emergency Food Procurement (OEFP), which was to handle indigenous purchasing for the rationing program. The OEFP undertook initially to procure from indigenous sources approximately 60 percent of the total food required for the operation of the rationing system, and ECA approximately 40 percent.

EMERGENCY FEEDING PROGRAMS

In addition to this rationing program for seven cities, a limited emergency feeding program for Mukden was developed while that city remained in Nationalist hands. Nearly one thousand tons of flour delivered under this emergency program were cooked and fed directly to key groups of workers with appropriate publicity. The resultant increase in morale was notable until, with the Communist assault on Mukden, the program had to be suspended. Some 400 tons of ECA flour in Chinchow awaiting airlift to Mukden were captured by the Communists during their rapid advance in that sector.

In order to cope with the heavy influx of refugees into Tsingtao from the war zones and to compensate for the reduced supplies of indigenous food coming into the city because of communist occupation of surrounding territory, the ECA China Mission has also provided, in that city, continuing support for a special Refugee Feeding Project originally instituted under the CRM program. This project, conducted outside the rationing program in cooperation with municipal authorities, consists of open-air kitchens which prepare and serve daily portions of rice congee to an estimated 100,000 refugees. Damaged rice, sweepings and poorer grades of rice unsuitable for rationing, which are received in ECA shipments from southeast Asia, are set aside for this project in Shanghai, for transshipment to Tsingtao. The bulk of shipments have been made via vessels of the U.S. Navy, which considers the project a necessary emergency measure effective in the maintenance of orderly conditions in Tsingtao. Requirements for the project are 1,300 tons per month.

AUGUST 19 REGULATIONS AND INDIGENOUS PROCUREMENT

An element of subsidy was inherent in the seven-city rationing plan. But it was never intended that the prices of rationed cereals would be allowed to fall far below open market prices. At first, prices for rationed foods were adjusted monthly to a level approximately 5 percent below prevailing open-market rates and held there throughout the ensuing month, regardless of price rises in the open market. Thus the Government was in a position to obtain much needed revenue from sales of rationed rice and flour, even though some slight subsidy accrued to the people, for the U.S. supplies thus sold cost the Government nothing and all local currency returns from this sale constituted a net gain.

Under the Government's August 19 reform measures, however, ration prices, particularly in the central and north China cities, were set well below market prices, with the result that the dependence of the program on governmental subsidies became heavy during the period until November when these measures were drastically revised. As the military, political and economic situation deteriorated, the Government deemed it expedient to use the rationing programs to provide an outright subsidy to all the people in the urban coastal cities in an effort to mitigate public discontent. At this time, wages were lagging so far behind essential commodity prices that the city populations began to be unable to purchase minimum requirements of daily necessities. ECA officials reluctantly acquiesced in the selling of U.S.-contributed food supplies along with indigenous supplies, at what to the Government were ruinously subsidized prices, but warned that the policy would prove exceedingly costly.

Since ECA funds for food procurement were limited, it appeared advisable at the outset to conserve them in large part to provide foodstuffs for the 1948–49 winter and spring months and thus assure rationing supplies at the time of the year when food is normally less plentiful. The Chinese Government agreed to find and deliver the foodstuffs needed for rationing during the last quarter of

1948, with the understanding that the ECA would undertake to supply a major portion of the ration during the first quarter of 1949 and to deliver additional food thereafter to the extent of availability of funds from the 1948 appropriation.

Difficulties developed in the implementation of this plan. The obtaining of indigenous supplies by the Chinese OEFP was slow and erratic; its attempts to purchase domestic food supplies were inspired by lack of sufficient appropriations and by the disparity between official and black-market prices. There was a failure to act quickly to procure domestic supplies in quantity when the harvests were in. Anticipated purchases of rice in Burma did not materialize. Some flour was collected at Shanghai for the ration in the cities of north China, but commandeering by the military of the ships selected for the transport of these supplies caused considerable delay in their movement. As indicated above, the unsuccessful economic regulations promulgated by the Government on August 19, 1948, resulted in the exclusion from China's major cities of normal free-market supplies of indigenous foods. The acute shortages, dramatized by all-night queues in front of food shops, were intensified by a partial breakdown of the rationing system during October. At the middle of October none of the cities except Canton and Tsingtao had even been able to start the October ration, and one city was still trying to fulfill the September ration commitment.

Throughout this period, the ECA China Mission pressed for the lifting of arbitrary food price ceilings in the cities, for a realistic pricing of rationed foods, and for more vigorous efforts by the OEFP to procure indigenous supplies.

SPEED-UP OF ECA DELIVERIES

Steps were also taken to speed up ECA deliveries of wheat, previously scheduled for the first quarter of 1949, in order to move up to November and December the resumption of ECA's contribution to the ration system. Some success was achieved in the acceleration of ECA shipments to China—which proved to be of crucial importance in allaying unrest in major cities—and in the development of more realistic pricing for rationed food, but indigenous procurement efforts by the Chinese Government continued to lag.

Reported shipments as of Decemer 31, 1948, under procurement programs 1, 2 and 3 (for the second, third and fourth quarters of 1943, were valued at approximately $37,000,000 for the purchase of 129,000 tons of rice and 107,000 tons of wheat and flour. In addition, about 25,000 tons of rice and flour had been received as residue from the China Relief Mission and 9,000 tons of rice had been borrowed from Hongkong to relieve a threatened November food shortage in Shanghai. Of these amounts, approximately 120,000 tons of rice and 30,000 tons of wheat and flour had before the end of December been released for the rationing programs. Additional Program 3 stocks either en route, loading or waiting for shipment, at the end of 1948, totaled 27,000 ton of rice from Siam and Burma and 56,000 tons of wheat and flour from the United States.

SUPERVISION OF RATIONING PROGRAM

Although administered by Chinese Government officials, the ECA food program in China has been carefully supervised by ECA representatives who have insisted upon the maintenance of high standards of performance and honesty. Mindful of the considerable pilfering and misuse of food supplies previously delivered under the UNRRA program, ECA has paid utmost attention to the problem of end-use control. Strict supervision and careful checking have been applied to every phase of distribution in order to assure that all ECA-financed food supplies allocated to the rationing program actually reach the end recipient. A detailed description of rationing and end-use control under the ECA food program is contained in the Appendix.

The United States has delivered its contributions to the rationing programs regularly and on time. ECA officials in China have manifested constant concern that the rationing program should be conducted for the benefit of the people as a whole. These facts are well known to the millions of persons affected, and has done much to sustain their faith in the friendship of the American people.

Cotton

The first step in the cotton program involved an easing of pressure upon China's strained foreign exchange resources by ECA financing of existing consignment contracts with early delivery dates; these contracts were between the China Textile Industries, Inc., and the agents in Shanghai of American cotton shippers. All of the cotton involved was programmed for supply from the United States. In the course of authorizing procurement of this cotton, provision was made for joint supervision, by the Government and the ECA China Mission, of processing and distribution of raw cotton after arrival in China.

The total cotton program developed under the current China Aid Program involved an expenditure of nearly $70 million. During October 1948, the first of this cotton reached the mills and the system of control and reporting of end use was perfected. As of December 31, cotton in the amount of 299,038 bales, costing approximately $52.7 million, had arrived in China and was being allocated and distributed to the mills; 51,000 bales of yarn and 557,000 bolts of cloth (40 yards each) had been received back from the mills.

Under the ECA China aid program, all cotton is procured through private trade channels. Cotton shipments to China are continuing under schedules designed to maintain production and employment while avoiding any undue advance stockpiling.

The Chinese textile industry with about 3,900,000 operable spindles is China's largest manufacturing industry and raw cotton is one of China's vital imports. Not only are the cloth and yarn produced of great significance to the Chinese economy, but a high level of employment among the textile workers is important to the maintenance of relative stability in industrial centers, particularly in Shanghai.

RAW COTTON SUPPLY PROBLEM

Before the war, cotton grown in China supplied the bulk of the fibre required to keep the textile mills in operation. Due to some reduction in cotton acreage and, more important, to the extensive disruption of internal transportation trade caused by the civil war (see accompanying map), indigenous cotton has gone largely into household use and China has had to depend on imports for more than a third of the cotton used in her mills. In the year 1947–1948, mill consumption was about 1,950,000 bales; imports of cotton were about 700,000 bales (as compared with a prewar level of imports of 340,000 bales). Procurement was in considerable part from India, and limited quantities were purchased also from British East Africa, Burma and Egypt.

Provision of the necessary foreign exchange for cotton importation has been for China a problem of increasing proportions. The ECA program, which financed 300,000 bales in 1948 and in January of 1949 was in process of financing an additional 100,000 bales, has been a major factor in the sustaining of production and employment in China's textile industry during the latter part of 1948.

USE AND CONTROL OF ECA COTTON IMPORTS

The plan developed for the use of ECA cotton imports called for the conversion of the cotton into yarn under arrangements involving processing or trading at a fixed ratio under which raw cotton is paid for by the processing and in most cases by conversion of the resulting yarn into cotton cloth. The Council for United States Aid (CUSA) and the ECA Mission to China agreed upon a division of the yarn and cloth produced from ECA cotton, with 50 percent to be used for domestic consumption and the rest to be exported—the proceeds to be used for purchase of additional raw cotton. Exports under this program had up to December 31, 1948, earned an equivalent of more than $4.5 million in foreign exchange, all sales being to countries of southeast Asia. Domestic distribution is largely by direct sale through commercial channels; some of the textiles, however, have been used in barter schemes, as described below, designed to bring more food into the cities. More than 2,000 bales of yarn and cloth made from ECA cotton were bartered in Nanking, Shanghai and Nanchang for 33,000 piculs of rice at a time when no other grain was moving into these cities from producing areas.

The arrangements adopted followed careful planning and careful negotiation by the Mission with the Chinese Government. The conversion, storage and disposition of ECA-financed cotton shipments to China are under the control of a Joint Management Board, and full records of each stage of the process are kept for end-use control purposes. Details of the end-use control mechanism developed are presented in the Appendix.

Petroleum

Since production of crude oil in China is negligible, the country is almost wholly dependent upon imports of petroleum products required in the operation of utilities, transport facilities, and manufacture and for household use. The cutting off of coal from north China, as a result of the civil war, increased greatly during the year the relative importance of petroleum products for power and industrial units in which they could be substituted for coal.

Taken as a whole, petroleum imports were vital to the operation of China's limited transport facilities and industrial plant. Diesel and fuel oil were essential to the operation of power plants and other utilities. These types, as well as motor and aviation gasoline and lubricants, were essential to the operation of water, rail and air transport. The use of kerosene, normally in wide demand for household lighting and fuel in rural districts and towns lacking electric power, has been restricted by disruptions in transport, but there has been continuing demand in the more accessible areas.

USE OF NORMAL TRADE CHANNELS

The petroleum program involved, at first, negotiations on the part which each of the petroleum distributing concerns and the large end users in China would play in the importation and distribution of the products. The problems involved were largely settled about the middle of 1948, and firm authorizations were thereupon prepared for issuance.

As a result, the importation and distribution of petroleum products under the ECA China Aid Program have been entirely through normal trade channels and the bulk of the business is handled by the Standard Vacuum Oil Co., the Shell Company of China, Ltd., the California Texas Oil Co., and the Chinese Petroleum

Corporation (an agency of the Chinese Government). A number of small importers and distributers have also participated in the program. The oil companies at first charged somewhat higher prices for petroleum products to China than to other destinations in order to recover thereby the foreign exchange component of internal distribution costs. Such price differentials were not satisfactory either to the Chinese Government or ECA: consequently ECA has indicated its willingness to finance only such petroleum shipments as are priced on a cost-and-freight basis and are within the U.S. market price as provided in Section 202 of the appropriation act (Public Law 793).

As of December 31, 1948, the Central Bank of China had financed petroleum brought into China under the ECA China Aid Program to a value of about $28 million, for which amount the Central Bank of China was to be reimbursed by ECA as rapidly as the requisite documentation is furnished ECA by the Central Bank of China.

In view of the Central Bank's straitened foreign exchange position, ECA Headquarters on November 26, 1948 authorized an advance of $15 million to the Central Bank to enable it, pending reimbursement by ECA, to continue financing the release and distribution of petroleum products in China. Shortly before the end of the year, the reimbursement procedure was abandoned, and arrangements were made to finance all future petroleum shipments (and releases from bonded tanks of products already in China) by letter of commitment to U.S. banks. In connection with the new procedure, the ECA Mission to China was given the responsibility of approving each shipment or release in advance, in order to avoid undue stockpiling of petroleum products in Chinese ports.

ADMINISTRATION OF PETROLEUM PROGRAM

Requirements programs have been prepared on a quarterly basis by the CUSA-ECA Petroleum Committee, which includes both active members and observers from CUSA and ECA. Up to the end of 1948, prices within China were determined by the Oil Allocation Committee, with approval of the Executive Yuan; the CUSA-ECA Petroleum Committee has sought Executive Yuan approval of a plan to authorize a CUSA-ECA-EIB (Export-Import Board) Price Adjustment Committee in Shanghai to make periodic reviews and price adjustments on its own initiative, in order to keep prices on a realistic basis and prevent the oil companies from sustaining losses because of currency fluctuations.

With ECA assistance, production has been continued at the Kao-hsiang refinery in Taiwan to which, at the end of 1948, 225,000 barrels of crude oil were being provided monthly, for conversion into motor gasoline, diesel and fuel oil and kerosene. The plan under which this assistance has been given was developed on the basis of recommendations by an independent firm of engineers engaged for the purpose by the Chinese Government upon the suggestion of ECA.

End-use control of the petroleum products imported into China has presented fewer administrative problems for the ECA than end-use control of other commodities. Distribution of ECA-financed petroleum products in China is generally of two types: distribution to large users (for example, fuel oil for the Shanghai Power Company) and distribution by individual companies to end users (for example, retail distribution of gasoline through filling stations to car owners). Since the companies are the distribution agents, and the major distributors are two American companies and one British company, these firms themselves provide a considerable measure of end-use control and are able to do most of the end-use reporting required, subject to necessary spot-checking by the ECA Mission.

Fertilizer

Procurement of fertilizer has proceeded within the limitation of availabilities for China from existing world supplies, as reflected in allocations by the International Emergency Food Council. Although increased use of fertilizers offers promise of substantial increases in indigenous food production, its widespread application during the postwar period has been impeded by a lack of extensive previous experience in the use of chemical fertilizers in China, except in Formosa; by a shortage of extension personnel and organization to train Chinese farmers in the effective application of modern fertilizers; and by the difficulty of devising effective distribution and end-use control systems within China. Under plans being perfected at the end of 1948, it was expected that substantial distribution to end users, particularly in Formosa and south China, would occur during the first quarter of 1949, and that a reasonable minimum of fertilizer could be made available in China for the spring planting.

ECA PROCUREMENT OF FERTILIZERS

Under the current China Program, ECA is financing the procurement of approximately 75,000 metric tons of chemical fertilizers, at a cost of approximately US$8.9 million; this should be of material benefit in increasing rice production in some districts, particularly in sections of Formosa and south China. It was at first planned to spend U.S. $13.8 million on fertilizers. Subsequently, arrangements were made whereby the Bank of China, the Central Bank and the Taiwan Provincial Government undertook to finance from their own resources the procurement of a portion of the nitrogenous fertilizers allocated to China by the International Emergency Food Committee; ECA thereupon reduced its fertilizer commitment by 4.9 million dollars. Under these arrangements China is in a position to acquire during 1948–49, through ECA and Government procurement, 116,000 metric tons of ammonium sulphate and ammonium phosphate. Having been used by Chinese farmers who have previously employed chemical fertilizers, these types are considered the most practical under prevailing agricultural practice.

AID TO FOOD PRODUCTION IN CHINA

Fertilizers provided by ECA are primarily for use in increasing yields of lowland rice, which should mean a corresponding decrease in dependence upon importations of rice from abroad.

It has been found, through scientific experimentation and practice, that one unit of nitrogenous fertilizer can produce an average increase in yield of at least 2 units of clean rice or about 3 units of paddy rice, all by weight. Theoretically, therefore, one dollar's worth of fertilizer should produce three dollars worth of grain (in terms of each equivalent to the import cost of an equal amount of food). However, owing to high transportation and internal handling costs and low price of rice at producing centers in China, a somewhat smaller gain is realized. Nevertheless, the use of chemical fertilizer is the most effective means known to augment food production in China.

The total annual domestic production of chemical fertilizers in China, at the 1948 rate, was only about 81,000 metric tons (36,000 ammonium sulphate, 35,000 superphosphate and 10,000 calcium cyanamide). A provisional allotment from ECA of $5.5 million to China's domestic fertilizer industry, aimed to increase substantially production capacity, had to be suspended at least temporarily, toward the end of the year, due to disturbed civil war conditions.

At the end of 1948, the first 10,000 tons of ECA fertilizer was scheduled to reach Shanghai in January 1949. This installment, on the basis of an agreement with the Farmer's Bank, was to be distributed to farmers who, during November and December, had advanced rice for the food rationing program. Plans were developed for the distribution, through commercial channels in south China and Taiwan and through the Joint Rural Reconstruction Commission, of additional shipments totalling about 61,000 tons.

Coal

China's principal coal-producing centers have been in north China and Manchuria. As indicated on the accompanying map, military developments together with the cutting of vital transportation routes during 1948 interrupted the flow of coal from north China producing areas to consuming areas in central China.

Arrangements were made, therefore, for ECA procurement on an emergency basis of limited stocks from Japan through the Supreme Command, Allied Powers, Pacific (SCAP) organization. Before the end of 1948, coal in the amount of 15,000 tons had been obtained from Japan at a cost of about $280,000, and there was a prospect that further emergency procurement would be required.

Medical Supplies

About $5 million worth of medical supplies were procured for China under Public Law 84, the U. S. Foreign Relief Program. Most of these supplies arrived in China after the expiration of the China Relief Mission on June 30, 1948; they became, therefore, an ECA responsibility. As of December, nearly 90 percent of the supplies programmed by the China Relief Mission had arrived in China.

The reception, storage and transportation phases of the medical supply program have worked smoothly and losses from pilferage and improper handling have been negligible. Special medical warehousing units established have operated with a high degree of efficiency. On the basis of careful allocation and distribution planning by the Council for U. S. Aid, the ECA Mission to China, the Ministry of Health and the International Relief Committee, the distribution of these supplies was proceeding regularly at the end of 1948.

Distribution from Shanghai was being accelerated in view of the rapidly changing political and military situations; additional warehouses were being stocked in Canton and Taipeh (on the island of Taiwan), leaving in Shanghai only supplies required in that area. It was expected that final distribution of medical supplies to end users would be completed by May 31, 1949.

Pesticides

ECA also took over from the China Relief Mission responsibility for $537,000 worth of pesticides which reached China during 1948; most of these supplies arrived too late for distribution during the lifetime of the China Relief Mission.

Plans were developed and agreed upon between ECA and the Chinese Government in September, for allocations of 35 percent of these pesticides to the Joint Rural Reconstruction Commission, 15 percent to the Ministry of Agriculture and Forestry for free distribution at agricultural demonstration centers, and the remaining 50 percent for sale through commercial channels. Sales during October and November were principally in south Kiangsu and north Chekian areas bordering the Shanghai district and were concluded in time to give needed protection to crops. When seasonal demand from farmers in these districts ceased, sales efforts were directed to south China where, with a long growing season, the need for insecticides continued during ensuing months. In Taiwan, where the use of agricultural insecticides is best known, the only channels through which farmers had been accustomed to obtain their supplies in the past had not, at the end of the year, been utilized in accordance with original plans due to lack of requisite cooperation in making supplies quickly available to consumers.

Special Barter Arrangements

A barter program, of an emergency nature, was developed initially on a small scale. Difficulties experienced by the Chinese in obtaining their quota of domestic food supplies for the rationing program were such that CUSA and ECA undertook to exchange limited quantities of cloth and yarn (maunfactured from aid cotton) for rice and other indigenous food grains.

About two hundred tons of cloth were sent to Nanking, for example, to be used in exchange for rice, about 150 pounds of rice being obtained for each piece of grey cloth 40 yards long.

In villages near Shanghai a similar type of exchange was developed, and in Changsha, commercial center of a large rice-producing area in northern Hunan, a beginning was made. Such exchanges up to the end of 1948, were experimental in character. The results attained indicated that considerable quantities of rice could be obtained in this manner, and it was planned that regular supplies of yarn and cloth to be used for this purpose would shortly be advanced to Office of Emergency Food Procurement, with ECA observing OEFP operations and ensuring strict end-use accounting.

In North China ECA representatives were, at the end of November, negotiating with representatives from General Fu Tso-yi's headquarters and local grain dealers. A contract was under consideration calling for 120,000 pieces of cloth to be used in exchange for domestic wheat, flour, and coarse grains, the foodstuffs to be used in a selective rationing plan for workers in essential services. This plan was disrupted by military developments in the Peiping-Tientsin area.

Two principal purposes were served by such barters of cloth and yarn for food: (a) the obtaining of additional supplies of food for use in the rationing programs and (2) the distribution of yarn and cloth in interior areas, in many cases direct to the farmers without passing through middlemen, thus reducing opportunities for cloth and yarn to fall into the hands of speculators.

Shipping

Mention has been made of the fact that more than 99 percent of ECA-financed commodities shipped from the United States to China during 1948 were carried in U.S. vessels.

Internal administrative rulings defining what types of transportation expenditures are eligible for reimbursing from ECA funds, written principally for application to Europe, are generally applied to China. However, due to emergency conditions in China the Administration has seen fit to depart from its general rules on special occasions. These departures involve the payment of partial freight in dollars to certain Chinese ships chartered to move rice from Siam and Burma. The rice, procured by U.S. representatives using ECA funds, has been moved to China on an exacting schedule to meet ECA's feeding program in principal Chinese cities. About $727,000 for freight thus provided before the end of December 1948 made possible the movement of 39 Chinese ships carrying about 155,000 metric tons of rice.

These movements of rice from southeast Asia to China have not taken place exclusively in Chinese ships; funds are made available to U.S. representatives to enable them to use American ships interested in the traffic. However, only one American ship was used for this purpose in 1948; the cost via this vessel was $7.50 per ton as compared with the current Chinese rate of $2.00 per ton from Siam. The Chinese rate toward the end of 1948 was $3.50 per ton from Burma as compared with an estimated $10.00 per ton in American vessels. It is considered doubtful whether the dollars provided the Chinese cover the out-of-pocket expenses of the ships involved, which do receive some additional compensation in Chinese currency from counterpart funds.

The reason for close scheduling of shipping carrying food into China has been to import sufficient amounts to prevent starvation and riots, at the same time avoiding stockpiling of quantities that might be lost as a result of the war. In addition to scheduling rice shipments, considerable authority was delegated to the ECA Mission in China to divert U.S. wheat and flour shipments, as well as shipments of other commodities, to meet changing situations. When the military situation in the vicinity of Tientsin deteriorated, several American ships about to discharge in ports serving that area were diverted to Tsingtao.

INDUSTRIAL RECONSTRUCTION AND REPLACEMENT PROGRAM

A total of $70 million was originally programmed for industrial reconstruction and replacement projects in China. The legislative history of the China Aid Act indicated considerable Congressional interest in this significant aspect of proposed assistance to China. Extensive, painstaking preparations were made, including the sending to China of a special Reconstruction Survey Group, in order to ensure the most productive use of the funds made available for industrial reconstruction and replacement purposes.

Necessity for Suspension

However, due to developments in the civil war situation in China, it became necessary for the Administrator, on December 21, 1948, to announce that work on the reconstruction and replacement program was, to a large extent, being suspended—exceptions being made in connection with the completion of certain pre-project engineering studies which had already reached an advanced stage of development. Preparatory work on some of the projects, located in areas of Manchuria or north China involved in or threatened by military developments, had already in fact been suspended. The series of defeats sustained by the Nationalist forces in the fall and early winter of 1948, jeopardizing the Government's position not only at its remaining bases in north China but also in the Yangtze Valley, had resulted in chaotic conditions and major uncertainties throughout many of the regions in which reconstruction and replacement projects had been planned.

The suspension did not eliminate the possibility of renewed activity on selected projects in areas remaining accessible, in the event that such a partial resumption of the reconstruction and replacement program should at any future time be deemed feasible and expedient. At the time of suspension, all of the projects were still in the pre-project engineering stage, no funds having as yet been actually committed for procurement.

The following paragraphs present a brief summary of the problems encountered in the field of industrial replacement and reconstruction, the planning and preparatory work undertaken, and the practical arrangements developed for the initiation and execution of replacement and reconstruction projects in China. A listing, with brief descriptions, of the projects for which "provisional allotments" were made prior to the suspension of this part of the program, appears in the Appendix.

Planning and Preparatory Work

Initial planning had called for an expenditure of $60 million for reconstruction and $10 million for replacement work; as a result of the work of the Reconstruction Survey Group, however, much greater proportionate emphasis was placed upon replacements needed to increase the productivity of existing enterprises.

Initial members of the Survey Group reached China on June 7, 1948. The Group, consisting of 4 engineers, 2 economists, a lawyer and a businessman (Charles L. Stillman) who served as its head, operated as a part of the ECA Mission to China. After several months' reviews of conditions in China by the members of this Group, the ECA Mission developed, in agreement with the Chinese Government, a tentative program designed to make a significant start toward the reconstruction or rehabilitation of certain railroads, electric power plants, fertilizer manufacturing units, and coal, tin and antimony mines—all in non-Communist China.

The program finally recommended by the Survey Group and tentatively approved by the Administrator prior to the enforced suspension of this aspect of ECA assistance to China, called for approximately $25 million worth of new reconstruction or development, $35 million to be spent for replacement assistance, and $7.5 million for engineering services and reserves, making a total of $67.5 million; the remaining $2.5 million was earmarked for foreign exchange expenditures required in connection with the rural reconstruction program. Most of the projects planned were in the fields of basic industry and transportation—approximately $13.5 million being provisionally allotted for railway rehabilitation, $17.25 million for power plants, $11 million for coal mines and $5.5 million for fertilizer manufacture.

Following extensive consideration within ECA of the possibility of extending assistance to certain types of replacement and reconstruction projects on a loan basis, and after subsequent consultation with the National Advisory Council, it was tentatively determined that projects currently under consideration would be provided on an outright grant basis, leaving open the possibility of future reconsideration of loan proposals.

Problems of Industrial Reconstruction in China

The Chinese, in taking back control of their country after eight long years faced many problems. The areas reoccupied had been swept over by Japanese armies, by Chinese armies, and by Chinese and American airforces. Communist raids and damage by armies of both sides in the civil war had continued in many regions. Nearly all existing industrial facilities were in deplorable condition due to a variety of causes dating back to the opening of the Sino-Japanese War in 1937. Railroads, partially restored during the UNRRA period, needed further assistance. Further problems were presented for foreign exchange shortages, internal economic and financial difficulties evidenced in extreme inflation, seriously inadequate transportation and a general disruption of Government and of industrial management, both public and private.

Elimination of much foreign participation in Chinese affairs, as a result of the war and the ending of extraterritoriality, inevitably left a gap in the nation's economic and industrial life. Particularly in the industrial areas, foreign participation in management and control of properties had been of significance in their development and effective operation. Following the war, foreign-flag shipping was excluded from Chinese river and coastal waters, resulting in higher transportation costs and less adequate services. The Chinese were unable to develop comparable services in a short time.

When Taiwan (the island of Formosa) was returned to *de facto* Chinese control after fifty years of Japanese occupation, U.S. military forces removed nearly all Japanese from the island. The removal of those who had exercised management control and possessed requisite technical knowledge meant that this relatively highly developed island had to be staffed at management and technical levels with Chinese personnel who lacked previous knowledge of the properties involved and who faced, in addition to normal maintenance problems, a large replacement problem resulting from bombing damage inflicted during the war by U.S. airforces.

Considerable quantities of industrial materials and equipment had been made available to China through previous aid programs, notably the UNRRA program, and through Chinese Government procurement from the Pacific islands of United States surplus supplies after the war. China had not been able to absorb all of these supplies during the first three post-war years. The ECA faced, therefore, the problem not only of making sure that equipment under the ECA China aid program was put to effective use, but of helping also to get into operation residual stockpiles of equipment already in China.

Most of China's industrial plant had been badly undermaintained throughout the long war years, and requisite training of personnel had been largely discontinued. Although China's industrial development was still in its early stages, the effective functioning of the nation's limited industrial plant was regarded as vital for the production of goods essential to the reducing of China's dependence upon external aid, and for an effective approach to the problem of inflation.

The essence of the problem facing ECA, then, was an extensive need for replacement and reconstruction equipment and a lack of the foreign assistance in engineering and management requisite to the effective absorption of such equipment into the Chinese economy. A solution to this problem required a unique approach. Engineering and management assistance would have to be furnished along with the equipment. The ECA, in approaching this problem, needed also to bear in mind objectives implicit in the legislative history of the ECA: to maximize the use of private trade channels, to encourage both internal production and international trade and to avoid impairment of the U.S. economy.

Insufficiency of technical knowledge and experience in management had been a recurrent problem encountered in efforts to help Chinese industry. This made necessary a provision of technical and managerial help along with material assistance. The Survey Group developed a unique plan of action for the meeting of this need. It recommended that each industrial project applying for, and receiving a tentative allotment for, ECA assistance be required to engage the services of a private engineering firm to help in surveying and planning the work needing to be done and in the procurement and installation of requisite equipment. The Survey Group further recommended that the Chinese Government and ECA jointly engage a high-grade American engineering management firm to assist in supervising the entire scheme, in order to ensure that this part of the China Aid Program would, as a whole, be conducted with the benefit of outstanding engineering talent and experience. These recommendations contemplated ECA payment for such engineering services under the "technical assistance" provision in Section 111 (a) (3) of the Foreign Assistance Act of 1948. These recommendations, in which the Chinese Government concurred, were approved by the Administrator as a tentative basis on which further development of the program might proceed.

In anticipating the types of firms best equipped to undertake, on behalf of provisionally approved projects, the requisite work of pre-project engineering analysis and subsequent assistance in procurement and installation, consideration was given both to engineering firms without previous experience in China and to concerns which had been active in developing production and trade in China. Some of the latter, with worldwide connections, extensive local experience and competent resident managers and staffs of engineers, both Chinese and foreign, could, it was believed, make valuable contributions, under appropriate safeguards, to the success of the program.

Practical Arrangements Developed

After consideration of all aspects of this complicated program, the Chinese Government and the ECA Mission to China agreed to form a non-voting consultative Joint Committee composed of three representatives of the Chinese Government and two representatives of the ECA Mission to supervise the carrying out of the replacement and reconstruction projects. This arrangement was in accord with the principles of the Economic Aid Agreement between China and the United States which specifies that programs are to be carried out by mutual agreement.

It was decided to engage the services of an outstanding American management engineering firm to assist the Joint Committee. This was a distinct change from methods hitherto employed for previous aid programs by either government or by the United Nations for the UNRRA program. Previous practice had involved efforts to coordinate the work of Chinese and non-Chinese staffs, without use in most cases of special engineering consultants or of normal business and trade channels for functions which might be performed efficiently and economically by private enterprise. The Joint Committee, representing both governments, decided to retain in a technical capacity the J. G. White Engineering Corporation of New York City. The principal function of this corporation, it was agreed, would be to furnish technical supervision, with a group of from six to ten U. S. engineers, of the projects approved under the tentatively authorized $70 million ECA replacement and reconstruction program in China. The staff was not itself to undertake any "projects", but to assist the Joint Committee in selecting, recommending for approval, and supervising a wide range of industrial projects.

The procedure adopted may be outlined briefly as follows:

Private or public enterprises desiring assistance under the program would present initial applications to the Joint Committee which would refer them to the J. G. White Corporation for analysis and recommendation; projects provisionally approved by the Joint Committee were to be given "provisional allotments".

As soon as a "provisional allotment" was made, the successful applicant was to select an engineering firm as its "project engineer", this selection requiring ratification by the Joint Committee set up by the Chinese Government and the ECA China Mission.

The project engineer would draw up a bill of materials with detailed specifications, search world markets for necessary equipment and supplies which could be procured on the most expeditious and economical terms, and present a fully justified "project" to the Joint Committee.

Upon approval of the project by the Joint Committee, the project engineer would arrange for the procurement and delivery of approved equipment and material, and assist the applicant in achieving prompt installation and use.

Financing was to be done by ECA by a letter of commitment to a U. S. bank, in effect guaranteeing letters of credit (a) to suppliers of equipment or materials under approved projects, and (b) to the project engineer for his approved fee.

At each stage of this procedure, the J. G. White Engineering Corporation was to act as technical staff to the Joint Committee, the Committee taking action only after receiving the recommendations of its technical staff on such matters as: approval of the selection of project engineering firms, approval of fees and charges by these firms, approval of the detailed specifications and sources of procurement of equipment for the projects, and approval of prices of materials to be procured. Before any program was approved, the applicant and the project engineer would be required to submit to the Joint Committee a sworn affidavit containing information with respect to their profit margins and their methods of seeking materials, including competitive bidding. Arrangements could be made for the technical staff of the Joint Committee to accept sealed bids on items where relationships between the project engineer and the supplier indicated that such protection would be desirable.

These procedures taken together represented a new pattern for publicly financed industrial projects in underdeveloped areas. As such, they provided a unique approach toward the solution of a large continuing problem, that of grafting branches of modern technology onto the great trunks of agrarian economy in Asia and other underdeveloped parts of the world. An uninterrupted testing of this approach was unfortunately precluded by events in China.

RURAL RECONSTRUCTION PROGRAM

During the deliberations of the House Foreign Affairs Committee in February and March of 1948 on prospective aid to China, consideration was given to the fundamental and extensive needs of the Chinese economy in the field of rural reconstruction. Some new light had been thrown on this problem by a special agricultural mission sent to China by the President in 1946. Valuable experience in dealing with certain aspects of the problem had been gained through the Chinese Mass Education Movement headed by Dr. James Y. C. Yen. Information from these and other sources was weighed by the Committee with the result that rural reconstruction was included in subsequent China aid legislation as a specific field in which program funds might be spent.

Section 407 of the China Aid Act

Authorization for inclusion of a special rural reconstruction program was provided in Section 407 of the China Aid Act of 1948—the full text of which appears in the Appendix. This Section authorized the Secretary of State, after consultation with the Administrator, "to conclude an agreement with China establishing a Joint Commission on Rural Reconstruction in China, to be composed of two citizens of the United States appointed by the President of the United States and three citizens of China appointed by the President of China." Such Commission, it was provided, subject to the direction and control of the Administrator, was to formulate and carry out a program for reconstruction in rural areas of China, including such research and training activities as might be necessary or appropriate for such reconstruction.

The Act authorized an expenditure, for this rural reconstruction program, of an amount equal to not more than 10 percent of the funds made available for economic aid to China under the China Aid Act. This placed an upper limit of $27.5 million upon the funds which could be used for the rural reconstruction program. It was stipulated that the amount could be made available in U.S. dollars, proceeds in Chinese currency from the sale of ECA commodities, or both.

Establishment of Rural Reconstruction Commission

Following a period of negotiation, notes were exchanged on August 5, 1948, between the United States Ambassador to China and the Chinese Government Ministry of Foreign Affairs, providing an agreement for the establishment of a Rural Reconstruction Commission in accordance with the terms of the China Aid Act of 1948. The texts of these notes are quoted in the section on Documents, below.

Following the conclusion of this agreement, appointments were made by the Chinese and the United States Governments to the Rural Reconstruction Commission, the Chinese members being Dr. Chiang Monlin (former President of the Peking National University, former Minister of Education, and recently Executive Secretary of the Chinese Government Executive Yuan), Chairman; Dr. James Y. C. Yen (for 25 years the leader of China's internationally known Mass Education Movement) ; and Dr. T. H. Shen (outstanding Chinese agriculturist). The United States members appointed by the President on September 19, 1948, were Dr. John Earl Baker (former Director of the China International Famine Relief Commission and former adviser to the Chinese Government), and Dr. Raymond T. Moyer (U.S. Department of Agriculture authority on Chinese agriculture). On October 1, the Commission held its first meeting.

Objectives and Principles

The problem of rural reconstruction in China is one of enormous magnitude and complexity. Intensive and lengthy discussion was required to reach general agreement among members of the Commission with respect to questions of aim, emphasis, organization and methods of work. On October 18, 1948, agreement was reached on a general statement of the objectives and principles of the Joint Commission on Rural Reconstruction. The text of this statement follows:

"I. *Objectives*
A. To improve the living conditions of the rural people.
B. To increase the production of food and other important crops.
C. To develop the potential power of the people to reconstruct their own communities and the nation, thus to lay the foundation of a strong and democratic China.
D. To help build up and strengthen appropriate services of government agencies—national, provincial and *hsien*—that are established to carry out measures pertaining to rural reconstruction.
E. To help stimulate and revitalize enterprises of the Rural Reconstruction Movement and other private agencies doing rural reconstruction work.
F. To offer liberals, educated youths and other constructive elements, opportunities to participate in a program of service.

"II. *Principles*
1. Relating to Program
A. The emergency nature of the present situation shall be given paramount consideration in deciding on the nature and location of program and projects.
B. First consideration shall be given to projects which will contribute most directly and immediately to the welfare of the rural people, with special emphasis to be given to the improvement of their economic conditions.
C. A literacy program, supplemented by audiovisual aids, shall be an essential

part of this program, as a means of furthering education, organizing the people, and developing and selecting rural leadership.
D. New projects in rural reconstruction deserve encouragement, but unless they can show evidence of self-help and self-support for a reasonable length of time, financial aid shall not be considered.
E. Projects which already have been proved successful, under rural conditions, and which are reasonably simple and inexpensive, shall be broadcast on a large scale.
F. In general, preference shall be given to those agencies engaged in rural reconstruction having a sound foundation and experienced staff and organization.

2. Relating to Procedure
A. The program formulated by the Commission shall be carried out in cooperation with existing agencies.
B. A correlated approach shall be adopted wherever possible, since the various aspects of rural reconstruction are interrelated, the success of one depending on the success of the other.
C. A direct extension-type of adult education shall be emphasized as the most effective and quickest means of promoting the understanding, acceptance and correct use of recommended practices.
D. Local initiative shall be fostered and local resources, both human and material, shall be mobilized for the purposes of the program.
E. Assistance to a project in any province shall be contingent upon the willingness of the provincial and local officials concerned to cooperate fully in efforts to carry it out, and to take other steps, themselves, that are essential to the attainment of results expected of the project." .

On October 26, 1948, "A Memorandum of Understanding Between the Economic Cooperation Administration and the Joint Commission on Rural Reconstruction in China, Defining Their Respective Spheres of Administrative Responsibility" was signed by the Chairman of the Joint Rural Reconstruction Commission and the Acting Chief of the ECA Mission to China. This agreement established procedures for the presentation of budget estimates by the Joint Commission and the allocation of U. S. dollar funds for material and technical assistance and of local currency from the counterpart funds for expenses incurred within China. And arrangements were agreed upon for the recruitment, administrative supervision and direction of Commission personnel.

Based on the objectives and principles quoted above, the Commission worked out the main outlines of a program, which was divided into four parts with the following aims:

To increase in supplying areas the domestic production of agricultural commodities currently in serious short supply in China and supplied in part by the United States ECA program, particularly foodstuffs;

To establish centers in which a broad integrated program would be started under appropriate agencies of the Government, through projects related to local government administration, land reform, agriculture, rural public health and rural social education;

To carry out a large-scale effort in adult education as a means of developing the potential power of the people and raising their level of understanding, thus enabling them to participate more intelligently in solving their present problems; and,

To assist significant projects in rural reconstruction established in numerous centers through local initiative and resources.

When Nanking became threatened by military action, it was decided to move the Commission's operational headquarters to Canton. At the same time, a decision was made to focus major attention first on the development of a program in provinces south of the Yangtze River, and to concentrate upon projects susceptible of prompt development and usefulness, in such fields as irrigation, dyke repair, public health, and the control of serious animal diseases.

Surveys and Organization

To put this initial program promptly into effect a trip was taken by members of the Commission to Szechwan and Hunan provinces to inspect existing efforts on behalf of the rural population and to consult with responsible persons concerning projects for which assistance had been requested. Steps also were taken to set up regional officers in Chungking (Szechwan), Changsha (Hunan), and Kweilin (Kwangsi), and a central office in Canton (Kwangtung), while retaining a regional office in Nanking. Tentative plans to carry out some phases of a rural program from two offices in north China had to be suspended on account of troubled civil war conditions there. Headquarters of the Commission were moved to Canton on December 5, 1948.

To assist the Commission in carrying out its plans, competent persons were selected as heads for three of the four divisions of work, and, at the end of the year, able appointees were under consideration for the fourth division and to represent the Commission in three of the most important regional offices. A staff of Chinese and American specialists was being assembled to advise the Commission and help carry out its program, although uncertainties in the general situation caused the Commission to proceed gradually in building up such a staff.

The impression gained by the Commission in visits to provinces in west and south China was that these provinces were at the time relatively free from the acute tension then felt in the lower Yangtze area, and that local officials and private agencies were anxious to proceed with rural reconstruction measures along the general lines formulated by the Joint Commission. Steps were taken, therefore, to get into operation, in an initial program, specific projects to which the Commission was prepared to allocate assistance.

Initial Projects

Projects for which detailed plans were being developed included the following:

A broad integrated program in rural reconstruction in the third prefecture of Szechwan province, initiated by the Mass Education Movement and local leaders, assistance to include grants for the development of educational, agricultural and farm organization projects, and loans for irrigation and weaving projects.

The completion of 11 irrigation projects already underway in Szechwan province, which would provide for the irrigation of 191,000 mow (about 30,000 acres) of land by the end of April 1949.

The establishment of a system to multiply and distribute improved rice, corn and cotton varieties in Szechwan province.

The repair of dykes in the Tung T'ing Lake area of Hunan province, which would restore to production and protect from flooding land normally producing around two-thirds of the amount of rice annually imported into China before the war, to be completed by the end of April 1949.

An integrated program of rural reconstruction in Hunan, for which definite plans were yet to be received and agreed upon.

The establishment in Hunan province, the "rice bowl" of central China, of the beginnings of an improved system of rice production and marketing, including the multiplication and distribution of improved seed varieties and the establishment of more modern milling and warehousing centers.

Projects involving cooperation with various Ministries of the National Government were being considered in consultation with these Ministries after specific project plans were reasonably well developed. Steps were being taken to set up appropriate committees of specialists to advise the Commission and to assist in carrying out phases of the rural reconstruction program; the first committee established was for work in the field of public health in rural areas, with a former Minister of Health as Chairman. In accordance with a request of the Rural Reconstruction Commission, a private public relations firm completed in November a special study of the facilities available for a widespread educational effort under the Commission's sponsorship.

Detailed plans for the irrigation projects in Szechwan, for the dyke repair project in Hunan, for certain parts of the program sponsored by the Mass Education Movement in Szechwan, and for several other projects were being reviewed in December with a view to early allocations of funds. The Commission also expected to make early announcement of projects to which it would initially allocate assistance in Kwangtung province, and trips were planned to Kwangsi, Fukien and Taiwan to study projects for which aid had been requested.

Specific plans for broader programs with a major emphasis on education, it was anticipated, might not be completed before the end of February 1949. Tentative planning, conditional upon developments, called for an extension of some assistance to such integrated programs during the spring of 1949. It was expected, however, under prevailing conditions, that available funds under the current program would necessarily be allocated principally to projects of a short-range nature, emphasizing increases in agricultural production and improvements in rural health conditions.

STRATEGIC MATERIALS

Article VI, paragraph 1, of the Economic Cooperation Agreement between the United States and the Republic of China (the full text of which is quoted in the section on Documents, below) provided that the Chinese Government would facilitate the transfer to the United States, for stockpiling or other purposes, "materials originating in China which are required by the United States of America as a result of deficiencies or potential deficiencies in its own resources upon such reasonable terms of sale, exchange, barter or otherwise and in such quantities and for such period of time as may be agreed to between the Government of the United States of America and of China for domestic use and commercial export of such materials." The Government of China agreed to undertake "such specific measures as may be necessary to carry out the provisions of this paragraph" and "when so requested by the Government of the United States of America, to enter into negotiations for detailed arrangements necessary to carry out the provisions of this paragraph."

Article V, paragraph 4, of the same agreement, provided that expenditures in Chinese currency from the Special Account (described below) would be "only for such purposes as may be agreed from time to time with the United States of America, including expenditures incident to the stimulation of production activity and the development of new sources of wealth including materials which may be required in the United States of America because of deficiencies or potential deficiencies in the resources of the United States of America."

A preliminary investigation was conducted by members of the Reconstruction Survey Group, with a view to promoting increased production and export to the United States of strategic materials available in China and required by the United States, particular attention being given to tin, antimony and tungsten in south and southwest China. Such procurement, it was felt—to the extent that it could be developed—would, in addition to increasing the supplies of minerals needed by the United States, serve the double purpose in China of increasing local employment and augmenting the country's slender foreign exchange resources.

Production and Procurement Problems

It was found that foreign exchange policies and controls connected therewith since V-J Day, related to the Government's attempts to deal with the inflation, had exerted a depressing influence upon the production and export of these minerals, making it impossible for exporters, by and large, to obtain by negotiations through official channels fair and realistic prices for their goods. Only on rare occasions, when official exchange rates were for short periods realistic, were such exporters able to secure reasonable returns upon their produce. Initial negotiations looking toward the acquisition of these materials were aimed in part at securing the agreement of the Chinese Government to changes of policy designed to remove some of the obstacles to the flow of materials through legitimate channels of trade to the U.S., at prices fair to the producers.

Additional difficulties in procurement and export of such materials to the United States were attributable to shortage of productive equipment in China and to lack of transportation facilities from relatively inaccessible parts of China where such materials existed. Efforts toward helping to meet both these needs were clearly needed if production and procurement were to be developed on any appreciable scale.

Initial Arrangements

Following the aforementioned survey, the ECA China Mission before the end of 1948 began to work out arrangements with Chinese tin interests to make their product available for export to the United States. After receipt of pertinent information from ECA, the Reconstruction Finance Corporation in Washington offered to purchase from China considerable quantities of tin concentrates, to be refined in the U.S. where efficient smelter operation could extract a maximum percentage of high-grade tin; and to buy some tin metal in China for stockpile purposes. Preliminary negotiations were in progress at the end of the year to effect procurement arrangements, which were complicated by the necessity of effecting purchases through barter by the use of commodities or silver, instead of depreciated local currency.

SPECIAL LOCAL CURRENCY ACCOUNT

Provision for the establishment of a special local currency account, or counterpart fund, was contained in Article V of the Economic Cooperation Agreement between the Governments of China and the United States; the full text of this Agreement appears in the section on Documents, below.[7]

---

[7] See annex 181.

Unique Provisions in the Bilateral Agreement

The article referred to provided for two unique features in connection with the special local currency account, or counterpart fund, in China. The first was a provision that deposits would be made in the account only when requested by the United States; thus deposits could be requested at a rate sufficient to cover actual expenses that had to be met currently, without the accumulation of large balances which would rapidly depreciate in value as a result of the inflation. The second was a provision that the Chinese Government would "maintain the value" of allotments made from the Special Account—for such important purposes as administrative costs, rural reconstruction and the internal expenses of industrial projects—by "depositing such additional amounts of currency as the Government of the United States of America may from time to time determine after consultation with the Government of China." The value of allotments, to be thus maintained, could be recorded in terms of such standard and relatively stable measures of value as quantities of cotton yarn, rice or American dollars.

Support for China Relief Mission Projects

Shortly after the establishment of the ECA Mission in China, discussions were initiated with the Chinese Government pertaining to the setting up and operation of the special local currency account. While these discussions were in progress, provisional arrangements were made for the use of counterpart funds made available by the Chinese Government in support of existing projects in the fields of medical services, relief and welfare, conservancy work, and agricultural improvement which had been previously supported from a local currency account created in connection with the operation of the U.S. China Relief Mission. These projects which had theretofore been regarded as ending on June 30, 1948, were in some cases selected by action of the Chinese Government in consultation with the ECA for continuation after that date.

Preliminary Studies and Proposals

After careful study of special questions involved in setting up the special local currency account in China, and in light of discussions with the Government, the ECA China Mission prepared in September 1948 a tentative proposed program of local currency utilization which outlined in some detail projected uses for the counterpart funds in the fields of conservancy, public works, agriculture, medical and health activities and welfare.

Concurrently, analysis was undertaken of the financial and economic problems in China which needed to be considered in determining the manner in which the counterpart funds would be utilized. These problems included: the extensive deficit spending of the Government, concomitant with the continued prosecution of the civil war; the inflationary effect of the enforcement of the Government's short-lived August 19 economic regulations; the continuation of certain inflationary practices of the Government; the progressive deterioration in economic production; the disruption of transportation in disturbed areas; and the loss of public confidence in the currency resulting in widespread hoarding of supplies and excessively rapid turnover of the currency.

Technical problems requiring study included determination of the exchange rates governing payments of local currency counterpart funds into the Special Account; the timing of deposits; and policies to be followed with regard to the disposition of Special Account funds.

Studies and proposals received from the Mission, in relation to these problems, were further analyzed in Washington prior to consultations with the National Advisory Council.

Establishment of the Special Account

Following these consultations, authorization was given to the ECA China Mission to negotiate with the Chinese Government on questions relating to the establishment of the Special Account, deposits into such account, and purposes for which funds from the account might be utilized.

The Special Account was established in the Central Bank of China. It was agreed that, in order to avoid depreciation of cash balances in the account as a result of the inflation, deposits would be made only as called for by the ECA China Mission, in most cases a short time before withdrawal and expenditure.

Utilization of Counterpart Funds

It was further agreed that withdrawals would be made to cover all mandatory expenditures from the account, as called for in the Bilateral Agreement, including the Chinese currency portion of the following expenses: administrative costs of the ECA China Mission; costs of delivering private relief gift packages in China; and costs of the Joint Commission on Rural Reconstruction. It was estimated that expenditures of these types would amount to roughly 12 percent of the total account.

From the outset, it was clear that "sterilization" of local currency Special Account funds could not of itself be the key to controlling the Chinese inflation. The basic cause of the inflation was the magnitude of the Government's deficit financing, which in turn was due to the exigencies of the civil war and shaken public confidence in the currency which led to excessively rapid rates of circulation of the note issue.

On the other hand, it was apparent that an easy money policy in the use of the Special Account would be inflationary, the effect of such a policy being similar to that of greatly increasing the Government's monthly budget deficit through excessive note issue.

The ECA China Mission, in the light of discussions of this problem with the National Advisory Council in Washington followed, therefore, a policy of agreeing only to expenditures from the account which could be regarded as of demonstrated urgency and which in many cases would have offsetting deflationary benefits. Broad categories of non-mandatory expenditures on which the ECA China Mission could agree with the Chinese Government as being appropriate uses for the Special Account included: emergency expenditures which, at the discretion of the Chief of the ECA China Mission, could be considered as consistent with the objectives of the China Aid Act—expenditures envisaged in this category being for such purposes as emergency procurement of indigenous food for the rationing programs; expenditures on certain carefully screened projects, chiefly in the fields of conservancy, health and welfare; and expenditures, when necessary, to insure prompt installation and proper utilization of capital equipment under the replacement and reconstruction program. The total of these expenditures, it was expected, should amount to less than half of the potential local currency account.

Exchange Rates

A persistent problem with respect to the Special Account has been that of agreeing with the Chinese Government upon appropriate rates at which deposits would be made in terms of U.S. currency—that is, rates reflecting commensurate value in Chinese currency, at given times, for U.S. dollar aid provided. A rapid decline in the value of the new gold yuan and reluctance of the Chinese Government to negotiate formally on a basis other than official exchange rates led, pending a settlement of this question, to deposits being made as advances, without final agreement before the end of 1948 on commensurate value in terms of U.S. dollars.

Deposits and Withdrawals

As of December 31, 1948, deposits into the Special Account totalled, in round numbers, 157,289,000 gold yuan, equivalent (on the basis of rough tentative estimates prior to agreement on applicable exchange rates) to US$9,543,000. Withdrawals on the same date totalled, in round numbers, 150,333,000 gold yuan, equivalent, according to similarly tentative estimates, to US$5,839,000—the equivalent of approximately $1,342,000 being for ECA administrative expenses in China, $2,498,000 for administrative expenses of the Chinese Council for United States Aid, $1,803,000 for special projects, $53,000 for engineering services, and $143,000 for expenses incurred by the Joint Commission on Rural Reconstruction.

Before the end of 1948, the local counterpart funds thus jointly managed by ECA and the Chinese Government had enabled many worthy institutions and projects to continue operations in spite of inflation and civil war.

185

Summary of United States Government Economic, Financial, and Military Aid Authorized for China Since 1937

[WASHINGTON,] *March 21, 1949*

Since the commencement of hostilities between China and Japan in 1937 the United States Government has authorized aid to China in the form of grants and credits totalling approximately $3,523 million, of which $2,422 million has been in the form of grants and $1,101 million as credits. About 40 percent of the total, or $1515.7 million, was authorized prior to V-J Day to contribute toward the stabilization of China's wartime economy and to enable the Chinese Government to obtain military, agricultural and industrial goods essential to the conduct of the war with Japan.

United States Government grants and credits to China authorized since V-J Day have amounted to approximately $2,007.7 million, representing sixty percent of the total, of which $1,596.7 million has been as grants and $411 million on credit terms. This aid was designed to assist the Chinese Government in the reoccupation of liberated areas and the repatriation of Japanese, to meet some of China's urgent relief and rehabilitation needs, and, in the case of the present ECA program, to help retard the rate of economic deterioration in China and to encourage the adoption of effective self-help measures on the part of the Chinese Government. The Chinese Government has elected to use $125 million authorized by the China Aid Act of 1948 (included in the total of grants above) to purchase items of a military nature.

The totals of United States aid given above do not include sales to the Chinese Government of United States Government military and civilian-type surplus property which have been made since V-J Day, except where these sales were made on credit terms. In such cases, the amount of the credit involved has been included in the total of United States credits authorized. Surplus property with a total estimated procurement cost of over $1,078.1 million has been sold China for an agreed realization to the United States of $232 million, of which $95.5 million is to be repaid on credit terms. There are no available estimates of the fair value of this surplus property at the time of its sale. Neither do the aid totals include certain ammunition transferred by the United States Marines in connection with their withdrawal from north China.

United States aid to China reviewed herein does not reflect assistance through provision of advisory personnel in cultural, economic and military fields; nor does it include United States contributions through certain United Nations' programs in China—the International Children's Emergency Fund, the International Refugee Organization, the World Health Organization, and advisory social welfare services.

The various measures of United States Government aid authorized for China since 1937, together with the miscellaneous sales to China of United States Government surplus property, are summarized in the table below and described briefly in the text that follows.

United States Government economic, financial and military aid to China since 1937

[In millions of U. S. dollars]

	Grants	Credits	Sales of U. S. Government Excess and Surplus Property		
			Procurement value	Realization by U. S.	
				Initial	Ultimate
	(1)	(2)	(3)	(4)	(5)
Pre-V-J Day:					
ECONOMIC					(Sum of Columns 2 & 4)
1. Export-Import Bank Credits Authorized	....	$120	....	....	....
2. Stabilization fund agreement, 1941	....	50	....	....	....
3. 1942 Treasury Credit (PL 442)	....	500	....	....	....
TOTAL ECONOMIC AID	....	$670	....	....	....
MILITARY					
4. Lend-lease ($845.7 million)	$825.7	20	....	....	....
TOTAL MILITARY AID	$825.7	20	....	....	....
TOTAL PRE-V-J DAY AID	$825.7	$690	....	....	....
Post-V-J Day:					
ECONOMIC					
5. Lend-lease "pipeline" credit	....	51.7	....	....	....
6. UNRRA—US Contribution	474.0	....	....	....	....
7. BOTRA—US Contribution	3.6	....	....	....	....
8. Export-Import Bank Credits Authorized	....	82.8	....	....	....
9. Civilian Surplus Property Transfers (Under August 30, 1946, bulk sale agreement)	....	55	$900	$120	$175
10. OFLC dockyard facilities sales	....	4.1	n. a.	....	4.1
11. Maritime Commission ship sales	....	$16.4	$77.3	$9.8	$26.2
12. U. S. Foreign Relief Program	$46.4	....	....	....	....
13. ECA Program	275	....	....	....	....
TOTAL ECONOMIC AID	$799.0	$210.0	$977.3	$129.8	$205.3

United States Government economic, financial and military aid to China since 1937—Continued

[In millions of U. S. dollars]

	Grants	Credits	Sales of U. S. Government Excess and Surplus Property		
			Procurement value	Realization by U. S.	
				Initial	Ultimate
	(1)	(2)	(3)	(4)	(5)
Post V–J Day—Continued					
MILITARY					
14. Lend-lease ($694.7 million)	513.7	181.0	. . . .	. . . .	. . . .
15. Military Aid Under SACO	17.7	. . . .	. . . .	. . . .	. . . .
16. Sale of excess stocks of U. S. Army in West China.	. . . .	20	n. a.	(ª)	(ª)20.0
17. Ammunition Abandoned and Transferred by U. S. Marines in North China (over 6,500 tons) .	(b)	. . . .	. . . .	. . . .	. . . .
18. Transfer of U. S. Navy Vessels (PL 512)	ᶜ 141.3	. . . .	. . . .	. . . .	. . . .
19. Sales of surplus military equipment (total accepted by Chinese Govt.)	. . . .	. . . .	100.8	6.7	6.7
20. $125 Million Grant Under China Aid Act of 1948.	125	. . . .	. . . .	. . . .	. . . .
TOTAL MILITARY AID	$797.7	$201.0	$100.8	$6.7	$26.7
TOTAL POST-V-J DAY AID	1,596.7	411.0	1,078.1	136.5	232.0
GRAND TOTAL	$2,422.4	$1,101.0	$1,078.1	$136.5	$232.0

ª Down payment covered under item 9. See textual explanation.
b No estimate of total value available.
c Vessels valued at procurement cost.

Description of Individual Categories of U.S. Aid

(Paragraph numbers correspond with numbers of items listed in table above)

1. *Pre–V–J Day Export-Import Bank Credits:* Export-Import Bank credits extended prior to V–J Day were general commodity credits, used to purchase a considerable variety of American industrial and agricultural products and services. Repayment was arranged by contracts between United States and Chinese Government agencies for the sale of strategic minerals or wood oil. Of the $120 million total authorized, $117 million was disbursed and the balance, approximately $3 million, expired. Of the amount disbursed, $112.8 million had been repaid as of December 31, 1948. Credit authorizations were as follows:

		Million
Universal Trading Corporation	12/13/38	$25.0
Universal Trading Corporation	3/7/40	20.0
Central Bank of China	10/17/40	25.0
Central Bank of China	11/30/40	50.0
Total		$120.0

2. On April 1, 1941, the Secretary of the Treasury entered into an agreement with the Government of China and the Central Bank of China to purchase Chinese Yuan up to an amount equivalent to U. S. $50 million to further the monetary and financial cooperation of the two governments and the stabilization of the United States dollar–Chinese Yuan rate of exchange. This agreement did not provide for collateralization of such purchases, as did a previous stabili-

zation agreement of 1937 which therefore cannot be considered as representing aid to the Chinese Government in the strict sense of the term. It was further agreed in connection with the 1941 agreement that a Stabilization Board be established, to which the Chinese Government banks were to contribute $20 million. Purchases of Chinese Yuan under this agreement amounted to U. S. $10 million and were repaid in April 1943.

3. *1942 Treasury Credit (PL 442)*: On February 7, 1942, Congress passed Public Law 442, authorizing the Secretary of the Treasury, with the approval of the President, to make available to China funds not to exceed $500 million and promptly made appropriations for this purpose. An agreement of March 21, 1942, between the United States and China established this amount as a credit in the name of the Chinese Government. Between the date of the agreement and V–J Day, the Chinese Government drew on this credit to the extent of $485 million, the balance having been drawn since V–J Day.

At the time of this congressional action, strategic bases of the United Nations were being lost to the Japanese offensive in the Pacific and southeast Asia, and effective land lines of communication with China were being severed. It was of vital importance to the United States Government that China, which had resisted Japanese aggression for 5 years, should be strengthened and encouraged to continue the war against Japan. Since opportunities for giving effective material aid to China, such as was being rendered to allies in more accessible areas through lend-lease, were not great, the $500 million credit was characterized by the Secretary of the Treasury and in House Report No. 1739 as "the financial counterpart of lend-leasing war materials."

Funds provided under the agreement of March 21, 1942, were used mainly by the Chinese Government to purchase gold for sale in China as an anti-inflationary measure and to provide reserves for the redemption of Chinese Government savings and victory bonds denominated in United States dollars. A total of $220 millions was withdrawn in gold, much of which was shipped to China, largely during 1945, to be sold internally in an effort to control inflation by reducing currency in circulation and keeping down the price of gold.

A total of $200 million was reserved out of the 1942 credit for the redemption of Chinese Government United States dollar security issues. A reserve of $100 million was established for payment of Chinese United States dollar savings certificates, and another $100 million was earmarked for the payment of Chinese United States dollar victory bonds. In 1946, this earmarking was abandoned, and the funds became available for imports and other foreign payments as measures were promulgated governing payment of foreign currency bonds held in China which provided that such bonds would be redeemed in Chinese currency. It was also provided, however, that registered bondholders outside China would be paid in foreign currency.

Of the balance of $80 millions of the credit, $55 million was spent for purchase of bank notes in the United States, and $25 million was used to import textiles into China.

Final settlement of the terms of this credit has not yet been negotiated.

4. *Pre-V–J Day Lend-Lease:* China was declared eligible for lend-lease aid on May 6, 1941. During that first year until the blocking of the Burma Road in April 1942, lend-lease aid was aimed especially at improving transport over the Burma Road, which, due to the Japanese blockade, was the only land route into China. Although amounts carried by this route were greatly increased, they were still small. Delivery by air cargo plane from Assam in India over the 18,000-foot hump of the Himalayas, begun in April 1942, was the only means of lend-lease

supply until the completion in January 1945 of the Ledo Road from India across Burma. Lend-lease materials supplied prior to V-J Day were primarily military in character, but included considerable quantities of industrial and transportation equipment essential to the Chinese war effort. All but approximately $20 million of the $845.7 million in lend-lease aid extended prior to V-J Day is considered to have been on a grant basis. Terms of settlement of the $20 million balance are subject to negotiation.

The following table presents a break-down by major categories of Pre-V-J Day lend-lease aid:

Ordnance and Ordnance Stores	$153,333,189.94
Aircraft and Aeronautical Material	187,339,849.94
Tanks and Other Vehicles	94,177,927.72
Vessels and Other Watercraft	35,561,264.12
Miscellaneous Military Equipment	47,085,115.94
Facilities and Equipment	9,928,803.33
Agricultural, Industrial and Other Commodities	46,505,983.26
Testing and Reconditioning of Defense Articles	204,393.63
Services and Expenses	271,611,693.00
Total	$845,748,220.88

These figures are compiled from reports received by the Treasury Department from United States Government agencies as of June 30, 1948.

5. *Lend-Lease "Pipeline" Credit:* An agreement between the United States and China dated June 14, 1946 authorized the delivery on 3 (c) credit terms of civilian-type equipment and supplies contracted for but undelivered on V-J Day under the wartime lend-lease program. It was subsequently determined that a total of $51.7 million in equipment and supplies could be furnished under contracts covered by this agreement. The Chinese Government had been billed for "pipeline" shipments totalling $50.3 million in value as of November 30, 1948.

6. *UNRRA:* The UNRRA program for China was estimated on December 31, 1947 to involve the procurement of goods valued at approximately $517.5 million, allocated as follows:

	(Millions)
Food	133.2
Clothing	113.4
Medical Supplies	31.7
Agricultural Rehabilitation	72.5
Industrial Rehabilitation	166.7
Total	517.5

The estimate of the total value of the goods procured under the UNRRA program has since been revised upward to $526.8 million. This figure does not include shipping and insurance costs, which, in the case of China, are roughly estimated to have added an average of about 25 percent. This brings the total estimated cost of the UNRRA China program to $658.4 million. Since the United States contribution to all UNRRA funds was approximately 72 percent, it may be said that the United States contribution to the China program amounted to 72 percent of $658.4 million, or $474.0 million.

7. *BOTRA:* $5 million of UNRRA funds were allocated to the Board of Trustees for Rehabilitation Affairs (BOTRA), an international body established by the Chinese Government to control the use of UNRRA supplies and funds remaining after the conclusion of its China program. Since the United States contribution to the entire UNRRA program was approximately 72 percent, it may be esti-

mated that the United States contribution to the BOTRA fund was $3.6 million.

8. *Post-V-J Day Export-Import Bank Credits:*

(a) *Credits Authorized for China:* Export-Import Bank credits have been authorized for China since V-J Day for specific rehabilitation purposes. Individual credits are as follows:

Borrower	To Finance	Date	Amount (Millions)
Yungli Chemical Industry	Machinery, equipment and services [1]	3/21/45	$16.0
Central Bank of China	Cotton	1/3/46	33.0
Republic of China	Cargo Vessels	2/20/46	4.2
Republic of China	" "		
Republic of China	Equipment, materials and engineering services	2/20/46	2.6
		2/20/46	8.8
Republic of China	Railway Repair Materials	2/20/46	16.7
Republic of China	Coal mining equipment, materials and supplies	3/13/46	1.5
TOTAL			$82.8

[1] Legal documents of guaranty not available until 1947.

Of the $82.8 million credit authorized since V-J Day, $65.4 million had been disbursed as of December 31, 1948. Thus a balance of $17.4 million remains undisbursed, including the $16 million credit to Yungli Chemical Industries, Ltd. Owing to the delay in concluding the detailed arrangements for disbursing the Yungli credit it was necessary for the Export-Import Bank to postpone the expiry date until December 31, 1950.

Of the total amount disbursed since V-J Day, 12.2 million had been repaid as of December 31, 1948, leaving 53.2 million outstanding.

(b) *The $500 Million Earmark for China:* In recognition of the magnitude of China's requirements for reconstruction and the possibilities for economic development under orderly conditions, the United States Government gave consideration after V-J Day to making available substantial funds for this purpose. In April 1946, following the recommendation of General Marshall and approval by the National Advisory Council, the Export-Import Bank authorized the earmarking until June 30, 1947 of $500 million of the Bank's funds for the possible extension of individual credits to the Chinese Government and private Chinese interests. It was contemplated that such credits would be confined to particular projects and would be subject to the usual criteria governing the Bank's lending operations. No implementing agreements were consummated between the Bank and the representatives of the Chinese Government.

During 1946 and the first half of 1947, the Chinese Government discussed numerous proposals for credits with the Export-Import Bank, for some of which General Marshall and the Department of State recommended favorable consideration. Most of the proposals were not adequately supported by economic and financial data and analysis, and many of them were overlapping and without any indication of priority. The principal reason, however, for the Bank's refusal to take favorable action on Chinese credit proposals was its inability to find reasonable assurances of repayment.

In accordance with the terms of its authorization, the earmarking of $500 million for China lapsed on June 30, 1947. However, on June 27, 1947, the Export-Import Bank announced that, the expiration of the earmarked funds notwithstanding, it was prepared to consider Chinese credit applications in accordance with its general policies. While the Chinese Government has subsequently applied for substantial credits, none have been extended by the Bank, primarily, again, because of inability to find reasonable assurances of repayment.

9. *Civilian-type Surplus Property Sales (Under August 30, 1946 Bulk Sale Agreement)*: The sale to China of United States surplus fixed installations and movable property located in India and China and on seventeen Pacific islands was authorized or recognized under an agreement between the two governments dated August 30, 1946. The property sold under this agreement included every type of supply used by an expeditionary force except combat matériel, vessels, and aircraft, all of which were specifically excluded from the contract. The total procurement cost of the property involved, initially computed at approximately $824 million, is now estimated at $900 million. Vehicles of all types account for about one-third of the total, construction equipment about one-sixth, and air force supplies and equipment about one-eighth. The remainder was composed principally of communication equipment, tools, shop equipment, industrial machinery, electrical equipment, medical equipment, and chemicals. Approximately $873.4 million at procurement cost had been declared surplus under this agreement as of September 30, 1948.

Property originally valued at $240 million, included in the above total, had been sold under a number of miscellaneous sales contracts prior to the conclusion of the agreement but incorporated in whole or in part in the consideration set forth in the agreement. This property consisted chiefly of fixed installations and stocks of equipment in China and India and small ships from the Pacific area. The sales value of this property was agreed in the contract as $74 million. It had been turned over, for the most part, to the Chinese Government prior to August 31, 1946, and consisted of the following individual transactions:

(a) The Calcutta stock pile, having a sales price of approximately $25,000,000. This group of property, which had been sold to China under an earlier agreement, was composed largely of trucks and spare parts together with other supplies related to the repair and maintenance of motor vehicles.

(b) The small-ship program, with the sales price of approximately $28,000,000. Ships included in this program cover all varieties of small noncombat types.

(c) Materials and supplies required for the support of air forces with a sales value of approximately $6,000,000. This package of equipment, originated as a part of the lend-lease program, had already been assembled for subsequent delivery to the Chinese when hostilities terminated.

(d) The Army's sale of property in west China, having a basic sales price of $25,000,000 (U.S.) plus $5,160,000,000 (Chinese) of which the $5,000,000 down payment is incorporated in the consideration covering the bulk sale. This sale was occasioned by the withdrawal of the Army from west China in 1945, and included a broad assortment of expeditionary supplies.

(e) Miscellaneous small sales with a sales value of approximately $10,000,000. These cover all types of property which had been purchased by the Chinese Government prior to the date of the bulk sale. Two major categories, which combined represent almost one-half the total, are railroad equipment purchased in France and an assortment of quartermaster supplies composed largely of mosquito bars, blankets, and bath towels.

The agreement of August 30, 1946 provided for a total realization by the United States of $175 million, as follows: 1) $150 million offset against the United States' wartime indebtedness to China, 2) the equivalent in Chinese currency of U.S. $20 million to be available over 20 years to the United States for research cultural, and educational activities in China, and 3) the equivalent in Chinese currency of U.S. $35 million to be available over 20 years for acquisition by the United States of property in China and for current governmental expenses. While these considerations total $205 million, the United States at the same time agreed to establish a $30 million fund to be used by China to cover the cost of shipping and technical services arising out of the property transfer. Thus the United States' net realization under the agreement was $175 million.

10. *OFLC Dockyard Facilities Sales:* On May 15, 1946 OFLC agreed to furnish the Chinese Government surplus supplies and equipment for dockyards at Shanghai and Tsingtao, with repayment to be made in thirty annual installments. However the agreement provided that the United States might, at its option, request of China certain goods and services for United States Navy and other Government-owned vessels, with the cost of such goods and services considered as part of China's annual payments of interest and principal. Transfers of United States surplus under this agreement have now been completed. As of October 31, 1948, OFLC sales totalled $4.1 million at fair value.

11. *Maritime Commission Ship Sales:* Since V-J Day the Maritime Commission has sold the Chinese Government 43 vessels with a total sales price of $26.2 million under the Merchant Ship Sales Act of 1946. Of this amount, $16.4 million was on Maritime Commission credit terms. The balance was paid in cash, obtained in part through an Export-Import Bank credit. (See item 8 above.) The total wartime procurement cost of the 43 vessels was $77.3 million. The following sales are included in the total:

No.	Type	Sales Price
10	N-3	$4,300,000
10	Liberty and	
8	N-3	9,300,000
8	C1-M-VI and	
4	C1-S-AY1	10,000,000
3	VC2-A-P2	2,600,000
TOTAL		$26,200,000

12. *U. S. Foreign Relief Program:* Public Law 84, approved May 31, 1947, authorized the initial appropriations for the United States Foreign Relief Program. China's allocation out of these appropriations amounted to approximately $28.4 million. A supplementary appropriation of $18 million for the China program was authorized under Public Law 393, approved December 23, 1947. Deliveries to China under the United States Foreign Relief Program were made during the first half of 1948, as follows:

Cereals	$35,412,900
Seeds	88,400
Pesticides	609,900
Medical Supplies	5,185,300
Estimated shipping costs	5,084,500
TOTAL	$46,381,000

13. *ECA Program:* The current program of economic aid for China was authorized on April 3, 1948, in the China Aid Act of 1948 (Title IV of the Foreign Assistance Act of 1948). This Act authorized to be appropriated $338,000,000 for economic assistance to China, to be available for obligation for a period of one year from the date of enactment. The Act further provided for creation

of a Joint Commission on Rural Reconstruction in China. It was specified that insofar as practicable a maximum of ten percent of the funds made available for economic assistance should be allotted to the Rural Reconstruction Program, in the form of United States dollars, proceeds in Chinese currency from the sale of ECA commodities, or both.

The appropriation act passed on June 28 (PL 793) appropriated $275,000,000 for economic aid to China of which not more than $1,200,000 was to be obligated for administrative expenses.

The original ECA Program for China consisted of the following four major categories of expenditures:

a) A commodity program, through which ECA finances the importation of food, petroleum, cotton, fertilizer, and coal into China, and supervises the use within China of these commodities	$203,800,000
b) Participation with the Chinese Government in a Joint Commission on Rural Reconstruction	2,500,000
c) A program of industrial replacement and reconstruction, together with related engineering services	67,500,000
d) Administration in Washington, D. C. and China	1,200,000
TOTAL	$275,000,000

The following amounts had been authorized for procurement under the ECA commodity program by March 11, 1949:

Rice	$44,580,000
Wheat/Flour	20,617,000
Petroleum	46,000,000
Cotton	69,790,000
Fertilizer	9,202,000
Coal	286,000
TOTAL	$190,475,000

Dollar expenditures for the rural reconstruction program to date have amounted to less than $50,000. The Commission's expenses have been met largely through withdrawals of Chinese currency from the "counterpart fund" provided by the Chinese Government.

Procurement authorizations under the industrial reconstruction and replacement program have been suspended due to the military situation in China, but pre-project engineering is continuing on a number of projects. A total of $1,550,500 had been authorized for expenditure as of March 11, 1949, mainly for engineering surveys.

14. *Post V-J Day Lend-Lease:* Lend-Lease aid was furnished China after V-J Day to assist the Chinese Government in the reoccupation of liberated areas and in the disarmament and evacuation of Japanese troops. Under the direction of General Wedemeyer, Chinese armies were moved by air to their new reoccupation assignments at a cost of approximately $300 million. Though the "thirty-nine division" program ceased as of V-J Day, transfers of army ground material and equipment were continued. Lend-lease transfers of aircraft and air equipment after V-J Day were effected in order to assist the Chinese in the creation of a modern air force. A military-aid agreemnt of June 28, 1946, provided for the continuation of military lend-lease on a reimbursable basis. This agreement authorized expenditures up to $25 million for the reoccupation of China between June 30 and October 31, 1946, and up to $15 million for training Chinese military, air force, and naval personnel between June 30, 1946, and December 31, 1947. Expenditures under these programs are included in the total figure of lend-lease aid.

As of June 30, 1948 a grand total of $781.0 million in post-V-J Day lend-lease transfers had been reported to the Treasury Department by United States Government agencies. Of this amount, $50.3 million represented deliveries on 3 (c) credit terms under the lend-lease "pipeline" agreement (see item 5 above), and $36 million covered United States Navy vessels originally lend-leased to China but subsequently transferred under the terms of PL 512 (see item 18 below). Of the balance of $694.7 million, $181.0 million is considered subject to payment. Settlement of this amount is now under negotiation.

Listed below are the major categories of Post-V-J Day Lend-Lease supplies:

Ordnance and Ordnance Stores	$117,869,076.94
Aircraft and Aeronautical Material	43,683,604.63
Tanks and Other Vehicles	96,009,610.08
Vessels and Other Watercraft	49,940,642.57
Miscellaneous Military Equipment	99,762,611.71
Facilities and Equipment	36,198.74
Agricultural, Industrial and Other Commodities	37,918,928.21
Testing and Reconditioning of Defense Articles	2,338.88
Services and Expenses	335,817,910.56
TOTAL	$781,040,922.32

15. *Military Aid Under SACO:* Supplies valued at $17,666,929.70, consisting primarily of ordnance, were furnished China between September 2, 1945 and March 2, 1946 by the United States Navy under the Sino-American Cooperative Organization agreement. The supplies were made available in exchange for certain services provided by the Chinese Government.

16. *Sale of Excess Stocks of United States Army in West China:* The sale of a broad assortment of military supplies in west China was made on the departure of United States forces from that area. This property was transferred for a sales price of $25 million (U. S.) plus $5.16 billion (Chinese). Down payments of $5.16 billion (Chinese) and $5 million (U. S.) were made in the form of offsets against the United States indebtedness to China. (The $5 million (U. S.) down payment was incorporated in the realized return to the United States under the surplus property sales agreement of August 30, 1946—see item 9 above.) It was agreed that $20 million (U. S.) would be paid over a period of time by China. The terms of repayment are subject to negotiation.

17. *Ammunition Abandoned and Transferred by U. S. Marines in North China:* Between April and September 1947 the United States Marines abandoned or transferred at no cost to the Chinese Government over 6,500 tons of ammunition in connection with their withdrawal from North China. Included was a wide variety of small arms and artillery ammunition, grenades, mines, bombs, and miscellaneous explosives. No estimate of the total value of this material is available.

18. *Transfer of United States Navy Vessels Under P. L. 512:* PL 512 authorized the President to transfer 271 naval vessels to the Chinese Government on such terms as he might prescribe. On December 8, 1947, an agreement was signed between the United States Government and the Republic of China relative to the implementation of this act. A total of 131 vessels with a procurement cost of $141.3 million had been transferred to the Chinese Navy under PL 512 as of December 31, 1948 on a grant basis. This figure includes approximately $36 million representing vessels originally lend-leased to China but subsequently transferred under P. L. 512.

19. *Sales of Surplus Military Equipment:* The United States continued to make military equipment available to the Chinese Government following the termination of lend-lease through the transfer of surplus U. S. equipment at a small fraction of its original procurement cost. As of November 30th, 1948, China had accepted declared military surplus totalling $100.8 million in value at procurement cost.

or $6.7 million at sales price. Of the total accepted, $99.8 million (procurement cost) had been shipped. The following is a listing, in summary form, of military surplus shipments:

	Procurement Cost	Sales Price
(1) 130 million rounds of 7.92 ammunition (sold by OFLC under contract dated June 25, 1947)	$6,564,992.58	$656,499.27
(2) 150 C–46 airplanes (sold by War Assets Administration under contract dated Dec. 22, 1947)	34,800,000.00	750,000.00
(3) OFLC transfers, Jan. 1, 1948–Nov. 30, 1948: Ammunition, Cal. .30 to 155 Howitzer	21,419,116.91	554,534.33
Air Force matériel and equipment, including 159 aircraft and 683 engines	34,895,332.52	4,365,929.29
Ordnance, signal, and other military equipment (10304 tons)	2,158,938.17	269,867.29
TOTAL	$99,838,380.18	[1] $6,596,830.18

[1] A portion of the total military surplus shipments was financed by the Chinese Government from the $125 million grants authorized under the China Aid Act of 1948 (see item 20 below).

20. *$125 Million Grant Under the China Aid Act of 1948:* Section 404 (b) of the China Aid Act of 1948 (Title IV of the Foreign Assistance Act of 1948) authorized to be appropriated to the President a sum not to exceed $125,000,000 for additional aid to China through grants, on such terms as the President might determine. The legislative history of the Act made it clear that the Congress intended that these funds should be made available to the Chinese Government for such purposes as it might specify. The grants have been used by China to purchase items of a military nature. As of March 11, 1949 the Department of the Treasury had paid a total of $124,148,891.99 of the $125 million appropriated. Disbursements were made to the Chinese Government direct or to United States Government agencies requested by the Chinese Government to engage in procurement activities, as follows:

Recipient	Materials Procured	Amount
U. S. Government Agencies:		
Department of the Army	Arms, ammunition, medical supplies, motor vehicles, spare parts, etc.	$64,437,061.68
Department of the Navy	Naval vessels, reconditioning of naval vessels, ammunition	6,892,020.00
Dept. of the Air Force	Miscellaneous air force equipment and aviation gasoline	7,750,000.00
Bureau of Federal Supply	Petroleum products, ordnance raw materials	13,765,522.12
Office of Foreign Liquidation Commissioner.	Surplus aircraft, aircraft spares, ammunition, etc.	[1] 2,690,910.88
Republic of China	Miscellaneous supplies and equipment, from commercial sources.	28,613,377.31
		$124,148,891.99

[1] In addition, OFLC has received by direct payment from the Chinese Government $1,045,693.80 of the $28,613,377.81 paid to the Chinese Government by the Treasury Department.

As of December 31, 1948, materials purchased for $60,958,791.38 under the $125 million grants had been shipped to China.

In accordance with the President's Directive of June 2, 1948, the Department of State examines the documentation submitted by the Chinese Government to determine that the request is not in excess of the total represented by the invoices or other supporting data, and authorizes the Treasury to make the appropriate payments to the Chinese Government. Under the President's Directive of July 28, 1948, the Chinese Government may arrange for the procurement or furnishing of supplies or services by any agency of the United States Government, subject to the approval of the Secretary of State as to the availability of funds. In such instances, the agency concerned is authorized to submit to the Department of State requests for reimbursement of appropriations or for advance payments. The Department has been able to certify fully documented requests for payment by the Treasury Department within a few days after receipt.

186

Secretary Acheson to Senator Tom Connally, Chairman of the Senate Committee on Foreign Relations

March 15, 1949.

The following comments on S. 1063 are offered in response to your request as conveyed by Mr. O'Day, Clerk of the Committee on Foreign Relations, in his letter of February 28, 1949. It is the Department's view that the Bill proposes aid of a magnitude and character unwarranted by present circumstances in China.

Despite the present aid program authorized by the last Congress, together with the very substantial other aid extended by the United States to China since V-J Day, aggregating over $2 billion, the economic and military position of the Chinese Government has deteriorated to the point where the Chinese Communists hold almost all important areas of China from Manchuria to the Yangtze River and have the military capability of expanding their control to the populous areas of the Yangtze Valley and of eventually dominating south China. The National Government does not have the military capability of maintaining a foothold in south China against a determined Communist advance. The Chinese Government forces have lost no battles during the past year because of lack of ammunition and equipment, while the Chinese Communists have captured the major portion of military supplies, exclusive of ammunition, furnished the Chinese Government by the United States since V-J Day. There is no evidence that the furnishing of additional military material would alter the pattern of current developments in China. There is, however, ample evidence that the Chinese people are weary of hostilities and that there is an overwhelming desire for peace at any price. To furnish solely military material and advice would only prolong hostilities and the suffering of the Chinese people and would arouse in them deep resentment against the United States. Yet, to furnish the military means for bringing about a reversal of the present deterioration and for providing some prospect of successful military resistance would require the use of an unpredictably large American armed force in actual combat, a course of action which would represent direct United States involvement in China's fratricidal warfare and would be contrary to our traditional policy toward China and the interests of this country.

In these circumstances, the extension of as much as $1.5 billion of credits to the Chinese Government, as proposed by the Bill, would embark this Government on an undertaking the eventual cost of which would be unpredictable but of great magnitude, and the outcome of which would almost surely be catastrophic. The field supervision of United States military aid, the pledging of revenue of major Chinese ports in payment of United States aid, United States administration and collection of Chinese customs in such ports, and United States participation in Chinese tax administration, all of which are called for by the Bill, would without question be deeply resented by the Chinese people as an extreme infringement of China's sovereignty and would arouse distrust in the minds of the Chinese people with respect to the motives of the United States in extending aid. While the use of up to $500 million in support of the Chinese currency, as proposed in the Bill, would undoubtedly ease temporarily the fiscal problem of the Chinese Government, stabilization of the Chinese currency cannot be considered feasible so long as the Government's monetary outlays exceed its income by a large margin. After the first $500 million had been expended, the United States would find it necessary to continue provision of funds to cover the Chinese Government's budgetary deficit if the inflationary spiral were not to be resumed. That China could be expected to repay United States financial, economic and military aid of the magnitude proposed, which the Bill indicates should all be on a credit basis, cannot be supported by realistic estimates of China's future ability to service foreign debts even under conditions of peace and economic stability.

The United States has in the past sought to encourage the Chinese Government to initiate those vital measures necessary to provide a basis for economic improvement and political stability. It has recognized that, in the absence of a Chinese Government capable of initiating such measures and winning popular support, United States aid of great magnitude would be dissipated and United States attempts to guide the operations of the Chinese Government would be ineffective and probably lead to direct involvement in China's fratricidal warfare. General Marshall reflected these considerations when he stated in February 1948 that an attempt to underwrite the Chinese economy and the Chinese Government's military effort represented a burden on the United States economy and a military responsibility which he could not recommend as a course of action for this Government.

Despite the above observations, it would be undesirable for the United States precipitously to cease aid to areas under the control of the Chinese Government which it continues to recognize. Future developments in China, including the outcome of political negotiations now being undertaken, are uncertain. Consideration is being given, therefore, to a request for Congressional action to extend the authority of the China Aid Act of 1948 to permit commitment of unobligated appropriations for a limited period beyond April 2, 1949, the present expiration date of the Act. If during such a period, the situation in China clarifies itself sufficiently, further recommendations might be made.

O